GW00371068

THE
MEDAL
YEARBOOK
2001

Edited by
James Mackay, MA, DLitt
John W. Mussell
and
the Editorial Team of MEDAL NEWS

ISBN 1 870 192 311
(Hardback edition 1 870 192 346)

Published by

TOKEN PUBLISHING LIMITED

Orchard House, Duchy Road, Heathpark, Honiton, Devon EX14 1YD, UK
Telephone: 01404 46972   Fax: 01404 44788
e-mail: info@medal-news.com   Website: www.medal-news.com

USA distributor: Steve Johnson, Worldwide Militaria Exchange Inc., PO Box 745, Batavia, IL 60510
Canadian distributor: Eugene G. Ursual, PO Box 8096, Ottawa, Ontario, K1G 3H6

Printed in Great Britain by Polestar Wheatons Ltd, Exeter, Devon

Regular Auctions of War Medals, Orders and Decorations

Contents

Index to advertisers

Preface

THIS IS the seventh annual edition of the MEDAL YEARBOOK. After our marathon efforts last year which resulted in a substantial increase in the number of pages, expansion this year has been on a more modest scale. Nevertheless, we have added no fewer than eleven medals to the main listing, and a further thirteen medals to the Australian section. In the first category come several entirely new awards, as the process of reforming the British honours system continues. Preliminary details of two new medals in the campaign series are also included, even though the final decisions regarding design and ribbon had not been completed at the time of going to press. Nevertheless, several medals of much earlier vintage have come to light and are now recorded for the first time, mainly in the "fringe" area of medals for coronations and royal visits but including a rather charming bronze medal awarded by Queen Alexandra in 1914 to the children of men on active service at the beginning of the First World War.

We are still very much committed to expanding the text to include the medals of Commonwealth countries and to this end we have included illustrations for the majority of the South African awards first included last year and, with the compliments of Professor Ed Haynes of Winthrop University we feature a detailed section on the medals of post-independence India. In due course we also hope to include a full list of the independence medals produced by the emergent nations of the Commonwealth and welcome information on these, together with photographs showing ribbons in colour if possible.

When we promised to include foreign orders and decorations which are found in British medal groups we had no idea what a gigantic can of worms this would turn out to be. It appears that virtually every foreign medal, at some time or another, has been awarded to British servicemen; there are even several instances on record of British personnel being awarded the Iron Cross. We are extremely reluctant to abandon this project, but now realise that to accord full coverage to all such foreign awards would swamp the rest of the catalogue. We are taking a long hard look at this problem and perhaps the solution may be to contiue with merely illustrations with an abbreviated listing. We welcome feedback from our readers on this topic.

As usual, we are considerably indebted to readers for helpful and constructive criticism as well as specific details of errors of omission or commission. We do take note of all readers' comments and do our best to act on them where practicable. Several readers have written asking if it would be possible to include a list of regimental numbers and their later county equivalents, this is an area that we are working on, and hope to include a comprehensive listing next year.

Several hundred amendments have been incorporated in this new edition, ranging from minor printers' errors to substantial revision of text. Our thanks to the many readers who sorted us out on our erroneous listing of the Silver War Badge which we had incorrectly listed as a wound badge. That entry has been completely rewritten and the award is now correctly captioned, with an amendment to the index accordingly. Similarly the unofficial medal from the First World War awarded to those who shot down the first Zeppelin has now been retitled the Lord Mayor of London's Gold Medal and the title of Dartford Medal dropped. The entry has also been completely rewritten in light of information submitted to us. Considerable interest in the salerooms in the past two or three years concerning the Suffragette Medal has also led to this poignant award being included for the first time.

Most importantly the medal ribbon charts have been completely updated with a great deal of assistance from the Ribbon Branch of the Orders and Medals Research Society. The extra ribbons have necessitated enlarging the charts by a further three pages this year.

What we have presented here is by no means the last word on the subject of British medals, and we may never reach that state of perfection, but we make every effort to ensure that the text and illustrations are as accurate and comprehensive as possible. We still require additional material and would welcome details of any medals so far unlisted, or having less than adequate descriptions. The merit of a yearbook is that it should show a marked improvement, year on year, and this is what we are constantly striving to achieve, with your help of course.

As in previous years we are deeply indebted to those many readers who have taken the trouble to give us corrections, amendments or additional material. In particular we would like to thank Chris Allen, Timothy Ash, Mark Barnard, Commander Antony Bateman, W. M. Benn, Dennis Blair, Colin Bruce III, Roger Campion, Howard Chamberlain, John Chidzey, Leon Clarke, Roger Colbourne, Malcolm Cook, Leopold de Coutere, Major J. C. Cowley, Martin Fuller, Major General Edward Fursdon, Colin Hole, Harvey R. Howland, Daniel Kington, Glenn and Wendy Mason, Irvin Mortenson, Frank Noonan, Ian Angus North, M. O'Brien, Jonathan Pittaway, Denis J. Poole, Malcolm Rouse, Marc J. Sherriff, Henry Tilling, Lieutenant Colonel Ashley Tinson, N. G. Tucker and Sam C. Warden. The universality of medal-collecting is reflected in the fact that our postbag has included letters from Canada, the United States, South Africa, Australia, New Zealand and even the war-torn Balkans.

Our special thanks are due to a number of dealers and collectors, but particularly Philip Burman, Mark Cline, Chris Dixon, John Millensted, Malcolm Rouse and John Wilson for checking the prices of medals and miniatures in light of auction results and dealers' lists in the course of the past twelve months.

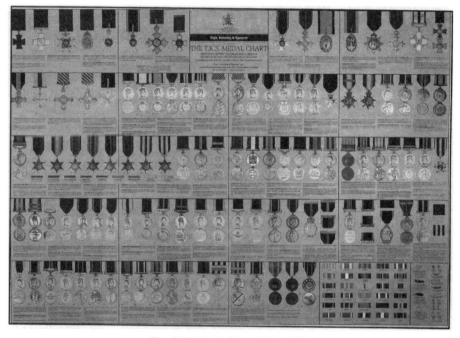

That was THE YEAR that was!

DECEMBER 31

An at-a-glance résumé of the main events and occurrences that affected the medal hobby during the past months, as reported in MEDAL NEWS . . .

July 1999

The Ministry of Defence turns down a plea from Andrew Bennett, MP, for the award of the Africa General Service Medal 1902–56 to veterans of the Suez campaign. No clasp for this medal has ever been issued for operations north of the Sahara, and Suez veterans must continue their fight for medallic recognition.

Arthur Daniels aged 101, formerly of the 1/Northamptons, and Marchant Bridgland aged 102, formerly of the KRRC, are invested with the Legion d'Honneur by the Lord Lieutenant of Kent at Dartford. Another veteran of the First World War, 101-year-old David Ireland, now resident in Stratheden Hospital near Dundee, is also awarded the Legion d'Honneur. He enlisted in March 1916, served with the Highland Cyclist Battalion and was wounded in 1916 and 1917.

An exhibition at the Victoria and Albert Museum, London devoted to the arts of the Sikh kingdoms includes a section focusing on the Sikhs as a martial force and includes a wide range of medals and militaria associated with them.

The UK internet auction site "Speedbid" (www.speedbid.com) exceeds 500 registered bidders and conducts sales of material from £2 to £2,000.

The annual exhibition of the Military Historical Society takes place on Sunday, July 4, at the Royal Military Academy, Sandhurst. Up to 25,000 visitors attend the military and sporting displays.

The twice-yearly journal *Standard Bearer* is launched, giving biographical and other background information on people who have displayed acts of bravery and dedication.

29-year-old Darren Restarick of the Royal Marines is awarded the MBE for his valuable contribution to the Royal Marines' transportation system over the past 11 years. This must be one of the youngest military awards of the MBE (other than the gallantry awards now discontinued).

Jemadar Ali Haidar, the only Pathan to win the Victoria Cross during the Second World War, dies. He won his VC as a sepoy in the 13th Frontier Force Rifles at the crossing of the Senio River in Italy.

Jungle tracking expert Winston Harris is awarded the MBE for his assistance to SAS soldiers in Belize.

August 1999

The School of Continuing Studies at the University of Birmingham offers a course leading to a Certificate of Higher Education in War Studies.

Proposals are mooted concerning a medal to recognise peacekeeping operations in Kosovo and Macedonia.

The OMRS decides to end London meetings at the Public Records Office, due to relative lack of support. Henceforward only the Society's AGM, Convention and auction will take place in the London area. Instead the Society will continue to support branch meetings in the provinces.

Major General A. S. H. Irwin, late of the Black Watch, is appointed chairman of the Joint-Service Operational Awards Committee

The first British sailor to receive the Legion d'Honneur in respect of service in the First World War is 101-year-old Royce McKenzie who fought at Gallipoli, the

---

Col. J. S. Wiliams, MBE, DCM (right) with Maj-Gen. P. R. Phillips, AO, MC, at the opening ceremony of the Gallantry Medallists' League muster in Queensland, on October 29.

Somme and Ypres with the Royal Naval Division. He was awarded the Military Medal in 1917.

Jim Lees and John Peters join forces to form a company entitled Empire Medals.

September 1999

Michael "Mick" Dalzell, a prominent member of the Orders and Medals Research Society, dies on September 7 after a long battle against cancer.

The Orders and Medals Research Society holds its annual Convention on September 18 at the New Connaught Rooms, London.

A new firm entitled Oceanwide Auctions Ltd of Ayr holds its first sale on September 22, and includes over 400 lots of medals.

The Aldershot Militaria Society holds its annual exhibition on September 26 at Farnham Maltings, Surrey. Members of the society exhibit items from their collections, but special emphasis is given to the Boer War as part of the centenary commemoration.

Proposals to establish a medal for firemen serving in Northern Ireland are rejected by HM Government, although the Northern Ireland Office maintains that it is keeping the matter under review.

The Royal Navy decides that officers who were formerly ratings are now eligible for the Naval Long Service Medal.

The Ministry of Defence gives approval for the unrestricted acceptance and wearing by UK service personnel of the United Nations Special Service Medal for service with the UN Special Commission in Iraq (UNSCOM). The bronze UN Special Service Medal has a ribbon of UN blue with a white stripe at each edge, and is worn with the clasp UNSCOM.

October 1999

On October 6 the Lord Lieutenant of Dorset awards the first eight medals to members of the Dorset Fire Authority for 20 years service.

The Stockport Militaria Collectors Society holds its 30th militaria fair on Saturday, October 9, at the Armoury Hall, Stockport.

The McCammon collection of numismatics, including militia and lifesaving medals, goes under the hammer at Baldwin's Auctions on October 11.

In the latest Operational List, published as a supplement to the *London Gazette* on October 28, 149 service personnel are awarded medals and citations for acts of bravery and dedication to service. The list includes awards for the liberation of Kosovo, comprising four DSOs, one MC, six DFCs, one QGM, 23 MIDs and seven QCVs. Awards for action in other parts of former Yugoslavia comprise two OBEs, five MBEs, two QGMs, one MC, two MIDs and 17 QCVs. Captain Lorraine Greasley, RAMC, becomes the first woman to earn the QGM, for her part in trying to save the lives of a helicopter crew after their machine crashed and burst into flames.

The first international muster of the Gallantry Medallists' League takes placed at Surfers Paradise, Queensland over the weekend of October 29 to November 1. Over 50 medallists and 100 honorary and associate members take part.

November 1999

Glenn Mason, formerly from Richmond, Yorkshire, establishes a medal research service in Australia, at PO Box 191, Virginia, Queensland 4014.

At an investiture at Buckingham Palace on November 4, Her Majesty the Queen presented the first of the newly created Queen's Volunteer Reserves Medal to Commander Kevin Kinsella, RNR, Lieutenant Colonel Nigel Beacon, TA, and Wing Commander Robert Kemp, RAAF.

At a military parade in Aldershot on November 8 the new *Kosovo* clasp to the NATO medal is presented for the first time. 100 soldiers from 101 Logistic Brigade receive the award.

A "Medal Weekend" is held at Banbury on November 6/7, with talks on subjects ranging from the German East African campaign to the 1980 siege of the Iranian Embassy in London.

The sale of militaria staged by Butterfield & Butterfield of San Francisco on November 15 realises a staggering total of $6,029,175. The top price of $442,500 was paid for a rare and experimental Colt Dragoon percussion revolver which realised more than four times the pre-sale estimate.

A special fair to mark the centenary of the opening of the Anglo-Boer War takes place at the Royal Engineers Museum, Chatham on November 28. The event, organised by World War Bookfairs, includes medals, militaria and ephemera of all conflicts from the Napoleonic War to the Second World War.

A Defence Council Instruction announces the award of three new medals for British service personnel. Troops involved in the liberation of Kosovo are eligible for NATO's Kosovo Medal. Her Majesty the Queen gives her approval for the Operational Service Medal (OSM) to replace the General Service Medal 1962 from January 1, 2000 onwards, as well as a medal for humanitarian or peacekeeping operations which do not warrant an OSM and do not attract the issue of a UN or NATO medal.

December 1999

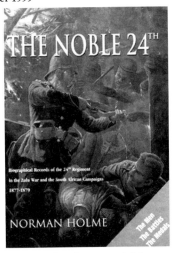

The South Wales Borderers and Monmouthshire Regimental Museum of the Royal Regiment of Wales host a reception on December 7 to launch *The Noble 24th*, a new book on the regiment, inaugurating a regimental website and bringing together two of the regiment's most famous Victoria Crosses.

January 2000

Reversing an earlier decision, the Australian Defence Minister announces that the Review Committee has agreed that officers and other ranks who were recommended for the Military Cross or Military Medal should now receive the equivalent Australian award, the Medal for Gallantry.

In the Millennium Honours List a number of awards go to service personnel for services in the liberation of Kosovo and include three CBs to senior officers. The Royal Navy receives three OBEs and six MBEs, the Army three CBEs, eight OBEs and 23 MBEs, and the Royal Air Force gets two CBEs, four OBEs and ten MBEs. In addition 50 QCVs were granted. Awards went to every rank between major general and private.

A plaque is erected in the Continental Ferry Port carpark at Portsmouth to mark the site of the pauper's grave of Seaman Thomas Reeves who won one of the first naval VCs during the Crimean War.

A further six veterans of the First World War receive the Legion d'Honneur. The six, who all live in Suffolk, are Charles Nugent (99), George Charles (99), Dennis Finbow (100), Reginald Crowther (100), Fred Leatherland (101) and Robert Richard Barron (103).

February 2000

A three-day seminar entitled "Gallantry at Sea" takes place at the National Maritime Museum on February 3–5.

Douglas Mitchell of Baldwin's dies on February 10 at the age of 93. He spent 64 years with the firm.

An exhibition marking the 60th anniversary of the Battle of Britain opens on February 18 at the Imperial War Museum under the title of "Spitfire Summer".

Sotheby, the world's oldest auctioneers, go on-line at sothebys.com.

The London Medal Club is formally inaugurated. Monthly meetings are held in a West End pub.

March 2000

Roger Colbourne becomes editor of the quarterly broadsheet of the Miniature Medals Branch of the Orders and Medals Research Society.

Spink and Son move, on March 20, to 69 Southampton Row, Bloomsbury, London. The first medal auction at the new premises takes place on April 27.

The New Zealand Cross, that country's highest civilian decoration, is awarded to Ms Jacinda Amey for saving a man from a shark in 1992. At the same ceremony, a posthumous award was made to Reg Dixon who died saving the passengers from a crashed airliner in 1995. The medals were presented by the Governor General, Sir Michael Hardie-Boys, at Government House, Wellington on March 8.

Captain Gaje Ghale, a Gurkha officer who won the Victoria Cross in Burma in 1943, dies on March 28. In 1990 he was one of the seven Gurkha VCs to attend the opening of the Gurkha Musuem at Peninsular Barracks, Winchester.

The George Medal is awarded posthumously to Bill Deacon and Anthony Doherty who both lost their lives during separate rescue operations in the North Sea.

Spink's new premises that opened on March 20.

An exhibition entitled "Go to it!" opens at the Imperial War Museum, commemorating the unsung heroes and heroines of the Home Front during the Second World War. The exhibition is accompanied by a book of the same title, by Lord Briggs.

George Mainwaring, GC, dies at the age of 83. He won his Edward Medal for outstanding bravery in rescuing trapped miners on January 30, 1949 and exchanged it for the George Cross in 1975.

April 2000

A permanent exhibition of medals and memorabilia of the Sandringham Company of the Norfolk Regiment opens at the Sandringham Estate Visitors Centre. It features a number of items which appeared in the television film "All the King's Men" starring David Jason as Captain Frank Beck who perished with his men in mysterious circumstances during the Gallipoli campaign.

Sotheby's team up with Amazon.com to focus on on-line auctions of all kinds of collectables including medals and decorations. The site is at www.sothebys.amazon.com. Lockdales, who regularly hold sales of medals and militaria, can be found at www.lockdales.co.uk

On April 12 Her Majesty the Queen presents the George Cross to the Royal Ulster Constabulary. This is only the second time that the GC has been awarded for acts of collective bravery, the first being in September 1940 when King George VI conferred the decoration on the people of Malta. The George Cross was accepted on behalf of the RUC by Constable Paul Slaine who lost both legs in an IRA rocket attack at Newry in 1992.

The 50th anniversary of the outbreak of war in Korea is marked by an exhibition at the Imperial War Museum which opens on April 14. Admission charges to the Museum go up from April 1.

The issue of the 80th Anniversary Armistice Remembrance Medal by Australia, together with the award of the Legion d'Honneur to surviving Allied participants on the Western Front, prompts a plea to the British Government to make a similar award to the few remaining British veterans of the First World War.

May 2000

The annual fair of the Victorian Military Society takes place at the Victory Services Club, London on May 7, with the special theme of the Boxer Rebellion to mark its centenary.

The annual auction of the Orders and Medals Research Society takes place at the Public Records Office, Kew on May 13.

Agansing Rai, VC, died on May 27. He was awarded the VC following action in Burma in June 1944.

The Duke of Edinburgh unveils a new headstone on the grave of Edward Robinson, VC, at Old Windsor cemetery. Robinson won his VC at the Residency at Lucknow during the Indian Mutiny in 1858.

June 2000

Service in new multinational operations can now count towards the Accumulated Campaign Service Medal.

A new exhibition opens at Keogh Barracks, Mytchett, Surrey dedicated to Victoria Cross winners of the Army Medical Services up to 1945.

Captain Ganju Lama, VC died on June 30 aged 77. His VC was won in Burma in the Imphal and Kohima area when he destroyed two enemy tanks single-handedly despite being badly wounded. His death reduces the number of living VC holders to 25.

An enduring image of the Korean War on display at the exhibition which opened on April 14.

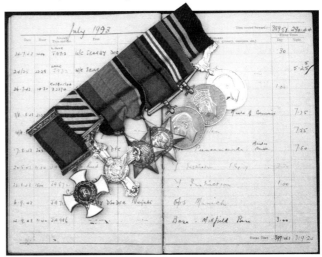

Market
trends

In the period under review (mid-1999 to early 2000), the pound continued very strong, especially against the Euro, although it tended to fluctuate against the US dollar to some extent. The policy of the British government in cutting interest rates continued, and for much of the period the annual rate of inflation was below 2 per cent. Towards the end of the period, however, the unemployment level began to rise again. Nevertheless the year in question was remarkably stable and London continued to be a good place for vendors to place material for sale. Market values were likewise stable and, if anything, one could detect a more discriminating approach, reflected in the prices realised for some medals being superficially disappointing, although on closer examination there were usually fairly cogent reasons why certain items failed to live up to the pre-sale expectations.

Although this was not a dull year at auction, sales lacked any truly spectacular pieces—the sort of thing that would hit the headlines in the national press. Eleven Victoria Crosses passed through the salerooms, but no George Crosses, and if there were very few of the very large groups of medals and decorations, there was a satisfying number of groups in the 10–14 range, with sufficient variety of British and foreign decorations, to add spice to the results. Furthermore, there were relatively few big "named" collections, although the appearance of the Feyver and Flatow collections in the saleroom excited considerable interest. Such collections invariably attract keen interest, partly because of their specialised nature and partly because they always contain a great deal of material that has not been on the market for many years.

During the year the centenary of the outbreak of the Anglo-Boer War was commemorated widely and considerable media interest helped to give zest to a number of sales which specialised in the medals and decorations of that conflict. Predictably some of the best results were achieved by medals whose recipients enjoyed some celebrity. In this category comes the medal to General Sir Almer Haldane who, as a captain, had been a comrade in arms (and fellow prisoner) of Winston Churchill. Conversely the previous year's *Titanic* bubble appears to have burst. Several *Titanic-Carpathia* medals and related memorabilia either sold well below estimate or failed to find a buyer at sales in the 1999–2000 season.

Corporal Wilcox and his VC group which Spink sold for £48,000 on April 27, 1999.

Although it may have seemed to be a fairly quiet year on the whole, the number of sales and the range of material on offer indicates that the market remains quite buoyant. The best indicators of the state of the market lies not in the spectacular gallantry awards and the flamboyant groups to admirals and generals, but the more run-of-the-mill material. Despite some disappointments, the market for First World War medals has shown a steady rise, with some quite startling results for individual Military Medals and DCMs and even the usual trio of 1914–15 Star, British War Medal and Victory Medal if there was particular interest in the recipient or his unit. This is a very healthy sign, pointing to increasing interest in regimental history and research into the service records of individual servicemen.

We should add, "and servicewomen too" for some of the best results achieved in the past year have concerned gallantry awards and campaign medals to members of the FANY and QARANC. Perhaps there is a feminist element in this, as is reflected in the very high prices fetched in the past year for suffragette medals (a category which we have hitherto ignored but which we are now listing in MEDAL YEARBOOK). Indeed, one of the spectacular results of the past year was the sale of the medal awarded by the Royal National Institution for the Preservation of Life from Shipwreck (forerunner of the RNLI) to the legendary heroine Grace Darling for her part in saving the survivors of the *Forfarshire* in September 1838. This was knocked down at Sotheby's in November 1999 for £34,000, against a pre-sale estimate of £15,000–£20,000.

Even Second World War medals and groups have shown a significant increase. Where they form part of a group in which one or more medals is named, demand has long been keen, but it is noticeable that even unnamed groups are yielding good prices where they

A number of World War I Memorial plaques to women surfaced during the season, including this one to Hilda May Bowman which realised £1,600.

are supported by research and collateral material that establishes their provenance. Interest in medal groups of more recent vintage remains high and prices continue to forge ahead, despite the fact that the vast majority of awards in the period from the Korean War onwards, and more especially recent conflicts such as the South Atlantic and Gulf War, are still in the hands of the recipients or their families. There is an interesting socio-economic factor involved in this; after both world wars there was a long period of slump and depression, unemployment was high, and many ex-servicemen were only too ready to sell their medals for a matter of shillings. Even Boer War QSAs with six or more clasps were fetching little more than their scrap value as late as the early 1950s, when medal collecting was still relatively in its infancy. But in this infinitely more affluent era there is not the same incentive to part with medals, in spite of the temptingly high prices which they fetch on the open market.

Interestingly there is an echo of postwar conditions in the continuing flood of medals and decorations from the former USSR and its satellites. Visitors to these countries will doubtless have been amazed at the vast quantities of these colourful medals which can be picked up on the spot for a song; but already the more enterprising dealers in Britain, western Europe and the United States have been steadily importing them and doubtless showing a handsome profit once the medals are marked up to the level obtaining outside the former Communist bloc. The interest (and therefore the long-term value) of these gongs is problematical, partly on account of the language barrier and partly because these medals were issued unnamed and thus lack the degree of personal interest attaching to British medals. But they are very colourful and on that score alone are attracting new recruits to the hobby, which is no bad thing. Despite the strength of sterling a number of important collections of foreign orders, decorations and medals have come under the hammer in London in the past twelve months and as most of these pieces are destined to be repatriated to their countries of origin, it proves what a magnet the London market continues to be globally.

Grace Darling and her famous medal.

A cross-section of notable medals sold at auction during the past year

GALLANTRY MEDALS AND GROUPS

Victoria Cross

Indian Mutiny, with IGSM, to Joseph Brennan, 1858, **£18,000,** *Spink, April 27, 1999.*

Crimea, to Bosun's Mate Henry Curtis, 1855, **£35,000,** *Spink April 27, 1999.*

World War I, in a group of five to Cpl. Wilcox, **£48,000,** *Spink, April 27, 1999.*

Indian Mutiny in group of six to General John Watson, 1857, **£80,000,** *Sotheby's, May 11, 1999.*

The medals and diary of General John Watson, VC, GCB, which realised £80,000. The VC was awarded for gallantry during the Indian Mutiny.

Indian Mutiny, with IGSM to L/Cpl William Goat, 1858, **£26,000,** *Sotheby's, May 11, 1999.*

Boer War in group of seven to Sgt J. J. Clements, **£65,000,** *Spink, October 20, 1999.*

Boer War, with QSA, to Sgt J. Firth, **£38,000,** *Spink, October 20, 1999.*

Boer War in group of five to Pte A. E. Curtis, **£40,000,** *Spink, October 20, 1999.*

Zulu War, with South Africa Medal, to Thomas Flawn, 1879, **£70,000,** *Sotheby's, November 26, 1999.*

Gwalior, to Lieut. William Waller, 1858, **£23,000,** *Spink, November 30, 1999.*

World War I, to Alfred Gill, 1916, with the campaign trio, **£60,000,** *Dix Noonan Webb, March 29, 2000.*

Conspicuous Gallantry Medal

World War I, in group of nine to J. F. McLaughlin, **£9,500,** *Dix Noonan Webb, June 22, 1999.*

World War II, to Flt/Sgt Preece, RAF, **£4,400,** *Glendining's, November 19, 1999.*

Police award to Barry Charles Court for his part in the Balcombe Street siege, 1975, **£2,400,** *Sotheby's, November 26, 1999.*

Gulf War, to Fusilier Bakkor, caught in "friendly fire", 1991, **£9,000,** *Sotheby's, November 26, 1999.*

World War I, Zeebrugge Raid, in group of seven to Leading Seaman Davis, **£5,200,** *Spink, November 30, 1999.*

Distinguished Service Order

DSO and MC group of seven, WWI, **£1,250,** *Bosleys, April 14, 1999.*

DSO and bar in group of 14 with CBE and MC to E. E. E. Cass, 1918–40, **£14,500,** *Spink, April 27, 1999.*

DSO group of five including the Croix de Guerre, RNAS/RFC, WWI, **£6,500,** *Sotheby's, May 11, 1999.*

DSO group of six, WWI, £1,200, Bosleys, June 9, 1999.

DSO group with WWI trio, **£1,180,** *Bosleys, June 16, 1999.*

DSO group of seven including OBE and TD, with KCMG neck badge, **£2,300,** *Bosleys, August 11, 1999.*

DSO and bar group of 11 with OBE and DCM, **£7,200,** *Dix Noonan Webb, September 17, 1999.*

DSO group of 12 with OBE and MC, WWI, **£4,000,** *Spink, October 20, 1999.*

DSO group of five, Boer War, to Hon. Harry White, **£4,000,** *Spink, October 20, 1999.*

DSO group to Lord Henry Cecil, Boer War, **£10,000,** *Spink, October 20, 1999.*

DSO group to C. F. Minchin, Boer War, **£1,900,** *Spink, October 20, 1999.*

DSO, MC and bar and DCM with WWI trio, to Major C. Gibbens, **£6,500,** *Dix Noonan Webb, March 29, 2000.*

Distinguished Conduct Medal

With WWI trio to L/Cpl H. Owens, **£400,** *Bosleys, April 14, 1999.*

Tel el Kebir, to C/Sgt Walkley, **£650,** *Spink, April 27, 1999.*

Abu Klea, to Sgt William Eaton, **£2,300,** *Spink, April 27, 1999.*

Suvla Bay, WWI group of eight, **£2,200,** *Sotheby's, May 11, 1999.*

WWI award, **£340,** *Bosleys, June 9, 1999.*

In group of six WWI to E. G. Port, **£620,** *Dix Noonan Webb, September 17, 1999.*

With WWI trio to V. R. Smith, **£600,** *Dix Noonan Webb, September 17, 1999.*

Six clasp MGSM to A. Poole, RA, which Bosleys sold for £600 on December 8, 1999.

DCM with MM and two bars, WWI group of six to L/Cpl W. R. Penistone, **£5,000,** *Dix Noonan Webb, September 17, 1999.*

Boer War group, including the MBE, to Sgt Rowland, **£3,200,** *Spink, October 20, 1999.*

Boer War group of three to Driver Felton, killed at Colenso, **£4,000,** *Spink, October 20, 1999.*

DCM and 8-clasp QSA to Gunner P. Noonan, **£3,500,** *Spink, October 20, 1999.*

Boer War group of four to Sgt W. Macdonald, **£2,700,** *Spink, October 20, 1999.*

In WWI group with the MBE, to Henry Woodlake, **£2,500,** *Dix Noonan Webb, December 9, 1999.*

DCM to an Australian warrant officer serving in Vietnam, **£4,600,** *Dix Noonan Webb, December 9, 1999.*

DCM and bar in SA/WWI group of six to Sgt Woods, **£2,500,** *Glendining's's, March 22, 2000.*

CAMPAIGN MEDALS

Naval General Service Medal

Single clasp, *1847,* **£300,** *Bosleys, April 14, 1999.*

Single clasp, *Navarino,* **£1,750,** *Dix Noonan Webb, June 22, 1999.*

Single clasp, *1794,* **£420,** *Spink, November 30, 1999.*

Single clasp, *Boat Service 14.12.1814,* **£1,400,** *Dix Noonan Webb, December 9, 1999.*

Single clasp, *Potomac 1814,* **£3,700,** *Dix Noonan Webb, March 29, 2000.*

Two clasps, *1794, 1795,* **£1,350,** *Dix Noonan Webb, June 22, 1999.*

Two clasps, *Pelagosa 28 Novr 1811* and *St Sebastian,* in original box, **£2,300,** *Glendining's's, March 22, 2000.*

Two clasps, *Basque Roads* and *Java,* **£1,300,** *Dix Noonan Webb, March 29, 2000.*

Military General Service Medal

Single clasp, *Egypt,* **£560,** *Sotheby's, November 26, 1999.*

Single clasp, *Busaco,* **£3,000,** *Spink, November 30, 1999.*

Single clasp, *Fort Detroit,* **£2,200,** *Spink, November 30, 1999.*

Single clasp, *Java,* **£6,000,** *Dix Noonan Webb, March 29, 2000.*

Two clasps, *Martinique* and *Guadeloupe,* **£950,** *Spink, November 30, 1999.*

Three clasps, **£4,600,** *Dix Noonan Webb, September 17, 1999.*

Five clasps, **£850,** *Baldwin, June 16, 1999.*

Six clasps, **£600,** *Bosleyss, December 8, 1999.*

Seven clasps, **£950,** *Sotheby's, May 11, 1999.*

Nine clasps, **£650,** *Bosleyss, August 11, 1999.*

Waterloo Medal

Lt. Col. Frederick von Wessell, King's German Legion, **£3,500,** *Spink, April 27, 1999.*

Lieut. James McConchy, **£2,600,** *Dix Noonan Webb, June 22, 1999.*

Lieut. James Mill, **£2,200,** *Dix Noonan Webb, June 22, 1999.*

Award to a soldier not involved in the action, **£600,** *Glendining's, July 25, 1999.*

Lieut. Henry Vane, **£1,850,** *Glendining's, November 10, 1999.*

William Robnson, **£1,300,** *Glendining's, November 10, 1999*

Timothy Greenhalgh, **£900,** *Sotheby's, November 26, 1999.*

With two-clasp MGSM to Lieut. W. Hill, **£2,600,** *Dix Noonan Webb, March 29, 2000.*

Waterloo Medal with a two-clasp MGSM to Lieut. W. Hill realised £2,600 at Dix Noonan Webb on March 29, 2000.

Beginner
beware

Medal collecting has its fair share of pitfalls to trap the unwary. Your best guarantee always is to purchase medals only from reputable dealers who will gladly refund your money should the medal turn out to be not quite what it seems. The main problem arises when you buy medals from general antique shops, street market stalls, swapmeets and collectors' fairs. Despite the Trades Descriptions Act and other legislation in recent years, in practice it is very difficult and expensive to win restitution. It is one thing to study a medal critically in the comfort of one's own home, with all the right tools and reference books at hand; and quite another matter to spot a fake or outright forgery while browsing in a dealer's stock. But a little care, and a better idea of the potential problems, may prevent you from making a costly mistake.

OUTRIGHT FORGERY

The traditional method of producing an outright forgery of a medal was to make moulds from a genuine example and then take casts from it. The most obvious telltale sign of forgery is the metal itself, for forgers seldom took the trouble to get exactly the right composition of alloy. A good example of this is the forgery of the India General Service Medal of 1854 which has a leaden appearance and a peculiarly soapy texture to the touch. On checking the diameter of the suspect medals, using callipers and a half-millimetre scale, it will invariably be found that the diameter is slightly smaller than the genuine medal. This is due to the fact that the plaster used in the mould shrinks slightly as it dries, with the result that any cast made subsequently will be correspondingly smaller and thinner.

Whether the alloy is suspect or not, it is strongly advised that you get into the habit of checking the dimensions of medals, suspension bars and clasps accurately. Both the thickness and diameter of medals should be measured as precisely as possible, the latter being checked at several points—for a reason which will become obvious later.

Apart from alloy and dimensions, the other telltale sign of forgery is the surface condition. Is every detail of the design sharp, or is there evidence of blurring? There are quite fundamental differences in the techniques of production, between a genuinely struck medal and a cast forgery. The latter will usually show some signs of microscopic surface pitting, caused by tiny air bubbles in the molten metal as it cools down. Some forgeries we have examined are actually unbelievably crude, and the wonder is that anyone could be deceived by them—but they frequently are! These forgeries were produced in simple sand moulds which, although lacking the shrinkage factor inherent

in plaster moulds, have a grainy quality. Sometimes attempts will be made to remove this grainy characteristic as well as other surface blemishes, by chasing—an ancient technique of metalsmiths which involves filing and scraping with fine chisels and burins. This technique inevitably leaves very fine marks which are absent in genuinely struck medals. Casts also exhibit fine lines on the rim, where the two halves of the mould join, and although they are invariably filed off this often leaves a slight ridge, often visible by holding the medal with the rim to the light and rotating it slowly.

In more recent years, as the value of medals has soared, forgers have been taking infinitely greater pains, even going to the length of having new dies made (by hubbing from a genuine original) and then striking them. Such struck forgeries are more difficult to detect, but usually there is some subtle difference in the design which betrays their true character. The Air Crew Europe Star, for example, has been a frequent target of the forger, and several counterfeits of varying quality have been recorded. These range from the easily detectable type, with three pearls instead of five on the central arch of the crown, to a very accurate design albeit slightly thinner than the genuine star and having the points noticeably rounded instead of cut square.

Unfortunately with today's computer-aided technology, forgeries are becoming more and more difficult to detect but hopefully the same technology will help us to combat the problem by making simple methods of detection available to everyone.

COPIES

Under this heading come all manner of reproductions and imitations, which are often much harder to detect, especially if their provenance leads you to believe them to be genuine—or at least to be not so wary. It was not uncommon in years gone by, when the wearing of medals was much more frequent than it is today, for generals, admirals, ambassadors and other high officials to have a second set of medals mounted for everyday wear. These copies were often produce by the firms who held the government contracts to manufacture the originals, and they were struck from the same dies, using the same materials. In this case, however, as a precaution, these medals were clearly marked COPY. Where this was stamped in incuse lettering there was little fear of erasure, but where raised capitals were employed these could be filed off. Again, it is advisable to check medals for any evidence of file-marks or erasure on the rim or in the field.

This problem becomes especially acute where gallantry medals and decorations are concerned. It has sometimes been the case that the recipient of a gallantry medal has been compelled, through straitened circumstances, to sell the medal while retaining the campaign medals which made up the rest of the group. Subsequently he obtains an official copy or duplicate medal to complete the set, and in the fulness of time this group comes on the market. In extreme cases the copy decoration may even be detached from the group and sold separately. Thus we have instances of gallantry awards appearing to sell twice over, when in fact only one was the genuine original and the second one was the replacement. This is a potential minefield, for there are also other reasons for replacement medals supplied by the official contractors for legitimate reasons. Gallantry awards, notably the Victoria Cross, have been replaced due to accidental loss or theft, and have then been worn just as proudly by the recipient. At the end of the day, however, the status of these replacements is somewhat less than that of the original medals, and is usually reflected in the market value. The question of status is something of a grey area which only the individual collector can decide for himself.

Campaign and general service medals, issued to serving soldiers to replace those lost or stolen are clearly marked "Replacement" at the time of issue and, as such, are not highly regarded by dealers or collectors. Unfortunately there have been numerous examples in recent years of these replacements having their true identity concealed by erasure. Be on your guard against such medals which appear to have been filed, rubbed or disfigured along the rim where the naming is found, as this could imply that the word "Replacement" has been removed for fraudulent purposes.

FAKES

These are genuine medals which have been tampered with in some way in order to convert a common (and relatively cheap) item into a rarity commanding a greatly enhanced price. Fakery is much harder to detect than forgery and each case has to be examined on its individual merits, but below (and in more depth, with regard to renaming, in the following section: "*Renaming*") we give a few pointers to look out for.

One common practice is to take a perfectly genuine medal and replace a common campaign clasp by one which is rare. Apart from the fact that the substitute will probably be an out and out forgery, detectable by the factors outlined above, a high-powered magnifier will usually show up evidence of tampering with the rivets securing the clasp to the medal. This in itself is not proof positive of substitution, for clasps can work loose for various reasons; but any sign of tampering with the rivets, or their replacement, should put you immediately on your guard. Examine the rivets closely for signs of file marks, soldering or any other form of tampering.

The chief ploy to improve the value of a medal, however, stems from the British practice of naming campaign medals to their recipients. This has given rise to a form of faking in which a medal named to someone in a plentiful regiment, or to a non-combatant, has had the original name erased by careful filing, and a new name, rank, number and regiment substituted. Some of these fakes were relatively crude in that the original name might be left intact and only the regiment altered; but as medal rolls and regimental muster rolls became more widely available to collectors and military historians, and fakers were forced to give closer attention to adding the name of a serviceman who would theoretically have been awarded such a medal.

This is where a careful measurement of the diameter, from several angles, is vital. Medals should be perfectly round and regular, so that any variation in diameter measured from different points will almost certainly indicate that the rim has been slightly shaved to remove the original impressed lettering. In some cases the original lettering may have been raised; filing this off may not materially affect the diameter, but the substitution of incuse or engraved lettering may be a dead giveaway. It is very important, therefore, to study the detailed catalogues of individual medals, and compare the method of naming with that found on your specimen. Even this is not always foolproof, for replacement medals issued to serving soldiers to make up for lost medals may be named in a manner which differed from the original issue. 19th century campaign medals were not always marked as clearly as they are nowadays to indicate that they were replacements, but the use of different lettering may provide a clue.

Of course, renaming or altering a medal in some way has not always been done to fool the collector; serving servicemen have been guilty of such practices over the years for a variety of reasons!

Any aspect of a medal which appears to differ from the norm should immediately put the collector on his guard. However, it is only fair to point out that many long-running general service medals differed in some subtle way in the fastenings of the clasps over a long period. In this case it is necessary to become fully acquainted with the different styles, including different shapes and sizes of rivets, types of solder and even twisted wire—all of which have been used quite legitimately at various times for the same medal.

Similarly differences in the lettering and numerals inscribed on campaign clasps may not betray the handiwork of the forger or faker, for such subtle variations may merely denote that the clasps were the work of one of the Royal Mint's sub-contractors. For example, India General Service Medals may be found with clasps manufactured at the branch mint in Calcutta, rather than in London. Once again, it is necessary for the collector to study all the available literature in his chosen field and thoroughly familiarise himself with the variants which may quite legitimately arise, as well as the difference between genuine and fake which have been recorded over the years.

RENAMING

Trying to determine whether a medal is correctly named is a problem that every collector has to face at some time or another. When checking for evidence of renaming always examine the medal with the aid of a magnifying glass. It is useful to bear in mind the following points:

1. Generally speaking, it is easier to re-name engraved medals than those that bear impressed namings. An engraved medal is relatively quick and easy to rename as it is necessary to remove less metal to erase the original naming.

   To rename a medal with an impressed naming requires special tools which are not easy to obtain.

   This having been said, it should be pointed out that many of the most notorious cases of renaming (especially with more expensive medals), done with the intention to deceive, have involved impressed medals.

2. Always consider whether the style of naming is correct for the particular medal under consideration, also for the particular clasp(s) concerned and for the regiment, etc. Sometimes medals issued for the same campaign are named in different styles depending on the unit involved and the clasp(s). A good example of this is the India General Service medal 1854–95. Such information can be acquired in part from books and articles, but these can be inaccurate or not sufficiently specialised. The best way to acquire knowledge is by examining as many medals as possible. Always take full advantage of medal fairs, auction viewings, visits to dealers' premises and chances to look at friends' medal collections to enhance your knowledge.

3. Before a medal can be renamed, the original naming must be removed and one can usually see some evidence of this, such as in the form of file marks. Figure 1 shows the results of an attempt to remove a recipient's name from a medal—notice the many scratch marks caused by the file.

Figure 1

Unless the removal of the original naming has been done extremely carefully the edge of the medal may have a "rounded" appearance, instead of being square and flat. Figure 2 shows a renamed medal with edge view silhouette. See how "rounded" the edge is when compared with the flat edge of a correctly named medal in Figure 3.

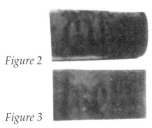

Figure 2

Figure 3

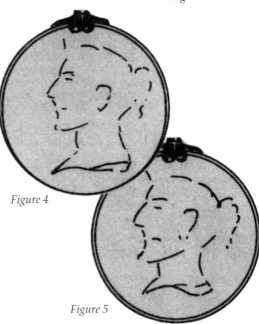

Figure 4

Figure 5

4. If the suspender on the medal is assumed to be the 12 o'clock position, the naming on most medals appears on the edge between 9 o'clock and 3 o'clock. When the original naming is removed this thins down the rim between these two points. This is well illustrated in Figures 4 and 5. The former (4) shows a renamed medal with a thin rim while the naming has been removed and the latter (5) shows a correct medal with an even rim all round. The removal of the original naming will also reduce the size of the medal and this can be checked by using either a micrometer or a vernier calliper. The diameter of the medal should be measured across the 9 o'clock to 3 o'clock position and then across the 1 o'clock to 7 o'clock position. If the medal is not renamed, the two measurements should be the same. A "suspect" medal can also be checked for size against a known genuine medal, although it should be noted that a random check of say 10 similar medals will show variations in size.

5. Traces of an original naming may be visible under the new naming. Figures 6, 7 and 8 show examples of this. In Figure 6, traces are seen under the new naming and also beyond the end of it. Figure 7 shows the outline of an impressed letter "A" under the new "S" and also shows traces of file marks. Figure 8 has a small impressed "T" appearing between the "L" and "A" of the new naming.

   To recap, always check a medal for the following points
   a. Is it named in the correct style?
   b. Does the edge show file marks?
   c. Is the edge flat?
   d. Is the rim thinned at any point?
   e. Is the diameter the same all round?
   f. Are there traces of the original naming?
   g. Has the medal been checked in all respects with a known correct medal?

A term which often appears in auction house and dealers' lists is "officially corrected" and "corrrected". Normally these expressions refer to instances where a single letter in the naming has been corrected by the issuing authority or by the recipient in order to rectify spelling mistakes, etc. Figures 9 and 10 show examples of "official" corrections. In both cases, traces of file marks can be seen and the corrected letter is impressed more heavily than the other letters.

Examples of privately corrected errors can be seen in Figures 11 and 12, here the new letters have been engraved rather than impressed and so do not match the rest of the naming. Traces of file marks are also visible. Figure 13 shows an example of where the correction is an "addition" due to the recipient's naming being incorrectly spelt. It is corrected by the addition of the letter "E", which is engraved and hence does not match the rest of the impressed naming. The engraved full-stop after the "K" can just be seen beneath the new "E". Figure 14 shows a Naval General Service medal 1793–1840, where the recipient has had his original rank removed and his later rank of "Lieut" added. Again this is engraved and does not match the rest of the naming, which is correctly impressed. Once more, notice the traces of file marks and the original impressed full-stop some way beyond the "Lieut".

These kinds of corrections to namings were necessary because of human error and hence cannot really be classified as renamings.

Why do renamed medals exist on the market? The majority were not produced to deceive medal collectors, but are the result of officers and men losing their own medals and having to find replacements. The obvious and easiest remedy was to buy someone else's medals and have them renamed. Servicemen out to impress their friends and family were not above adding an extra medal to their rows and what better proof of entitlement than to see that the medal had their name on it. Many such medals were renamed by local jewellers.

Most collectors shun renamed medals and they are not usually offered for sale. An "official" correction unfortunately mars the appeal of a medal and hence affects the price. However some medals are very skilfully renamed with the sole intention of deceiving the unwary collector and dealer. This is especially so with rare and, therefore more expensive medals. The best advice is to use the check list given in this article and then, if still in doubt, consult a competent authority.

Figure 6

Figure 7

Figure 8

Figure 9

Figure 10

Figure 11

Figure 12

Figure 13

Figure 14

Taking
precautions

Like any other form of property, a collection of medals presents its owner with a variety of problems and responsibilities. No one in his right mind would rest easy, knowing that his house or motorcar were not protected by insurance. Indeed, in the latter case, insurance is both a wise precaution and a legal necessity. Yet, how often do we hear of numismatists who possess a really fine, often quite valuable, collection of medals but who have never taken the trouble to get it insured?

The usual argument is that insurance companies place so many obstacles in the way of the insurer, or that premiums are too high, or sometimes that it is just not worth the fuss and bother.

In many cases the antipathy towards insurance stems from a casual attitude. "This is my hobby," they say, "and it's only a bit of fun, a relaxation. If I have to start messing about with such boring matters as insurance, it would rob me of the pleasure of it." This cavalier approach is akin to the attitude of people, on being asked why they have not made a will, responding with some asperity, "Because I'm not at death's door". This completely misses the point, that the main object of making a will is because you have some property and wish to make some provision for its disposal in the (unlikely or hopefully long deferred) event of your death.

The emphasis should be on property and a sense of responsibility for it, rather than dwelling on eventualities that may never happen, or may not occur in the foreseeable future.

So, too, in the matter of insurance. People do not take out house or car insurance because they think their house is going to burn down or that they will be in a motorway pile-up. But these things do happen, and usually without any forewarning. Insurance is one of the methods we adopt to give ourselves some peace of mind.

The argument that premiums are too high is utterly fallacious. At most, they represent a very small percentage of the value of the items insured. It is an amazing fact that some collectors will happily fork out thousands of pounds on a single rarity, yet cavil at paying annual premiums of three figures on a collection worth a hundred times as much.

Normally those companies with whom you have your household contents insured will also extend cover to medal collections, provided that the value of the latter in proportion to other goods and chattels is not above a certain percentage. The practice in this regard varies from one company to another, so it pays to shop around and see what appears to be the most cost-effective deal on offer.

Where a collection of medals is coverable by the normal household policy there is usually a limit on the value of any single item. If you have a few medals which each exceed 10 per cent of the value of the

collection as a whole it will usually be necessary to get a special numismatic insurance policy to cover these items adequately. Many of the larger dealers and some auctioneers also act as valuers and insurance brokers, so it is worth while to consult them for precise details of terms and costs in each case.

The insurance company may then require an independent valuation set on the collection, particularly if it is a large and valuable one, and will appoint one of their accredited experts to carry out the assessment. The cost of these valuations is calculated either on the time involved or, more usually, as a percentage of the final value.

Valuations and insurance premiums are not cheap but, with medal thefts on the increase, no collector can afford to do without some safeguard against loss. Money may be small compensation for the loss of a collection which has taken a lifetime to build up and which contains so many irreplaceable items, but it is better than nothing at all and with the insurance money collected one can always start all over again.

In most cases, where the medal collection is of moderate value, no restriction will be placed by the insurance company on how it is stored, but in cases of very valuable collections or, more likely that relatively small portion of the collection wherein lies the greatest value, the insurer may insist on that part being kept in a fireproof steel safe, or even in a bank vault. This and other aspects of security will be discussed in much greater detail in a subsequent article in this series.

If the collection is a more modest one the insurance company may accept the owner's own valuation. In arriving at this figure it is important to remember that it is the replacement value of the collection which is required. A valuation based on the catalogue prices quoted in the *Medal Yearbook* or other price guides could be regarded as a starting point; on the other hand, some collectors tend to forget that medal values rise steadily and inexorably as the value of money falls, due to inflation, and thus they neglect to keep their valuations up to date.

This leads to the side issue of maintaining records which are invaluable for many purposes other than insurance. Not so long ago, keeping tabs on one's collection was a tedious and time-consuming process, involving notebooks and ledgers in which one could enter the details of each new acquisition, with a description noting the name and personal details of the recipient, bars or clasps and comments on condition or any distinguishing marks, catalogue number where relevant, price paid and date of purchase. A detailed record of this sort served as an inventory and, in the case of probate, would also help to establish whether any items were liable to estate duty.

In recent years, however, home computers have greatly simplified this task, to the point at which it is an easy matter to keep very detailed records and there is now no excuse for not compiling an accurate inventory which can quickly be duplicated in the dread event of burglary. It is also possible to reproduce medals and their ribbons by scanner accurately enough for identification purposes, and this is far cheaper than, and just as effective as, taking photographs of the more important items. Medal photography is a skill in itself, requiring a great deal of time and patience, apart from expensive equipment; so the modern system of digital cameras and computer scanners which enable you to store visual material on floppy disks is extremely useful for this purpose.

In the "bad old days", even the most detailed inventory was probably only revalued every five or six years, but now it is a simple matter to update it annually, thanks to the miracle of the personal computer. It is even possible to build into the program an automatic increase to cope with the annual rate of inflation or according to the Retail Price Index (RPI).

Even if you have not embraced the new technology, some form of inventory is a prerequisite. In its most basic form this might consist of a notebook, giving a brief description of the items, whether individual medals or groups, with catalogue numbers, and condition and physical peculiarities, if any. The date and cost of purchase should also be noted where practicable and such supporting documentation as auction descriptions and auctioneer's or dealer's invoices are useful.

This may not be necessary for items of moderate or low value, but where valuable items are concerned (say from £500 upwards and particularly for items costing £1,000 or more) there is a statutory requirement, under successive Finance Acts, to maintain records. This may become crucial in the event of subsequent disposal and the question of a possible capital gain arises. This is not just a matter of deducting the purchase price from the eventual selling price, but has to take account of such factors as the length of time the coin was in your possession, and variations in the RPI over that period, to arrive at the true value today, adjusted for inflation over the intervening period. For this reason it is advisable to obtain a bill of sale and to keep a file of all receipts where the sums involved are fairly large.

Apart from their usefulness to the insurance companies, medal inventories are of vital importance to executors. Many collectors, extremely efficient in their business or profession, have unfortunately been quite unbusinesslike where their hobby was concerned. Non-collectors seldom know how much money their partners lavish on their medals. In many cases they have regarded their partner's pastime with amused indulgence, partly condescending and partly tolerant, with little realisation of the value or importance of the asset which is being built up.

Taking out a fully comprehensive insurance policy to safeguard your collection, and revising the contents listing on a regular basis, is a good discipline, not only for the here and now but also for the hereafter.

Few people ever take a real interest in their partner's hobby and consequently when a collector dies, the surviving partner is often at a loss (a) to appreciate the value of the collection and (b) to know what to do with it. If you have spent a lot of money on your medals you owe it to your dependants to make an inventory (a copy of which should be kept with the collection and another filed somewhere safe and separate as a precaution in case of theft). A copy of the inventory should ideally be filed with your will and instructions to your executor regarding the eventual disposal of the collection. If possible, a numismatic executor should be appointed specifically for this purpose. In the "big league" those dealers who have given a great deal of time to building up a collection for a client often act as numismatic executors; but usually some close friend who shares the hobby will suffice. A few numismatic societies even provide a service to the families of deceased members, to ensure that the collection is properly disposed of.

If the collection is to be sold or auctioned off after the death of the owner, written instructions to that effect should be left with the numismatic executor and, if possible, a dealer or auctioneer nominated to handle the negotiations.

Glossary of
medal terms

There are a number of words used specifically by the medal collecting hobby, whilst others are borrowed from other areas. Some can cause confusion and many can be misunderstood by the beginner. To help the novice collector DENNIS G. BLAIR has listed some of the words which are regularly used in connection with medals.

Bar
(Sometimes referred to as clasp). An attachment indicating either : (a) campaigns—place, action or date; (b) service—duration or type; (c) gallantry decorations—a subsequent award. Usually attached to the medal suspender or preceding bar but sometimes direct to ribbon as on 1914 Star and WWII Stars.

Beading
String of embossed dots usually lining the rim, as on the Arctic Medal 1818–55.

Boxed
Within the original box of issue.

Brooch (fastening)
For securing a medal to clothing, e.g. buckle, as used with Royal Humane Society medals.

Brooched
A medal spoilt by having a pin soldered to its flan to convert it for wear as a brooch.

Campaign awards
Medal to participants in a campaign or battle.

Carriage
Back plate to a bar or clasp to contain the ribbon.

Cartouche
Ornamental plaque containing an inscription as on the Colonial Auxiliary Forces Long Service Medal.

Bars or clasps as affixed to the Crimea Medal (top), and the Indian Mutiny Medal.

Cast
Technique of forming a medal through the use of a mould and molten metal.

Centre stem
The pivot about which a swivel suspender turns.

Citation
Description of action accompanying an award for bravery.

Clasp
See "bar". Term also used to describe the bottom straight ribbon support used in conjunction with certain awards that have ring attachment, e.g. Victoria Cross.

Claw
Ornate connection between medal flan and suspender via a centre stem.

Clip
Plain link crimped on to a medal rim to which a ring suspender connects, e.g. Waterloo Medal.

Coat of Arms
Heraldic shield, with or without crest, mantling and supporters.

Coinage head
Monarch's portrait as occurring on respective contemporary coins, e.g. George V on the Mercantile Marine Medal 1914–19 obverse.

Commemorative
In honour of an occasion or person, e.g. Visit to Ireland 1900 Medal.

Conjoined
Two overlapping busts, as on the obverse of the Jubilee Medal 1935 (sometimes termed jugate).

Contact mark
Impact scar, usually caused by one medal jangling against another on the wearer's chest.

Converted
Having a pin or clip added to provide direct brooch fixing.

Copy
Replica made to replace a medal lost or stolen.

Cross
Device having four equal arms set at right angles. Most frequent forms being Greek (plain), Maltese (with flared sides and double points to the arms) or pattée (with flared sides).

Cord circlet
Rope like encircling ring as on the Royal Naval Long Service & Good Conduct Medal 2nd type.

Crowned effigy
Portrait of the monarch wearing a crown, as occurring on most British medal obverses.

Decoration
Award for meritorious or gallant conduct, e.g. Distinguished Service Order.

Defective
Not in original state, i.e. incomplete, renamed, damaged or otherwise spoilt.

Device
Symbolic emblem forming part of a design.

Documented
Formally recorded with details.

Duplicate
Official replacement for a lost medal.

Ears
Lugs at the ends of bars to receive a subsequent bar.

Edge
Outer rim of the flan, usually bearing recipient's details.

Edge-knock
Impact scar on the edge.

Emblem attachment
Attachment to the suspension ribbon to indicate class, or other distinction e.g. oak leaf denoting mentioned in despatches.

Embossed
With raised inscription/design.

Enamelled
Inlaid with a fired coloured vitreous coating, as embodied on the neck badge of the Most Eminent Order of the Indian Empire.

Engraved
With an incuse inscription added by hand or machine.

Erased
The deliberate removal of the naming or details from a medal's edge.

Essay Piece
Trial specimen taken during manufacture.

The exergue of the China Medal 1900.

Exergue
Segment below the reverse design often containing the date or an inscription.

Expedition Medals
Issued to those involved in an undertaking such as Polar exploration.

Faked
Having falsified details, e.g. renamed over erasure to convert an apparent common award to a rarity.

Field
Background area of the flan.

Filler Piece
"Temporary" specimen included in a collection pending a replacement proper.

Fishtail bar
Description given to the distinctively-shaped bars of the Second China War and Indian Mutiny medals.

Flan
The "disc body" of a medal.

Flaw
Defect in manufacture.

Forgery
A copy made to deceive.

Frosted
Matt finish often used on the field to contrast with polished highlighting.

Gallantry Award
For bravery, e.g. Military Medal.

Gazetted
Publicised in the *London Gazette*, official journal of the British government.

Ghost dates
Where dates have been officially removed but are still discernible, as on certain early Queen's South Africa Medals.

Grade
The condition in respect of wear. The symbols used are the same as those used for coin grading, e.g. EF, VF, etc.

Group
A number of medals awarded to one person.

Hallmark
The official impressed assay mark denoting gold or silver.

Impressed
Indented details applied usually to the edge or a panel on the reverse.

Incuse
Legend or design formed by indentation.

Inscription
Wording as part of or added to the design .

Jewel
Name applied to masonic medals.

Jugate
Another term for conjoined.

KIA
Abbreviation showing that the recipient was "Killed in Action".

Lacquered
Having a coating of clear lacquer added to protect the surface from oxidation.

Late issue
Deferred award (often due to delayed claim); may consequently not possess the original style or naming used.

Laureated
With laurel leaves design, e.g. as on reverse of the New Zealand Medals 1845–66.

Legend
Inscription on medal, usually round the circumference.

Long Service Award
An award for a period of unbroken service, often coupled with the requirement of Good Conduct in continuity.

Loop
Ring affixed to the rim of a medal for ribbon or cord attachment, e.g. as on Coorg Medal 1837.

Lunette contained
Within a watch style casing.

Medalet
Refers to pieces of 25mm diameter or less.

Medallion
Large piece not intended to be worn; often a prize or commemorative item.

Mention in Despatches
Recorded conduct from the theatre of war.

Miniature Medal
Piece reproduced approximately half full size, worn when full dress is inappropriate.

Moiré
Description given to watered silk ribbon, as used with the South Atlantic Medal.

Monogrammed
Embellished with representative initials, as upon the Second World War stars.

Motto
An inscribed maxim as on the Royal Humane Society medal for life saving.

Mounted
Method of wearing medals (in order of precedence) may be either "standard" whereby medals hang freely, or "royal style" (also termed court style), whereby medals are sewn to a back piece with the ribbons extending below their suspenders.

Named
Having the recipient's name, etc. (usually edge-impressed or engraved).

Native award
Issue to a native as against a member of Home Forces.

Oak leaf *indicating a Queen's Commendation for Valuable Service.*

Oak leaf
Emblem affixed to the ribbon to indicate extra merit, e.g. "mentioned in despatches".

Obverse
The side on display when being worn, usually bearing the Sovereign's effigy.

Officially corrected
When the name or other details have been amended by the issuing body.

Order
Insignia of certain revered brotherhoods, e.g. Most Honourable Order of the Bath.

Order badges
Insignia emblems worn in the manner of medals, also upon regalia accoutrements.

Ornament
Added embellishment to provide design balance.

Pair
Two medals awarded to one person.

Patinated
Oxidation formed on the surface of bronze and copper medals in particular.

Pattern
Model used to enable the making of moulds and dies.

Pierced
With a hole drilled through, usually for unofficial suspension fitting.

Pitted
Surface spoiling by minute holes, caused by chemical attack or contact from another medal.

Planchet
Blank metal disc from which a medal is struck.

Plated
With a thin coating of metal applied, usually silver or gold.

Plugged
Having a hole made good by filling.

Polished
Excessively shined-up, resulting in loss of highlight detail.

Posthumous award
Issued after death.

Privately engraved
Engraved unofficially.

Prize medal
Award for personal achievement (e.g. academic) or competition success (e.g. sport).

Proficiency medal
Award for achieving a recognised standard in a particular specialisation, e.g. those awarded by the British Red Cross Society.

Radiant star
Formed with emanating rays, as upon the Most Noble Order of the Garter star.

Regimentally named
Engraved or impressed after issue through the recipient's regiment.

Relief
Raised design or legend/inscription.

Renamed
When original naming has been removed and other naming substituted.

Researched
Checked out against roll and records.

Restored
When a defective medal has been fully repaired or any missing parts replaced.

Restrike
Copy produced from original dies subsequent to original issue.

Reverse
The back of a medal not seen when being worn.

Riband bar
Strip (10mm deep) faced with medal ribbons worn to show medals awarded.

Ribbon
Strip of fabric for suspender attachment, and of respective colour/s to suit each particular medal.

Ribbon roller
The rod of a suspender over which the ribbon passes.

Rim
Raised outer ring to a medal's edge.

Rimless
When the edge is on the same plane as the field, e.g. Victory Medal of World War I.

Roll
Official list of those to whom a medal/bar has been awarded.

Roses
Ornamental florets on certain bars serving to conceal rivet fixings, as on Indian General Service Medals.

Rosette
Rose emblem attached to ribbons of medals to indicate distinguishing factor, as on the South Atlantic Medal denoting close action involvement.

Roundel
Design contained within a circle, as on the Order of Burma.

Saltire
A diagonal cross, as on the sash badge of the Most Illustrious Order of St Patrick.

Scroll
Ribbon-like device containing an inscription, often a date, as on the 1914 Star.

Series
An ordered succession of medals of like category, e.g. the Indian General Service Medals.

Set
A complete assembly of a theme of collection, e.g. all combinations of bars issued for one campaign.

Shaded ribbon
Description of the colours merging into each other, instead of appearing as separate stripes, e.g. Scinde Campaign medals 1843.

Skeletal
Of open design, e.g. the Territorial Decoration.

Specimen
Medal struck contemporary with the original manufacture but not intended for issue.

Stain
Localised permanent surface discoloration.

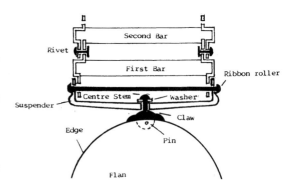

Diagram of medal with swivel suspender, showing assembly of components.

Star
Stellar shaped award, e.g. Kimberley Star 1899–1900.

Struck
Technique of medal manufacture by stamping the blank piece between two dies.

Suspender
Means by which a medal is attached to its ribbon. It may be swivel or fixed, straight, horn or scroll shaped, floreate or otherwise ornate.

Tablet
Inscribed plaque panel, often integrated as a base for a design, as on the Queen's Sudan Medal.

Tailor's copy
Also referred as jeweller's copy, a fair reproduction made up as a dress piece.

Temperance medal
Reward for recorded abstinence to encourage continuance.

Toning
The natural darkening of silver occurring with age and exposure.

Tooled
Touch-up work effected with a chasing tool.

Tressure
An ornamental border following the rim as on the reverse of George V Coronation Medals.

Trio
Three medals awarded to the one person and usually referring to First World War medals.

Trophy of arms
Design showing an assembly of armaments representative of the defeated enemy's weaponry.

Uniface
With design on one side only.

Unnamed
Issued without indication of the recipient's name.

Verdigris
Damaging greenish deposit which can form on copper in particular.

Wreath
Representing a ring of foliage, e.g. as on the reverse of the Territorial Force War Medal 1914–19.

Wearing awards

The wearing of Orders, Decorations and Medals is a complex subject too complicated to cover in a publication such as this. However, there a number of questions that collectors frequently ask, so we have attempted to deal with these as fully as possible.

Full-size Awards Mounted for Wear

Orders, decorations and medals are worn on the left breast in a line suspended from a single brooch mount or a rectangular frame (court mounted), the latter gives a firmer grip which occasions less damage than medals hanging more loosely from a brooch. The brooch/frame is covered by the medal ribbons. The most senior medal (see the following Order of Precedence) is furthest from the left shoulder. The obverse of the medals should show (this will usually be the sovereign's head, coat of arms, cypher, etc.).

If more than five medals are worn (three for the Navy), they should not be suspended side by side, but overlapped, the senior medal and ribbon is the one to be positioned so it can be seen completely. Medals should be lined up straight by the bottom rim/point, the length of ribbon should be one and a quarter inches (33mm) from the top of the mount to the first clasp or the suspension, which ever is appropriate (one and three quarters (45mm) for the Navy). Where the awards differ in size then a ribbon adjustment will be necessary to ensure a straight line.

Mentions-in-Despatches emblems should be worn on the relevant campaign medal, for example on the Victory Medal for the First World War and the War Medal 1939–45 for the Second World War. Where a recipient has no relevant campaign medal, the MID emblem is worn directly on the coat after any medal ribbons, or if no ribbons then in the position of a single ribbon.

There are a number of awards for which the sovereign has granted permission that they be worn on the right breast:

Royal Humane Society Medals
Stanhope Gold Medal
Royal National Lifeboat Institution Medal
Order of St John of Jerusalem Life Saving Medal.

Foreign Order, Decorations and Medals

The British sovereign's subjects are not permitted to accept and wear the orders, decorations and medals of a foreign country of which the sovereign is not head of state. Application can be made for wear and permission is of two types: (a) restricted, that is instructions are given as to the exact occasions on which the award(s) may be worn; (b) unrestricted which allows the item(s) to be worn on all occasions according to the Order of Precedence, that is, generally speaking, arranged after British awards by date—first orders, then decorations, followed by medals (there are exceptions for the members of the armed services serving in an overseas force and receive that country's awards).

Awards are worn on a variety of State, evening or other occasions and the rules governing the wearing of orders according to dress are quite detailed. The subject is covered fully in Medals Will Be Worn *by Lieutenant Colonel Ashley R. Tinson (Token Publishing Ltd., 1999) and in* Spink's Guide to the Wearing of Orders, Decorations and Medals *(Spink, 1990).*

The order of precedence

The Order of Precedence, or the order in which decorations and medals should be worn in the United Kingdom and the Commonwealth, is set out below, as announced by the Central Chancery of the Orders of Knighthood.

Victoria Cross
George Cross
Most Noble Order of the Garter
Most Ancient and Most Noble Order of the Thistle
Most Illustrious Order of St. Patrick
Knights Grand Cross, The Most Honourable Order of the Bath (GCB)
Order of Merit
Baronet's Badge
Knight Grand Commander, The Most Exalted Order of the Star of India (GCSI)
Knights Grand Cross, The Most Distinguished Order of St. Michael and St. George (GCMG)
Knight Grand Commander, The Most Eminent Order of the Indian Empire (GCIE)
The Order of the Crown of India
Knights Grand Cross, The Royal Victorian Order (GCVO)
Knights Grand Cross, The Most Excellent Order of the British Empire (GBE)
Order of the Companions of Honour (CH)
Knight Commander, The Most Honourable Order of the Bath (KCB)
Knight Commander, The Most Exalted Order of the Star of India (KCSI)
Knight Commander, The Most Distinguished Order of St. Michael and St. George (KCMG)
Knight Commander, The Most Eminent Order of the Indian Empire (KCIE)
Knight Commander, The Royal Victorian Order (KCVO)
Knight Commander, The Most Excellent Order of the British Empire (KBE)
Knight Bachelor's Badge
Companion, The Most Honourable Order of the Bath (CB)
Companion, The Most Exalted Order of the Star of India (CSI)
Companion, The Most Distinguished Order of St. Michael and St. George (CMG)
Companion, The Most Eminent Order of the Indian Empire (CIE)
Commander, The Royal Victorian Order (CVO)
Commander, The Most Excellent Order of the British Empire (CBE)
Distinguished Service Order (DSO)
Lieutenant, The Royal Victorian Order (LVO)
Officer, The Most Excellent Order of the British Empire (OBE)

Imperial Service Order (ISO)
Member, The Royal Victorian Order (MVO)
Member, The Most Excellent Order of the British Empire (MBE)
Indian Order of Merit—Military

DECORATIONS
Conspicuous Gallantry Cross
Royal Red Cross, Class 1
Distinguished Service Cross
Military Cross
Distinguished Flying Cross
Air Force Cross
Royal Red Cross, Class II
Order of British India
Kaisar-I-Hind Medal
Order of St John

GALLANTRY AND DISTINGUISHED CONDUCT MEDALS
Union of South Africa Queen's Medal for Bravery in gold
Distinguished Conduct Medal
Conspicuous Gallantry Medal
Conspicuous Gallantry Medal (Flying)
George Medal
Queen's Police Medal for Gallantry
Queen's Fire Service Medal for Gallantry
Royal West African Frontier Force Distinguished Conduct Medal
King's African Rifles Distinguished Conduct Medal
Indian Distinguished Service Medal
Union of South Africa Queen's Medal for Bravery in silver
Distinguished Service Medal
Military Medal
Distinguished Flying Medal
Air Force Medal
Medal for Saving Life at Sea
Indian Order of Merit (Civil)
Indian Police Medal for Gallantry
Ceylon Police Medal for Gallantry
Sierra Leone Police Medal for Gallantry
Sierra Leone Fire Brigades Medal for Gallantry
Colonial Police Medal for Gallantry
Queen's Gallantry Medal
Royal Victorian Medal (gold, silver and bronze)
British Empire Medal
Canada Medal

43

Queen's Police Medal for Distinguished Service
Queen's Fire Service Medal for Distinguished Service
Queen's Medal for Chiefs
War Medals, including the UN Medals—in order of
date of campaign for which awarded
Polar Medals—in order of date of award
Imperial Service Medal

POLICE MEDALS FOR VALUABLE SERVICE

Indian Police Medal for Meritorious Service
Ceylon Police Medal for Merit
Sierra Leone Police Medal for Meritorious Service
Sierra Leone Fire Brigades Medal for Meritorious
Service
Colonial Police Medal for Meritorious Service
Badge of Honour

JUBILEE, CORONATION, DURBAR MEDALS

Queen Victoria's Jubilee Medal 1887 (gold, silver and
bronze)
Queen Victoria's Police Jubilee Medal 1887
Queen Victoria's Jubilee Medal 1897 (gold, silver and
bronze)
Queen Victoria's Police Jubilee Medal 1897
Queen Victoria's Commemoration Medal 1900
(Ireland)
King Edward VII's Coronation 1902
King Edward VII's Police Coronation 1902
King Edward VII's Durbar 1903 (gold, silver and
bronze)
King Edward VII's Police Medal 1903 (Scotland)
King's Visit Commemoration Medal 1903 (Ireland)
King George V's Coronation Medal 1911
King George V's Police Coronation Medal 1911
King George V's Visit Police Commemoration Medal
1911 (Ireland)
King George V's Durbar Medal 1911 (gold, silver and
bronze)
King George V's Silver Jubilee Medal 1935
King George VI's Coronation Medal 1937
Queen Elizabeth II's Coronation Medal 1953
Queen Elizabeth II's Silver Jubilee Medal 1977
King George V's Long and Faithful Service Medal
King George VI's Long and Faithful Service Medal
Queen Elizabeth II's Long and Faithful Service
Medal

EFFICIENCY AND LONG SERVICE
DECORATIONS AND MEDALS

Medal for Meritorious Service
Accumulated Campaign Service Medal
The Medal for Long Service and Good Conduct,
Army
Naval Long Service and Good Conduct Medal
Medal for Meritorious Service (Royal Navy 1918–28)
Indian Long Service and Good Conduct Medal (for
Europeans of Indian Army)
Indian Meritorious Service Medal (for Europeans of
Indian Army)
Royal Marines Meritorious Service Medal (1849–1947
Royal Air Force Meritorious Service Medal 1918–28
Royal Air Force Long Service and Good Conduct
Medal
Ulster Defence Regiment Long Service and Good
Conduct Medal

Indian Long Service and Good Conduct Medal
(Indian Army)
Royal West African Frontier Force Long Service and
Good Conduct Medal
Royal Sierra Leone Military Forces Long Service and
Good Conduct Medal
King's African Rifles Long Service and Good Conduct
Medal
Indian Meritorious Service Medal (for Indian Army)
Police Long Service and Good Conduct Medal
Fire Brigade Long Service and Good Conduct Medal
African Police Medal for Meritorious Service
Royal Canadian Mounted Police Long Service Medal
Ceylon Police Long Service Medal
Ceylon Fire Services Long Service Medal
Sierra Leone Police Long Service Medal
Colonial Police Long Service Medal
Sierra Leone Fire Brigade Long Service Medal
Mauritius Police Long Service and Good Conduct
Medal
Mauritius Fire Service Long Service and Good
Conduct Medal
Mauritius Prisons Service Long Service and Good
Conduct Medal
Colonial Fire Brigades Long Service Medal
Colonial Prison Service Medal
Army Emergency Reserve Decoration
Volunteer Officers' Decoration
Volunteer Long Service Medal
Volunteer Officers' Decoration (for India and the
Colonies)
Volunteer Long Service Medal (for India and the
Colonies)
Colonial Auxiliary Forces Officers' Decoration
Colonial Auxiliary Forces Long Service Medal
Medal for Good Shooting (Naval)
Militia Long Service Medal
Imperial Yeomanry Long Service Medal
Territorial Decoration
Ceylon Armed Service Long Service Medal
Efficiency Decoration
Territorial Efficiency Medal
Efficiency Medal
Special Reserve Long Service and Good Conduct Medal
Decoration for Officers of the Royal Naval Reserve
Decoration for Officers of the Royal Naval Volunteer
Reserve
Royal Naval Reserve Long Service and Good
Conduct Medal
Royal Naval Volunteer Reserve Long Service and
Good Conduct Medal
Royal Naval Auxiliary Sick Berth Reserve Long
Service and Good Conduct Medal
Royal Fleet Reserve Long Service and Good Conduct
Medal
Royal Naval Wireless Auxiliary Reserve Long Service
and Good Conduct Medal
Royal Naval Auxiliary Service Medal
Air Efficiency Award
Ulster Defence Regiment Medal
Queen's Medal (for Champion Shots of the Royal
Navy and Royal Marines)
Queen's Medal (for Champion Shots of the New
Zealand Naval Forces)
Queen's Medal (for Champion Shots in the Military
Forces)

Queen's Medal (for Champion Shots of the Air Force)
Cadet Forces Medal
Coast Guard Auxiliary Service Long Service Medal
Special Constabulary Long Service Medal
Canadian Forces Decoration
Royal Observer Corps Medal
Civil Defence Long Service Medal
Rhodesia Medal
Royal Ulster Constabulary Service Medal
Union of South Africa Commemoration Medal
Indian Independence Medal
Pakistan Medal
Ceylon Armed Services Inauguration Medal
Ceylon Police Independence Medal (1948)
Sierra Leone Independence Medal
Jamaica Independence Medal
Uganda Independence Medal
Malawi Independence Medal

Fiji Independence Medal
Papua New Guinea Independence Medal
Solomon Islands Independence Medal
Service Medal of the Order of St. John
Badge of the Order of the League of Mercy
Voluntary medical Service Medal
Women's Voluntary Service Medal
South African Medal for War Services
Colonial Special Constabulary Medal
Honorary Membership of Commonwealth Orders
    (instituted by the Sovereign, in order of date of award)
Other Commonwealth Members, orders, Decorations
    and Medals (instituted since 1949 otherwise than
    by the Sovereign, and awards by States of
    Malaysia and Brunei in order of date of award)
Foreign Orders in order of date of award
Foreign Decorations in order of date of award
Foreign Medals in order of date of award

THE ORDER IN WHICH CAMPAIGN STARS AND MEDALS AWARDED FOR SERVICE DURING WORLD WAR I AND II ARE WORN

1914 Star with dated "Mons" clasp "15th AUGUST–
    22nd NOVEMBER 1914"
1914 Star
1914/15 Star
British War Medal
Mercantile Marine Medal
Victory Medal
Territorial Force War Medal

1939/45 Star
Atlantic Star
Air Crew Europe Star
Africa Star

Pacific Star
Burma Star
Italy Star
France and Germany Star
Defence Medal
Canadian/Newfoundland Volunteer Service Medal
1939/45 War Medal
1939/45 Africa Service Medal of the Union of South
    Africa
India Service Medal
New Zealand War Service Medal
Southern Rhodesia Service Medal
Australian Service Medal

POST-NOMINAL LETTERS

Recipients of some awards are entitled to use post-nominal letters including the following:

VC	Victoria Cross
GC	George Cross
KG	Knight, Most Noble Order of the Garter
KT	Knight, Most Ancient and Most Noble Order of the Thistle
KP	Knight, Most Illustrious Order of St Patrick
GCB	Knight Grand Cross, The Most Honourable Order of the Bath
OM	Order of Merit
GCSI	Knight Grand Commander, The Most Exalted Order of the Star of India
GCMG	Knight Grant Cross—The Most Distinguished Order of St Michael and St George
GCIE	Knight Grand Commander. The Most Eminent Order of the Indian Empire
CI	The Order of the Crown of India (women only)
GCVO	Knight Grand Cross, The Royal Victorian Order
GBE	Knight Grand Cross, The Most Excellent Order of the British Empire
CH	Order of the Companion of Honour
KCB	Knight Commander, The Most Honourable Order of the Bath

DCB	Dame Commander, The Most Honourable Order of the Bath
KCSI	Knight Commander, The Most Exalted Order of the Star of India
KCMG	Knight Commander, The Most Distinguished Order of St Michael and St George
DCMG	Dame Commander, The Most Distinguished Order of St Michael and St George
KCIE	Knight Commander, The Most Eminent Order of the Indian Empire
KCVO	Knight Commander, The Royal Victorian Order
DCVO	Dame Commander, The Royal Victorian Order
KBE	Knight Commander, The Most Excellent Order of the British Empire
DBE	Dame Commander, The Most Excellent Order of the British Empire
CB	Companion, The Most Honourable Order of the Bath
CSI	Companion, The Most Exalted Order of the Star of India

CMG	Companion, The Most Distinguished Order of St Michael and St George	DCM	Distinguished Conduct Medal (West Africa Frontier Force)
CIE	Companion, The Most Eminent Order of the Indian Empire	DCM	Distinguished Conduct Medal (King's African Rifles)
CVO	Commander, The Royal Victorian Order	IDSM	Indian Distinguished Service Medal
CBE	Commander, The Most Excellent Order of the British Empire	BGM	Burma Gallantry Medal
		DSM	Distinguished Service Medal
DSO	Distinguished Service Order	MM	Military Medal
LVO	Lieutenant, The Royal Victorian Order	DFM	Distinguished Flying Medal
OBE	Officer, The Most Excellent Order of the British Empire	AFM	Air Force Medal
		SGM	Sea Gallantry Medal
QSO	Queen's Service Order (NZ)	IOM	Indian Order of Merit (civil)
ISO	Imperial Service Order	CPM	Colonial Police Medal (gallantry)
MVO	Member, The Royal Victorian Order	QGM	Queen's Gallantry Medal
MBE	Member, The Most Excellent Order of the British Empire	QSM	Queen's Service Medal
		RVM	Royal Victorian Medal
IOM	Indian Order of Merit (military)	BEM	British Empire Medal
OB	Order of Burma (gallantry)	CM/M DU C	Canada Medal
CGC	Conspicuous Gallantry Cross	QPM	Queen's Police Medal (distinguished service)
RRC	Royal Red Cross First Class		
DSC	Distinguished Service Cross	QFSM	Queen's Fire Service Medal (distinguished service)
MC	Military Cross		
DFC	Distinguished Flying Cross	CPMSM	Colonial Police Medal for Meritorious Service
AFC	Air Force Cross		
ARRC	Royal Red Cross, Second Class	MSM	Meritorious Service Medal (Navy, awards up to 20.7.28)
OBI	Order of British India		
OB	Order of Burma (distinguished service)	ERD	Army Emergency Reserve Decoration
AM	Albert Medal	VD	Volunteer Officers' Decoration
DCM	Distinguished Conduct Medal	TD	Territorial Decoration
CGM	Conspicuous Gallantry Medal	ED	Efficiency Decoration
GM	George Medal	RD	Royal Naval Reserve Decoration
KPM	King's Police Medal (gallantry)	VRD	Royal Naval Volunteer Reserve Decoration
QPM	Queen's Police Medal (gallantry)	AE	Air Efficiency Award (officers)
KFSM	King's Fire Service Medal (gallantry)	UD	Ulster Defence Regiment Medal (officers)
QFSM	Queen's Fire Service Medal (gallantry)	CD	Canadian (Forces) Decoration
EM	Edward Medal	QVRM	Queen's Volunter Reserves Medal
		VRSM	Volunter Reserves Service Medal

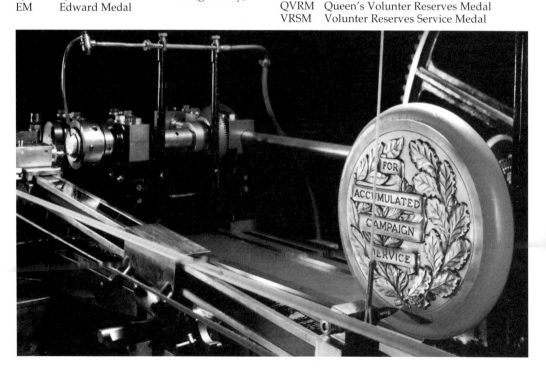

Collecting
medal ribbons

There is nothing new or old about collecting medal ribbons, in fact the founders of the present Orders and Medals Research Society originally set out as medal ribbon collectors. The ribbon has, ever since the early 18th century, been an important complement to the medal or badge of an order and its importance has grown over the years. Since those early orders of chivalry when it was deemed necessary to identify the various religious or secular orders one belonged to by the colour of its ribbon, the emphasis has been on the ribbon to identify the order or medal. This practice has continued down through the centuries, even to today when the avid enthusiast can recognise a warriors medals simply be identifying his ribbons.

However, times are changing. The practice of wearing medals is on the decline, reserved only for ceremonial occasions, whilst the wearing of ribbon bars and the awarding of a single campaign or service medal with different ribbons to denote specific operations is on the increase. Our very own Operational Service Medal (OSM), the NATO medal and of course the plethora of United Nations medals are all classic examples of today's expansion of the medal ribbon. There is of course the growing cost of collecting medals and decorations compared to that of medal ribbons. There is also the down side to all of this, as the opportunity to acquire medal ribbons has become a challenge to many, as sources such as tailor shops, small ribbon manufacturers or numerous regimental or quartermasters stores have all gone into decline, if not altogether vanished.

Before one can collect ribbons properly one must first be able to identify them. It is therefore important to have a reasonable reference library— nothing elaborate or expansive is needed. It is probably wise to start collecting ribbons of the United Kingdom before branching out into those of other countries. There are several good books on the subject and ribbons can be obtained quite easily.

The more one handles ribbons the quicker one starts to get a feel for the subject and gets to know which colours are used by certain countries or organisations, whether they always use silk or fine cottons, prefer moiré (watered) or corded ribbons whether they use wide or narrow ribbons, all are skills one picks up along the way, though sadly this art is slowly dying as the quality of many modern manufactured ribbons is really quite poor compared to the silk watered ribbons of bygone days.

Once over the initial teething problems of deciding how to store ribbons and ultimately mount or display them, the desire to expand and even specialise creeps in. Do you collect ribbons from just one country, state or organisation such as the Red Cross or the United Nations? Campaign medals and their numerous emblems? Famous chests? Regimental battle streamers? Religious or chivalric orders past and present? British or foreign orders and their various rosettes? The choice can be endless. Whatever the path you choose, you will almost certainly have to do a little research to obtain the reason for the award and the colours adopted for the ribbon. In reality, a true ribbon collector will know just as much about the medal or decoration as they will about the ribbon. Depending on the amount of time you have, research can lead you to museums, reading rooms or even portrait galleries, as well as societies such as the Ribbon Branch of the Orders and Medals Research Society. But whatever path is chosen you will be in awe of the sacrifices made by mankind down the centuries.

Miniature medals and decorations

The collecting of miniature medals has gained in popularity over the past few years and as a result groups and single miniatures that were once sold with their full-size counterparts, as an added extra, are now being traded in their own right. The market prices for these attractive and often superbly-produced little pieces are included in the catalogue section. Collectors wishing to learn more about miniature medals are invited to contact the Miniature Medals Branch of the Orders & Medals Research Society whose address can be found opposite.

Miniatures are small versions of orders, decorations and medals designed for formal evening wear. The custom appears to have developed in Continental Europe in the early years of the 18th century, but is now more or less universal, although the actual practice varies from country to country. In the United Kingdom, for example, miniatures are confined to mess kit and evening dress (white tie and tails), whereas in the United States it is quite common to see miniatures worn with dinner jackets. In Europe, miniatures are often worn without ribbons, suspended from a tiny chain, but in Britain and elsewhere miniatures are worn with exact replicas of the appropriate ribbons correspondingly reduced in size.

The scale of miniatures likewise varies from country to country. In Britain miniatures are usually half the size of the full-sized medals, but the Scandinavian countries use a 17mm size, while France and the Low Countries prefer a 14mm size, calculated from the diameter of medals or the badges of orders.

In the 18th and early 19th centuries the breast stars of orders were also worn in miniature, but nowadays only the badges of the orders are miniaturised. In Europe the higher classes of orders are designated by placing wings in silver, gold and silver, or gold, according to the class, below the rosette on the riband of the Officer Class. In Britain, however, miniatures are exact replicas of the badges they represent, and no additional rosettes or emblems are added to the ribands to denote a particular class.

Miniatures differ in one major respect from the full-scale; whereas the latter were produced by specific contractors, the former have been manufactured by many jewellers and goldsmiths. Consequently, the quality may vary considerably, from a very faithful replica (doubtless produced by the same firm that made the originals and using scaled-down dies for the purpose), to quite crude imitations that differ in many details from the full sized version. In many instances, miniature medal groups may be found with the original case as supplied by the jeweller, so that identification is not a problem. Many other groups, however, have long since parted company from their presentation cases, and identification is then only possible from other factors, either stylistic or from marks. Some miniatures are hallmarked (i.e. they bear the punches of an assay office and the mark of the manufacturer), and in such cases the miniature can not only be identified, but even the date of manufacture adduced from the year letter. Not all miniatures by any means are hallmarked, especially if they fall below the statutory minimum weight, so that this aid to identification is not always present.

The value placed on miniatures is governed by condition, of course, but other factors that must be taken into consideration are the provenance and authenticity of the medal or group. Miniatures which are contemporary with the original award are rated more highly than replacements procured many years later. And miniature groups which can definitely be assigned to a particular recipient are worth a premium over those whose original owner cannot be determined. Unlike the full-scale originals, miniatures very seldom bear the name of the recipient. Nevertheless, this is a fascinating aspect of medal collecting, much less expensive than the full-size medals but often as rewarding for the human interest which miniatures represent.

A note on the pricing of miniatures

HAPPILY, I am able to say that the collecting of Miniature Medals continues apace, with a steady flow of new collectors coming on stream. An interesting adjunct is the growing number of people wanting to replicate, in miniature, the medals awarded to fathers or grandfathers in the last two world conflicts. As these do not include 19th century miniatures, they do not come within the scope of my warning, given in the 1999 issue of the MEDAL YEARBOOK, of made up groups being offered for sale. Alarmingly, however, miniature VC groups continue to appear and should be treated with caution.

Prices continue to vary widely, so shopping around, if not physically, by at least scanning the various price lists, would be prudent practice, as a difference as much as £100 can be found on a miniature of comparable quality valued at £20. A further disturbing observation is the appearance of good quality reproductions of early miniatures and scarce clasps in silver which are not easy to detect unless compared against a genuine item. So be aware.

Prices generally have stabilised over this last year and shopping around is recommended to get the best value for money. In spite of the above warnings, do collect for enjoyment and not solely as an investment.

Mark Cline
Proprietor of MC Miniature Medals
Immediate Past President, Miniature Medals Branch, OMRS

For further information on the collecting of miniature medals, readers are invited to contact:

The Honorary Secretary
The Miniature Medals Branch
Orders and Medals Research Society
54 Priory Bridge Road
Taunton
Somerset
TA1 1QB

Orders
of Chivalry

The most colourful and romantic of all awards are those connected with the orders of chivalry. Many of them have their origins in the Middle Ages, when knights in armour formed the elite fighting force in every European country. This was the period when knights jousted in tournaments as a pastime, between going off to the Holy Land on the wars of Christendom known as the Crusades. This was the era of such popular heroes as Richard the Lionheart, William the Lion, Robert the Bruce, the Black Prince, Pepin of Herstal and John the Blind King of Bohemia. Their exploits have passed into the folklore of Europe, together with the legends of Roland and his Paladins or King Arthur and the Knights of the Round Table.

From the idea of a select band of knights, pledged to the support of a king or an ideal (usually religious), sprang the orders of chivalry. Many of these existed in the Middle Ages but most of them died out as feudalism went into decline. In some cases they survived; in others they disappeared for centuries, only to be resurrected at a later date. Still others were devised and instituted in relatively modern times, and indeed, continue to evolve. For example, Canada instituted the Order of Canada in 1967 and both Australia and New Zealand introduced their own orders in 1975.

In their original form membership of the orders of chivalry were just as highly coveted as they are today, but the insignia was usually simple or even non-existent. The complicated system of insignia which now surrounds these orders is fairly modern, dating from the 16th century or later. Nowadays most orders also exist in several classes, with the insignia becoming increasingly elaborate with each higher class.

Britain's senior order is the Garter, and although it consists of one class only it provides a good example of the pomp and ceremony which often surrounds these awards. It was founded by King Edward III and is said to derive its name from the fact that the King was attending a dance one day, when a lady's garter slipped from her leg and fell to the floor. To save her the embarrassment of retrieving her garter—and thus letting everyone know it was hers—the King himself picked it up and tied it round his own leg. Lest anyone should doubt that it was his garter he said, in court French, "Let evil be to him who evil thinks". From this curious incident came the idea of a very exclusive order of knighthood, consisting of the sovereign and 26 knights.

The insignia of this order consists of a Garter, a mantle of blue velvet lined with taffeta with the star of the Order embroidered on the left breast, a hood of crimson velvet, a surcoat of crimson velvet lined with white taffeta, a hat of black velvet lined with white taffeta, with a plume of white ostrich and black heron feathers fastened by a band of diamonds, a collar of gold composed of buckled garters and lovers' knots with red roses, the George (an enamelled figure of St George slaying the dragon) suspended from the collar, the

Lesser George or badge, worn from a broad blue sash passing over the left shoulder to the right hip, and the star, a silver eight-pointed decoration bearing the red cross of St George surrounded by the garter and motto.

The insignia is exceptionally elaborate, the other orders of chivalry varying considerably in their complexity according to the class of the order. The full insignia is only worn on special occasions. In the case of the Garter usually the Lesser George and the breast star are worn on their own.

On the death of a Knight of the Garter the insignia must be returned to the Central Chancery of Orders of Knighthood, and therefore few examples of the Garter ever come on to the market. Those that do are usually examples from the 17th and 18th centuries when regulations regarding the return of insignia were not so strict. In the case of the lesser orders, insignia is returnable on promotion to a higher class. All collar chains are returnable, although that of the Order of St Michael and St George could be retained prior to 1948.

British orders are manufactured by firms holding contracts from the Central Chancery of Orders of Knighthood, and the values quoted in this Yearbook are for the official issues. It should be noted, however, that holders of orders frequently have replicas of breast stars made for use on different uniforms and it is sometimes difficult to tell these replicas from the originals as in many cases the replicas were made by the court jewellers responsible for making the originals. In addition, many jewellers in such European capitals as Vienna, Berlin and Paris have a long tradition of manufacturing the insignia of orders for sale to collectors.

The badges and breast stars of orders of chivalry are very seldom named to the recipient and therefore lack the personal interest of campaign medals and many gallantry awards. For this reason they do not command the same interest or respect of collectors. Nevertheless, in cases where the insignia of orders can be definitely proved to have belonged to some famous person, the interest and value are enhanced. In any case, these orders are invariably very attractive examples of the jeweller's art, and they often possess titles and stories as colourful and romantic as their appearance.

1. THE MOST NOBLE ORDER OF THE GARTER

KG Star
(a Victorian example)

Instituted: 1348.

Ribbon: 100mm plain dark blue. Not worn in undress uniform.

Garter: Dark blue velvet. Two versions may be encountered, with embroidered lettering and other details, or with gold lettering, buckle and tab. Worn on the left leg by gentlemen and on the left forearm by laides.

Collar Chain: Gold composed of alternate buckled garters, each encircling a red enamelled rose, and lovers' knots in gold although sometimes enamelled white.

Collar badge: An enamelled figure of St George fighting the dragon.

Star: Originally always embroidered in metal thread, a style which continues in the mantle to this day. Prior to 1858 knights often purchased metal stars in addition and since that date metal stars have been officially issued. These consist of a silver eight-pointed radiate star bearing in its centre and red cross of St George on a white ground, surrounded by the garter and motto HONI SOIT QUI MAL Y PENSE (evil be who evil thinks).

Sash Badge: The Lesser George, similar to the collar badge but encircled by an oval garter bearing the motto.

Comments: *Membership of the Order of the Garter is confined to the reigning sovereign, the Prince of Wales and 25 other Knights, and is the personal gift of the monarch. In addition to the 25 Knights there have, from time to time, been extra Knights, occasionally non-Christians such as the Sultans of Turkey or the Emperor of Japan. The Emperor Hirohito, incidentally had the dubious distinction of being the only person awarded the Garter twice: in 1922 and again in 1971, having forfieted the original award as a result of the Japanese entry into the Second World War in 1941. Sir Winston Churchill was invested with the insignia originally presented in 1702 to his illustrious ancestor, the Duke of Marlborough. All official insignia is returnable to the Central Chancery of Knighthood on the death of the holder. Ladies (other than royalty) are now eligible for the Order.*

Lesser George
(this early example has the garter enamelled in blue)

VALUE:

Collar chain	Rare
Collar badge (the George)	£50,000–100,000*
Star (in metal)	£1500–5000
Star (embroidered)	£400–1000
Mantle star	£500–600
Sash badge (Lesser George)	£3000–40,000
Garter (embroidered)	£300–500
Garter (gold lettering and buckle)	£1200–2500

Miniature

Star (metal)	£150–200

*Prices are for privately made examples many of which are jewelled and enamelled.

2. THE MOST ANCIENT AND MOST NOBLE ORDER OF THE THISTLE

KT Star

Instituted: 1687.

Ribbon: 100mm plain dark green. Not worn in undress uniform.

Collar Chain: Gold of alternate thistles and sprigs of rue enamelled in proper colours.

Collar Badge: The jewel is a gold and enamelled figure of St Andrew in a green gown and purple surcoat, bearing before him a white saltire cross, the whole surrounded by rays of gold.

Star: Silver, consisting of a St Andrew's cross, with other rays issuing between the points of the cross and, in the centre, on a gold background, a thistle enamelled in proper colours surrounded by a green circle bearing the Latin motto NEMO ME IMPUNE LACESSIT (no one assails me with impunity)

Sash Badge: The medal of the Order is a gold figure of St Andrew bearing before him a saltire cross, surrounded by an oval collar bearing the motto, surmounted by a gold cord fitted with a ring for suspension. Examples are found in plain gold, or with enamelling and/or set with jewels.

Comments: *This order is said to have been founded in AD 787, alluding to barefoot enemy soldiers who cried out when they trod on thistles and thus alerted the Scots of an imminent attack. The order had long been defunct when it was revived by King James VII and II and re-established in December 1703 by Queen Anne. It now consists of the sovereign and 16 Knights, making it the most exclusive of the orders of chivalry. At death, the official insignia is returned to the Central Chancery. Ladies (other than royalty) are now eligible for the Order.*

VALUE:

Collar chain	Rare
Collar badge	Rare
Star (metal)	£1500–4000
Star (embroidered)	£400–600
Mantle star	£500–1000
Sash badge	£5000–8000
Miniature	
Star (metal)	£250–300

Examples of Sash Badges

3. THE MOST ILLUSTRIOUS ORDER OF ST PATRICK

KP Star

Sash badge

Instituted: February 5, 1783.

Ribbon: 100 mm sky-blue. Not worn in undress uniform.

Collar Chain: Gold, composed of five roses and six harps alternating, each tied together with a gold knot. The roses are enamelled alternately white petals within red and red within white.

Collar Badge: An imperial crown enamelled in proper colours from which is suspended by two rings a gold harp and from this a circular badge with a white enamelled centre embellished with the red saltire cross on which is surmounted a green three-petalled shamrock its leaves decorated with gold crowns, the whole surrounded by a gold collar bearing the Latin motto QUIS SEPARABIT (who shall separate us?) with the date of foundation in roman numerals round the foot MDCCLXXXIII.

Star: A silver eight-pointed star, having in its centre, on a white field, the saltire cross of St Parick in red enamel charged with a green trefoil bearing a gold crown on each leaf.

Sash Badge: The saltire cross in red enamel surmounted by a green shamrock with gold crowns as above, surrounded by an oval collar of pale blue with the Latin motto round the top and the date of foundation round the foot, the whole enclosed by a gold and white enamel surround charged with 32 shamrocks.

Comments: *Founded by King George III to reward the loyalty of Irish peers during the American War of Independence, it originally comprised the monarch and 15 Knights. In 1833 it was extended to include the Lord-Lieutenant of Ireland and 22 Knights, with certain extra and honorary knights. Appointments of non-royal Knights to the Order ceased with the partition of Ireland in 1922, although three of the sons of King George V were appointed after that date—the Prince of Wales (1927), the Duke of York (1936) and the Duke of Gloucester (1934). It became obsolete in 1974 with the death of the last holder. All items of official insignia were returned at death. Unlike the other two great orders, the sash for this Order is worn in the manner of the lesser orders, over the right shoulder.*

VALUE:

Collar chain	Rare
Collar badge	£8000–12,000
Star (metal)	£1500–3000
Star (embroidered)	£400–600
Mantle star	£500–1000
Sash badge	£5000–7000
Miniature	
Star (metal)	£200–250

4. THE MOST HONOURABLE ORDER OF THE BATH

GCB Star (Military)

Instituted: 1725.

Ribbon: 38mm.

Collar Chain: Gold composed of nine crowns and eight devices, each consisting of a rose, a thistle and a shamrock issuing from a sceptre all enamelled in their proper colours. The crowns and devices are joined by gold, white-enamelled knots.

Collar Badge: A skeletal gold badge with an oval collar inscribed TRIA JUNCTA IN UNO (three joined in one) in white enamelled letters, enclosing a thistle, rose and shamrock issuing from a sceptre, with a crown above the sceptre and two crowns below, at the sides.

Star: A silver flaming star surmounted by a circular gold band enamelled red bearing the motto round the top and having a laurel spray round the foot, enclosing three gold crowns enamelled in red.

Sash Badge: As the Collar Badge but smaller and without white enamelling.

Comments: *Established by King George I, this was a single-class Order comprising the monarch, a prince of the blood royal, a Great Master and 35 Knights of Companions (KB). It was re-organised at the conclusion of the Napoleonic Wars (see below). Ladies (other than royalty) are now eligible for the Order.*

VALUE:

Collar chain	£18,000–25,000
Collar badge	Rare
Star (metal)	£2000–3500
Star (embroidered)	£400–800
Sash badge	£2000–3000

KNIGHT GRAND CROSS

The Order was re-organised in 1815 in two divisions, Military and Civil. The Military Division had three classes: Knight Grand Cross (GCB), Knight Commander (KCB) and Companion (CB), while the Civil Division continued with the single class of Knight Grand Cross. In 1847 the Civil Division came into line with the Military, and divided into three classes.

Metal: Gold (1815–87): silver-gilt (since 1887).

Collar Badge: The Military Badge is a gold Maltese cross of eight points, each point tipped with a small gold ball, and in each angle between the arms of the cross is a gold lion. In the centre of the cross is a device comprising a rose, thistle and shamrock issuing from a sceptre, and three imperial crowns . This device is surrounded by a red enamelled circle on which appears the Latin motto TRIA JUNCTA IN UNO (three joined in one) in gold lettering. The circle is surrounded by two branches of laurel, enamelled green, and below is a blue enamelled scroll with the German motto ICH DIEN (I serve) in gold.

The Civil Badge is of gold filigree work, and oval in shape. It consists of a bandlet bearing the motto, and in the centre is the usual device of the rose, thistle and shamrock issuing from a sceptre, together with the three crowns.

Star: A gold Maltese cross of the same pattern as the Military Badge, mounted on a silver flaming star (Military); or a silver eight-pointed star with a central device of three crowns on a silver ground, encircled by the motto on a red enamelled ribbon (Civil).

Sash Badges: Similar to the Collar Badges, they were originally made in gold but since 1887 silver-gilt has been substituted.

VALUE:	Military	Civil
Collar chain (gold)	£18,000–25,000	£18,000–25,000
Collar chain (silver gilt)	£8000–10,000	£8000–10,000
Collar badge (gold)	£2000–3500	£800–1000
Star (metal)	£500–1000	£300–400
Star (embroidered)	£300–500	£200–300
Mantle star	£500–700	£400–600
Sash badge (gold)	£1800–3000	£800–1000
Sash badge (gilt)	£800–1000	£400–600

4. THE MOST HONOURABLE ORDER OF THE BATH *continued*

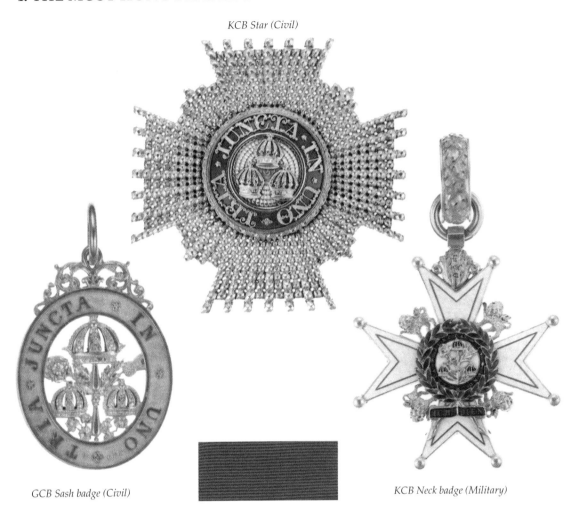

KCB Star (Civil)

GCB Sash badge (Civil)

KCB Neck badge (Military)

KNIGHTS COMMANDERS (KCB) AND COMPANIONS (CB)

Holders of the KCB wear a neck badge suspended by a ribbon as well as a breast star. Prior to 1917 Companions wore a breast badge, the same way as a medal: but in that year it was converted into a neck badge.

Star: (KCB): (Military) a star with the gold Maltese cross omitted, and in the shape of a cross pattée, the three crowns and motto in the centre surrounded by a green enamelled laurel wreath. (Civil) similar but omitting the laurel wreath.

Breast Badge (CB): Similar to the Star but smaller.

Neck Badge (KCB): Similar to the Collar badges of the GCB but smaller, in Military and Civil versions as above.

Neck Badge (CB): Similar to the above, but smaller.

VALUE:	Military	Miniature	Civil	Miniature
Knight Commander				
Star (metal)	£300–500		£200–400	
Star (embroidered)	£150–400		£100–250	
Neck badge (gold)	£700–1200		£400–500	
Neck badge (gilt)	£350–450		£200–250	
Companion				
Breast badge (gold)	£600–1200	£100–150	£350–400	£80–100
Breast badge (gilt)	£350–450	£30–50	£180–220	£30–50
Neck badge (gilt)	£300–400		£140–180	

5. THE ROYAL GUELPHIC ORDER

Instituted: 1815.
Ribbon: 44mm light blue watered silk.

KNIGHTS GRAND CROSS (GCH)

KCH Star (Military)

Collar Chain: Gold, with lions and crowns alternating, linked by scrolled royal cyphers.
Collar Badge: An eight-pointed Maltese cross with balls on each point and a lion passant gardant in each angle. (Obverse) in the centre, on a ground of red enamel, is a white horse of Hanover surrounded by a circle of light blue enamel with the motto in gold lettering NEC ASPERA TERRENT (difficulties do not terrify). Surrounding this circle is a green enamelled laurel wreath. (Reverse) the monogram GR in gold letters on a red ground, surmounted by the British crown and surrounded by a gold circle with the date of the institution MDCCCXV. In the Military version two crossed swords are mounted above the cross and below a Hanoverian crown. In the Civil version the swords are omited, and the wreath is of oak-leaves instead of laurel.
Star: A radiate star with rays grouped into eight points, the centre being similar to the Collar Badge. Behind the laurel wreathed centre are two crossed swords (Military); in the Civil version the swords are omitted and the wreath is of oak leaves.
Sash Badge: Similar to the Collar Badge but smaller.

Comments: *Founded by HRH the Prince Regent (later King George IV), it took its name from the family surname of the British sovereigns from George I onwards and was awarded by the crown of Hanover to both British and Hanverian subjects for distinguished services to Hanover. Under Salic Law, a woman could not succeed to the Hanoverian throne, so on the death of King William IV in 1837 Hanover passed to Prince Augustus, Duke of Cumberland, and thereafter the Guelphic Order became a purely Hanoverian award.*

VALUE:

	Military	Civil
Collar chain (gold)	£7000–9000	£7000–9000
Collar chain (silver gilt)	£4000–5000	£4000–5000
Collar Chain (copper gilt)	£2000–5000	£2000–3000
Collar badge	£5000–6000	£2500–3500
Star	£1000–2000	£500–1000
Sash badge	£6000–8000	£3000–4000

KNIGHTS COMMANDERS (KCH) AND KNIGHTS (KH)

Knights Commanders wore a neck badge suspended by a ribbon, and a breast star, while Knights wore a breast badge only.
Star: As above, but smaller.
Neck Badge: Similar to the Collar Badge but smaller.
Breast Badge: Two versions, in gold and enamel or silver and enamel.

VALUE:

	Military	Miniature	Civil	Miniature
Star	£000–1000		£400–600	
Neck badge	£1500–2000		£800–1200	
Breast badge (gold)	£800–1200	£250–300	£500–700	£200–250

KH Breast Badge (Military)

6. THE MOST DISTINGUISHED ORDER OF ST MICHAEL AND ST GEORGE

Instituted: 1818.
Ribbon: 38mm three equal bands of Saxon blue, scarlet and Saxon blue.

KNIGHTS GRAND CROSS (GCMG)

Knights Grand Cross wear a mantle of Saxon blue lined with scarlet silk tied with cords of blue and scarlet silk and gold, and having on the left side the star of the Order. The chapeau or hat is of blue satin, lined with scarlet and surmounted by black and white ostrich feathers. The collar, mantle and chapeau are only worn on special occasions or when commanded by the sovereign, but in ordinary full dress the badge is worn on the left hip from a broad ribbon passing over the right shoulder and the star on the left breast.

Collar Chain: Silver gilt formed alternately on lions of England, Maltese crosses enamelled in white, and the cyphers SM and SG with, in the centre, two winged lions of St Mark each holding a book and seven arrows.

Star: A silver star of seven groups of rays, with a gold ray between each group, surmounted overall by the cross of St George in red enamel. In the centre is a representation of St Michael encountering Satan within a blue circular riband bearing the motto AUSPICIUM MELIORIS AEVI (A token of a better age).

Sash Badge: A gold seven-pointed star with V-shaped extremities, enamelled white and edged with gold, surmounted by an imperial crown. In the centre on one side is a representation in enamel of St Michael encountering Satan and on the other St George on horseback fighting the dragon. This device is surrounded by a circle of blue enamel bearing the Latin motto in gold lettering. Silver-gilt was substituted for gold in 1887.

Comments: *Founded by HRH the Prince Regent and awarded originally to citizens of Malta and the Ionian Islands in the Adriatic Sea, both of which had been ceded to Britain during the Napoleonic Wars. The Ionian Islands were transferred to Greece in 1859. Towards the end of the 19th century, however, the Order was awarded to those who had performed distinguished service in the colonies and protectorates of the British Empire and in more recent times it has been widely used as an award to ambassadors and senior diplomats as well as colonial governors. Ladies are now eligible for this Order.*

VALUE:	
Collar chain	£1400–1800
Star	£500–600
Sash badge (gold)	£3000–4000
Sash badge (gilt)	£600–800

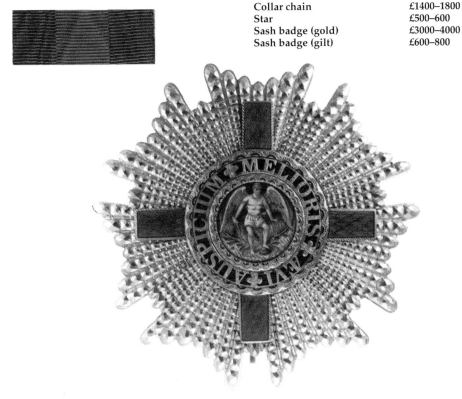

GCMG Star

6. THE MOST DISTINGUISHED ORDER OF ST MICHAEL AND ST GEORGE *continued*

KCMG Star

KNIGHTS COMMANDERS (KCMG) AND COMPANIONS (CMG)

Knights Commanders wear the badge suspended round the neck from a narrower ribbon of the same colours, and a breast star; Companions wear a neck badge. In undress uniform Knights Grand Cross and Knights Commanders wear the ribbon of Companions of the Order. Prior to 1917 Companions wore a breast badge, worn the same way as a medal, but this was then changed to a neck badge.

Star: A silver eight-pointed star charged with the red St George's cross and having the same central device as the GCMG Star. This was introduced in 1859.

Neck Badge: Similar to the sash badge of the GCMG but smaller. Those worn by KCMG were of gold and enamel until 1887 but silver-gilt and enamel thereafter. The CMG neck badges are invariably of enamel and silver-gilt.

Breast Badge: Similar to the star of the KCMG but smaller and made of gold and enamel till 1887, and silver gilt and enamel from then till 1917.

VALUE:		*Miniature*
Knight Commander		
Star	£300–400	
Neck badge (gold)	£800–900	
Neck badge (gilt)	£350–450	
Companion		
Breast badge (gold)	£500–600	£80–100
Breast badge (gilt)	£350–400	£30–50
Neck badge (gilt)	£250–350	

7. THE MOST EXALTED ORDER OF THE STAR OF INDIA

Instituted: 1861.
Ribbon: Broad light blue with white edges (GCSI); 50mm plain white (KCSI); 38mm plain white (CSI).

KNIGHTS GRAND COMMANDERS (GCSI)

KCSI Neck badge

The insignia consisted of a gold collar and badge, a mantle of light blue satin with a representation of the star on the left side and tied with a white silk cord with blue and silver tassels. The collar and mantle were only worn on special occasions and in ordinary full dress uniform a GCSI wore the star on the left breast and the badge on the left hip from a broad sash of light blue edged in white.

Collar Chain: Gold formed of lotus flowers, palm branches and united red and white roses.

Badge: An onyx cameo bearing the left-facing bust of Queen Victoria wearing an imperial crown, set in a gold ornamental oval containing the motto of the Order HEAVEN'S LIGHT OUR GUIDE in diamonds, on a pale blue ground surmounted by a five-pointed star in chased silver.

Star: A five-pointed star in diamonds resting on a circular riband of light blue enamel bearing the motto in diamonds, the whole set on a circular star of golden rays.

Comments: *Founded by Queen Victoria a few years after the British Crown took over the administration of India from the Honourable East India Company, it was intended primarily as an award to loyal Indian princes. The highest class was designated Knight Grand Commander, rather than Cross, because the majority of recipient were not Christians (either Hindus or Muslims). The Order at first consisted of the sovereign, a Grand Master (the Viceroy of India), 36 Knights Grand Commanders (18 British and 18 Indian), 85 Knights Commanders and 170 Companions. The GCSI was the most lavish of all British orders. It lapsed in 1947 when the sub-continent attained independence. Until then all insignia of this Order was returnable on the death of recipients. After 1947, however, recipients or their heirs were allowed in certain cases to purchase the star and badges of any of the three applicable classes, but not the collar chain of the Knight Grand Commander.*

VALUE:

Collar chain	Rare
Star and badge	£25,000–30,000

KNIGHTS COMMANDERS (KCSI) AND COMPANIONS (CSI)

Knights Commanders wore a badge round the neck and a star on the left breast, while Companions originally had a breast badge which was transmuted into a neck badge from 1917 onwards.

Star: Similar to that of the GCSI but in silver.

Neck Badge: Similar to the collar badge of the GCSI but smaller and less ornate.

Breast Badge: Similar to the above but smaller and less ornate and fitted with a straight bar suspender. Subtle differences in the ornament at the foot of the blue border and the external ornament at the sides and foot of the oval.

Comments: *The second and third classes of the Order were awarded to Indian and British subjects of the armed forces and Indian Civil Service for distinguished service of not less than 30 years' duration.*

VALUE:		*Miniature*
Star and Neck badge (KCSI)	£4000–6000	
Breast badge (CSI)	£2500–3000	£150–200 (gold), £80–100 (gilt)
Neck badge (CSI)	£1750–2000	

8. THE MOST EMINENT ORDER OF THE INDIAN EMPIRE

Instituted: 1878.
Ribbon: Broad of imperial purple (GCIE); 50mm imperial purple (KCIE); 38mm imperial purple (CIE).

KNIGHTS GRAND COMMANDERS (GCIE)

KCIE Neck badge

The insignia consisted of a collar, badge and mantle of imperial purple or dark blue satin lined with white silk and fastened with a white silk cord with gold tassels, and having on the left side a representation of the Star of the Order. On ordinary full-dress occasions, however, Knights Grand Commanders wore the badge on the left hip from a broad sash, and a star on the left breast.

Collar Chain: Silver-gilt, composed of elephants, lotus flowers, peacocks in their pride and Indian roses with, in the centre, the imperial crown, the whole linked together by chains.

Badge: A gold five-petalled rose, enamelled crimson and with a green barb between each petal. In the centre is an effigy of Queen Victoria on a gold ground, surrounded by a purple riband originally inscribed VICTORIA IMPERATRIX but from 1901 onwards inscribed IMPERATRICIS AUSPICIIS (under the auspices of the Empress). The letters I N D I A are inscribed on the petals in the first version, but omitted in the second.

Star: Composed of fine silver rays with smaller gold rays between them, the whole alternately plain and scaled. In the centre, within a purple circle bearing the motto and surmounted by the imperial crown in gold, is the effigy of Queen Victoria on a gold ground.

Comments: *Founded by Queen Victoria after assuming the title of Empress of India, it was originally confined to Companions only, together with the Sovereign and Grand Master. Members of the Council of the Governor-General were admitted ex officio as Companions. It was intended for award in respect of meritorious services in India but from the outset it was regarded as a junior alternative to the Star of India. In 1886 the Order was expanded to two classes by the addition of Knights Commanders up to a maximum of 50 in number. In 1887, however, it was again re-organised into three classes: up to 25 Knights Grand Commanders (GCIE), up to 50 Knights Commanders (KCIE) and an unlimited number of Companions (CIE). The Order has been in abeyance since 1947.*

VALUE:

Collar chain	Rare
Star and badge	£4000–5000

KNIGHTS COMMANDERS (KCIE) AND COMPANIONS (CIE)

The insignia of Knights Commanders consisted of a neck badge and a breast star, while that of Companions was originally a breast badge, converted to a neck badge in 1917.

Star: Similar to that of the GCIE but fashioned entirely in silver.

Neck badge: Similar to the collar or sash badge of the GCIE but in correspondingly smaller sizes and differing in minor details.

Breast badge: Similar to the sash badge of the GCIE but differing in minor details, notably the spacing ornament at the foot of the blue circle. Two versions exist, with or without INDIA on the petals of the lotus flower.

VALUE:

		Miniature
Knights Commanders		
Star and Neck badge	£1400–2000	
Companions		
Breast badge (INDIA)	£800–1000	£150–200 (gold)
Breast badge (smaller, without INDIA)	£400–450	£100–150 (gold), £30–80 (gilt)
Neck badge	£300–350	

9. THE ROYAL FAMILY ORDER

Instituted: 1820.
Ribbon: 50mm sky blue moire (1820); 38mm dark blue bordered by narrow stripes of yellow and broader stripes of crimson with narrow black edges (1902); 50mm pale blue moire (1911); 50mm pink moire (1937); 50mm pale yellow silk moire (1953). These ribbons are tied in a bow and worn on the left shoulder.
Descriptions: An upright oval heavily bordered by diamonds and surmounted by a crown, also embellished in diamonds. The oval contains a miniature portrait of the sovereign in enamels.
Comments: *Awarded to the Queen and female relatives of the reigning monarch. It was instituted by King George IV who conferred such orders on his sister, Princess Charlotte Augusta, wife of Frederick William, King of Wurttemberg, and his niece Princess Augusta Caroline, who married the Grand Duke of Mecklenburg-Strelitz. Queen Victoria instituted a separate Order (see next entry), but this Order was revived by King Edward VII in 1902 and continued by successive sovereigns ever since. Special badges are given to ladies-in-waiting. The insignia of these Family Orders very seldom appear on the market and on account of their immense rarity they are unpriced here.*

VALUE:
George IV	Rare
Edward VIII	Rare
George V	Rare
George VI	Rare
Elizabeth II	Rare
Ladies-in-waiting badges	From £1000

10. THE ROYAL ORDER OF VICTORIA AND ALBERT

Instituted: 1862.
Ribbon: 38mm white moire, in the form of a bow worn on the left shoulder.
Description: An upright oval onyx cameo bearing conjoined profiles of HRH Prince Albert, the Prince Consort and Queen Victoria. The badges of the First and Second Classes are set in diamonds and surmounted by an imperial crown similarly embellished, the badge of the Second Class being rather smaller. The badge of the Third Class is set in pearls, while that of the Fourth Class takes the form of a monogram "V & A" set with pearls and surmounted by an imperial crown.

VALUE:
First Class	£24,000–26,000
Second Class	£16,000–18,000
Third Class	£10,000–12,000
Fourth Class	£4000–5000

11. THE IMPERIAL ORDER OF THE CROWN OF INDIA

Instituted: January 1, 1878.
Ribbon: 38mm light blue watered silk with narrow white stripes towards the edges, formed in a bow worn on the left shoulder.
Description: A badge consisting of the royal and imperial monogram VRI in diamonds, turquoises and pearls, surrounded by an oval frame and surmounted by a jewelled imperial crown.
Comments: *Awarded by Queen Victoria to the princesses of the royal and imperial house, the wives or other female relatives of Indian princes and other Indian ladies, and of the wives or other female relatives of any of the persons who had held or were holding the offices of Viceroy and Governor-General of India, Governors of Madras or Bombay, or of Principal Secretary of State for India, as the sovereign might think fit to appoint. This order, conferred on females only, became obsolete in 1947.*

VALUE:
Breast badge	£6000–10,000

12. THE ROYAL VICTORIAN ORDER

Instituted: April 1896.
Ribbon: Dark blue with borders of narrow red, white and red stripes on either side.

KNIGHTS GRAND CROSS AND DAMES GRAND CROSS (GCVO)

The insignia consists of a mantle of dark blue silk, edged with red satin, lined with white silk, and fastened by a cordon of dark blue silk and gold; a gold collar and a badge, worn only on special occasions. Knights wear the badge on the left hip from a broad ribbon worn over the right shoulder, with a star on the left breast, while Dames wear a somewhat narrower ribbon over the right shoulder with the badge, and a star similar to that of the Knights. Dames' insignia are smaller than those of the Knights.

Collar: Silver gilt composed of octagonal pieces and oblong perforated and ornamental frames alternately linked together with gold. The pieces are edged and ornamented with gold, and each contains on a blue-enamelled ground a gold rose jewellerd with a carbuncle. The frames are gold and each contains a portion of inscription VICTORIA BRITT. DEF. FID. IND. IMP. in letters of white enamel. In the centre of the collar, within a perforated and ornamental frame of gold, is an octagonal piece enamelled blue, edged with red, and charged with a white saltire, superimposed by a gold medallion of Queen Victoria's effigy fromwhich is suspended the badge.

Badge: A white-enamelled Maltese cross of eight points, in the centre of which is an oval of crimson enamel bearing the cypher VRI in gold letters. Encircling this is a blue enamel riband with the name VICTORIA in gold letters, and above this is the imperial crown enamelled in proper colours.

Star: Of chipped silver of eight points on which is mounted a white-enamelled Maltese cross with VRI in an oval at the centre.

Comments: *Awarded for extraordinary, important or personal services to the sovereign of the Royal Family. Ladies became eligible for the Order in 1936. Most of the badges of the Royal Victorian Order are numbered on the reverse and are returnable on promotion. Honourary awards are unnumbered.*

VALUE:

	Knights	Dames
Collar	£5000–6000	£6000–7000
Star and Badge	£900–1200	£1000–1200

KNIGHTS COMMANDERS (KCVO), DAMES COMMANDERS (DCVO), COMMANDERS (CVO), LIEUTENANTS (LVO) AND MEMBERS (MVO)

The insignia of the Second, Third, Fourth and Fifth Classes follows the usual pattern. Knights wear a neck badge and a breast star, Dames a breast star and a badge on the left shoulder from a ribbon tied in a bow, Commanders the same neck badge (men) or shoulder badge (women), Lieutenants a somewhat smaller breast badge worn in line with other medals and decorations (men) or a shoulder badge (women) and Members breast or shoulder badges in frosted silver instead of white enamel. The two lowest classes of the Order were originally designated member Fourth Class or member Fifth Class (MVO), but in 1988 the Fourth Class was renamed Lieutenant (LVO) and the Fifth Class simply Member (MVO).

GCVO star

VALUE:

	Gentlemen	*Miniature*	Ladies
Neck badge and breast star	£400–600		£500–600
Neck badge (CVO)	£300–350	£30–50	£400–450
Breast or shoulder badge (LVO)	£200–250	£30–50	£250–300
Breast or shoulder badge (MVO)	£190–230	£15–25	£220–250

13. ROYAL VICTORIAN MEDAL

Instituted: April 1896.
Ribbon: As for the Royal Victorian Order (above); foreign Associates, however, wear a ribbon with a central white stripe added.
Metal: Silver-gilt, silver or bronze.
Size: 36mm.
Description: (Obverse) the effigy of the reigning sovereign; (reverse) the royal cypher on an ornamental shield within a laurel wreath.
Comments: *Awarded to those below the rank of officers who perform personal services to the sovereign or to members of the Royal Family. Originally awarded in silver or bronze, a higher class, in silver-gilt, was instituted by King George V. Only two medals (both silver) were issued in the brief reign of King Edward VIII (1936) and only four bronze medals were issued in the reign of King George VI. Any person in possession of the bronze medal to whom a silver medal is awarded, can wear both, and the silver-gilt medal in addition if such be conferred upon him or her. Clasps are awarded for further services to each class of the medal, while the medals may be worn in addition to the insignia of the Order if the latter is subsequently conferred. To distinguish between British and foreign recipients, King George VI decreed in 1951 that the ribbon worn by the latter should have an additional stripe, these recipients to be designated Associates. In 1983 the order for wearing this medal was altered, and it was no longer to be worn after campaign medals but took precedence over them.*

VALUE:

	Silver-gilt	Miniature	Silver	Miniature	Bronze	Miniature
Victoria	—	£45–50	£100–120	£25–35	£80–100	£25–35
Edward VII	£250–300		£120–150	£15–20	£80–100	£20–30
George V	£250–300		£100–120	£10–15	£250–300	£15–20
Edward VIII	—		Rare		—	
George VI	£120–140		£100–120	£10–15	Rare	£10–15
Elizabeth II	£140–160		£130–150	£10–15	£140–180	£10–15

14. THE ROYAL VICTORIAN CHAIN

Instituted: 1902.
Ribbon: None.
Metal: Silver gilt
Description: A chain consisting of three Tudor roses, two thistles, two shamrocks and two lotus flowers (the heraldic flowers of England, Scotland, Ireland and India respectively), connected by a slender double trace of gold chain. At the bottom of the front loop is a centre piece consisting of the royal cypher in enamel surrounded by a wreath and surmounted by a crown. From this centrepiece hangs a replica of the badge of a Knight Grand Cross of the Royal Victorian order. Ladies were the insignia in the form of a shoulder badge suspended from a miniature chain with links leading to a rose, thistle, shamrock and lotus. An even more elaborate collar, with diamonds encrusting the crown and cypher, was adopted in 1921 and there is a ladies' version of this as well.
Comments: *Sometimes regarded as the highest grade of the Royal Victorian Order, it is actually a quite separate Order and was introduced by King Edward VII for conferment as a special mark of the sovereign's favour, and then only very rarely, upon Royalty, or other especially distinguished personages, both foreign and British.*

VALUE

	Gentlemen	Ladies
Chain (1902–21)	Rare	Rare
Chain with diamonds	Rare	Rare

15. ORDER OF MERIT

Order of Merit obverse

Order of Merit reverse

Instituted: 1902.

Ribbon: 50mm half blue, half crimson.

Metal: Gold.

Size: Height 50mm; max. width 35mm.

Description: A pattée convexed cross, enamelled red, edged blue. (Obverse) FOR MERIT in the centre surrounded by a white band and a laurel wreath enamelled in proper colours. (Reverse) the royal cypher in gold on a blue ground with a white surround and a laurel wreath as above. The cross is surmounted by a Tudor crown to which is attached a ring for suspension. Naval and military recipients have crossed swords in the angles of the cross.

Comments: *This highly prestigious Order consists of the sovereign and a maximum of 24 members in one class only. There is, however, no limit on the number of foreign honorary members, although only ten have so far been admitted to the Order. It was intended for award to those whose achievements in the fields of art, music and literature were outstanding, but it was later extended to naval and military leaders in wartime. To date, fewer than 160 awards have been made, including a mere five ladies, from Florence Nightingale (1907) to Baroness Thatcher. The insignia of those appointed since 1991 have to be returned on the death of the recipient. The insignia of members appointed prior to that date is retained, but understandably few items have come on to the market.*

VALUE:

	Military	Civil
Edward VII	£5000–6000	£3500–4500
George V	£5000–6000	£3000–4000
George VI	Rare	£4000–5000
Elizabeth II	Rare	£3500–4500
Miniature (crude example)		£100–150

16. THE MOST EXCELLENT ORDER OF THE BRITISH EMPIRE

GBE Star (2nd type)

CBE Badge (2nd type)

Instituted: June 1917.

Ribbon: 38mm originally purple, with a narrow central scarlet stripe for the Military Division; rose-pink edged with pearl grey, with a narrow central stripe of pearl-grey for the Military Division (since 1936). A silver crossed oakleaf emblem for gallantry was instituted in 1957.

Comments: *Founded by King George V during the First World War for services to the Empire at home, in India and in the overseas dominions and colonies, other than those rendered by the Navy and Army, although it could be conferred upon officers of the armed forces for services of a non-combatant character. A Military Division was created in December 1918 and awards made to commissioned officers and warrant officers in respect of distinguished service in action. The insignia of the Civil and Military Divisions is identical, distinguished only by the respective ribbons.*

KNIGHTS AND DAMES GRAND CROSS (GBE)

The insignia includes a mantle of rose-pink satin lined with pearl-grey silk, tied by a cord of pearl-grey silk, with two rose-pink and silver tassels attached. On the left side of the mantle is a representation of the star of the First Class of the Order. The mantle, collar and collar badge are only worn on special occasions. In dress uniform, however, the badge is worn over the left hip from a broad (96mm) riband passing over the right shoulder, while Dames wear the badge from a narrower (57mm) ribbon in a bow on the left shoulder; both with the breast star of the Order.

Collar: Silver-gilt with medallions of the royal arms and of the royal and imperial cypher of King George V alternately linked together with cables. In the centre is the imperial crown between two sea lions. The collar for Dames is somewhat narrower than that for Knights.

Badge: A cross patonce in silver-gilt the arms enamelled pearl-grey. In the centre, within a circle enamelled crimson, the figure of Britannia, replaced since 1936 by the conjoined left-facing crowned busts of King George V and Queen Mary, surrounded by a circle inscribed FOR GOD AND THE EMPIRE.

Star: An eight-pointed star of silver chips on which is superimposed the enamelled medallion as for the badge (Britannia or George V and Queen Mary). The star worn by Dames is smaller.

VALUE:

	Britannia	King and Queen
Knights Grand Cross		
Collar	£5000–6000	£5000–6000
Badge and star	£900–1000	£1000–1200
Dames Grand Cross		
Collar	£6000–7000	£6000–7000
Badge and star	£1000–1200	£1200–1400

16. THE MOST EXCELLENT ORDER OF THE BRITISH EMPIRE *continued*
KNIGHTS COMMANDERS (KBE),
DAMES COMMANDERS (DBE),
COMMANDERS (CBE) AND
MEMBERS (MBE)

KBE Star

The insignia of these four Classes follows the same pattern as other Orders. Both Britannia and King and Queen medallion types have been issued.

Star: A star of four large points and four minor points in chipped silver, with the enamelled medallion superimposed. The star worn by Dames is smaller.

Neck Badge: Similar to the badge of the GBE but smaller and worn from a 44mm ribbon round the neck (men) or from a shoulder bow (ladies). Worn by KBE, DBE and CBE.

Breast Badge: As above, but in silver-gilt (OBE) or frosted silver (MBE), with shoulder versions for ladies, worn with a 38mm ribbon.

Gallantry Award: An emblem of silver crossed oak leaves was added to the ribbon of the CBE, OBE and MBE (1957–74).

VALUE:

	Britannia	Miniature	King and Queen	Miniature
Badge and Star (KBE,)	£380–450		£380–450	
Badge and Star (DBE)	£380–450		£450–550	
Neck badge (CBE)	£150–170	£15–20	£150–180	£15–20
Shoulder badge (CBE)	£140–160		£180–220	
Breast badge (OBE)	£60–65	£10–15	£60–65	£10–15
Shoulder badge (OBE)	£55–65		£60–65	
Breast badge (MBE)	£55–65	£8–10	£55–65	£8–10
Shoulder badge (MBE)	£55–65		£55–65	

OBE badge (silver-gilt) and reverse of the MBE badge (frosted silver).

Ribbons: (top to bottom) OBE (Civil) 1st type, OBE (Civil) 2nd type, OBE (Military) 1st type and OBE (Military) 2nd type.

17. MEDAL OF THE ORDER OF THE BRITISH EMPIRE

Civil ribbon

Instituted: June 1917.
Ribbon: 32mm plain purple (Civil), with a narrow scarlet central stripe (Military).
Medal: Silver.
Size: 30mm.
Description: (Obverse) a seated figure of Britannia facing right, her left arm extended and her right holding a trident, with the inscription FOR GOD AND THE EMPIRE round the upper part of the circumference; (reverse) the royal and imperial cypher GRI surmounted by a Tudor crown, the whole enclosed in a cable circle. Fitted with a plain ring for suspension.
Comments: *Instituted as a lower award connected with the Order, it consisted originally of a Civil Division, but a Military Division, distinguishable solely by the ribbon, was added in December 1918. This medal was issued unnamed but many were subsequently engraved or impressed on the rim privately. Fewer than 2000 medals were awarded before they were discontinued in 1922.*

VALUE:

		Miniature
Medal unnamed as issued	£80–90	£30–40
Military award with named medal group	£150–200	
Civil award with supporting documents	£100–150	

18. EMPIRE GALLANTRY MEDAL

1st type rev.

Instituted: December 29, 1922.
Ribbon: Originally plain purple (Civil), with a thin scarlet central stripe (Military; from July 1937 rose-pink with pearl-grey edges (Civil) and a central pearl-grey stripe (Military). A silver laurel branch was added to the ribbon (1933), with a smaller version for wear on the ribbon alone.
Metal: Silver.
Size: 36mm.
Description: (Obverse) the seated figure of Britannia, her left hand resting on a shield and her right holding a trident, with a blazing sun upper right. The words FOR GOD AND THE EMPIRE inscribed round the upper part of the circumference, with FOR in the wave lower left above the exergue which bears the word GALLANTRY. (Reverse) 1st type has six lions passant gardant, with the Royal cypher in the centre surmounted by an imperial crown. The George VI issue has four lions, two either side and round the foot, in two concentric arcs, the words INSTITUTED BY KING GEORGE V. It is suspended from a straight bar ornamented with laurel leaves. Named in seriffed capitals engraved round the rim.
Comments: *This medal, officially known as the Medal of the Order of the British Empire for Gallantry, replaced the Medal of the Order of the British Empire and was awarded for specific acts of gallantry. It was abolished on the institution of the George Cross in September 1940, while it was announced in the London Gazette of April 22, 1941 that a recipient still living on September 24, 1940 should return it to the Central Chancery of the Orders of Knighthood and become a holder of the George Cross instead. Not all EGMs, however, were exchanged or returned. Only 130 medals were issued, 64 being civil, 62 military and 4 honorary.*

VALUE:

		Miniature
George V	£3000–3500	£30–40
George VI	£3000–3500	£30–40

19. BRITISH EMPIRE MEDAL

BEM (MIlitary) 2nd type

Instituted: December 1922.
Ribbon: As above, but without the silver laurel branch.
Metal: Silver.
Size: 36mm.
Description: As above, but with the words MERITORIOUS SERVICE in the exergue. Suspended from a straight bar ornamented with oak leaves. A silver bar decorated with oak leaves was introduced in March 1941 for further acts, and is denoted by a silver rosette on the ribbon worn on its own. An emblem of crossed silver oak leaves was introduced in December 1957 to denote a gallantry award, a smaller version being worn on the ribbon alone. Named in engraved capitals round the rim.
Comments: *Formally entitled the Medal of the Order of the British Empire for Meritorious Service, it is generally known simply as the British Empire Medal. It is awarded for meritorious service by both civil and military personnel. The medal may be worn even if the recipient is promoted to a higher grade of the Order. The gallantry awards, instituted in December 1957, ceased in 1974 on the introduction of the Queen's Gallantry Medal. No British awards have been made for the BEM since 1995 but Commonwealth awards are still being made.*

VALUE:

	Military	Civil	Miniature
George V	£150–180	£100–120	£10–15
George VI GRI cypher	£120–175	£70–80	£10–15
George VI GVIR cypher	£120–175	£70–80	£10–15
Elizabeth II	£120–175	£80–100	£10–15
Elizabeth II with gallantry emblem	£300–600	£250–350	

19A. QUEEN'S VOLUNTEER RESERVES MEDAL

Instituted: 1999.
Ribbon: Dark green with three narrow gold stripes.
Metal: Silver.
Size: 36mm.
Description: (Obverse) effigy of Queen Elizabeth II; (reverse) five ribbons containing the words THE QUEEN'S VOLUNTEER RESERVES MEDAL. The medal is fitted with a large ring for suspension.
Comments: *Awarded to men and women of any rank in the volunteer reserves of all three services, in recognition of outstanding service which formerly would have merited an award within the Order of the British Empire. Holders are entitled to the post-nominal letters QVRM.*

VALUE: —

20. THE ORDER OF THE COMPANIONS OF HONOUR

Instituted: June 1917
Ribbon: 38mm carmine with borders of gold thread.
Metal: Silver gilt.
Size: Height 48mm; max. width 29mm.
Description: An oval badge consisting of a medallion with an oak tree, a shield bearing the royal arms hanging from one branch, and on the left a knight armed and in armour, mounted on a horse. The badge has a blue border with the motto IN ACTION FAITHFUL AND IN HONOUR CLEAR in gold letters. The oval is surmounted by an imperial crown. Gentlemen wear the badge round their necks, while ladies wear it from a bow at the left shoulder.
Comments: *Instituted at the same time as the Order of the British Empire, it carries no title or precedence althought the post-nominal letters CH are used. The Order consists of the sovereign and one class of members. Not more than 50 men or women who have rendered conspicuous service of national importance were admitted, but in 1943 this was increased to 65. The Order is awarded in Britain and the Commonwealth on a quota basis: UK (45), Australia (7), New Zealand (2), other countries (11). It is awarded for outstanding achievements in the arts, literature, music, science, politics, industry and religion.*

VALUE

Gentlemen	£1800–2000
Ladies	£1800–2000

21. THE BARONET'S BADGE

Instituted: 1629
Ribbon: 30mm orange watered silk (Nova Scotia); 44mm orange bordered with narrow blue edges (other Baronets).
Metal: Gold or silver-gilt.
Size: Height 55mm; max. width 41mm(Nova Scotia) or 44mm (later badges).
Description: An upright oval badge with a plain ring suspension. The badge of the Baronets of Nova Scotia was originally skeletal, with a shield bearing the lion rempant of Scotland, decorated with pearls and enamels, surmounted by a Scottish crown and surrounded by a blue border inscribed in gold FAX MENTIS HONESTAE GLORIA. The remaining badges (authorised in 1929) have a solid ground and a central shield with the red hand of Ulster surmounted by a crown and a border of gold and blue enamel decorated with roses (England), shamrocks (Ireland), roses and thistles combined (Great Britain) or roses, thistles and shamrocks combined (United Kingdom). Engraved on the reverse with the recipient's title and date of creation.
Comments: *In an ingenious attempt to raise money without recourse to Parliament, King James I sold grants of land in Nova Scotia. Five years later King Charles I conferred on holders of this land the dignity and rank of Baronets of Nava Scotia, with the title Sir, and decreed that such baronets should wear round their necks "an orange tawny ribbon whereon shall be pendent an escutcheon". After the Union of 1707 Baronets of Scotland properly charged their arms with the badge of Ulster, the red hand, being created Baronets of the United Kingdom. No Baronets of Scotland have been created since 1707, or of Ireland since 1801. Later baronets are of Great Britain, or of the United Kingdom. Badges for the latter were not introduced until 1929, the tercentenary year of the original institution.*

Baronet's badge—United Kingdom

VALUE:	Gold	Silver-gilt
Nova Scotia, 18th–early 19th centuries	£1500–3000	£500–800
Nova Scotia, late 19th and 20th centuries	£1400–1600	£400–600
England (rose surround)	£700–900	£400–600
Ireland (shamrock surround)	£700–900	£400–600
Great Britain (roses and thistles)	£700–900	£400–600
United Kingdom (roses, thistles and shamrocks)	£700–900	£400–600

22. THE KNIGHT BACHELOR'S BADGE

Instituted: 1929.

Ribbon: 38mm scarlet with broad yellow borders.

Metal: Silver-gilt and enamels.

Size: Height 81mm; max. width 60mm. Reduced in 1933 and 1974.

Description: An upright oval medallion enclosed by a scroll, bearing a cross-hilted sword, belted and sheathed, pommel upwards, between two spurs, rowels upwards, the whole set about with the sword-belt.

Comments: *The title Knight Bachelor (KB) was introduced by King Henry III to signify that the title would die with the holder, and not be transmitted to the holder's heir. The badge was authorised by King George V at the same time as the Baronet's Badge, in response to a request from the Imperial Society of Knights Bachelors who wished to have a distinctive badge denoting their rank. The original badge was of the dimensions given above and affixed to the breast by means of a pin on the reverse. This badge was reduced in size in 1933 and again in 1974 when it was fitted with a ring for suspension by a ribbon round the neck.*

VALUE:

		Miniature
First type (1929)	£200–220	£20–30
Smaller type (1933)	£200–220	(Skeletal type
Neck badge (1974)	£220–250	£10–20)

Knight Bachelor's badge

23. THE ORDER OF ST JOHN

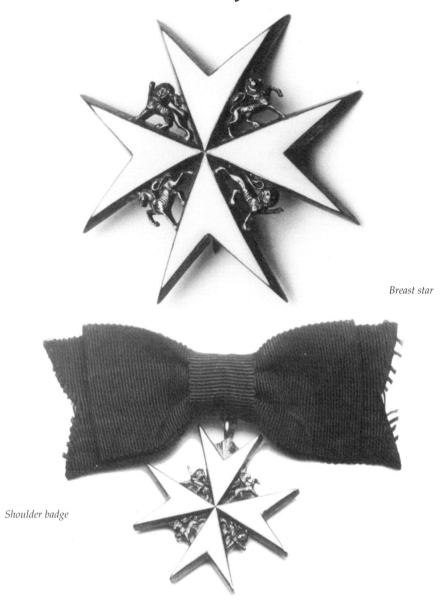

Breast star

Shoulder badge

Instituted: May 14, 1888.
Ribbon: Plain black watered silk. Sash ribbons for Bailiffs, 100mm; Dames Grand Cross, 65mm. Ribbons for Chaplains and Knights, 50mm; Dames 32mm in a bow. Ribbons for Commanders, Officers and Serving Brothers, 38mm for men and 32mm for ladies. Donats have a white central stripe.
Metal: Gold, silver-gilt and silver, or base metal.
Sash badge: An eight-pointed gold Maltese cross in white enamel with two lions and two unicorns in the angles. Confined to Bailiffs and Dames Grand Cross.
Neck badge: Worn by Knights of Justice and Chaplains in gold and Knights of Grace and Commanders (Brothers) in silver. These neck badges are all of the same size.
Star: The eight-pointed Maltese cross in white enamel without the lions and unicorns (Grand Cross and Justice) or with lions and unicorns (Grace and Sub-Prelate). A sub-Prelate is an Order Chaplain (so his badge is included above) who holds high rank in the Church as distinct from the Order.
Shoulder badge: Worn by Dames of Justice in gold and Dames of Grace, Commanders (Sisters) and Officers (Sisters) in silver. The badge is the same size for Dame and Commander but smaller for Officers.

Breast badges: Officers (Brothers) is the Order badge with animals, in silver (1926–36) and in silver and enamel subsequently. Those worn by Serving Brothers, and as shoulder badges by Serving Sisters, have undergone six main phases:

    1892–1939: a circular badge with crosses and animals raised above the surface of the medal.

    1939–1949: circular skeletal badge with ring suspension and the eight-point cross set in a silver rim.

    1949–1974: the first badge resumed.

    1974–1984: a badge of the same design but with the cross and animals flush with their background.

    1984–1991: the cross and animals in white metal, slightly smaller than the Officer (Brother) cross and the whole convex on the obverse.

    Since 1991: Cross and animals thicker, with each arm raised and shaped on both sides of a central channel, the whole in rhodium.

Donats' badges: Gold, silver or bronze, consisting of the badge of the Order with the upper arm of the cross replaced by an ornamental piece of metal for suspension.

Comments: *The Most Venerable Order of the Hospital of St John of Jerusalem was incorporated by Royal Charter of Queen Victoria and granted the epithet Venerable in 1926 and Most in 1955; despite its title, it has no connection with the Knights Hospitallers of Jerusalem, who were subsequently based at Rhodes and Malta and are now located at Rome. In 1926 the Order was reorganised into five Classes like certain other Orders. A sixth class was added later. Both men and women are eligible for membership. Her Majesty the Queen is the Sovereign Head of the Order. Next in authority is the Grand Prior, followed by Bailiffs and Dames Grand Cross, Chaplains, Knights and Dames of Justice, Knights and Dames of Grace, Commanders, Officers, Serving Brothers and Sisters and Esquires. Associates are people who are not citizens of the United Kingdom, the British Commonwealth or the Republic of Ireland, or are non-Christians, who have rendered conspicuous service to the Order and may be attached to any grade of the Order. They wear the insignia of that grade, at one time distinguished only by a central narrow white stripe on the ribbon, but now all ribbons are identical. Donats are people who have made generous contributions to the funds of the Order. They are not enrolled as members of the Order but receive badges in gold, silver or bronze. The category of Associate was abolished in 1999, all Associates being regraded as Members.*

VALUE:

	Gold	Silver/Gilt	Bronze	*Miniature*
Bailiff badge and star	£1500–2200	£800–1000	—	
Dame Grand Cross	£1500–2000	£500–600	—	
Knight of Justice				
neck badge and star	£800–900	£400–500	£150–250	
Dame of Justice				
shoulder badge and star	£800–900	£400–500	£200–300	
Knight of Grace				
neck badge and star	—	£350–400	£150–250	
Dame of Grace				
shoulder badge and star	—	£350–400	£150–250	
Commander (Brother) neck badge	—	£130–180	£60–80	
Commander (Sister) shoulder badge	—	£35–50	£30–50	
Officer breast badge, plain silver	—	£35–50	—	£10–15
Office breast badge, enamelled	—	£40–60	£30–50	£15–20
Officer (Sister) enamelled badge	—	£40–60	£30–50	
Serving Brother/Sister 1926–39	—	£50–60	£30–50	£10–12
Serving Brother/Sister 1939–49	—	£40–60	£40–60	£10–12
Serving Brother/Sister 1949–	—	—	£30–50	
Donat's badge	£80–100	£40–50	£30–40	£25–30

KIWI SCORPIONS

. . . New Zealanders in the Long Range Desert Group in World War II

£29.95 *(plus £3.50p&p)*

A profusely illustrated, hardbound publication featuring the deeds and actions of New Zealanders of the Long Range Desert Group of World War II. With information that cannot be found anywhere else and illustrations never before published, this extensive publication deserves a place on the bookshelf of any serious military historian. The men, the weapons, the vehicles and the uniforms are all fully described together with the battles and the conditions under which these brave men fought.

ORDER YOUR COPY OF "KIWI SCORPIONS"
Simply write, fax or email your order to the address and numbers below. Remittance of £29.95 (plus £3.50 p&p) payable by cheque, credit card or dollar cheque secures your copy. Strictly limited print run.

TOKEN PUBLISHING LTD
ORCHARD HOUSE, DUCHY ROAD, HEATHPARK, HONITON, DEVON EX14 1YD
TEL: 01404 44166   FAX: 01404 44788   e-mail: info@medal-news.com

Decorations

The award of decorations for distinguished military service is an ancient institution. In his *Antiquities of the Jews*, the historian Josephus relates that, in the third century BC, King Alexander was so pleased with Jonathan the High Priest that he sent him a gold button as a mark of favour for his skill in leading the Jews in battle. Subsequently Jonathan was presented with a second gold button for his gallant conduct in the field, making these incidents among the earliest recorded for which specific military awards were granted. The award of jewels, gold buttons and badges for valour was carried on in most European countries on a sporadic basis but the present system of decorations is essentially a modern one dating back no farther than the middle of the seventeenth century. Earlier medals were quasi-commemorative and include the famous Armada Medal of 1588. A few medals in silver or gold were awarded to officers for distinguished service during the English Civil War, although the first "official" rewards in Britain were probably those issued by Parliament to naval officers following their victories over the Dutch fleet in 1653.

Decorations may be divided into those awarded for individual acts of heroism and those conferred in recognition of distinguished military, political or social service. In general terms collectors prefer a decoration awarded for bravery in the field rather than a political honour given automatically to a civil servant, just because he happens to have been in a particular grade for a certain number of years. The debasement of civil awards, such as the OBE and MBE, is reflected in the relative lack of interest shown by collectors.

It is generally true to say that military decorations are more desirable, but it is important to note that one decoration may be more highly prized than another, while the same decoration may well be more valuable to collectors when issued in one period rather than in another. At one extreme is the greatly coveted Victoria Cross, only 1354 of which (including three bars) have been awarded since its inception. VCs won during the Crimean War (111 awarded) are usually less highly regarded than Crosses awarded during the First World War, where, although numerically greater (633) they were far more dearly won. Second World War Crosses are correspondingly more expensive as only 182 were awarded and even now comparatively few of them have ever come on to the market. Today, while pre-1914 Crosses would rate at least £10,000 and those from the First World War slightly more, Second World War Crosses start around £20,000 but have been known to fetch several times as much, depending on the precise circumstances and the branch of the services.

At the other extreme is the Military Medal, of which no fewer than 115,589 were awarded during the First World War alone. For this reason a MM from this period can still be picked up for under £100, whereas one from the Second World War would usually fetch about four times as much, and awards made during the minor campaigns of the 1930s or the Korean War often rate at least ten times as much.

The value of a decoration, where its provenance can

be unquestionably established, depends largely on the decoration itself, whether awarded to an officer or an enlisted man, the individual circumstances of the award, the campaign or action concerned, the regiment, unit or ship involved, and the often very personal details of the act or acts of bravery. These factors are extraordinarily difficult to quantify, hence the frequent large discrepancies in the prices fetched by decorations at auction.

The addition of even relatively common decorations, such as the Military Cross or the Military Medal to the average First World War campaign medal group, invariably enhances its value very considerably while the addition of bars for subsequent awards likewise rates a good premium. Decorations awarded to officers tend to fetch more than those awarded to other ranks, mainly because they are proportionately rarer but also because it is usually easier to trace the career details of an officer.

Sometimes the rank of the recipient may have a bearing on the demand for a particular decoration: e.g. Military Crosses awarded to warrant officers are scarcer than those awarded to subalterns and captains. The branch of the armed services may also have some bearing. Thus a Military Medal awarded to a member of the RAF rates far higher than one awarded to a soldier, while a medal awarded to a seaman in one of the naval battalions which fought on the Western Front is also equally desirable.

Initially the Distinguished Service Order could be won by commissioned officers of any rank but after 1914, when the Military Cross was instituted, it was usually restricted to officers of field rank. DSOs awarded to lieutenants and captains in the Army in both World Wars are therefore comparatively rare and invariably expensive, usually as they were awarded for acts of heroism which in earlier campaigns might have merited the VC.

The opportunity for individual acts of bravery varied

from service to service, and in different conflicts. Thus sailors in the Second World War generally had less scope than air crew. Consequently specifically naval awards, such as the Conspicuous Gallantry Medal and the Distinguished Service Cross, are much more scarce than the corresponding RAF awards for Conspicuous Gallantry and the Distinguished Flying Cross.

The addition of bars to gallantry decorations greatly enhances the scarcity and value of such medals. The VC, for example, has been won by only three men on two occasions; none of these VC and bar combinations has ever come on the market, but should one come up for sale, it is certain that the price would be spectacular. The average First World War MM is today worth around £60, but with a bar for second award its value immediately jumps to about three times as much, while MMs with two or more bars are very much more expensive.

It is important to note that in some cases (the DSO for example) decorations were issued unnamed; for this reason the citation or any other supporting documents relevant to the award should be kept with the decoration wherever possible to confirm its attribution.

Engraving of Gallantry Decorations

After the special investiture for the South Atlantic campaign held on February 8, 1983, the question as to why certain awards were engraved with the date only was raised within the Ministry of Defence. A joint service working party considered the matter and recommended that procedures for all decorations and medals for gallantry in the face of the enemy and for the Air Force Cross when awarded for a specific act of gallantry should be brought into line. A submission was accordingly made to the Queen by the Committee on the Grant of Honours, Decorations and Medals and in April 1984 Her Majesty approved the following:

(i) That the Distinguished Service Cross, Military Cross, Distinguished Flying Cross and Air Force Cross when awarded for gallantry should be engraved with the personal details of the recipient with effect from January 1, 1984.
(ii) That there should be no retrospection;
(iii) That the badge of a Companion of the Distinguished Service Order should not be engraved (in common with the badges of other orders); and
(iv) That the Royal Red Cross (RRC and ARRC) and the Air Force Cross when awarded for meritorious service should not be engraved.

Condition

The same terms are applied to describe the condition of medals and decorations as apply to coins, although the wear to which they are put is caused by other factors. In modern times, when the number of occasions on which medals are worn are relatively few and far between, the condition of most items will be found to be Very Fine (VF) to Extremely Fine (EF). Indeed, in many cases, the medals may never have been worn at all. A good proportion of Second World War medals and decorations are found in almost mint condition as they were not issued till long after the war, by which time their recipients had been demobilised. In some cases they even turn up still in the original cardboard box in which they were posted to the recipients or their next-of-kin.

Before the First World War, however, the wearing of medals was customary on all but the most informal occasions and when actually serving on active duty. Thus medals could be, and often were, subject to a great deal of wear. Medals worn by cavalrymen are often found in poor condition, with scratches and edge knocks occasioned by the constant jangling of one medal against another while on horseback. Often the medals in a group have an abrasive effect on each other. For this reason the Queen's Medal for Egypt (1882) is comparatively rare in excellent condition, as it was usually worn in juxtaposition to the bronze Khedive's Star whose points were capable of doing considerable damage to its silver companion. Apart from these factors it should also be remembered that part of the ritual of "spit and polish" involved cleaning one's medals and they were therefore submitted to vigorous cleaning with metal polish over long periods of service.

For these reasons medals are often sold by dealers "as worn"—a euphemism which conceals a lifetime of hardy service on the chest of some grizzled veteran. Because of the strong personal element involved in medal-collecting, however, genuine wear does not affect the value of a medal to the same degree that it would in other branches of numismatics. There is a school of thought which considers that such signs enhance the interest and value of a medal or group.

This line of thinking also explains the controversy over medal ribbons. Some military outfitters still carry extensive stocks of medal ribbons covering every campaign from Waterloo onwards, so that it is a very easy matter to obtain a fresh length of ribbon for any medal requiring it, and there is no doubt that the appearance of a piece is greatly improved by a clean, bright new ribbon. On the other hand, that ribbon was not the one actually worn by Corporal Bloggs on parade and, to the purist, it would spoil the total effect of the medal. Some collectors therefore retain the original ribbon, even though it may be faded and frayed. As ribbons are things which one cannot authenticate, however, there seems to be little material benefit to be gained from clinging rigidly to a tattered strip of silk when an identical piece can be obtained relatively cheaply. In reality, most collectors compromise by obtaining new ribbons while preserving the old lengths out of sentiment.

Pricing

The prices quoted are *average* figures for medals and decorations as individual items. Combinations with other decorations and campaign medals will produce a value usually well in excess of the aggregate of the individual items. Value will depend to a large extent on the personal factors and circumstances of the award, but where general factors are involved (age, the design of the medal, the period of issue or the campaign concerned, or in some cases the branch of the services) these are itemised separately. "—" indicates that either no examples have come onto the market or no examples have been issued. The figure in brackets (where available) is the *approximate* number awarded.

In the lists which follow, it should be assumed that decorations were instituted by Royal Warrant, unless otherwise stated.

24. THE VICTORIA CROSS

Instituted: January 1856.

Ribbon: Crimson. Originally naval crosses used a blue ribbon, but since 1918 the crimson (Army) ribbon has been used for all awards. A miniature cross emblem is worn on the ribbon alone in undress uniform.

Metal: Bronze, originally from Russian guns captured in the Crimea. Modern research, however, reveals that guns captured in other conflicts, e.g. China, have also been used at various periods.

Size: Height 41mm; max. width 36mm.

Description: A cross pattée. (Obverse) a lion statant gardant on the royal crown, with the words FOR VALOUR on a semi-circular scroll. (Reverse) a circular panel on which is engraved the date of the act for which the decoration was awarded. The Cross is suspended by a ring from a seriffed "V" attached to a suspension bar decorated with laurel leaves. The reverse of the suspension bar is engraved with the name, rank and ship, regiment or squadron of the recipient.

Comments: *Introduced as the premier award for gallantry, available for all ranks, to cover all actions since the outbreak of the Crimean War in 1854, it was allegedly created on the suggestion of Prince Albert, the Prince Consort. Of the 1354 awards since 1856, 832 have gone to the Army, 107 to the Navy, 31 to the RAF, ten to the Royal Marines and four to civilians. Second award bars have been awarded three times. The facility for posthumous awards, made retrospective to 1856, began in 1902 and was confirmed in 1907, while the early practice of forfeitures (eight between 1863 and 1908) was discontinued after the First World War.*

VALUE:	Royal Navy	Army	RFC/RAF	Miniature
1856–1914 (522)	£24,000–30,000	£25,000–30,000	—	Victorian
1914–18 (633)	£25,000–28,000	£28,000–35,000	£80,000–120,000	£50–80
1920–45 (187)	£30,000–40,000	£28,000–50,000	£40,000–120,000	
post-1945 (12)	—	From £50,000	—	£10–20

NB These prices can only be construed as a general guide. Quite a few awards would exceed these price ranges, particularly Commonwealth examples or those appertaining to well known actions.

25. NEW ZEALAND CROSS

Instituted: 10 March 1869 (by an Order in Council, Wellington).
Ribbon: 38mm crimson.
Metal: Silver with gold appliqué.
Size: Height 52mm; max. width 38mm.
Description: A silver cross pattée with a six-pointed gold star on each limb. In the centre are the words NEW ZEALAND within a gold laurel wreath. The cross is surmounted by a gold Tudor crown which is attached by a ring and a seriffed "V" to a silver bar ornamented with gold laurel leaves, through which the ribbon passes. The recipient's name and details are engraved on the reverse.
Comments: *The rarest of all gallantry awards, it was conferred for bravery during the second series of Maori Wars (1860-72). Only 23 Crosses were awarded, the last being authorised in 1910. This medal was called into being solely because local volunteer forces were not eligible for the VC. Replicas of the Cross have been authorised by the New Zealand government.*

VALUE: £15,000–20,000   *Miniature* £250–750
                    Official copy £650–750   (depending on the quality which is extremely varied)

26. GEORGE CROSS

Instituted: 24 September 1940.
Ribbon: 38mm dark blue. A silver miniature cross emblem is worn on the ribbon alone.
Metal: Silver.
Size: Height 48mm; max. width 45mm.
Description: A plain bordered cross with a circular medallion in the centre depicting the effigy of St George and the Dragon after Benedetto Pistrucci, surrounded by the words FOR GALLANTRY. In the angle of each limb is the Royal cypher GVI. The plain reverse bears in the centre the name of the recipient and date of the award. The Cross hangs by a ring from a bar adorned with laurel leaves.
Comments: *The highest gallantry award for civilians, as well as for members of the armed forces in actions for which purely military honours would not normally be granted. It superseded the Empire Gallantry Medal whose holders were then required to return it and receive the GC in exchange. By Warrant of December 1971 suviving recipients of the Albert and Edward Medals were also invited to exchange their awards for the GC—a move which created a controversy which is still continuing, particularly among those who received the Albert Medal. Perhaps the most famous Cross was that conferred on the island of Malta in recognition of its gallantry during the Second World War. Apart from exchange awards, between 1940 and 1947 the GC was awarded to 102 men and four women; since 1947 a further 40 awards have been made. To date no second award bars have been awarded.*

VALUE:

Service awards 1940 to date	£5000–8000
Civilian awards 1940 to date	£2500–3500
Service exchange pre-1940	£2500–3000
Civilian exchange pre-1940	£2000–3000
Miniature	£10-15

26A. CONSPICUOUS GALLANTRY CROSS

Instituted: October 1993.
Ribbon: White with blue edges and a red central stripe.
Metal: Silver.
Size: Max. width 36mm
Description: A cross pattée imposed on a wreath of laurel, with the royal crown in a circular panel in the centre. Suspended by a ring from a plain suspension bar.
Comments: *As part of the decision to remove distinctions of rank in awards for bravery this decoration replaced the DSO for gallantry as well as the Conspicuous Gallantry Medal and the Distinguished Conduct Medal. It was first awarded in 1995 to Corporal Wayne Mills of the Duke of Wellington's Regiment and in 1996 to Colour Sergeant Peter Humphreys of the Royal Welch Fusiliers, both for gallantry in action during service with the UN Peacekeeping Forces in Bosnia.*

VALUE:	Rare	*Miniature*	£15–18

27. DISTINGUISHED SERVICE ORDER

Instituted: 1886.
Ribbon: 29mm crimson with dark blue edges.
Metal: Originally gold; silver-gilt (since 1889).
Size: Height 44mm; max. width 41.5mm.
Description: A cross with curved ends, overlaid with white enamel. (Obverse) a green enamel laurel wreath enclosing an imperial crown; (reverse) the royal monogram within a similar wreath. It is suspended from its ribbon by a swivel ring and a straight laureated bar. Additional awards are denoted by bars ornamented by a crown. Silver rosettes on the ribbon alone are worn in undress uniform. Since its inception, the DSO has been issued unnamed, but since 1938 the year of award has been engraved on the reverse of the lower suspension bar as well as the reverse of the bars for second or subsequent awards.
Comments: *Intended to reward commissioned officers below field rank for distinguished service in time of war, and for which the VC would not be appropriate. Previously the CB had sometimes been awarded to junior officers, although intended mainly for those of field rank. It was also available to officers in both the other armed services. In September 1942 the regulations were relaxed to permit award of the DSO to officers of the Merchant Navy who performed acts of gallantry in the presence of the enemy. As a result of the 1993 Review of gallantry awards and resultant changes to the operational gallantry award system, the DSO is now awarded for "Leadership" only—theoretically to all ranks (it is not awarded posthumously). It has been replaced by the Conspicuous Gallantry Cross as the reward for gallantry.*

VALUE:	Unnamed single	Attributable group	*Miniature*
Victoria, gold (153)	£1500–2000	£2800–4000	£60
Victoria, silver-gilt (1170)	£700–800	£1500–2000	£40
Edward VII (78)	£900–1100	£2500–5500	£60 (gold)
George V (9900)	£450–500	£650–950	£25 (gilt), £50 (gold)
George VI 1st type 1938–48 (4880)	£550–650	£1500–1800	£40 (gilt)
George VI 2nd type 1948–52 (63)	£800–1200	£2500–3500	£40 (gilt)
Elizabeth II (110)	£800–1200	£2500–4500	£30

28. IMPERIAL SERVICE ORDER

Instituted: August 1902.
Ribbon: 38mm three equal sections of blue, crimson and blue.
Metal: Silver with gold overlay.
Size: Height 61mm; max. width 55mm.
Description: The badge consists of a circular gold plaque bearing the royal cypher and surrounded by the words FOR FAITHFUL SERVICE. This plaque is then superimposed on a seven-pointed silver star surmounted by a crown and ring for suspension. The badge of the ISO awarded to women is similar but has a laurel wreath instead of the star-shaped base.
Comments: *Instituted by King Edward VII as a means of rewarding long and faithful service in the Administrative and Clerical grades of the Civil Service at home and overseas. Women were admitted to the order in 1908. The order was awarded after at least 25 years service at home, 20 years and 6 months (India) and 16 years in the tropics, but in exceptional cases awards were made for "eminently meritorious service" irrespective of qualifying period. No UK awards have been made since 1995 but some Commonwealth awards continue to this day.*

VALUE:			Miniature
Edward VII	Gentleman (489)	£100–120	£25–30
	Lady (3)	£280–350	£50–60
George V	Gentleman (909)	£110–120	£20–25
	Lady (2)	£280–350	£45–50
George VI	Gentleman (608)	£110–120	£15–20
	Lady (8)	£280–350	£30–35
Elizabeth II	Gentleman (2,153)*	£120–150	£10–15
	Lady (114)*	£280–350	£20–25

*1953–94

29. IMPERIAL SERVICE MEDAL

Instituted: August 1902.
Ribbon: Same as above.
Metal: Silver and bronze.
Description: Originally similar to the ISO but with a silver plaque and bronze star or wreath. In 1920 the ISM was transformed into a circular medal of silver with the sovereign's effigy on the obverse and a reverse depicting a naked man resting from his labours, with FOR FAITHFUL SERVICE in the exergue.
Comments: *Instituted at the same time as the ISO but intended for junior grades of the Civil Service.*

VALUE:

		Miniature
Edward VII, 1903–10 (c. 4,500) Star (Gentleman)	£45–55	£15–20
Wreath (Lady)	£200–250	£30–40
George V, 1911-20 (c. 6,000) Star (Gentleman)	£35–45	£12–15
Wreath (Lady)	£200–250	£30–40
George V Circular type		
Coinage profile, 1920–31 (c. 20,000)	£12–15	£10–12
Crowned bust, 1931–37 (c. 16,000)	£12–15	£10–12
George VI		
Crowned bust INDIAE:IMP, 1938–48 (c. 36,000)	£12–15	£8–10
Crowned bust FID:DEF, 1949–52 (c. 16,000)	£12–15	£8–10
Elizabeth II		
Tudor crown BRITT:OMN, 1953–54 (c. 9,000)	£12–15	£8–10
Tudor crown DEI:GRATIA, 1955– (c. 150,000)	£12–15	£8–10

30. INDIAN ORDER OF MERIT

Instituted: 1837 (by the Honourable East India Company).

Ribbon: Dark blue with crimson edges (military) or crimson with dark blue edges (civil).

Metal: Silver and gold.

Size: Height 41mm; max. width 40mm.

Description: An eight-pointed star with a circular centre surrounded by a laurel wreath and containing crossed sabres and the relevant inscription. The star is suspended by a curvilinear suspension bar. The different classes were denoted by the composition of the star, noted below.

Comments: *The oldest gallantry award of the British Empire, it was founded in 1837 by the Honourable East India Company. Twenty years later it became an official British award when the administration of India passed to the Crown after the Sepoy Mutiny. Originally known simply as the Order of Merit, it was renamed in 1902 following the introduction of the prestigious British order of that name. There were three classes of the order, promotion from one class to the next being the reward for further acts of bravery. A civil division (also in three classes) was introduced in 1902. Ten years later the military division was reduced to two classes, when troops of the Indian Army became eligible for the VC. The civil division became a single class in 1939 and the military in 1945. Both divisions came to an end with the British Raj in 1947.*

VALUE:

Military Division	
1837-1912 Reward of Valor	
1st class in gold (42)	£1400–1600
2nd class in silver and gold (130)	£450–650
3rd class in silver (2740)	£250–450
1912-39 Reward of Valor	
1st class in silver and gold (26)	£750–1000
2nd class in silver (1215)	£250–450
1939-44 Reward for Gallantry	
1st class in silver and gold (2)	Rare
2nd class in silver (332)	£400–650
1945-47 Reward for Gallantry (44mm diameter)	£800–1000
Civil Division	
1902-39 For Bravery (35mm diameter)	
1st class in gold (0)	—
2nd class in silver and gold (0)	—
3rd class in silver (39)	£600–800
1939-47 For Bravery (26mm diameter)	
Single class (10)	Rare
Miniature	£150–200

NB These priÉes represent unattrieutable pieces. Values can climb rapidly when in company with related campaign medals, particularly for the Victorian era.

31. ROYAL RED CROSS

First Class obverse

2nd Class reverse

Instituted: 27 April 1883.
Ribbon: 25mm dark blue edged with crimson, in a bow.
Metal: Gold (later silver-gilt) and silver.
Size: Height 41mm; max. width 35mm.
Description: (Obverse) The *1st class* badge was originally a gold cross
pattée, enamelled red with gold edges, but from 1889 silver-gilt was
substituted for gold. At the centre was a crowned and veiled
portrait, with the words FAITH, HOPE and CHARITY inscribed on
three arms, and the date 1883 on the lower arm. Subsequently the
effigy of the reigning monarch was substituted for the allegorical
profile; (reverse) crowned royal cypher. *2nd Class:* in silver, design
as the 1st class but the inscriptions on the arms appear on the
reverse. Awards from 1938 have the year of issue engraved on the
reverse of the lower arm.
Comments: *This decoration had the distinction of being confined to females
until 1976. It is conferred on members of the nursing services regardless of
rank. A second class award was introduced in November 1915. Bars for the
first class were introduced in 1917. Holders of the second class are
promoted to the first class on second awards. Holders of the first class
decoration are known as Members (RRC) while recipients of the second
class are Associates (ARRC).*

VALUE:	First class (RRC)	Miniature	Second class (ARRC)	Miniature
Victoria, gold	£800–1000	—		£90–100
Victoria, silver-gilt	£400–500	—		£60–70
Edward VII	£500–550	—		£90–100
George V	£200–250	£20–30	£40–50	£10–20
George V, with bar	£300–350		—	
George VI GRI	£250–300	£20–30	£100–150	£10–20
George VI GVIR	£300–350	£20–30	£150–180	£10–20
Elizabeth II	£300–350	£20–30	£100–150	£10–20

32. DISTINGUISHED SERVICE CROSS

Instituted: June 1901.
Ribbon: 36mm three equal parts of dark blue, white and dark blue.
Metal: Silver.
Size: Height 43mm; max. width 43mm.
Description: A plain cross with rounded ends. (Obverse) crowned
royal cypher in the centre, suspended by a ring; (reverse) plain apart
from the hallmark. From 1940 onwards the year of issue was
engraved on the reverse of the lower limb.
Comments: *Known as the Conspicuous Service Cross when instituted, it was
awarded to warrant and subordinate officers of the Royal Navy who were
ineligible for the DSO. In October 1914 it was renamed the Distinguished
Service Cross and thrown open to all naval officers below the rank of
lieutenant-commander. Bars for second awards were authorised in 1916
and in 1931 eligibility for the award was enlarged to include officers of the
Merchant Navy. In 1940 Army and RAF officers serving aboard naval
vessels also became eligible for the award. Since 1945 fewer than 100 DSCs
have been awarded. As a result of the 1993 Review of gallantry awards and
resultant changes to the operational gallantry award system, this award is
now available to both officers and other ranks, the DSM having been
discontinued.*

VALUE:	Unnamed single	Attributable group	Miniature
Edward VII	Rare	£5000–7000	£150–200
George V	£325–375	£500–650	£10–12
George VI GRI	£350–380	£450–600	£10–12
George VI GVIR	Rare	£2000–2500	£30–50
Elizabeth II	Rare	£2000–3000	£10–12

33. MILITARY CROSS

Instituted: 31 December 1914.

Ribbon: 38mm three equal bars of white, deep purple and white.

Metal: Silver.

Size: Height 46mm; max. width 44mm.

Description: An ornamental cross with straight arms terminating in broad finials decorated with imperial crowns. The royal cypher appears at the centre and the cross is suspended from a plain silver suspension bar.

Comments: *There was no gallantry award, lesser than the VC and DSO, for junior Army officers and warrant officers until shortly after the outbreak of the First World War when the MC was instituted. Originally awarded to captains, lieutenants and warrant officers of the Army (including RFC), it was subsequently extended to include equivalent ranks of the RAF when performing acts of bravery on the ground and there was even provision for the Royal Naval Division and the Royal Marines during the First World War. Awards were extended to majors by an amending warrant of 1931. Bars for second and subsequent awards have a crown at the centre. The MC is always issued unnamed, although since about 1938 the reverse of the cross or bar is officially dated with the year of issue. As a result of the 1993 Review of gallantry awards and resultant changes to the operational gallantry award system, this award is now available to both officers and other ranks, the Military Medal having been discontinued.*

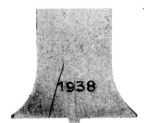

VALUE:	Unnamed single	Attributable group	*Miniature*
George V 1914-1920 (37,000)	£200–250	£350–1000	£15–20
George V 1914-1920 one bar (3000)	£350–400	£800–1000	
George V 1914-1920 two bars (170)	£450–500	£2500–3500	
George V 1914-1920 three bars (4)	Rare	Rare	
George V 1921-1936 (350)	Rare	£400–800	
George V 1921-1936 one bar (31)	Rare	£800–1200	
George VI GRI 1939-1946 (11,000)	£275–350	£600–800	£10–15
George VI GRI one bar (500)	£400–450	£600–800	
George VI GVIR (158)	Rare	£1500–2000	£10–15
Elizabeth II	£500–600	£2000–3000	£8–10
Elizabeth II one bar	Rare	Rare	

34. DISTINGUISHED FLYING CROSS

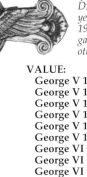

Instituted: June 1918.

Ribbon: 30mm diagonal alternate stripes of white and deep purple.

Metal: Silver.

Size: Height 60mm; max. width 54mm.

Description: (Obverse) a cross flory terminating with a rose, surmounted by another cross made of propeller blades charged in the centre with a roundel within a laurel wreath. The horizontal arms bear wings and the crowned RAF monogram at the centre; (reverse) the royal cypher above the date 1918. The cross is suspended from a bar decorated with a sprig of laurel.

Comments: *Established for officers and warrant officers of the RAF in respect of acts of valour while flying in active operations against the enemy. The DFC is issued unnamed, but Second World War crosses usually have the year of issue engraved on the reverse of the lower limb. As a result of the 1993 Review of gallantry awards and resultant changes to the operational gallantry award system, this award is now available to both officers and other ranks, the Distinguished Flying Medal having been discontinued.*

VALUE:	Unnamed single	Attributable group	*Miniature*
George V 1918-20 (1100)	£550–600	£700–900	£20–25
George V 1918-20 one bar (70)	£700–800	£1000–1500	
George V 1918-20 two bars (3)	Rare	Rare	
George V 1920-36 (130)	Rare	£800–1000	
George V 1920-36 one bar (20)	Rare	£1400–1800	
George V 1920-36 two bars (4)	Rare	Rare	
George VI GRI 1939-45 (20,000)	£400–450	£500–2500	£15–20
George VI 1939-45 one bar (1550)	£500–580	£650–3500	
George VI 1939-45 two bars (42)	Rare	£1600–5000	
George VI GVIR 1948-52 (65)	Rare	£800–2000	£15–20
Elizabeth II (260)	Rare	£1200–3000	£12–15

(in silver add £5)

35. AIR FORCE CROSS

Instituted: June 1918.
Ribbon: 30mm originally horizontal but since June 1919 diagonal alternate stripes of white and crimson.
Metal: Silver.
Size: eight 60mm; max. width 54mm.
Description: (Obverse) the cross consists of a thunderbolt, the arms conjoined by wings, base bar terminating in a bomb, surmounted by another cross of aeroplane propellers, the finials inscribed with the royal cypher. A central roundel depicts Hermes mounted on a hawk bestowing a wreath; (reverse) the royal cypher and the date 1918.
Comments: *This decoration, awarded to officers and warrant officers of the RAF, was instituted in June 1918 for gallantry on non-operational missions and for meritorious service on flying duties. Since the 1993 Review of gallantry awards it is now available to all ranks (the Air Force Medal having been discontinued) for non-operational gallantry in the air only (no longer for meritorious service also).*

VALUE:	Unnamed single	Attributable group	*Miniature*
George V 1918-20 (680)	£550–600	£700–900	£15–20
George V 1918-20 one bar (12)	Rare	Rare	
George V 1918-20 two bars (3)	Rare	Rare	
George V 1920-36 (160)	Rare	£700–800	
George VI GRI (2000)	£550–600	£600–700	£15–20
George VI one bar (26)	£550–600	£1000–1200	
George VI two bars (1)	Rare	Rare	
George VI GVIR (980)	£550–650	£800–1000	£15–20
Elizabeth II	£550–650	£800–1000	£10–12

(in silver add £5)

36. ORDER OF BRITISH INDIA

Instituted: 1837 by the Honourable East India Company.
Ribbon: Worn around the neck, the base colour of the ribbon was originally sky blue but this was altered to crimson in 1838, allegedly because the hair oil favoured by Indians of all classes would soon have soiled a light ribbon. From 1939 onwards the first class ribbon had two thin vertical lines of light blue at the centre, while the second class ribbon had a single vertical line. Originally these distinctive ribbons were only worn in undress uniform (without the insignia itself), but from 1945 they replaced the plain crimson ribbons when worn with the decoration.
Metal: Gold.
Size: Height 42mm; max. width 38mm.
Description: The first class badge consists of a gold star with a crown between the upper two points and a blue enamelled centre bearing a lion surrounded by the words ORDER OF BRITISH INDIA enclosed in a laurel wreath. The second class badge is smaller, with dark blue enamel in the centre and with no crown.
Comments: *Intended for long and faithful service by native officers of the Indian Army, it was thrown open in 1939 to officers of the armed forces, frontier guards, military police and officers of the Indian native states. There were two classes, promotion to the first being made from the second. Recipients of both classes were entitled to the letters OBI after their names, but holders of the first class had the rank of Sardar Bahadur, while those of the second were merely Bahadur. A few awards were made by Pakistan to British officers seconded to the Pakistan forces at the time of independence.*

VALUE:		Miniature
1st class, light blue centre and		
dark blue surround	£350–450	£150–200
1st class, sky blue centre and		
surround (1939)	£350–450	£150–200
2nd class	£350–400	£150–200

NB The prices quoted are for unattributable awards.

37. ORDER OF BURMA

Instituted 1940.
Ribbon: 38mm dark green with light blue edges.
Metal: Gold.
Size: Height 52mm; max. width 38mm.
Description: The badge consists of a gold-rayed circle with a central roundel charged with a peacock in his pride azure, surmounted by an imperial crown.
Comments: *Instituted by King George VI, three years after Burma became independent of British India. Only 24 awards were made, to Governor's Commissioned Officers for long, faithful and honourable service in the army, frontier force and military police of Burma. By an amendment of 1945 the order could also be awarded for individual acts of heroism or particularly meritorious service. It was abolished in 1947.*

VALUE: £3500–4500   *Miniature* £50–100

38. KAISAR-I-HIND MEDAL

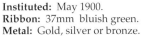

Instituted: May 1900.
Ribbon: 37mm bluish green.
Metal: Gold, silver or bronze.
Size: Height 61mm; max. width 34mm.
Description: An oval badge surmounted by the imperial crown. (Obverse) the royal cypher set within a wreath; (reverse) FOR PUBLIC SERVICE IN INDIA round the edge and KAISAR-I-HIND (Emperor of India) on a scroll across the centre against a floral background.
Comments: *Queen Victoria founded this medal for award to those, regardless of colour, creed or sex, who had performed public service in India. Originally in two classes George V introduced a 3rd Class in bronze. The medals were originally large and hollow but were changed to smaller in diameter and solid during the reign of George V.*

Victoria obv.

VALUE:	1st class (gold)	*Miniature*	2nd class (silver)	*Miniature*	3rd class (bronze)
Victoria	£575–700	£120–150	£200–250	£80–100	—
Edward VII	£575–650	£120–150	£180–220	£80–100	—
George V 1st	£475–600	£50–100	£150–180	£25–50	—
George V 2nd	£425–500	£50–100	£100–120	£25–50	£80–100
George VI	£475–600	£120–150	£100–120	£50–80	£80–100

Victoria rev.

George VI   obv.

rev.

39. ALBERT MEDAL

Instituted: 7 March 1866.

Ribbons: Originally 16mm blue with two white stripes (gold 1st class), changed on introduction of the 2nd class to 35mm blue with four white stripes. The 2nd class remained 16mm blue with two white stripes until 1904 when it was changed to 35mm blue with two white stripes. For the gold 1st class medal the ribbon was 35mm crimson with four white stripes, that for the 2nd class originally 16mm crimson with two white stripes, changing in 1904 to a 35mm ribbon.

Metal: Gold (early issues gold and bronze); bronze.

Size: Height 57mm; max. width 30mm.

Description: The badge consists of an oval enclosing the entwined initials V and A. The sea medals have, in addition, an anchor. The oval is enclosed by a bronze garter with the words FOR GALLANTRY IN SAVING LIFE, with AT SEA or ON LAND as appropriate, and enamelled in blue or crimson respectively. The whole is surmounted by a crown pierced by a ring for suspension. The first class medal was originally worked in gold and bronze and later in gold alone, the second class in bronze alone.

Comments: *Named in memory of the Prince Consort who died in 1861, this series of medals was instituted for gallantry in saving life at sea. An amendment of 1867 created two classes of medal and ten years later awards were extended to gallantry in saving life on land. In 1917 the title of the awards was altered, the first class becoming the Albert Medal in Gold and the second class merely the Albert Medal. It was last awarded to a living recipient in April 1943, the last posthumous award being in May 1945. The last bronze medal awarded to a living recipient was in January 1949, and posthumous in August 1970. In 1949 the Medal in Gold was abolished and replaced by the George Cross and henceforward the Albert Medal (second class) was only awarded posthumously. In 1971 the award of the medal ceased and holders were invited to exchange their medals for the George Cross. Of the 64 eligible to exchange, 49 did so.*

VALUE:

	Civilian	Service	Miniature
Gold Sea (25)	£3500–4500	£4500–5500	£40–60*
Bronze Sea (216)	£2200–2500	£2500–3000	£30–50
Gold Land (45)	£2500–3000	£3000–4000	£40–60*
Bronze Land (282)	£1800–2000	£2000–2500	£30–50

*assumed gilt

40. UNION OF SOUTH AFRICA KING'S/ QUEEN'S MEDAL FOR BRAVERY (WOLTEMADE MEDAL)

Instituted: 1939 by the Government of the Union of South Africa.

Ribbon: Royal blue with narrow orange edges.

Metal: Gold or silver.

Size: 37mm.

Description: (Obverse) an effigy of the reigning sovereign; (reverse) a celebrated act of heroism by Wolraad Woltemade who rescued sailors from the wreck of the East Indiaman *De Jong Thomas* which ran aground in Table Bay on 17 June 1773. Seven times Woltemade rode into the raging surf to save fourteen seamen from drowning, but on the eighth attempt both rider and horse perished.

Comments: *This medal was awarded to citizens of the Union of South Africa and dependent territories who endangered their lives in saving the lives of others. It was awarded very sparingly, in gold or silver.*

VALUE: George VI Gold (1) — Rare
George VI Silver (34) — Rare
Elizabeth II Silver (1) — Rare

41. DISTINGUISHED CONDUCT MEDAL

1st type obv.

Instituted: 1854.
Ribbon: 32mm crimson with a dark blue central stripe.
Metal: Silver.
Size: 36mm.
Description: (Obverse) originally a trophy of arms but, since 1902, the effigy of the reigning sovereign; (reverse) a four-line inscription across the field FOR DISTINGUISHED CONDUCT IN THE FIELD.
Comments: *The need for a gallantry medal for other ranks was first recognised during the Crimean War, although previously the Meritorious Service Medal (qv) had very occasionally been awarded for gallantry in the field. The medals have always been issued named, and carry the number, rank and name of the recipient on the rim, together with the date of the act of gallantry from 1881 until about 1901. Bars are given for subsequent awards and these too were dated from the first issued in 1881 until 1916 when the more usual laurelled bars were adopted. Since 1916 it has ranked as a superior decoration to the Military Medal. As a result of the 1993 Review of gallantry awards and resultant changes to the operational gallantry award system, the decoration has been replaced by the Conspicuous Gallantry Cross.*

VALUE:

Crimea (800)	£600–4000
Indian Mutiny (17)	£5500–7000
India general service 1854-95	£1500–3000
Abyssinia 1867-8 (7)	£2000–3000
Ashantee 1873-4 (33)	£1800–2000
Zulu War 1877-9 (16)	£3000–7000
Afghanistan 1878-80 (61)	£1800–2500
First Boer War 1880-1 (20)	£2500–5000
Egypt & Sudan 1882-9 (134)	£2500–3000
India 1895-1901	£1500–2200
Sudan 1896-7	£1500–5500
Second Boer War 1899-1902 (2090)	£500–1200
Boxer Rebellion 1900	£3000–7000
Edward VII	Many rarities
George V 1st type (25,000)	£300–1000
George V 2nd type 1930-7 (14)	£2500–3500
George VI, IND IMP 1937-47	£1500–4000
George VI, 2nd type 1948-52 (25)	£1800–4000
Elizabeth II, BR: OMN:	£3000–4000
Elizabeth II, DEI GRATIA	£3000–6000
Miniature	
Victoria	£25–30
Edward VII	£25–30
George V	£15–20
George VI	£10–15
Elizabeth II	£10–15

42. DISTINGUISHED CONDUCT MEDAL (DOMINION & COLONIAL)

Instituted: 31 May 1895.
Ribbon: 32mm crimson with a dark blue central stripe.
Metal: Silver.
Size: 36mm.
Description: As above, but the reverse bears the name of the issuing country or colony round the top.
Comments: *A separate DCM for warrant officers, NCOs and men of the colonial forces. Medals were struck for the Cape of Good Hope, New Zealand, New South Wales, Queensland, Tasmania, Natal and Canada, but only the last two actually issued them and the others are known only as specimens.*

VALUE:

Victoria Canada (1)	Rare
Victoria Natal (1)	Rare
Edward VII Natal (9)	Rare

43. DISTINGUISHED CONDUCT MEDAL (KAR & WAFF)

Instituted: early 1900s.
Ribbon: Dark blue with a central green stripe flanked by crimson stripes.
Metal: Silver.
Size: 3mm
Description: As no. 42, with either King's African Rifles or West Africa Frontier Force around the top of the reverse.
Comments: *Separate awards for gallantry were instituted in respect of the King's African Rifles (East Africa) and the West Africa Frontier Force (Nigeria, Sierra Leone, Gambia and the Gold Coast). These were issued until 1942 when they were superseded by the British DCM.*

VALUE:	Attributable groups
Edward VII KAR (2)	Rare
Edward VII WAFF (55)	Rare
George V KAR (190)	£300–450
George V WAFF (165)	£400–500

44. CONSPICUOUS GALLANTRY MEDAL

Instituted: 1855.
Ribbon: 31mm white (RN) or sky blue (RAF) with dark blue edges.
Metal: Silver.
Size: 36mm.
Description: (Obverse) the effigy of the reigning monarch; (reverse) the words FOR CONSPICUOUS GALLANTRY in three lines within a crowned laurel wreath.
Comments: *Conceived as the naval counterpart to the DCM, it was instituted for award to petty officers and seamen of the Royal Navy and to NCOs and other ranks of the Royal Marines. Originally awarded only for gallantry during the Crimean War, it was revived in 1874 to recognise heroism during the Ashantee War and has since been awarded, albeit sparingly, for other wars and campaigns. The Crimean issue utilised the dies of the Meritorious Service Medal which had the date 1848 below the truncation of the Queen's neck on the obverse. The raised relief inscription MERITORIOUS SERVICE on the reverse was erased and the words CONSPICUOUS GALLANTRY engraved in their place. When the decoration was revived in 1874 a new obverse was designed without a date while a new die, with the entire inscription in raised relief, was employed for the reverse. In 1943 the CGM was extended to NCOs and other ranks of the RAF. Both naval and RAF medals are identical, but the naval medal has a white ribbon with dark blue edges, whereas the RAF award has a pale blue ribbon with dark blue edges. It ranks as one of the rarest decorations: the only three medals issued in the present reign were awarded to an airman in the RAAF for gallantry in Vietnam (1968), to Staff-Sergeant James Prescott, RE, during the South Atlantic War (1982) (posthumous) and to CPO Diver Philip Hammond, RN, during the Gulf War (1991). As a result of the 1993 Review and resultant changes to the operational gallantry award system, the decoration has been replaced by the Conspicuous Gallantry Cross.*

VALUE:	Attributable groups
Victoria 1st type (11)	£2500–3000
Victoria 2nd type (51)	£2000–5000
Edward VII (2)	£8000–9000
George V (110)	£2500–4000
George VI Navy (2)	£3000–10,000
George VI RAF (111)	£3500–5000
Elizabeth II (3)	Rare
Miniature	
Victoria	£50–80
Edward VII	£50–80
George V	£20–30
George VI	£15–20
Elizabeth II	£15–20

45. GEORGE MEDAL

Instituted: 1940.

Ribbon: 32mm crimson with five narrow blue stripes.

Metal: Silver.

Size: 36mm.

Description: (Obverse) the effigy of the reigning monarch; (reverse) St George and the Dragon, modelled by George Kruger Gray, after the bookplate by Stephen Gooden for the Royal Library, Windsor.

Comments: *Awarded for acts of bravery where the services were not so outstanding as to merit the George Cross. Though primarily a civilian award, it has also been given to service personnel for heroism not in the face of the enemy. Of the approximately 2000 medals awarded, 1030 have been to civilians.*

VALUE:	Civilian	Service
George VI 1st type 1940-47	£600–750	£700–900
George VI 2nd type 1948-52	£600–750	£800–900
Elizabeth II 1st type 1953	£600–800	£1000–1500
Elizabeth II 2nd type	£800–900	£1200–1600

Miniature	
George VI	£10–15 (Silver £20–25)
Elizabeth II	£10–15 (Silver £20–25)

46. KING'S POLICE MEDAL

Instituted: 7 July 1909.

Ribbons: 36mm Originally deep blue with silver edges, but in 1916 a central silver stripe was added. Gallantry awards have thin crimson stripes superimposed on the silver stripes.

Metal: Silver.

Size: 36mm.

Description: (Obverse) the monarch's effigy; (reverse) a standing figure with sword and shield inscribed TO GUARD MY PEOPLE. The first issue had a laurel spray in the exergue, but in 1933 two separate reverses were introduced and the words FOR GALLANTRY or FOR DISTINGUISHED SERVICE were placed in the exergue.

Comments: *Instituted to reward "courage and devotion to duty" in the police and fire services of the UK and overseas dominions. Recognising the bravery of the firemen during the Blitz, the medal was retitled the King's Police and Fire Services Medal in 1940, but no change was made in the design of the medal itself. From 1950, the gallantry medals were only awarded posthumously and all medals were discontinued in 1954 when seperate awards were established for the two services (see numbers 47 and 48).*

VALUE:		*Miniature*
Edward VII (100)	£600–800	£25–30
George V 1st type coinage head (1900)	£150–300	£20–25
George V 2nd type crowned head	£200–300	£20–25
George V for Gallantry (350)	£350–450	£15–20
George V for Distinguished Service	£200–250	£15–20
George VI 1st type for Gallantry (440)	£450–550	£10–15
George VI 2nd type for Gallantry (50)	£500–700	£10–15
George VI 1st type for Distinguished Service	£200–250	£10–15
George VI 2nd type for Distinguished Service	£200–250	£10–15

47. QUEEN'S POLICE MEDAL

Instituted: 19 May 1954.
Ribbon: Three silver stripes and two broad dark blue stripes.
Metal: Silver.
Size: 36mm.
Description: (Obverse) effigy of the reigning sovereign; (reverse) a standing figure (as on the KPM) but the laurel spray has been restored to the exergue and the words FOR GALLANTRY or FOR DISTINGUISHED POLICE SERVICE are inscribed round the circumference.
Comments: *The QPM for Gallantry has been effectively redundant since November 1977 when it was made possible to award the George Medal posthumously. Prior to this the QPM was the posthumous equivalent of the GM for police officers.*

VALUE:

Elizabeth II for Gallantry (23)	£500–600
Elizabeth II for Distinguished Service (1100)	£250–350
Miniature	£10–15

48. QUEEN'S FIRE SERVICE MEDAL

Instituted: 19 May 1954.
Ribbon: Red with three yellow stripes (distiguished service) or similar, with thin dark blue stripes bisecting the yellow stripes (gallantry).
Metal: Silver.
Size: 36mm
Description: (Obverse) effigy of the reigning monarch; (reverse) standing figure with sword and shield (as on KPM), laurel spray in the exergue, and inscription round the circumference FOR GALLANTRY or FOR DISTINGUISHED FIRE SERVICE.

VALUE:

Elizabeth II for Gallantry	Rare
Elizabeth II for Distinguished Service	£350–450
Miniature	£10–12

49. KING'S POLICE MEDAL (SOUTH AFRICA)

Instituted: 24 September 1937.
Ribbon: Silver with two broad dark blue stripes. Red stripes are added for gallantry awards.
Metal: Silver.
Size: 36mm.
Description: (Obverse) effigy of George VI and title including the words ET IMPERATOR (1937-49), George VI minus IMPERATOR (1950-52) and Queen Elizabeth II (1953-60). (Reverse) as UK (no. 47 above) but inscribed in English and Afrikaans. Inscribed FOR BRAVERY VIR DAPPERHEID or FOR DISTINGUISHED SERVICE VIR VOORTREFLIKE DIENS.
Comments: *Awarded to members of the South Africa Police for courage and devotion to duty. In 1938 it was extended to cover the constabulary of South West Africa.*

VALUE:

George VI 1st type 1937-49	
for Gallantry (10)	Rare
for Distinguished Service (13)	Rare
George VI 2nd type 1950-52	
for Distinguished Service (13)	Rare
Elizabeth II 1953-60	
for Gallantry (20)	Rare
Elizabeth II 1953-69	
for Distinguished Service (3)	Rare

50. EDWARD MEDAL (MINES)

Instituted: July 1907.

Ribbon: Dark blue edged with yellow.

Metal: Silver or bronze.

Size: 33mm.

Description: (Obverse) the monarch's effigy; (reverse) a miner rescuing a stricken comrade, with the caption FOR COURAGE across the top (designed by W. Reynolds-Stephens).

Comments: *Awarded for life-saving in mines and quarries, in two grades: first class (silver) and second class (bronze). Interestingly, the cost of these medals was borne not by the State but from a fund created by a group of philanthropic individuals led by A. Hewlett, a leading mine-owner. Medals were engraved with the names of the recipient from the outset, but since the 1930s the date and sometimes the place of the action have also been inscribed. The medal is now only granted posthumously, living recipients having been invited to exchange their medals for the GC, under Royal Warrant of 1971. Two silver and seven bronze medallists elected not to do so. This is one of the rarest gallantry awards, only 77 silver and 318 bronze medals having been granted since its inception. The last awards to living recipients were made in 1949.*

VALUE:	Silver	Bronze
Edward VII	£650–850	£550–650
George V 1st type	£650–850	£650–750
George V 2nd type	£1200–1500	£650–850
George VI 1st type	£1500–1800	£1200–1400
George VI 2nd type	—	Rare
Elizabeth II	Not issued	From £1800
Miniature		
Edward VII	£60–80	
George V	£50–60	
George VI	£70–80	

51. EDWARD MEDAL (INDUSTRY)

1st type rev.

2nd type rev.

Instituted: December 1909.

Ribbon: As above.

Metal: Silver or bronze.

Size: 33mm.

Description: (Obverse) effigy of the reigning monarch; (reverse) originally a worker helping an injured workmate with a factory in the background and the words FOR COURAGE inscribed diagonally across the top. A second reverse, depicting a standing female figure with a laurel branch and a factory skyline in the background, was introduced in 1912.

Comments: *Awarded for acts of bravery in factory accidents and disasters. Like the Mines medal it was also available in two classes, but no first class medals have been awarded since 1948. This medal is now only awarded posthumously, living recipients having been invited to exchange their medals for the GC, under Royal Warrant of 1971. A total of 25 silver and 163 bronze awards have been issued.*

VALUE:	Silver	Bronze
Edward VII	Rare	Rare
George V 1st Obv, 1st Rev	—	£1500–1800
George V 1st Obv, 2nd Rev	£1400–1500	£600–800
George V 2nd Obv, 2nd Rev	Rare	£1200–1400
George VI 1st type	—	£1000–1200
George VI 2nd type	Not issued	Rare
Elizabeth II 1st type	Not issued	Rare
Elizabeth II 2nd type	Not issued	Rare
Miniature		
George V	£60–80	
George VI (modern)	£15–20	

52. INDIAN DISTINGUISHED SERVICE MEDAL

Instituted: 25 June 1907.
Ribbon: Crimson with broad dark blue edges.
Metal: Silver.
Size: 36mm.
Description: (Obverse) the sovereign's effigy; (reverse) the words FOR DISTINGUISHED SERVICE in a laurel wreath.
Comments: *Awarded for distinguished service in the field by Indian commissioned and non-commissioned officers and men of the Indian Army, the reserve forces, border militia and levies, military police and troops employed by the Indian Government. An amendment of 1917 extended the award to Indian non-combatants engaged on field service, bars for subsequent awards being authorised at the same time. It was formally extended to the Royal Indian Marine in 1929 and members of the Indian Air Force in 1940. Finally it was extended in 1944 to include non-European personnel of the Hong Kong and Singapore Royal Artillery although it became obsolete in 1947.*

VALUE:

		Miniature
Edward VII (140)	£500–650	£40–50
George V KAISAR-I-HIND (3800)	£130–250	£30–40
George V 2nd type (140)	£350–450	£30–40
George VI (1190)	£250–550	£20–30

53. BURMA GALLANTRY MEDAL

Instituted: 10 May 1940.
Ribbon: Jungle green with a broad crimson stripe in the centre.
Metal: Silver.
Size: 36mm.
Description: (Obverse) the effigy of King George VI; (reverse) the words BURMA at the top and FOR GALLANTRY in a laurel wreath.
Comments: *As Burma ceased to be part of the Indian Empire in April 1937 a separate gallantry award was required for its armed services. The Burma Gallantry Medal was awarded by the Governor to officers and men of the Burma Army, frontier forces, military police, Burma RNVR and Burma AAF, although by an amendment of 1945 subsequent awards were restricted to NCOs and men. The medal became obsolete in 1947 when Burma became an independent republic and left the Commonwealth. Just over 200 medals and three bars were awarded, mainly for heroism in operations behind the Japanese lines.*

VALUE: | *Miniature*
£2000–3000 | £35–50

54. DISTINGUISHED SERVICE MEDAL

Instituted: 14 October 1914.
Ribbon: Dark blue with two white stripes towards the centre.
Metal: Silver.
Size: 36mm.
Description: (Obverse) the sovereign's effigy; (reverse) a crowned wreath inscribed FOR DISTINGUISHED SERVICE.
Comments: *Awarded to petty officers and ratings of the Royal Navy, NCOs and other ranks of the Royal Marines and all other persons holding corresponding ranks or positions in the naval forces, for acts of bravery in face of the enemy not sufficiently meritorious to make them eligible for the CGM. It was later extended to cover the Merchant Navy and Army, the WRNS and RAF personnel serving aboard ships in the Second World War. Of particular interest and desirability are medals awarded for outstanding actions, e.g. Jutland, Q-Ships, the Murmansk convoys, the Yangtze incident and the Falklands War. First World War bars for subsequent awards are dated on the reverse, but Second World War bars are undated. As a result of the 1993 Review of gallantry awards and resultant changes to the operational gallantry award system, this award has been replaced by the DSC which is now available both to officers and other ranks.*

VALUE:		*Miniature*
George V uncrowned head 1914-30 (4100)	£200–1000	£15–18
George VI IND IMP 1938-49 (7100)	£200–750	£10–15
George VI 2nd type 1949-53	£800–2000	£10–15
Elizabeth II BR OMN 1953-7	£2000–3000	£8–10
Elizabeth II 2nd type	£2000–4000	£8–10

55. MILITARY MEDAL

Instituted: 25 March 1916.
Ribbon: Broad dark blue edges flanking a central section of three narrow white and two narrow crimson stripes.
Metal: Silver.
Size: 36mm.
Description: (Obverse) the sovereign's effigy—six types; (reverse) the crowned royal cypher above the inscription FOR BRAVERY IN THE FIELD, enclosed in a wreath.
Comments: *Awarded to NCOs and men of the Army (including RFC and RND) for individual or associated acts of bravery not of sufficient heroism as to merit the DCM. In June 1916 it was extended to women, two of the earliest awards being to civilian ladies for their conduct during the Easter Rising in Dublin that year. Some 115,600 medals were awarded during the First World War alone, together with 5796 first bars, 180 second bars and 1 third bar. Over 15,000 medals were conferred during the Second World War, with 177 first bars and 1 second bar. About 300 medals and 4 first bars were awarded for bravery in minor campaigns between the two world wars, while some 932 medals and 8 first bars have been conferred since 1947. As a result of the 1993 Review of gallantry awards and resultant changes to the operational gallantry award system, this award has been replaced by the MC which is now available both to officers and other ranks.*

VALUE:		*Miniature*
George V uncrowned head 1916-30	£100–200*	£10–12
named to a woman	£800–1500
George V crowned head 1930-38	£2500–4000	£15–20
George VI IND IMP 1938-48	£400–1200	£8–10
George VI 2nd type 1948-53	£800–2000	£8–10
Elizabeth II BR: OMN 1953-8	£1800–3000	£8–10
Elizabeth II 2nd type	£2500–6000	£8–10

*Groups to RFC and RND will be considerably higher.

56. DISTINGUISHED FLYING MEDAL

Instituted: 1918.

Ribbon: Originally purple and white horizontal stripes but since 1919 thirteen narrow diagonal stripes alternationg white and purple.

Metal: Silver.

Size: 42mm tall; 34mm wide.

Description: An oval medal, (obverse) the sovereign's effigy; (reverse) Athena Nike seated on an aeroplane, with a hawk rising from her hand. Originally undated, but the date 1918 was added to the reverse with the advent of the George VI obverse. The medal is suspended by a pair of wings from a straight bar.

Comments: *Introduced at the same time as the DFC, it was awarded to NCOs and men of the RAF for courage or devotion to duty while flying on active operations against the enemy. During the Second World War it was extended to the equivalent ranks of the Army and Fleet Air Arm personnel engaged in similar operations. First World War medals have the names of recipients impressed in large seriffed lettering, whereas Second World War medals are rather coarsely engraved. Approximately 150 medals have been awarded since 1945. As a result of the 1993 Review of gallantry awards and resultant changes to the operational gallantry award system, this award has been replaced by the DFC which is now available both to officers and other ranks.*

Example of WWI impressed naming

WWII engraved naming

VALUE:

		Miniature
George V uncrowned head 1918-30 (105)	£900–2000	£15–18
George V crowned head 1930-38	£2000–3500	£25–30
George VI IND IMP 1938-49 (6500)	£600–2000	£8–10
George VI 2nd type 1949-53	£1500–2500	£8–10
Elizabeth II	£1500–2500	£8–10

(in silver add £5)

57. AIR FORCE MEDAL

Instituted: 1918.

Ribbon: Originally horizontal narrow stripes of white and crimson but since July 1919 diagonal narrow stripes of the same colours.

Metal: Silver.

Size: 42mm tall; 32mm wide.

Description: An oval medal with a laurel border. (Obverse) the sovereign's effigy; (reverse) Hermes mounted on a hawk bestowing a laurel wreath. The medal is suspended by a pair of wings from a straight bar, like the DFM.

Comments: *Instituted at the same time as the AFC, it was awarded to NCOs and men of the RAF for courage or devotion to duty while flying, but not on active operations against the enemy. About 100 medals and 2 first bars were awarded during the First World War, 106 medals and 3 bars between the wars and 259 medals during the Second World War. After the 1993 Review of gallantry awards the AFM was discontinued; the AFC is now available both to officers and other ranks.*

VALUE:

		Miniature
George V uncrowned head 1918-30	£800–1000	£12–15
George V crowned head 1930-38	£2000–3000	£20–25
George VI IND IMP 1939-49	£700–800	£8–10
George VI 2nd type 1949-53	£700–800	£8–10
Elizabeth II	£700–800	£8–10

(in silver add £5)

58. CONSTABULARY MEDAL (IRELAND)

1st type obv.

2nd type obv.

Instituted: 1842.
Ribbon: Originally light blue, but changed to green in 1872.
Metal: Silver.
Size: 36mm.
Description: (Obverse) a crowned harp within a wreath of oak leaves and shamrocks, with REWARD OF MERIT round the top and IRISH CONSTABULARY round the foot. In the first version the front of the harp took the form of a female figure but later variants had a plain harp and the shape of the crown and details of the wreath were also altered. These changes theoretically came in 1867 when the Constabulary acquired the epithet Royal, which was then added to the inscription round the top, although some medals issued as late as 1921 had the pre-1867 title. (Reverse) a wreath of laurel and shamrock, within which are engraved the recipient's name, rank, number, date and sometimes the location of the action.
Comments: *Originally awarded for gallantry and meritorious service by members of the Irish Constabulary. From 1872, however, it was awarded only for gallantry. It was first conferred in 1848 and became obsolete in 1922 when the Irish Free State was established. Bars for second awards were authorised in 1920. About 315 medals and 7 bars were awarded (or, in some cases, second medals—the records are inconclusive), mostly for actions in connection with the Easter Rising of 1916 (23) or the subsequent Anglo-Irish War of 1920 (180) and 1921 (55).*

VALUE:

First type	Rare
Second type	£800–1200

59. INDIAN POLICE MEDAL

1st type

2nd type (after 1944)

Instituted: 23 February 1932.
Ribbon: Crimson flanked by bands of dark blue and silver grey. From 1942 onwards an additional silver stripe appeared in the centre of the ribbon intended for the gallantry medal.
Metal: Bronze.
Size: 36mm.
Description: (Obverse) the King Emperor; (reverse) a crowned wreath inscribed INDIAN POLICE, with the words FOR DISTINGUISHED CONDUCT across the centre. In December 1944 the reverse was re-designed in two types, with the words FOR GALLANTRY or FOR MERITORIOUS SERVICE in place of the previous legend.
Comments: *Intended for members of the Indian police forces and fire brigades as a reward for gallantry or meritorious service. The medal became obsolete in 1950 when India became a republic.*

VALUE:

		Miniature
George V	£200–300	£20–25
George VI Distinguished Conduct	£250–300	£20–25
George VI for Gallantry	£300–400	£20–25
George VI for Meritorious Service	£200–300	£20–25

60. BURMA POLICE MEDAL

Instituted: 14 December 1937.
Ribbon: A wide central blue stripe flanked by broad black stripes and white edges.
Metal: Bronze.
Size: 36mm.
Description: (Obverse) the effigy of George VI; (reverse) similar to the Indian medal (first type)and inscribed FOR DISTINGUISHED CONDUCT, irrespective of whether awarded for gallantry or distinguished service.
Comments: *Introduced following the separation of Burma from India, it was abolished in 1948. All ranks of the police, frontier force and fire brigades, both European and Burmese, were eligible.*

VALUE:		MIniature
For Gallantry (53)	£750–1000	£20–25
For Meritorious Service (80)	£600–800	£10–15

61. COLONIAL POLICE MEDAL

Instituted: 10 May 1938
Ribbon: Blue with green edges and a thin silver stripe separating the colours, but the gallantry award had an additional thin red line through the centre of each green edge stripe.
Metal: Silver.
Size: 36mm.
Description: (Obverse) the sovereign's effigy; (reverse) a policeman's truncheon superimposed on a laurel wreath. The left side of the circumference is inscribed COLONIAL POLICE FORCES and the right either FOR GALLANTRY or FOR MERITORIOUS SERVICE.
Comments: *Intended to reward all ranks of the police throughout the Empire for acts of conspicuous bravery or for meritorious service. The number to be issued was limited to 150 in any one year. Only 450 were awarded for gallantry, whilst almost 3000 were issued for meritorious service.*

VALUE:		Miniature
George VI GRI for Gallantry	£500–1200	£10–12
George VI GRI for Meritorious Service	£200–350	£12–15
George VI GVIR for Gallantry	£500–1000	£12–15
George VI GVIR for Meritorious Service	£200–350	£12–15
Elizabeth II 1st type for Gallantry	£500–1000	£15–20
Elizabeth II 1st type for Meritorious Service	£200–300	£15–20
Elizabeth II 2nd type for Gallantry	£500–1000	£15–20
Elizabeth II 2nd type for Meritorious Service	£200–300	£15–20

62. COLONIAL FIRE BRIGADE MEDAL

Instituted: 10 May 1938.
Ribbon: As above.
Metal: Silver.
Size: 36mm.
Description: (Obverse) the effigy of the reigning sovereign; (reverse) a fireman's helmet and axe, with the inscription COLONIAL FIRE BRIGADES FOR GALLANTRY or FOR MERITORIOUS SERVICE.
Comments: *As No. 59 this medal was intended to reward all ranks of the Colonial fire brigades but very few were awarded for gallantry.*

VALUE:		Miniature
George VI GRI for Gallantry	Rare	£12–15
George VI GRI for Meritorious Service	Rare	£12–15
George VI GVIR for Gallantry	Rare	£12–15
George VI GVIR for Meritorious Service	£200–300	£12–15
Elizabeth II 1st type for Gallantry	From £750	£10–12
Elizabeth II 1st type for Meritorious Service	£200–300	£10–12
Elizabeth II 2nd type for Gallantry	£400–600	£10–12
Elizabeth II 2nd type for Meritorious Service	£150–250	£10–12

63. QUEEN'S GALLANTRY MEDAL

Instituted: 20 June 1974.

Ribbon: Blue with a central pearl-grey stripe bisected by a narrow rose-pink stripe.

Metal: Silver.

Size: 36mm.

Description: (Obverse) the Queen's effigy; (reverse) an imperial crown above THE QUEEN'S GALLANTRY MEDAL flanked by laurel sprigs.

Comments: *Awarded for exemplary acts of bravery. Although intended primarily for civilians, it is also awarded to members of the armed forces for actions which would not be deemed suitable for a military decoration. With the introduction of the QGM the gallantry awards in the Order of the British Empire came to an end. A bar is added for a second award. A post-1990 SAS QGM and bar group sold at a recent auction for £26,000.*

VALUE:		Miniature
Service award	£1400–2000	£10
Civilian award	£600–800	

64. ALLIED SUBJECTS' MEDAL

Instituted: November 1920.

Ribbon: Bright red with a light blue centre, flanked by narrow stripes of yellow, black and white (thus incorporating the Belgian and French national colours).

Metal: Silver or bronze.

Size: 36mm.

Description: (Obverse) the effigy of King George V; (reverse) designed by Edmund Dulac, the female allegory of Humanity offering a cup to a British soldier resting on the ground, with ruined buildings in the background.

Comment: *Shortly after the cessation of the First World War it was proposed that services rendered to the Allied cause, specifically by those who had helped British prisoners of war to escape, should be rewarded by a medal. The decision to go ahead was delayed on account of disagreement between the War Office and the Foreign Office, but eventually the first awards were announced in November 1920, with supplementary lists in 1921 and 1922. Medals were issued unnamed and almost half of the total issue, namely 56 silver and 247 bronze medals, were issued to women.*

VALUE:		Miniature
Silver (134)	£500–700	£35–40
Bronze (574)	£300–400	£40–45

NB These prices are for unattributable awards.

65. KING'S MEDAL FOR COURAGE IN THE CAUSE OF FREEDOM

Instituted: 23 August 1945

Ribbon: White with two narrow dark blue stripes in the centre and broad red stripes at the edges.

Metal: Silver.

Size: 36mm.

Description: (Obverse) the crowned profile of King George VI; (reverse) inscribed, within a chain link, THE KING'S MEDAL FOR COURAGE IN THE CAUSE OF FREEDOM.

Comments: *Introduced to acknowledge acts of courage by foreign civilians or members of the armed services "in the furtherance of the British Commonwealth in the Allied cause" during the Second World War. Like its First World War counterpart, it was intended mainly to reward those who had assisted British escapees in enemy-occupied territories. About 3200 medals were issued, commencing in 1947.*

VALUE: £250–300 (unattributable)   *Miniature* £20–30

66. KING'S MEDAL FOR SERVICE IN THE CAUSE OF FREEDOM

Instituted: 23 August 1945.
Ribbon: White with a central red bar flanked by dark blue stripes.
Metal: Silver.
Size: 36mm.
Description: (Obverse) effigy of King George VI; (reverse) a medieval warrior in armour carrying a broken lance, receiving nourishment from a female.
Comments: *Introduced at the same time as the foregoing, it was intended for foreign civilians who had helped the Allied cause in other less dangerous ways, such as fund-raising and organising ambulance services. 2490 medals were issued.*

VALUE: £200–250 (unattributable)   *Miniatur e* £10–15

67. SEA GALLANTRY MEDAL

Instituted: 1855, under the Merchant Shipping Acts of 1854 and 1894.
Ribbon: Bright red with narrow white stripes towards the edges.
Metal: Silver or bronze.
Size: 58mm or 33mm.
Description: (Obverse) Profile of Queen Victoria; (reverse) a family on a storm-tossed shore reviving a drowning sailor. Both obverse and reverse were sculpted by Bernard Wyon.
Comments: *Exceptionally, this group of medals was authorised not by Royal Warrant but by Parliamentary legislation, under the terms of the Merchant Shipping Acts of 1854 and 1894. The 1854 Act made provision for monetary rewards for life saving at sea, but in 1855 this was transmuted into medals, in gold, silver or bronze, in two categories, for gallantry (where the rescuer placed his own life at risk) and for humanity (where the risks were minimal). The gold medal, if ever awarded, must have been of the greatest rarity. These medals, issued by the Board of Trade, were 58mm in diameter and not intended for wearing. The only difference between the medals lay in the wording of the inscription round the circumference of the obverse. Later medals were issued by the Ministry of Transport. In 1903 Edward VII ordered that the medal be reduced to 1.27 inches (33mm) in diameter and fitted with a suspension bar and ribbon for wearing. Both large and small medals were always issued with the recipient's name round the rim.*

VALUE:

	Silver	Bronze	Miniature
Victoria Gallantry	£400–500	£250–350	£100–150
Victoria Humanity (to 1893)	Rare	Rare	
Edward VII Gallantry (large)	£1400–1800	£1150–1400	
Edward VII Gallantry (small)	£450–600	£400–450	£100–150
Edward VII (2nd small type)	£450–600	£400–450	
George V	£300–450	£250–400	£50–75
George VI 1st type	Rare	Rare	
George VI 2nd type	—	Rare	
Elizabeth II	Rare	Rare	

68. SEA GALLANTRY MEDAL (FOREIGN SERVICES)

Type 4 rev.

Instituted: 1841.
Ribbon: Plain crimson till 1922, thereafter the same ribbon as the SGM above.
Metal: Gold, silver or bronze.
Size: 36mm or 33mm.
Description: The large medal had Victoria's effigy (young head) on the obverse, but there were five reverse types showing a crowned wreath with PRESENTED BY (or FROM) THE BRITISH GOVERNMENT inside the wreath. Outside the wreath were the following variants:
1. Individually struck inscriptions (1841-49 but sometimes later).
2. FOR SAVING THE LIFE OF A BRITISH SUBJECT (1849-54)
3. FOR ASSISTING A BRITISH VESSEL IN DISTRESS (1849-54)
4. FOR SAVING THE LIVES OF BRITISH SUBJECTS (1850-54)
There are also unissued specimens or patterns with a Latin inscription within the wreath VICTORIA REGINA CUDI JUSSIT MDCCCXLI.
The small medal, intended for wear, has five obverse types combined with four reverse types: as 2 above (1854-1906), as 3 above (1854-1896), as 4 above (1854-1926), or FOR GALLANTRY AND HUMANITY (1858 to the present day).
Comments: *Although intended to reward foreigners who rendered assistance to British subjects in distress some early awards were actually made for rescues on dry land. Originally a special reverse was struck for each incident, but this was found to be unnecessarily expensive, so a standard reverse was devised in 1849. Medals before 1854 had a diameter of 45mm and were not fitted with suspension. After 1854 the diameter was reduced to 33mm and scrolled suspension bars were fitted. Of the large medals about 100 gold, 120 silver and 14 bronze were issued, while some 10 gold and 24 bronze specimens have been recorded.*

VALUE:

	Gold	Silver	Bronze
Victoria large	Rare	£400–500	£400–500
Victoria small	£1000–1200	£250–350	—
Edward VII	£1000–1500	£400–500	—
George V	£1000–1200	£250–350	—
George VI	—	Rare	—
Elizabeth II	Rare	Rare	—
Miniature			£50–60

69. BRITISH NORTH BORNEO COMPANY'S BRAVERY CROSS

Instituted: 1890 by the British North Borneo Company.
Ribbon: Yellow watered silk.
Metal: Silver or bronze.
Size: 36mm.
Description: The cross pattée has a central medallion bearing a lion passant gardant with the Company motto PERGO ET PERAGO (I carry on and accomplish) within a garter. The arms of the cross are inscribed BRITISH NORTH BORNEO with FOR BRAVERY in the lower limb.
Comments: *Both silver and bronze crosses were manufactured by Joseph Moore of Birmingham. Both silver and bronze medals were issued unnamed. The only genuine striking of silver medals bears the Birmingham hallmark for 1890. Examples with the word STERLING on the reverse are modern copies. The reverse of the bronze medal is smooth, with no marks.*

VALUE:

Silver	£300–350
Bronze	£150–200

70. NATIVE CHIEF'S MEDAL

Instituted: 1920.
Ribbon: Yellow with two white central stripes (silver-gilt) or a single white stripe (silver).
Metal: Silver or silver-gilt.
Size: 40mm x 34mm (oval) or 36mm (circular).
Description: Originally an oval badge with collar. (Obverse) the crowned effigy of the monarch; (reverse) a warship, symbolic of imperial power. The Queen's Medal for Chiefs is circular with a beaded frame and has a crowned effigy of Elizabeth II entitled QUEEN ELIZABETH THE SECOND. It is fitted with a plain ring for suspension.

Comments: *Various large silver medals were struck for award to native chiefs in various parts of the world, from the eighteenth century onwards, and of these the awards to American Indian chiefs are probably the best known. In 1920, however, a standard King's Medal for Chiefs was instituted. It was awarded exceptionally in silver-gilt (first class), and usually in silver (second class). The oval medal was worn round the neck from a silver collar. The more modern issues, however, are intended for wear with a ribbon from the breast.*

VALUE:		Silver-gilt	Silver
	George V	£800–1000	£700–800
	George VI	£800–1000	£500–600
	Elizabeth II	£800–1000	£600–700

Mentions and
Commendations

A description of the various emblems denoting Mentions in Despatches and King's (or later Queen's) Commendations was published as a Supplement to the *London Gazette,* July 27, 1951. A special clasp to signify a Mention in Despatches was instituted during the First World War and continued to be awarded for active service up to August 10, 1920. It was worn on the ribbon of the Victory Medal (no. 170) and consisted of a bronze spray of oak leaves.

For Mentions in Despatches after August 10, 1920, or a King's Commendation for brave conduct or valuable service in the air, a bronze emblem consisting of a single oak leaf was worn on the appropriate medal ribbon, either a General Service Medal or the War Medal, 1939–45. King's or Queen's Commendations for brave conduct or valuable service in the air, in cases where no campaign or war medal was awarded, were worn on the breast in the position where an appropriate medal ribbon would

have been worn, generally on the uniform tunic after any medal ribbons.

King's or Queen's Commendations in respect of bravery, granted to civilians for acts during or since the Second World War, are denoted by a silver emblem in the form of a spray of laurel leaves (this was originally a plastic oval badge). For service during the Second World War this emblem was worn on the ribbon of the Defence Medal (no. 185). Where no medal was awarded, it was sewn directly on to the coat, after any medal ribbons.

For civilians the King's or Queen's Commendation for Valuable Service in the Air, during the Second World War and subsequently, consisted of an oval silver badge, worn on the coat below any medals or medal ribbons, or in civil airline uniform, on the panel of the left breast pocket.

The emblems denoting Mentions and Commendations were revised on August 12, 1994, as shown in the table below.

Mention in Despatches emblem pre-1920

Mention in Despatches emblem 1920–94

FOR GALLANTRY			FOR VALUABLE SERVICE
IN ACTION WITH THE ENEMY (ALL ENVIRONMENTS)	NOT IN ACTION WITH THE ENEMY or OUT OF THEATRE (EXCEPT FLYING)	NOT IN ACTION WITH THE ENEMY or OUT OF THEATRE (FLYING)	IN-THEATRE BUT NOT IN ACTION WITH THE ENEMY
MENTION IN DESPATCHES	QUEEN'S COMMENDATION FOR BRAVERY	QUEEN'S COMMENDATION FOR BRAVERY IN THE AIR	QUEEN'S COMMENDATION FOR VALUABLE SERVICE
A single oak leaf in SILVER	A spray of laurel leaves in SILVER	A new emblem in SILVER	A spray of oak leaves in SILVER

Campaign medals

The evolution of medals struck to commemorate, and later to reward participants in, a battle or campaign was a very gradual process. The forerunner of the modern campaign medal was the Armada Medal, cast in gold or silver, which appears to have been awarded to naval officers and distinguished persons after the abortive Spanish invasion of 1588. The obverse bears a flattering portrait of Queen Elizabeth (thought to have been designed by Nicholas Hilliard, the celebrated miniaturist) with a Latin inscription signifying "enclosing the most precious treasure in the world" (i.e. the Queen herself). On the reverse, the safety of the kingdom is represented by a bay tree growing on a little island, immune from the flashes of lightning which seem to strike it. This medal, and a similar type depicting the Ark floating calmly on a stormy sea, bore loops at the top so that a chain or cord could be passed through it for suspension from the neck of the recipient.

The Civil War produced a number of gallantry medals, mentioned in the previous section; but in 1650 Parliament authorised a medal which was struck in silver, bronze or lead to celebrate Cromwell's miraculous victory over the Scots at Dunbar. This was the first medal granted to all the participants on the Parliamentary side, and not restricted to high-ranking officers, or given for individual acts of heroism.

The Dunbar Medal thus established several useful precedents, which were eventually to form the criteria of the campaign medal as we know it today. After this promising start, however, the pattern of medals and their issue were much more restrictive. Naval medals were struck in gold for award to admirals and captains during the First Dutch War (1650–53), while the battle of Culloden (1746) was marked by a medal portraying the "Butcher" Duke of Cumberland, and granted to officers who took part in the defeat of the Jacobites.

In the second half of the eighteenth century there were a number of medals, but these were of a private or semi-official nature. The Honourable East India Company took the lead in awarding medals to its troops. These medals were often struck in two sizes and in gold as well as silver, for award to different ranks. The siege of Gibraltar (1779–83) was marked by an issue of medals to the defenders, but this was made on the initiative (and at the expense) of the garrison commanders, Generals Eliott and Picton, themselves.

During the French Revolutionary and Napoleonic Wars several medals were produced by private individuals for issue to combatants. Alexander Davison and Matthew Boulton were responsible for the medals granted to the officers and men who fought the battles of the Nile (1798) and Trafalgar (1805). Davison also produced a Trafalgar medal in pewter surrounded by a copper rim; it is recorded that the seamen who received it were so disgusted at the base metal that they threw it into the sea! At the same time, however, Government

recognition was given to senior officers who had distinguished themselves in certain battles and engagements and a number of gold medals were awarded. The events thus marked included the capture of Ceylon (1795–96) and the battles of Maida, Bagur and Palamos.

Towards the end of the Napoleonic Wars an Army Gold Medal was instituted in two sizes—large (generals) and small (field officers). Clasps for second and third battles and campaigns were added to the medal, but when an officer became eligible for a third clasp the medal was exchanged for a Gold Cross with the names of the four battles engraved on its arms. Clasps for subsequent campaigns were then added to the cross (the Duke of Wellington receiving the Gold Cross with nine clasps). A total of 163 crosses, 85 large and 599 small medals was awarded, so that, apart from their intrinsic value, these decorations command very high prices when they appear in the saleroom.

The first medal awarded to all ranks of the Army was the Waterloo Medal, issued in 1816 shortly after the battle which brought the Napoleonic Wars to an end. No action was taken to grant medals for the other campaigns in the Napoleonic Wars until 1847 when Military and Naval General Service Medals were awarded retrospectively to veterans who were then still alive. As applications were made, in some cases, in respect of campaigns more than fifty years earlier, it is hardly surprising that the number of medals awarded was comparatively small, while the number of clasps awarded for certain engagements was quite minute. The Military General Service Medal was restricted to land campaigns during the Peninsular War (1808–13), the American War (1812–14) and isolated actions in the West Indies, Egypt and Java, whereas the Naval GSM covered a far longer period, ranging from the capture of the French frigate *La Cleopatra* by HMS *Nymphe* in June 1793, to the naval blockade of the Syrian coast in 1840, during the British operations against Mehemet Ali. Thus Naval Medals with the clasp for Syria are relatively plentiful (7057 awarded) while in several cases clasps were awarded to one man alone, and in seven cases there were no claimants for clasps at all. It is worth bearing in mind that applications for the medals and clasps resulted mainly from the publicity given by printed advertisements and notices posted up all over the country. With the poor general standard of literacy prevalent at the time, many people who were entitled to the medals would have been quite unaware of their existence.

The Naming of Medals

The Military and Naval GSMs, with their multitudinous combinations of clasps, have long been popular with collectors, but the other campaign medals of the past century and a half have a strong following as well. With the exception of the stars and medals awarded during the Second World War, all British campaign medals have usually borne the name of the recipient and usually his (or her) number, rank and regiment, unit or ship as well. This brings a personal element into the study of medals which is lacking in most other branches of numismatics. The name on a medal is very important for two reasons. It is a means of testing the genuineness, not only of the medal itself, but its bar combination, and secondly it enables the collector to link the medal not only with the man who earned it, but with his unit or formation, and thus plays a vital part in the development of naval or military history, if only a small part in most cases.

Much of the potential value of a medal depends on the man who won it, or the unit to which he belonged. To form a coherent collection as opposed to a random accumulation of medals, the collector would be well advised to specialise in some aspect of the subject, restricting his interests perhaps to one medal (the Naval GSM) or a single group (British campaigns in India), or to medals awarded to the men of a particular regiment. The information given on the rim or back of a medal is therefore important in helping to identify it and assign it to its correct place. Even this has to be qualified to some extent. Some regiments are more popular than others with collectors and much depends on the part, active or passive, played by a unit in a particular battle or campaign for which the medal was awarded. Then again, the combination of event with the corps or regiment of the recipient must also be considered.

At one extreme we find the Royal Regiment of Artillery living up to its motto *Ubique* (everywhere) by being represented in virtually every land action (and not a few naval actions, as witness the Atlantic Star worn by former Maritime Gunners), so that a comprehensive collection of medals awarded to the RA would be a formidable feat.

At the other extreme one finds odd detachments, sometimes consisting of one or two men only, seconded from a regiment for service with another unit. The Indian GSM, with bar for Hazara (1891), is usually found named to personnel of the 11th Bengal Lancers and various battalions of the Bengal Infantry, but according to the medal rolls it was also given to six men of the 2nd Manchester Regiment, two men of the Queen's Regiment and one each to troopers of the 2nd and 7th Dragoon Guards. Whereas a specimen of the IGS medal with this bar is not hard to find named to a soldier in one of the Bengal units, it constitutes a major rarity when awarded to one of the "odd men" and its value is correspondingly high.

As the personal details given on a medal regarding the recipient are so important, it is necessary for the collector to verify two facts—that the person whose name is on the medal was actually present at the action for which either the medal or its bars were awarded, and secondly, that the naming of the bar and the attachment of the bars is correct and not tampered with in any way. As regards the first, the Public Record Office at Kew, London is a goldmine of information for all naval and military campaigns. Apart from despatches, reports and muster rolls covering the actions, there are the medal rolls compiled from the applications for medals and bars. Transcriptions of the medal rolls are held by regimental museums and also by such bodies as the Military Historical Association and the Orders and Medals Research Society. Details of these and other clubs and societies devoted to medal collecting can be found in the later chapters.

The presence of a name on the roll does not mean that a medal or clasp was inevitably awarded; conversely authenticated medals are known to exist named to persons not listed on the medal roll. There are often divergences between the muster and medal rolls. Moreover, discrepancies in the spelling of recipients' names are not uncommon and bars are sometimes found listed for regiments which were not even in existence when the battle was fought! This is explained, however, by the fact that a man may have been serving with one unit which took part in the campaign and subsequently transferred to another regiment. When claiming his medal he probably gave his *present* unit, rather than the one in which he was serving at the time of the action.

Unfortunately cases of medals having been tampered with are by no means rare, so it is necessary to be able to recognise evidence of fakery. A favourite device of the faker is to alter the name and personal details of the recipient and to substitute another name in order to enhance the medal's value. This is done simply by filing the inscription off the rim and adding a new one. In order to check for such alterations a similar medal of proven genuineness should be compared with a pair of fine callipers. Take the measurements at several points round the rim so that any unevenness should soon be apparent.

We cannot stress too much the importance of being closely familiar with the various styles of naming medals. Over the past 150 years an incredible variety of lettering— roman, italic, script, sans-serif, seriffed in all shapes and sizes—has been used at one time or another. In some cases the inscription was applied by impressing in raised relief; in others the inscription was punched in or engraved by hand. If a medal is normally impressed and you come across an engraved example you should immediately be on your guard. This is not an infallible test, however, as medals have been known with more than one style of naming, particularly if duplicates were issued at a much later date to replace medals lost or destroyed.

A rather more subtle approach was adopted by some fakers in respect of the Naval GSM. The three commonest clasps—*Algiers* (1362), *Navarino* (1137) and *Syria* (7057)— were awarded to many recipients possessing common names such as Jones or Smith which can be matched with recipients of some very rare clasps. In the case of the Naval GSM the ship on which the recipient served is not given, thus aiding the fraudulent substitution of clasps. It is necessary, therefore, to check the condition of clasps, even if the naming appears to be correct. Points to watch for are file or solder marks on the rivets which secure the clasps to each other and to the suspender of the medal. This test is not infallible as clasps *do* occasionally work loose if subject to constant wear (particularly if the recipient was a cavalryman, for obvious reasons). But clasps whose rivets appear to have been hammered should automatically be suspect, until a check of the medal rolls pass them as authentic. Examples of the earlier medals, particularly those awarded to officers, may be found with unorthodox coupling. Major L. L. Gordon, in his definitive work *British Battles and Medals*, mentions a Naval GSM awarded to one of his ancestors, with clasps for *Guadaloupe* and *Anse la Barque* in a large rectangular style which must have been unofficial. The medal is quite authentic, so it must be presumed that officers were allowed a certain degree of latitude in the manner in which they altered their medals.

Medals with clasps awarded for participation in subsequent engagements are invariably worth much more than the basic medal. In general, the greater number of clasps, the more valuable the medal, although, conversely, there are a few instances in which single-clasp medals are scarcer than twin-clasp medals. There is no short answer to this and individual rare clasps can enhance the value of an otherwise common medal out of all proportion. Thus the Naval GSM with clasp for *Syria* currently rates £230–280, but one of the two medals known to have been issued with the *Acheron* clasp of 1805 would easily rate twelve times as much. Again, relative value can only be determined by reference to all the circumstances of the award.

The person to whom a medal was issued has considerable bearing on its value. If the recipient belonged to a regiment which played a spectacular part in a battle, this generally rates a premium. The rank of the recipient also has some bearing; in general the higher the rank, the more valuable the medal. Medals to commissioned officers rate more than those awarded to NCOs and other ranks, and the medals of British servicemen rate more as a rule than those awarded to native troops. Medals granted to women usually command a relatively good premium. Another grim aspect is that medals issued to personnel who were wounded or killed in the campaign also rate more highly than those issued to servicemen who came through unscathed.

With the collector of British campaign medals the person to whom the medal was awarded tends to become almost as important as the medal itself. It is often not sufficient to collect the medal and leave it at that. The collector feels that he must investigate it and delve into the archives to find out all that he can about the recipient. The Public Record Office and regimental museums have already been mentioned, but do not overlook the usefulness of such reference tools as the monumental Mormon International Genealogical Index (now on microfiche and available in good public libraries and county record offices). All of these should help you to flesh out the bare bones of the details given in the muster and medal rolls.

Medal Groups

Apart from the combination of clasps on a medal and the significance of the recipient, there is a third factor to be considered in assessing the value of medals, namely the relationship of one medal to another in a group awarded to one person. Just as the number of clasps on a medal is not in itself a significant factor, so also the number of medals in a group is not necessarily important *per se*. Groups of five or more medals, whose recipient can be identified, are by no means uncommon. For example, a fairly common five medal group would consist of 1914–15 Medal, War Medal and Victory Medal (for the First World War) and the Defence Medal and War Medal (for the Second World War). Thousands of men served throughout the first war to do duty, in a less active role, during a part at least of the second, long enough to qualify for the latter pair of medals.

It should be noted that none of the medals awarded for service in the Second World War was named to the recipient, so that groups comprising such medals alone cannot be readily identified and are thus lacking in the interest possessed by those containing named medals. Six-medal groups for service in the Second World War are not uncommon, particularly the combination of 1939–45 Star, Africa Star, Italy Star, France and Germany Star, Defence Medal and War Medal awarded to Army personnel who served from any time up to late 1942 and took part in the campaigns of North Africa and Europe.

Conversely it would be possible for troops to have served over a longer period and seen more action, and only been awarded the 1939–45 Star, Burma Star (with Pacific bar) and the War Medal. Naval groups consisting of the 1939–45 Star, Atlantic Star (with bar for France and Germany), Italy Star and War Medal are less common and therefore more desirable (with, of course, the rider that it must be possible to identify the recipient), while the most desirable of all is the three-medal group of 1939–45 Star (with Battle of Britain bar), Air Crew Europe Star (with bar for France and Germany) and the War Medal. Such a group, together with a Distinguished Flying Cross awarded to one of The Few, is a highly coveted set indeed, providing, as always, that one can prove its authenticity. In any event, the addition of a named medal to a Second World War group (e.g. a long service award, a gallantry medal, or some other category of medal named to the recipient), together with supporting collateral material (citations, log-books, pay-books, service records, newspaper cuttings, etc), should help to establish the provenance of the group.

71. LOUISBURG MEDAL

Date: 1758.
Campaign: Canada (Seven Years War).
Branch of Service: British Army and Navy.
Ribbon: 32mm half yellow, half black, although not originally intended for wear and therefore not fitted with suspension or ribbon.
Metals: Gold, silver or bronze.
Size: 42mm.
Description: (Obverse) the globe surrounded by allegorical figures of victory and flanked by servicemen; (reverse) burning ships in the harbour.
Comments: *More in the nature of a decoration, this medal was only given to certain recipients for acts of bravery or distinguished service in the capture in July 1758 of Louisburg in Canada during the Seven Years War. James Wolfe and Jeffrey Amherst commanded the land forces and Edward Boscawen the fleet.*

VALUE:

Gold	Rare
Silver	£2000–4000
Bronze	£800–1100

72. CARIB WAR MEDAL

Date: 1773.
Campaign: Carib rebellion, St Vincent.
Branch of Service: Local militia or volunteers.
Ribbon: None.
Metal: Silver.
Size: 52mm.
Description: (Obverse) bust of George III in armour; (reverse) Britannia offering an olive branch to a defeated Carib, the date MDCCLXXIII in the exergue.
Comments: *The Legislative Assembly of St Vincent in the West Indies instituted this award to members of the militia and volunteers who served in the campaign of 1773 which put down a native rebellion that had been fomented by the French.*

VALUE:

Silver	£800–900

73. DECCAN MEDAL

Date: 1784.
Campaign: Western India and Gujerat 1778-84.
Branch of Service: HEIC forces.
Ribbon: Yellow cord.
Metals: Gold or silver.
Size: 40.5mm or 32mm.
Description: (Obverse) a rather languid Britannia with a trophy of arms, thrusting a laurel wreath towards a distant fort. (Reverse) an inscription in Farsi signifying "As coins are current in the world, so shall be the bravery and exploits of these heroes by whom the name of the victorious English nation was carried from Bengal to the Deccan. Presented in AH 1199 [1784] by the East India Company's Calcutta Government".
Comments: *The first medals struck by order of the Honourable East India Company were conferred on Indian troops for service in western India and Gujerat under the command of Warren Hastings. They were struck at Calcutta in two sizes; both gold and silver exist in the larger size but only silver medals in the smaller diameter.*

VALUE:

40.5mm gold	£4000–6000
40.5mm silver	£1000–1200
32mm silver	£550–650

74. DEFENCE OF GIBRALTAR

Date: 1783.

Eliott's medal   *Picton's medal*

Campaign: Siege of Gibraltar 1779-83.
Branch of Service: British and Hanoverian forces.
Ribbon: None.
Metal: Silver.
Size: 59mm (Picton) and 49mm (Eliott).
Description: Eliott's medal was confined to the Hanoverian troops, hence the reverse inscribed
BRUDERSCHAFT (German for "brotherhood") above a wreath containing the names of the three
Hanoverian commanders and General Eliott. The obverse, by Lewis Pingo, shows a view of the Rock and
the naval attack of 13 September 1782 which was the climax of the siege. Picton's medal, awarded to the
British forces, has a larger than usual diameter, with a map of the Rock on the obverse and a 22-line text—the
most verbose British medal—above a recumbent lion clutching a shield bearing the castle and key emblem of
Gibraltar on the reverse.
Comments: *Several medals of a private nature were struck to commemorate the defence of Gibraltar during the Franco-Spanish siege of 1779–83, but those most commonly encountered are the silver medals which were provided by George Augustus Eliott and Sir Thomas Picton, the military commanders.*

VALUE:

Picton medal	£450–550
Eliott medal	£400–500

75. MYSORE MEDAL

Date: 1792.
Campaign: Mysore 1790-92.
Branch of Service: HEIC forces.
Ribbon: Yellow cord.
Metal: Gold or silver.
Size: 43mm or 38mm.
Description: (Obverse) a sepoy of the HEIC Army holding British and Company flags over a trophy of arms with the fortress of Seringapatam in the background; (reverse) a bilingual inscription (in English and Farsi). The medal has a ring for suspension round the neck by a cord.
Comments: *Indian officers and men who served under Marquis Cornwallis and Generals Abercromby and Meadows received this medal for service in the campaign which brought about the downfall of Tippoo Sultan of Mysore.*

VALUE:

43mm gold (subadars)	£5000–7000
43mm silver (jemadars)	£800–1200
38mm silver (other ranks)	£550–600

76. ST VINCENTS BLACK CORPS MEDAL

Date: 1795.
Campaign: Carib rebellion 1795.
Branch of Service: Local militia volunteers.
Ribbon: None.
Metal: Bronze.
Size: 48.5mm.
Description: (Obverse) the winged figure of Victory brandishing a sword over a fallen foe who has abandoned his musket; (reverse) native holding musket and bayonet, BOLD LOYAL OBEDIENT around and H.G.FEC. in exergue.
Comments: *Awarded to the officers and NCOs of the Corps of Natives raised by Major Seton from among the island's slaves for service against the rebellious Caribs and French forces.*

VALUE:

Bronze	£600–700

77. CAPTURE OF CEYLON MEDAL

Date: 1796.
Campaign: Ceylon 1795.
Branch of Service: HEIC forces.
Ribbon: Yellow cord.
Metal: Gold or silver.
Size: 50mm.
Description: The plain design has an English inscription on the obverse, and the Farsi equivalent on the reverse.
Comments: *Awarded for service in the capture of Ceylon (Sri Lanka) from the Dutch during the French Revolutionary Wars. It is generally believed that the gold medals were awarded to Captains Barton and Clarke while the silver medals went to the native gunners of the Bengal Artillery.*

VALUE:

Gold (2)	—
Silver (121)	£750–850

78. DAVISON'S NILE MEDAL

Date: 1798.   **Campaign:** Battle of the Nile 1798.
Branch of Service: Royal Navy.
Ribbon: None, but unofficially 32mm, deep navy blue.
Metal: Gold, silver, gilt-bronze and bronze.   **Size:** 47mm.
Description: (Obverse) Peace caressing a shield decorated with the portrait of Horatio Nelson; (reverse) the
British fleet at Aboukir Bay.
Comments: *Nelson's victory at the mouth of the Nile on 1 August 1798 was celebrated in a novel manner by his prize
agent, Alexander Davison, whose name and London address appear in the edge inscription of the medal designed by
Kuchler. Originally issued without a suspender, many recipients added a ring to enable the medal to be worn. Admiral
Nelson's medal was stolen in 1900 and is believed to have been melted down. If it ever came on the market and proved
to be genuine the price would undoubtedly be in the £40,000–50,000 price range. Prices quoted below are for unnamed
specimens, contemporary engraved medals are usually worth about twice as much.*

VALUE:

Gold (Nelson and his captains)	£4000–6000	Gilt-bronze (petty officers)	£250–300
Silver (junior officers)	£450–500	Bronze (ratings)	£125–175

79. SERINGAPATAM MEDAL

Date: 1808.   **Campaign:** Seringapatam, India, 1799.
Branch of Service: HEIC forces.
Ribbon: 38mm gold.
Metal: Gold, silver-gilt, silver, bronze and pewter.   **Size:** 48mm or 45mm.
Description: (Obverse) the British lion defeating Tiger of Mysore (Tippoo Sultan) with the date of the capture
of the fortress IV MAY MDCCXCIX (1799) in the exergue; (reverse) the assault on Seringapatam.
Comments: *The British and native troops who took part in the renewed campaign against Tippoo Sultan were awarded
this medal in 1808 in various metals without suspension (a number of different types of suspenders and rings were
subsequently fitted by individual recipients). The medal was designed by Kuchler and struck in England and Calcutta,
the latter version being slightly smaller. There are several different strikings of these medals.*

VALUE:

Gold 48mm (113)	£3000–4000	Silver 45mm	£300–350
Gold 45mm	£2500–3000	Bronze 48mm (5000)	£200–240
Silver-gilt 48mm (185)	£400–500	Pewter 48mm (45,000)	£200–220
Silver 48mm (3636)	£350–450		

80. EARL ST. VINCENT'S MEDAL

Date: 1800.　**Campaign:** Mediterranean.
Branch of Service: Royal Navy.
Ribbon: None.
Metal. Gold or silver.　**Size:** 48mm
Description: (Obverse) left-facing bust of the Earl in Admiral's uniform; (reverse) a sailor and marine.
Comments: *A private medal presented by Earl St Vincent, when he struck his flag and came ashore in 1800, to the petty officers and men of his flagship* Ville de Paris *as a token of appreciation to his old shipmates. Contemporary engraved and named pieces with researched provenance are worth at least twice as much as unnamed specimens.*

VALUE:
Gold	£3000–4000
Silver	£350–450

81. EGYPT MEDAL 1801

Date: 1801.　**Campaign:** Egypt 1801.
Branch of Service: HEIC forces.
Ribbon: Yellow cord.
Metal: Gold or silver.　**Size:** 48mm.
Description: (Obverse) a sepoy holding a Union Jack, with an encampment in the background. A four-line Farsi text occupies the exergue; (reverse) a warship and the Pyramids.
Comments: *Issued by the Honourable East India Company to British and Indian troops in the Company's service who took part in the conquest of Egypt under Generals Baird and Abercromby.*

VALUE:
Gold (16)	Rare
Silver (2200)	£500–600

82. SULTAN'S MEDAL FOR EGYPT

Date: 1801.
Campaign: Egypt 1801.
Branch of Service: British forces.
Ribbon: The gold medals were originally suspended by gold hook and chain as shown. The silver medals were hung from a sand-coloured ribbon.
Metals: Gold or silver.
Size: Various (see below).
Description: The very thin discs have an elaborate arabesque border enclosing the *toughra* or sign manual of the Sultan.
Comments: *This medal was conferred by Sultan Selim III of Turkey on the British officers and NCOs who took part in the campaign against the French. It was produced in five gold versions for award to different ranks of commissioned officers, as well as one in silver for award to sergeants and corporals.*

VALUE:

Gold 54mm studded with jewels	Rare
Gold 54mm plain	£3000–3500
Gold 48mm	£2000–2300
Gold 43mm	£1400–1600
Gold 36mm	£1000–1350
Silver 36mm	£600–700
Miniature	
Gold	£100–150
Silver	£50–80

83. HIGHLAND SOCIETY'S MEDAL FOR EGYPT 1801

Date: 1801.
Campaign: Egypt 1801.
Branch of Service: British forces.
Ribbon: None.
Metals: Gold, silver and bronze.
Size: 49mm.
Description: The medal was designed by Pidgeon. (Obverse) the right-facing bust of General Sir Ralph Abercromby, with a Latin inscription alluding to his death in Egypt; (reverse) a Highlander and the date 21 MAR. 1801 with the Gaelic inscription NA FIR A CHOISIN BUAIDH (These are the heroes who achieved victory in Egypt).
Comments: *The Highland and Agricultural Society (now Royal) was founded in 1784 to promote the development of agriculture in Scotland generally and the Highlands in particular. General Abercromby (born at Tullibody, 1734) commanded the British expedition to Egypt, and the landing at Aboukir Bay on 2 March 1801 in the face of strenuous French opposition, is justly regarded as one of the most brilliant and daring exploits of all time. The French made a surprise attack on the British camp on the night of 21 March and Abercromby was struck by a ricochet; he died aboard the flagship seven days later. Medals in gold were presented to the Prince Regent and Abercromby's sons, but silver and bronze medals were later struck and awarded to senior officers of the expedition as well as soldiers who had distinguished themselves in the campaign.*

VALUE:

Gold	—
Silver	£500–600
Bronze	£200–250

84. BOULTON'S TRAFALGAR MEDAL

Date: 1805.
Campaign: Battle of Trafalgar 1805.
Branch of Service: Royal Navy.
Ribbon: None, but unofficially 32mm navy blue (originally issued without suspension).
Metals: Gold, silver, white metal, gilt-bronze or bronze.   **Size:** 48mm.
Description: (Obverse) bust of Nelson; (reverse) a battle scene.
Comments: *Matthew Boulton of the Soho Mint, Birmingham, struck this medal on his own initiative for presentation to the survivors of the battle of Trafalgar. It was awarded in white metal, but bronze and gilt-bronze specimens also exist. It was subsequently restruck on at least two occasions, the first and second strikings have the inscription impressed in large capitals around the rim TO THE HEROES OF TRAFALGAR FROM M:BOULTON, the last having the inscription omitted. As the original dies were used for each striking, they had to be polished before reuse, so the fine detail on Nelson's uniform and in the battle scene is less pronounced in the second and subsequent strikings. Examples of the original striking can sometimes be found engraved in various styles, but great care should be taken over checking the authenticity of such pieces. All gold specimens are restrikes. Silver medals were not awarded but were later ordered from Boulton or his descendants by officers who wished to have a medal to form a group with the 1848 NGS.*

VALUE:

Gold (c. 1905)	£1000	Gilt-bronze	£500–700
Silver (1820–50)	£1000–1500	Bronze	£150–300
White metal	£150–300		

NB These prices are based on medals ssued from the original striking and are dependent on attribution.

85. DAVISON'S TRAFALGAR MEDAL

Date: 1805.
Campaign: Battle of Trafalgar 1805.
Branch of Service: Royal Navy.
Ribbon: None, but unofficially 32mm navy blue.
Metal: Pewter with a copper rim.   **Size:** 52mm.
Description: (Obverse) bust of Nelson; (reverse) a man-of-war with an appropriate biblical quotation from Exodus "The Lord is a Man-of-War".
Comments: *Alexander Davison, Nelson's prize agent, had this medal struck for award to the ratings of HMS Victory who took part in the battle.*

VALUE: £650–850

86. CAPTURE OF RODRIGUEZ, ISLE OF BOURBON AND ISLE OF FRANCE

Date: 1810.
Campaign: Indian Ocean 1809-10.
Branch of Service: HEIC forces.
Ribbon: Yellow cord.
Metal: Gold or silver.
Size: 49mm.
Description: (Obverse) a sepoy in front of a cannon with the Union Jack; (reverse) a wreath with inscriptions in English and Farsi.
Comments: *The East India Company awarded this medal to native troops of the Bengal and Bombay Armies for the capture of three French islands in the Indian Ocean (the latter two being better known today as Mauritius and Reunion) between July 1809 and December 1810.*

VALUE:

Gold (50)	£4000–6000
Silver (2200)	£550–650

87. BAGUR AND PALAMOS MEDAL

Date: 1811.
Campaign: Peninsular War 1810.
Branch of Service: Royal Navy.
Ribbon: Red with yellow edges.
Metal: Gold or silver.
Size: 45mm.
Description: (Obverse) the conjoined crowned shields of Britain and Spain in a wreath with ALIANZA ETERNA (eternal alliance) round the foot; (reverse) inscription in Spanish GRATITUDE OF SPAIN TO THE BRAVE BRITISH AT BAGUR 10 SEPT. 1810, PALAMOS 14 SEPT. 1810.
Comments: *Awarded by the Spanish government to the crews of the British warships* Ajax, Cambrian *and* Kent *who landed at Bagur and Palamos to seize French ships. The British force was, in fact, driven back with very heavy losses.*

VALUE:

Gold (8)	£3000–4000
Silver (600)	£600–800

88. JAVA MEDAL

Date: 1811.
Campaign: Java 1811.
Branch of Service: HEIC forces.
Ribbon: Yellow cord.
Metals: Gold or silver.
Size: 49mm.
Description: (Obverse) the assault on Fort Cornelis; (reverse) inscriptions in English and Farsi.
Comments: *Awarded by the HEIC for the seizure of Java from the Dutch. The 750 British officers and men who took part in the operation were not only awarded this medal but were eligible for the Military GSM with Java clasp, issued 38 years later. Senior officers of the Company were given the gold medal, while junior officers, NCOs and sepoys received the silver version.*

VALUE:

Gold (133)	£3500–4500
Silver (6519)	£550–650

89. NEPAUL MEDAL

Date: 1816.
Campaign: Nepal 1814-16.
Branch of Service: HEIC native troops.
Ribbon: Yellow cord.
Metal: Silver.
Size: 51mm.
Description: (Obverse) a fortified mountain-top with a cannon in the foreground; (reverse) Farsi inscription.
Comments: *This medal marked the campaign to pacify Nepal led by Generals Marley, Ochterlony and Gillespie (the last named being killed in action). At the conclusion of the war Ochterlony began recruiting Gurkha mercenaries, a policy which has continued in the British Army to this day. The clasp "Nepaul" was granted with the Army of India Medal to British forces in 1851.*

VALUE: £550–650

90. CEYLON MEDAL

Date: 1818.
Campaign: Ceylon (Sri Lanka) 1818.
Branch of Service: British and HEIC forces.
Ribbon: 38mm deep navy blue.
Metal: Gold or silver.
Size: 35mm.
Description: The very plain design has "Ceylon 1818" within a wreath (obverse) and REWARD OF MERIT at top and bottom of the reverse, the personal details being engraved in the centre.
Comments: *Awarded by the Ceylon government for gallant conduct during the Kandian rebellion. Only selected officers and men of the 19th, 73rd and 83rd Foot, the 1st and 2nd Ceylon Regiments and 7th, 15th and 18th Madras Native Infantry received this medal.*

VALUE:

Gold (2)	—
Silver (45)	£1500–2000

91. BURMA MEDAL

Date: 1826.
Campaign: Burma 1824-26.
Branch of Service: HEIC native forces.
Ribbon: 38mm crimson edged with navy blue.
Metals: Gold or silver.
Size: 39mm.
Description: (Obverse) the Burmese elephant kneeling in submission before the British lion; (reverse) the epic assault on Rangoon by the Irrawaddy Flotilla.
Comments: *Granted to native officers and men who participated in the campaign for the subjugation of Burma. This was the first of the HEIC campaign medals in what was to become a standard 1.5 inch (38mm) diameter. The medal was fitted with a large steel ring for suspension and issued unnamed. British troops in this campaign were belatedly (1851) given the clasp "Ava" to the Army of India Medal.*

VALUE: *Miniature*

Gold (750)	£2000–2500	—
Silver-gilt	£450–500	—
Silver (24,000)	£350–450	£250–300

92. COORG MEDAL

Date: 1837.
Campaign: Coorg rebellion 1837.
Branch of Service: HEIC loyal Coorg forces.
Ribbon: Yellow cord.
Metals: Gold, silver or bronze.
Size: 50mm.
Description: (Obverse) a Coorg holding a musket, with kukri upraised; (reverse) weapons in a wreath with the inscription FOR DISTINGUISHED CONDUCT AND LOYALTY TO THE BRITISH GOVERNMENT COORG APRIL 1837, the equivalent in Canarese appearing on the obverse.
Comments: *Native troops who remained loyal during the Canara rebellion of April-May 1837 were awarded this medal by the HEIC the following August. Bronze specimens were also struck but not officially issued and may have been restrikes or later copies. Bronzed and silvered electrotype copies are also known.*

VALUE:

Gold (44)	£4000–6000	
Silver (300)	£550–650	
Bronze	£200–300	

93. NAVAL GOLD MEDAL

Date: 1795.
Campaign: Naval actions 1795-1815.
Branch of Service: Royal Navy.
Ribbon: 44mm white with broad dark blue edges.
Metal: Gold.
Size: 51mm and 38mm.
Description: The medals were glazed on both sides and individually engraved on the reverse with the name of the recipient and details of the engagement in a wreath of laurel and oak leaves. (Obverse) the winged figure of Victory bestowing a laurel wreath on the head of Britannia standing in the prow of a galley with a Union Jack shield behind her, her right foot on a helmet, her left hand holding a spear.
Comments: *Instituted in 1795, a year after Lord Howe's naval victory on "the glorious First of June", this medal was awarded continually till 1815 when the Order of the Bath was expanded into three classes. Large medals were awarded to admirals and small medals went to captains. As medals were awarded for separate actions it was possible for officers to wear more than one; Lord Nelson himself had three. Two miniatures are recorded and would probably fetch at least £1000 if they came onto the market.*

VALUE:

Large medal (22)	From £25,000
Small medal (117)	From £12,000

94. NAVAL GENERAL SERVICE MEDAL

Date: 1847.

Campaign: Naval battles and boat actions 1793-1840.

Branch of Service: Royal Navy.

Ribbon: 32mm white with dark blue edges.

Metal: Silver.

Size: 36mm.

Description: (Obverse) the Young Head profile of Queen Victoria by William Wyon; (reverse) Britannia with her trident seated on a sea horse.

Clasps: No fewer than 230 different clasps for major battles, minor engagements, cutting-out operations and boat service were authorised. These either have the name or date of the action, the name of a ship capturing or defeating an enemy vessel, or the words BOAT SERVICE followed by a date. No fewer than 20,933 medals were awarded but most of them had a single clasp. Multi-clasp medals are worth very considerably more. The greatest number of clasps to a single medal was seven (two awards made); four medals had six clasps and fourteen medals had five clasps. For reasons of space only those clasps which are met with fairly often in the salerooms are listed below. At the other end of the scale it should be noted that only one recipient claimed the clasps for *Hussar* (17 May 1795), *Dido* (24 June 1795), *Spider* (25 August 1795), *Espoir* (7 August 1798), *Viper* (26 December 1799), *Loire* (5 February 1800), *Louisa* (28 October 1807), *Carrier* (4 November 1807), *Superieure* (10 February 1809), *Growler* (22 May 1812) and the boat actions of 15 March 1793, 4 November 1803, 4 November 1810 and 3-6 September 1814. In several cases no claimants came forward at all. The numbers of clasps awarded are not an accurate guide to value, as some actions are rated more highly than others, and clasps associated with actions in the War of 1812 have a very strong following in the USA as well as Britain. Clasps for famous battles, such as Trafalgar, likewise command a high premium out of all proportion to the number of clasps awarded. A medal to HMS *Victory* would be worth in excess of £5000.

Comments: *Instituted in 1847 and issued to* **surviving** *claimants in 1848, this medal was originally intended to cover naval engagements of the French Revolutionary and Napoleonic Wars (1793-1815) but was almost immediately extended to cover all naval actions of a more recent date, down to the expedition to Syria in 1840. It was fitted with a straight suspender.*

VALUE:

Fleet Actions

1 June 1794 (540)	£600–650
14 March 1795 (95)	£750–850
23 June 1795 (177)	£600–700
St Vincent (348)	£600–650
Camperdown (298)	£600–700
Nile (326)	£600–700
12 Octr 1798 (78)	£700–800
Egypt (618)	£380–450
Copenhagen (555)	£700–800
Gut of Gibraltar (142)	£550–650
Trafalgar (1710)	£1500–1800
4 Novr 1805 (296)	£650–750
St Domingo (396)	£400–450
Martinique (486)	£400–450
Basque Roads (529)	£500–550
Guadaloupe (483)	£400–450
Java (665)	£400–450
St Sebastian (293)	£400–450
Algiers (1328)	£350–400
Navarino (1142)	£475–550
Syria (6978)	£230–280

Ship Actions

Mars 21 April 1798 (26)	£1200–1400
Lion 15 July 1798 (23)	£1200–1400
Acre 30 May 1799 (41)	£800–1000
London 13 March 1806 (27)	£1200–1500
Curacao 1 Jany 1807 (65)	£800–1000
Stately 22 March 1808 (31)	£900–1000
Lissa (124)	£700–800
Shannon with Chesapeake (42)	£3000–3500
Gluckstadt 5 Jany 1814 (44)	£900–1000
Gaieta 24 July 1815 (88)	£600–700

Boat Service

16 July 1806 (51)	£850–950
1 Novr 1809 (110)	£650–750
28 June 1810 (25)	£900–1000
29 Sepr 1812 (25)	£1000–1200
8 Ap and May 1813 (57)	£1700–1900
2 May 1813 (48)	£700–800
8 April 1814 (24)	£1800–2000
24 May 1814 (12)	£1000–1200
14 Decr 1814 (205)	£800–1000

Miniature

Without clasp £100–150, for each clasp add £50+ depending on the action.

95. ARMY GOLD CROSS

Date: 1813.
Campaigns: Peninsular War and War of 1812.
Branch of Service: British Army.
Ribbon: 38mm crimson edged with dark blue.
Metal: Gold. **Size:** 38mm.
Description: A cross pattée with a laurel border having a rose at the centre on each of the four flat ends. At the centre of the cross appears a British lion statant. The scrolled top of the cross is fitted with an elaborate ring decorated with laurel leaves looped through a plain swivel ring fitted to the suspender. The arms of the cross on both obverse and reverse bear the names of four battles in relief.
Clasps: Large borders of laurel leaves enclosing the name of a battle in raised relief within an elliptical frame, awarded for fifth and subsequent battles.
Comments: *Arguably the most prestigious award in the campaign series, the Army Gold Cross was approved by the Prince Regent in 1813. It was granted to generals and officers of field rank for service in four or more battles of the Peninsular War. Three crosses had six clasps, two had seven, while the Duke of Wellington himself had the unique cross with nine clasps, representing participation in thirteen battles.*

VALUE:

Gold cross without clasp (61)	From £18,000
Miniature	£350–450

Battle of Vimiera.

96. MAIDA GOLD MEDAL

Date: 1806.
Campaign: Peninsular War, Battle of Maida 1806.
Branch of Service: British Army.
Ribbon: 38mm crimson edged with navy blue.
Metal: Gold. **Size:** 39mm.
Description: (Obverse) laureated profile of George III; (reverse) winged figure of Victory hovering with a laurel wreath over the head of Britannia, shield upraised, in the act of throwing a spear. The name and date of the battle appears on Britannia's left, with the *trinacria* or three-legged emblem on the right.
Clasps: None.
Comments: *This small gold medal was authorised in 1806 and awarded to the thirteen senior officers involved in the battle of Maida in Calabria when a small British force under General Sir John Stuart defeated a much larger French army with heavy loss. A small unknown number of gold and silver specimens are known to exist.*

VALUE: from £25,000

97. ARMY GOLD MEDAL

Date: 1810.
Campaigns: Peninsular War 1806-14 and War of 1812.
Branch of Service: British Army.
Ribbon: 38mm crimson edged with navy blue.
Metal: Gold.
Size: 54mm and 33mm.
Description: (Obverse) Britannia seated on a globe, holding a laurel wreath over the British lion and holding a palm branch in her left hand while resting on a shield embellished with the Union Jack. The name of the first action is generally engraved on the reverse.
Clasps: For second and third actions.
Comments: *The Maida medal (no. 96) established a precedent for the series of medals instituted in 1810. The name of the battle was inscribed on the reverse, usually engraved, though that for Barossa was die-struck. These medals were struck in two sizes, the larger being conferred on generals and the smaller on officers of field rank. Second or third battles were denoted by a clasp appropriately inscribed, while those who qualified for a fourth award exchanged their medal and bars for a gold cross. The award of these gold medals and crosses ceased in 1814 when the Companion of the Bath was instituted.*

VALUE:

Large medal	From £12,000
Small medal	From £5,500

98. MILITARY GENERAL SERVICE MEDAL

Date: 1847.

Campaigns: French Revolutionary and Napoleonic Wars 1793-1814.

Branch of Service: British Army.

Ribbon: 31mm crimson edged with dark blue.

Metal: Silver.

Size: 36mm.

Description: (Obverse) the Wyon profile of Queen Victoria; (reverse) a standing figure of the Queen bestowing victor's laurels on a kneeling Duke of Wellington. The simple inscription TO THE BRITISH ARMY appears round the circumference, while the dates 1793-1814 are placed in the exergue. Despite this, the earliest action for which a clasp was issued took place in 1801 (Abercromby's Egyptian campaign).

Clasps: Only 29 battle or campaign clasps were issued but multiple awards are much commoner than in the naval medal, the maximum being fifteen. While it is generally true to say that multi-clasp medals are worth more than single-clasp medals, there are many in the latter category (noted below) which command higher prices. The figures quoted below are based on the commonest regiments. Clasps awarded to specialists and small detached forces rate more highly than medals to the principal regiment in a battle or campaign. In particular, it should be noted that one naval officer, Lieut. Carroll, received the Military GSM and clasp for Maida, while a few other officers of the Royal Navy and Royal Marines received the medal with the clasps for Guadaloupe, Martinique or Java, and these, naturally, are now very much sought after. Paradoxically, the clasps for Sahagun and Benevente alone are very much scarcer than the clasp inscribed Sahagun and Benevente, awarded to surviving veterans who had participated in both battles. The clasps are listed below in chronological order. Medals to officers rate a premium.

Comments: *Like the Naval GSM, this medal was not sanctioned till 1847 and awarded the following year. Unlike the Naval medal, however, the Military GSM was confined to land actions up to the defeat of Napoleon in 1814 and the conclusion of the war with the United States. The regiment is now having a bearing on price, with medals to the 52nd, 88th or 95th Foot worth a good premium.*

VALUE:

Egypt	£500–600	Chateauguay	£1700–2000
Maida	£550–600	Chrystler's Farm	£1600–1800
Roleia	£550–600	Vittoria	£375–450
Vimiera	£350–400	Pyrenees	£375–450
Sahagun	£650–750	St Sebastian	£450–500
Benevente	£4500–5500	Nivelle	£375–450
Sahagun and Benevente	£650–750	Nive	£375–450
Corunna	£400–450	Orthes	£375–450
Martinique	£450–500	Toulouse	£375–450
Talavera	£350–400	2 clasps	£450–500
Guadaloupe	£450–500	3 clasps	£480–550
Busaco	£400–450	4 clasps	£550–650
Barrosa	£400–450	5 clasps	£650–750
Fuentes D'Onor	£450–500	6 clasps	£775–900
Albuhera	£550–650	7 clasps	£950–1050
Java	£550–650	8 clasps	£1100–1250
Ciudad Rodrigo	£450–500	9 clasps	£1300–1550
Badajoz	£500–600	10 clasps	£1600–1800
Salamanca	£400–500	11 clasps	£1850–2300
Fort Detroit	£1600–2000	12 or more clasps	From £2500

Miniature **without clasp** £100–150, for each clasp add £50+ depending on the action.

99. WATERLOO MEDAL

Date: 1815.
Campaign: Waterloo 1815.
Branch of Service: British Army.
Ribbon: 38mm, crimson edged in dark blue.
Metal: Silver.
Size: 37mm.
Description: (Obverse) the profile of the Prince Regent; (reverse) the seated figure of Victory above a tablet simply inscribed WATERLOO with the date of the battle in the exergue.
Comments: *This was the first medal awarded and officially named to all ranks who took part in a particular campaign. It was also issued, however, to those who had taken part in one or more of the other battles of the campaign, at Ligny and Quatre Bras two days earlier. The ribbon was intended to be worn with an iron clip and split suspension ring but many recipients subsequently replaced these with a more practical silver mount which would not rust and spoil the uniform. Some 39,000 medals were issued. The value of a Waterloo medal depends to a large extent on the regiment of the recipient. Medals awarded to those formations which saw the heaviest action and bore the brunt of the losses are in the greatest demand, whereas medals named to soldiers in General Colville's reserve division which did not take part in the fighting, are the least highly rated.*

VALUE:

Heavy Cavalry	£600–750
Scots Greys	£1400–1600
Light Cavalry	£500–600
Royal Artillery	£450–550
Royal Horse Artillery	£500–650
Foot Guards	£650–750
1st, 27th, 28th, 30th, 42nd, 44th, 52nd, 73rd, 79th, 92nd, 95th Foot	£650–1200
Other Foot regiments	£550–650
Colville's division (35th, 54th, 59th, 91st Foot)	£450–500
King's German Legion	£500–650
Miniature	£50–200

100. BRUNSWICK MEDAL FOR WATERLOO

Date: 1815.
Campaign: Battle of Waterloo 1815.
Branch of Service: Brunswick troops.
Ribbon: Cream with light blue stripes towards the edges.
Metal: Bronze.
Description: (Obverse) Duke Friedrich Wilhelm of Brunswick who was killed in the battle; (reverse) a wreath of laurel and oak leaves enclosing the German text "Braunschweig Seinen Kriegern" (Brunswick to its warriors) and the names of Quatre Bras and Waterloo.
Comments: *The Prince Regent authorised this medal for issue to the contingent from the Duchy of Brunswick.*

VALUE: £240–280

101. HANOVERIAN MEDAL FOR WATERLOO

Date: 1815.
Campaign: Battle of Waterloo 1815.
Branch of Service: Hanoverian troops.
Ribbon: Crimson edged with light blue.
Metal: Silver.
Description: (Obverse) the Prince Regent, his name and title being rendered in German. (Reverse) a trophy of arms below the legend HANNOVERSCHER TAPFERKEIT (Hanoverian bravery), with the name and date of the battle wreathed in the centre.
Comments: *The Prince Regent authorised this medal on behalf of his father George III in his capacity as Elector of Hanover and this was conferred on survivors of the battle. Suspension was by iron clip and ring similar to the British Waterloo Medal.*

VALUE: £300–350

102. NASSAU MEDAL FOR WATERLOO

Date: 1815.
Campaign: Battle of Waterloo 1815.
Branch of Service: Nassau forces.
Ribbon: Dark blue edged in yellow.
Metal: Silver.
Size: 25mm.
Description: (Obverse) Duke Friedrich of Nassau; (reverse) the winged figure of Victory crowning a soldier with laurels, the date of the action being in the exergue.
Comments: *Friedrich Duke of Nassau distributed this medal on 23 December 1815 to all of his own troops who had been present at the battle.*

VALUE: £200–220

103. SAXE-GOTHA-ALTENBURG MEDAL

Date: 1815.
Campaign: Germany and Waterloo 1814-15.
Branch of Service: Saxe-Gotha-Altenburg Foreign Legion.
Ribbon: Green with black edges and gold stripes.
Metal: Gilt bronze or bronze.
Size: 42mm.
Description: (Obverse) a crown with the legend IM KAMPFE FUER DAS RECHT (in the struggle for the right); (reverse) an ornate rose motif with the name of the duchy and the dates of the campaign in roman numerals.
Comments: *Gilded medals were issued to officers, but other ranks received a bronze version.*

VALUE:

Gilt-bronze	£220–260	
Bronze	£200–240	

104. ARMY OF INDIA MEDAL

Date: 1851.

Campaigns: India 1803–26.

Branch of Service: British and HEIC troops.

Ribbon: 32mm pale blue.

Metal: Silver.

Size: 35mm.

Description: (Obverse) the Wyon profile of Queen Victoria; (reverse) the seated figure of Victory beside a palm tree, with a wreath in one hand and a laurel crown in the other. The medal is fitted with an ornamental scroll suspender.

Clasps: The medal was not awarded without a campaign clasp and, unusually, in multi-clasp medals, the last clasp awarded was mounted closest to the medal itself, so that the battle roll has to be read downwards. There were two dies of the reverse, leading to the long- or short-hyphen varieties, both of comparable value. In all, some 4500 medals were awarded, but there is a very wide divergence between the commonest and rarest bars. Multi-clasp medals are rare, and medals awarded to Europeans are much scarcer than those to Indian troops.

Comments: *The last of the medals authorised in connection with the Napoleonic Wars, it was instituted and paid for by the Honourable East India Company in March 1851 for award to surviving veterans of the battles and campaigns in India and Burma between 1803 and 1826. Despite the dates 1799–1826 in the exergue, the medal was in fact awarded for service in one or other of four wars: the Second Mahratta War (1803–4), the Nepal War (1814–16), the Pindaree or Third Mahratta War (1817–18) and the Burmese War (1824–26), together with the siege of Bhurtpoor (1825–26). The medal is scarce, and examples with the clasps for the Second Mahratta War are much sought after, partly because few veterans were still alive 48 years after the event to claim their medals, and partly because of the war's association with Arthur Wellesley, the Duke of Wellington, who died in the very year in which the medal was awarded. Medals to the Royal Navy with the Ava clasp are very rare.*

VALUE:

Prices for medals bearing the following clasps are for European recipients. Medals to Indians are generally less expensive.

Rev. die a, short hyphen

Rev. die b, long hyphen

Allighur (66)	£2000–2500
Battle of Delhi (40)	£2500–2800
Assye (87)	£2000–2500
Asseerghur (48)	£2000–2500
Laswarree (100)	£1000–1200
Argaum (126)	£2000–2500
Gawilghur (110)	£2000–2500
Defence of Delhi (5)	Rare
Battle of Deig (47)	£2200–2500
Capture of Deig (103)	£1800–2200
Nepaul (505)	£700–800
Kirkee (5)	Rare
Poona (75)	£900–1100
Kirkee and Poona (88)	£950–1200
Seetabuldee (2)	Rare
Nagpore (155)	£800–900
Seetabuldee and Nagpore (21)	Rare
Maheidpoor (75)	£1000–1200
Corygaum (4)	Rare
Ava (2325)	£500–600
Bhurtpoor (1059)	£650–800
2 clasps (300)	Rare
3 clasps (150)	Rare
4 clasps (23)	Rare
5 or more clasps (10 x 5, 2 x 6, 1 x 7)	Rare
Glazed gilt specimen	£400
*Miniature**	
One clasp Ava	£100–150
Further clasps	£100–150 each

*Note there are many silver reproductions on the market, value £10–20.

105. GHUZNEE MEDAL

Date: 1839.
Campaign: Ghuznee 1839.
Branch of Service: British and HEIC forces.
Ribbon: 35mm half crimson, half dark green.
Metal: Silver.
Size: 37mm.
Description: (Obverse) the impressive gateway of the fortress of Ghuznee; (reverse) a mural crown enclosed in a laurel wreath with the date of capture.
Comments: *This was the second medal awarded for a particular campaign (after Waterloo) and was granted to both British and Indian troops who took part in the assault on Ghuznee in July 1839 which brought the first Afghan War to a close, overthrew the pro-Russian Dost Mohamed and restored Shah Soojah who instituted the Order of the Dooranie Empire (awarded to British generals and field officers) in appreciation. The Ghuznee medal was issued unnamed by the Honourable East India Company, but many recipients subsequently had their names impressed or engraved in various styles. No clasps were issued officially, but unauthorised clasps are occasionally encountered.*

VALUE:
British recipient	£250–450
Indian recipient	£200–250
Unnamed as issued	£200–250
Miniature	£150–300

106. ST. JEAN D'ACRE MEDAL

Date: 1840.
Campaign: Syria 1840.
Branch of Service: Royal Navy, Royal Marines and British Army.
Ribbon: Red with white edges.
Metal: Gold, silver or copper (bronzed).
Size: 30mm.
Description: (Obverse) a fortress flying the Ottoman flag, with six five-pointed stars round the top. A commemorative inscription and date in Arabic appear at the foot; (reverse) the Toughra of the Sultan in a laurel wreath.
Comments: *Awarded by the Sultan of Turkey to British, Austrian and Turkish forces under Sir Charles Napier, taking part in the liberation of this important city on the Syrian coast after eight years of Egyptian occupation. The medal has a plain ring suspension. The clasp "Syria" to the Naval GSM was awarded in 1848 in respect to this operation, and this medal generally accompanies the St Jean d'Acre medal.*

VALUE:
		Miniature
Gold (captains and field officers)	£500–700	—
Silver (junior officers)	£120–150	£150–200
Copper (petty officers, NCOs and other ranks)	£50–65	—

107. CANDAHAR, GHUZNEE, CABUL MEDAL

Date: 1842.

Campaign: Afghanistan 1841–42.

Branch of Service: British and HEIC troops.

Ribbon: 40mm watered silk of red, white, yellow, white and blue.

Metal: Silver.

Size: 35mm.

Description: Although the medals have a uniform obverse, a profile of the Queen captioned VICTORIA VINDEX, reverses are inscribed with the names of individual battles, or combinations thereof, within wreaths surmounted by a crown.

Comments: *The Honourable East India Company instituted this series of medals in 1842 for award to both HEIC and British troops who took part in the First Afghan War. The issue of this medal to units of the British Army, to Europeans serving in the Company's forces, and to Indian troops is further complicated by the fact that unnamed medals are generally common. In addition, the medal for Cabul is known in two versions, with the inscription CABUL or CABVL, the latter being a major rarity as only fifteen were issued. Beware of modern copies of the Candahar and Cabul medals.*

VALUE:	Imperial Regiments	Indian Units	Unnamed
Candahar	£400–500	£200–250	£220–250
Cabul	£300–350	£180–200	£180–230
Cabvl (15)	Rare	Rare	Rare
Ghuznee/Cabul	£400–600	£250–300	£200–250
Candahar/Ghuznee/ Cabul	£300–400	£200–250	£200–240
Miniature	from £200		

108. JELLALABAD MEDALS

Type 2 rev.

Type 1 obv.

Date: 1842.

Campaign: Afghanistan 1841-42.

Branch of Service: British and HEIC forces.

Ribbon: 44mm watered silk red, white, yellow, white and blue.

Metal: Silver.

Size: 39mm and 35mm.

Description: There are two different types of this medal, awarded by the HEIC to surviving defenders of the fortress of Jellalabad between 12 November 1841 and 7 April 1842. The first, struck in Calcutta, has a mural crown and JELLALABAD on the obverse, with the date of the relief of the garrison on the reverse; the second type shows the Wyon profile of Victoria (obverse) and the winged Victory with mountain scenery in the background and JELLALABAD VII APRIL round the top and the year in roman numerals in the exergue (reverse).

Comment: *The first type, struck in Calcutta, was considered to be unsuitable and holders were invited to exchange their medals for the second, more attractive, issue which was produced in London, although very few recipients took up the offer. The latter type was also awarded to the next of kin of soldiers killed in action.*

VALUE:	Imperial Regiments	Indian Units	Unnamed	*Miniature*
First type (Crown)	£450–550	£350–450	£350–400	£150–250
Second type (Victory)	£600–800	—	£450–550	£150–250

109. MEDAL FOR THE DEFENCE OF KELAT-I-GHILZIE

Date: 1842.
Campaign: Afghanistan 1842.
Branch of Service: European and native troops, HEIC.
Ribbon: 40mm watered silk red, white, yellow, white and blue.
Metal: Silver.
Size: 36mm.
Description: (Obverse) a shield bearing the name of the fort, surmounted by a mural crown and encircled by laurels; (reverse) a trophy of arms above a tablet inscribed INVICTA (unbeaten) and the date in roman numerals.
Comments: *Awarded to those who took part Qn the defence of the fort at Kelat-i-Ghilzie in May 1842, it is the rarest medal of the First Afghan War. No British imperial regiments took part, but 55 Europeans in the Company's service received the medal. It was also awarded to 877 native troops (including a contingent supplied by Shah Soojah) but few of their medals appear to have survived.*

VALUE:

European recipients	£4500–5500
Indian recipients	£1800–2300
Unnamed	£800–1000
Miniature	£250–300

110. CHINA WAR MEDAL

Issued reverse

Date: 1842.
Campaign: China 1841-42.
Branch of Service: British and HEIC forces.
Ribbon: 39mm crimson with yellow edges.
Metal: Silver.
Size: 36mm.
Description: The medal has the usual Wyon obverse, but the reverse was to have shown a British lion with its forepaws on a dragon. This was deemed to be offensive to the Chinese and was replaced by an oval shield bearing the royal arms and a palm tree flanked by a capstan, anchor and naval cannon representing the Royal Navy (left) and a field gun, drum and regimental flag representing the Army (right), with the Latin motto ARMIS EXPOSCERE PACEM (to pray for peace by force of arms) round the top and CHINA 1842 at the foot.
Comments: *Originally intended for issue to all ranks of the Honourable East India Company, it was subsequently awarded by the British government in 1843 to all who had taken part in the campaign in China popularly known as the First Opium War which ended with the seizure of Nanking.*

VALUE:

Royal Navy	£220–275
Indian and Bengal marine units	£240–300
British imperial regiments	£250–300
Indian Army	£175–200
Specimens of the original reverse	From £500
Miniature	£150–250

111. SCINDE MEDAL

Date: 1843.
Campaign: Scinde 1843.
Branch of Service: HEIC forces and 22nd Foot.
Ribbon: 44mm watered silk red, white, yellow, white and blue.
Metal: Silver.
Size: 36mm.
Description: The usual Wyon profile obverse was married to three different reverse types showing a crowned laurel wreath inscribed with the name of one or two campaigns and the date.
Comments: *Authorised in September 1843, this silver medal marked Sir Charles Napier's conquest of Scinde. The two major battles in the campaign, at Meeanee and Hyderabad, accomplished the complete rout of the forces of the Amirs of Scinde. The medals were originally issued with steel suspenders but the commanding officer of the 22nd Foot had the medals awarded to his men fitted with silver suspenders, at his own expense. Medals to the Indus Flotilla are particularly sought after by collectors.*

VALUE:

	22nd Foot	Indian units	HEIC ships
Meeanee	£600–850	£275–400	£1000–1250 (38)
Hyderabad	£550–650	£200–250	£1000–1250 (52)
Meeanee/Hyderabad	£450–550	£200–250	
Miniature	£150–250		

112. GWALIOR STAR

Date: 1843.
Campaign: Gwalior 1843.
Branch of Service: British and HEIC forces.
Ribbon: 44mm watered silk red, white, yellow, white and blue.
Metals: Bronze, with a silver centre.
Size: Max. width 45mm; max. height 52mm.
Description: Six-pointed bronze star with a silver centre star. The silver stars in the centre bear the name of one or other of the battles and the date 29 December 1843 on which both battles were fought. The plain reverse bears the name and regiment of the recipient.
Comments: *Bronze from guns captured at the battles of Maharajpoor and Punniar during the Gwalior campaign was used in the manufacture of these stars, thus anticipating the production of the Victoria Cross in the same manner. They were presented by the Indian government to all ranks who took part in these actions. When first issued, these stars were fitted with hooks to be worn like a breast decoration, but later ornate bar or ring suspensions were fitted to individual fancy and worn with the standard Indian ribbon of the period.*

VALUE:

		Miniature
Maharajpoor	£250–325	£100–150
Punniar	£280–340	£150–200

*Awards to Indian recipients are usually somewhat less.

113. SUTLEJ MEDAL

Date: 1846.
Campaign: Sutlej 1845-46.
Branch of Service: British and HEIC forces.
Ribbon: Dark blue with crimson edges.
Metal: Silver.
Size: 36mm.
Description: (Obverse) Wyon profile of Queen Victoria; (reverse) standing figure of Victory holding aloft a laurel crown, with a pile of captured weapons at her feet. The legend ARMY OF THE SUTLEJ appears round the top. The medal was fitted with an ornamental scroll suspender.
Clasps: Mounted above the suspender with roses between: Ferozeshuhur, Aliwal or Sobraon.
Comments: *The practice of issuing medals inscribed with different battles now gave way to the style of medals with specific battle or campaign clasps which set the precedent for the Naval and Military GSMs and later awards. As a compromise, however, the exergue of the reverse bears the name and date of the action for which the medal was first granted, and thus several different types are known.*

VALUE:	British regiments	Europeans in HEIC units	Indian units
Moodkee	£180–200	£140–180	£120–140
Moodkee 1 clasp	£220–250	£180–230	£160–180
Moodkee 2 clasps	£350–400	£240–280	£220–280
Moodkee 3 clasps	£500–600	£400–500	£300–350
Ferozeshuhur	£180–200	£150–200	£140–180
Ferozeshuhur 1 clasp	£250–280	£180–220	£180–200
Ferozeshuhur 2 clasps	£320–380	£300–350	£220–280
Aliwal	£180–200	£160–180	£140–180
Aliwal 1 clasp	£220–260	£200–240	£160–180
Sobraon	£250–300	£180–200	£120–150
Glazed gilt specimen	£250–300		
Miniature	£100–150, for each clasp add £50		

114. PUNJAB MEDAL

Date: 1849.
Campaign: Punjab 1848-49.
Branch of Service: British and HEIC forces.
Ribbon: Dark blue with yellow stripes towards the edges.
Metal: Silver.
Size: 36mm.
Description: (Obverse) Wyon profile of Queen Victoria; (reverse) Sir Walter Gilbert receiving the Sikh surrender. TO THE ARMY OF THE PUNJAB appears round the top and the year in roman numerals in the exergue. The medal has a scroll suspender.
Clasps: Mooltan, Chilianwala, Goojerat. Unusually the clasps read downwards from top to bottom
Comments: *This medal was granted to troops taking part in the campaigns which ended in the annexation of the Punjab. Unlike the Sutlej medal, however, this silver medal had a standard design. Large numbers of this medal were awarded to native troops, however many were melted down and therefore surprisingly few remain on the market in comparison with medals to European recipients.*

VALUE:	British units	Europeans in HEIC units	Indian units
No clasp	£150–170	£120–150	£80–100
Mooltan	£190–220	£180–200	£120–150
Chilianwala	£200–230	£180–200	£120–150
Goojerat	£190–200	£180–200	£140–160
Mooltan/Goojerat	£250–300	£240–280	£180–200
Chilianwala/Goojerat	£250–300	£240–280	£180–200
24th Foot casualty at Chilianwala	£550–650	—	—
Glazed gilt specimen	£250–300		
Miniature	£50–75, for each clasp add £25		

115. SOUTH AFRICA MEDAL

Date: 1854.
Campaigns: Southern Africa 1834–53.
Branch of Service: Royal Navy and Army.
Ribbon: Gold with broad and narrow deep blue stripes towards each end.
Metal: Silver.
Size: 36mm.
Description: (Obverse) Wyon profile of Queen Victoria; (reverse) a British lion drinking at a waterhole beside a protea shrub, the date 1853 being in the exergue.
Clasps: None.
Comments: *Authorised in November 1854, this medal was awarded in respect of three campaigns in southern Africa: 1834–35, 1846–47 and 1850–53, but as the medal was issued with a standard reverse and no campaign clasps it is impossible to tell when and where the recipient served without reference to the medal rolls. The majority of recipients were British troops but several hundred sailors of the Royal Navy also received the medal and a much smaller number of local forces. Of particular interest are medals awarded to men who survived the sinking of the troopship Birkenhead on its way to the Eastern Cape from Simons Town.*

VALUE:

	1834–35	1846–47	1850–53
British Army	£250–300	£220–270	£200–230
Royal Navy	—	£250–290	£180–220
HMS *Birkenhead*			From £500
Local forces	£260–280	£230–250	£180–220
Miniature	£50–65	£50–65	£50–65

116. SIR HARRY SMITH'S MEDAL FOR GALLANTRY

Date: 1851.
Campaign: Eighth Kaffir War 1850-51.
Branch of Service: Cape Mounted Rifles.
Ribbon: Dark blue with crimson edges.
Metal: Silver.
Size: 34mm.
Description: (Obverse) British lion passant gardant with a laurel wreath over its head; date 1851 in the exergue. (Reverse) PRESENTED BY round top and FOR GALLANTRY IN THE FIELD round the foot. HIS EXCELLENCY SIR H. G. SMITH and the name of the recipient appear across the centre.
Comments: *Sir Harry Smith (1787–1860) served with distinction in the Kaffir War of 1834–35, gained his KCB in the Gwalior campaign and a baronetcy for his decisive victory at Aliwal in the Sikh War. In 1847 he returned to South Africa as governor of Cape Colony. Although short of troops he conducted the eighth Frontier War (1850–53) with great resourcefulness but was recalled to England in 1852 before the Xhosas had been subdued. Harrismith in the Orange Free State was named in his honour, while Ladysmith in Natal was named after his beautiful and spirited Spanish wife Juanita, the forces' sweetheart of her day. Sir Harry had this medal struck at his own expense and awarded to troopers of the Cape Mounted Rifles who took part in the epic ride through the enemy lines from Fort Cox to Kingwilliamstown in 1851. Only 31 medals were presented, of which 22 are believed to be still extant.*

VALUE:

Unnamed	£1400–1800
Named	£2000–3000

117. INDIA GENERAL SERVICE MEDAL

Date: 1854.

Campaigns: Indian 1854-95.

Branch of Service: British and Indian forces.

Ribbon: Three crimson and two dark blue bars of equal width.

Metal: Silver or bronze.

Size: 36mm.

Description: (Obverse) Wyon profile of Queen Victoria; (reverse) Victory crowning a semi-nude seated warrior.

Clasps: 24 (see below).

Comments: *This medal was the first of five general service medals issued to cover minor campaigns in India. It was instituted in 1854 and continued for forty-one years, retaining the original Wyon profile of Queen Victoria throughout the entire period. Although the medal itself is quite common, some of its clasps are very rare, notably Kachin Hills 1892–93 awarded to the Yorkshire Regiment and Chin Hills 1892–93 awarded to the Norfolk Regiment. The maximum number of clasps to one medal recorded is seven. At first the medal was awarded in silver to all ranks regardless of race or branch of the services, but from 1885 onwards it was issued in bronze to native support personnel such as bearers, sweepers and drivers.*

VALUE:

	RN/RM	British Army	Indian Army	Bronze
Pegu	£100–120	£110–130	—	—
Persia	—	£110–130	£65–75	—
North West Frontier	—	£110–100	£60–70	—
Umbeyla	—	£100–110	£65–75	—
Bhootan	—	£110–120	£60–70	—
Looshai	—	—	£110–120	—
Perak	£100–150	£120–140	£80–100	—
Jowaki 1877–78	—	£100–120	£70–80	—
Naga 1879–80	—	—	£130–150	—
Burma 1885–87	£80–100	£80–100	£55–65	£50–60
Sikkim 1888	—	£120–140	£60–70	£80–100
Hazara 1888	—	£100–110	£90–100	£75–90
Burma 1887–89	—	£80–100	£50–60	£60–70
Burma 1887–9	—	£100–110	—	—
Chin Lushai 1889–90	—	£120–130	£60–70	£110–130
Lushai 1889-92	—	£300–350	£120–150	£170–190
Samana 1891	—	£110–120	£60–70	£60–70
Hazara 1891	—	£100–110	£50–60	£50–60
NE Frontier 1891	—	£120–140	£50–60	£80–90
Hunza 1891	—	—	£180–200	£350–380
Burma 1889–92	—	£90–110	£65–70	£50–60
Chin Hills 1892-93	—	£500–600	£110–130	£320–350
Kachin Hills 1892-93	—	£450–500	£180–200	£700–750
Waziristan 1894-95	—	£100–110	£50–60	£40–50

Miniature   £20–30, for each clasp add £10 (*Hunza*, *Chin Hills* and *Kachin Hills* clasps are rare)

118. BALTIC MEDAL

Date: 1856.

Campaign: Baltic Sea 1854–55.

Branch of Service: Royal Navy, Royal Marines and Royal Sappers and Miners.

Ribbon: Yellow with light blue edges.

Metal: Silver.

Size: 36mm.

Description: (Obverse) Wyon profile of Queen Victoria; (reverse) Britannia seated on a plinth decorated by a cannon, with a coastal scene in the background and BALTIC round the top.

Comments: *Authorised in 1856, this medal was granted to officers and men of the Royal Navy and Royal Marines for operations against Russia in the Baltic at the same time as the war in the Crimea. It was also awarded to about 100 members of the Royal Sappers and Miners engaged in the demolition of Russian fortifications of Bomarsund and Sveaborg. Medals were generally issued unnamed but often privately named afterwards, the exception being medals to the Sappers and Miners which were officially impressed.*

VALUE:

Unnamed	£80–90
Privately named	£90–100
Officially impressed to Sappers and Miners	£800–1000
Miniature	£15–20

119. CRIMEA MEDAL

Date: 1854.

Campaign: Crimea 1854–56.

Branch of Service: British Army, Navy and Marines.

Ribbon: Pale blue with yellow edges.

Metal: Silver.

Size: 36mm.

Description: (Obverse) Wyon profile of Queen Victoria; (reverse) a Roman soldier, armed with circular shield and short sword, being crowned by a flying Victory.

Clasps: Unusually ornate, being shaped like oak leaves with acorn finials: Alma, Inkerman, Azoff, Balaklava, Sebastopol, but the maximum found on any medal is four. Unofficial clasps for Traktir, Mamelon Vert, Malakoff, Mer d'Azoff and Kinburn are sometimes found on medals awarded to French troops.

Comments: *Medals may be found unnamed, unofficially or regimentally named, or officially impressed. Medals awarded to participants in the most famous actions of the war—the Thin Red Line (93rd Foot) and the Charge of the Light and Heavy Brigades—rate a very high premium. The prices quoted are for medals officially impressed to the Army. Clasps awarded to the Royal Navy and Royal Marines (Azoff, Balaklava, Inkerman, Sebastopol) rate a good premium, especially those named to personnel on board HM Ships London, Niger, Rodney and Wasp.*

VALUE:	Unnamed	Engraved	Regimentally impressed	Officially impressed Army
No clasp	£50–70	£50–70	£60–80	£90–150
Alma	£100–120	£100–120	£100–120	£160–180
Inkerman	£75–100	£90–120	£90–110	£150–170
Azoff	£130–150	£180–200	—	£350–400
Balaklava	£90–100	£110–130	£120–150	£160–180
93rd Foot*	—	£350–400	£600–700	£800–900
Heavy Brigade*	—	£350–400	£450–500	£700–800
Light Brigade (Charger)*	—	£1200–1500	£1400–1800	£4500–5500
Sebastopol	£80–110	£70–90	£100–125	£100–140
2 clasps	£120–140	£100–130	£120–150	£170–200
3 clasps	£170–200	£150–200	£220–250	£275–350
4 clasps	£200–250	£200–250	£250–300	£450–500
Miniature	£15–20, for each clasp add £10			

It is always difficult to price scarce or rare medals such as those marked as we have seen many engraved or Depot-style impressing that were probably named in the past 30 to 40 years. Also an engraved Crimea, together with a Mutiny and/or LS&GC would be worth considerably more than the prices indicated. Buyer beware!

120. TURKISH CRIMEA MEDAL

Date: 1855.
Campaign: Crimea 1855-56.
Branch of Service: British, French and Sardinian forces.
Ribbon: Crimson with green edges.
Metal: Silver.
Size: 36mm.
Description: (Obverse) a cannon, weapons and the four Allied flags with the name and date in the exergue; (reverse) the Toughra and Arabic date according to the Moslem calendar.
Clasps: None.
Comments: *Instituted by the Sultan of Turkey, this silver medal was conferred on troops of the three Allies who fought in the Crimea. The obverse types differed in the arrangement of the flags, corrsponding with the inscription in English, French or Italian in the exergue. Although the medals were intended to be issued to British, French and Sardinian troops respectively, they were issued haphazardly. They were unnamed, but many were privately engraved or impressed later. There is a dangerous copy emanating from the West Country of the UK.*

VALUE:			*Miniature*
CRIMEA (British Issue)		£65–85	£20–25
LA CRIMEE (French Issue)		£125–185	Rare
LA CRIMEA (Sardinia Issue)		£55–65	£10–15

121. INDIAN MUTINY MEDAL

Date: 1858.
Campaign: Sepoy mutiny, India 1857-58.
Branch of Service: British Army, Navy and Indian forces. It was also awarded to many civilians who took part in suppressing the Mutiny.
Ribbon: White with two red stripes.
Metal: Silver.
Size: 36mm.
Description: (Obverse) Wyon profile of Queen Victoria; (reverse) the standing figure of Britannia bestowing victor's laurels, with the British lion alongside. INDIA appears round the top with the dates 1857-1858 in the exergue.
Clasps: Delhi, Defence of Lucknow, Relief of Lucknow, Lucknow, Central India. The maximum recorded for a single medal is four (Bengal Artillery) or three (imperial troops, 9th Lancers).
Comments: *This medal was awarded to troops who took part in operations to quell the Sepoy mutiny which had been the immediate cause of the uprising, although it also served to focus attention on the Honourable East India Company's conduct of affairs and led directly to the transfer of the administration of India to the Crown. Medals with the clasp for the defence of Lucknow awarded to the original defenders rate a considerable premium, as do medals awarded to members of the Naval Brigade which witnessed most of the fighting in the mopping-up operations. Medals to Indian recipients although scarcer on the market, generally bring a little less than their British counterparts. Four-clasp medals to the Bengal Artillery bring from £800 if verified.*

VALUE:	British Navy	British Army	*Miniature*
No clasp	£350–450*	£110–120	£12–15
Delhi	—	£160–180	£15–25
Defence of Lucknow			
original defender	—	£600–700	£35–45
first relief force	—	£300–350	
Relief of Lucknow	£500–600	£180–200	£15–25
Lucknow	£500–600	£150–180	£15–25
Central India	—	£150–180	£15–20, add
2 clasps	£600–700	£250–280	£10 for each
3 clasps (9th Lancers)	—	£500–600	additional clasp

*The 66 medals to HMS Shannon *and the 253 to HMS* Pearl *rate an even higher premium.*

122. SECOND CHINA WAR MEDAL

Date: 1861.

Campaign: Second China War 1857-60.

Branch of Service: British Army and Navy.

Ribbon: 33mm crimson with yellow edges.

Metal: Silver.

Size: 36mm.

Description: As the First China War Medal (no. 110), but without the year 1842 at the foot.

Clasps: Fatshan 1857, Canton 1857, Taku Forts, Pekin 1860.

Comments: *This medal was awarded to British sevicemen who took part, alongside the French, in the campaign against China which had been provoked by hostile acts against European nationals. The Royal Navy, under Admiral Sir Michael Seymour, destroyed a Chinese flotilla at Fatshan Creek, preparing the way for the attack on Canton whose capture brought the first phase to an end in June 1858. Reinforcements were meanwhile diverted to help put down the Indian mutiny. Fighting broke out again and this time large numbers of troops were involved in the assault on the Taku forts and the sack of Pekin (Beijing). Examples of the China medal of 1842, with or without clasps for 1857-60, have been recorded to recipients who fought in the Second China War. Medals may be found unnamed or with names officially engraved (Indian Army) or impressed (British Army, Indian Navy). Although those to the Navy were all issued unnamed, they are occasionally encountered unofficially named. Awards to Army and Navy personnel are other factors governing values.*

VALUE:	Unnamed	Army/Navy officially impressed	Miniature
No clasp	£70–80	£100–120	£18
China 1842	Rare	Rare	—
Fatshan 1857	£90–100	£130–150	£45
Canton 1857	£90–100	£140–170	£35
Taku Forts 1858	£90–100	£120–150	£30
Taku Forts 1860	£90–100	£140–170	£40
Pekin 1860	£90–100	£140–170	£30
2 clasps	£130–150	£200–240	£55
3 clasps	£160–180	£350–400	£65
4 clasps	£190–220		
5 clasps	£240–280		

123. NEW ZEALAND MEDALS

Date: 1869.

Campaigns: First and Second Maori Wars 1845–47 and 1860–66.

Branch of Service: Army, Navy and local volunteers.

Ribbon: Blue with a central orange stripe.

Metal: Silver.

Size: 36mm.

Description: (Obverse) Veiled head of Queen Victoria. (Reverse) Date of service in a wreath, with NEW ZEALAND round the top and VIRTUTIS HONOR (honour of valour) round the foot. Suspender ornamented with New Zealand wattle.

Comments: *These medals were unusual in having the recipient's dates of service die-struck on the centre of the reverse, though medals were also issued without dates. As the medal was only awarded to surviving veterans, the numbers issued in respect of the earlier conflict are understandably small. Many of the dates are very scarce, especially those issued to naval personnel in the first war. Only naval personnel received dated medals in the first war.*

VALUE:	Army	Navy/Royal Marines
First war		
Undated	£300–325	—
1845–46 (155)	—	£325–350
1845–47 (36)	—	£375–425
1846–47 (69)	—	£475–525
1846 (10)	—	£575–625
1847 (20)	£500–550	£465–500
Second war		
Undated	£150–165	—
1860	£600–650	Rare
1860-61	£350–380	£260–325
1860-63	From £1500	—
1860-64	£220–260	—
1860-65	£240–275	—
1860-66	£225–265	—
1861	Rare	—
1861-63	Rare	—
1861-64	£250–300	—
1861-65	Rare	—
1861-66	£210–250	—
1862-66	Rare	—
1863	£260–275	Rare
1863-64	£240–265	£250–275
1863-65	£210–250	Scarce
1863-66	£210–250	Rare
1864	£230–260	Rare
1864-65	£210–225	—
1864-66	£210–225	—
1865	£275–325	£380–420
1865-66	£220–225	—
1866	£210–225	—
Miniature		
Undated	£45	
Dated	£60+	

124. ABYSSINIAN WAR MEDAL

Date: 1869.
Campaign: Abyssinia (Ethiopia) 1867–68.
Branch of Service: Royal Navy, British and Indian Armies.
Ribbon: Red with broad white edges.
Metal: Silver.
Size: 33mm diameter.
Description: (Obverse) the veiled portrait of Victoria framed by a
zigzag pattern with floral ornament alternating with the letters of
the name ABYSSINIA. The recipient's name and unit were
embossed in the centre of the reverse except most to Indian troops
which were impressed. Suspension is by a ring via a large crown
standing proud from the top of the medal.
Clasps: None.
Comments: *The imprisonment of British subjects by King Theodore of
Abyssinia precipitated a punitive expedition under General Sir Robert
Napier involving ships of the Royal Navy, a naval brigade and troops of the
British and Indian armies. Because casualties were unusually light (only
two killed and 27 wounded), medals from this campaign are not so highly
rated as those from other nineteenth century wars.*

VALUE:

British troops	£140–180
Royal Navy	£140–160
RN Rocket Brigade	£300–350
Indian troops	£80–120
Miniature	£55–65

125. CANADA GENERAL SERVICE MEDAL

Date: 1899.
Campaign: Canada 1866–70.
Branch of Service: Royal Navy, British Army and Canadian units.
Ribbon: Red, white and red.
Metal: Silver.
Size: 36mm.
Description: (Obverse) crowned and veiled Old Head bust of Queen
Victoria by Sir Thomas Brock (reflecting the very late issue of the
medal). (Reverse) Canadian flag surrounded by maple leaves.
Clasps: Fenian Raid 1866, Fenian Raid 1870, Red River 1870.
Comments: *This medal was not authorised until January 1899, thirty years
after the event, and was issued by the Canadian government to British and
Canadian local forces who took part in operations to put down the Fenian
raids of 1866 and 1870 and the Red River rebellion of the latter year. Of
the 16,100 medals awarded, 15,000 went to local forces. Naval medals
command a premium.*

VALUE:

	Canadian forces	British Army	Royal Navy	*Miniature*
Fenian Raid 1866	£140–160	£180–200	£180–220	£60
Fenian Raid 1870	£140–160	£180–200	£300–400	£65
Red River 1870	£550–650	£650–800	£850–1000	£85
2 clasps	£220–250	—	—	£80
3 clasps	Rare	—	—	—

126. ASHANTEE MEDAL

Date: 1874.

Campaign: Gold Coast 1873–74.

Branch of Service: Royal Navy, Army and native troops.

Ribbon: Orange with black stripes at the sides and two narrow black stripes towards the centre.

Metal: Silver.

Size: 36mm.

Description: The obverse and reverse are similar to the East and West Africa Medal of 1887–1900, differing solely in thickness and the method of naming. The veiled profile of Victoria graces the obverse while the reverse, designed by Sir Edwin Poynter, shows a skirmish in the jungle between British soldiers and Ashantee warriors.

Clasps: Coomassie.

Comments: *All ranks who took part in operations against King Kalkali of Ashantee, Gold Coast, were awarded this medal, approved in June 1874. The campaign lasted only four weeks but was fought with great ferocity and resulted in the award of four VCs. There was also a very high incidence of sickness and disease among the troops, notably the naval contingent. Unusually the medals are named in engraved capitals filled in with black.*

VALUE:

	Navy	Army	Natives	*Miniature*
No clasp	£110–120	£120–140	£70–90	£30
Coomassie	£180–220	£220–240	£100–130	£65

127. SOUTH AFRICA MEDAL

Date: 1879.

Campaign: South Africa 1877-79.

Branch of Service: Royal Navy, Army and colonial units.

Ribbon: As no. 115.

Metal: Silver.

Size: 36mm.

Description: The same design as no. 115, except that the date 1853 in the exergue is replaced by a Zulu shield and four crossed assegais.

Clasps: 1877, 1877–8, 1877–9, 1877–8–9, 1878, 1878–9, 1879.

Comments: *The campaign began in 1877 with an attack on the Fingoes by the Galeka and Gaika tribes and culminated in the showdown between the Zulus and the British when Lord Chelmsford's column was annihilated at Isandhlwana. When the 3000 Zulus advanced on Rorke's Drift, however, they were checked with heavy losses by a tiny garrison of 139 men. During the defence no fewer than eleven VCs were won—the largest number for a single action. The campaign concluded with the defeat of Dinizulu and his warriors at Ulundi.*

VALUE:

	Navy	Army	Colonial	*Miniature*
No clasp	£120–140	£120–150	£100–110	£25
1877	—	Rare	£1100–1300	—
1877–8	£400–500	£200–250	£200–240	£40
1877–9	—	Unique	£4000–5000	—
1877–8–9	£350–450	£260–280	£190–220	£35
1878	—	£250–300	£200–220	£40
1878–9	—	£250–280	£200–220	£35
1879	£180–200	£240–270	£180–200	£35

Isandhlwana casualty	£2000–3000
Rorke's Drift participant	From £7500

128. AFGHANISTAN MEDAL

Date: 1881.

Campaign: Afghanistan 1878–80.

Branch of Service: British and Indian Armies.

Ribbon: Dark green with broad crimson edges.

Metal: Silver or bronze.

Size: 36mm.

Description: (Obverse) veiled profile of Queen Victoria. (Reverse) a column on the march, with an elephant carrying cannon. The dates 1878–79–80 appear in the exergue.

Clasps: Ali Musjid, Peiwar Kotal, Charasia, Kabul, Ahmed Kel, Kandahar. Maximum number of clasps per medal is four.

Comments: *This medal was awarded to all who took part in the campaigns against Afghanistan known as the Second Afghan War. In 1877 the Amir refused to accept a British resident and the following year raised an army which began harrassing the Indian frontier. A treaty with Russia, however, granting it protective rights in Afghanistan, precipitated an armed response from Britain. In 1880 General Roberts led a column from Kabul to Kandahar to relieve General Burrows and the resulting battle led to the defeat of the Afghans and the conclusion of the war. Medals awarded to the 66th Foot (Berkshire regiment) and E Battery of B Brigade, Royal Artillery rate a high premium as these units sustained the heaviest casualties at the battle of Maiwand in July 1880.*

VALUE:	British units	Indian units	*Miniature*
No clasp bronze	—	£140–180	—
No clasp silver	£65–90	£40–60	£20
Ali Musjid	£120–140	£60–80	£30
Peiwar Kotal	£140–150	£60–80	£40
Charasia	£120–140	£60–80	£30
Kabul	£120–140	£60–80	£25
Ahmed Khel	£120–140	£60–80	£30
Kandahar	£120–140	£60–80	£30
2 clasps	£150–200	£70–95	£50
3 clasps	£250–300	£110–135	£65
4 clasps	£350–450	£150–200	£80
Maiwand casualties:			
66th Foot	£550–650	—	
E Bty, B Bde RHA	£500–600	—	

129. KABUL TO KANDAHAR STAR

Date: 1881.

Campaign: Afghanistan 1878–80.

Branch of Service: British and Indian Armies.

Ribbon: Watered silk red, white, yellow, white and blue.

Metal: Bronze from captured guns.

Size: Height 60mm, width 45mm.

Description: (Obverse) a rayed five-pointed star surmounted by a crown with a ring for suspension. The centre is inscribed KABUL TO KANDAHAR with 1880 at the foot and the VRI monogram of the Queen Empress in the centre. Stars were either issued unnamed, or had the recipient's name impressed (to British) or engraved (to Indian troops) on the reverse.

Clasps: None.

Comments: *This star, struck by Jenkins of Birmingham, was awarded to those who took part in the epic 300-mile march from the Afghan capital to Kandahar, led by General Roberts to relieve the beleaguered forces of General Burrows.*

VALUE:	
Unnamed	£80–90
Impressed (British troops)	£145–165
Engraved (Indian troops)	£100–125
Miniature	£40–65

Maiwand (see no. 128)

130. CAPE OF GOOD HOPE GENERAL SERVICE MEDAL

Date: 1900.
Campaign: Uprisings in Transkei, Basutoland and Bechuanaland 1880-97.
Branch of Service: Local forces and volunteers.
Ribbon: Dark blue with a central yellow stripe.
Metal: Silver.
Size: 36mm.
Description: (Obverse) Jubilee bust of Queen Victoria by Sir Joseph Boehm; (reverse) arms of Cape Colony.
Clasps: Transkei, Basutoland, Bechuanaland.
Comments: *Instituted by the Cape government, this medal acknowledged service in putting down the Transkei (1880-1) and Bechuana (1896-7) rebellions and dealing with the unrest that erupted sporadically in Basutoland for much of this period. The medal was awarded, with one or more campaign clasps, to local forces and volunteer regiments. Ten medals were, however, officially awarded without a clasp.*

VALUE:		*Miniature*
Transkei (1070)	£220–260	£50
Basutoland (2150)	£120–140	£50
Bechuanaland (2580)	£120–140	£45
2 clasps	£220–250	£65
3 clasps (23)	Rare	—
No clasp	Very rare	

131. EGYPT MEDAL 1882–89

Date: 1882.
Campaign: Egypt 1882–89.
Branch of Service: Royal Navy and Army.
Ribbon: Three blue and two white stripes.
Metal: Silver.
Size: 36mm.
Description: (Obverse) the veiled profile of Queen Victoria; (reverse) the Sphinx.
Clasps: 13, listed below. Maximum number for one medal is 7, but only one such award was made. Common two-clasp combinations are denoted below by /.
Comments: *British involvement in Egypt deepened after the opening of the Suez Canal in 1869, many British officers being seconded to the Khedive's Army. When the Army mutinied in 1882 and triggered off a general anti-European uprising, an Anglo-French expedition was mounted. Subsequently the French withdrew before a landing was effected. Trouble erupted in the Sudan (under Anglo-Egyptian administration) in 1884 where General Gordon was besieged at Khartoum. Further campaigns aimed at the overthrow of the Mahdi and the reconquest of the Sudan. These prolonged operations created immense logistical problems. Nile transportation in particular was a matter resolved only when Canadian voyageurs were recruited to handle the river-boats. In addition, a contingent of troops from New South Wales "answered the Empire's call" and medals awarded to them for the Suakin campaign of 1885 are much sought after. Except where noted, the prices quoted below are for medals awarded to British Army personnel. Medals awarded to Indian or Egyptian troops are generally worth about 25 per cent less than comparable awards to British Army units. Medals to Royal Navy are rare.*

Dated rev.

VALUE:		*Miniature*
No clasp (dated)	£70–80	£15
No clasp (undated)	£70–80	£20
Alexandria 11th July	£100–120	£22
Tel-el-Kebir	£100–120	£22
El-Teb	£120–140	£35
Tamaai	£130–150	£30
El-Teb/Tamaai	£120–130	£30
Suakin 1884	£100–120	£25
The Nile 1884-85	£100–120	£25
The Nile 1884-85/Abu Klea	£450–550	£30
The Nile 1884-85/Kirbekan	£140–155	£30
Suakin 1885	£100–120	£25
Suakin 1885/Tofrek	£140–160	£35
Gemaizah 1888	£125–145	£40
Toski 1889	£135–165	£50
2 clasps	£120–160	£40
3 clasps	£200–240	£50
4 clasps	£270–320	£60
5 clasps	£450–550	—
Canadian boatmen	£900–1000	
NSW units (Suakin 1885)	From £700	

Undated rev.

132. KHEDIVE'S STAR

Date: 1882.
Campaign: Egypt 1892-91.
Branch of Service: Royal Navy and Army.
Ribbon: 37mm deep blue.
Metal: Bronze.
Size: Height 60mm; width 45mm.
Description: A five-pointed star with a circular centre showing the Sphinx and Pyramids surrounded by a band inscribed EGYPT followed by a year round the top, with 'Khedive of Egypt' and the year in the Moslem calendar in Arabic at the foot. (Reverse) the Khedive's monogram surmounted by a crown. The star is suspended by a ring from an ornamental clasp in the centre of which is a star and crescent.
Clasps: Tokar.
Comments: *This star, struck by Jenkins of Birmingham, was conferred by Khedive Tewfik of Egypt on those who qualified for the Egypt medal and it was invariably worn alongside, to the detriment of the silver medal which suffered abrasion from the points of the star. There was also an undated version found with or without a campaign clasp for Tokar, awarded in 1891. These stars were issued unnamed.*

VALUE:		Miniature
1882	£40–45	£10
1884	£45–50	£12
1884-86	£40–50	£12
Undated	£45–60	£12
Undated with Tokar bar	£120–140	£60

133. GENERAL GORDON'S STAR FOR THE SIEGE OF KHARTOUM

Date: 1884.
Campaign: Mahdist uprising, Sudan 1884.
Branch of Service: British and Sudanese forces.
Ribbon: Deep blue.
Metal: Silver or pewter.
Size: Height 80mm; maximum width 54mm.
Description: Star with three concentric circles and seven groups of rays on which are superimposed seven crescents and stars. Suspension by a ring from a Crescent and Star ornament.
Clasps: None.
Comments: *To boost the morale of the defenders Charles Gordon, commanding the garrison at Khartoum, had this star cast locally in a sand mould, using his own breast star of the Order of Mejidieh as the model. Exceptionally, recipients had to purchase their medals, the proceeds going to a fund to feed the poor.*

VALUE:	
Silver gilt	£900–1200
Silver	£600–800
Pewter	£350–400

134. NORTH WEST CANADA MEDAL

Date: 1885.

Campaign: Riel's rebellion 1885.

Branch of Service: Mainly local forces.

Ribbon: Blue-grey with red stripes towards the edges.

Metal: Silver.

Size: 36mm.

Description: (Obverse) bust of Queen Victoria; (reverse) the inscription NORTH WEST CANADA 1885 within a frame of maple leaves.

Clasps: Saskatchewan,

Comments: *Paradoxically, while the medal for the Fenian Raids of 1866–70 was not sanctioned till 1899, this medal for service in the North West was authorised immediately after the conclusion of operations against the Metis led by Louis Riel. It was issued unnamed, with or without the clasp for Saskatchewan where the bulk of the action took place. Of particular interest are medals to officers and men aboard the steamship Northcote involved in a boat action; exceptionally, their medals were impressed. Other medals may be encountered with unofficial naming. The medal was awarded to sixteen British staff officers but the majority of medals (5600 in all) went to local forces.*

VALUE:		Miniature
No clasp	£165–200	£35
Saskatchewan	£420–460	£65
Northcote recipient	£650–700	

135. ROYAL NIGER COMPANY'S MEDAL

Date: 1899.

Campaign: Nigeria 1886–97.

Branch of Service: Officers and men of the Company's forces.

Ribbon: Three equal stripes of yellow, black and white.

Metal: Silver or bronze.

Size: 39.5mm.

Description: (Obverse) the Boehm bust of Queen Victoria; (reverse) the Company's arms in a laurel wreath.

Clasps: Nigeria 1886-97 (silver), Nigeria (bronze).

Comments: *This medal was issued in silver to Europeans and bronze to natives for service in the vast territories administered by the Royal Niger chartered company. Silver medals were impressed in capitals, but those in bronze were more usually stamped with the recipient's service (constabulary) number. Specimens of both versions were later struck from the original dies but these lack name or number.*

VALUE:		Miniature
Silver named (85)	£1500–2000	
Original Silver specimen	£80–100	£130–150
Bronze named (250)	£450–500	
Original Bronze specimen	£60–80	

136. IMPERIAL BRITISH EAST AFRICA COMPANY'S MEDAL

Date: 1890.
Campaign: East Africa (Kenya and Uganda) 1888–95.
Branch of Service: Company forces.
Ribbon: Plain blue.
Metal: Silver.
Size: 39mm.
Description: (Obverse) the Company badge, a crowned and radiant sun, with a Suaheli inscription in Arabic round the foot signifying "the reward of bravery"; (reverse) plain except for a wreath. Suspension is by a plain ring or an ornamental scroll.
Comments: *The rarest of the medals awarded by the chartered companies, this medal was originally intended solely as a gallantry award; but after the BEA Company was wound up in 1895 further issues were authorised by the Foreign Office for service in Witu (1890) and the Ugandan civil war (1890-91). Less than thirty medals are known.*

VALUE: From £600   *Miniature* £150–200

137. EAST AND WEST AFRICA MEDAL

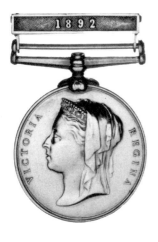

Date: 1892.
Campaigns: East and West Africa 1887–1900.
Branch of Service: Royal Navy, Army and native forces.
Ribbon: As 126.
Metal: Silver or bronze.
Size: 36mm.
Description: As for the Ashantee Medal (q.v.), distinguished only by its clasps.
Clasps: 21 (see below). A 22nd operation (Mwele, 1895–96) was denoted by engraving on the rim of the medal.
Comments: *This medal was awarded for general service in a number of small campaigns and punitive expeditions. Though usually awarded in silver, it was sometimes struck in bronze for issue to native servants, bearers and drivers. British regiments as such were not involved in any of the actions, but individual officers and NCOs were seconded as staff officers and instructors and their medals bear the names of their regiments. Units of the Royal Navy were also involved in many of the coastal or river actions. Especially sought after are naval medals with the bar for Lake Nyassa 1893 in which the ships* Pioneer *and* Adventure *were hauled in sections overland through 200 miles of jungle.*

VALUE:

	Royal Navy	Europeans	Natives	*Miniature*
1887–8	£350–450	£130–140	£100–120	£40
Witu 1890	£120–140	£130–160	£80–100	£40
1891–2	£170–190	£140–160	£100–120	£40
1892 (8)	£700–900	£160–180	£100–120	£40
Witu August 1893	£150–180	—	£110–130	£60
Liwondi 1893	£1500–2000	—	—	—
Juba River 1893	£1500–2000	—	—	—
Lake Nyassa 1893	£1500–2000	—	—	—
1893–94	£600–800	£140–160	£90–110	£50
Gambia 1894	£140–160	—	£100–120	£45
Benin River 1894	£140–160	£120–140	£90–110	£40
Brass River 1895	£180–200	—	—	£45
M'wele 1895–6	£100–120	£100–120	£80–100	£100
1896–98	—	£300–350	£150–200	£30
Niger 1897	—	£250–300	£150–200	£30
Benin 1897	£100–120	£100–120	£150–200	£35
Dawkita 1897	£800–1000	Rare	Rare	—
1897–98	—	£130–150	£120–130	£40
1898	£600–800	£140–170	£120–140	£40
Sierra Leone 1898–99	£140–180	£130–160	£80–100	£30
1899	£800–1000	£220–250	£150–170	£35
1900	—	£200–220	£130–150	£35

138. BRITISH SOUTH AFRICA COMPANY'S MEDAL

1st type rev.

Mashonaland (2nd) obv.

Date: 1896.
Campaign: South Africa 1890-97.
Branch of Service: British Army and colonial units.
Ribbon: Seven equal stripes, four yellow and three dark blue.
Metal: Silver.
Size: 36mm.
Description: (Obverse) the Old Head bust of Queen Victoria; (reverse) a charging lion impaled by a spear, with a mimosa bush in the background and a litter of assegais and a shield on the ground.
Clasps: Mashonaland 1890, Matabeleland 1893, Rhodesia 1896, Mashonaland 1897.
Comments: *Originally instituted in 1896 for award to troops taking part in the suppression of the Matabele rebellion, it was later extended to cover operations in Rhodesia (1896) and Mashonaland (1897). The medal, as originally issued, had the inscription MATABELELAND 1893 at the top of the reverse. The medal was re-issued with RHODESIA 1896 or MASHONALAND 1897 inscribed on the reverse, but holders of medals for their first campaign only added clasps for subsequent campaigns. Rather belatedly, it was decided in 1927 to issue medals retrospectively for the Mashonaland campaign of 1890; in this instance the name and date of the campaign were not inscribed on the reverse though the details appeared on the clasp. An unusually ornate suspender has roses, thistles, shamrocks and leeks entwined. Only two medals are known with all four clasps, while only fifteen medals had three clasps.*

VALUE:

		Miniature
Mashonaland 1890	From £500	£30
Matabeleland 1893	£150–200	£30
with 1 clasp	£250–280	£50
with 2 clasps	From £450	£65
Rhodesia 1896	£150–170	£30
with 1 clasp	£250–280	£50
Mashonaland 1897	£150–200	£30

139. HUNZA NAGAR BADGE

Date: 1891.
Campaign: Hunza and Nagar 1891.
Branch of Service: Jammu and Kashmir forces.
Ribbon: Large (46mm x 32mm) with a broad red diagonal band and white centre stripe and green upper left and lower right corners.
Metal: Bronze.
Size: 55mm x 27mm.
Description: A uniface rectangular plaque featuring three soldiers advancing on the crenellated hill fort of Nilt, with mountains in the background. The inscription HUNZA NAGAR 1891 appears lower right. It was intended to be worn as a brooch at the neck but subsequently many were fitted with a suspender for wear with a red and green ribbon.
Clasps: None.

Comments: *Gurney of London manufactured this badge which was awarded by the Maharajah of Jammu and Kashmir to his own troops who served in the operation against the border states of Hunza and Nagar and qualified for the Indian general service medal with clasp for Hunza 1891. The punitive expedition was led by Colonel A. Durand in response to the defiant attitude of the Hunza and Nagar chiefs towards the British agency at Gilgit.*

VALUE: £450–500

140. CENTRAL AFRICA MEDAL

Date: 1895.
Campaigns: Central Africa 1891–98.
Branch of Service: Mainly local forces.
Ribbon: Three equal stripes of black, white and terracotta representing the Africans, Europeans and Indians.
Metal: Silver or bronze.
Size: 36mm.
Description: Obverse and reverse as the East and West Africa (Ashantee) medal, distinguished only by its ribbon.
Clasps: Originally issued without a clasp but one for Central Africa 1894–98 was subsequently authorised.
Comment: *Though generally issued in silver, a bronze version was awarded to native servants. The first issue of this medal had a simple ring suspension and no clasp. For the second issue a clasp, Central Africa 1894–98 was authorised and the medal was issued with a straight bar suspender, which is very rare.*

VALUE:

		Miniature
Without clasp (ring)	£250–300	£80
Clasp and ring suspension	£350–400	—
Clasp and bar suspension	£500–550	£40
Bronze	From £1000	—

141. HONG KONG PLAGUE MEDAL

Date: 1894.
Campaign: Hong Kong, May-September 1894.
Branch of Service: Royal Navy, Royal Engineers, KSLI and local personnel.
Ribbon: Red with yellow edges and two narrow yellow stripes in the centre.
Metal: Silver.
Size: 36mm.
Description: (Obverse) a Chinese lying on a trestle table being supported by a man warding off the winged figure of Death while a woman tends to the sick man. The year 1894 appears on a scroll in the exergue, while the name of the colony in Chinese pictograms is inscribed on the left of the field. (Reverse) inscribed PRESENTED BY THE HONG KONG COMMUNITY round the circumference, and FOR SERVICES RENDERED DURING THE PLAGUE OF 1894 in seven lines across the centre. It was fitted with a plain ring for suspension.
Clasps: None.
Comments: *The colonial authorities in Hong Kong awarded this medal to nurses, civil servants, police, British Army and Royal Navy personnel who rendered assistance when the crown colony was stricken by a severe epidemic of bubonic plague in May 1894. Despite stringent measures, over 2500 people died in the ensuing three months. About 400 medals were issued in silver and awarded to 300 men of the King's Shropshire Light Infantry, 50 petty officers and ratings of the Royal Navy and NCOs and other ranks of the Royal Engineers, as well as about the same number of police and junior officials, while 45 were struck in gold for award to officers, nursing sisters and senior officials.*

VALUE:

		Miniature
Gold (45)	From £4000	—
Silver (400)	£850–1200	£50–65

142. INDIA MEDAL

Date: 1896.
Campaign: India 1895–1902.
Branch of Service: British and Indian forces.
Ribbon: Crimson with two dark green stripes.
Metal: Silver or bronze.
Size: 36mm.
Description: Issued with two different obverses, portraying Queen Victoria (1895–1901) and King Edward VII in field marshal's uniform (1901–02). (Reverse) British and Indian soldiers supporting a standard.
Clasps: Seven, mainly for actions on the North West Frontier (see below).
Comments: *This medal replaced the India GSM which had been awarded for various minor campaigns over a period of four decades from 1854. Combatant troops were given the medal in silver but native bearers and servants received a bronze version. Although the clasp Waziristan 1901–2 is rare to British recipients it was awarded to a number of regiments.*

VALUE:

	British regiments	Indian	Bronze	Miniature
Defence of Chitral 1895	—	£700–800	Rare	£60
Relief of Chitral 1895	£75–85	£50–60	£50–60	£20
Punjab Frontier 1897-98	£70–80	£50–60	£65–75	£15
pair with Malakand 1897	£80–90	£60–75	£60–70	£20–25
pair with Samana 1897	£80–90	£60–75	£70–80	£20–25
pair with Tirah 1897-98	£90–100	£50–65	£50–60	£20–25
Waziristan 1901-2	£230–280	£70–80	£60–70	£20–25
3 clasps	£135–150	£85–115	£80–115	£50–60
4 clasps	—	£115–130	—	£60–80

143. JUMMOO AND KASHMIR MEDAL

Date: 1895.
Campaign: Defence of Chitral 1895.
Branch of Service: Native levies.
Ribbon: White with red stripes at the edges and a broad central green stripe.
Metal: Bronze, silver.
Size: 35mm high; 38mm wide.
Description: This medal, by Gurney of London, has a unique kidney shape showing the arms of Jummoo (Jammu) and Kashmir on the obverse. (Reverse) a view of Chitral fort with troops in the foreground.
Clasps: Chitral 1895.
Comments: *Awarded by the Maharajah of Jummoo (Jammu) and Kashmir to the Indian troops who participated in the defence of Chitral (a dependency of Kashmir) during the siege of 4 March to 20 April by Chitralis and Afghans led by Umra Khan and Sher Afzul.*

VALUE:

Named	£350–400
Unnamed	£240–280
Silver	Rare

144. ASHANTI STAR

Date: 1896.
Campaign: Gold Coast 1896.
Branch of Service: British forces.
Ribbon: Yellow with two black stripes.
Metal: Bronze.
Size: 44mm.
Description: A saltire cross with a four-pointed star in the angles, surmounted by a circular belt inscribed ASHANTI 1896 around a British crown. The plain reverse is simply inscribed FROM THE QUEEN.
Clasps: None.
Comments: *Issued unnamed, but the colonel of the West Yorkshire Regiment had the medals of the second battalion engraved at his own expense. Some 2000 stars were awarded to officers and men serving in the expedition led by Major-General F.C. Scott against the tyrannical King Prempeh. It is believed that the star was designed by Princess Henry of Battenberg whose husband died of fever during the campaign.*

VALUE:

Unnamed	£120–130
Named to West Yorkshire Regiment	£240–280
Miniature	£35–40

INTERIOR OF CHITRAL FORT

(see nos. 142 & 143)

147

145. QUEEN'S SUDAN MEDAL

Date: 1899.
Campaign: Reconquest of the Sudan 1896–97.
Branch of Service: Royal Navy, Army and local forces.
Ribbon: Half-yellow and half-black representing the desert and the
    Sudanese nation, divided by a thin crimson stripe representing the
    British forces.
Metal: Silver or bronze.
Size: 36mm.
Description: (Obverse) the Jubilee bust of Queen Victoria. (Reverse) a
    seated figure of Victory holding palms and laurels with flags in the
    background, the word SUDAN appearing on a tablet at her feet.
Clasps: None.
Comments: *Unusually, no clasps were granted for individual actions which*
    included the celebrated battle of Omdurman in which young Winston
    Churchill charged with the cavalry. Medals named to the 21st Lancers are
    especially desirable on that account.

VALUE:

Bronze named	£160–180
Silver named to British Regt	£140–175
Indian Regt	£125–140
21st Lancers (confirmed charger)	From £750
RN/RM (46)	£700–950
Miniature	£25–30

146. KHEDIVE'S SUDAN MEDAL 1896–1908

(reverse)

Date: 1897.
Campaign: Sudan 1896-1908.
Branch of Service: Royal Navy and British and Egyptian Armies.
Ribbon: 38mm yellow with a broad central deep blue stripe, symbolising
    the desert and the River Nile.
Metal: Silver or bronze.
Size: 39mm.
Description: (Obverse) an elaborate Arabic inscription translating as
    'Abbas Hilmi the Second' and the date 1314 (AD 1897); (reverse) an
    oval shield surrounded by flags and a trophy of arms. Bar suspender.
Clasps: Fifteen (see below) but medals with more than the two clasps
    'The Atbara' and 'Khartoum' are unusual. Inscribed in English and
    Arabic.
Comments: *Instituted by the Khedive of Egypt in February 1897 and granted*
    to those who served in the reconquest of Dongola province in the Sudan
    (1896-8) as well as in subsequent operations for the pacification of the
    southern provinces. It was awarded to officers and men of the British and
    Egyptian Armies and Royal Navy personnel who served on the Nile
    steamboats. In addition, the crews of the Royal Naval ships HMS Melita
    (139) and HMS Scout *(149) were awarded silver medals with no clasps for*
    Dongola 1896 (but were not *awarded the Queen's Sudan Medal 1896–98).*
    Medals to Royal Naval personnel with clasps are rare and command a high
    premium: Hafir (16), The Atbara (6), Sudan 1897 (12), Khartoum (33),
    Gedaref (9), Gedid (5) and Sudan 1899 (6).

VALUE:

		Miniature			*Miniature*
No clasp silver	£60–70	£20	Jerok	£90–100	£45
No clasp silver (RN)	£90–120	—	Nyam-Nyam	£110–120	£40
No clasp bronze	£70–80	—	Talodi	£110–120	£45
Firket	£90–100	£30	Katfia	£110–120	£45
Hafir	£90–100	£30	Nyima	£100–110	£35
Abu Hamed	£90–100	£35			
Sudan 1897	£90–100	£35	2 clasps	£110–120	Add £10–15
The Atbara	£90–100	£25	3 clasps	£120–140	per clasp
Khartoum	£100–110	£25	4 clasps	£140–160	
Gedaref	£90–100	£40	5 clasps	£150–170	
Gedid	£90–100	£40	6 clasps	£160–180	
Sudan 1899	£90–100	£25	7 clasps	£180–200	
Bahr-el-Ghazal 1900-2	£120–150	£45	8 clasps	£200–240	

147. EAST AND CENTRAL AFRICA MEDAL

Date: 1899.
Campaigns: East and Central Africa 1897–99.
Branch of Service: British, Indian and local forces.
Ribbon: Half yellow, half red.
Metal: Silver or bronze.
Size: 36mm.
Description: (Obverse) the Jubilee bust of Queen Victoria; (reverse) a standing figure of Britannia with the British lion alongside.
Clasps: Five (see below).
Comments: *Instituted for service in operations in Uganda and the southern Sudan, it was awarded in silver to combatants and in bronze to camp followers. Most of the medals were awarded to troops of the Uganda Rifles and various Indian regiments. The few British officers and NCOs were troop commanders and instructors seconded from their regiments and their medals are worth very much more than the prices quoted, which are for native awards.*

VALUE:

	Europeans	Natives	Miniature
No clasp silver	—	£180–200	£20
Lubwa's (with clasp Uganda 1897-98)	—	£250–280	£35
Uganda 1897-98	£350–400	£220–250	£35
1898 (silver)	—	£230–260	£35
1898 (bronze)	—	£350–400	—
Uganda 1899	—	£230–260	£35

147A. UGANDA STAR

Instituted: 1897–98.
Campaign: Mutiny of Sudanese troops in Uganda.
Branch of Service: African civilians and soldiers.
Ribbon: None.
Metal: Silver.
Description: An eight-pointed uniface star surmounted by a crown, with the dates 1897 and 1898 on a circular rim enclosing the Old Head or Veiled Bust of Queen Victoria. Brooch-mounted. Manufactured by Carrington of London and issued in a blue plush-lined case.
Comments: *This award, approved by the Foreign Office and sanctioned by Queen Victoria, acknowledged the loyalty of African tribal leaders but, in a few cases, was also awarded to Sudanese troops (one, in fact, a Tunisian) who fought gallantly in quelling the serious mutiny of Sudanese troops of the Uganda Rifles. It was for this action that British, Indian and Local forces were awarded the East and Central Africa Medal with the bar for Lubwa's (see above). Only 39 stars were awarded.*

VALUE: £2500–3000

148. BRITISH NORTH BORNEO COMPANY'S MEDALS

1st type obv.

1st type rev.

Date: 1897.

Campaign: North Borneo 1897–1915.

Branch of Service: Company forces.

Ribbon: (i) 36mm gold watered silk, (ii) 32mm yellow with maroon edges and a central blue stripe (Punitive Expeditions and Rundum) or (iii) 32mm yellow with a central green stripe (Tambunan).

Metal: Silver or bronze.

Size: 39mm.

Description: (Obverse) the Company arms; (reverse) the British lion standing in front of a bush adorned by the Company flag, with a small wreath in the exergue.

Clasps: Four (see below).

Comments: *This series of medals was made by the British North Borneo Company for service in what is now Sabah. The medals, struck by Spink and Son of London, were issued in silver and bronze (except for Rundum) to British and Bornean officials, Sikh troops and a small number of servants. The first obverse showed the Company arms with supporters, crest and motto. This medal was issued unnamed and unnumbered. Specimens from the original dies are known with the S of Spink or Son erased and the word "Copy" on the rim. The medal was re-issued for a second expedition in 1898 and on this occasion it was named and numbered to the recipient. For a third expedition, in 1899–1900, the second obverse was used, showing the Company shield without supporters, motto or crest, but inscribed BRITISH NORTH BORNEO and with the date 1900 round the foot. This was used in conjunction with a new reverse showing the Company crest, two arms supporting a flag. This medal had a yellow ribbon with a central green stripe. In 1915 an expedition to raise the siege of Rundum was marked by the issue of a silver medal, similar to the 1897 medal but only struck in silver and fitted with a* Rundum *clasp.*

VALUE:

	Silver	Bronze	Miniature
Punitive Expedition (1897)	£60–80	£40–60	£40
Punitive Expeditions (1898)	£70–80	£40–60	£45
Tambunan	£70–80	£50–60	£45
Rundum	£80–100	—	£50
Originally named and numbered	from £1500	£650–850	

2nd type obv.

2nd type rev.

149. SULTAN OF ZANZIBAR'S MEDAL

Date: 1896.
Campaign: East Africa 1896.
Branch of Service: Sultan's forces.
Ribbon: Plain bright scarlet.
Metal: Silver.
Size: 36mm.
Description: (Obverse) a facing bust of Sultan Hamid bin Thwain surrounded by a Suaheli inscription in Arabic; (reverse) same inscription set in four lines.
Clasps: Pumwani, Jongeni, Takaungu, Mwele (inscribed only in Arabic).
Comments: *Awarded to the Zanzibari contingent who served under Lieut. Lloyd-Matthews RN in East Africa alongside British and Imperial forces.*

VALUE: £250–300   *Miniature* £60

150. QUEEN'S SOUTH AFRICA MEDAL

Date: 1899.
Campaign: Anglo-Boer War 1899-1902.
Branch of Service: British and Imperial forces.
Ribbon: Red with two narrow blue stripes and a broad central orange stripe.
Metal: Silver or bronze.
Size: 36mm.
Description: (Obverse) the Jubilee bust of Queen Victoria; (reverse) Britannia holding the flag and a laurel crown towards a large group of soldiers, with warships offshore. The words SOUTH AFRICA are inscribed round the top.
Clasps: 26 authorised but the maximum recorded for a single medal is nine to the Army and eight to the Navy.
Comments: *Because of the large number of British and imperial forces which took part and the numerous campaign and battle clasps awarded, this is one of the most popular and closely studied of all medals, offering immense scope to the collector. A total of 178,000 medals were awarded. Numerous specialist units were involved for the first time, as well as locally raised units and contingents from India, Canada, Australia and New Zealand. Of particular interest are the medals awarded to war correspondents and nurses which set precedents for later wars. Although nurses received the medal they were not issued with clasps to which they were entitled. A small number of bronze medals without a clasp were issued to bearers and servants in Indian units. The original issue of the QSA depicts Britannia's outstretched hand pointing towards the R of AFRICA and bears the dates 1899–1900 on the reverse field. Less than 70 of these were issued to Lord Strathcona's Horse who had returned to Canada before the war ended, but as the war dragged on the date was removed before any other medals were issued, although some medals can be found with a "ghost" of this date still to be seen. On the third type reverse there is again no date but Britannia's hand points towards the F. The prices for clasps given below are for clasps issued in combination with others. Some clasps are much scarcer when issued singly than combined with other clasps and conversely some clasps are not recorded on their own. Verified ten-clasp medals to South African units are known.*

1st type rev.

continued overleaf

150. QUEEN'S SOUTH AFRICA MEDAL *continued*

VALUE:

	RN	British	SA/Indian	Aus/NZ	Canadian
No clasp bronze	—	—	£80–100	—	—
No clasp silver	£80–100	£30–40	£60–80	£75–85	£110–120
Cape Colony	£85–100	£40–50	£35–45	£45–50	£110–120
Rhodesia	£1000	£80–120	£90–100	£150–200	£260–280
Relief of Mafeking	—	—	£130–150	£150–160	£350–370
Defence of Kimberley	—	£100–125	£90–100	—	—
Talana	—	£140–150	£90–120	—	—
Elandslaagte	—	£130–150	—	—	—
Defence of Ladysmith	£160–185	£70–90	£70–80	—	—
Belmont	£95–120	£50–70	—	£180–200	—
Modder River	£95–120	£50–70	—	£180–200	—
Tugela Heights	£350–500	£40–50	—	—	—
Natal	£250–300	£70–95	£60–70	—	£180–200
Relief of Kimberley	£750–900	£45–65	£40–50	£100–120	—
Paardeberg	£90–110	£40–50	£55–60	£90–100	£130–140
Orange Free State	£120–130	£40–45	£35–40	£50–60	£120–140
Relief of Ladysmith	£250–400	£45–65	£60–70	—	—
Driefontein	£90–110	£40–50	—	£40–50	£180–200
Wepener	—	£250–300	£220–250	—	—
Defence of Mafeking	—	—	£650–800	—	—
Transvaal	£450–600	£35–45	£35–45	£50–60	£180–200
Johannesburg	£100–120	£45–55	£50–60	£50–60	£120–130
Laing's Nek	£500–650	£60–75	—	—	—
Diamond Hill	£110–130	£45–55	£55–65	£60–75	£180–200
Wittebergen	£1000	£40–50	£90–100	£65–75	—
Belfast	£120–140	£60–70	£50–60	£60–75	£120–140
South Africa 1901	£60–75	£40–50	£40–50	£60–75	£140–150
South Africa 1902	£750–850	£40–50	£40–50	£60–75	£120–130
2 clasps	£110–140	£40–50	£40–50	£90–100	£120–130
3 clasps	£130–160	£50–80	£50–60	£100–125	£120–130
4 clasps	£150–200	£60–85	£50–70	£130–160	£140–150
5 clasps	£200–400	£75–120	£55–75	£160–200	£200–220
6 clasps	£300–500	£110–130	£100–130	£250–300	£250–300
7 clasps	£400–600	£180–250	£180–240	£450–600	—
8 clasps	£650–1000	£450–550	£400–450	—	—
Relief dates on reverse	—	—	—	—	£1900–2200
Nurses	—	£100–200	—	—	—
War Correspondents	—	£1200–1500	—	—	—

Miniature
From £5 with no clasp to £45 with 6 fixed clasps—"slip-on" style clasps approx. 20% less.

2nd type rev.   *3rd type rev.*

151. QUEEN'S MEDITERRANEAN MEDAL

Date: 1899.
Campaign: Mediterranean garrisons 1899-1902.
Branch of Service: British militia forces.
Ribbon: Red with two narrow dark blue stripes and a central broad orange stripe (as for Queen's South Africa Medal).
Metal: Silver.
Size: 36mm.
Description: Similar to the Queen's South Africa Medal but inscribed MEDITERRANEAN at the top of the reverse.
Clasps: None.
Comments: *Awarded to officers and men of the militia battalions which were sent to Malta and Gibraltar to take over garrison duty from the regular forces who were drafted to the Cape.*

VALUE:

Silver (5000)	£140–180	*Miniature* £45–55

152. KING'S SOUTH AFRICA MEDAL

Date: 1902.
Campaign: South Africa 1901–02.
Branch of Service: British and imperial forces.
Ribbon: Three equal stripes of green, white and orange.
Metal: Silver.
Size: 36mm.
Description: (Obverse) bust of King Edward VII in field marshal's uniform; (reverse) as for Queen's medal.
Clasps: Two: South Africa 1901, South Africa 1902.
Comments: *This medal was never issued without the Queen's medal and was awarded to all personnel engaged in operations in South Africa in 1901–02 when fighting was actually confined to numerous skirmishes with isolated guerrilla bands. Very few medals were awarded to RN personnel as the naval brigades had been disbanded in 1901. Apart from about 600 nurses and a few odd men who received the medal without a clasp, this medal was awarded with campaign clasps—most men were entitled to both clasps, single clasp medals being very rare.*

VALUE:

No clasp (nurses)	£75–100
1901 / 1902 (RN) (33)	£750–1000
1901 / 1902 (Army)	£35–45
1901 / 1902 (Canada)	£50–60
1901 / 1902 (Aus, NZ)	£40–50
1901 alone	From £100
1902 alone	From £100
Miniature	£5–6

153. ST JOHN AMBULANCE BRIGADE MEDAL FOR SOUTH AFRICA

Date: 1902.
Campaign: South Africa 1899–1902.
Branch of Service: St John Ambulance Brigade.
Ribbon: Black with narrow white edges.
Metal: Bronze.
Size: 37mm.
Description: (Obverse) King Edward VII; (reverse) the arms of the Order with a legend in Latin, SOUTH AFRICA and the dates 1899 and 1902.
Clasps: None.
Comments: *Issued by the Order of St John of Jerusalem to the members of its ambulance brigade who served during the Boer War or who played an active part in the organisation, mobilisation and supply roles. Medals were engraved on the edge with the recipient's name and unit. It is most often associated with the two South Africa medals, but fourteen members who went on from South Africa to serve during the Boxer Rebellion were also awarded the China Medal.*

VALUE: Bronze (1,871) £180–220   *Miniature* £50–60

154. KIMBERLEY STAR

Date: 1900.
Campaign: Defence of Kimberley 1899–1902.
Branch of Service: British and local forces.
Ribbon: Half yellow, half black, separated by narrow stripes of red, white and blue.
Metal: Silver.
Size: Height 43mm; max. width 41mm.
Description: A six-pointed star with ball finials and a circular centre inscribed KIMBERLEY 1899–1900 with the civic arms in the middle. (Reverse) plain, but for the inscription MAYOR'S SIEGE MEDAL 1900. Suspended by a plain ring from a scrolled bar.
Clasps: None
Comments: *The Mayor and council of Kimberley awarded this and the following medal to the defenders of the mining town against the Boer forces. Two medals were struck in gold but about 5000 were produced in silver. Those with the "a" Birmingham hallmark for 1900 rate a premium over stars with later date letters.*

VALUE:
hallmark "a"	£110–125
later date letters	£90–110

Miniature £60–80

155. KIMBERLEY MEDAL

Date: 1900.
Campaign: Defence of Kimberley 1899–1900.
Branch of Service: Local forces.
Ribbon: As above.
Metal: Silver
Size: 38mm.
Description: (Obverse) the figure of Victory above the Kimberley Town Hall, with the dates 1899–1900 in the exergue. (Reverse) two shields inscribed INVESTED 15 OCT. 1899 and RELIEVED 15 FEB. 1900. The imperial crown appears above and the royal cypher underneath, with the legend TO THE GALLANT DEFENDERS OF KIMBERLEY round the circumference.
Clasps: None.
Comments: *Although awarded for the same purpose as the above, this silver medal is a much scarcer award.*

VALUE:
Silver   £500–650

156. YORKSHIRE IMPERIAL YEOMANRY MEDAL

Date: 1900.
Campaign: South Africa 1900–02.
Branch of Service: Yorkshire Imperial Yeomanry.
Ribbon: Yellow.
Metal: Silver.
Size: 38mm.
Description: Three versions were produced. The first two had the numeral 3 below the Prince of Wales's feathers and may be found with the dates 1900–1901 or 1901–1902, while the third type has the figures 66, denoting the two battalions involved. The uniform reverse has the white rose of Yorkshire surmounted by an imperial crown and enclosed in a laurel wreath with the legend A TRIBUTE FROM YORKSHIRE.
Clasps: None.
Comments: *Many medals wre produced locally and awarded to officers and men of county regiments. The medals struck by Spink and Son for the Yorkshire Imperial Yeomanry, however, are generally more highly regarded as they were much more extensively issued, and therefore more commonly met with, than the others.*

VALUE:

3rd Battalion 1900–1901	£70–80
3rd Battalion 1901–1902	£80–100
66th Battalion 1900–1901	£120–150

157. MEDAL FOR THE DEFENCE OF OOKIEP

Date: 1902.
Campaign: Defence of Ookiep 1902.
Branch of Service: British and colonial forces.
Ribbon: Dark brown with a central green stripe.
Metal: Silver or bronze.
Size: 36mm.
Description: (Obverse) a miner and copper-waggon, with the Company name and date of foundation (1888) round the circumference; (reverse) a thirteen-line text. Fitted with a scroll suspender.
Clasps: None.
Comments: *This medal was awarded by the Cape Copper Company to those who defended the mining town of Ookiep in Namaqualand when it was besieged from 4 April to 4 May 1902 by a Boer commando led by Jan Christian Smuts, later Field Marshal, Prime Minister of South Africa and a member of the Imperial War Cabinet. The defence was conducted by Lieut. Colonel Sheldon, DSO and Major Dean, the Company's manager. The garrison consisted of 206 European miners, 660 Cape Coloureds, 44 men of the 5th Warwickshire militia and twelve men of the Cape Garrison Artillery.*

VALUE:

Silver (officers)	Rare
Bronze (other ranks)	£500–600

158. CHINA WAR MEDAL 1900

Date: 1901.
Campaign: Boxer Rebellion 1900.
Branch of Service: British and imperial forces.
Ribbon: Crimson with yellow edges.
Metal: Silver or bronze.
Size: 36mm.
Description: (Obverse) bust of Queen Victoria; (reverse) trophy of arms, similar to the 1857-60 China Medal but inscribed CHINA 1900 at the foot.
Clasps: Taku Forts, Defence of Legations, Relief of Pekin.
Comments: *Instituted for service during the Boxer Rebellion and the subsequent punitive expeditions, this medal was similar to that of 1857-60 with the date in the exergue altered to 1900. There are three types of naming: in small, impressed capitals for European troops, in large impressed capitals for naval recipients, and in engraved cursive script for Indian forces. The medal was issued in silver to combatants and in bronze to native bearers, drivers and servants. The international community was besieged by the Boxers, members of a secret society, aided and abetted by the Dowager Empress. The relieving force, consisting of contingents from Britain, France, Italy, Russia, Germany and Japan, was under the command of the German field marshal, Count von Waldersee. The British Legation Guard, comprising 80 Royal Marines and a number of 'odd men', won the clasp for Defence of Legations, the most desirable of the campaign bars in this conflict.*

VALUE:

	Royal Navy	Army	Indian units	Miniature
Silver no clasp	£90–110	£100–120	£50–75	£10–15
Bronze no clasp	—	—	£70–90	—
Taku Forts	£300–320	—	—	£20–25
Defence of Legations	£3000–4000	—	—	£50–60
Relief of Pekin (silver)	£190–220	£200–220	£120–140	£20–25
Relief of Pekin (bronze)	—	—	£150–175	—
2 clasps	£400–450	—	—	£40–50
No-clasp medal to a nurse	£1000–1100			
To a War correspondent	£1000–1100			

159. TRANSPORT MEDAL

Date: 1903.
Campaigns: Boer War 1899-1902 and Boxer Rebellion 1900.
Branch of Service: Mercantile Marine.
Ribbon: Red with two blue stripes.
Metal: Silver.
Size: 36mm.
Description: (Obverse) bust of King Edward VII in the uniform of an Admiral of the Fleet; (reverse) HMS *Ophir* below a map of the world.
Clasps: S. Africa 1899-1902, China 1900.
Comments: *The last of the medals associated with the major conflicts at the turn of the century, it was instituted for award to the officers and men of the merchant vessels used to carry troops and supplies to the wars in South Africa and China.*

VALUE:

		Miniature
South Africa 1899–1902 (1219)	£260–280	£40–60
China 1900 (322)	£380–420	£50–70
Both clasps (178)	£450–550	£80–100

160. ASHANTI MEDAL

Date: 1901.
Campaign: Gold Coast 1900.
Branch of Service: British and local forces.
Ribbon: Black with two broad green stripes.
Metal: Silver or bronze.
Size: 36mm.
Description: (Obverse) bust of King Edward VII in field marshal's uniform. (Reverse) a lion on the edge of an escarpment looking towards the sunrise, with a native shield and spears in the foreground. The name ASHANTI appeared on a scroll at the foot.
Clasps: Kumassi.
Comments: *A high-handed action by the colonial governor provoked a native uprising and the siege of the garrison at Kumassi. The medal was awarded to the defenders as well as personnel of the two relieving columns. Very few Europeans were involved as most were in South Africa fighting the Boers. The medal was awarded in silver to combatants and bronze to native transport personnel and servants.*

VALUE:

	Silver	Bronze	*Miniature*
No clasp	£150–170	£250–300	£20–25
Kumassi	£320–350	Rare	£40–50

161. AFRICA GENERAL SERVICE MEDAL

Date: 1902.
Campaigns: Minor campaigns in Africa 1902 to 1956.
Branch of Service: British and colonial forces.
Ribbon: Yellow with black edges and two thin central green stripes.
Metal: Silver or bronze.
Size: 36mm.
Description: (Obverse) effigies of Edward VII, George V and Elizabeth II; (reverse) similar to that of the East and Central Africa medal of 1897–99, with AFRICA in the exergue.
Clasps: 34 awarded in the reign of Edward VII, ten George V and only one Elizabeth II (see below).
Comments: *This medal replaced the East and West Africa Medal 1887–1900, to which 21 clasps had already been issued. In turn, it remained in use for 54 years, the longest-running British service medal. Medals to combatants were in silver, but a few bronze medals were issued during the 1903–04 operations in Northern Nigeria and the Somaliland campaigns of 1902 and 1908 to transport personnel and these are now much sought after, as are any medals with the effigy of George V on the obverse. With the exception of the 1902–04 Somali campaign and the campaign against the Mau Mau of Kenya (1952–56) European troops were not involved in any numbers, such personnel consisting mostly of detached officers and specialists.*

VALUE:	RN	British units	African/Indian regiments
N. Nigeria	—	—	£120–140
N. Nigeria 1902	—	—	£110–130
N. Nigeria 1903	—	—	£100–120
N. Nigeria 1903-04	—	—	£150–170
N. Nigeria 1903-04 (bronze)	—	—	£130–150
N. Nigeria 1904	—	—	£130–150
N. Nigeria 1906	—	—	£130–150
S. Nigeria	—	—	£180–200
S. Nigeria 1902	—	—	£130–150
S. Nigeria 1902-03	—	—	£130–150

continued overleaf

161. AFRICA GENERAL SERVICE MEDAL *continued*

S. Nigeria 1903	—	—	£120–140
S. Nigeria 1903-04	—	—	£150–170
S. Nigeria 1904	—	—	£120–140
S. Nigeria 1904-05	—	—	£150–170
S. Nigeria 1905	—	—	£250–300
S. Nigeria 1905-06	—	—	£140–160
Nigeria 1918	—	—	£110–130
East Africa 1902	—	—	£300-350
East Africa 1904	—	—	£170–190
East Africa 1905	—	—	£170–190
East Africa 1906	—	—	£170–190
East Africa 1913	—	—	£180–220
East Africa 1913-14	—	—	£170–190
East Africa 1914	—	—	£180–220
East Africa 1915	—	—	£200–250
East Africa 1918	—	—	£170–190
West Africa 1906	—	—	£170–190
West Africa 1908	—	—	£180–220
West Africa 1909-10	—	—	£180–200
Somaliland 1901	—	—	£250–300
Somaliland 1901 (bronze)	—	—	£200–250
Somaliland 1902-04	£75–85	£80–100	£50–60
Somaliland 1902-04 (bronze)	—	—	£220–250
Somaliland 1908-10	£80–90	—	£65–75
Somaliland 1908-10 (bronze)	—	—	£80–90
Somaliland 1920	£180–200	—	£80–90
as above but RAF	—	£320–350	—
Jidballi (with Somaliland 1902–04)	—	£150–180	£110–130
Uganda 1900	—	—	£170–190
B.C.A. 1899-1900	—	—	£120–150
Jubaland	£200–220	—	£90–110
Jubaland (bronze)	—	—	£275–325
Jubaland 1917-18	—	—	£160–180
Jubaland 1917-18 (bronze)	—	—	£125–150
Gambia	£600–800	—	£120–140
Aro 1901-1902	£500–650	—	£130–150
Lango 1901	—	—	£200–250
Kissi 1905	—	—	£350–400
Nandi 1905-06	—	—	£80–120
Shimber Berris 1914-15	—	—	£200–220
Nyasaland 1915	—	—	£120–150
Kenya	£350–500	£50–70	£40–50
Kenya (to RAF)	—	£55–60	—
2 clasps	£80–120	£100–150	£100–250
3 clasps	—	—	£200–400
4 clasps	—	—	£300–450
5 clasps	—	—	£350–500
6 clasps	—	—	£350–550

Miniature
   Range from £10 to £60 depending upon clasp. "Slip-on" clasps are approx. 20% cheaper. Add £5 for
   each additional clasp.

162. TIBET MEDAL

Date: 1905.
Campaign: Tibet 1903–04.
Branch of Service: British and Indian regiments.
Ribbon: Green with two white stripes and a broad maroon central stripe.
Metal: Silver or bronze.
Size: 36mm.
Description: (Obverse) bust of King Edward VII; (reverse) the fortified hill city of Lhasa with TIBET 1903–04 at the foot.
Clasps: Gyantse.
Comments: *The trade mission led by Colonel Sir Francis Younghusband to Tibet was held up by hostile forces, against whom a punitive expedition was mounted in 1903. This medal was awarded mainly to Indian troops who took part in the expedition, camp followers being awarded the medal in bronze. A clasp was awarded to those who took part in the operations near Gyantse beteen 3 May and 6 July 1904.*

VALUE:

	British	Indian	Bronze	*Miniature*
Without clasp	£250–300	£140–160	£75–85	£20–25
Gyantse	£500–600	£200–240	£170–190	£50–60

163. NATAL REBELLION MEDAL

Date: 1907.
Campaign: Natal 1906.
Branch of Service: Local forces.
Ribbon: Crimson with black edges.
Metal: Silver.
Size: 36mm.
Description: (Obverse) right-facing profile of King Edward VII. (Reverse) an erect female figure representing Natal with the sword of justice in her right hand and a palm branch in the left. She treads on a heap of Zulu weapons and is supported by Britannia who holds the orb of empire in her hand. In the background, the sun emerges from behind storm clouds.
Clasp: 1906.
Comments: *The Natal government instituted this medal for services in the operations following the Zulu rebellion. Local volunteer units bore the brunt of the action and it is interesting to note that one of the recipients was Sergeant-Major M. K. Gandhi who later led India to independence.*

VALUE:

		Miniature
without clasp (2000)	£80–110	£15–20
clasp 1906 (8000)	£100–120	£30–40
Natal Naval Corps		
without clasp (67)	£150–200	
clasp 1906 (136)	£250–300	

163A. MESSINA EARTHQUAKE COMMEMORATIVE MEDAL

Date: 1908.

Campaign: Messina earthquake relief.

Branch of Service: Royal Navy.

Ribbon: Green with white edges and central white stripe.

Metal: Silver.

Size: 31.5mm.

Description: (Obverse) left-facing profile of King Victor Emanuel III; (reverse) A wreath of oak leaves within which are the words MEDAGLIA COMMEMORATIVA/TERREMOTO CALABRO SICULO 28 DICEMBRE 1908.

Clasp: —

Comments: *The King of Italy rewarded Royal Naval and other personnel who went to the aid of victims of the tragic earthquake that hit Messina in December 1908 with this silver medal. Officers and men serving on certain ships were eligible for the award as well as members of the Mercantile Marine and others who were engaged in relief operations. The Admiralty's published list of RN ships is as follows: HMS Duncan, HMS Euralyus, HMS Exmouth, HMS Lancaster, HMS Minerva and HMS Sutlej. However 52 medals were also awarded to personnel from HMS Boxer, which was omitted from the original list and a further 35 medals were awarded to the officers and men of HMS Philomel who had actually 'been engaged in work which was directly attributable to the rescue operations'. In addition to the commemorative medal a special Messina Earthquake Merit Medal was awarded in two sizes (40mm and 30mm) bronze, silver and gold to organisations, vessels and various key individuals who played a part in the rescue operations.*

VALUE:		Miniature
Royal Navy (c. 3500)	£100–120	£20–30
Royal Marines (481)	£120–140	
Mercantile Marine (c. 400)	£120–140	
Other	Rare	

164. INDIA GENERAL SERVICE MEDAL

Date: 1909.

Campaigns: India 1908 to 1935.

Branch of Service: British and Indian forces.

Ribbon: Green with a broad blue central band.

Metal: Silver.

Size: 36mm.

Description: Three obverse types were used: Edward VII (1908–10), George V Kaisar-i-Hind (1910–30) and George V Indiae Imp (1930–35). (Reverse) the fortress at Jamrud in the Khyber Pass, with the name INDIA in a wreath at the foot.

Clasps: Fourteen, some in bronze (see below).

Comments: *This medal was awarded for a number of minor campaigns and operations in India before and after the First World War. The medals were struck at the Royal Mint in London and by the Indian government in Calcutta, the only difference being in the claw suspenders, the former being ornate and the latter plain. Medals with the bars North West Frontier 1908 and Abor 1911–12 were also issued in bronze to native bearers.*

VALUE:

	British Army	RAF	Indian regiments	Miniature
NW Frontier 1908	£55–65	—	£30–40	£20
bronze	—	—	£50–60	—
Abor 1911–12	—	—	£140–180	£20
bronze	—	—	£250–300	—
Afghanistan NWF 1919	£40–60	£100–120	£18–25	£10
*Mahsud 1919–20				
& Waziristan 1919–21	£70–90	£120–150	£30–40	£10
Malabar 1921–22	£80–100	—	£35–55	£30
Waziristan 1921–24	£35–45	£70–90	£20–30	£12
Waziristan 1925	—	£500–600	—	£12
NW Frontier 1930–31	£35–45	£70–80	£18–25	£10
Burma 1930–32	£40–50	Rare	£25–30	£10
Mohmand 1933	£100–120	£180–200	£25–35	£10
NW Frontier 1935	£50–60	£80–100	£20–25	£10

*Usually found in combination with Waziristan 1919-21, but 10 medals were awarded either with this clasp alone or with the Afganistan NWF clasp.

165. KHEDIVE'S SUDAN MEDAL 1910

Date: 1911.

Campaign: Sudan 1910 to 1922

Branch of Service: British and Egyptian forces.

Ribbon: Black with thin red and green stripes on either side.

Metal: Silver or bronze.

Size: 36mm.

Description: (Obverse) an Arabic inscription signifying the name of Khedive Abbas Hilmi and the date 1328 in the Moslem calendar (1910 AD). He was deposed in December 1914 when Egypt was declared a British protectorate, and succeeded by his nephew who was proclaimed Sultan. Sultan Hussein Kamil changed the Arabic inscription and date to AH 1335 (1916–17) on later issues of the medal. (Reverse) a lion poised on a plinth with the sunrise in the background.

Clasps: 16, inscribed in English and Arabic.

Comments: *Introduced in June 1911 as a replacement for the previous Khedive's Sudan medal of 1896–1908, it was awarded for minor operations in the southern Sudan between 1910 and 1922. The silver medal was issued with clasps to combatants, and without a clasp to non-combatants, while the bronze version was granted to camp followers. The medal is usually found unnamed although a few British recipient's medals are found named in small impressed capitals or arabic script. The prices below are for unnamed examples.*

VALUE:

Silver without clasp type I	£100–120		
Silver without clasp type II	£130–150	Darfur 1916	£220–250
Bronze without clasp type I	£400–450	Fasher	£220–240
Bronze without clasp type II	£160–180	Lau Nuer	£240–260
Atwot	£220–240	Nyima 1917-18	£220–240
S. Kordofan 1910	£220–240	Atwot 1918	£220–240
Sudan 1912	£240–260	Garjak Nuer	£240–260
Zeraf 1913-14	£260–280	Aliab Dinka	£260–280
Mandal	£260–280	Nyala	£260–280
Miri	£260–280	Darfur 1921	£280–320
Mongalla 1915-16	£260–280	2 clasps	£280–300

Miniature
  Silver   £20. Prices for clasps vary between £10 and £30.

The Camel Corps in the Sudan.

FIRST WORLD WAR MEDALS

The various combinations of WWI medals that are found makes them still fairly easy to value. There are however large differences in price when it comes to casualties, for example medals to those who were killed on the first day of the battle of the Somme command a far higher price than to someone who was killed several days before. Regiments also alter the price greatly: recently a 1914–15 star trio without Memorial Plaque to a Welsh Guardsman who was killed in action realised over £700 in auction. A trio to the Royal Welsh Fusliiers in similar circumstances may sell for around £80. Purchasing the medals, plaque and scroll is far harder than ever before. Scrolls and plaques tended to become separated from the medals as relatives generally did not view them with as great a significance as the medals.

Valuations for casualty groups are usually made without including the Memorial Scroll. For those fortunate to have the scroll with their group of medals then add £20 minimum to the group.

166. 1914 STAR

Date: 1917.
Campaign: France and Belgium 1914.
Branch of Service: British forces.
Ribbon: Watered silk red, white and blue.
Metal: Bronze.
Size: Height 50mm; max. width 45mm.
Description: A crowned four-pointed star with crossed swords and a wreath of oak leaves, having the royal cypher at the foot and a central scroll inscribed AUG NOV 1914. Uniface, the naming being inscribed incuse on the plain reverse.
Clasps: 5th Aug. - 22nd Nov. 1914. The clasp was sewn on to the ribbon, the first of this type.
Comments: *Awarded to all those who had served in France and Belgium between 5 August and 22 November 1914. In 1919 King George V authorised a clasp bearing these dates for those who had actually been under fire during that period. The majority of the 400,000 recipients of the star were officers and men of the prewar British Army, the "Old Contemptibles" who landed in France soon after the outbreak of the First World War and who took part in the retreat from Mons, hence the popular nickname of Mons Star by which this medal is often known.*

VALUE:

		Miniature
1914 Star	£25–35	£2–3
With "Mons" clasp	£45–55	£3–4
To RN or RM	£40–60	
1914 Star trio	from £55	
Trio with plaque (no. 172)	from £100	

167. 1914–15 STAR

Date: 1918.
Campaign: First World War 1914–15.
Branch of Service: British and imperial forces.
Ribbon: Watered silk red, white and blue (as above).
Metal: Bronze.
Size: Height 50mm; max. width 45mm.
Description: As above, but AUG and NOV omitted and scroll across the centre inscribed 1914–15.
Clasps: None.
Comments: *Awarded to those who saw service in any theatre of war between 5 August 1914 and 31 December 1915, other than those who had already qualified for the 1914 Star. No fewer than 2,350,000 were awarded, making it the commonest British campaign medal up to that time.*

VALUE:

1914–15 Star	£10–15	Miniature	£2–3
1914–15 Star trio	from £30		
Trio with plaque (no. 172)	from £75		

168. BRITISH WAR MEDAL 1914–20

Date: 1919.
Campaign: First World War, 1914–20.
Branch of Service: British and imperial forces.
Ribbon: Orange watered centre with stripes of white and black at each side and borders of royal blue.
Metal: Silver or bronze.
Size: 36mm.
Description: (Obverse) the uncrowned left-facing profile of King George V by Sir Bertram Mackennal. (Reverse) St George on horseback trampling underfoot the eagle shield of the Central Powers and a skull and cross-bones, the emblems of death. Above, the sun has risen in victory. The figure is mounted on horseback to symbolise man's mind controlling a force of greater strength than his own, and thus alludes to the scientific and mechanical appliances which helped to win the war.
Clasps: None.
Comments: *This medal was instituted to record the successful conclusion of the First World War, but it was later extended to cover the period 1919–20 and service in mine-clearing at sea as well as participation in operations in North and South Russia, the eastern Baltic, Siberia, the Black Sea and Caspian. Some 6,500,000 medals were awarded in silver, but about 110,000 in bronze were issued mainly to Chinese, Indian and Maltese personnel in labour battalions. It was originally intended to award campaign clasps, but 79 were recommended by the Army and 68 by the Navy, so the scheme was abandoned as impractical. The naval clasps were actually authorised (7 July 1920) and miniatures are known with them, though the actual clasps were never issued.*

VALUE:		Miniature
Silver (6,500,000)	**£8–10**	£3–4
Bronze (110,000)	**£50–60**	£10–15
BWM/Victory pair	**from £14**	
Pair with plaque (no. 172)	**from £60**	

169. MERCANTILE MARINE WAR MEDAL

Date: 1919.
Campaign: First World War 1914–18.
Branch of Service: Mercantile Marine.
Ribbon: Green and red with a central white stripe, symbolising port and starboard navigation lights.
Metal: Bronze.
Size: 36mm.
Description: (Obverse) Mackennal profile of King George V; (reverse) a steamship ploughing through an angry sea, with a sinking submarine and a sailing vessel in the background, the whole enclosed in a laurel wreath.
Clasps: None.
Comments: *Awarded by the Board of Trade to members of the Merchant Navy who had undertaken one or more voyages through a war or danger zone.*

VALUE:			
Bronze (133,000)	£14–16	*Miniature*	£3–5
BWM/Mercantile Marine pair	from £25		

170. VICTORY MEDAL

Date: 1919.

Campaign: First World War 1914–19.

Branch of Service: British forces.

Ribbon: 38mm double rainbow (indigo at edges and red in centre).

Metal: Yellow bronze.

Size: 36mm.

Description: (Obverse) the standing figure of Victory holding a palm branch in her right hand and stretching out her left hand. (Reverse) a laurel wreath containing a four-line inscription THE GREAT WAR FOR CIVILISATION 1914–1919.

Clasps: None.

Comments: *Issued to all who had already got the 1914 or 1914–15 Stars and most of those who had the British War Medal, some six million are believed to have been produced. It is often known as the Allied War Medal because the same basic design and double rainbow ribbon were adopted by thirteen other Allied nations (though the USA alone issued it with campaign clasps). The Union of South Africa produced a version with a reverse text in English and Dutch (not Afrikaans as is often stated).*

VALUE:

British pattern	£6–10
South African pattern	£12–15
Miniature	
Normal	£1–2
"CIVILIZATION" variety	£3–4

171. TERRITORIAL FORCE WAR MEDAL

Date: 1919.

Campaign: First World War 1914–19.

Branch of Service: Territorial forces.

Ribbon: Watered gold silk with two dark green stripes towards the edges.

Metal: Bronze.

Size: 36mm.

Description: (Obverse) effigy of King George V; (reverse) a wreath enclosing the text FOR VOLUNTARY SERVICE OVERSEAS 1914–19.

Clasps: None.

Comments: *Granted to all members of the Territorial Force embodied before 30 September 1914, who had completed four years service by that date, and who had served outside the United Kingdom between 4 August 1914 and 11 November 1918. Those who had already qualified for the 1914 or 1914–15 Stars, however, were excluded. Only 34,000 medals were awarded, making it by far the scarcest of the First World War medals. The value of individual medals depends on the regiment or formation of the recipient.*

VALUE:

Infantry	£80–90
RA, RE or support units	£60–75
Yeomanry	£100–150
RFC or RAF	Rare
Nursing sisters	£100–150
Miniature	£5–6

172. MEMORIAL PLAQUE

Date: 1919.
Campaign: First World War.
Branch of Service: British forces.
Ribbon: None.
Metal: Bronze.
Size: 120mm.
Description: The plaque shows Britannia bestowing a laurel crown on a rectangular tablet bearing the full name of the dead in raised lettering. In front stands the British lion, with dolphins in the upper field, an oak branch lower right, and a lion cub clutching a fallen eagle in the exergue. The inscription round the circumference reads HE (or SHE) DIED FOR FREEDOM AND HONOVR. A parchment scroll was issued with each plaque giving the deceased's name and unit.
Comments: *Awarded to the next of kin of those who lost their lives on active service during the War. Plaques issued to the Army and the Navy can usually be differentiated by the size of the H in "HE". Those issued to the Navy have a narrower H when compared with the H of "HONOUR", whereas those to the Army are of equal size.*

VALUE: He died (1,355,000) £25–35 She died (600) £800–1600 Parchment scroll (male) £20–30
(female) £400–600

172A. SILVER WAR BADGE

Date: 12 September 1916.
Campaign: First World War.
Ribbon: None.
Metal: Silver.
Size: 33mm.
Description: A brooch-mounted circular badge with the crowned royal monogram in the centre and edge inscription FOR KING AND EMPIRE + SERVICES RENDERED +.
Comments: *Awarded to service personnel who sustained a wound or contracted sickness or disability in the course of the war as a result of which they were invalided out. It was worn on the lapel in civilian clothes. Each badge was numbered on the reverse. The purpose of the badge was to prevent men of military age but not in uniform from being harassed by women pursuing them with white feathers.*

VALUE: £8–10

172B. CEYLON VOLUNTEER SERVICE MEDAL

Date: 1919.
Campaign: First World War.
Branch of Service: Ceylon volunteer forces.
Ribbon: None.
Metal: Bronze.
Size: 48mm x 44mm.
Description: An upright oval medal. (Obverse) a seated female figure bestowing a laurel crown on a kneeling soldier, with a radiant sun on the horizon; above, a six-line inscription: PRESENTED BY THE GOVERNMENT OF CEYLON TO THOSE WHO VOLUNTARILY GAVE THEIR SERVICES OVERSEAS IN THE GREAT WAR OF with the dates 1914 1919 in two lines on the right of the field; (reverse) the winged figure of Victory seated on a throne above a tablet inscribed with the name of the recipient.
Comments: *Awarded to the 450 volunteers from the Ceylon forces who served abroad during the war. Ceylon (now Sri Lanka) was the only British colony to issue such a medal for war service.*

VALUE: £100–200

173. NAVAL GENERAL SERVICE MEDAL 1915–62

Date: 1915.
Campaigns: Naval actions 1915 to 1962.
Branch of Service: Royal Navy.
Ribbon: White with broad crimson edges and two narrow crimson stripes towards the centre.
Metal: Silver.
Size: 36mm.
Description: (Obverse) effigy of the reigning monarch (see below). (Reverse) Britannia and two seahorses travelling through the sea.
Clasps: Seventeen (see below).
Comments: *Instituted for service in minor operations for which no separate medal might be issued, it remained in use for almost half a century. In that period five different obverses were employed: George V (1915-36), George VI Ind Imp (1936-49), George VI Fid Def (1949-52), Elizabeth II Br Omn (1952-53) and Elizabeth II Dei Gratia (1953-62). Medals issued with the first clasp include the name of the recipient's ship but this lapsed in later awards. The Malaya clasp was issued with three types of medal: the George VI Fid Def and Elizabeth II Dei Gratia being the most common, the Elizabeth II Br Omn type being awarded mainly to SBS for special duties. The clasp Bomb & Mine Clearance 1945–46 is very rare as it was apparently only awarded to the Royal Australian Navy.*

VALUE:		*Miniature*
Persian Gulf 1909-1914		*(in silver add £5)*
RN (7,127)	£70–80	
Army (37)	£200–250	£10
Iraq 1919-20 (116)	£800–1000	£15
NW Persia 1919-20 (4)*	Rare	£15
Palestine 1936-39 (13,600)	£60–70	£10
SE Asia 1945-46 (2,000)	£100–135	£10
Minesweeping 1945-51 (4,750)	£90–100	£10
Palestine 1945-48 (7,900)	£55–65	£10
Malaya (George VI, Elizabeth II		
2nd type) (7,800)	£55–65	£10
(Elizabeth II 1st type)	£120–130	£10
Yangtze 1949 (1,450)	£250–300	£10
to HMS *Amethyst*	£500–600	
Bomb and Mine Clearance		
1945-53 (117)	£450–475	£10
Bomb and Mine Clearance 1945–56	Very rare	—
Bomb and Mine Clearance		
Mediterranean (60)	£900–1000	£10
Cyprus (4,300)	£70–80	£10
Near East (17,800)	£60–65	£10
Arabian Peninsula (1,200)	£140–180	£10
Brunei (900)	£140–160	£10

* The clasp NW Persia 1920 was withdrawn in favour of the clasp NW Persia 1919–20. Recipients were supposed to return their first clasp in exchange for the latter.

174. GENERAL SERVICE MEDAL 1918–62

Date: 1923.
Campaigns: Minor campaigns 1918 to 1962.
Branch of Service: Army and RAF.
Ribbon: Purple with a central green band.
Metal: Silver.
Size: 36mm
Description: (Obverse) five different effigies of the reigning monarch (see preceding entry). (Reverse) a standing figure of Victory in a Greek helmet and carrying a trident, bestowing palms on a winged sword.
Clasps: Sixteen (see below).
Comments: *Awarded to military and RAF personnel for numerous campaigns and operations that fell short of full-scale war. It did not cover areas already catered for in the Africa and India general service medals.*

VALUE:

	British units	RAF	Indian and local units	Miniature *(in silver add £5)*
S. Persia (Brit. officers)	£140–170	Rare	£30–40	£12
Kurdistan	£65–75	£130–150	£20–30	£12
Iraq	£35–45	£100–130	£20–25	£10
N.W. Persia	£65–75	£180–220	£25–35	£10
Southern Desert Iraq	—	£250–275	£80–100	£10
Northern Kurdistan	£150–175	£650–850	£120–150	£10
Palestine	£40–50	£30–40	£20–30	£10
S.E. Asia 1945-46	£60–70	£50–60	£25–35	£10
Bomb and Mine Clearance 1945-49	£280–300	£280–300	—	£10
Bomb and Mine Clearance 1945-56	£400–500	£400–500	—	£10
Palestine 1945-48	£30–35	£30–50	£20–25	£10
Malaya (George VI)	£25–35	£25–30	£20–25	£10
Malaya (Elizabeth II)	£25–35	£25–30	£20–25	£10
Cyprus	£35–45	£35–45	£20–25	£10
Near East	£45–55	£40–60	—	£10
Arabian Peninsular	£35–45	£30–40	£25–30	£10
Brunei	£120–150	£100–120	£60–80	£10

175. INDIA GENERAL SERVICE MEDAL 1936–39

Date: 1938.
Campaign: India 1936–39.
Branch of Service: British and Indian Armies and RAF.
Ribbon: Grey flanked by narrow red stripes, with broad green stripes at the edges.
Metal: Silver.
Size: 36mm
Description: (Obverse) crowned effigy of King George VI; (reverse) a tiger with the word INDIA across the top.
Clasps: North-West Frontier 1936–37, North-West Frontier 1937–39.
Comments: *The fifth and last of the IGS series, it was introduced when the change of effigy from George V to George VI became necessary, anticipating a similarly long life. It was not awarded after the outbreak of the Second World War, while the partition and independence of the Indian sub-continent afterwards rendered it obsolete. The medal was struck at the Royal Mint, London for award to British Army troops and RAF personnel, but the Calcutta Mint struck the medals awarded to the Indian Army.*

VALUE:	British Army	RAF	Indian Army	*Miniature*
North West Frontier				
1936-37	£50–60	£80–90	£20–25	£10
1937-39	£55–65	£80–90	£25–30	£10
2 clasps	£80–90	£120–140	£30–40	£12

Cherat as sketched by Lt C. A. Souper, RA (later Captain, Army Pay Corps), November 1880.

176. NORTH BORNEO GENERAL SERVICE MEDAL

Date: 1937.
Campaign: British North Borneo 1937-41.
Branch of Service: British North Borneo Company Staff, Constabulary and Residents.
Ribbon: Half dark green, half yellow for general awards, with provision for a thin red central stripe in the case of awards for bravery.
Metal: Silver.
Size: 37mm.
Description: (Obverse) the seated figure of Britannia with shield and trident, and a laurel spray in the exergue; (reverse) the arms of the Company.
Clasps: None.
Comments: *Although it could be granted for meritorious service or individual acts of gallantry, as a rule it was granted for at least eighteen years service. The medal was no longer awarded after the Japanese occupation of North Borneo, January 19, 1942. 50 medals were manufactured in 1937. Between 1937 and 1941 a total of 44 were awarded, including one for bravery (1939). In 1947 one officially-named medal was issued to replace one lost during the Japanese occupation. Total issued was therefore 45, and all were officially named prior to issue.*

VALUE: **Rare**

176A. SUDAN DEFENCE FORCE GENERAL SERVICE MEDAL

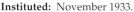

Instituted: November 1933.
Campaign: Minor campaigns in the Sudan after 1933.
Branch of Service: Sudan Defence Force (SDF) and Police.
Ribbon: Central stripe of royal blue, edged by two yellow stripes and two black stripes at the edges.
Metal: Silver.
Size: 36mm.
Description: (Obverse) the seal of the Governor-General of the Sudan; (reverse) a stationary group of Sudanese soldiers, with "The Sudan" in Arabic below.
Clasps: None.
Comments: *The medal was awarded on the recommendation of the Kaid el'Amm (SDF Commander) to native personnel of the SDF, Police and other approved Sudanese who served in the field on such operations as might be considered by the Governor-General as being of sufficient importance to warrant the grant of the medal. It was also awarded for action against Italian forces in the southern Sudan from June 1940 to November 1941.*

VALUE: (700) £150–£200

SECOND WORLD WAR STARS

Eight different campaign stars were issued for the Second World War. Apart from some Commonwealth issues, these were issued unnamed. It was decided that the maximum number of stars that could be earned by any one person was five, while those who qualified for more received a clasp to be sewn on the ribbon of the appropriate star. Only one clasp per ribbon was permitted. Thus the stars could bear the following clasps:

1 1939-45 (Battle of Britain)
2 Atlantic (Air Crew Europe or France and Germany)
3 Air Crew Europe (Atlantic or France and Germany)
4 Africa (North Africa 1942-43, 8th Army or 1st Army)
5 Pacific (Burma)
6 Burma (Pacific)
7 Italy
8 France and Germany (Atlantic)

The ribbons are believed to have been designed by King George VI personally and have symbolic significance in each case.

When ribbons alone are worn, the clasp is denoted by a silver rosette, the Battle of Britain being represented by a gilt rosette. As the clasps were sewn on to the ribbon and the stars issued unnamed, it is difficult to put valuations on examples with campaign clasps, however, the prices quoted are for medals with the *original* clasps. When purchasing expensive groups it is advisable that the medals be supported by documentary provenance or form part of a group in which at least one of the medals is named to the recipient.

Many of the medals and stars of the Second World War are still being produced, therefore there are a number of different die varieties available. There are also a number of dangerous forgeries in existence so care should be taken when purchasing expensive items.

177. 1939–1945 STAR

Date: 1945.
Campaign: Second World War 1939–45.
Branch of Service: British and Commonwealth forces.
Ribbon: Equal stripes of dark blue, red and light blue symbolising the Royal Navy, Army and RAF respectively.
Metal: Bronze.
Size: Height 44mm; max. width 38mm.
Description: The six-pointed star has a circular centre with the GRI/VI monogram, surmounted by a crown and inscribed THE 1939-1945 STAR round the foot.
Clasps: Battle of Britain, sewn directly on to the ribbon.
Comments: *The first in a series of eight bronze stars issued for service in the Second World War, it was awarded to personnel who had completed six months' service in specified operational commands overseas, between 3 September 1939 and 2 September 1945, though in certain cases the minimum period was shortened. Any service curtailed by death, injury or capture also qualified, as did the award of a decoration or a mention in despatches. The clasp awarded to RAF aircrew for action during the Battle of Britain was denoted by a gilt rosette when the ribbon was worn alone.*

VALUE:		Miniature
1939-45 Star	£8–10	£3
With Battle of Britain clasp	£400–450	£8

178. ATLANTIC STAR

Campaign: Atlantic 1939-45.
Branch of Service: Mainly Royal and Commonwealth Navies.
Ribbon: Watered silk blue, white and green representing the ocean.
Metal: Bronze.
Size: Height 44mm; max. width 38mm.
Description: As above, but inscribed THE ATLANTIC STAR.
Clasps: Air Crew Europe, France and Germany.
Comments: *This star was awarded in the Royal Navy for six months' service afloat between 3 September 1939 and 8 May 1945 in the Atlantic or home waters, and to personnel employed in the convoys to North Russia and the South Atlantic. Personnel must have already qualified for the 1939–45 Star with the qualifying period for this not counting towards the Atlantic Star. Merchant Navy personnel also qualified, as did RAF and Army (maritime gunners and air crews—the latter only requiring 2 months service) who served afloat. In the case of Merchant seamen who served in the last six months of operational service up to 8 May 1945, the Atlantic Star was awarded but not the 1939–45 Star. Entitlement to the France and Germany or Air Crew Europe stars was denoted by clasps to that effect, if the Atlantic Star was previously awarded.*

VALUE:		*Miniature*
Atlantic Star	£25–30	£3
Air Crew Europe clasp	£50–60	£8
France and Germany clasp	£35–40	£6

179. AIR CREW EUROPE STAR

Campaign: Air operations over Europe 1939-44.
Branch of Service: RAF and Commonwealth aircrew.
Ribbon: Pale blue (the sky) with black edges (night flying) and a narrow yellow stripe on either side (enemy searchlights).
Metal: Bronze.
Size: Height 44mm; max. width 38mm.
Description: As above, but inscribed THE AIR CREW EUROPE STAR.
Clasps: Atlantic or France and Germany.
Comments: *Awarded for operational flying from UK bases over Europe, for a period of two months between 3 September 1939 and 4 June 1944. Entitlement to either the Atlantic Star or France and Germany Star was denoted by the appropriate bar. This star is by far the most coveted of all the Second World War stars. The officially named South African star is the rarest of all the Second World War medals.*

VALUE:		*Miniature*
Air Crew Europe Star	£100–120	£3
Atlantic Clasp	£150–155	£6
France and Germany Clasp	£100–110	£6

180. AFRICA STAR

Campaign: Africa 1940-43.
Branch of Service: British and Commonwealth forces.
Ribbon: Pale buff symbolising the sand of the desert, with a broad red central stripe, a dark blue stripe on the left and a light blue stripe on the right symbolising the three services.
Metal: Bronze.
Size: Height 44mm; max. width 38mm.
Description: As above, but inscribed THE AFRICA STAR.
Clasps: North Africa 1942-43, 8th Army, 1st Army.
Comments: *Awarded for entry into an operational area in North Africa between 10 June 1940 (the date of Italy's declaration of war) and 12 May 1943 (the end of operations in North Africa), but service in Abyssinia (Ethiopia), Somaliland, Eritrea and Malta also qualified for the award. A silver numeral 1 or 8 worn on the ribbon denoted service with the First or Eighth Army between 23 October 1942 and 23 May 1943. A clasp inscribed North Africa 1942-43 was awarded to personnel of the Royal Navy Inshore Squadrons and Merchant Navy vessels which worked inshore between these dates. RAF personnel also qualified for this clasp, denoted by a silver rosette on the ribbon alone.*

VALUE:		*Miniature*
Africa Star	£10–15	£3
8th Army clasp	£15–20	£8
1st Army clasp	£15–20	£8
North Africa 1942-43 clasp	£15–20	£10

181. PACIFIC STAR

Campaign: Pacific area 1941-45.
Branch of Service: British and Commonwealth forces.
Ribbon: Dark green (the jungle) with a central yellow stripe (the beaches), narrow stripes of dark and light blue (Royal Navy and RAF) and wider stripes of red (Army) at the edges.
Metal: Bronze.
Size: Height 44mm; max. width 38mm.
Description: As above, but inscribed THE PACIFIC STAR.
Clasps: Burma.
Comments: *Awarded for operational service in the Pacific theatre of war from 8 December 1941 to 15 August 1945. Service with the Royal and Merchant navies in the Pacific Ocean, Indian Ocean and South China Sea and land service in these areas also qualified. Personnel qualifying for both Pacific and Burma Stars got the first star and a clasp in respect of the second.*

VALUE: *Miniature*
Pacific Star £25–30 £3
Burma clasp £35–40 £6

182. BURMA STAR

Campaign: Burma 1941-45.
Branch of Service: British and Commonwealth forces.
Ribbon: Three equal bands of dark blue (British forces), red (Commonwealth forces) and dark blue. The dark blue bands each have at their centres a stripe of bright orange (the sun).
Metal: Bronze.
Size: Height 44mm; max. width 38mm.
Description: As above, but inscribed THE BURMA STAR.
Clasps: Pacific
Comments: *Qualifying service in the Burma campaign counted from 11 December 1941 and included service in Bengal or Assam from 1 May 1942 to 31 December 1943, and from 1 January 1944 onwards in these parts of Bengal or Assam east of the Brahmaputra. Naval service in the eastern Bay of Bengal, off the coasts of Sumatra, Sunda and Malacca also counted.*

VALUE: *Miniature*
Burma Star £20–25 £3
Pacific Clasp £30–35 £6

183. ITALY STAR

Campaign: Italy 1943-45.
Branch of Service: British and Commonwealth forces.
Ribbon: Five equal stripes of red, white, green, white and red (the Italian national colours).
Metal: Bronze.
Size: Height 44mm; max. width 38mm.
Description: As above, but inscribed THE ITALY STAR.
Clasps: None.
Comments: *Awarded for operational service on land in Italy, Sicily, Greece, Yugoslavia, the Aegean area and Dodecanese islands, Corsica, Sardinia and Elba at any time between 11 June 1943 and 8 May 1945.*

VALUE: *Miniature*
Italy Star £10–12 £3

184. FRANCE AND GERMANY STAR

Date: 1945.
Campaign: France and Germany 1944-45.
Branch of Service: British and Commonwealth forces.
Ribbon: Five equal stripes of blue, white, red, white and blue (the national colours of the United Kingdom, France and the Netherlands).
Metal: Bronze.
Size: Height 44mm; max. width 38mm.
Description: As above, but inscribed THE FRANCE AND GERMANY STAR.
Clasps: Atlantic.
Comments: *Awarded for operational service in France, Belgium, the Netherlands or Germany from 6 June 1944 to 8 May 1945. Service in the North Sea, English Channel and Bay of Biscay in connection with the campaign in northern Europe also qualified. Prior eligibility for the Atlantic or Air Crew Europe Stars entitled personnel only to a bar for France and Germany. Conversely a first award of the France and Germany Star could earn an Atlantic bar.*

VALUE:		Miniature
France and Germany Star	£18–20	£3
Atlantic Clasp	£70–80	£6

185. DEFENCE MEDAL

Date: 1945.
Campaign: Second World War 1939-45.
Branch of Service: British and Commonwealth forces.
Ribbon: Two broad bars of green (this green and pleasant land) superimposed by narrow stripes of black (the black-out), with a wide band of orange (fire-bombing) in the centre.
Metal: Cupro-nickel or silver.
Size: 36mm.
Description: (Obverse) the uncrowned effigy of King George VI; (reverse) two lions flanking an oak sapling crowned with the dates at the sides and wavy lines representing the sea below. The words THE DEFENCE MEDAL appear in the exergue.
Clasps: None.
Comments: *Awarded to service personnel for three years' service at home or six months' service overseas in territories subjected to air attack or otherwise closely threatened. Personnel of Anti-Aircraft Command, RAF ground crews, Dominion forces stationed in the UK, the Home Guard, Civil Defence, National Fire Service and many other civilian units* qualified for the medal. The medal was generally issued unnamed in cupro-nickel, but the Canadian version was struck in silver.*

VALUE:		Miniature
Cupro-nickel	£12–14	£8
Silver (Canadian)	£15–18	£12

*The definitive list of eligible recipients was published by the Ministry of Defence in 1992—Form DM1/DM2 and Annexe. This lists 50 different organisations and 90 sub-divisions of eligible personnel.

186. WAR MEDAL 1939–45

Date: 1945.
Campaign: Second World War 1939-45.
Branch of Service: British and Commonwealth forces.
Ribbon: Narrow red stripe in the centre, with a narrow white stripe on either side, broad red stripes at either edge and two intervening stripes of blue.
Metal: Cupro-nickel or silver.
Size: 36mm.
Description: (Obverse) effigy of King George VI; (reverse) a triumphant lion trampling on a dragon symbolising the Axis powers.
Clasps: None.
Comments: *All fulltime personnel of the armed forces wherever they were serving, so long as they had served for at least 28 days between 3 September 1939 and 2 September 1945 were eligible for this medal. It was granted in addition to the campaign stars and the Defence Medal. A few categories of civilians, such as war correspondents and ferry pilots who had flown in operational theatres, also qualified. No clasps were issued with this medal but a bronze oak leaf denoted a mention in despatches. The medal was struck in cupro-nickel and issued unnamed, but those issued to Australian and South African personnel were officially named. The Canadian version of the medal was struck in silver.*

VALUE:		*Miniature*
Cupro-nickel	£7–10	£8
Named (Australian or South African)	£8–12	
Silver (Canadian)	£10–14	£12

186A. KING'S BADGE FOR WAR SERVICE

Date: 1945.
Campaign: Second World War.
Ribbon: None.
Metal: Silver.
Size: 26mm.
Description: A circular buttonhole badge with the crowned monogram GRI in script capitals in the centre, inscribed FOR LOYAL SERVICE.
Comments: *Awarded to personnel who did not qualify for one or other of the service medals or campaign stars, and who had been invalided out of the services. The badges are not numbered or named.*

VALUE: £8

187. INDIA SERVICE MEDAL

Date: 1945.
Campaign: India 1939-45.
Branch of Service: Indian forces.
Ribbon: Dark blue with two wide and one central thin pale blue stripes.
Metal: Cupro-nickel.
Size: 36mm.
Description: (Obverse) the effigy of the King Emperor; (reverse) a map of the Indian sub-continent with INDIA at the top and 1939-45 at foot.
Clasps: None.
Comments: *Awarded to officers and men of the Indian forces for three years' non-operational service in India. In effect, it took the place of the Defence Medal in respect of Indian forces.*

VALUE: £10–12   *Miniature*   £10–12

188. CANADIAN VOLUNTEER SERVICE MEDAL

Date: 1943.
Campaign: Second World War 1939-45.
Branch of Service: Canadian forces.
Ribbon: Narrow stripes of green and red flanking a broad central stripe of dark blue.
Metal: Silver.
Size: 36mm.
Description: (Obverse) seven men and women in the uniforms of the various services, marching in step; (reverse) the Canadian national arms.
Clasps: Maple leaf. A clasp inscribed DIEPPE and surmounted by the Combined Operations emblem, was instituted in 1994 for award to all servicemen who took part in the Dieppe raid of 1942.
Comments: *Awarded for eighteen months' voluntary service in the Canadian forces. The clasp denoted overseas service. The seven marching personnel are based on real people taken from National Defence photographs, representing the land, sea and air forces plus a nurse. The individuals are: first row: centre, 3780 Leading Seaman P. G. Colbeck, RCN, left, C52819 Pte D. E. Dolan, 1 Can. Para Bn; right, R95505 F/Sgt K. M. Morgan, RCAF. Second row: centre, W4901 Wren P. Mathie, WRCNS; left, 12885 L/Cpl J. M. Dann, CWAC; right, W315563 LAW O. M. Salmon, RCAF; back row: Lt N/S E. M. Lowe, RCAMC.*

VALUE:		Miniature
Silver medal	£14–16	£8
Maple leaf clasp	£18–22	£12
Dieppe clasp	£35–45	£15

188A. CANADIAN MEMORIAL CROSS

Instituted: 1914.
Branch of Service: Relative of Canadian forces.
Ribbon: Violet 11mm (ring suspension), 32mm (bar suspension).
Metal: Dull silver.
Size: 32mm.
Description: A Greek cross with the royal Cypher at the centre, superimposed on another with arms slightly flared at the ends. Maple leaves adorn three of the arms while the top arm has a crown surmounted by a suspension ring. (Reverse): details of the award. Four versions of the cross exist: the original, with GVR cypher (1914–19), with GVIR cypher and ring suspension (1940–45), GVIR cypher with suspension bar (1945–52) and an EIIR version for Korea and later conflicts.
Comments: *Issued to wives and mothers of servicemen who had died during World War I. A second version was introduced in August 1940 for award to widows and mothers of World War II servicemen, but this was extended to include those of merchant seamen and civilian firefighters. Newfoundland service personnel became eligible after April 1, 1949.*

VALUE:	
GVR, ring suspension	£50–£70
GVIR, ring suspension	£40–£60
GVIR, bar suspension	£60–£80
EIIR, bar suspension	£120–160

189. AFRICA SERVICE MEDAL

Date: 1943.
Campaign: Second World War 1939-45.
Branch of Service: South African forces.
Ribbon: A central orange stripe, with green and gold stripes on either side.
Metal: Silver.
Size: 36mm.
Description: (Obverse) depicts a map of the African Continent; (reverse) bears a leaping Springbok. Inscribed AFRICA SERVICE MEDAL on the left and AFRIKADIENS-MEDALJE on the right.
Clasps: None.
Comments: *Awarded to Union service personnel who served at home and abroad during the War for at least thirty days. Medals were fully named and gave the service serial number of the recipient, prefixed by the letters N (Native Military Corps), C (Cape Corps) or M (Indian and Malay Corps), no prefix indicated a white volunteer—a curious example of racism at work.*

VALUE:
    Silver medal (190,000)   £10–12   *Miniature* £10

190. AUSTRALIA SERVICE MEDAL

Date: 1949.
Campaign: Second World War 1939-45.
Branch of Service: Australian forces.
Ribbon: A broad central band of khaki bordered in red, with a dark blue and a light blue bar at either edge.
Metal: Cupro-nickel.
Size: 36mm.
Description: (Obverse) the effigy of King George VI; (reverse) the Australian arms supported by a kangaroo and an emu.
Clasps: None.
Comments: *Awarded to all Australian personnel who had seen eighteen months' overseas or three years' home service. The medals were named to the recipients. In the case of Army personnel, their service numbers were prefixed by the initial of their state: N (New South Wales), Q (Queensland), S (South Australia), T (Tasmania), V (Victoria) and W (Western Australia). In 1999 the time served for eligibility was reduced.*

VALUE:
    Cupro-nickel medal (180,000)   £25–30   *Miniature*   £12

191. NEW ZEALAND WAR SERVICE MEDAL

Date: 1946.
Campaign: Second World War 1939-45.
Branch of Service: New Zealand forces.
Ribbon: Black with white edges.
Metal: Cupro-nickel.
Size: 36mm.
Description: (Obverse) effigy of King George VI; (reverse) the text FOR SERVICE TO NEW ZEALAND 1939-45 with a fern leaf below. Suspension was by a pair of fern leaves attached to a straight bar.
Clasps: None.
Comments: *Issued unnamed, to all members of the New Zealand forces who completed one month full-time or six months part-time service between September 1939 and September 1945.*

VALUE:
    Cupro-nickel medal (240,000)   £20–25   *Miniature*   £7

191A. NEW ZEALAND MEMORIAL CROSS

Instituted: 1960.
Campaign: Second World War, 1939–45.
Branch of Service: Relatives of New Zealand forces.
Ribbon: 12mm royal purple
Metal: Dull Silver.
Size: 32 mm.
Description: A cross surmounted by a St Edward Crown, with fern leaves on each arm, in the centre, within a wreath, the Royal Cypher; (reverse) details of the person in respect of whose death the cross is granted.
Comments: *Granted to the next-of-kin of persons who had lost their lives on active service with the New Zealand forces during the Second World War, or who had subsequently died of wounds or illness contracted during that conflict. Provision was made for the grant of crosses to the parent(s) as well as the wife or eldest surviving daughter or son.*
VALUE:
Silver £60–£80

192. SOUTH AFRICAN MEDAL FOR WAR SERVICE

Date: 1946.
Campaign: Second World War 1939-46.
Branch of Service: South African forces.
Ribbon: Three equal stripes of orange, white and blue, the South African national colours.
Metal: Silver.
Size: 36mm.
Description: (Obverse) South African arms; (reverse) a wreath of protea flowers enclosing the dates 1939 and 1945. Inscribed in English and Afrikaans: SOUTH AFRICA FOR WAR SERVICES on the left and SUID AFRIKA VIR OORLOGDIENSTE on the right.
Clasps: None.
Comments: *Men and women who served for at least two years in any official voluntary organisation in South Africa or overseas qualified for this medal so long as the service was both voluntary and unpaid. Those who already had the South African War Service Medal were ineligible.*

VALUE:
Silver (17,500) £30–40 *Miniature* £14

193. SOUTHERN RHODESIA WAR SERVICE MEDAL

Date: 1946.
Campaign: Second World War 1939-45.
Branch of Service: Southern Rhodesian forces.
Ribbon: Dark green with black and red stripes at each edge.
Metal: Cupro-nickel.
Size: 36mm.
Description: (Obverse) King George VI; (reverse) the Rhodesian national arms. FOR SERVICE IN SOUTHERN RHODESIA round the top and the dates 1939-1945 at the foot.
Clasps: None.
Comments: *This very scarce medal was awarded only to those who served in Southern Rhodesia during the period of the War but who were ineligible for one of the campaign stars or war medals.*

VALUE:
Cupro-nickel (1700) £160–175 *Miniature* £16

194. NEWFOUNDLAND VOLUNTEER WAR SERVICE MEDAL

Date: 1981.
Campaign: Second World War 1939-45.
Branch of Service: Newfoundland forces.
Ribbon: Deep claret with edges of red, white and blue.
Metal: Bronze.
Size: 37mm.
Description: (Obverse) the royal cypher of George VI surmounted by a crown topped by a caribou, the Newfoundland national emblem; (reverse) Britannia on a scallop shell background guarded by two lions.
Clasps:
Comments: *While the Second World War was being fought, Newfoundland was still a separate British colony which did not enter the Canadian Confederation till 1947. Consequently Newfoundland servicemen did not qualify for the Canadian Volunteer Service medal, and this deficiency was not remedied until July 1981 when the Newfoundland provincial government instituted this medal. Those who had served with the Canadian forces, on the other hand, and already held the Canadian medal, were not eligible for this award. The medal could be claimed by next-of-kin of those who died in or since the war.*

VALUE: Bronze (7,500) £350–450   *Miniature*   £35

195. KOREA MEDAL

Date: July 1951.
Campaign: Korean War 1950-53.
Branch of Service: British and Commonwealth forces.
Ribbon: Yellow, with two blue stripes .
Metal: Cupro-nickel or silver.
Size: 36mm.
Description: (Obverse) Right-facing bust of Queen Elizabeth II by Mary Gillick; there are two obverse types, with or without BR: OMN; (reverse) Hercules wrestling with the Hydra, KOREA in the exergue.
Clasps: None.
Comments: *Awarded to all British and Commonwealth forces who took part in the Korean War between July 1950 and July 27, 1953. British medals were issued in cupro-nickel impressed in small capitals, medals to Australian and New Zealand forces were impressed in large capitals and the Canadian version was struck in silver and has CANADA below the Queen's bust. Particularly prized are medals issued to the 'Glorious Gloucesters' who played a gallant part in the battle of the Imjin River.*

VALUE:		*Miniature*
British, first obverse	£60–70	£7
British, second obverse	£100–150	£7
To Gloucester Regiment	£250–300	
Australian or New Zealand naming	£70–90	
Canadian, silver (27,000)	£60–70	£9

196. SOUTH AFRICAN MEDAL FOR KOREA

Date: 1953.
Campaign: Korea 1950-53.
Branch of Service: South African forces.
Ribbon: Sky blue central band flanked by dark blue stripes and edges of orange.
Metal: Silver.
Size: 38mm.
Description: (Obverse) maps of South Africa and Korea with an arrow linking them and the words VRYWILLIGERS and VOLUNTEERS in the field. (Reverse) the then South African arms surmounted by the crowned EIIR.
Clasps: None.
Comments: *Awarded to the 800 personnel in the contingent sent to Korea by the Union of South Africa. Suspension is by a ring and claw.*

VALUE:

Silver (800)	£280–300	*Miniature*	£25
Pilot's issue	£1000–1500		

197. UNITED NATIONS KOREA MEDAL

Date: December 1950.
Campaign: Korea 1950-53.
Branch of Service: All UN forces.
Ribbon: Seventeen narrow stripes alternating pale blue and white.
Metal: Bronze.
Size: 35mm.
Description: (Obverse) the wreathed globe emblem of the UN; (reverse) inscribed FOR SERVICE IN DEFENCE OF THE PRINCIPLES OF THE CHARTER OF THE UNITED NATIONS.
Clasps: Korea.
Comments: *National variants were produced, but the British type was granted to all personnel of the British and Commonwealth forces who had served at least one full day in Korea or in support units in Japan. Moreover, as those who served in Korea after the armistice in July 1953 were also entitled to the UN medal it is sometimes found in groups without the corresponding British medal. The award was extended to cover the period up to July 27, 1954, the first anniversary of the Panmunjom Truce. Issues to South African personnel were named on the rim.*

VALUE: £25–30   *Miniature*   £6

If you know of a British or Commonwealth medal that is not included in the MEDAL YEARBOOK we would be delighted to hear from you.

Or if you can supply us with a photograph of any of the medals not illustrated in this publication we would be pleased to include it next year.

If you can help, please contact the Managing Editor, John Mussell, telephone 01404 46972 or at the address on page 1. Thank you!

198. GENERAL SERVICE MEDAL 1962

Date: 1964.
Campaign: Minor campaigns and operations since 1962.
Branch of Service: British forces.
Ribbon: Deep purple edged with green.
Metal: Silver.
Size: 36mm.
Description: (Obverse) a crowned bust of Queen Elizabeth II; (reverse) an oak wreath enclosing a crown and the words FOR CAMPAIGN SERVICE. It has a beaded and curved suspension above which are mounted campaign clasps.
Clasps: Twelve to date (see below); the maximum clasps awarded so far seems to be six.
Comments: *This medal was instituted for award to personnel of all services, and thus did away with the need for separate Army and Navy general service medals. Awards range from a mere 70 for South Vietnam to over 130,000 for service in Northern Ireland.*

VALUE:

		Miniature
Borneo	£30–40	£8–10
Radfan	£45–55	£8–10
South Arabia	£30–40	£8–10
Malay Peninsula	£30–40	£8–10
South Vietnam	Rare	£8–10
Northern Ireland	£35–45	£8–10
Dhofar	£120–140	£8–10
Lebanon	£400–450	£8–10
Mine Clearance	£650–800	£8–10
Gulf	£150–200	£8–10
Kuwait	£300–400	£8–10
N. Iraq & S. Turkey	£300–400	£8–10
Air Operations Iraq	£400–600	£10–12
2 clasps	£40–60	£12–16
3 clasps	£80–120	£14–18
4 clasps	From £140	£16–20

198A. OPERATIONAL SERVICE MEDAL

Date: 1999.
Campaign: Operations after 1 January 2000.
Branch of Service: All branches of the armed forces.
Ribbon: Basic colours with a varying number of thin stripes for each operation.
Metal: Silver.
Size: 36mm.
Description: Not yet available.
Clasps: None.
Comments: *To be awarded for minor campaigns for which a separate medal is not issued, and operations for which the award of a UN or NATO medal is not merited. It replaces the General Service Medal 1962, except for Northern Ireland and Air Operations Iraq.*

VALUE: —

199. UNITED NATIONS EMERGENCY FORCE MEDAL

Date: 1957.
Campaign: Israel and Egypt 1956–57.
Branch of Service: All UN forces.
Ribbon: Sand-coloured with a central light blue stripe and narrow dark blue and green stripes towards each edge.
Metal: Bronze.
Size: 35mm.
Description: (Obverse) the UN wreathed globe emblem with UNEF at the top; (reverse) inscribed IN THE SERVICE OF PEACE. Ring suspension.
Clasps: None.
Comments: *Awarded to all personnel who served with the UN peace-keeping forces on the border between Israel and Egypt following the Sinai Campaign of 1956. These medals were awarded to troops from Brazil, Canada, Colombia, Denmark, Finland, Indonesia, Norway, Sweden and Yugoslavia.*

VALUE:

Bronze	£20–25	*Miniature*	£7

200. VIETNAM MEDAL

Date: July 1968.
Campaign: Vietnam 1964-68.
Branch of Service: Australian and New Zealand forces.
Ribbon: A broad central band of bright yellow surmounted by three thin red stripes (the Vietnamese national colours) and bordered by broader red stripes, with dark and light blue stripes at the edges, representing the three services.
Metal: Silver.
Size: 36mm.
Description: (Obverse) the crowned bust of Queen Elizabeth II; (reverse) a nude male figure pushing apart two spheres representing different ideologies.
Clasps: None.
Comments: *Awarded to personnel who served in Vietnam a minimum of one day on land or 28 days at sea after 28 May 1964. The medal was impressed in large capitals (Australian) or small capitals (New Zealand).*

VALUE:

Australian recipient (18,000)	£140–160
New Zealand recipient (3,312)	£170–200
Miniature	£10–12

200A. VIETNAM LOGISTIC AND SUPPORT MEDAL

Instituted: 1993.
Campaign: Vietnam 1964–68.
Branch of Service: Australian and New Zealand forces.
Ribbon: A broad central band of yellow with three narrow red stripes superimposed. On the left are stripes of red and dark blue and on the right stripes of dark brown and light blue.
Metal: Nickel-silver.
Size: 36mm.
Description: (Obverse) crowned effigy of Queen Elizabeth and titles; (reverse) as MY200 above but with a cartouche containing a ram's head (Royal Australian Mint's mark) near the man's right foot. The suspension bar also differs from MY200 with graduated straight sides.
Clasps: None.
Comments: *Awarded to personnel who served in the Vietnam War but who did not qualify for the Vietnam Medal. It is estimated that about 20,000 individuals are eligible for this award. Recipients include Qantas air crew who took troop flights to Saigon, and civilian entertainers.*

VALUE:

Australian recipient (5121)	£150–300
New Zealand recipient	£250–350
Miniature	£10–12

201. SOUTH VIETNAM CAMPAIGN MEDAL

Date: 1964.
Campaign: Vietnam 1960–68.
Branch of Service: Allied forces in Vietnam.
Ribbon: White with two broad green stripes towards the centre and narrow green edges.
Metal: Bronze.
Size: Height 42mm; max. width 36mm.
Description: A six-pointed star, with gold rays in the angles. The gilt enamelled centre shows a map of Vietnam engulfed in flames; (reverse) a Vietnamese inscription in the centre.
Comments: *Awarded by the government of South Vietnam to Australian and New Zealand forces who served at least six months in Vietnam. The original issue, of Vietnamese manufacture, was relatively crude and issued unnamed. Subsequently medals were produced in Australia and these are not only of a better quality but bear the name of the recipient.*

VALUE:

Unnamed	£10–15
Named	£20–30
Miniature	£6–10

202. RHODESIA MEDAL

Date: 1980.
Campaign: Rhodesia 1979–80.
Branch of Service: British and Rhodesian forces.
Ribbon: Sky blue, with a narrow band of red, white and dark blue in the centre.
Metal: Rhodium-plated cupro-nickel.
Size: 36mm.
Description: (Obverse) the crowned bust of Queen Elizabeth II; (reverse) a sable antelope with the name of the medal and the year of issue.
Clasps: None.
Comments: *This medal was awarded to personnel serving in Rhodesia for fourteen days between 1 December 1979 and 20 March 1980, pending the elections and the emergence of the independent republic of Zimbabwe. Medals were issued unnamed or named in impressed capitals. Examples with the word COPY in raised capitals immediately below the suspension fitment are believed to have been issued as replacements for lost medals, although examples with "R" for replacement are also known to exist.*

VALUE:

Cupro-nickel (2500)	£300–350	*Miniature*	£9

203. SOUTH ATLANTIC MEDAL

Date: 1982.
Campaign: Falkland Islands and South Georgia 1982.
Branch of Service: British forces.
Ribbon: Watered silk blue, white, green, white and blue.
Metal: Cupro-nickel.
Size: 36mm.
Description: (Obverse) crowned profile of Queen Elizabeth II;
(reverse) laurel wreath below the arms of the Falkland Islands with
SOUTH ATLANTIC MEDAL inscribed round the top.
Clasps: None, but a rosette denoting service in the combat zone.
Comments: *Awarded to all personnel who took part in operations in the
South Atlantic for the liberation of South Georgia and the Falkland Islands
following the Argentinian invasion. To qualify, the recipient had to have at
least one full day's service in the Falklands or South Georgia, or 30 days in
the operational zone including Ascension Island. Those who qualified
under the first condition were additionally awarded a large rosette for wear
on the ribbon.*

VALUE:

Army (7000)	£180–220
Royal Navy (13,000)	£170–190
Royal Marines (3700)	£200–240
Royal Fleet Auxiliary (2000)	£120–150
RAF (2000)	£140–160
Merchant Navy and civilians (2000)	£115–140
Miniature	£6
with rosette	£9

203A. SOVIET 40th ANNIVERSARY MEDAL

Date: 1985.
Campaign: Second World War.
Branch of Service: British and Canadian forces who served
mainly in RN or MN ships on Arctic convoys.
Ribbon: One half red, the other orange with three black
stripes, edged with pale blue. Worn in the Russian
style.
Metal: Bronze.
Size: 32mm.
Description: (Obverse) Group of servicemen and women
in front of a five-pointed star flanked by oak leaves and
the dates 1945–1985 above; (reverse) 40th anniversary of
the Victory in the Great Patriotic War 1941–1945, in
Russian.
Clasps: None.
Comments: *In 1994 Her Majesty the Queen approved the
wearing of this medal awarded by the Soviet Government to
selected ex-Servicemen, bearing in mind the changed
circumstances in Russia since the award was first issued.*

VALUE:	British striking	£16–20
	Russian striking	£16–20

Miniature (unofficial) £9

204. GULF MEDAL

Date: 1992.
Campaign: Kuwait and Saudi Arabia 1990-91.
Branch of Service: British forces.
Ribbon: Sand-coloured broad central band flanked by narrow stripes of dark blue, red and light blue (left) or light blue, red and dark blue (right) representing the sands of the desert and the three armed services.
Metal: Cupro-nickel.
Size: 36mm.
Description: (Obverse) crowned profile of Queen Elizabeth II; (reverse) an eagle and automatic rifle superimposed on an anchor, symbolising the three armed services. The dates of the Gulf War appear at the foot.
Clasps: 2 Aug 1990, 16 Jan–28 Feb 1991.
Comments: *Awarded to personnel who had thirty days continuous service in the Middle East (including Cyprus) between 2 August 1990 and 7 March 1991, or seven days between 16 January 1991 and 28 February 1991, or service with the Kuwait Liaison Team on 2 August 1990, the date of the Iraqi invasion. Two clasps were sanctioned and awarded to personnel who qualified for active service with the Liaison Team or in the operations to liberate Kuwait. A rosette is worn on the ribbon alone to denote the campaign clasps. Naming is in impressed capitals. More than 45,000 medals were awarded. See also the Kuwait and Iraq-Turkey clasps awarded to the General Service Medal 1962. About 1,500 civilians, including members of British Aerospace working at Dahran, also received the medal with the clasp 16 Jan to 28 Feb 1991.*

VALUE:

No clasp		£90–110
16 Jan to 28 Feb 1991		
	Regiments/RN/RAF	£140–200
	Corps and Artillery	£100–120
	Civilians	£90–120
2 Aug 1990		£1200–1600
Miniature		£10

204A. HUMANITARIAN PEACEKEEPING MEDAL

Date: 1999.
Campaign: Humanitarian or peacekeeping operations.
Branch of Service: Military and civilian personnel.
Ribbon: Details not yet available.
Metal: Details not yet available.
Size: Details not yet available.
Description: Details not yet available.
Clasps: Details not yet available.
Comment: *To be issued to military and civilian personnel engaged in operations of a humanitarian or peacekeeping character which do not warrant the issue of an Operational Service Medal and which do not attract the award of a UN medal.*

205. SAUDI ARABIAN MEDAL FOR THE LIBERATION OF KUWAIT

Date: 1991.
Campaign: Gulf War 1991.
Branch of Service: British and Allied forces.
Ribbon: Green with edges of red, black and white (the Saudi national colours).
Metal: White metal.
Size: approx. 45mm across
Description: The white metal medal has a star of fifteen long and fifteen short round-tipped rays, surmounted by a bronze circle bearing a crowned and enwreathed globe on which appears a map of Arabia. Above the circle is a palm tree with crossed scimitars, the state emblem of Saudi Arabia. A scroll inscribed in Arabic and English LIBERATION OF KUWAIT appears round the foot of the circle.
Clasps: None.
Comments: *Awarded by the government of Saudi Arabia to all Allied personnel who took part in the campaign for the liberation of Kuwait, although only a few of the 45,000 British servicemen were subsequently given permission by the Foreign and Commonwealth Office to wear it. The contract for production was shared between Spink and a Swiss company, but subsequently a flatter version, more practicable for wear with other medals, was manufactured in the United States.*

VALUE: £15–20   *Miniature*   £12

205A. MULTINATIONAL FORCE AND OBSERVERS MEDAL

Date: March 1982.
Campaign: Sinai Peninsula.
Ribbon: 36mm with 10mm central white stripe, flanked by 3mm dark green stripes and 10mm orange stripes on the outside.
Metal: Bronze.
Size: 30mm.
Description: (Obverse) a dove clutching an olive branch surrounded by the inscription MULTINATIONAL FORCE & OBSERVERS; (reverse) UNITED IN SERVICE FOR PEACE in five lines.
Comments: *Awarded to personnel of the Multinational Force and Observers (MFO) created in 1979 to monitor the peace agreement between Egypt and Israel. Eligibility for the medal was originally 90 days continuous service in the force, but this was raised to 170 days in March 1985. Subsequent awards for each completed six-month tour is indicated by a silver numeral affixed to the ribbon. It was originally awarded personally by the MFO's first commander, the Norwegian General Fredrik Bull-Hansen. The Force has 3,000 personnel drawn from the armed services of Australia, Canada, Colombia, Fiji, France, Italy, the Netherlands, New Zealand, UK, USA and Uruguay.*

VALUE: £25–30   *Miniature* £7

206. KUWAITI LIBERATION MEDALS

4th grade

Date: 1991.
Campaign: Liberation of Kuwait 1991.
Branch of Service: Allied forces.
Ribbon: Equal stripes of green, white and red (the Kuwaiti national colours) with a black quadrilateral at the upper edge.
Metal: Various.
Size: Various.
Description: The circular medals have different decorative treatments of the Kuwaiti state emblem on the obverse, enshrined in a five-petalled flower (Second Grade), a five-pointed star with radiate background (Third Grade) and a plain medallic treatment (Fourth Grade). All grades, however, have a straight bar suspender of different designs.
Clasps: None.
Comments: *This medal was issued in five grades and awarded according to the rank of the recipient. The Excellent Grade was only conferred on the most senior Allied commanders, the First Grade went to brigadiers and major-generals, the Second Grade to officers of field rank (colonels and majors), the Third Grade to junior officers (captains, lieutenants and equivalent ranks in the other services), and the Fourth Grade to all other ranks. HM Government has decreed that British personnel may accept their medals as a keepsake but permission to wear them in uniform has so far been refused. The Canadian Government has followed the same policy, but the personnel of other Allied nations are permitted to wear their medals.*

VALUE:		*Miniature*
2nd grade	—	
3rd grade	—	
4th grade	£10–15	£12 (silver)

206A. NATO MEDAL

Instituted: December 20, 1994.
Campaigns: Any theatre or area of operations in the service of the North Atlantic Treaty Organization.
Branch of Service: NATO military and service personnel.
Ribbon: NATO blue with a narrow white stripe towards each edge (Former Yugoslavia) or blue with a white central stripe and white edges (Kosovo).
Metal: Bronze
Size: 36mm
Description: (Obverse) the NATO star emblem set in a wreath of olive leaves; (reverse) the title NORTH ATLANTIC TREATY ORGANIZATION and the words IN SERVICE OF PEACE AND FREEDOM in English and French.
Clasps: Former Yugoslavia, Kosovo.
Comments: *The NATO medal was first instituted to reward personnel who took part in the Alliance operations in the former Yugoslavia. Any person serving under NATO command or operational control is eligible for the award. UK Service personnel cannot qualify for the NATO Medal and the UNPROFOR Medal (no. 207) in respect of the same period of service. The qualifying period for the medal is to be designated by the Secretary-General, however, for the operations in the former Yugoslavia the period has been set as 30 days continuous or accumulated service within the theatre of operations inside the former Yugoslavia and the Adriatic, or 90 days within the area of operations but outside the territory of the former Yugoslavia. The medal takes precedence equal to the General Service Medal in order of date of award. Numerals are worn on the ribbon to denote multiple tours.*

VALUE: £20 *Miniature* £8

206B. OMANI 25th NATIONAL DAY MEDAL

Date: November 18, 1995.
Branch of Service: British personnel seconded to the service of the Sultan of Oman.
Ribbon:
Metal:
Size:
Description:
Comments: *This medal was instituted to celebrate the 25th anniversary of the National Day of Oman (November 18). In December 1998 Her Majesty the Queen granted permission for members of the British armed forces to wear this medal.*

VALUE: —

206C. EUROPEAN COMMUNITY MONITORING MISSION MEDAL

Date: 1995.
Campaigns: Former Yugoslavia.
Branch of Service: EC Community Peacekeeping.
Ribbon: Navy with stripes of white and red and thin yellow.
Metal: Silver.
Size: 36mm.
Description: (Obverse) Outline map of Yugoslavia surmounted by the words EC MONITOR MISSION surrounded by a ring of stars; (reverse) a dove of peace.
Comments: *Awarded or 21 days service between July 27, 1991 and June 30, 1993, in and around the former Yugoslavia.*

VALUE: —

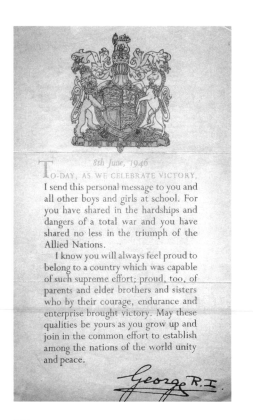

8th June, 1946

TO-DAY, AS WE CELEBRATE VICTORY, I send this personal message to you and all other boys and girls at school. For you have shared in the hardships and dangers of a total war and you have shared no less in the triumph of the Allied Nations.

I know you will always feel proud to belong to a country which was capable of such supreme effort; proud, too, of parents and elder brothers and sisters who by their courage, endurance and enterprise brought victory. May these qualities be yours as you grow up and join in the common effort to establish among the nations of the world unity and peace.

George R.I.

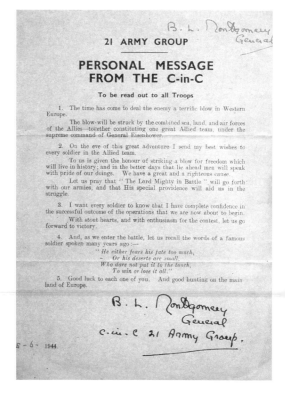

21 ARMY GROUP

B. L. *Montgomery*
General

PERSONAL MESSAGE FROM THE C-in-C

To be read out to all Troops

1. The time has come to deal the enemy a terrific blow in Western Europe.

The blow will be struck by the combined sea, land, and air forces of the Allies—together constituting one great Allied team, under the supreme command of General Eisenhower.

2. On the eve of this great adventure I send my best wishes to every soldier in the Allied team.

To us is given the honour of striking a blow for freedom which will live in history; and in the better days that lie ahead men will speak with pride of our doings. We have a great and a righteous cause.

Let us pray that "The Lord Mighty in Battle" will go forth with our armies, and that His special providence will aid us in the struggle.

3. I want every soldier to know that I have complete confidence in the successful outcome of the operations that we are now about to begin.

With stout hearts, and with enthusiasm for the contest, let us go forward to victory.

4. And, as we enter the battle, let us recall the words of a famous soldier spoken many years ago:—

" *He either fears his fate too much,*
Or his deserts are small,
Who dare not put it to the touch,
To win or lose it all."

5. Good luck to each one of you. And good hunting on the main land of Europe.

B. L. *Montgomery*
General
c-in-c 21 Army Group.

5-6-1944

207. UNITED NATIONS MEDAL

Date: 1951.
Campaigns: Various supervisory or observation roles since 1948.
Branch of Service: UN forces.
Ribbons: Various (see below).
Metal: Bronze.
Size: 35mm.
Description: (Obverse) the wreathed globe emblem surmounted by the letters UN; (reverse) plain.
Clasps: CONGO, UNGOMAP, OSGAP.
Comments: *Apart from the UN Korea and UNEF medals, there have been numerous awards to personnel who served in one or other of the UN peace-keeping actions around the world since the end of the Second World War. The all-purpose medal has been awarded with various distinctive ribbons for service in many of the world's trouble spots.*

UNTSO   United Nations Truce Supervision Organization (Israel, Egypt, Syria since 1948).
Blue ribbon with two narrow white stripes towards the edges.
UNOGIL   United Nations Observation Group in Lebanon (1958).
Same ribbon as UNTSO.
ONUC   Organisation des Nations Unies au Congo (1960–64).
Originally the same ribbon as UNTSO with clasp CONGO, but a green ribbon, with white and blue edges was substituted in 1963.
UNTEA   United Nations Temporary Executive Authority (Netherlands New Guinea, 1962).
Blue ribbon with a white central stripe bordered green.
UNMOGIP   United Nations Military Observer Group in India and Pakistan since 1949.
Dark green ribbon shading to light green with white and blue edges.
UNIPOM   United Nations India Pakistan Observation Mission (1965–66).
Ribbon as UNMOGIP.
UNYOM   United Nations Yemen Observation Mission (1963–64).
Ribbon with brown centre, yellow stripes and light blue edges.
UNFICYP   United Nations Force in Cyprus (1964–).
Pale blue ribbon with central white stripe bordered in dark blue.
UNEF 2   United Nations Emergency Force 2 patrolling Israeli-Egyptian cease-fire (1973–).
Pale blue ribbon with sand centre and two dark blue stripes.
UNDOF   United Nations Disengagement Observer Force, Golan Heights (1974–).
Ribbon of red, white, black and pale blue.
UNIFIL   United Nations Interim Force in Lebanon (1978–).
Pale blue ribbon with green centre bordered white and red.
UNGOMAP   United Nations Good Offices in Afghanistan and Pakistan.
A bronze bar inscribed UNGOMAP was issued but as the mission was made up from observers from three other missions it can only be found on these ribbons: UNTSO, UNIFIL, UNDOF.
UNIIMOG   United Nations Iran-Iraq Monitoring Observation Group.
Pale blue with red, white and green edges.
UNAVEM   United Nations Angola Verification Missions: I (1989–91), II (1991–95), III (1995–).
Pale blue ribbon with yellow edges separated by narrow stripes of red, white and black (same for all three).
ONUCA   Observadores de las Naciones Unidas en Centro America (Nicaragua and Guatemala).
Pale blue ribbon with dark blue edges and nine thin central green or white stripes.
UNTAG   United Nations Transitional Assistance Group (Namibia, 1990).
Sand ribbon with pale blue edges and thin central stripes of blue, green, red, sand and deep blue.
ONUSAL   Observadores de las Naciones Unidas en El Salvador.
Pale blue ribbon with a white central stripe bordered dark blue.
UNIKOM   United Nations Iraq Kuwait Observation Mission.
Sand ribbon with a narrow central stripe of pale blue.
MINURSO   Mission des Nations Unies pour la Referendum dans le Sahara Occidental (UN Mission for the Referendum in Western Sahara).
Ribbon has a broad sandy centre flanked by stripes of UN blue.
UNAMIC   United Nations Advanced Mission in Cambodia (Oct. 1991–March 1992).
Pale blue ribbon with central white stripe bordered with dark blue, yellow and red stripes.
UNTAC   United Nations Transitional Authority in Cambodia (March 1992–Sept. 1993).
Green ribbon with central white stripe edged with red, pale blue and dark blue.

UNOSOM   United Nations Operations in Somalia (I: 1992–93 and II: 1993–95).
Pale yellow ribbon with central blue stripe edged with green.
UNMIH   United Nations Mission in Haiti
Pale blue ribbon with dark blue and red central stripes edged with white.
UNIMOZ   United Nations Operations in Mozambique (1992–).
Pale blue ribbon edged with white and green stripes.
UNPROFOR   United Nations Protection Force (1992–) operating in the former Yugoslavia, especially Bosnia.
Blue ribbon with central red stripe edged in white and green or brown edges.
UNOMIL   United Nations Observer Mission in Liberia (1993–).
Pale blue ribbon flanked with white stripes with dark blue or red edges.
UNOMUR   United Nations Observer Mission in Uganda/Rwanda (1993–).
Pale blue central stripe edged by white and flanked by equal stripes of black, orange and red.
UNOMIG   United Nations Observer Mission in Georgia (1993–).
Pale blue central stripe flanked by equal stripes of white, green and dark blue.
UNAMIR   United Nations Assistance Mission in Rwanda (1993–).
Pale blue central stripe edged with white and flanked by equal stripes of black, green and red.
UNHQ   General service at UN headquarters, New York.
Plain ribbon of pale blue, the UN colour.
UNPREDEP   United Nations Preventative Deployment in Yugoslavia.
Blue ribbon with central red stripe bearing four yellow lines and flanked by white edging.
UNMOP   United Nations Mission of Observers in Pravlaka.
Dark blue ribbon with central yellow stripe edged with white, and two pale blue stripes.
UNTAES   United Nations Transitional Authority in Eastern Slavonia.
Pale blue ribbon with yellow, red edged with white, and green stripes.
UNMOT   United Nations Peacekeeping Force in Tadjikistan.
Blue ribbon with central green stripe flanked by white stripes.
UNMIBH   United Nations Mission in Bosnia Herzegovina.
Blue ribbon with white central stripe, edged with one green and one red stripe.
UNMOGUA   United Nations Military Observers in Guatemala.
Purple with central blue stripe and two white stripes each with central green line.
UNSMIH   United Nations Support Mission in Haiti (July 1996 –).
Same ribbon as UNMIH above, but with clasp UNSMIH.
UNCRO   United Nations Confidence Restoration Operation in Croatia (1995–96).
Same ribbon as UNPROFOR above, but with clasp UNCRO.
MINUGUA   Mision de las Naciones Unidas en Guatemala.
Same ribbon as UNMOGUA but clasp with initials in Spanish.
ONUMOZ   Operation des Nations Unies pour le referendum dans Mozambique.
Same ribbon as UNIMOZ above. Clasp with French initials.
UNSSM   United Nations Special Service Medal.
Awarded to personal serving at least 90 consecutive days under UN control in operations for which no other UN award is authorised. Blue ribbon with white edges.
OSGAP   Office of the Secretary General for Afghanistan and Pakistan.
Silver clasp worn by Canadian personnel on the ribbons of UNTSO, UNDOF or UNIFIL.
UNOMSIL United Nations Observer Mission in Sierra Leone.
Awarded for 90 days service. White ribbon with blue edges and the Sierra Leone colours (light blue flanked by green stripes) in the centre.
UNPSG United Nations Police Support Group Medal.
A support group of 180 police monitors created in January 1998 initially to supervise the Croatian police in the return of displaced persons. 90 days qualifying service. White ribbon with a broad blue central stripe and narrow dark grey (left) and bright yellow (right) stripes towards the edges.
MINURCA United Nations Verification Mission in the Central African Republic.
Mission instituted April 15, 1998 to monitor the restoration of peace following the Bangui agreement. 90 days qualifying service. Ribbon has a broad blue central stripe flanked by yellow, green, red, white and dark blue stripes on either side.
UNSCOM United Nations Special Service Medal
The UN Special Service Medal with UNSCOM clasp is awarded to personnel with a minimum of 90 days consecutive service or 180 days in all, with UNSCOM in Iraq. Ribbon is UN blue with a white stripe at each edge.
UNMIK United Nations Mission in Kosovo
Pale blue ribbon with wide central dark blue stripe edged with white.

VALUE:

Any current issue medal regardless of ribbon	**£10–15**
Original striking for Cyprus	**£25–30**
Miniature	**£6–8**

Long and Meritorious Service Medals

A large, varied but until recently relatively neglected category comprises the medals awarded for long service and good conduct or meritorious service. Their common denominator is that the grant of such awards is made in respect of a minimum number of years of unblemished service—"undetected crime" is how it is often described in the armed forces. As their title implies, long service and good conduct medals combine the elements of lengthy service with no transgressions of the rules and regulations. Meritorious service, on the other hand, implies rather more. Apart from a brief period (1916-28) when awards were made for single acts of gallantry, MSMs have generally been granted to warrant officers and senior NCOs as a rather superior form of long service medal.

Long service and good conduct medals do not appear to excite the same interest among collectors as campaign medals. Perhaps this may be accounted for by their image of stolid devotion to duty rather than the romantic connotations of a medal with an unusual clasp awarded for service in some remote and all but forgotten outpost of the Empire. Nevertheless their importance should not be overlooked. Especially in regard to groups consisting primarily of the Second World War medals, they serve a useful purpose in establishing the provenance of the group, on account of the fact that they are invariably named to the recipient.

Service medals include not only such well known types as the Army LSGC (known affectionately as "the mark of the beast" on account of its high incidence on the chests of sergeant-majors), but also awards to the Territorial and Reserve forces, the auxiliary forces, the nursing services, and organisations such as the Royal Observer Corps and the Cadet Force, the Police, the Red Cross and St John's Ambulance Brigade. The Special Constabulary and Fire Brigades also have their own medals bestowed according to length of service and distinguished conduct. These medals may lack the glamour of naval and military awards but in recent years they have become increasingly fashionable with collectors and will certainly repay further study in their own right.

As many of these medals have been in use for eighty years or more with a standard reverse, variation usually lies in the obverse, changed for each successive sovereign. In addition, considerable variety has been imparted by the use of crowned or uncrowned profiles and busts, and changes in titles.

The following is a summary of the principal obverse types which may be encountered, referred to in the text by their type letters in brackets:

Queen Victoria (A) Young Head by William Wyon 1838–60
Queen Victoria (B) Veiled Head by Leonard C. Wyon 1860–87
Queen Victoria (C) Jubilee Head by Sir Joseph E. Boehm 1887–93
Queen Victoria (D) Old Head by Sir Thomas Brock 1893–1901
Edward VII (A) Bareheaded bust in Field Marshal's uniform
Edward VII (B) Bareheaded bust in Admiral's uniform
Edward VII (C) Coinage profile by George W. de Saulles
George V (A) Bareheaded bust in Field Marshal's uniform
George V (B) Bareheaded bust in Admiral's uniform
George V (C) Crowned bust in Coronation robes
George V (D) Crowned bust in Delhi Durbar robes
George V (E) Coinage profile by Bertram Mackennal 1931–36
George VI (A) Crowned bust in Coronation robes
George VI (B) Crowned profile IND: IMP 1937–48
George VI (C) Crowned profile FID: DEF 1949–52
George VI (D) Coinage profile IND: IMP 1937–48
George VI (E) Coinage profile FID: DEF 1949–52
Elizabeth II (A) Tudor crown 1953–80
Elizabeth II (B) St Edward crown 1980–
Elizabeth II (C) Coinage bust BR: OMN 1953–54
Elizabeth II (D) Coinage bust without BR: OMN 1955–

PRINCIPAL OBVERSE TYPES:

Queen Victoria (A) Young Head

Queen Victoria (B) Veiled Head

Queen Victoria (C) Jubilee Head

Queen Victoria (D) Old Head

Edward VII (A) Bareheaded bust in Field Marshal's uniform

Edward VII (B) Bareheaded bust in Admiral's uniform

George V (A) Bareheaded bust in Field Marshal's uniform

George V (B) Bareheaded bust in Admiral's uniform

George V (C) Crowned bust in Coronation robes

George V (E) Coinage profile by Bertram Mackennal

George VI (B) Crowned profile with IND: IMP in legend 1937–48

George VI (C) Crowned profile with FID: DEF 1949–52

George VI (D) Coinage profile with IND: IMP 1937–48

George VI (E) Coinage profile with FID: DEF 1949–52

Elizabeth II (A) Tudor crown 1953–80

Elizabeth II (B) St Edward crown 1980–

Elizabeth II (C) Coinage bust with BR: OMN 1953–54

Elizabeth II (D) Coinage bust without BR: OMN.

208. ROYAL NAVAL MERITORIOUS SERVICE MEDAL

Instituted: 14 January 1919, by Order in Council.
Branch of Service: Royal Navy.
Ribbon: Crimson edged in white, with a central white stripe.
Metal: Silver
Size: 36mm.
Description: (Obverse) effigy of the reigning monarch; (reverse) imperial crown surmounting a wreath containing the words FOR MERITORIOUS SERVICE. The medal was named in large seriffed capitals round the rim.
Comments: *Awarded without annuity or pension to petty officers and ratings of the Royal Navy. Originally it was awarded either for specific acts of gallantry not in the presence of the enemy or for arduous and specially meritorious service afloat or ashore in action with the enemy. Bars were granted for second awards. It was superseded in 1928 by the British Empire Medal for Gallantry or Meritorious Service, but re-instated on 1 December 1977. In this guise it has been awarded to senior petty officers of the Royal Navy, warrant officers and senior NCOs of the Royal Marines, and equivalent ranks in the WRNS and QARNNS, who have at least 27 years service and are already holders of the LSGC medal and three good conduct badges. The medal is not awarded automatically when these criteria are satisfied, as no more than 59 medals may be awarded annually. The revived medal is identical to the Army MSM and can only be distinguished by the naming giving rank and name of ship.*

VALUE:		Miniature
George V (B)	Rare	—
George V (B) (1020)	£200–250	£10–12
Elizabeth II (D)	£240–300	£10–12

209. ROYAL MARINES MERITORIOUS SERVICE MEDAL

Instituted: 15 January 1849, by Order in Council.
Branch of Service: Royal Marines.
Ribbon: Plain dark blue.
Metal: Silver.
Size: 36mm.
Description: (Obverse) effigy of the monarch; (reverse) a crowned laurel wreath enclosing the words FOR MERITORIOUS SERVICE.
Comments: *Annuities not exceeding £20 a year might be granted in addition to the medal for distinguished service. Sergeants with a minimum of 24 years service (the last fourteen as a sergeant), 'with an irreproachable and meritorious character' were considered eligible for the award which was extended to discharged sergeants in 1872 when the service qualification was reduced to 21 years. The award of the MSM for gallantry was discontinued in 1874 when the Conspicuous Gallantry Medal was reconstituted. Only six MSMs for gallantry were ever awarded. The medal was identical with the Army MSM, distinguished solely by its ribbon and the naming to the recipient. Under the royal warrants of 1916-19 Marine NCOs became eligible for immediate awards of the MSM for arduous or specially meritorious service. The medals in this case were worn with crimson ribbons with three white stripes and had the obverse showing the King in the uniform of an Admiral or a Field Marshal, depending on whether the award was for services afloat, or with the naval brigades on the Western Front. The use of this medal ceased in 1928 when the BEM for Gallantry was instituted. The Royal Marines MSM was revived in 1977 solely as a long service award and is the same as the naval MSM already noted, differing only in the details of the recipient.*

VALUE: Rare   *Miniature*   £40–50

210. ARMY MERITORIOUS SERVICE MEDAL

Instituted: 19 December 1845.
Branch of Service: Army.
Ribbon: Plain crimson (till 1916), white edges added (1916-17), three white stripes (since August 1917).
Metal: Silver.
Size: 36mm.
Description: (Obverse) effigy of the monarch; (reverse) a crowned laurel wreath inscribed FOR MERITORIOUS SERVICE.
Comments: *A sum of £2000 a year was set aside for distribution to recipients in the form of annuities not exceeding £20, paid for life to NCOs of the rank of sergeant and above for distinguished or meritorious service. The number of medals awarded was thus limited by the amount of money available in the annuity fund, so that medals and annuities were only granted on the death of previous recipients or when the fund was increased. Until November 1902 holders were not allowed to wear the LSGC as well as the MSM, but thereafter both medals could be worn, the LSGC taking precedence. In 1979, however, the order of precedence was reversed. Until 1951 the MSM could only be awarded when an annuity became available, but since then it has often been awarded without the annuity, the latter becoming payable as funds permit. Since 1956 recipients must have at least 27 years service to become eligible. What was, in effect, a second type of MSM was introduced in October 1916 when immediate awards for exceptionally valuable and meritorious service were introduced. In January 1917 this was extended to include individual acts of gallantry not in the presence of the enemy. No annuities were paid with the immediate awards which terminated in 1928 with the institution of the Gallantry BEM. Bars for subsequent acts of gallantry or life-saving were introduced in 1916, seven being awarded up to 1928. The standard crown and wreath reverse was used but in addition to the wide range of obverse types swivelling suspension was used until 1926, and immediate and non-immediate awards may be distinguished by the presence or absence respectively of the recipient's regimental number. Recent awards of the Elizabethan second bust medals have reverted to swivelling suspension.*

VALUE:

		Miniature
Victoria (A) 1847 on edge (110)	£300–500	—
Victoria (A) 1848 below bust (10)	£1500–1850	—
Victoria (A) (990)	£250–350	£30
Edward VII (725)	£100–150	£25
George V (A) swivel (1050)	£80–120	£10–18
George V (A) non-swivel (400)	£80–120	£10–18
George V (A) Immediate awards 1916–28 (26,211+7 bars):		
For Gallantry (366+1 bar)	£200–250	—
Meritorious services (25,845+6 bars)	£80–120	—
George V (E) (550)	£150–200	£10–18
George VI (D) (1090)	£100–150	£10–18
George VI (E) (5600)	£75–90	£10–18
George VI (B) (55)	£800–1000	£10–18
Elizabeth II (C) (125)	£160–180	£10–18
Elizabeth II (D) (2750)	£120–150	£10–18

211. ROYAL AIR FORCE MERITORIOUS SERVICE MEDAL

Instituted: June 1918
Branch of Service: Royal Air Force.
Ribbon: Half crimson, half light blue, with white stripes at the centre and edges.
Metal: Silver.
Size: 36mm.
Description: (Obverse) effigy of the monarch; (reverse) a crowned laurel wreath enclosing the words FOR MERITORIOUS SERVICE. Originally medals were named in large seriffed capitals and were issued in respect of the First World War and service in Russia (1918-20), but later medals were impressed in thin block capitals. The RAF version had a swivelling suspension, unlike its military counterpart.
Comments: *Awarded for valuable services in the field, as opposed to actual flying service. This medal was replaced by the BEM in 1928, but revived in December 1977 under the same conditions as the military MSM. No more than 70 medals are awarded annually. The current issue is similar to the naval and military MSMs, differing only in the naming which includes RAF after the service number.*

VALUE:		Miniature
George V (E) (854)	£240–280	£10–15
Elizabeth II (D)	£240–280	£10–15

212. COLONIAL MERITORIOUS SERVICE MEDALS

Instituted: 31 May 1895.
Branch of Service: Colonial forces.
Ribbon: According to issuing territory (see below).
Metal: Silver.
Size: 36mm.
Description: (Obverse) as British counterparts; (reverse) as British type, but with the name of the dominion or colony round the top.
Comments: *Awarded for service in the British dominions, colonies and protectorates.*

Canada: Ribbon as for British Army MSM. CANADA on reverse till 1936; imperial version used from then until 1958. No medals with the Victorian obverse were awarded, but specimens exist.
Cape of Good Hope: Crimson ribbon with central orange stripe. Only one or two Edward VII medals issued.
Natal: Crimson ribbon with a central yellow stripe. Exceptionally, it was awarded to volunteers in the Natal Militia. Fifteen Edward VII medals awarded.
Commonwealth of Australia: Crimson ribbon with two dark green central stripes. Issued between 1903 and 1975.
New South Wales: Crimson ribbon with a dark blue central stripe. Issued till 1903.
Queensland: Crimson ribbon with light blue central stripe. Issued till 1903.
South Australia: Plain crimson ribbon. Issued till 1903.
Tasmania: Crimson ribbon with a pink central stripe. Issued till 1903.
New Zealand: Crimson ribbon with a light green central stripe. Issued since 1898.

VALUE	Rare	Miniature £30–40

213. INDIAN ARMY MERITORIOUS SERVICE MEDAL 1848

Instituted: 20 May 1848, by General Order of the Indian government.
Branch of Service: Forces of the Honourable East India Company and later the Indian armed services.
Ribbon: Plain crimson.
Metal: Silver.
Size: 36mm.
Description: (Obverse) the Wyon profile of Queen Victoria; (reverse) the arms and motto of the Honourable East India Company.
Comments: *Awarded with an annuity up to £20 to European sergeants, serving or discharged, for meritorious service. It was discontinued in 1873.*

VALUE: £250–350   *Miniature* £100–150

214. INDIAN ARMY MERITORIOUS SERVICE MEDAL 1888

Instituted: 1888.
Branch of Service: Indian Army.
Ribbon: Plain crimson (till 1917); three white stripes added (1917).
Metal: Silver.
Size: 36mm.
Description: (Obverse) the sovereign's effigy; (reverse) a central wreath enclosing the word INDIA surrounded by the legend FOR MERITORIOUS SERVICE with a continuous border of lotus flowers and leaves round the circumference.
Comments: *For award to Indian warrant officers and senior NCOs (havildars, dafadars and equivalent band ranks). Eighteen years of exceptionally meritorious service was the minimum requirement, subject to the availability of funds in the annuity. At first only one medal was set aside for each regiment and thereafter awards were only made on the death, promotion or reduction of existing recipients. On promotion the medal was retained but the annuity ceased. It became obsolete in 1947.*

VALUE:		*Miniature*
Victoria (B)	£80–100	£65
Edward VII (A)	£60–80	£50
George V (D)	£30–40	£45
George V (C)	£30–50	£45
George VI (B)	£30–40	£25

215. AFRICAN POLICE MEDAL FOR MERITORIOUS SERVICE

Instituted: 14 July 1915.
Branch of Service Non-European NCOs and men of the colonial police forces in East and West Africa.
Ribbon: Sand-coloured with red edges.
Metal: Silver.
Size: 36mm
Description: (Obverse) effigy of the sovereign; (reverse) a crown surmounted by a lion passant gardant within a palm wreath and having the legend FOR MERITORIOUS SERVICE IN THE POLICE and AFRICA at the foot.
Comments: *Awarded for both individual acts of gallantry and distinguished, meritorious or long service. In respect of the lastnamed, a minimum of 15 years exemplary service was required. It was superseded by the Colonial Police Medal in 1938.*

VALUE:

George V (A) IND: IMP 1915-31	£300–400	
George V (A) INDIAE IMP 1931-7	£250–350	
George VI (B) 1938	Rare	

216. UNION OF SOUTH AFRICA MERITORIOUS SERVICE MEDAL

Instituted: 24 October 1914, by Government gazette.
Branch of Service: Service personnel of South Africa, Southern Rhodesia and Swaziland.
Ribbon: Crimson with blue edges and a central white, blue and white band.
Metal: Silver.
Size: 36mm.
Description: As British military MSM.
Comments: *A total of 46 gallantry and 300 meritorious service awards were made up to 1952 when the medal was discontinued. Of these only two were awarded to South Africans in the RNVR.*

VALUE: Rare

216A. ACCUMULATED CAMPAIGN SERVICE MEDAL

Instituted: January 1994.
Branch of Service: All branches of the armed services.
Ribbon: Purple and green with a gold stripe.
Metal: Silver.
Size: 36mm.
Description: (Obverse) crowned effigy of Queen Elizabeth; (reverse) the inscription FOR ACCUMULATED CAMPAIGN SERVICE set within a four-part ribbon surrounded by a branch of oak leaves with laurel and olive leaves woven through the motto ribbon.
Comments: *Awarded to holders of the General Service Medal 1962 on completion of 36 months* accumulated *campaign service since August 14, 1969. Further periods of 36 months accumulated campaign service will be denoted by a clasp, indicated as a silver rosette when the ribbon alone is worn.*

VALUE: £100–125 *Miniature* £8

217. ROYAL HOUSEHOLD FAITHFUL SERVICE MEDALS

1st type obv.

1st type rev.

Instituted: 1872 by Queen Victoria.
Branch of Service: Royal Household.
Ribbon: Originally Royal Stuart tartan; later, a different ribbon for each monarch: dark blue and red diagonal stripes descending from left to right (George V), the same but descending from right to left (George VI) or dark blue with three red stripes (Elizabeth II).
Metal: Silver.
Size: 27mm (Victoria); 29mm (later awards).
Description: (Obverse) the sovereign's effigy; (reverse) the personal details of the recipient engraved on it. The Victorian medal has a very elaborate suspension ornamented with the crowned royal monogram, with a laurel bar brooch fitting at the top. This medal was not originally intended to be worn with a ribbon, although it had a strip of Royal Stuart tartan behind it. The same medal, but struck in 22 carat gold, was presented to John Brown, the Queen's personal servant. The concept was revived by George V, a silver medal of more conventional appearance being struck with the text FOR LONG AND FAITHFUL SERVICE on the reverse. Thirty, forty and fifty year service bars were also awarded.
Comments: *Intended as a reward to servants of the Royal Household for long and faithful service of at least 25 years. A further 10 years merited a bar. Different ribbons were used for each monarch, corresponding to the crowned cypher joining the medal to the suspension bar on either side of which the recipient's years of service were inscribed. Only two medals have been recorded with the profile of Edward VIII (1936).*

VALUE:		Miniature
Victoria	From £500	£100–150
George V (E)	£200–250	£30–40
Edward VIII	Rare	—
George VI (D)	£240–280	£30–40
Elizabeth II (C)	£250–300	£30–40

2nd type obv. (George V).

2nd type rev.

218. ROYAL NAVAL LONG SERVICE AND GOOD CONDUCT MEDAL

1st type obv.

1st type rev.

Instituted: 24 August 1831, by Order in Council.
Branch of Service: Royal Navy.
Ribbon: Plain dark blue (1831); dark blue with white edges (1848).
Metal: Silver.
Size: 34mm (1831); 36mm (1848).
Description: First type: (Obverse) an anchor surmounted by a crown and enclosed in an oak wreath; (reverse) the recipient's details. Plain ring for suspension.

Second type, adopted in 1848: (Obverse) the sovereign's effigy; (reverse) a three-masted man-of-war surrounded by a rope tied at the foot with a reef knot and having the legend FOR LONG SERVICE AND GOOD CONDUCT round the circumference. This medal originally had a wide suspender bar 38mm, but a narrow suspender was substituted in 1874. Normally the obverse was undated, but about 100 medals were issued in 1849-50 with the obverse of the Naval GSM, with the date 1848 below the Queen's bust. Between 1875 and 1877 a number of medals had the years of service added to the recipient's details, either engraved or impressed on the edge—these medals (about 60 known) are now sought after by collectors. Engraved naming was used from 1875 to 1877, but from then until 1901 impressed naming was adopted. Later medals used the various obverse effigies noted below.

Comments: *Originally awarded for 21 years exemplary conduct, but the period was reduced to 10 years in 1874, then later increased to 15 years. Bars for additional periods of 15 years were instituted by George V. In March 1981 commissioned officers of the naval services became eligible after 15 years service, provided at least 12 years were served in the ranks.*

VALUE:

		Miniature
Anchor 1831-47 (644)	£355–475	—
Victoria (A) wide suspender (3572)	£160–225	—
1848 type (100)	£1000–1200	—
Victoria (A) narrow suspender (4400)	£50–85	£30–40
Year on edge variety (c. 40)	£180–200	
impressed naming (18,200)	£45–55	
Year on edge variety (c. 20)	£180–200	
Edward VII (B)	£30–45	—
George V (B) 1910-20 swivel	£20–30	£5–10
1920–30 non-swivelling bar	£20–30	£5–10
George V (E) 1931-36	£30–50	£5–10
George VI (D) 1937-48	£30–50	£5–10
George VI (E) 1949-52	£30–50	£5–10
Elizabeth II (C) 1953-54	£30–45	£5–10
Elizabeth II (D) 1954-	£30–45	£5–10

2nd type rev. wide suspender

2nd type rev. narrow suspender

2nd type obv. George V

219. ROYAL NAVAL RESERVE DECORATION

Instituted: 1908.
Branch of Service: Royal Naval Reserve.
Ribbon: Plain green ribbon, white edges being added from 1941 onwards.
Metal: Silver and silver-gilt.
Size: Height 54mm; max. width 33mm.
Description: A skeletal badge with the royal cypher in silver surrounded by an oval cable and reef knot in silver-gilt, surmounted by a crown and suspension ring.
Comments: *Granted for 15 years commissioned service (sub-lieutenant and above) in the Royal Naval Reserve, active service in wartime counting double. Bars are awarded for additional periods of 15 years. Recipients were entitled to the letters RD after their name, altered to VRD since 1966. This decoration was replaced by the VRSM (No. 242A) in 2000.*

VALUE:		Miniature
Edward VII	£100–120	£12–15
George V	£80–90	£10–12
George VI (GRI)	£80–90	£10–12
George VI (GVIR)	£80–90	£10–12
Elizabeth II	£120–130	£10–12

220. ROYAL NAVAL RESERVE LONG SERVICE AND GOOD CONDUCT MEDAL

Instituted: 1908.
Branch of Service: Royal Naval Reserve.
Ribbon: Plain green, white edges and a central white stripe being added in 1941. On the amalgamation of the RNR and RNVR in 1958 the ribbon was changed to five equal stripes of blue, white, green, white and blue.
Metal: Silver.
Size: 36mm.
Description: (Obverse) effigy of the monarch; (reverse) a battleship with the motto DIUTERNE FIDELIS (faithful for ever) at the foot.
Comments: *Awarded to petty officers and ratings of the RNR for 15 years service, war service counting double, with bars for additional 15 year periods. This medal was replaced by the VRSM (No. 242A) in 2000.*

VALUE:		Miniature
Edward VII (B)	£20–25	£15–25
George V (B)	£20–25	£10–15
George V (E)	£20–25	£10–15
George VI (D)	£20–25	£10–15
George VI (E)	£20–25	£10–15
Elizabeth II (C)	£40–50	£10–15
Elizabeth II (D)	£30–40	£10–15

221. ROYAL NAVAL VOLUNTEER RESERVE DECORATION

Instituted: 1908.
Branch of Service: Royal Naval Volunteer Reserve.
Ribbon: 38mm originally plain dark green; dark blue with a central green stripe flanked by narrow red stripes (since 1919).
Metal: Silver and silver-gilt.
Size: Height 54mm; max. width 33mm.
Description: Similar to RNR decoration.
Comments: *Awarded to commissioned officers of the RNVR. The qualifying period was 20 years, service in the ranks counting half and war service counting double. In 1966 the decoration was replaced by the RD following the merger of the RNR and RNVR.*

VALUE:		Miniature
Edward VII	£100–120	£15–20
George V	£90–100	£10–12
George VI GRI	£80–90	£10–12
George VI GVIR	£80–90	£10–12
Elizabeth II	£120–130	£10–12

222. ROYAL NAVAL VOLUNTEER RESERVE LONG SERVICE AND GOOD CONDUCT MEDAL

Instituted: 1908.
Branch of Service: Royal Naval Volunteer Reserve.
Ribbon: Originally plain green, but subsequently a broad central green bar edged in red with blue stripes at the ends was adopted.
Metal: Silver.
Size: 36mm.
Description: Identical to the RNR medal, but distinguished by the ribbon and the naming which includes the letters RNVR, RCNVR (Canada), RSANVR (South Africa), etc.
Comments: *Awarded to petty officers and ratings for 12 years service with the necessary training, character assessed as "very good" or better throughout the period. War service counted double. The award was extended to the Colonial Navies during the Second World War.*

VALUE:		Miniature
Edward VII (B)	Rare	£15–25
George V (B)	£30–40	£10–15
George V (E)	£40–50	£10–15
George VI (D)	£30–40	£10–15
George VI (E)	£30–40	£10–15
Elizabeth II (D)	£50–70	£10–15

223. ROYAL FLEET RESERVE LONG SERVICE AND GOOD CONDUCT MEDAL

Instituted: 1919.
Branch of Service: Royal Fleet Reserve.
Ribbon: Blue bordered with thin red stripes and white edges.
Metal: Silver.
Size: 36mm.
Description: Similar to the RNR LSGC but with ring suspension instead of a bar suspender.
Comments: *Awarded for 15 years service in the Fleet Reserve.*

VALUE:		*Miniature*
George V (B)	£20–25	£12–15
George V (E)	£20–25	£8–10
George VI (D)	£20–25	£8–10
George VI (E)	£20–25	£8–10
Elizabeth II (C)	£40–50	£8–10
Elizabeth II (D)	£30–40	£8–10

224. ROYAL NAVAL AUXILIARY SICK BERTH RESERVE LONG SERVICE AND GOOD CONDUCT MEDAL

Instituted: 1919.
Branch of Service: Royal Naval Auxiliary Sick Berth Reserve.
Ribbon: Plain green but later green with a white central stripe and white edges.
Metal: Silver.
Size: 36mm.
Description: Identical to the RNR equivalent, but the letters RNASBR appear after the recipient's name.
Comments: *Arguably the longest title of any British medal, it continued until the RNASBR was disbanded in 1949. The Auxiliary Sick Berth Reserve was created in 1903, members being recruited from the St John Ambulance Brigade. About 780 medals were granted prior to the Second World War and a further 715 between 1939 and 1949.*

VALUE:		*Miniature*
George V (B)	£70–90	£10–15
George V (E)	£80–100	£10–15
George VI (D)	£70–90	£10–15

225. ROYAL NAVAL WIRELESS AUXILIARY RESERVE LONG SERVICE AND GOOD CONDUCT MEDAL

Instituted: 1939.
Branch of Service: Royal Naval Wireless Auxiliary Reserve.
Ribbon: Broad green stripe with narrow red stripes on either side and blue edges.
Metal: Silver.
Size: 36mm.
Description: Identical to the RNR equivalent, but the letters RNWAR after the recipient's name. The last of the service medals with a battleship reverse.
Comments: *Issued till 1957 when the RNWAR was disbanded. It was awarded for 12 years service, only about 200 having been issued.*

VALUE:		*Miniature*
George VI (D)	£140–160	£10–15
Elizabeth II (C)	£140–160	£10–15

226. ROYAL NAVAL AUXILIARY LONG SERVICE MEDAL

Instituted: July 1965.
Branch of Service: Royal Naval Auxiliary Service (RNXS), formerly the Royal Naval Minewatching Service.
Ribbon: Dark blue with a narrow green central stripe and broad white bars at the edges bisected by thin dark green stripes.
Metal: Cupro-nickel.
Size: 36mm.
Description: (Obverse) the Queen's effigy; (reverse) a fouled anchor in an oak wreath surmounted by a naval crown.
Comments: *Awarded for 12 years service.*

VALUE: Elizabeth II (D)   £120–160   *Miniature*   £8–10

227. ROCKET APPARATUS VOLUNTEER LONG SERVICE MEDAL

Instituted: 1911 by the Board of Trade.
Branch of Service: Rocket Life Saving Apparatus Volunteers,
Ribbon: Watered blue silk with broad scarlet edges.
Metal: Silver.
Size: 36mm.
Description: (Obverse) the effigy of the reigning monarch with the date 1911 below the truncation. (Reverse) exists in four types. The first refers to the Board of Trade but when that department handed over responsibility to the Ministry of Transport in 1942 the wording was amended to read ROCKET APPARATUS VOLUNTEER MEDAL round the circumference. In 1953 the inscription was changed to COAST LIFE SAVING CORPS and then in 1968 to COASTGUARD AUXILIARY SERVICE.
Comments: *Awarded for 20 years service with the Rocket Life Saving Apparatus Volunteers. The RLSAV became the Coast Life Saving Corps in 1953 and the Coastguard Auxiliary Service in 1968, these titles being reflected in the wording on the reverse.*

VALUE:

George V (E)	£40–50
George VI (D) BoT	£60–65
George VI (D) Rocket Apparatus	£60–65
Elizabeth II (E) Coast Life Saving	£100–120
Elizabeth II (E) Coastguard Auxiliary	£100–120

229. ARMY LONG SERVICE AND GOOD CONDUCT MEDAL

1st type obv. Trophy of Arms with badge of Hanover.

2nd type obv. with badge of Hanover omitted and swivel suspender.

Instituted: 1830.
Branch of Service: Army.
Ribbon: Plain crimson was used till 1917 when white stripes were added to the edges.
Metal: Silver.
Size: 36mm.
Description: Over the long period in which this medal has been in use it has undergone a number of changes. Until 1901 the obverse bore a trophy of arms with the royal arms in an oval shield in the centre while the reverse bore the inscription FOR LONG SERVICE AND GOOD CONDUCT. The first issue had the royal arms with the badge of Hanover on the obverse and small suspension ring with a plain crimson ribbon. A large ring was substituted in 1831. On the accession of Queen Victoria in 1837 the Hanoverian emblem was dropped from the arms. In 1855 a swivelling scroll suspension was substituted and in 1874 small lettering replaced the original large lettering on the reverse. From 1901, however, the effigy of the reigning sovereign was placed on the obverse although the reverse remained the same. In 1920 the swivelling scroll suspension gave way to a fixed suspender. In 1930 the title of the medal was changed to the Long Service and Good Conduct (Military) Medal; at the same time the design was modified. A fixed suspension bar was added, bearing the words REGULAR ARMY or the name of a dominion (India, Canada, Australia, New Zealand or South Africa). This replaced the Permanent Forces of the Empire LSGC Medal (see below).
Comments: *Originally awarded to soldiers of exemplary conduct for 21 years service in the infantry or 24 years in the cavalry, but in 1870 the qualifying period was reduced to 18 years. During the Second World War commissioned officers were permitted to acquire this medal so long as they had completed at least 12 of their 18 years service in the ranks. Canada discontinued the LSGC medal in 1950 when the Canadian Forces Decoration was instituted, while South Africa replaced it with the John Chard Medal later the same year. From 1930 onwards the lettering of the reverse inscription was in tall, thin letters. In 1940 bars for further periods of service were authorised. The LSGC is invariably named to the recipient. The William IV and early Victorian issues (to 1854) were impressed in the style of the Waterloo Medal and also bore the date of discharge and award. The 1855 issue was not dated, while lettering was impressed in the style of the Military General Service Medal. Later Victorian issues, however, were engraved in various styles, while medals from 1901 onwards are impressed in small capitals of various types. Medals to Europeans in the Indian Army are engraved in cursive script. Recent research by Irvin Mortensen, however, reveals that some medals after 1850 were issued unnamed, and this also accounts for various unofficial styles of naming found on later medals*

1st type rev. large letters

2nd type rev. small letters with swivel suspender

3rd type obv. (George V).

229. ARMY LONG SERVICE & GOOD CONDUCT MEDAL *continued*

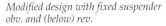

Modified design with fixed suspender obv. and (below) rev.

VALUE:		Miniature
William IV small ring 1830–31	£420–450	—
William IV large ring 1831–37	£380–420	—
Victoria without Hanoverian arms 1837–55	£120–150	—
Victoria swivelling scroll suspension 1855–74	£80–100	—
Victoria small reverse lettering 1874–1901	£50–75	£25–30
Edward VII (A) 1902–10	£40–50	£25–30
George V (A) 1911–20	£30–40	£6–10
George V (A) fixed suspender 1920–30	£30–40	£6–10
George V (C) 1930–36	£30–40	£6–10
Commonwealth bar	From £75	£10–20
George VI (D) 1937–48	£25–35	£6–10
Commonwealth bar	From £75	£10–20
George VI (E) 1949–52	£25–35	£6–10
Elizabeth II (C) 1953–54	£40–50	£6–10
Elizabeth II (D) 1954–	£40–50	£6–10
Commonwealth bar	From £100	£12–15

230. ULSTER DEFENCE REGIMENT MEDAL FOR LONG SERVICE AND GOOD CONDUCT

Instituted: 1982.
Branch of Service: Ulster Defence Regiment.
Ribbon: Similar to the Military LSGC medal but with a central green stripe in addition.
Metal: Silver.
Size: 36mm.
Description: (Obverse) the imperial crowned bust of Queen Elizabeth II; (reverse) similar to the Military LSGC medal. Fitted with a fixed suspension bar inscribed UDR.
Comments: *Granted to personnel for 15 years exemplary service after 1 April 1970, with bars for additional 15-year periods. It is also awarded to officers provided that at least 12 of their 15 years service was in the ranks.*

VALUE:
Elizabeth II (B)	£80–100	*Miniature*	£8–10	

231. VOLUNTEER OFFICER'S DECORATION

Instituted: 25 July 1892.
Branch of Service: Volunteer Force.
Ribbon: Plain green.
Metal: Silver and silver-gilt.
Size: Height 42mm; max. width 35mm.
Description: An oval skeletal badge in silver and silver-gilt, with the royal cypher and crown in the centre, within a wreath of oak leaves. It is suspended by a plain ring with a laurel bar brooch fitted to the top of the ribbon. Although issued unnamed, many examples were subsequently engraved or impressed privately. Two versions of the Victorian decoration were produced, differing in the monogram—VR for United Kingdom recipients and VRI for recipients in the dominions and colonies.
Comments: *The basic qualification was 20 years commissioned service in the Volunteer Force, a precursor of the Territorial Army, non-commissioned service counting half. By Royal Warrant of 24 May 1894 the decoration was extended to comparable forces overseas, the qualifying period for service in India being reduced to 18 years. The colonial VD was superseded in 1899 by the Colonial Auxiliary Forces Officers Decoration and the Indian Volunteer Forces Officers Decoration. In the United Kingdom it was superseded by the Territorial Decoration, on the formation of the TF In 1908. A total of 4,710 decorations were awarded. Awards in Bermuda continued until 1930.*

VALUE:		*Miniature*
Victoria VR	£60–70	£10–20
Victoria VRI	£250–300	£25–35
Edward VII	£60–80	£15–25
George V	£75–85	£25–40

232. VOLUNTEER FORCE LONG SERVICE AND GOOD CONDUCT MEDAL

Instituted: 1894.
Branch of Service: Volunteer Force.
Ribbon: Plain green, but members of the Honourable Artillery Company were granted a distinctive ribbon in 1906, half scarlet, half dark blue with yellow edges—King Edward's racing colours.
Metal: Silver.
Size: 36mm.
Description: (Obverse) effigy of the reigning monarch; (reverse) a laurel wreath on which is superimposed ribbons inscribed FOR LONG SERVICE IN THE VOLUNTEER FORCE.
Comments: *This medal was awarded for 20 years service in the ranks. Officers could also receive the medal, being eligible on account of their non-commissioned service. Many officers then gained sufficient commission service to be awarded either the Volunteer Decoration or (from 1908) the Territorial Decoration. The medal was extended to Colonial Forces in June 1896, the titles of the monarch being appropriately expanded for this version. This medal was superseded by the Territorial Force Efficiency Medal in 1908, although it continued to be awarded until 1930 in Bermuda, India, Isle of Man (Isle of Man Vols.) and the 7th Volunteer Battalion of the King's (Liverpool) Regiment.*

VALUE:		*Miniature*
Victoria Regina (C) (UK)	£35–45	
Unnamed	£25	£20–25
Victoria Regina et Imperatrix (C) (overseas)	£55–85	£20–25
Edwardus Rex (A)	£35–45	£15–25
Edwardus Rex et Imperator (A) (colonial)	£35–45	£15–25
Edwardus Kaisar-i-Hind (A) (India)	£60–80	£15–25
George V (A) (India)	£20–25	£15–20
George V (A) (Isle of Man)	£120–150	£15–20

233. TERRITORIAL DECORATION

Instituted: 29 September 1908.
Branch of Service: Territorial Force, later Territorial Army.
Ribbon: 38mm plain dark green with a central yellow stripe.
Metal: Silver and silver-gilt.
Size: Height 46mm; max. width 35mm.
Description: A skeletal badge with the crowned monogram of the sovereign surrounded by an oval oak wreath, fitted with a ring for suspension.
Comments: *Awarded for 20 years commissioned service, service in the ranks counting half and war service double. It was superseded by the Efficiency Decoration in 1930. A total of 4,783 decorations were awarded.*

VALUE:		Miniature
Edward VII (585)	£65–75	£15–20
George V (4,198)	£65–75	£10–12

234. TERRITORIAL FORCE EFFICIENCY MEDAL

Instituted: 1908.
Branch of Service: Territorial Force.
Ribbon: 32mm plain dark green with a central yellow stripe.
Metal: Silver.
Size: Height 38mm; max. width 31mm.
Description: An oval medal fitted with claw and ring suspension. (Obverse) the sovereign's effigy; (reverse) inscribed with the name of the medal in four lines.
Comments: *Granted for a minimum of 12 years service in the Territorial Force. It was superseded in 1921 by the Territorial Efficiency Medal when the service was renamed.*

VALUE:		Miniature
Edward VII (A) (10,812)	£60–80	£15–20
George V (A) (37,726)	£30–40	£15–20
George V first clasps (362)	£40–50	

235. TERRITORIAL EFFICIENCY MEDAL

Instituted: 1921.
Branch of Service: Territorial Army.
Ribbon: 32mm plain dark green with yellow edges.
Metal: Silver.
Size: Height 38mm; max. width 31mm.
Description: As above, but with the name amended and inscribed in three lines.
Comments: *Introduced following the elevation of the Territorial Force to become the Territorial Army. It was superseded by the Efficiency Medal in 1930.*

VALUE:			
George V (A)	£20–35	Miniature	£10–15

236. EFFICIENCY DECORATION

Instituted: 17 October 1930.
Branch of Service: Territorial Army (UK), the Indian Volunteer Forces and the Colonial Auxiliary Forces.
Ribbon: 38mm plain dark green with a central yellow stripe.
Metal: Silver and silver-gilt.
Size: Height 54mm; max. width 37mm.
Description: An oval skeletal badge in silver and silver-gilt with the crowned monogram in an oak wreath, the ring for suspension being fitted to the top of the crown. It differs also from the previous decorations in having a suspender bar denoting the area of service: Territorial (UK), India, Canada, Fiji or other overseas country being inscribed as appropriate, but the previous ribbon was retained.
Comments: *Recipients in Britain were allowed to continue using the letters TD after their names, but in the Commonwealth the letters ED were used instead. The 20-year qualification was reduced to 12 years in 1949, bars for each additional 6 years being added. In 1969 the British bar was changed to T & AVR, on the establishment of the Territorial and Army Volunteer Reserve, the ribbon being then altered to half green, half blue, with a central yellow stripe. In 1982 the title of Territorial Army was resumed, so the inscription on the bar reverted to TERRITORIAL but the blue, yellow and green ribbon was retained. This decoration was superseded by the VRSM (No. 242A) in 2000.*

VALUE:

	Territorial	T&AVR	Commonwealth
George V	£65–70	—	£80–100
George VI (GRI)	£60–70	—	£80–100
George VI (GVIR)	£60–70	—	—
Elizabeth II	£70–80	£100–120	—

Miniature £8–20

237. EFFICIENCY MEDAL

Instituted: 17 October 1930.
Branch of Service: Territorial Army (UK), Indian Volunteer Forces and Colonial Auxiliary Forces.
Ribbon: 32mm green with yellow edges. Members of the HAC wear the medal with the scarlet and blue ribbon edged in yellow.
Metal: Silver.
Size: Height 39mm; max. width 32mm.

237. EFFICIENCY MEDAL *continued*

Description: An oval silver medal. (Obverse) the monarch's effigy; (reverse) inscribed FOR EFFICIENT
SERVICE. In place of the simple ring suspension, however, there was now a fixed suspender bar decorated
with a pair of palm leaves surmounted by a scroll inscribed TERRITORIAL or MILITIA (for UK volunteer
forces), while overseas forces had the name of the country.

Comments: *This medal consolidated the awards to other ranks throughout the volunteer forces of Britain and the
Commonwealth. The basic qualification was 12 years service, but war service and peacetime service in West Africa
counted double. The Militia bar was granted to certain categories of the Supplementary Reserve until the formation of
the Army Emergency Reserve in 1951. In 1969 the bar inscribed T & AVR was introduced, along with a ribbon half
blue, half green, with yellow edges. The bar TERRITORIAL was resumed in 1982 but the ribbon remained the same.
For the distinctive medal awarded in the Union of South Africa see number 254. Instead of the second obverse of Queen
Elizabeth II, Canada adopted a type showing the Queen wearing the Imperial Crown. This medal was superseded by the
VRSM (No. 242A) in 2000.*

VALUE:	Territorial	Militia	T&AVR	Commonwealth
George V (C)	£25–35	£40–50	—	£40–50*
George VI (A)	£20–25	£40–50	—	£80–90*
George VI (C)	£20–25	£40–50	—	£60–75*
Elizabeth II (A)	£45–50	—	—	*
Elizabeth II (B)	£45 –50	—	£60–80	*

Miniature from £15

*These prices are for the commoner Commonwealth types. However, some are extremely rare as can be seen
in the table below where the issue numbers are indicated in brackets.

George V (C)	*George VI (A)*	*George VI (C)*	*Elizabeth II (A)*	*Elizabeth II (B)*
—	—	—	Antigua (3)	—
Australia	Australia	Australia	Australia	Australia
Barbados	Barbados	Barbados	Barbados	Barbados
Bermuda	Bermuda	Bermuda	Bermuda	Bermuda
British Guiana (15)	British Guiana	British Guiana	British Guiana	—
British Honduras (1)	British Honduras (23)	British Honduras (3)	British Honduras (13)	—
—	Burma (111)	—	—	—
Canada	Canada	Canada	Canada (Rare)	Canada (Rare)
Ceylon	Ceylon	Ceylon	Ceylon (69)	—
—	Dominica (130)	—	—	—
Falkland Islands (29)	Falkland Islands (29)	—	Falkland Islands	Falkland Islands
Fiji (29)	Fiji (35)	Fiji (9)	Fiji (7)	Fiji (33)
—	—	Gibraltar (15)	Gibraltar	Gibraltar
—	Gold Coast (275)	Gold Coast (35)	—	—
—	Grenada (1)	—	—	—
—	Guernsey (3)	Guernsey (4)	Guernsey (3)	Guernsey (35)
Hong Kong (21)	Hong Kong (50)	Hong Kong (224)	Hong Kong (145)	Hong Kong (268)
India	India	—	—	—
Jamaica	Jamaica	Jamaica	Jamaica	—
—	Jersey (40)	Jersey (7)	—	Jersey (1)

237. EFFICIENCY MEDAL *continued*

George V (C)	George VI (A)	George VI (C)	Elizabeth II (A)	Elizabeth II (B)
—	Kenya (1)	Kenya (159)	Kenya (36)	—
—	Leeward Islands (49)	Leeward Islands (14)	Leeward Islands (2)	—
—	Malaya	Malaya	Malaya (54)	—
—	Malta (320)	Malta (84)	Malta (7)	Malta (36)
—	—	—	Mauritius (71)	—
—	—	—	—	Montserrat (6)
New Zealand (71)	New Zealand (34)	New Zealand	New Zealand	New Zealand
Nigeria (1)	—	Nigeria (7)	Nigeria (3)	—
—	—	—	Rhodesia/Nyasaland (7)	—
—	—	—	St Christopher Nevis (13)	—
—	St Lucia (2)	—	—	—
—	St Vincent (1)	—	—	—
S. Rhodesia (17)	S. Rhodesia (230)	S. Rhodesia (24)	S. Rhodesia (6)	—
—	Trinidad/Tobago (228)	Trinidad/Tobago (46)	Trinidad/Tobago (5)	—

238. ARMY EMERGENCY RESERVE DECORATION

Instituted: 17 November 1952.
Branch of Service Army Emergency Reserve.
Ribbon: 38mm dark blue with a central yellow stripe.
Metal: Silver and silver-gilt.
Size: Height 55mm; max. width 37mm.
Description: An oval skeletal badge, with the monarch's cypher surmounted by a crown in an oak wreath. Suspension is by a ring through the top of the crown and it is worn with a brooch bar inscribed ARMY EMERGENCY RESERVE.
Comments: *Awarded for 12 years commissioned service. Officers commissioned in the Army Supplementary Reserve or Army Emergency Reserve of Offices between 8 August 1942 and 15 May 1948 who transferred to the Regular Army Reserve of Officers after 10 years service were also eligible. War service counts double and previous service in the ranks counts half. The ERD was abolished in 1967 on the formation of the Territorial and Army Volunteer Reserve.*

VALUE:

Elizabeth II	£110–130	*Miniature*	£10–14

239. ARMY EMERGENCY RESERVE EFFICIENCY MEDAL

Instituted: 1 September 1953.
Branch of Service: Army Emergency Reserve.
Ribbon: 32mm dark blue with three central yellow stripes.
Metal: Silver.
Size: Height 39mm; max. width 31mm.
Description: This oval medal is similar to the Efficiency Medal previously noted, but has a scroll bar inscribed ARMY EMERGENCY RESERVE.
Comments: *Awarded for 12 years service in the ranks or for service in the Supplementary Reserve between 1924 and 1948 prior to transferring to the Army Emergency Reserve. War service counted double. It was abolished in 1967, following the formation of the Territorial and Army Volunteer Reserve.*

VALUE:

Elizabeth II	£140–160	*Miniature*	£10–12

240. IMPERIAL YEOMANRY LONG SERVICE AND GOOD CONDUCT MEDAL

Instituted: December 1904, by Army Order number 211.
Branch of Service: Imperial Yeomanry.
Ribbon: 32mm plain yellow.
Metal: Silver.
Size: Height 38mm; max. width 31mm.
Description: Upright oval. (Obverse) the sovereign's effigy; (reverse) inscribed IMPERIAL YEOMANRY round the top and the usual long service and good conduct inscription in four lines across the middle.
Comments: *Awarded to NCOs and troopers of the Imperial Yeomanry for 10 years exemplary service. It became obsolete in 1908 when the Territorial Force was created. Nevertheless 48 medals were awarded in 1909, one in 1910, one in 1914 and one in 1917. All medals were issued with the bust of King Edward VII on the obverse.*

VALUE:

Edward VII (A) (1674)	£200–240	*Miniature*	£50–60

241. MILITIA LONG SERVICE AND GOOD CONDUCT MEDAL

Instituted: December 1904, by Army Order number 211.
Branch of Service: Militia.
Ribbon: 32mm plain light blue.
Metal: Silver.
Size: Height 38mm; max. width 31mm.
Description: An upright oval medal. (Obverse) the effigy of the monarch; (reverse) similar to the preceding but inscribed MILITIA at the top of the reverse.
Comments: *Qualifying service was 18 years and 15 annual camps. It was superseded by the Efficiency Medal with the Militia bar in 1930.*

VALUE:

		Miniature
Edward VII (A) (1446)	£150–200	£35–50
George V (C) (141)	£160–200	£35–50

242. SPECIAL RESERVE LONG SERVICE AND GOOD CONDUCT MEDAL

Instituted: June 1908, by Army Order.
Branch of Service: Special Reserve.
Ribbon: Dark blue with a central light blue stripe.
Metal: Silver.
Size: Height 38mm; max. width 31mm.
Description: As the foregoing but inscribed SPECIAL RESERVE round the top of the reverse.
Comments: *Awarded to NCOs and men of the Special Reserve who completed 15 years service and attended 15 camps. A total of 1078 medals were awarded between 1908 and 1936, with solitary awards in 1947 and 1953.*

VALUE:

		Miniature
Edward VII (A)	£155–185	£35–50
George V (C)	£150–175	£35–50

242A. VOLUNTEER RESERVES SERVICE MEDAL

Instituted: 1999.
Branch of Service: Volunteer reserves of all three armed services.
Ribbon: Dark green with three narrow central stripes of dark blue, scarlet and light blue, separated from the green by two narrow bands of gold.
Metal: Silver.
Size: Height 38mm; width 32mm.
Description: An oval medal. (Obverse)the sovereign's effigy; (reverse) inscribed FOR SERVICE IN THE VOLUNTEER RESERVES above a spray of aok.
Comments: *Awarded to all ranks of the volunteer reserves who complete ten years of continuous service. Bars for additional five-year periods of efficient service are also awarded. This medal replaces the Royal Naval Reserve Decoration, the Royal Naval Reserve Long Service and Good Conduct Medal, the Efficiency Decoration, the Efficiency Medal and the Air Efficiency Award. Holders are entitled to the post-nominal letters VRSM.*

243. INDIAN ARMY LONG SERVICE AND GOOD CONDUCT MEDAL FOR EUROPEANS 1848

Instituted: 20 May 1848, by General Order of the Indian government.
Branch of Service: Indian Army.
Ribbon: Plain crimson.
Metal: Silver.
Size: 36mm.
Description: (Obverse) a trophy of arms, not unlike its British counterpart, but a shield bearing the arms of the Honourable East India Company was placed in the centre. (Reverse) engraved with the recipient's name and service details. In 1859 some 100 medals were sent to India by mistake, with the Wyon profile of Queen Victoria on the obverse and a reverse inscribed FOR LONG SERVICE AND GOOD CONDUCT within an oak wreath with a crown at the top and a fouled anchor at the foot.
Comments: *Awarded to European NCOs and other ranks of the Indian Army on discharge after 21 years meritorious service. It was discontinued in 1873 after which the standard Army LSGC medal was granted.*

VALUE:			*Miniature*
HEIC arms	£275–365	£100–150
Victoria (A) (100)	£350–465	£80–100

HEIC arms type.

Victoria type.

244. INDIAN ARMY LONG SERVICE AND GOOD CONDUCT MEDAL (INDIAN)

Instituted: 1888.
Branch of Service: Indian Army.
Ribbon: Originally plain crimson but white edges were added in 1917.
Metal: Silver.
Size: 36mm.
Description: (Obverse) the sovereign's effigy; (reverse) the word INDIA set within a palm wreath surrounded by a border of lotus flowers and leaves. The inscription FOR LONG SERVICE AND GOOD CONDUCT appears between the wreath and the lotus flowers.
Comments: *Awarded to native Indian NCOs and other ranks for 20 years meritorious service. The medal became obsolete in 1947 when India achieved independence.*

VALUE:

		Miniature
Victoria (B) Kaisar-i-Hind	£70–90	£40–50
Edward VII (A) Kaisar-i-Hind	£40–50	£40–50
George V (D) Kaisar-i-Hind	£20–30	£25–30
George V (C) Rex Et Indiae Imp	£30–40	£25–30
George VI (B)	£20–30	£15-20

245. INDIAN VOLUNTEER FORCES OFFICERS' DECORATION

Instituted: May 1899, but not issued until 1903.
Branch of Service: Indian Volunteer Forces.
Ribbon: Plain green.
Metal: Silver and silver-gilt.
Size: Height 65mm; max. width 35mm.
Description: An oval skeletal badge with the royal monogram within an oval band inscribed INDIAN VOLUNTEER FORCES surmounted by a crown fitted with a suspension bar and an elaborate silver brooch.
Comments: *Awarded for 18 years commissioned service, with any service in the ranks counting half. It was superseded by the Efficiency Decoration with India bar in 1930, although the first awards were not gazetted until 1933. A total of 1,165 decorations were awarded, the last in 1934.*

VALUE:

		Miniature
Edward VII	£130–150	£20–25
George V	£130–150	£15–20

246. COLONIAL AUXILIARY FORCES OFFICERS' DECORATION

Instituted: 18 May 1899.
Branch of Service: Colonial Auxiliary Forces.
Ribbon: Plain green.
Metal: Silver and silver-gilt.
Size: Height 66mm; max. width 35mm.
Description: Similar to the previous decoration, with an oval band inscribed COLONIAL AUXILIARY FORCES.
Comments: *Awarded to officers of auxiliary forces everywhere except in India, service in West Africa counting double. Although issued unnamed, it was usually impressed or engraved privately. Examples to officers in the smaller colonies command a considerable premium. It became obsolete in 1930.*

VALUE:		*Miniature*
Victoria	£200–220	£20–30
Edward VII	£180–200	£15–25
George V	£120–140	£12–18

247. COLONIAL AUXILIARY FORCES LONG SERVICE MEDAL

Instituted: 18 May 1899.
Branch of Service: Colonial Auxiliary Forces.
Ribbon: Plain green.
Metal: Silver.
Size: 36mm.
Description: (Obverse) the effigy of the reigning monarch; (reverse) an elaborate rococo frame surmounted by a crown and enclosing the five-line text FOR LONG SERVICE IN THE COLONIAL AUXILIARY FORCES.
Comments: *Awarded for 20 years service in the ranks, West African service counting double. It was superseded in 1930 by the Efficiency Medal with the appropriate colonial or dominion bar.*

VALUE:		*Miniature*
Victoria (D)	£90–100	£25–35
Edward VII (A)	£80–90	£20–25
George V (A)	£70–80	£12–15

If you know of a British or Commonwealth medal that is not included in the MEDAL YEARBOOK we would be delighted to hear from you.

Or if you can supply us with a photograph of any of the medals not illustrated in this publication we would be pleased to include it next year.

If you can help, please contact the Managing Editor, John Mussell, telephone 01404 46972 or at the address on page 1. Thank you!

248. COLONIAL LONG SERVICE AND GOOD CONDUCT MEDALS

Instituted: May 1895.
Branch of Service: Indian and Colonial forces.
Ribbon: Crimson with a central stripe denoting the country of service (see no. 212).
Metal: Silver.
Size: 36mm.
Description: Similar to its British counterpart except that the name of the country appeared on the reverse.
Comments: *Awarded to warrant officers, NCOs and other ranks for distinguished conduct in the field, meritorious service and long service and good conduct. Medals of the individual Australian colonies were superseded in 1902 by those inscribed COMMONWEALTH OF AUSTRALIA. The Colonial LSGC medal was replaced in 1909 by the Permanent Forces of the Empire Beyond the Seas LSGC award.*

VALUE: Rare   *Miniature*   £35–50

249. PERMANENT FORCES OF THE EMPIRE BEYOND THE SEAS LONG SERVICE AND GOOD CONDUCT MEDAL

Instituted: 1909.
Branch of Service: Colonial and Dominion forces.
Ribbon: Maroon bearing a broad white central stripe with a narrow black stripe at its centre.
Metal: Silver.
Size: 36mm.
Description: (Obverse) the effigy of the reigning sovereign; (reverse) the legend PERMANENT FORCES OF THE EMPIRE BEYOND THE SEAS round the circumference, with FOR LONG SERVICE AND GOOD CONDUCT in four lines across the centre.
Comments: *This award replaced the various colonial LSGC medals, being itself superseded in 1930 by the LSGC (Military) Medal with appropriate dominion or colonial bar. It was awarded for 18 years exemplary service.*

VALUE: *Miniature*

Edward VII (A)	Rare	£50–60
George V (C)	£80–100	£40–50

250. ROYAL WEST AFRICA FRONTIER FORCE LONG SERVICE & GOOD CONDUCT MEDAL

Instituted: September 1903.
Branch of Service: Royal West Africa Frontier Force.
Ribbon: Crimson with a relatively broad green central stripe.
Metal: Silver.
Size: 36mm.
Description: (Obverse) the effigy of the reigning monarch. Two reverse types were used, the word ROYAL being added to the regimental title in June 1928.
Comments: *Awarded to native NCOs and other ranks for 18 years exemplary service.*

VALUE: Rare   *Miniature*   £25–30

251. KING'S AFRICAN RIFLES LONG SERVICE & GOOD CONDUCT MEDAL

Instituted: March 1907.
Branch of Service: King's African Rifles.
Ribbon: Crimson with a broad green central stripe.
Metal: Silver.
Size: 36mm.
Description: Very similar to the foregoing, apart from the regimental name round the top of the reverse.
Comments: *Awarded to native NCOs and other ranks for 18 years exemplary service.*

VALUE:			Miniature
	George V	Rare	£15–25
	George VI (B)	£220–250	£15–25

252. TRANS-JORDAN FRONTIER FORCE LONG SERVICE & GOOD CONDUCT MEDAL

Instituted: 20 May 1938.
Branch of Service: Trans-Jordan Frontier Force.
Ribbon: Crimson with a green central stripe.
Metal: Silver.
Size: 36mm.
Description: Similar to the previous medals, with the name of the Force round the circumference.
Comments: *This rare silver medal was awarded for 16 years service in the ranks of the Trans-Jordan Frontier Force. Service in the Palestine Gendarmerie or Arab Legion counted, so long as the recipient transferred to the Frontier Force without a break in service. Only 112 medals were awarded before it was abolished in 1948.*

VALUE: Rare

253. SOUTH AFRICA PERMANENT FORCE LONG SERVICE AND GOOD CONDUCT MEDAL

Instituted: 29 December 1939.
Branch of Service: South African forces.
Ribbon:
Metal: Silver.
Size: 36mm.
Description: (Obverse) Crowned effigy of King George VI; (reverse) FOR LONG SERVICE AND GOOD CONDUCT in four lines across the upper half and VIR LANGDURIGE DIENS EN GOEIE GEDRAG in four lines across the lower half. It also differs from its British counterpart in having a bilingual suspension bar.
Comments: *Awarded to NCOs and other ranks with a minimum of 18 years service.*

VALUE:			Miniature
	George VI (B)	£120–140	£10–15
	George VI (C)	£150–170	£10–15

253A. UNION MEDAL

Instituted: 1952.
Branch of Service: Union of South Africa Permanent Defence Force.
Ribbon: Nine stripes of blue, white and orange.
Metal: Silver.
Size: 38mm.
Description: A scalloped medal with an ornamental suspension bar. (Obverse) arms of South Africa; (reverse) Royal Cypher.
Comments: *Awarded to all ranks for a total of 18 years service. Clasp were awarded for further periods of 12 years service. It was superseded in 1961 by the Permanent Force Good Service Medal.*

VALUE:		Miniature
George VI cypher	£50–£60	£10–£20
Elizabeth II cypher	£30–£40	£10–£20

254. EFFICIENCY MEDAL (SOUTH AFRICA)

Instituted: December 1939.
Branch of Service: Coast Garrison and Active Citizen Forces of South Africa.
Ribbon: 32mm plain dark green with yellow edges.
Metal: Silver.
Size: Height 38mm; max. width 30mm.
Description: An oval silver medal rather similar to the Efficiency Medal (number 237) but having a scroll bar inscribed UNION OF SOUTH AFRICA with its Afrikaans equivalent below. The reverse likewise bears a bilingual inscription.
Comments: *Awarded for 12 years non-commissioned service in the Coast Garrison and Active Citizen Forces. It was replaced in 1952 by the John Chard Medal.*

VALUE:	£55–65	Miniature	£10–20

254A. ROYAL HONG KONG REGIMENT DISBANDMENT MEDAL

Instituted: 1995.
Branch of Service: Royal Hong Kong Regiment (Volunteers).
Ribbon: Half red and half blue with a central yellow stripe.
Metal: Cupro-nickel.
Size: 38mm.
Description: (Obverse) Regimental badge with dates 1854 and 1995 either side and ROYAL HONG KONG REGIMENT THE VOLUNTEERS around. (Reverse) Coat of Arms of Hong Kong with DISBANDMENT MEDAL 3rdSEPTEMBER 1995 (date of disbandment) around.
Comment: *Available to those serving with the Regiment as the end of the Crown Colony became imminent. Recipients, however, had to purchase their medals.*

VALUE:	—	Miniature	—

255. CANADIAN FORCES DECORATION

Instituted: 15 December 1949.
Branch of Service: Canadian Forces.
Ribbon: 38mm orange-red divided into four equal parts by three thin white stripes.
Metal: Silver-gilt (George VI) or gilded tombac brass (Elizabeth II).
Size: Height 35mm; max. width 37mm.
Description: A decagonal (ten-sided) medal. The George VI issue has a suspension bar inscribed CANADA and the recipient's details engraved on the reverse, whereas the Elizabethan issue has no bar, the recipient's details being impressed on the rim. The reverse has a naval crown at the top, three maple leaves across the middle and an eagle in flight across the foot. In the George VI version the royal cypher is superimposed on the maple leaves.
Comments: *Awarded to both officers and men of the Canadian regular and reserve forces for 12 years exemplary service, with a bar for each additional 10 years.*

VALUE:			*Miniature*
George VI (E)	£50–60		£10–20
Elizabeth II (D)	£30–40		£10–20

256. VICTORIA VOLUNTEER LONG AND EFFICIENT SERVICE MEDAL

1st type obv.

Instituted: 26 January 1881 but not given royal sanction until 21 April 1882.
Branch of Service: Volunteer Forces, Victoria.
Ribbon: White, with broad crimson bars at the sides.
Metal: Silver.
Size: 39mm.
Description: (Obverse) the crowned badge of Victoria with LOCAL FORCES VICTORIA round the circumference; (reverse) inscribed FOR LONG AND EFFICIENT SERVICE. Two types of obverse exist, differing in the motto surrounding the colonial emblem. The first version has AUT PACE AUT BELLO (both in peace and war) while the second version is inscribed PRO DEO ET PATRIA (for God and country).
Comments: *Awarded to officers and men of the Volunteers in the colony of Victoria for 15 years service. Awards to officers ended in 1894 with the introduction of the Volunteer Officers Decoration. This medal was replaced by the Commonwealth of Australia LSGC medal in 1902.*

VALUE: Rare

2nd type obv.

257. NEW ZEALAND LONG AND EFFICIENT SERVICE MEDAL

Instituted: 1 January 1887.
Branch of Service: Volunteer and Permanent Militia Forces of New Zealand.
Ribbon: Originally plain crimson, but two white central stripes were added in 1917.
Metal: Silver.
Size: 36mm.
Description: (Obverse) an imperial crown on a cushion with crossed sword and sceptre and NZ below, within a wreath of oak-leaves (left) and wattle (right) and having four five-pointed stars, representing the constellation Southern Cross, spaced in the field; (reverse) inscribed FOR LONG AND EFFICIENT SERVICE. Plain ring suspension.
Comments: *Awarded for 16 years continuous or 20 years non-continuous service in the Volunteer and Permanent Militia Forces of New Zealand. It became obsolete in 1931 following the introduction of the LSGC (Military) medal with bar for New Zealand.*

VALUE: 1887-1931   £75–100   *Miniature*   £10–15

258. NEW ZEALAND VOLUNTEER SERVICE MEDAL

Instituted: 1902.
Branch of Service: Volunteer Forces, New Zealand.
Ribbon: Plain drab khaki.
Metal: Silver.
Size: 36mm
Description: (Obverse) a right-facing profile of King Edward VII with NEW ZEALAND VOLUNTEER round the top and 12 YEARS SERVICE MEDAL round the foot; (reverse) a kiwi surrounded by a wreath. Plain ring suspension.
Comments: *This rare silver medal (obsolete by 1912) was awarded for 12 years service. Two reverse dies were used. In type I (1902–04) the kiwi's beak almost touches the ground, whereas in Type II (1905–12) there is a space between the tip of the beak and the ground. Only about 100 of Type I were produced, but 636 of Type II.*

VALUE: Type I   £250–350   *Miniature*   —
             Type II   £180–220

259. NEW ZEALAND TERRITORIAL SERVICE MEDAL

Instituted: 1912.
Branch of Service: Territorial Force, New Zealand.
Ribbon: Originally as above, but replaced in 1917 by a ribbon of dark khaki edged with crimson.
Metal: Silver.
Size: 36mm.
Description: (Obverse) left-facing bust of King George V in field marshal's uniform; (reverse) similar to the above.
Comments: *It replaced the foregoing but became obsolete itself in 1931 when the Efficiency Medal with New Zealand bar was adopted.*

VALUE:
       George V   £75–100   *Miniature*   £10–15

261. ULSTER DEFENCE REGIMENT MEDAL

Instituted: 1982.
Branch of Service: Ulster Defence Regiment.
Ribbon: Dark green with a yellow central stripe edged in red.
Metal: Silver.
Size: 36mm.
Description: (Obverse) crowned head of Elizabeth II (B); (reverse) crowned harp and inscription ULSTER DEFENCE REGIMENT with a suspender of laurel leaves surmounted by a scroll bar bearing the regiment's initials.
Comments: *Awarded to part-time officers and men of the Ulster Defence Regiment with 12 years continuous service since 1 April 1970. A bar for each additional six-year period is awarded. Officers are permitted to add the letters UD after their names. This medal is to be superseded by the Northern Ireland Home Service Medal.*

VALUE:

Elizabeth II (B)	£150–200	*Miniature*	£6–8

261A. ULSTER DEFENCE REGIMENT MEDALLION

Instituted: 1987.
Branch of Service: Relatives of the Ulster Defence Regiment.
Ribbon: Dark green with a central yellow stripe, flanked by two narrow red stripes.
Metal: Silver.
Size: 36mm.
Description: Uniface medal showing a crowned Irish harp flanked by sprays of shamrocks. Ring suspension. Ribbons of awards to widows and other female relatives mounted as a bow with a brooch fitment.
Comments: *Designed by Colour Sergeant Win Clark and struck by Spink & Son, it was commissioned by the Regiment for presentation to the families of UDR personnel killed during the conflict in Northern Ireland as a token of appreciation.*

VALUE: —

262. CADET FORCES MEDAL

Instituted: February 1950.
Branch of Service: Cadet Forces.
Ribbon: A broad green central band bordered by thin red stripes flanked by a dark blue stripe (left) and light blue stripe (right, with yellow edges).
Metal: Cupro-nickel.
Size: 36mm.
Description: (Obverse) the effigy of the reigning monarch; (reverse) a hand holding aloft the torch of learning. Medals are named to recipients on the rim, in impressed capitals (Army and Navy) or engraved lettering (RAF).
Comments: *Awarded to commissioned officers and adult NCOs for 12 years service in the Cadet Forces. A bar is awarded for each additional 8 years.*

VALUE:		*Miniature*
George VI (C)	£60–70	£8–12
Elizabeth II (A, BRITT: OMN)	£60–80	£8–12
Elizabeth II (A, DEI GRATIA)	£60–70	£8–12

263. ROYAL OBSERVER CORPS MEDAL

Instituted: 31 January 1950 but not awarded until 1953.

Branch of Service: Royal Observer Corps.

Ribbon: Pale blue with a broad central silver-grey stripe edged in dark blue.

Metal: Cupro-nickel.

Size: 36mm.

Description: (Obverse) effigy of the reigning monarch; (reverse) an artist's impression of a coast-watcher of Elizabethan times, holding a torch aloft alongside a signal fire, with other signal fires on hilltops in the background. The medal hangs from a suspender of two wings. An obverse die with the effigy of George VI was engraved, but no medals were struck from it.

Comments: *Awarded to part-time officers and observers who have completed 12 years satisfactory service and full-time members for 24 years service. A bar is awarded for each additional 12-year period. Home Office scientific officers and other non Royal Observer Corps members of the United Kingdom Warning and Monitoring Organisation were eligible for the Civil Defence Medal (no. 264) until being stood down on September 30, 1991. This entailed serving for 15 years alongside ROC members who received their own medal for 12 years' service.*

VALUE:		*Miniature*
Elizabeth II (C)	£60–70	£8–12
Elizabeth II (D)	£60–70	£8–12

264. CIVIL DEFENCE LONG SERVICE MEDAL

Instituted: March 1961.

Branch of Service: Civil Defence and other auxiliary forces.

Ribbon: Blue bearing three narrow stripes of yellow, red and green.

Metal: Cupro-nickel.

Size: 36mm.

Description: (Obverse) the effigy of the reigning monarch; (reverse) two types. Both featured three shields flanked by sprigs of acorns and oak leaves. The upper shield in both cases is inscribed CD but the initials on the lower shields differ, according to the organisations in Britain and Northern Ireland respectively—AFS and NHSR (British) or AERS and HSR (Northern Ireland).

Comments: *Issued unnamed to those who had completed 15 years service in a wide range of Civil Defence organisations. It was extended to Civil Defence personnel in Gibraltar, Hong Kong and Malta in 1965. The medal became obsolescent in the UK after the Civil Defence Corps and Auxiliary Fire Service were disbanded in 1968, but members of the CD Corps in the Isle of Man and Channel Islands are still eligible.*

VALUE:		*Miniature*
British version	£15–20	£8–12
Northern Ireland version	£70–90	—

British rev.

Northern Ireland rev.

264A. AMBULANCE SERVICE (EMERGENCY DUTIES) LONG SERVICE AND GOOD CONDUCT MEDAL

Instituted: 5 July 1996.

Branch of Service: Ambulance services in England and Wales, Scotland, Northern Ireland, the Isle of Man and the Channel Islands.

Ribbon: Green with, on either side, a white stripe on which is superimposed a narrow green stripe.

Metal: Cupro-nickel.

Size: 36mm.

Description: (Obverse) crowned effigy of the reigning monarch, ELIZABETH II DEI GRATIA REGINA F.D.; (reverse) FOR EXEMPLARY SERVICE round the top, with either the emblem of the Ambulance Services of Scotland or the remainder of the United Kingdom in the centre below. Fitted with a ring for suspension.

Comments: *Both full- and part-time members of Ambulance Services are eligible provided they are employed on emergency duties. Service prior to 1974 in ambulance services maintained by local authorities counts. For paramedics and technicians the qualifying service is 20 years. For ambulance officers and other management grades, at least seven of their 20 years' service must have been spent on emergency duties.*

VALUE:	UK version	£20–30	*Miniature*	£35–40
	Scottish version	£30–40		

264B. ASSOCIATION OF CHIEF AMBULANCE OFFICERS SERVICE MEDAL

Instituted: —.

Branch of Service: Members of the Ambulance Service.

Ribbon: Dark green with twin central red stripe edged with yellow.

Metal: Bronze.

Size: 36mm.

Description: (Obverse) symbol of the Association (caduceus on a wheel) surrounded by ASSOCIATION OF CHIEF AMBULANCE OFFICERS; (reverse) FOR SERVICE surrounded by a laurel wreath.

Comments: *Issued by members of the Association to ambulancemen who have performed exemplary service.*

VALUE:	£30–40	Miniature	—

265. WOMEN'S VOLUNTARY SERVICE LONG SERVICE MEDAL

Instituted: 1961.

Branch of Service: Women's Royal Voluntary Service.

Ribbon: Dark green with twin white stripes towards the end and broad red edges.

Metal: Cupro-nickel.

Size: 36mm.

Description: (Obverse) the interlocking initials WVS in an ivy wreath (although the WVS acquired the Royal title in 1966 only one obverse has so far been used); (reverse) three flowers, inscribed SERVICE BEYOND SELF round the circumference.

Comments: *Issued unnamed and awarded for 15 years service. Bars for additional 15 year periods are awarded. Although the majority of the 35,000 (approx.) medals have been awarded to women there has also been a substantial number of male recipients.*

VALUE:	£10–15	*Miniature*	£25–30

266. VOLUNTARY MEDICAL SERVICE MEDAL

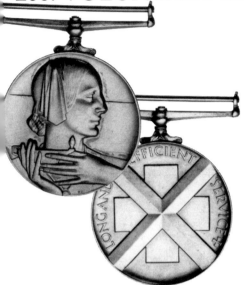

Instituted: 1932.

Branch of Service: British Red Cross Society and the St Andrew's Ambulance Corps (Scotland).

Ribbon: Red with yellow and white stripes.

Metal: Originally struck in silver but since the 1960s it has been produced in cupro-nickel.

Size: 36mm.

Description: (Obverse) the veiled bust of a female holding an oil lamp, symbolic of Florence Nightingale; (reverse) the crosses of Geneva and St Andrew, with the inscription FOR LONG AND EFFICIENT SERVICE.

Comments: *Awarded for 15 years service, with a bar for each additional period of five years. The service bars are embellished with a Geneva cross or saltire (St Andrew) cross, whichever is the more appropriate.*

VALUE:	Silver	£14–18
	Cupro-nickel	£8–12
	Miniature	£8–10

267. SERVICE MEDAL OF THE ORDER OF ST JOHN

Instituted: 1898.

Branch of Service: The Most Venerable Order of the Hospital of St John of Jerusalem.

Ribbon: Three black and two white stripes of equal width.

Metal: Silver (1898–1947), silvered base metal (1947–60), silvered cupro-nickel (1960–66) and rhodium-plated cupro-nickel (since 1966).

Size: 38mm.

Description: (Obverse) an unusual veiled bust of Queen Victoria with her name and abbreviated Latin titles round the circumference. A new obverse was adopted in 1960 with a slightly reduced effigy of Queen Victoria and less ornate lettering. (Reverse) the royal arms within a garter surrounded by four circles containing the imperial crown, the Prince of Wales's feathers and the armorial bearings of the Order and of HRH the Duke of Clarence and Avondale, the first Sub-Prior of the Order. Between the circles are sprigs of St John's Wort. Round the circumference is the Latin inscription MAGNUS PRIORATUS ORDINIS HOSPITALIS SANCTI JOHANNIS JERUSALEM IN ANGLIA in Old English lettering.

Comments: *Originally awarded for 15 years service to the Order in the United Kingdom (12 in the Dominions and 10 in the Colonies) but the qualifying period has now been reduced to 12 years service, except that overseas service outside South Africa, New Zealand, Canada and Australia remains 10 years. A silver bar was introduced in 1911 for additional periods of five years. From then until 1924 the bar was inscribed 5 YEARS SERVICE but then a design showing a Maltese cross flanked by sprays of St John's Wort was substituted. Bars for 20 years service were subsequently instituted in silver-gilt. Suspension by a ring was changed in 1913 to a straight bar suspender. The medal is worn on the left breast. Although awarded for long service this medal should not be solely referred to as a long service award as it can also be awarded for conspicuous service—when so awarded it was distinguished by the addition of a silver palm leaf on the ribbon. The silver palm was discontinued in 1949, after only three years. It is believed to be the only medal still issued bearing the bust of Queen Victoria (the effigy was first sculptured by HRH Princess Louise, daughter of Queen Victoria).*

Ribbon embellishments:

5-year cross

Palm leaf for conspicuous service

Voluntary Aid Detachment

Military Hospital Reserve

Ribbon bars:

5-year bar (second type)

VAD (or MHR)

VALUE:		*Miniature*
Silver, ring suspension	£15–20	£15–20
Silver, straight bar suspension	£12–16	£12–15
Base metal, first obverse	£8–12	£6–10
Base metal, second obverse	£8–12	£6–10

268. ROYAL AIR FORCE LONG SERVICE AND GOOD CONDUCT MEDAL

Instituted: 1 July 1919.
Branch of Service: Royal Air Force.
Ribbon: Dark blue and maroon with white edges.
Metal: Silver/silver-plated.
Size: 36mm.
Description: (Obverse) the effigy of the reigning monarch; (reverse) the RAF eagle and crown insignia.
Comments: *Awarded to NCOs and other ranks of the RAF for 18 years exemplary service, reduced in 1977 to 15 years. Provision for bars for further periods of service was made from 1944 onwards. Before 1945 conduct below the required standard was permitted to count if the airman had displayed higher exemplary conduct against the enemy, gallantry or some special service in times of emergency. From 1944 prior service in the Navy and Army up to a maximum of four years could be counted. In 1947 officers became eligible for the medal provided they had had at least 12 years service in the ranks. Recipients' details are inscribed on the rim. The later issues are of silver-plated base metal.*

VALUE:		*Miniature*
George V (E)	£60–70	£15–20
George VI (D)	£25–35	£10–15
George VI (E)	£30–40	£10–15
Elizabeth II (C)	£30–40	£8–10
Elizabeth II (D)	£30–40	£8–10

269. ROYAL AIR FORCE LEVIES LONG SERVICE AND GOOD CONDUCT MEDAL

Instituted: 1948.
Branch of Service: RAF Levies, Iraq.
Ribbon: As the preceding.
Metal: Silver.
Size: 36mm.
Description: Similar to the previous type but was fitted with a clasp inscribed ROYAL AIR FORCE LEVIES IRAQ.
Comments: *Awarded to the locally commissioned officers and men of the RAF Levies in Iraq, for 18 years service (the last 12 to be of an exemplary nature). The Iraq Levies were raised in 1919 and became the responsibility of the RAF in 1922, maintaining law and order by means of light aircraft and armoured cars. The force was disbanded in 1955 when the RAF withdrew from Iraq. Only about 300 medals were issued.*

VALUE:	
George VI (E)	£800–1000
Elizabeth II (C)	£900–1100
Elizabeth II (D)	£900–1100

270. AIR EFFICIENCY AWARD

Instituted: September 1942
Branch of Service: Royal Air Force.
Ribbon: Green with two light blue stripes towards the centre.
Metal: Silver.
Size: Height 38mm; max. width 32mm.
Description: An oval medal with a suspender in the form of an eagle with wings outspread. (Obverse) the effigy of the reigning monarch; (reverse) inscribed AIR EFFICIENCY AWARD in three lines.
Comments: *Granted for 10 years efficient service in the Auxiliary and Volunteer Air Forces of the United Kingdom and Commonwealth. A bar was awarded for a further ten-year period. Officers are permitted to add the letters AE after their name. This award was replaced in 2000 by the VRSM (No. 242A).*

VALUE:

George VI (D)	£70–90
George VI (E)	£70–90
Elizabeth II (C)	£80–90
Elizabeth II (D)	£70–90
Miniature (all)	£8–12

271. POLICE LONG SERVICE AND GOOD CONDUCT MEDAL

Instituted: 14 June 1951.
Branch of Service: Police Forces.
Ribbon: Dark blue with twin white stripes towards each end.
Metal: Cupro-nickel
Size: 36mm.
Description: (Obverse) the effigy of the reigning monarch; (reverse) a standing female allegorical figure of Justice, with scales in one hand and a wreath in the other.
Comments: *awarded for 22 years full-time service in any UK constabulary. By a Royal Warrant of 1 May 1956 it was extended to police forces in Australia, Papua New Guinea and Nauru. The Australian award was replaced in 1976 by the National Medal.*

VALUE:		*Miniature*
George VI (C)	£30–35	£5–8
Elizabeth II (A)	£40–50	£5–8
Elizabeth II (D)	£30–35	£5–8

272. SPECIAL CONSTABULARY LONG SERVICE MEDAL

Instituted: 30 August 1919.
Branch of Service: Special Constabulary.
Ribbon: A broad red stripe in the centre flanked by black and white stripes.
Metal: Bronze.
Size: 36mm.
Description: (Obverse) the effigy of the reigning monarch; (reverse) a partial laurel wreath with a six-line text inscribed FOR FAITHFUL SERVICE IN THE SPECIAL CONSTABULARY. A second reverse was introduced by 1970 for 15 years service in the Ulster Special Constabulary, the text being modified to permit the inclusion of the word ULSTER. A third type was introduced in 1982 for 15 years service in the RUC Reserve and is thus inscribed.
Comments: *Awarded to all ranks in the Special Constabulary for 9 years unpaid service, with more than 50 duties per annum. War service with at least 50 duties counted triple. A clasp inscribed THE GREAT WAR 1914-18 was awarded to those who qualified for the medal during that conflict. Clasps inscribed LONG SERVICE, with the date, were awarded for additional ten-year periods.*

VALUE:		Miniature
George V (C)	£8–10	£3–5
George V (E)	£8–10	£3–5
George VI (D)	£8–10	£3–5
George VI (E)	£50–75	£4–8
Elizabeth II (C)	£20–30	£4–8
Elizabeth II (D)	£20–30	£4–8
Elizabeth II (D) Ulster	£100–120	£8–12
Elizabeth II (D) RUC Reserve	£120–140	£8–12

273. ROYAL ULSTER CONSTABULARY SERVICE MEDAL

Instituted: 1982.
Branch of Service: RUC and its Reserve.
Ribbon: Green, with narrow central stripes of red, black and dark blue.
Metal: Cupro-nickel.
Size: 36mm.
Description: (Obverse) the effigy of Queen Elizabeth II; (reverse) the crowned harp insignia of the RUC with the words FOR SERVICE round the foot.
Comments: *Awarded for 18 months continuous service since 1 January 1971, but the award was made immediate on the recipient also being awarded a gallantry decoration or a Queen's commendation.*

VALUE:
Elizabeth II (D)	£80–100	*Miniature*	£10–15

274. COLONIAL POLICE LONG SERVICE MEDAL

Instituted: 1934.
Branch of Service: Colonial police forces.
Ribbon: Green centre bordered with white and broad blue bars towards the edges.
Metal: Silver.
Size: 36mm.
Description: (Obverse) the effigy of the reigning monarch; (reverse) a police truncheon superimposed on a laurel wreath.
Comments: *Originally awarded to junior officers who had completed 18 years exemplary service but latterly awarded to officers of all ranks who have the required service qualification. A bar is awarded on completing 25 years service and a second bar after 30 years. These are represented on the ribbon bar in working dress by silver rosettes. The number (where applicable), rank and name as well as (for George VI and later issues) the relevant force in which the recipient is serving at the time of the award is engraved on the rim, often locally and therefore in a variety of styles.*

VALUE:		*Miniature*
George V (C)	£80–100	£12–18
George VI (B)	£45–50	£10–15
George VI (C)	£45–50	£10–15
Elizabeth II (A)	£45–50	£10–15
Elizabeth II (B)	£45–50	£10–15

275. COLONIAL SPECIAL CONSTABULARY LONG SERVICE MEDAL

Instituted: 1957.
Branch of Service: Colonial Special Constabulary.
Ribbon: Two thin white stripes on a broad green centre, with broad blue edges.
Metal: Silver.
Size: 36mm.
Description: (Obverse) the effigy of the reigning monarch; (reverse) the crowned royal cypher above the words FOR FAITHFUL SERVICE in a laurel wreath.
Comments: *Awarded for nine years unpaid or 15 years paid service in a colonial special constabulary. A bar is awarded for further ten-year periods.*

VALUE:
Elizabeth II (A)   £180–220   *Miniature*   £15–20

LOOKING FOR A SPECIAL MEDAL?
WHY NOT USE THE MEDAL TRACKER SERVICE IN
MEDAL NEWS . . . **IT'S FREE TO SUBSCRIBERS!**

276. ROYAL CANADIAN MOUNTED POLICE LONG SERVICE MEDAL

Instituted: 14 January 1933, by Order in Council.
Branch of Service: Royal Canadian Mounted Police.
Ribbon: Dark blue with two gold stripes towards the edges.
Metal: Silver.
Size: 36mm.
Description: (Obverse) the effigy of the reigning monarch; (reverse) the RCMP insignia with the legend FOR LONG SERVICE AND GOOD CONDUCT.
Comments: *Awarded to all ranks of the RCMP who had served 20 years. Bronze, silver or gold bars were awarded for 25, 30 or 35 years further service. A French language version of the later issue also exists.*

VALUE:		*Miniature*
George V (C)	£500–600	£15–25
George V (E)	£500–600	£15–25
George VI (B)	£450–500	£8–10
George VI (C)	£450–500	£5–10
Elizabeth II (A)	£250–300	£5–10
Elizabeth II (French)	£500–600	£5–10

277. CEYLON POLICE LONG SERVICE AND GOOD CONDUCT MEDAL (I)

Instituted: 1925.
Branch of Service: Ceylon Police.
Ribbon: Very similar to that of the Special Constabulary Long Service Medal.
Metal: Silver.
Size: 36mm.
Description: (Obverse) coinage profile of King George V by Sir Bertram Mackennal; (reverse) an elephant surmounted by a crown. Ring suspension.
Comments: *Awarded for 15 years active service. It was superseded in 1934 by the Colonial Police Long Service Medal.*

VALUE:			
George V (E)	£300–350	*Miniature*	—

278. CEYLON POLICE LONG SERVICE AND GOOD CONDUCT MEDAL (II)

Instituted: 1950.
Branch of Service: Ceylon Police.
Ribbon: Dark blue edged with khaki, white and pale blue.
Metal: Cupro-nickel.
Size: 36mm.
Description: (Obverse) the effigy of the reigning monarch; (reverse) similar to the foregoing, but without the crown above the elephant, to permit the longer inscription CEYLON POLICE SERVICE. Straight bar suspender.
Comments: *Awarded for 18 years exemplary service. Bars for 25 and 30 years service were also awarded. It became obsolete when Ceylon (now Sri Lanka) became a republic in 1972.*

VALUE:		*Miniature*
George VI (C)	£280–320	£15–20
Elizabeth II (A)	£250–300	£10–15

279. CYPRUS MILITARY POLICE LONG SERVICE & GOOD CONDUCT MEDAL

Instituted: October 1929.
Branch of Service: Cyprus Military Police.
Ribbon: Yellow, dark green and yellow in equal bands.
Metal: Silver.
Size: 36mm.
Description: (Obverse) King George V; (reverse) the title of the police round the circumference and the words LONG AND GOOD SERVICE in four lines across the middle.
Comments: *Awarded to those who had three good conduct badges, plus six years exemplary service since the award of the third badge, no more than four entries in the defaulters' book and a minimum of 15 years service. Officers who had been promoted from the ranks were also eligible. No more than 7 officers and 54 other ranks were awarded this medal during its brief life before it was superseded in 1934 by the Colonial Police Long Service Medal.*

VALUE: George V   Rare

279A. ROYAL FALKLAND ISLANDS POLICE JUBILEE MEDAL

Date: 1996
Branch of Service: Royal Falkland Islands Police
Ribbon: Blue with a central white stripe edged in black and a thin red central stripe.
Metal: Silver.
Size: 36mm.
Description: (Obverse) Elizabeth II (A); (reverse) arms of the colony; ROYAL FALKLAND ISLANDS POLICE round top and double dated 1846-1996 round foot. Fitted with ring suspension and a brooch clasp at the top of the ribbon.
Comments: *Awarded to all officers serving in the Royal Falkland Islands Police on 15 October 1996. Only 27 medals were awarded.*

VALUE: Rare

280. HONG KONG POLICE MEDAL FOR MERIT

Instituted: May 3, 1862.
Branch of Service: Hong Kong Police.
Ribbon: Various, according to class (see below).
Metal: Gold, silver or bronze.
Size: 36mm.
Description: (Obverse) the effigy of the reigning monarch; (reverse) inscribed in three lines HONG KONG POLICE FORCE FOR MERIT within a laurel wreath and beaded circle. Examples have been recorded with the effigy of Queen Victoria as on the Abyssinian and New Zealand Medals (123–124), and King George V types C and E.
Comment: *Exceptionally awarded in five different classes according to the length and type of service. The 1st Class medal was struck in gold and worn with a maroon (VC) ribbon, the 2nd Class in silver with a plain yellow ribbon, the 3rd Class in bronze with a central black stripe on the yellow ribbon, the 4th Class in bronze with two central black stripes in the yellow ribbon, and the 5th Class (confined to the Police Reserve) in bronze had a green ribbon with two black central stripes. The 4th Class was engraved on the reverse above the wreath. These medals were superseded in April 1937 by the Hong Kong Police Silver Medal, only four of which was awarded before it was replaced by the Colonial Police Medal for Meritorious Service 1938.*

VALUE:	1st class	2nd class	3rd class	4th class
Victoria	—	£450–500	£400–450	£250–300
Edward VII	Rare	£450–500	£350–450	£250–300
George V (B)	Rare	£400–450	£300–350	£225–275
George V (C)	Rare	£$00–450	£300–350	£225–275

280A. HONG KONG DISTRICT WATCH FORCE MERIT MEDAL

Instituted: 1868.
Branch of Service: District Watch Force.
Ribbon: Very dark green with a central deep red stripe.
Metal: Silver.
Size: 31mm with a prominent rim.
Description: (Obverse) four Chinese characters "Great Britain Hong Kong" above a watchman's lamp, superimposed on a cutlass and police baton, with the Chinese characters for "District Watch Force" and "Medal" at the sides; (reverse) DISTRICT WATCHMEN'S FORCE FOR MERIT within a laurel wreath.
Comment: *While the Hong Kong Police was principally a mixed force of Europeans and Indians, operated in the business and higher class residential areas, and was paid for out of the colony's revenues, the District Watch Force was a purely Chinese organisation, raised by prominent citizens of the colony to patrol and police the Chinese parts of the city. Its members had statutory powers, were uniformed and were trained and functioned in the style of the old parish constables, rather than in the gendarmerie style of the Hong Kong Police which was colonial in nature and imposed on society rather than integrated with it. The District Watch Force ceased to function at the time of the Japanese invasion in 1941 and was not revived on liberation.*

VALUE: £500

280B. ROYAL HONG KONG POLICE COMMEMORATION MEDAL

Instituted: 1996.
Branch of Service: Royal Hong Kong Police.
Ribbon: Black, magenta and old gold (colours of the turban worn by the original Punjabi constables).
Metal: Silver.
Size: 38mm.
Description: (Obverse) the RHKP crest; (reverse) crossed tipstaves inside a laurel wreath with the dates 1844 and 1997.
Comment: *The medal, approved by Commissioner Eddie Hui Kion, is available on purchase (HK$1,000, about £80) to those who served in the Hong Kong Police (1844–1969) and the Royal Hong Kong Police (1969–97). Made by Spink & Son and cased. Apparently only about 2,000 of the 40,000 eligible have purchased the medal owing to the cost. Purchasers' details are engraved in bold upright capitals in a variety of formats. The medal, worn on the right breast, has the same status as the Royal Hong Kong Regiment Disbandment Medal (254A).*

VALUE: £100   *Miniature*   £30

280C. ROYAL HONG KONG AUXILIARY POLICE COMMEMORATION MEDAL

Instituted: 1996.
Branch of Service: Royal Hong Kong Auxiliary Police.
Ribbon: Black, magenta and old gold (colours of the turban worn by the original Punjabi constables).
Metal: Silver.
Size: 38mm.
Description: Similar to the above, but inscribed ROYAL HONG KONG AUXILIARY POLICE FORCE.
Comment: *Similar to the above this medal is available for purchase. Some 5,000 auxiliary policemen and women being eligible for the award.*

VALUE: £120   *Miniature*   £30

281. HONG KONG ROYAL NAVAL DOCKYARD POLICE LONG SERVICE MEDAL

Instituted: 1920.
Branch of Service: Hong Kong Royal Naval Dockyard Police.
Ribbon: Yellow with two royal blue stripes towards the centre.
Metal: Gilt bronze or silver.
Size: 31mm.
Description: (Obverse) the effigy of the reigning monarch; (reverse) the title of the Police within a laurel wreath. Swivel ring suspension.
Comments: *Awarded for 15 years service. Although the Dockyard closed in 1961 men who transferred to other police divisions continued to be awarded the medal up to 1973. About 280 medals in all were issued.*

VALUE:		Miniature
George V (E)	£200–250	—
George VI (C)	£160–180	—
George VI (D)	£200–250	—
Elizabeth II (C)	£200–250	—

281A. HONG KONG DISCIPLINED SERVICES MEDAL

Instituted: 1986.
Branch of Service: Hong Kong Customs & Excise and Immigration Service.
Ribbon: Green bordered by vertical stripes of dark blue with a strip of sky blue at each edge.
Metal: Silver.
Size: 36mm.
Description: (Obverse) crowned effigy of Queen Elizabeth II (B); (reverse) armorial bearings of Hong Kong, with the inscription "For Long Service and Good Conduct".
Clasps: Awarded after 25 and 30 years, denoted by silver rosettes on ribband in working dress.
Comments: *Awarded after 18 years continuous service. Engraved with name and rank on rim. Some 1,739 medals were awarded between 1987 and the return of Hong Kong to China on June 30, 1997. This appears to have been the only medal awarded to Customs officers.*

VALUE:		Customs	Immigration
	Medal	£100–£150	£250–£300
	1st clasp	£250–£300	£500–£700
	2nd clasp	£400–£500	Unique

282. MALTA POLICE LONG SERVICE AND GOOD CONDUCT MEDAL

Instituted: 1921.
Branch of Service: Malta Police.
Ribbon: Dark blue with a narrow central silver stripe.
Metal: Silver.
Size: 36mm.
Description: (Obverse) the effigy of King George V; (reverse) an eight-pointed Maltese cross in a laurel wreath with the title of the service and FOR LONG SERVICE AND GOOD CONDUCT round the circumference.
Comments: *Awarded to sergeants and constables with 18 years exemplary service. Officers who had had 18 years in the ranks were also eligible for the award. It was superseded by the Colonial Police Long Service Medal in 1934. No more than 99 medals were awarded.*

VALUE:		Miniature
George V (E)	£300–350	£50–75
George V (C)	£350–400	£50–75

282A. MAURITIUS POLICE LONG SERVICE AND GOOD CONDUCT MEDAL: I

Instituted: —.
Branch of Service: Mauritius Police.
Ribbon: Three types: (a) 36mm half black, half white; (b) 33mm white with a broad royal blue central stripe; (c) blue with two narrow white stripes towards the edges.
Metal: Bronze.
Size: Oval, 40x33mm or 39x31mm.
Description: (Obverse) crown surmounting crossed tipstaves with the motto PAX VOBISCUM (Peace be with you) and the legend POLICE DEPARTMENT round the top and MAURITIUS at the foot; (reverse) palm fronds enclosing a theee-line inscription FOR GOOD CONDUCT. Fitted with a ring for suspension. Medals with 33mm ribbon fitted at top with a pin brooch by Hunt & Roskill.
Comment: *It is believed that the different ribbons indicated different periods of service, but confirmation is sought. It is presumed that this medal was superseded by no. 282B.*

VALUE;   £100–150   *Miniature*   —

282B. MAURITIUS POLICE LONG SERVICE AND GOOD CONDUCT MEDAL: II

Instituted: —.
Branch of Service: Mauritius Police
Ribbon: Green centre flanked by white stripes and broad blue stripes towards the edges.
Metal: Silver.
Size: 36mm.
Description: (Obverse) the effigy of Queen Elizabeth II; (reverse) police truncheon on a laurel wreath.
Comments: *This medal is identical to the Colonial Police Long Service Medal (no. 274) except that the inscription substituted the name MAURITIUS for COLONIAL. It has been recorded in a medal group of 1976 and may have been introduced in or about 1968 when Mauritius attained independence.*

VALUE: £75–85

283. NEW ZEALAND POLICE LONG SERVICE & GOOD CONDUCT MEDAL

Instituted: 1886.
Branch of Service: New Zealand Police.
Ribbon: Originally plain crimson but in 1917 it was changed to a pattern very similar to that of the Permanent Forces of the Empire Beyond the Seas LSGC medal.
Metal: Silver.
Size: 36mm.
Description: The original obverse was very similar to that of the NZ Long and Efficient Service Medal, with the crown, crossed sword and sceptre motif within a wreath of oak and fern leaves. Two types of suspension for this medal are known: the normal type has a bar suspender but a very rare variant has a ring suspender. By Royal Warrant of 8 September 1976 an obverse portraying Queen Elizabeth was introduced. The reverse was plain with the words FOR LONG SERVICE AND GOOD CONDUCT across the field.
Comments: *Awarded for 14 years service. Bars for further eight-year periods were added in 1959, reduced to seven years in 1963, the total length of service being indicated on the bar. A new medal, introduced in 1994 but retaining the original name, will be found in the New Zealand section (no. NZ16).*

VALUE:		*Miniature*
Regalia obverse, bar suspension	£100–120	£10–15
Regalia obverse, ring suspension	Rare	—
Elizabeth II	£90–110	£10–15

283A. SEYCHELLES POLICE LONG SERVICE AND GOOD CONDUCT MEDAL

Instituted: —.
Branch of Service: Seychelles Police.
Ribbon: Crimson.
Metal: Bronze.
Size: Oval, 40x33mm.
Description: (Obverse) crown surmounting crossed tipstaves with legend POLICE DEPARTMENT round the top and SEYCHELLES at the foot; (reverse) palm fronds enclosing a three-line inscription FOR GOOD CONDUCT. Fitted with a ring for suspension.
Comments: *Like the Mauritius Police Medal (282A) it is presumed that this medal became obsolete on the introduction of the Colonial Police Long Service Medal in 1934. Details of qualifying terms of service and other regulations are sought.*

VALUE: £100–150   *Miniature*   —

284. SOUTH AFRICA POLICE GOOD SERVICE MEDAL

Instituted: 1923.
Branch of Service: South Africa Police.
Ribbon: Broad black centre, flanked by white stripes and green borders.
Metal: Silver.
Size: 36mm.
Description: (Obverse) South African coat of arms; (reverse) bilingual inscriptions separated by a horizontal line. Three versions of the medal have been recorded. In the first version inscriptions were in English and Dutch, the latter reading POLITIE DIENST with VOOR TROUWE DIENST (for faithful service) on the reverse. In the second, introduced in 1932, Afrikaans replaced Dutch and read POLISIE DIENS and VIR GETROUE DIENS respectively. In the third version, current from 1951 to 1963, the Afrikaans was modified to read POLISIEDIENS and VIR TROUE DIENS respectively.
Comments: *Awarded to other ranks for 18 years exemplary service or for service of a gallant or particularly distinguished character. In the latter instance a bar inscribed MERIT-VERDIENSTE was awarded. The medal was replaced by the South African Medal for Faithful Service.*

VALUE:		
	1st type	£20–30
	2nd type	£15–25
	3rd type	£15–25
	Miniature	£10–12

285. SOUTH AFRICAN RAILWAYS AND HARBOUR POLICE LONG SERVICE AND GOOD CONDUCT MEDAL

Instituted: 1934.
Branch of Service: South African Railways and Harbour Police.
Ribbon: Similar to the Police Good Service Medal but with the colours reversed—a green central stripe flanked by white stripes and blue edges.
Metal: Silver.
Size: 36mm.
Description: (Obverse) the Union arms with S.A.R. & H. POLICE at the top and S.A.S.- EN HAWE POLISIE round the foot, but this was changed in 1953 to S.A.S. POLISIE at the top and S.A.R. POLICE at the foot. (Reverse) six line bilingual inscription.
Comments: *Awarded for 18 years unblemished service. Immediate awards for gallant or especially meritorious service earned a bar inscribed MERIT - VERDIENSTE (later with the words transposed). The medal was superseded in 1960 by the Railways Police Good Service Medal.*

VALUE: 1st type   £30–40   2nd type   £20–30

286. FIRE BRIGADE LONG SERVICE MEDAL

Instituted: 1 June 1954.
Branch of Service: Fire Services.
Ribbon: Red with narrow yellow stripes towards the end and yellow borders.
Metal: Cupro-nickel.
Size: 36mm.
Description: (Obverse) the Queen's effigy; (reverse) two firemen manning a hose. Ring suspension.
Comments: *Awarded to all ranks of local authority fire brigades, whether full- or part-time for 20 years exemplary service.*

VALUE:
      Elizabeth II   £35–40   *Miniature*   £4–8

286A. ASSOCIATION OF PROFESSIONAL FIRE BRIGADE OFFICERS LONG SERVICE MEDAL

Branch of Service: Association of Professional Fire Brigade Officers.
Ribbon: A red central stripe flanked by narrow white stripes and broad black edges (silver medal) or grey edges (bronze medal).
Metal: Silver or bronze.
Size: 38mm.
Description: (Obverse) allegorical female figure carrying a palm frond and bestowing a laurel crown on a kneeling fireman; an early fire appliance in the background; blank exergue; (reverse) an oak wreath enclosing a four-line inscription ASSOCIATION OF PROFESSIONAL FIRE BRIGADE OFFICERS FOR LONG SERVICE. Fitted with a swivelling bar suspension.
Comments: *The medal in silver was awarded to professional fire brigade officers for a minimum of 20 years full time service and in bronze for lesser periods. Engraved on the rim with the rank and name of the officer, together with the year of the award.*

VALUE: —

287. COLONIAL FIRE BRIGADE LONG SERVICE MEDAL

Instituted: 1934.
Branch of Service: Colonial Fire Services.
Ribbon: Blue with twin green central stripes separated and bordered by thin white stripes.
Metal: Silver.
Size: 36mm.
Description: (Obverse) the effigy of the reigning monarch; (reverse) a fireman's helmet and axe. Ring suspension.
Comments: *Awarded to junior officers for 18 years full-time exemplary service. Bars are awarded for further periods of service.*

VALUE:		*Miniature*
George V (E)	£300–350	£15–20
George VI (D)	£250–300	£10–15
George VI (E)	£250–300	£10–15
Elizabeth II (C)	£250–300	£10–15
Elizabeth II (D)	£250–300	£10–15

288. CEYLON FIRE BRIGADE LONG SERVICE & GOOD CONDUCT MEDAL

Instituted: 1950.
Branch of Service: Ceylon Fire Service.
Ribbon: Similar to the Police Medal, but with a thin central white stripe through the dark blue band.
Metal: Silver.
Size: 36mm.
Description: As the Police Medal, but with a reverse inscribed CEYLON FIRE SERVICES.

VALUE:
		Miniature
George VI	£300–400	—
Elizabeth II	£300–400	—

289. COLONIAL PRISON SERVICE LONG SERVICE MEDAL

Instituted: October 1955.
Branch of Service: Colonial Prison Services.
Ribbon: Green with dark blue edges and a thin silver stripe in the centre.
Metal: Silver.
Size: 36mm.
Description: (Obverse) Queen Elizabeth II; (reverse) a phoenix rising from the flames and striving towards the sun.
Comments: *Awarded to ranks of Assistant Superintendent and below for 18 years exemplary service. Bars are awarded for further periods of 25 or 30 years service.*

VALUE:
Elizabeth II	£225–250		*Miniature*	£8–12

290. SOUTH AFRICAN PRISON SERVICE FAITHFUL SERVICE MEDAL

Instituted: September 1922.
Branch of Service: South African Prison Service.
Ribbon: Broad green centre flanked by white stripes and blue edges.
Metal: Silver.
Size: 36mm.
Description: (Obverse) arms of the Union of South Africa, with GEVANGENIS DIENST round the top and PRISONS SERVICE round the foot. (Reverse) inscribed FOR FAITHFUL SERVICE across the upper half and in Dutch VOOR TROUWE DIENST across the lower half.
Comments: *Awarded to prison officers with 18 years exemplary service. Immediate awards for gallantry or exceptionally meritorious service received the Merit bar. In 1959 this medal was superseded by a version inscribed in Afrikaans.*

VALUE: £30–40 *Miniature* —

291. SOUTH AFRICA PRISONS DEPARTMENT FAITHFUL SERVICE MEDAL

Instituted: 1959.
Branch of Service: South African Prisons Department.
Ribbon: Broad blue centre flanked by white stripes and green edges.
Metal: Silver.
Size: 36mm.
Description: (Obverse) arms of the Union of South Africa, with DEPARTEMENT VAN GEVANGENISSE round the top and PRISONS DEPARTMENT round the foot. (Reverse) VIR TROUE DIENS across the upper half and FOR FAITHFUL SERVICE across the lower half.
Comments: *The conditions of the award were similar to the previous medal, the main difference being the change of title and the substitution of Afrikaans inscriptions for Dutch. This medal was superseded by the Prisons Department Faithful Service Medal of the Republic of South Africa, instituted in 1966.*

VALUE: £30–40 *Miniature* —

Coronation and Jubilee Medals

The first official royal medal was that cast by Henry Basse in 1547 for the accession of the young King Edward VI. It is known cast in gold or silver and is a curious example of bad design and poor workmanship for such an august occasion. No coronation medals were produced in honour of either Mary or Elizabeth I, but under James VI and I there was a small silver medal struck at the Royal Mint to mark the king's accession in 1603. These early medals celebrated the accession of the new sovereign, rather than the act of crowning itself.

To mark the coronation of James I, however, a small silver medalet was struck for distribution among the people who attended the ceremony, and this may be regarded as the forerunner of the modern series. This bore a Latin title signifying that James was Caesar Augustus of Britain and Heir to the Caesars. Thereafter medals in gold, silver or base metals were regularly struck in connection with the coronations of British monarchs. These were purely commemorative and not intended for wear, so they lack rings or bars for suspension.

By the early 19th century medals were being struck by many medallists for sale as souvenirs to the general public. At least fifteen different medals greeted the coronation of William IV in 1830 and more than twice that number appeared seven years later for the coronation of Queen Victoria. That paled into insignificance compared with the number produced for the coronation of Edward VII in 1902. On that occasion numerous civic authorities, organizations, industrial concerns and business firms issued medals in celebration—well over a hundred different medals and medalets were produced.

Sir George Frampton designed two silver medals, and one of these was mounted with a suspender and a blue ribbon with a thin white stripe and scarlet edges. This medal was distributed to notable personages attending the ceremony and established the precedent for subsequent coronation medals which came to be regarded as an award in recognition of services rendered in connection with the coronation, from the Earl Marshal of England to the

private soldiers taking part in the ceremonial parades. In more recent times the coronation medal has even been given to people who were not present at the ceremony but who performed notable public service in the coronation year.

Many other royal events have been commemorated by medals over the centuries. Royal weddings and the birth of the heir to the throne were regularly celebrated in this manner. Important anniversaries in long reigns have been the subject of numerous commemorative medals. The Golden Jubilee of George III in 1809-10, for example, resulted in over 30 different medals. Five times that number greeted the Golden Jubilee of Queen Victoria in 1887, but among them was an official medal intended for wear by those on whom it was conferred.

Even this, however, was not the first of the royal medals intended to be worn. This honour goes to a very large medal celebrating the proclamation of Victoria as Empress of India in 1877. Although fitted with a suspender bar and worn from a ribbon round the neck, it was not permitted for officers and men to wear this medal while in uniform. Later medals, however, were permitted to be worn when in uniform, but after other orders, decorations and campaign medals.

In the following listing (291A–291N) are the official Coronation Medals of James I, 1603, to Victoria, 1838. All were originally non-wearing, i.e. without suspension or ribbon, although some were later pierced or fitted with suspension for wearing. **Values are for silver medals only.**

291A. JAMES I CORONATION MEDAL

Date: 1603.
Metal: Silver.
Size: 28mm.
Description: (Obverse) Bust of King James I facing right.
Legend: IAC: I: BRIT: CAE: AVG: HAE CAESArum cae
D.D. (Reverse) Lion rampant facing left. Legend: ECCE
PHA(R)OS POPVLIQ(VE) SALVS (Behold a lighthouse
and safety of the people)

VALUE:
Silver: £250–400

291B. CHARLES I CORONATION MEDAL

Date: 1626.
Metal: Gold, silver.
Size: 28mm.
Designer: Nicholas Briot.
Description: Bust of Charles I facing right. Legend:
CAROLVS. I. DG. MAG. BRITAN. FRAN. ET. HIB.
REX. (Reverse) An arm issuing from a cloud and
holding a sword. Legend: DONEC. PAX. REDDITA.
TERRIS. (As long as Peace returns to the lands).

VALUE: £280–300

291C. CHARLES I CORONATION MEDAL

Date: 1633 (Scottish Coronation)
Metal: Gold, silver.
Size: 28mm.
Designer: Nicholas Briot.
Mintage: Gold (3), silver (Unknown)
Description: Bust of Charles I facing left. Legend:
CAROLVS DG SCOTIAE. ANGLIAE. FR. ET. HIB.
REX. (Reverse) A rose bush surmounted by a thistle.
Legend: HINC. NOSTRAE. CREVERE. ROSAE (From
this our roses abound). Exergue: CORON. 18 JVNII
1633

VALUE: £300–350

291D. CHARLES II CORONATION MEDAL

Date: 1651 (Scottish Coronation).
Metal: Gold, silver.
Size: 31mm.
Designer: Sir James Balfour.
Description: Bust of Charles II facing right. Legend:
CAROLVS.2. D.G. SCO. ANG. FRA. ET. HI. REX. FI.
DE. cor. i. ia. scon. 1651. (Reverse) Lion rampant
facing left, holding a thistle. Legend: NEMO. ME.
IMPVNE. LACESSET (No one touches me with
impunity).

VALUE: £100–125

291E. CHARLES II CORONATION MEDAL

Date: 1661 (English Coronation).
Metal: Gold, silver.
Size: 30mm.
Designer: Thomas Simon.
Description: Bust of Charles II facing right. Legend:
CAROLVS .II.DG ANG. SCO. FR. ET. HI REX.
(Reverse) Charles II, wearing royal robe, seated on
throne facing left, holding sceptre. Angel hovering
over him placing crown on his head. Legend:
EVERSO. MISSVS. SVCCVRRERE. SECLO. XXIII APR.
1661 (the times having been turned upside down, he
has been sent to succour us)

VALUE: £100–130

291F. JAMES II CORONATION MEDAL

Date: 1685.
Metal: Gold, silver, copper (?)
Size: 34mm.
Designer: John Roettier.
Mintage: Gold (200), silver (800), copper
(Unknown).
Description: Bust of James II facing right, laureate.
Legend: JACOBVS. II. D.G. ANG. SCO. FR. ET.
HI. REX. (Reverse) Hand holding the crown
above a laurel branch resting on a pillow.
Legend: A. MILITARI. AD. REGIAM. (from
soldiering to the palace). Exergue:
INAVGVRAT. 23. AP. 1685.

VALUE: £250–300

291G. WILLIAM AND MARY CORONATION MEDAL

Date: 1689.
Metal: Gold, silver, lead.
Size: 34mm.
Designer: John Roettier.
Mintage: Gold (515), silver (1,200), lead
(Unknown).
Description: Conjoint busts of William and Mary
facing right. Legend: GVLIELMVS. ET. MARIA.
REX. ET. REGINA. (Reverse) Two-horse vehicle
lower left, Jove in cloud above right. Legend:
NE TOTVS ABSVMATVR. (let not the whole be
consumed). Exergue: INAVGVRAT. II. AP.
1689.

VALUE: £280–320

291H. ANNE CORONATION MEDAL

Date: 1702.
Metal: Gold, silver, base metal.
Size: 34mm.
Designer: John Croker.
Mintage: Gold (858), silver (1,200), base metal (Unknown).
Description: Bust of Queen Anne facing left. Legend: ANNA. D:G: MAG: BR. FR. ET. HIB: REGINA. (Reverse) Pallas Athene, left, with shield and lightning bolts, attacking recumbent monster, right. Legend: VICEM GERIT. ILLA. TONANTIS. Exergue: INAVGVRAT. XXIII. AP. MDCCII. (As, making sounds, she conducts herself).

VALUE: £125–150

291I. GEORGE I CORONATION MEDAL

Date: 1714.
Metal: Gold, silver, base metal.
Size: 34mm.
Designer: John Croker
Mintage: Gold (330), silver (1,200), base metal (Unknown).
Description: Bust of George I facing right. Legend: GEORGIVS. DG. MAG. BR. FR. ET. HIB. REX. (Reverse) Seated King, left, being crowned by Britannia standing right. Exergue: INAVGVRAT. XX. OCT. MDCCXIIII.

VALUE: £125–150

291J. GEORGE II CORONATION MEDAL

Date: 1727.
Metal: Gold, silver, base metal.
Size: 34mm.
Designer: John Croker
Mintage: Gold (238), silver (800), base metal (Unknown)
Description: Bust of George II facing left. Legend: GEORGIVS. II. D.G. MAG. BR. FR. ET. HIB. REX. (Reverse) King seated on throne, left being crowned by Britannia, standing right. Legend: VOLENTES. PER. POVLOS (through the will of the people) Exergue: CORON. XI. OCTOB. MDCCXXVII.

VALUE: £125–150

291K. GEORGE III CORONATION MEDAL

Date: 1761.
Metal: Gold, silver, bronze
Size: 34mm.
Designer: Lorenz Natter.
Mintage: Gold (858), silver (800), bronze (unknown)
Description: Bust of George III facing right. Legend: GEORGIVS. III. D.G. M. BRI. FRA. ET. HIB. REX. F.D. (Reverse) Britannia standing left, crowning King seated right. Legend: PATRIAE. OVANTI. (Crowned as the country rejoices). Exergue: CORONAT. XXII. SEPT. CI ƆIƆ CCLXI

VALUE: £280–320

291L. GEORGE IV CORONATION MEDAL

Date: 1821.
Metal: Gold, silver, bronze
Size: 35mm.
Designer: Benedetto Pistrucci.
Mintage: Gold (1,060), silver (800), bronze (unknown, over 1,525)
Description: Bust of George IV, laureate, facing left. Legend: GEORGIVS IIII D.G. BRITANNIARUM REX F.D. (Reverse) Three standing ladies, left, facing seated King, right. Behind King stands angel holding crown above his head. Legend: PROPRIO JAM JURE ANIMO PATERNO (already by special right, inaugurated in the spirit of his father). Exergue: INAUGURATUS DIE JULII. XIX ANNO. MDCCXXI.
Comments: *A slightly smaller and thinner version of this medal was struck and pierced for suspension from a plain maroon ribbon. These medals are invariably named to members of the Buckinghamshire Yeomanry Cavalry Hussars who took part in lining the route of the procession. This is believed to be the first coronation medal designed to be worn.*

VALUE: £90–110

291M. WILLIAM IV CORONATION MEDAL

Date: 1831.
Metal: Gold, silver, bronze
Size: 34mm.
Designer: William Wyon
Mintage: Gold (1,000), silver (2,000), bronze (1,133)
Description: Head of William IV facing right. Legend: WILLIAM THE FOURTH CROWNED SEP: 8 1831 (Reverse) Head of Queen Adelaide facing right. Legend: ADELAIDE. QUEEN CONSORT. CROWNED SEP: 8 1831.

VALUE: £100–125

291N. VICTORIA CORONATION MEDAL

Date: 1838.
Metal: Gold, silver, bronze.
Size: 36mm.
Designer: Benedetto Pistrucci.
Mintage: Gold (1,369), silver (2,209), bronze (1,871)
Description: Head of Queen Victoria facing left. Legend: VICTORIA D.G. BRITANNIARUM REGINA F.D. (Reverse) Three ladies symbolic of England, Scotland and Ireland, standing left, presenting crown to Queen, seated on a dais, right. A lion lies behind her chair. Legend: ERIMUS TIBI NOBILE REGNUM (We shall be a noble Kingdom to you). Exergue: INAUGURATA DIE JUNII XXVIII MDCCCXXXVIII.

VALUE: £115–135

292. EMPRESS OF INDIA MEDAL

Date: 1877.
Ribbon: 42mm crimson edged in gold.
Metal: Gold or silver.
Size: 58mm.
Description: (Obverse) a left-facing bust of Queen Victoria wearing a veil and a coronet, her name and the date of her elevation being inscribed round the circumference. (Reverse) a broad zigzag border enclosing the words EMPRESS OF INDIA and its equivalent in Punjabi and Hindi across the field.
Comments: *Issued to celebrate the proclamation of Victoria as Empress of India on 1 January 1877. It was awarded in gold to Indian princes and high-ranking British officials. Indian civilians and selected officers and men of the various British and Indian regiments serving in India at the time were awarded the silver medal. It was issued unnamed but many examples were subsequently engraved or impressed privately.*

VALUE: *Miniature*

Gold	£2000–2500	£250–350
Silver	£285–375	£100–150

292A. VISIT OF THE PRINCE OF WALES TO INDIA MEDAL 1875

Date: 1875–76.
Ribbon: 38mm plain white.
Metal: Gold, silver or white metal with a silver crown.
Size: Oval 48mmx77mm.
Description: (Obverse) left-facing effigy of the Prince of Wales (later King Edward VII) surrounded by a laurel wreath and surmounted by a crown fitted to a suspension ring; (reverse) Prince of Wales's emblem surrounded by the chain of the GCSI.
Comments: *A large oval medal was struck to commemorate the state visit of HRH the Prince of Wales to India. Some 48 medals were struck in gold, 165 in silver and an unknown number in white metal. The gold medals are impressed on the rim with a small numeral, and engraved with the recipient's name in block capitals. The medals were numbered and named in strict order of precedence. The silver medal has a frosted relief on a mirror table, serially numbered on the edge but not named. 13 small silver badges were also presented. In addition a small silver medalet was issued with an obverse similar to the reverse of the large medal but with the initials A and E either side and a reverse inscribed HRH ALBERT EDWARD PRINCE OF WALES 1875–76.*

VALUE:

Gold (48)	£7000–8000
Silver (165)	£1000–1500
White metal	£200–250
Silver badge (13)	Rare
Silver medalet	—

293. JUBILEE MEDAL 1887

Date: 1887.
Ribbon: Broad central blue band with wide white stripes at the edges.
Metal: Gold, silver or bronze.
Size: 30mm.
Description: (Obverse) the bust of Queen Victoria by Sir Joseph Edgar Boehm; (reverse) an elaborate wreath in which are entwined the heraldic flowers of the United Kingdom. This encloses an eight-line inscription surmounted by a crown: IN COMMEMORATION OF THE 50th YEAR OF THE REIGN OF QUEEN VICTORIA 21 JUNE 1887. The reverse was designed by Clemens Emptmayer
Comments: *Struck to celebrate the 50th anniversary of Victoria's accession to the throne. The medal in gold was given to members of the Royal Family and their personal guests. The silver medal was given to members of the Royal Household, government ministers, senior officials, distinguished foreign visitors, naval and military officers involved in the Jubilee parade on 21 June 1887 and the captains of vessels taking part in the great Naval Review at Spithead. The bronze medal was given to selected NCOs and men who took part in the parade or the Spithead Review. All medals were issued unnamed with a ring for suspension. When the Diamond Jubilee was celebrated ten years later holders of the 1887 medal were given a clasp in the form of a cable entwined around the date 1897 and surmounted by an imperial crown. Twin loops at the ends enabled the clasp to be sewn on to the ribbon.*

VALUE:

	without clasp	with clasp	*Miniature*
Gold	£1100–1300	Rare	—
Silver	£75–85	£110–120	£10–15 (add £30 for clasp)
Bronze	£65–75	£100–110	£10–15 (add £30 for clasp)

294. JUBILEE (POLICE) MEDAL 1887

Date: 1887.
Ribbon: Plain dark blue.
Metal: Bronze.
Size: 36mm.
Description: (Obverse) the veiled profile of Queen Victoria; (reverse) a wreath surmounted by a crown and enclosing the inscription: JUBILEE OF HER MAJESTY QUEEN VICTORIA. The year appears at the foot and the name of the force round the top.
Comments: *Issued to all ranks of the Metropolitan and City of London Police involved in the parades and celebrations on 21 June 1887. Medals are believed to have been issued with the inscription POLICE AMBULANCE round the top but confirmation of this is required. Clasps for 1897 were likewise issued ten years later.*

VALUE:

	without clasp	with clasp	*Miniature*
Metropolitan Police (1400)	£20–25	£25–35	£8–12
City of London Police (900)	£40–50	£30–40	£10–15
			(add £5 for clasp)

295. JUBILEE MEDAL 1897

Date: 1897.
Ribbon: Dark blue with two broad white bands and dark blue edges.
Metal: Gold, silver or bronze.
Size: 30mm.
Description: This medal is very similar to the 1887 issue, differing solely in the date and anniversary on the reverse. Around 980 medals were awarded to army officers.

VALUE:

		Miniature
Gold (73)	£850–1000	—
Silver (3040)	£75–80	£8–12
Bronze (890)	£75–80	£8–12

296. JUBILEE MEDAL (MAYORS AND PROVOSTS) 1897

Date: 1897.
Ribbon: White with two broad dark blue bands and white edges.
Metal: Gold or silver.
Size: Height 48mm; max. width 40mm.
Description: A diamond-shaped medal with ring suspension, reminiscent of the *Klippe* coinage of central Europe. Both sides had circular centres with trefoil ornaments occupying the angles. (Obverse) the Wyon profile of the young Victoria at the time of her accession; (reverse) Sir Thomas Brock's Old Head veiled bust of the Queen.
Comments: *The gold version was presented to Lord Mayors and Lord Provosts while the silver medal was granted to Mayors and Provosts. Small silver medals of more conventional circular format were produced with these motifs and sold as souvenirs of the occasion.*

VALUE:

		Miniature
Gold (14)	Rare	£180–200
Silver (512)	£250–300	£80–120

297. JUBILEE (POLICE) MEDAL 1897

Date: 1897.
Ribbon: Plain dark blue.
Metal: Bronze.
Size: 36mm.
Description: Very similar to the 1887 issue with the dates suitably amended and the name of the service round the top of the reverse.
Comments: *Separate issues were made in respect of the Police Ambulance service, St John Ambulance Brigade and the Metropolitan Fire Brigade. Holders of the previous medal merely received the 1897 clasp.*

VALUE:		Miniature
Metropolitan Police (7500)	£16–20	£10–15
City of London Police (535)	£40–50	£10–15
Police Ambulance (210)	£180–200	£25–30
St John Ambulance Brigade (910)	£60–70	£20–25
Metropolitan Fire Brigade (950)	£60–70	£30–35

298. CEYLON DIAMOND JUBILEE MEDAL 1897

Date: 1897.
Ribbon: Plain red.
Metal: Gold or silver.
Size: 35mm.
Description: (Obverse) the Boehm bust of Queen Victoria with the dates 1837-1897 at the foot. (Reverse) an elephant and a stupa (dome-shaped Buddhist shrine), with two lines of concentric inscriptions: TO COMMEMORATE SIXTY YEARS OF HER MAJESTY'S REIGN and, unusually, THE RT. HON. SIR J. WEST RIDGEWAY K.C.B., K.C.M.G., GOVERNOR. A crown above the rim was fixed to a ring for suspension.
Comments: *Awarded to local dignitaries and leading officials in the Ceylon government.*

VALUE:		Miniature
Gold	Rare	£300–350
Silver	£200–250	£100–120

299. HONG KONG DIAMOND JUBILEE MEDAL

Date: 1897.
Ribbon: Three equal bands of dark blue, maroon and dark blue.
Metal Silver, possibly also bronze.
Size: 36mm.
Description: (Obverse) the Boehm bust of Queen Victoria with the date 1897 at the foot; (reverse) a seascape with a British three-masted sailing ship and a Chinese junk in the background and two figures shaking hands in the foreground. The name of the colony appears at the top, while two concentric inscriptions read SIR WILLIAM ROBINSON G.C.M.G. GOVERNOR and TO COMMEMORATE SIXTY YEARS OF HER MAJESTY'S REIGN 1837-1897.
Comments: *Very little is known for certainty about this medal, on account of the fact that the colonial records were destroyed during the Japanese occupation.*

VALUE:	
Silver	£300–400
Bronze	£180–230

299A. LAGOS DIAMOND JUBILEE MEDAL

Date: 1897.
Ribbon: Dark blue with two broad white stripes towards the edges.
Metal Silver.
Size: 34mm.
Description: (Obverse) the veiled crowned profile of Queen Victoria (similar to the Egypt Medal 1882, No. 131) inscribed VICTORIA QUEEN AND EMPRESS with a Tudor rose at the foot; (reverse) QUEEN'S DIAMOND JUBILEE LAGOS round the circumference, with JUNE 22ND 1897 in the centre.
Comments: *Issued to civil and military personnel associated with the Diamond Jubilee celebrations in the crown colony of Lagos (1886–1906 when it was incorporated in the colony and protectorate of Southern Nigeria).*

VALUE: Rare

300. VISIT TO IRELAND MEDAL 1900

Date: 1900.
Ribbon: Plain dark blue.
Metal: Bronze.
Size: 36mm.
Description: (Obverse) a half-length version of the Boehm bust of Queen Victoria; (reverse) the female allegorical figure of Hibernia looking out over Kingstown (Dun Laoghaire) harbour in which the Royal Yacht can be seen (far left). Unusually, the medal was mounted with a suspension bar decorated with shamrocks.
Comments: *The medal designed by G. W. de Saulles commemorated Queen Victoria's visit to Ireland in 1900. It was awarded to officers of the Royal Irish Constabulary and Dublin Metropolitan Police who were involved in security and policing the various events connected with the visit. The medal was worn with the same ribbon as the Jubilee Police medals.*

VALUE:
    Bronze (2285)   £60–70   *Miniature*   £25–35

300A. VISIT TO THE COLONIES MEDAL 1901

Date: 1901.
Ribbon: Unknown.
Metal: Silver.
Size: Oval 20 x 24mm.
Description: (Obverse) a crowned anchor with the royal garter and rose emblem inset; (reverse) inscribed T.R.H. DUKE & DUCHESS OF CORNWALL & YORK—BRITISH COLONIES 1901 H.M.S. OPHIR.
Comments: *This small medalet was issued to commemorate the visit of the Duke and Duchess of Cornwall and York to the British Colonies aboard HMS Ophir in 1901.*

VALUE: —

301. CORONATION MEDAL 1902

Date: 1902.
Ribbon: Dark blue with a central red stripe and white edges.
Metal: Silver or bronze.
Size: Height 42mm; max. width 30mm.
Description: (Obverse) the left-facing conjoined busts of King Edward VII and Queen Alexandra, both crowned and wearing coronation robes. (Reverse) the crowned royal cypher above the date of the actual ceremony. The medal has an elaborate raised rim decorated with a wreath culminating in a crown through which the ring for suspension was looped.
Comments: *This medal, designed by Emil Fuchs and struck by Messrs. Elkington & Co., celebrated the coronation of King Edward VII on 9 August 1902. It was presented in silver to members of the Royal Family, foreign dignitaries, high officials of the government, senior officials and service officers involved in the celebrations. Selected NCOs and other ranks of the Army and Navy taking part in the parades were awarded the medal in bronze. Both versions were issued unnamed.*

VALUE:		Miniature
Silver (3493)	£60–65	£5–10
Bronze (6054)	£40–50	£5–10

302. CORONATION MEDAL (MAYORS AND PROVOSTS) 1902

Date: 1902.
Ribbon: Dark blue with a narrow white central stripe and crimson borders.
Metal: Silver.
Size: 32mm.
Description: (Obverse) conjoined right-facing busts of the King and Queen; (reverse) the crowned cypher and date. It differed from the ordinary medal by having flat, broad borders decorated with the heraldic flowers of the United Kingdom culminating at the top in a simple suspension ring.
Comments: *The medal was designed by Emil Fuchs and struck by Messrs. Elkington & Co.*

VALUE:			
Silver	£120–130	Miniature	£30–40

303. CORONATION (POLICE) MEDAL 1902

Date: 1902.
Ribbon: Red, with a narrow dark blue central stripe.
Metal: Silver or bronze.
Size: 36mm.
Description: (Obverse) the left-facing bust of King Edward VII; (reverse) a crown above a nosegay of heraldic flowers with the words CORONATION OF HIS MAJESTY KING EDWARD VII 1902 in the upper field. The name or initials of the service appeared round the top, LCC MFB signifying London County Council Metropolitan Fire Brigade.
Comments: *Issued to all ranks of the police and associated services involved in the coronation celebrations, and awarded in silver or bronze to officers and other ranks respectively. Thje medal was designed by G. W. de Saulles.*

VALUE:	Silver	Miniature	Bronze	Miniature
Metropolitan Police	£250–300 (51)	£15–20	£12–15 (16,700)	£12–15
City of London Police	£500–600 (5)	£15–20	£40–45 (1060)	£12–15
LCC MFB	£350–400 (9)	£30–35	£40–50 (1000)	£30–35
St John Ambulance Brigade	—	£15–20	£40–50 (912)	£15–20
Police Ambulance Service	—	£30–35	£200–220 (204)	£30–35

304. CEYLON CORONATION MEDAL 1902

Date: 1902.
Ribbon: Plain blue.
Metal: Gold.
Size: 35mm.
Description: (Obverse) a crowned left-facing bust of King Edward VII; (reverse) the elephant and stupa motif previously used. The concentric inscription on the reverse now tactfully omitted any reference to the governor: IN COMMEMORATION OF THE CORONATION OF H.M. KING EDWARD VII 1902. The medal was fitted with a ring for suspension.
Comments: *Like its predecessor, this rare medal was struck for presentation to local dignitaries and government officials.*

VALUE:
    Gold   Rare   *Miniature*   —

305. HONG KONG CORONATION MEDAL 1902

Date: 1902.
Ribbon: None officially designated.
Metal: Silver and Bronze.
Size: 36mm.
Description: (Obverse) conjoined right-facing busts of King Edward VII and Queen Alexandra with their names round the circumference; (reverse) the maritime motif of the Diamond Jubilee medal with new inscriptions in two concentric curves: SIR HENRY A. BLAKE G.C.M.G. GOVERNOR (inner) and TO COMMEMORATE THE CORONATION OF THEIR MAJESTIES THE KING & QUEEN (outer). Fitted with a suspension ring.
Comments: *Issued to all British and Indian officers and other ranks serving in the colony as well as local police. Some 6,000 medals were produced by Edmonds & Son, London, and issued in cases.*

VALUE:
    Bronze   £45–65
    Silver   £140–180

305A. NATAL CORONATION MEDAL 1902

Date: 1902.
Ribbon: Dark blue with a central claret stripe.
Metal: Silver.
Size: 29mm and 51mm.
Description: (Obverse) a right-facing crowned bust of King Edward VII with the inscription TO COMMEMORATE THE CORONATION OF KING EDWARD VII: (reverse) Royal coat of arms above two running springbok, inscribed (round top) EDWARDUS DEI GRATIA BRITANNIAR REX F:D and (round bottom) COLONY OF NATAL 26 JUNE 1902. Ring suspension.
Comments: *Issued unnamed to native chiefs. The larger medal was issued without suspension.*

VALUE: 29mm   £100–150
               51mm   £300–400

306. DELHI DURBAR MEDAL 1903

Date: 1903.
Ribbon: Pale blue with three dark blue stripes.
Metal: Gold or silver.
Size: 38.5mm.
Description: (Obverse) a right-facing crowned bust of the King Emperor with DELHI DARBAR 1903 on the right side; (reverse) a three-line inscription in Farsi across the field, which translates as "By grace of the Lord of the Realm, Edward, King, Emperor of India, 1901", with an elaborate border of roses, thistles, shamrocks and Indian flowers. Ring suspension.
Comments: *Struck to celebrate the Durbar of the King Emperor at Delhi on 1 January 1903. It was awarded in gold to the rulers of the Indian princely states and in silver to lesser dignitaries, government officials, and officers and other ranks of the armed services actually involved in the celebrations.*

VALUE: *Miniature*

Gold (140)	£800–1000	—
Silver (2567)	£80–100	£10–15

307. VISIT TO SCOTLAND MEDAL 1903

Date: 1903.
Ribbon: Plain red.
Metal: Bronze.
Size: 36mm.
Description: Very similar to the Police Coronation medal but the year was changed to 1903 and the inscription SCOTTISH POLICE appeared round the top of the reverse. The medal was named to the recipient on the rim. An ornate clasp decorated with a thistle was worn above the suspension bar.
Comments: *This medal was designed by G. W. de Saulles and struck to commemorate Their Majesties' post-coronation tour of Scotland in May 1903. It was awarded to the police and troops involved in parades and escort duties, as well as the ancillary services such as the Fire Brigade and the St Andrew's Ambulance Association.*

VALUE:
Bronze (2957)   £55–60   *Miniature*   £25–30

308. VISIT TO IRELAND MEDAL 1903

Date: 1903.
Ribbon: Pale blue.
Metal: Bronze.
Size: 36mm.
Description: (Obverse) bust of King Edward VII; (reverse) as 1900 medal with the date altered at the foot. The suspension brooch is ornamented with shamrocks.
Comments: *This medal was designed by G. W. de Saulles and struck to mark the King's visit to Ireland in July 1903. It was awarded on the same terms as the Visit to Ireland Medal 1900.*

VALUE:
Bronze (7757)   £60–70   *Miniature*   £35–45

308A. VISIT OF THE PRINCE AND PRINCESS OF WALES TO INDIA

Instituted: 1905–06
Ribbon: Neck ribbon 55mm wide, maroon with wide blue stripes towards each edge.
Metal: Frosted silver.
Size: 46mm.
Description: (Obverse) conjoined busts of the Prince and Princess of Wales (later King George V and Queen Mary), facing right. ELKINGTON (manufacturers) inscribed below busts. (Reverse) badge of the Prince of Wales surrounded by the chain of the GCSI, with legend T.R.H. THE PRINCE & PRINCESS OF WALES VISIT TO INDIA 1905–6.
Comments: *Only 72 medals were struck, 70 of which were bestowed on British and Indian officials.*

VALUE: £300–400

308B. GEORGE PRINCE OF WALES MEDAL

Instituted: 1905-06.
Ribbon: 15mm, red, white and blue in equal parts.
Metal: Silver or gold.
Size: Oval 20 x 24mm.
Description: (Obverse) the Prince of Wales's plumes surrounded by the Garter and the chain and badge of the GCSI, flanked in the field by the letters G and M; (reverse) inscription T.R.H. GEORGE PRINCE OF WALES & VICTORIA MARY PRINCESS OF WALES with INDIA 1905-6 in the upper centre.
Comments: *The 26 gold medals were given by Their Royal Highnesses to their personal staff, while a total of 1,625 silver medals were presented to all hands aboard HMS* Renown *and* Terrible *and the Royal Yacht* Osborne.

VALUE:
Gold (26)	£800–1000
Silver (1625)	£80–120

309. CORONATION MEDAL 1911

Date: 1911.
Ribbon: Dark blue with two thin red stripes in the centre.
Metal: Silver.
Size: 32mm.
Description: (Obverse) conjoined left-facing busts of King George V and Queen Mary in their coronation robes within a floral wreath; (reverse) the crowned royal cypher above the date of the coronation itself. Plain ring suspension.
Comments: *Designed by Sir Bertram McKennal, MVO, ARA, these medals were issued unnamed but may sometimes be found with unofficial engraving. Those who were also entitled to the Delhi Darbar Medal received a crowned clasp inscribed DELHI if they had previously been awarded the coronation medal. This was the first occasion that the medal might be awarded to those not actually present at the ceremony itself.*

VALUE:
Silver (15,901)	£30–35	*Miniature*	£4–8
Clasp Delhi (134)	£80–100		

310. CORONATION (POLICE) MEDAL 1911

Date: 1911.

Ribbon: Red with three narrow blue stripes.

Metal: Silver.

Size: 32mm.

Description: (Obverse) a crowned left-facing bust of King George V; (reverse) an imperial crown with an ornate surround. The inscription CORONATION 1911 appears at the foot and the name of the service at the top. Ring suspension.

Comments: *By now the number of police and ancillary services had grown considerably, as witness the various reverse types which may be encountered in this medal. The medal was designed by Sir Bertram McKennal, MVO, ARA.*

VALUE: *Miniature*

Metropolitan Police (19,783)	£10–15	£10–12
City of London Police (1400)	£40–50	£10–12
County and Borough Police (2565)	£65–75	£12–15
Police Ambulance Service*	£280–320	£30–35
London Fire Brigade (1374)	£40–50	£20–25
Royal Irish Constabulary (585)	£70–80	£20–25
Scottish Police (280)	£90–100	£20–25
St John Ambulance Brigade*	£40–50	£10–12
St Andrew's Ambulance Corps*	£120–150	£40–50
Royal Parks (109)	£210–280	£40–50

* A total of 2623 medals was awarded to these three services, the Police Ambulance medal being the scarcest and St John Ambulance medal the commonest.

311. VISIT TO IRELAND MEDAL 1911

Date: 1911.

Ribbon: Dark green with thin red stripes towards either end.

Metal: Silver.

Size: 36mm.

Description: Very similar to the foregoing, distinguished only by the reverse which is inscribed CORONATION 1911 round the top, with the actual date of the visit round the foot.

Comments: *This medal was designed by Sir Bertram McKennal, MVO, ARA and was granted to prominent civic dignitaries and members of the Irish police forces involved in the royal visit to Ireland which took place on 7-12 July 1911.*

VALUE:

Silver (2477)	£50–75	*Miniature*	£25–30

311A. EAST INDIAN RAILWAY COMPANY ROYAL VISIT TO INDIA MEDAL 1911

Date: 1911.

Ribbon: Dark blue with a central maroon stripe flanked by narrow gold stripes.

Metal: Gilded bronze.

Size: 32mm.

Description: (Obverse) the arms of the East Indian Railway Company surrounded by the inscription EAST INDIAN RAILWAY COMPANY with a winged wheel at the foot; (reverse) a ten-line inscription FOR SERVICES RENDERED DURING THE RAILWAY JOURNEYS OF THEIR MAJESTIES THE KING EMPEROR AND QUEEN EMPRESS IN INDIA 1911.

Comments: *Very little is known about this rare medal, but it is believed to have been awarded to members of the Honour Guard of the East Indian Railway Volunteer Rifle Corps and employees of the company present during the tour of India undertaken in 1911 by King George V and Queen Mary. It is believed that no more than 30 medals were issued.*

VALUE: £100–£120

312. DELHI DURBAR MEDAL 1911

Date: 1911.
Ribbon: Dark blue with two narrow red stripes in the middle.
Metal: Gold or silver.
Size: 38.5mm.
Description: (Obverse) the conjoined crowned busts of King George V and Queen Mary in a floral wreath; (reverse) an elaborate Farsi text which translates as "The Durbar of George V, Emperor of India, Master of the British Lands".
Comments: *This medal marked the Delhi Durbar held in the King Emperor's honour in December 1911. Most of the gold medals went to the Indian princely rulers and top government officials, 10,000 of the 30,000 silver medals were awarded to officers and other ranks of the British and Indian Armies for exemplary service, without their necessarily being present at the Durbar itself.*

VALUE:		*Miniature*
Gold (200)	£800–850	—
Silver (30,000)	£35–45	£6–10

312A. VISIT OF KING GEORGE V AND QUEEN MARY TO INDIA 1911–12

Date: 1911–12.
Ribbon: None.
Metal: Silver.
Size: Oval 20 x 24mm.
Description: (Obverse): GRI entwined initials as a monogram above the dsatews 1911–12; (reverse) MRI monogram and dates, suspended from a bar by a simple ring and scroll suspender.

VALUE: £40–60

312B. VISIT OF THE PRINCE OF WALES TO INDIA 1921–22

Date: 1921–22.
Ribbon: Neck ribbon 55mm maroon with broad blue stripes towards each edge.
Metal: Frosted silver.
Size: 50mm.
Description: (Obverse) bust of Prince of Wales facing left with inscription EDWARD PRINCE OF WALES INDIA 1921–1922; (reverse) badge of the Prince of Wales surrounded by the chain of the GCSI. Fitted with a plain suspension ring.
Comments: *Only 84 medals were awarded in connection with the visit of HRH the Prince of Wales (later King Edward VIII and Duke of Windsor) to India in the course of his world tour aboard HMS Renown.*

VALUE: £500–650	*Miniature*	£40–60

312C. WELCOME HOME MEDAL FOR THE PRINCE OF WALES

Date: 1922.
Ribbon: Green with red central stripe.
Metal: Bronze.
Size: 35mm.
Description: Oval.
Comments: *Struck by F. Bowcher to mark the return of the Prince of Wales to England after his world tour.*

VALUE: £50–65

312D. VISIT OF THE PRINCE OF WALES TO BOMBAY MEDAL 1921

Date: 1921.
Ribbon: Not known.
Metal: Bronze.
Size: Oval 38mm x 30mm.
Description: An oval medal. (Obverse) bust of the Prince of Wales facing right, with the inscription EDWARD PRINCE OF WALES and surmounted by the Prince of Wales's feathes and motto ICH DIEN; (reverse) VISIT OF HIS ROYAL HIGHNESS BOMBAY NOVEMBER 1921 in six lines.
Comment: *Presented to the leading military and civil dignitaries present during the visit of the Prince of Wales. The number issues is not known but is believed to be very small.*

VALUE: £60–£80

313. JUBILEE MEDAL 1935

Date: 1935.
Ribbon: Red with two dark blue and one white stripes at the edges.
Metal: Silver.
Size: 32mm.
Description: (Obverse) left-facing conjoined half-length busts of King George V and Queen Mary in crowns and robes of state; (reverse) a crowned GRI monogram flanked by the dates of the accession and the jubilee.
Comments: *This medal, designed by Sir William Goscombe John, RA, was issued to celebrate the Silver Jubilee of King George V and widely distributed to the great and good throughout the Empire.*

VALUE:
Silver (85,234)   £20–25   *Miniature*   £3–6

313A. ISLE OF MAN SILVER JUBILEE MEDAL 1935

Date: 1935.
Ribbon: Three equal stripes of red, white and blue. However some medals had their ribbons substituted with black to mark the death of the King in 1936.
Metal: Silver.
Size: 32mm.
Description: (Obverse) conjoined busts of King George V and Queen Mary in an inner circle surrounded by the legend KING GEORGE V & QUEEN MARY REIGNED 25 YEARS; (reverse) Triskelion emblem with the legend IN COMMEMORATION OF THE SILVER JUBILEE 1935. Suspended from a brooch bar of seven overlapping panels. The centre panel has the royal cypher GvR while the outer panels have two leaves in each.
Comments: *This medal is an unofficial issue struck to celebrate the Silver Jubilee. It is included here as it was apparently presented to civic dignitaries and officials in the island.*

VALUE: £100–120

314. CORONATION MEDAL 1937

Date: 1937.
Ribbon: Blue edged with one red and two white stripes.
Metal: Silver.
Size: 32mm.
Description: (Obverse) conjoined busts of King George VI and Queen Elizabeth in their robes of state without any inscription. The stark simplicity of this motif was matched by a reverse showing the crowned GRI over the inscription CROWNED 12 MAY 1937, with the names of the King and Queen in block capitals round the circumference.
Comments: *Issued to celebrate the coronation of King George VI on 12 May 1937.*

VALUE:
    Silver (90,000)   £20–25   *Miniature*   **£3–6**

315. CORONATION MEDAL 1953

Date: 1953.
Ribbon: Dark red with two narrow blue stripes in the centre and narrow white edges.
Metal: Silver.
Size: 32mm.
Description: (Obverse) a right-facing bust of Queen Elizabeth II in a Tudor crown and robes of state, the field being otherwise plain. (Reverse) a similar crown over the royal monogram EIIR with the legend QUEEN ELIZABETH II CROWNED 2ND JUNE 1953 round the circumference. Ring suspension.
Comments: *This medal celebrated the coronation of Queen Elizabeth II on 2 June 1953. News that Edmund Hillary and Sherpa Tenzing had successfully attained the summit of Everest reached London on the morning of the Coronation. Subsequently the members of the Hunt Expedition were invited to Buckingham Palace on 16 July 1953 where, on Her Majesty's own initiative, they were presented with coronation medals engraved MOUNT EVEREST EXPEDITION on the rim, following the precedent of the Mwele medals of 1895–96.*

VALUE: *Miniature*
    Silver (129,000)   £25–30   £5–10
    Mount Everest Expedition (37)   £600

315A. ROYAL VISIT TO NEW ZEALAND MEDAL 1953-54

Date: 1953.
Ribbon: Dark blue.
Metal: Copper-coloured alloy.
Size: 38mm.
Description: (Obverse) right-facing crowned bust of Queen Elizabeth II wearing Tudor crown; (reverse) the crowned New Zealand coat of arms surrounded by sprays of flowers and the inscription ELIZABETH II ROYAL VISIT 1953–54. The copper-coloured medal is hung by a ring from a scalloped suspender as illustrated.
Comment: *This origin of this medal is unknown but it is believed that a number were presented to various dignitaries and others involved in the arrangements for the royal visit.*

316. JUBILEE MEDAL 1977

Date: 1977.
Ribbon: White with thin red stripes at the edges, a broad blue stripe in the centre and a thin red stripe down the middle of it.
Metal: Silver.
Size: 32mm.
Description: (Obverse) Right-facing profile of Queen Elizabeth II wearing the St Edward's crown—the first time this design was employed; (reverse) a crown and wreath enclosing the words THE 25TH YEAR OF THE REIGN OF QUEEN ELIZABETH II 6 FEBRUARY 1977. A distinctive reverse was used in Canada, showing the dates of the reign flanking the royal monogram round the foot, CANADA round the top and a large stylised maple leaf in the centre.
Comments: *The 25th anniversary of the Queen's accession was marked by the release of this unnamed medal.*

VALUE:		*Miniature*
General issue (30,000)	£130–150	£6–10
Canadian issue (30,000)	£70–90	£6–10

316A. QUEEN ALEXANDRA'S CHILDREN'S BANQUET MEDAL 1914

Date: 28 December 1914.
Ribbon: White, with red stripes at each edge.
Metal: Bronze.
Size: 38mm.
Description: (Obverse) bust of Queen Alexandra facing right with the inscription A GIFT FROM QUEEN ALEXANDRA; (reverse) central inscription FEAR GOD, HONOUR THE KING surrounded by the legend GUILDHALL BANQUET TO OUR SOLDIERS' & SAILORS' CHILDREN 28th DEC. 1914. The suspension is ornate and has the arms of the City of London superimposed.
Comments: *This medal, designed and manufactured by Elkington, was issued unnamed to 1,300 children and a small number of Chelsea pensioners who attended a banquet at the Guildhall on 28 December 1914. The children, between the ages of eight and thirteen, were the sons and daughters of men in the Fleet or on the Western Front. One child was chosen from each family by Sir James Gildea of the Soldiers' and Sailors' Families' Association. Relatively few medals appear to have survived.*

VALUE: £50–£70

Medals for Saving Life

Until the establishment of the government's own gallantry awards for the saving of life (the Sea Gallantry Medal (Foreign Services), instituted in 1841 and the Sea Gallantry Medal of 1854 and the Albert Medal of 1866), it was left entirely to private individuals and organizations to reward those who risked their own lives to save the lives of others. Although the medals granted from the late eighteenth century onwards are unofficial, they are of considerable human interest and are now very much sought after, preferably with the citations, diplomas, printed testimonials and other collateral material. The most commonly found of these medals are listed in broadly chronological order of their institution. However, listed below is the very wide range of Institutions and other bodies who have issued or continue awards for life saving as currently known to the Life Saving Awards Research Society. The Society would be very pleased to hear from readers of this Yearbook of any that are not on the list. Many of the following awards are as yet incompletely researched, and it is our intention to include many of these in this section when the research has been completed by the Life Saving Awards Research Society.

LIFE SAVING SOCIETY / FUNDS

Royal Humane Society
Bolton & District Humane Society
Bristol Humane Society
Carnegie Hero Fund Trust
Fleetwood Humane Society
Glasgow Humane Society
Grimsby Humane Society
The Hundred of Salford Humane Society
Jersey Humane Society
Liverpool Shipwreck & Humane Society
Norfolk Humane Society
Northants Humane Society
Port of Plymouth Humane Society
The Royal National Lifeboat Institution
The (Royal) Society for the Protection of Life from Fire
The Royal Life Saving Society (Mountbatten Medal)
Shipwrecked Fishermen & Mariners Royal Benevolent Society
Suffolk Humane Society
Tayleur Fund
Tynemouth Trust

NEWSPAPERS/MAGAZINES

The Quiver Medal
Answers Medal
Associated Newspapers Medal
Daily Herald (Order of Industrial Heroism)
Daily Sketch Medal
Fleet (For Merit) Medal
Golden Penny Medal

Pluck Medal
Post Office Magazine (St. Martin's Medal)
Ally Sloper's Medal
To-Day (Gallantry Fund) Medal

MUNICIPAL AUTHORITIES

Birmingham Fire Medal
Dundee Corporation Medal for Bravery
Folkestone Bravery Medal
The Corporation of Glasgow Bravery Medal
Liverpool Corporation Medal for Bravery
Metropolitan/LCC/London Fire Brigade Bravery Medal
Plymouth City Police Bravery Medal
Southend-on-Sea Pier Department Life Saving Medal
The Strathclyde Bravery Medal

The Golden Penny Award and the Liverpool Corporation Medal for Bravery

257

YOUTH ORGANISATIONS

The Boys Brigade
The Girl Guides Association
The Scouts Association

ANIMAL SOCIETIES

Dumb Friends League
National Canine Defence League
Peoples Dispensary for Sick Animals
Royal Society for the Prevention of Cruelty to
    Animals

COMMERCIAL ORGANISATIONS

Castle Mail Steam Packet Co.
Imperial Chemical Industries
Lever Brothers
Lloyds
Silk Cut Awards

NON-COMMERCIAL ORGANISATIONS

Imperial Merchant Services Guild
Mercantile Marine Service Association
St. Andrews Ambulance Association Bravery Medal
Order of St. John of Jerusalem Life Saving Medal
Shipping Federation

SPECIFIC RESCUES

Indian Chief Medal (Ramsgate Medal)
CQD Medal
SS Drummond Castle
SS Lusitania (Wanderer)
Osip Medal
HMS Niger Meda (Deal)
Henry Vernon Crew Fund Medal

COLLIERY DISASTERS

Little Hulton 1866
Hamstead Colliery 1908
Hartley Colliery 1862
Hulton Coliery 1910
Sacriston Colliery 1903

OTHER DISASTERS

Glasgow Plague Medal 1900
Maidstone Typhoid Medal 1897
Moray Floods Medal 1829

RAILWAYS

London, Midland & Scottish Railway
London & North Eastern Railway
London Passenger Transport Board
Midland Railway
Southern Railway

PRIVATE AWARDS

Too numerous to mention—but each a tale of heroism in
its own right!

Illustrated are just some of the medals that are currently being researched by the Life Saving Awards Research Society and which it is hoped will feature in forthcoming issues of the MEDAL YEARBOOK.

317. ROYAL HUMANE SOCIETY MEDALS

Date: 1774.

Ribbon: None (1774-1869); plain navy blue (1869); thin central yellow stripe and white edges added (silver medal, 1921).

Metal: Gold, silver or bronze.

Size: 51mm (1774-1869); 38mm (1869-).

Description: (Obverse) a cherub, nude but for a flowing cloak, blowing on a burnt-out torch explained by the Latin legend LATEAT SCINTILLVLA FORSAN (perhaps a tiny spark may be concealed). A three-line Latin text across the exergue reads SOC. LOND. IN RESUSCITAT INTERMORTUORUM INSTIT. with the date in roman numerals. (Reverse) an oak wreath containing the engraved details of the recipient and the date of the life-saving act. Round the circumference is a Latin motto HOC PRETIVM CIVE SERVATO TVLIT (He has obtained this reward for saving the life of a citizen). When the rescue attempt was unsuccessful, however, the medal was granted without this inscription. Later medals of similar design were struck also in bronze.

Comments: *The society was formed in 1774 for the specific purpose of diffusing knowledge about the techniques of resuscitation and saving life from drowning. From the society's inception large medals were struck in gold or silver. Monetary rewards, medals, clasps and testimonials were granted to those who saved life, or attempted to save life from drowning, but later the society's remit was broadened to include "all cases of exceptional bravery in rescuing or attempting to rescue persons from asphyxia in mines, wells, blasting furnaces or in sewers where foul air may endanger life".*

Although not intended for wear, the large medals were often pierced or fitted with a ring or bar for suspension from a ribbon. The details of the recipient and the act were engraved on the reverse.

In 1869 permission was given for the medals to be worn. As a result the diameter was reduced to 38mm and a scroll suspension was fitted for wear with a navy blue ribbon. At the same time the Latin text of the "unsuccessful" and "successful" medals was altered to read VIT. PERIC. EXPOS. D.D. SOC REG. HVM. (the Royal Humane Society presented this gift, his life having been exposed to danger) and VIT. OB. SERV. D.D. SOC, REG. HVM. (the Royal Humane Society presented this gift for saving life) respectively. Details of the recipient and the act were engraved on the rim. In 1921 the ribbon of the silver medal was changed to navy blue with a central yellow stripe and white edges, but the plain navy blue ribbon was retained for the bronze medal. Scrolled clasps with the initials R.H.S. were awarded for subsequent acts of lifesaving.

In 1873 the Stanhope Gold Medal, in memory of Captain C.S.S. Stanhope, RN, was instituted for award to the person performing the bravest act of life-saving during the year. The first Stanhope medals were similar to the society's small silver medal, differing only in the addition of a clasp inscribed STANHOPE MEDAL and the year, but since 1937 the Stanhope Medal has been identical to the other medals, differing solely in the metal. In 1921, however, the ribbon for the Stanhope Gold Medal was changed to one of navy blue with yellow and black edges.

VALUE:	Gold	Silver	Bronze
Large successful	—	£175–250	£75–120
Large unsuccessful	—	£250–320	£80–120
Small successful	—	£140–180	£45–90
Small unsuccessful	—	£150–200	£45–90
Stanhope Gold Medal	£1500–2000	—	—
Miniature	£250–300	£20–25	£15–20

317A. GLASGOW HUMANE SOCIETY MEDAL

Instituted: 1780.
Ribbon:
Metal: Gold or silver.
Size: 42mm.
Description: (Obverse) a naturalistic treatment of the elements of the Glasgow civic arms: the tree that never grew, the bird that never flew, the fish that never swam and the bell than never rang, with edge inscription GLASGOW HUMANE SOCIETY INSTITUTED 1780; (reverse) PRESENTED BY THE GLASGOW HUMANE SOCIETY TO above a horizontal tablet engraved with the name of the recipient; below: FOR INTREPIDITY OF COURAGE AND SUCCESS IN SAVING THE LIFE OF A FELLOW CITIZEN.
Comments: *Awarded mainly for saving people from drowning in the Clyde and Kelvin rivers, but also for rescues in the Firth of Clyde.*

VALUE:

Gold:	Rare
Silver:	£500–700

318. HUNDRED OF SALFORD HUMANE SOCIETY MEDALS

Date: 1824.
Ribbon: Plain dark blue.
Metal: Gold, silver or bronze.
Size: 32mm (circular type); height 49mm; max. width 41mm (cruciform type).
Description: Circular silver or bronze medals were awarded from 1824 onwards, with the recipient's name and details engraved on the reverse, and featuring a cherub kindling a spark similar to the Royal Humane Society's medal, on the obverse. Around the time of the society's centenary in 1889, however, a more elaborate type of medal was devised, with the circular medal superimposed on a cross of distinctive shape, so that the society's name could be inscribed on the arms. The recipient's details are again found on the reverse.
Comments: *This society was formed in 1789 to serve the needs of the Salford and Manchester area. After a few years it was dissolved, but was revived again in 1824. These awards ceased in 1922.*

VALUE:

	Gold	Silver	Bronze	*Miniature*
Circular medal	Rare	£120–140	£95–125	—
Cruciform medal	—	£65–85	—	—

If you know of a British Life Saving medal that is not included in the MEDAL YEARBOOK we would be delighted to hear from you.

Or if you can supply us with a photograph of any of the medals not illustrated in this publication we would be pleased to include it next year.

If you can help, please contact the Managing Editor, John Mussell, telephone 01404 46972 or at the address on page 1.
Thank you!

319. ROYAL NATIONAL LIFEBOAT INSTITUTION MEDAL

Date: 1825.
Ribbon: Plain blue.
Metal: Gold, silver or bronze.
Size: 36mm.
Description: The first medals bore the effigy of George IV on the obverse and it was not until 1862 that this was replaced by a garlanded profile of Victoria by Leonard C. Wyon. Medals portraying Edward VII and George V were introduced in 1902 and 1911 respectively, but when permission to portray George VI was refused in 1937 the RNLI adopted a profile of its founder, Sir William Hillary, instead. All but the Edwardian medals have a reverse showing a drowning seaman being rescued by three men in a boat with the motto LET NOT THE DEEP SWALLOW ME UP. The Edwardian medals have the seated figure of Hope adjusting the lifejacket on a lifeboatman. The twin-dolphin suspension (first fitted in the 1850s) has a plain blue ribbon, and clasps inscribed SECOND SERVICE, THIRD SERVICE and so on are awarded for subsequent acts of gallantry.
Comments: *The RNLI was founded, as the Royal National Institution for the Preservation of Life from Shipwreck, on 1 March 1824 and began awarding medals the following year to "persons whose humane and intrepid exertions in saving life from shipwreck on our coasts are deemed sufficiently conspicuous to merit honourable distinction". Its title changed to the Royal National Lifeboat Institution in 1854.*

VALUE:	Gold	Silver	Bronze
George IV	£1200–1500	£200–250	—
Victoria	£1200–1500	£250–300	—
Edward VII	£1500–1800	£700–800	—
George V	£1400–1800	£400–500	£250–350
Hillary	£1000–1500	£500–600	£300–400

320. MEDALS OF THE SOCIETY FOR THE PROTECTION OF LIFE FROM FIRE

Date: 1836.
Ribbon: Plain scarlet.
Metal: Silver or bronze.
Size: 52mm (I and II), 45mm (III), 42mm (IV &V) and 40mm (VI).
Description: The first medal (type I) had a radiate eye in garter on the obverse and a reverse giving the recipient's details in an oak-leaf wreath. They were fitted with a ring suspender. The Society was granted the Royal title in 1843 and a new medal (type II) was adopted the following year, with the word ROYAL added and the date at the foot of the obverse changed to 1844. In the early 1850s type III was introduced, with an obverse of a man carrying a woman away from a fire. This and type IV (1892) were struck in silver or bronze. As royal patronage ended with the death of Queen Victoria, a new medal (type V) was required in 1902 without the Royal title. Types IV and V show a man rescuing a woman and two children from a fire. The reverse of this medal has the words DUTY AND HONOR within a wreath, the recipient's details being placed on the rim. Type VI , awarded from 1984, is a bronze medal without suspension with the recipient's details engraved on the reverse.

VALUE:		Silver	Bronze
I	Eye and garter (1836)	£350–400	—
II	Eye and garter (1844)	£350–400	—
III	Man and woman (1850s)	£150–200	Rare
IV	Man, woman and children (1892)	£350–450	Rare
V	As type IV but "Royal" removed (1902)	£150–200	£100–150
VI	As type IV but details on rev.	—	Rare
Miniature (type IV)		£60–80	—

321. LLOYD'S MEDAL FOR SAVING LIFE AT SEA

Date: 1836.
Ribbon: Blue, striped white, red and white in the centre.
Metal: Gold, silver or bronze.
Size: 73mm or 36mm.
Description: Both large and small medals had similar motifs. (Obverse) the rescue of Ulysses by Leucothoe; (reverse) an ornate wreath.
Comments: *The first medals, introduced in 1836, had a diameter of 73mm and were not intended for wear, but in 1896 the diameter was reduced to 36mm and a ring fitted for suspension with a ribbon.*

VALUE:

		Miniature
Large silver	£400–500	—
Large bronze	£250–300	—
Small silver	£250–300	£60–80
Small bronze	£150–200	£40–50

322. LIVERPOOL SHIPWRECK AND HUMANE SOCIETY'S MARINE MEDALS

Date: 1839.
Ribbon: Plain dark blue.
Metal: Gold, silver or bronze.
Size: 54mm (type I), 45mm x 36mm (oval, type II) or 38mm (type III).
Description: (Obverse) a man on a spar of wreckage, taking an inert child from its drowning mother, with the stark legend LORD SAVE US, WE PERISH. This motif was retained for smaller, oval medals (type II) introduced around 1867 with the name of the Society round the edge, and a simple wreath reverse. The suspender was mounted with the Liver Bird emblem. A smaller circular version (type III) was adopted in 1874/75 and fitted with a scroll suspender. In this type the Liver Bird appeared in a wreath on the reverse. Bars engraved with the details were awarded for subsequent acts of life-saving. In addition to the general Marine medals there were distinctive awards in connection with specific marine rescues and funded separately. These had the type III obverse, but the reverse was inscribed CAMP & VILLAVERDE or BRAMLEY-MOORE. A glazed silver medal inscribed IN MEMORIAM was granted to the next of kin of those who lost their lives while attempting to save the lives of others.
Comments: *The Society was formed in 1839 to administer funds raised to help and reward those who distinguished themselves in saving life as a result of a hurricane which swept the Irish Sea in January of that year. The first medals were struck in 1844 and presented for rescues dating back to November 1839. They were large (54mm) in diameter, without suspension.*

VALUE:

	Gold	Silver	Bronze
Large (54mm) 1844	Rare	£250–300	—
Oval 1867	—	£400–450	—
Small (38mm) 1874/5	£800–1200	£60–150	£50–100
Camp & Villaverde	—	£450–600	£400–450
Bramley-Moore	—	£450–600	£400–450
In Memoriam	—	£500–600	—
Miniature (type III)	—	£90–100	—

323. SHIPWRECKED FISHERMEN AND MARINERS ROYAL BENEVOLENT SOCIETY MEDAL

Date: 1851.
Ribbon: Navy blue.
Metal: Gold or silver.
Size: 36mm.
Description: (Obverse) the Society's arms; (reverse) inscribed PRESENTED FOR HEROIC EXERTIONS IN SAVING LIFE FROM DROWNING with a quotation from Job 29: 13 at the foot. The circumference is inscribed ENGLAND EXPECTS EVERY MAN WILL DO HIS DUTY, a quotation from Lord Nelson's signal to the fleet at Trafalgar, 1805. The first medals had a straight suspender but by 1857 a double dolphin suspender had been adopted (five variations of this suspender can be identified). Details of the recipient's name and the date of the rescue are engraved on the edge.
Comments: *The Society was founded in 1839 to raise funds for shipwrecked fishermen and mariners and the families of those lost at sea.*

VALUE	Gold	Silver
Straight suspender	Rare	£150–200
Dolphin suspender	Rare	£150–200
Miniature	—	£90–100

324. TAYLEUR FUND MEDAL

Date: 1854.
Ribbon: Dark blue.
Metal: Gold (2) or silver.
Size: 45mm.
Description: (Obverse) a sinking ship with the legend TAYLEUR FUND FOR THE SUCCOUR OF SHIPWRECKED STRANGERS; (reverse) details of the award engraved.
Comments: *In January 1854 the emigrant ship* Tayleur *foundered in Bantry Bay, Ireland. A fund was started for the relief of the survivors and the surplus used to issue silver life-saving medals. The first awards were made in 1861. Medals are known to have been awarded for eight separate rescues, the last in 1875. In December 1913 the residue of the Tayleur Fund was transferred to the RNLI and the issue of medals terminated.*

VALUE:

Gold (2)	Rare
Silver (39)	£250–350

325. HARTLEY COLLIERY MEDAL

Date: 1862.
Ribbon: None.
Metal: Gold (1) or silver.
Size: 53mm
Description: (Obverse) an angel with mine rescuers and disaster victims. Details of the award were engraved on the reverse.
Comments: *Some 204 miners perished in the disaster which overtook the Hartley Colliery, Northumberland on 10 January 1862. This medal was awarded to those involved in the rescue operations.*

VALUE:

Gold (1)	Rare
Silver (37)	£250–350

325A. MERCANTILE MARINE SERVICE ASSOCIATION MEDAL

Date: 1872.
Ribbon: Blue.
Metal: Gold (2) and silver (74).
Size: 38mm.
Description: The obverse has a border with the legend "MERCANTILE MARINE SERVICE ASSOCIATION". In the centre are two seated figures of Neptune and Britannia. Neptune has a shield decorated with an anchor; Britannia a shield decorated with a sailing ship. Between the two figures are Cornucopias, Mercury's staff and a Liver bird. Beneath the two figures are the words "INCORPORATED BY SPECIAL ACT OF PARLIAMENT", and the maker's name Elkington & Co. Liverpool. The reverse bears a wreath containing the engraved details of the incident and the recipient's name.
Comments: *The medal was instituted by the MMSA in 1875 but the first awards were made retrospectively for rescues in 1872. The award was generally given to the Master and senior officers of ships engaged in life saving actions, but towards the end of its issuance some of the recipients were not officers. The last known award was made in 1906.*

VALUE:

Gold	Silver
—	£400–500

326. LIFE SAVING MEDAL OF THE ORDER OF ST JOHN

Date: 1874.
Ribbon: Black, embroidered with the eight-point cross in white (1874), black watered silk (1888), white inner and red outer stripes added, separated by a black line(1950) which was subsequently removed in 1954.
Metal: Gold, silver or bronze.
Size: 36mm.
Description: The first medals had a plain eight-pointed cross of the Order on the obverse with the legend AWARDED BY THE ORDER OF ST JOHN OF JERUSALEM IN ENGLAND. A second type of medal was adopted in 1888 and showed two tiny lions and two tiny unicorns in the interstices of the cross, the reverse shows sprigs of St John's wort and the legend FOR SERVICE IN THE CAUSE OF HUMANITY. Clasps for further awards were instituted in 1892.
Comments: *Instituted on 15 December 1874 and awarded for gallantry in saving life, these medals were originally granted in bronze or silver, but gold medals were also struck from 1907.*

VALUE:

	Gold	Silver	Bronze
1st type 1874	—	£600–800	£400–500
2nd type 1888	Rare	£600–800	£400–500
Miniature	—	£40–50	£30–40

327. LIVERPOOL SHIPWRECK AND HUMANE SOCIETY'S FIRE MEDAL

Date: 1883.
Ribbon: Plain scarlet.
Metal: Gold, silver or bronze.
Size: 38mm.
Description: (Obverse) a fireman descending the stairs of a burning house carrying three children to their kneeling mother, her arms outstretched to receive them. (Reverse) the wreathed Liver Bird previously noted for the third type of Marine medal. The medal is fitted with a scroll suspender. Clasps engraved with the details are awarded for subsquent acts.
Comments: *The first recipient was William Oversly in November 1883, for rescuing a child from a burning house. The first woman recipient was Miss Julia Keogh (12 February 1895) who saved two children in a house fire.*

VALUE:

	Gold	Silver	Bronze
Fire medal	Rare	£250–300	£150–180
Miniature	—	£40–50	£40–50

328. LLOYD'S MEDALS FOR MERITORIOUS SERVICE

Date: 1893.
Ribbon: Red with blue stripes towards the edges (1893); blue with broad white stripes towards the edges (since 1900).
Metal: Silver or bronze.
Size: 36mm x 38mm (star), 39mm x 29mm (oval), 36mm (circular).
Description: The original medal was a nine-pointed rayed star in bronze with the arms of Lloyd's on the obverse, suspended by a ring from a red ribbon with blue stripes towards the edge. A silver oval medal was introduced in 1900 with Lloyd's arms on the obverse and details of the recipient engraved on the reverse. This medal was fitted with a twin dolphin suspender and a blue ribbon with broad white stripes towards the edge. A third type, introduced in 1913, was a circular medal, struck in silver or bronze, with Lloyd's shield on the obverse. The fourth type, still current, was introduced in 1936 and has the full arms, with crest, motto and supporters, on the obverse. The ribbon is suspended by a ring.
Comments: *These medals have been awarded to officers and men for extraordinary services in the preservation of vessels and cargoes from peril.*

VALUE:

	Silver	Bronze
Star 1893	—	£100–120
Oval 1900	£400–450	—
Circular 1913	£320–350	£280–320
Circular 1936	—	—
Miniature (circular)	£60–80	—

329. LIVERPOOL SHIPWRECK AND HUMANE SOCIETY'S GENERAL MEDAL

Date: 1894.
Ribbon: Five equal stripes, three red and two white.
Metal: Gold, silver or bronze.
Size: 38mm.
Description: (Obverse) a cross pattee with a wreathed crown at the centre and the legend FOR BRAVERY IN SAVING LIFE with the date 1894 at the foot; (reverse) the wreathed Liver Bird of the Marine medal, type III. Fitted with an ornate bar suspender. Bars for subsequent awards are granted.
Comments: *The first award was made on 9 June 1894 to Constables Twizell and Dean who were both injured whilst stopping runaway horses.*

VALUE:

	Gold	Silver	Bronze
General medal	Rare	£140–180	£80–120
Miniature	—	£80–100	—

329A. QUIVER MEDAL

Date: c.1897.
Ribbon: Dark blue, with a broad diagonal white stripe.
Metal: Silver.
Size: 38mm.
Description: A thick medal weighing two ounces. (Obverse) a naked figure holding a rescued child, with the winged skeletal figure of Death hovering over a stormy sea in the background; (reverse) a laureated tablet bearing the name of the recipient and the date of the act. The circumference is inscribed round the top: FOR HEROIC CONDUCT IN THE SAVING OF LIFE and THE QUIVER MEDAL round the foot. The very elaborate suspension ring is in the form of a laurel wreath and is fitted to the suspender bar by means of a scroll inscribed THE QUIVER MEDAL. Brooch mounting at top of ribbon.
Comments: *The popular Victorian magazine* Quiver *took a keen interest in promoting safety at sea and organised a Lifeboat Fund which provided not only a number of lifeboats named* Quiver *but also this gallantry award. It is not known how many medals were awarded but four were presented to the survivors of the Margate surf boat disaster on December 2, 1897.*

VALUE: £200–250

330. DRUMMOND CASTLE MEDAL

Date: 1896.
Ribbon: Plain crimson.
Metal: Silver.
Size: 38mm.
Description: (Obverse) the veiled profile of Queen Victoria; (reverse) a wreath enclosing the name of the ship and the date of its sinking with the legend FROM QUEEN VICTORIA A TOKEN OF GRATITUDE. Fitted with a scrolled suspender.
Comments: *Presented on behalf of Queen Victoria by officials from the British Embassy in Paris to inhabitants of Brest, Ushant and Molene for their generosity and humanity in rescuing and succouring the survivors of the SS* Drummond Castle *which struck a reef off Ushant on 16 June 1896. Of the 143 passengers and 104 crew, all but three perished. 282 medals were struck and 271 of these were awarded to those who helped save the living and assisted in the recovery and burial of the victims.*

VALUE:

Silver (282)	£180–220	*Miniature*	—

331. CARNEGIE HERO FUND MEDAL

Date: 1908.
Ribbon: None.
Metal: Bronze.
Size: 90mm.
Description: (Obverse) an angel and a nude male figure surrounded by an inscription "HE SERVES GOD BEST WHO MOST NOBLY SERVES HUMANITY"; (reverse) two wreaths surrounding a central tablet inscribed "FOR HEROIC ENDEAVOUR TO SAVE HUMAN LIFE 19…" surrounding a further inscription "PRESENTED BY THE TRUSTEES OF THE CARNEGIE HERO FUND". Details of the recipient are engraved on the rim.
Comments: *The Carnegie Hero Fund Trust was established in Scotland by Andrew Carnegie in 1908. The first medallion was awarded posthumously on 26 November 1909 to Thomas Wright for a life saving act on 23 September 1908. To date 174 medallions have been awarded.*

VALUE:
    Bronze   £500–700

332. C.Q.D. MEDAL

Date: 1909.
Ribbon: Plain dark blue.
Metal: Silver.
Size: 45mm.
Description: (Obverse) the SS Republic with the initials C.Q.D. at the top; (reverse) the words FOR GALLANTRY across the middle, with a very verbose inscription round the circumference and continued in eight lines across the field. Ring suspension.
Comments: *This medal takes its curious name from the CQD signal (Come Quick Danger) sent out by the Italian steamer* Florida *when it collided in thick fog with the White Star liner* Republic *on 21 January 1909. The liner* Baltic *responded to the call. The* Republic *was the more severely damaged vessel, but all of her passengers and crew were transferred, first to the* Florida *and then to the* Baltic, *before she sank. The saloon passengers of the* Baltic *and* Republic *subscribed to a fund to provide medals to the crews of all three ships in saving more than 1700 lives.*

VALUE:
    Silver   £180–230

333. RSPCA MARGARET WHEATLEY CROSS

Date: 1936.

Ribbon: 32mm blue with a white stripe towards each edge.

Metal: Bronze.

Size: 33mm square.

Description: Cross pattee with a central circular cross with rounded ends superimposed. R.S.P.C.A. across the top arm of the outer cross and INSTD. 1936 across the lower arm. THE MARGARET WHEATLEY CROSS inscribed in four lines across the centre. (Reverse) central circle inscribed FOR BRAVING DEATH ON BEHALF OF ANIMALS, above and below a raised horizontal panel engraved with the details of the award. Fixed ring for suspension.

Comments: *The RSPCA's highest award, it was named in memory of 16 year-old Margaret Wheatley who was killed by a train at Grange-over-Sands on June 4, 1936 while saving her dog who had got trapped on the railway line. She was posthumously awarded the RSPCA's Silver Medal and was also the first recipient of the cross named in her honour. To date, a total of 70 crosses have been awarded, at least 32 of them posthumously.*

VALUE: Rare

333A. RSPCA LIFE-SAVING MEDAL

Date: 1909.

Ribbon: Blue with three white stripes in the centre, the central stripe being narrower than the others (silver); blue with a central white stripe flanked by narrow red and white stripes (bronze).

Metal: Silver or bronze.

Size: 36mm.

Description: (Obverse) a seated female figure surrounded by a cow, sheep, cat, dog, goat and horse; (reverse) plain, with an inscription. The recipient's name usually appears on the rim. Both medals have a brooch bar inscribed FOR HUMANITY.

Comments: *Instituted in 1909 by the Royal Society for the Prevention of Cruelty to Animals, this medal is awarded in silver or bronze for acts of gallantry in saving the lives of animals.*

VALUE:		*Miniature*
Silver	£90–120	£20–25
Bronze	£60–70	£15–20

334. SCOUT ASSOCIATION GALLANTRY MEDAL

Date: 1909.

Ribbon: Red (bronze), blue (silver) or half red, half blue (gilt).

Metal: Bronze, silver and gilt.

Size: 33mm.

Description: A cross pattée with the Scout fleur-de-lis emblem at the centre with the motto "BE PREPARED" and the words "FOR GALLANTRY" or "FOR SAVING LIFE". The name and details of the recipient are engraved on the plain reverse. Suspension is by a ring or straight bar. A plain bar is awarded for additional acts of gallantry.

Comments: *The Scout movement began informally in 1907 and the Boy Scouts Association was founded a year later. Gallantry awards were instituted in 1908 and 1909. The bronze cross is the highest award of the Association for gallantry, granted for special heroism or action in the favce of extraordinary risk. The silver cross is awarded for gallantry in circumstances of considerable risk. The gilt cross is awarded for gallantry in circumstances of moderate risk. A bar may be awarded to the holder of any gallantry award for further acts of gallantry in circumstances of similar risk.*

VALUE:	Bronze	£350–450
	Silver	£300–400
	Gilt	£200–300

334A. BOYS' BRIGADE CROSS FOR HEROISM

Date: September 1902.

Ribbon: Originally royal blue with two equal white stripes, but changed to plain royal blue in 1941.

Metal: Bronze.

Description: A cross pattee formed of four V-shaped finials linked to a circular disc inscribed the BOYS' BRIGADE CROSS FOR HEROISM and enclosing the emblem of the Boys' Brigade. The cross has a suspension ring and a plain brooch bar at the top of ribbon. There are two types, with or without a plain Greek cross behind the anchor in the emblem (added in 1926 when the Boys' Life Brigade amalgamated with the Boys' Brigade).

Comments: *First awarded in 1904, the cross was awarded only 194 times up to the end of 1985, including five posthumous awards.*

VALUE:		
First type (without central cross)		Rare
Second type (with central cross)		£500

335. CARPATHIA AND TITANIC MEDAL

Date: 1912.

Ribbon: Maroon.

Metal: Gold, silver or bronze.

Size: Height 40mm; max. width 35mm.

Description: The ornately shaped medal, in the best Art Nouveau style, has the suspension ring threaded through the head of Neptune whose long beard flows into two dolphins terminating in a fouled anchor and ship's spars. (Obverse) the Carpathia steaming between icebergs; (reverse) a twelve-line inscription, with the name of the manufacturer at the foot. It was worn from a straight bar suspender.

Comments: *This medal recalls one of the greatest tragedies at sea, when the White Star liner Titanic struck an iceberg on her maiden voyage and sank with the loss of 1490 lives. The 711 survivors were picked up by the Carpathia whose officers and men were subsequently awarded this medal in gold, silver or bronze according to the rank of the recipient.*

VALUE:		
Gold (14)		£7000–10,000
Silver (110)		£5000–7000
Bronze (180)		£3500–5000

336. CORPORATION OF GLASGOW BRAVERY MEDAL

Date: 1924

Ribbon: Green with red edges.

Metal: Gold, silver or bronze.

Size: 38mm (type I) or 33mm (type II).

Description: Type I: (obverse) Fame blowing a trumpet and holding a laurel wreath in front of a circular scrolled cartouche inscribed FOR BRAVERY; (reverse) plain, engraved with the name and details of the recipient. Type II: (obverse) wreath enclosing the words"FOR BRAVERY"; (reverse) Arms of the Corporation of Glasgow and details of the recipient. Fitted with a ring suspension and an ornate thistle brooch inscribed GALLANTRY in a scroll.

Comments: *Following the reorganisation of local government in Scotland in 1975, the award ceased and was replaced by the Strathclyde Regional Council Medal for Bravery.*

VALUE:	Type I	Type II
Gold	£200–250	£200–250
Silver	£100–150	£80–100
Bronze	£80–100	—

337. LLOYD'S MEDAL FOR SERVICES TO LLOYDS

Date: November 1913.
Ribbon: Blue with broad white stripes towards the edge.
Metal: Silver.
Size: 36mm.
Description: (Obverse) Neptune in a chariot drawn by four horses; (reverse) an oak-leaf wreath enclosing a scroll inscribed FOR SERVICES TO LLOYD'S. Fitted with ring suspension.
Comments: *Instituted by Lloyd's Committee, this medal was intended to reward services of a general nature.*

VALUE:			*Miniature*
Gold (14)	£1500–2000	—
Silver (10)	£800–1000	£65–70

338. LLOYD'S MEDAL FOR BRAVERY AT SEA

Date: 1940.
Ribbon: White with broad blue stripes at the sides.
Metal: Silver.
Size: 36mm.
Description: (Obverse) a seated nude male figure holding a laurel wreath, extending his hand towards a ship on the horizon; (reverse) a trident surmounted by a scroll inscribed BRAVERY, enclosed in a wreath of oak leaves. It has a ring suspender.
Comments: *Instituted by Lloyd's Committee, it was awarded to officers and men of the Merchant Navy and fishing fleets for exceptional bravery at sea in time of war. A total of 523 medals was awarded up to December 1947 when it was discontinued.*

VALUE:
Silver	£500–700	*Miniature*	£65–75

339. LIVERPOOL SHIPWRECK AND HUMANE SOCIETY'S SWIMMING MEDAL

Date: 1885
Ribbon: Five equal bars, three blue and two white.
Metal: Silver or bronze.
Size: Height 44mm; max. width 30mm.
Description: This extremely ornate medal has a twin dolphin suspender and a free form. (Obverse) a wreath surmounted by crossed oars and a trident, with a lifebelt at the centre enclosing the Liver Bird emblem on a shield; (reverse) plain, engraved with the recipient's name and details.
Comments: *Not granted for life-saving as such, but for proficiency in swimming and life-saving techniques.*

VALUE:
Silver	£30–50
Bronze	£20–40

340. BINNEY MEMORIAL MEDAL

Date: 1947.
Ribbon: None.
Metal: Bronze.
Size: 48mm.
Description: (Obverse) a bust of Captain R.D. Binney, CBE, RN; (reverse) inscription FOR COURAGE IN SUPPORT OF LAW AND ORDER and AWARDED TO above the recipient's name on a raised tablet.
Comments: *Instituted in memory of Captain Ralph Douglas Binney who was killed on 8 December 1944 in the City of London while attempting to apprehend two armed robbers single-handedly. It is awarded annually to the British citizen who displays the greatest courage in support of law and order within the areas under the jurisdiction of the Metropolitan Police and the City of London Police. The medal is not intended for wear. See MEDAL NEWS, August 1998 for a detailed article on the medal by Victor Knight.*

VALUE: Bronze   £400–600

340A. ORDER OF INDUSTRIAL HEROISM

Date: 1923.
Ribbon: Bright watered red.
Metal: Bronze.
Size: 28mm.
Description: (Obverse) a modern interpretation of St Christopher carrying Christ (by Eric Gill); (reverse) inscription ORDER OF INDUSTRIAL HEROISM around the perimeter and in the upper half AWARDED BY THE DAILY HERALD above the recipient's name and date of award.
Comments: *Created by the* Daily Herald *and first issued in 1923. It was given as a reward to the "workers" who demonstrated bravery in the workplace and was initially only to be awarded to members of a Trade Union. However, there are numerous examples of the awards being given to non Union members and the definition of "workplace" was wide. The award was intimately associated with the* Daily Herald *throughout the lifetime of the newspaper and when it ceased publication in 1963 the award was discontinued. The medal was always awarded with a cerificate and a monetary award. 440 were awarded.*

VALUE: Bronze   £400–600

340B. TYNEMOUTH MEDAL

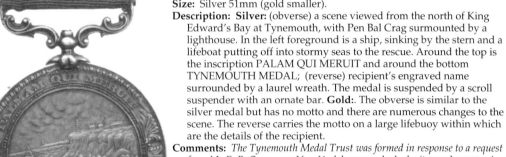

Date: 1895.
Ribbon: Dark blue.
Metal: Gold or silver.
Size: Silver 51mm (gold smaller).
Description: **Silver:** (obverse) a scene viewed from the north of King Edward's Bay at Tynemouth, with Pen Bal Crag surmounted by a lighthouse. In the left foreground is a ship, sinking by the stern and a lifeboat putting off into stormy seas to the rescue. Around the top is the inscription PALAM QUI MERUIT and around the bottom TYNEMOUTH MEDAL; (reverse) recipient's engraved name surrounded by a laurel wreath. The medal is suspended by a scroll suspender with an ornate bar. **Gold:.** The obverse is similar to the silver medal but has no motto and there are numerous changes to the scene. The reverse carries the motto on a large lifebuoy within which are the details of the recipient.
Comments: *The Tynemouth Medal Trust was formed in response to a request from Mr E. B. Convers, a New York lawyer, who had witnessed a rescue in the Tynemouth area. He was so impressed that he had a medal designed and produced and sent 100 silver medals to the Trustees to be awarded for acts of heroism to Tynesiders worldwide, or for acts of heroism in the Tyne and the surrounding area. A variant to the silver medal exists in which the reverse of the medal is inverted in relation to the suspender—this is known as the Tynemouth Extension Medal.*

VALUE: Silver (approx. 100) £250–350   Gold   Rare

Miscellaneous Medals

Under this heading are grouped a very disparate range of medals whose only common denominator is that they do not fit conveniently into one or other of the preceding categories. They are not without considerable interest, the polar medals in particular having a very keen following and a buoyant market.

341. KING'S AND QUEEN'S MESSENGER BADGE

Instituted: 1485.
Ribbon: Plain blue.
Metal: Silver.
Size: 45mm x 35mm.
Description: An upright oval fitted with a plain suspension ring and having a greyhound suspended by a ring from the foot of the rim. (Obverse) the Garter inscribed HONI SOIT QUI MAL Y PENSE enclosing the crowned royal cypher. (Reverse) plain, engraved with dates of service. Occasionally found with additional dates and monarchs' details, indicating re-issue to other messengers.
Comments: *John Norman was the first gentleman messenger formally appointed by King Richard III. Henry VIII expanded the service into a corps of 40 King's Messengers under the control of the Lord Chamberlain. Nowadays the corps is controlled by the Foreign and Commonwealth Office. Originally the badge was worn at all times by messengers on duty; today it is only worn on formal occasions.*

VALUE: Rare

342. ARCTIC MEDAL

Instituted: 30 January 1857.
Ribbon: 38mm plain white.
Metal: Silver.
Size: Height 46mm; max. width 32mm.
Description: An octagonal medal with a beaded rim, surmounted by a nine-pointed star (representing the Pole Star) through which the suspension ring is fitted. (Obverse) an unusual profile of Queen Victoria, her hair in a loose chignon secured with a ribbon. (Reverse) a three-masted sailing vessel amid icebergs with a sledge party in the foreground and the dates 1818-1855 in the exergue. The medal was issued unnamed, but is often found privately engraved.
Comments: *Awarded retrospectively to all officers and men engaged in expeditions to the polar regions from 1818 to 1855, including those involved in the on-going search for the ill-fated Franklin Expedition of 1845-8. Thus the medal was granted to civilians, scientists, personnel of the French and US Navies and employees of the Hudson's Bay Company who took part in a number of abortive search parties for Sir John Franklin and his crew. Some 1106 medals, out of 1486 in all, were awarded to officers and ratings of the Royal Navy.*

VALUE:
    Silver   £300–375   *Miniature* £150–200

343. ARCTIC MEDAL

Instituted: 28 November 1876.
Ribbon: 32mm plain white.
Metal: Silver.
Size: 36mm
Description: A circular medal with a raised beaded rim and a straight bar suspender. (Obverse) a veiled bust of Queen Victoria wearing a small crown, dated 1877 at the foot; (reverse) a three-masted ship icebound.

Comments: *Granted to officers and men of HM ships* Alert *and* Discovery *who served in the Arctic Expedition between 17 July 1875 and 2 November 1876. The medal was later extended to include the crew of the private yacht* Pandora *commanded by Allen Young which cruised in polar waters between 25 June and 19 October 1875 and from 3 June to 2 November 1876. Medals were impressed with the name and rank of the recipient. Only 170 medals were awarded.*

VALUE:
    Silver £900–1250 *Miniature* £200–250

344. POLAR MEDAL

Instituted: 1904.
Ribbon: 32mm plain white.
Metal: Silver or bronze.
Size: 33mm octagonal.
Description: (Obverse) the effigy of the reigning sovereign; (reverse) a view of the Royal Research Ship *Discovery* with a man-handling sledge party in the foreground.
Comments: *Originally issued in silver to officers and in bronze to petty officers and ratings, but the bronze medals were discontinued in 1939 and since then only silver medals have been awarded. Apart from the 1904 issue of bronze medals, all Polar Medals have been fitted with a clasp giving details of the service for which they were awarded. However, those receiving the bronze medal for the first time (21) in 1917 also had no clasp, the date being on the rim. Those already having a bronze medal (3) received a 1917 dated clasp. The 1904 bronze issue included four dated 1902–03, 23 dated 1902–04 and 33 1903–04. Only two women have received the Polar Medal: Lady Virginia Fiennes and the NZ scientist Mary Bradshaw. Medals are named to the recipient, engraved on the earlier and most recent issues and impressed in small capitals on the earlier Elizabethan issues. Clasps for subsequent expeditions are awarded. Altogether some 880 silver and 245 bronze medals for the Antarctic and 73 silver medals for the Arctic have been awarded to date. Of these almost 670 have been awarded in the present reign alone. 8 medals have been awarded for service in both the Arctic and Antarctic and 3 for Antarctic and Arctic (differentiating where first service took place). No bronze medals were issued for Arctic service.*

VALUE:	Silver	Miniature (no clasp)	Bronze	Miniature (no clasp)
Edward VII	from £1,250	£40–50	from £1,000	£20–30
George V (B)	from £1,000	£30–40	from £750	£20–30
George V (C)	—	£30–40	from £750	£20–30
George V (E)	from £1,000	£30–40	—	£20–30
George VI	from £800	£20–25	from £750	£15–20
Elizabeth II	from £800	£15–20	—	£15–20

345. KING EDWARD VII MEDAL FOR SCIENCE, ART AND MUSIC

Instituted: 1904
Ribbon: 35mm scarlet with a broad central band of dark blue and thin white stripes towards the edges.
Metal: Silver.
Size: 32mm.
Description: The raised rim consisted of a laurel wreath and has a ring for suspension. (Obverse) the conjoined busts of King Edward VII and Queen Alexandra; (reverse) the Three Graces engaged in various cultural pursuits.
Comments: *This short-lived medal was discontinued only two years later. It was awarded in recognition of distinguished services in the arts, sciences and music.*

VALUE:
Silver   £700–800

346. ORDER OF THE LEAGUE OF MERCY

Date: 1900.
Ribbon: 38mm watered white silk with a central broad stripe of dark blue.
Metal: Silver.
Size: Height 51mm; max. width 39mm.
Description: An enamelled red cross surmounted by the Prince of Wales's plumes enfiladed by a coronet, with a central medallion depicting a group of figures representing Charity, set within a laurel wreath.
Comments: *Appointments to the Order were sanctioned and approved by the sovereign on the recommendation of the Grand President of the League of Mercy as a reward for distinguished personal service to the League in assisting the support of hospitals. Ladies and gentlemen who rendered such aid for at least five years were eligible for the award. In 1917 King George V instituted a bar to be awarded to those who gave continuing service over a period of many years after receiving the Order itself. The Order was last awarded in 1946, the League itself ceasing to exist in 1947.*

VALUE:

Badge of the Order	£30–50	*Miniature* £15–20

347. INDIAN TITLE BADGE

Instituted: 12 December 1911.
Ribbon: Light blue edged with dark blue (1st class); red edged with dark red (2nd class); or dark blue edged with light blue (3rd class).
Metal: Silver or silver-gilt.
Size: Height 58mm; max. width 45mm.
Description: A radiate star topped by an imperial crown with a curved laurel wreath below the crown and cutting across the top of a central medallion surrounded by a collar inscribed with the appropriate title. The medallion bears the left-facing crowned profile of King George V or the right-facing crowned bust of King George VI. (Reverse) plain, but engraved with the name of the recipient.
Comments: *Introduced by King George V on the occasion of the Delhi Durbar of 1911 and awarded in three classes to civilians and Viceroy's commissioned officers of the Indian Army for faithful service or acts of public welfare. Recipients proceeded from the lowest grade to higher grades, each accompanied by a distinctive title. Each grade was issued in Hindu and Muslim versions, differing in title: Diwan Bahadur (Muslim) or Sardar Bahadur (Hindu), Khan Bahadur (Muslim) or Rai or Rao Bahadur (Hindu) and Khan Sahib (Muslim) or Rai or Rao Sahib (Hindu), in descending order of grade. These title badges took precedence after all British and Indian orders and decorations, and before campaign medals.*

VALUE:

Diwan Bahadur	£60–70
Sardar Bahadur	£60–70
Khan Bahadur	£50–60
Rao Bahadur	£50–60
Khan Sahib	£40–50
Rao Sahib	£40–50
Miniature	£20–30

348. BADGES OF HONOUR (AFRICAN COUNTRIES)

Instituted: 1922.
Ribbon: Plain yellow, 38mm (neck) or 32mm (breast).
Metal: Bronze.
Size: 65mm x 48mm (neck); 45mm x 33mm (breast).
Description: Oval badges with a raised rim of laurel leaves terminating at the top in an imperial crown flanked by two lions. (Obverse) a crowned effigy of the reigning monarch; (reverse) the crowned cypher of the monarch or some emblem symbolic of the particular country with the country name in the exergue.
Comments: *The badge accompanied a certificate of honour awarded to chiefs and other persons of non-European descent who had rendered loyal and valuable service to the government of the territory. The original award was a neck badge suspended by a ribbon, but from 1954 onwards recipients were given the option of taking the award as a neck or breast badge. These awards were quite distinct from the decorations known as the Native Chiefs Medals (see number 70). They were first awarded to Ugandans but later extended to other British territories in East and West Africa. They are believed to have fallen into abeyance in the early 1980s.*

VALUE:

George V	Rare
George VI	Rare
Elizabeth II (neck)	Rare
Elizabeth II (breast)	Rare

348A. BADGES OF HONOUR (NON-AFRICAN COUNTRIES)

Instituted: 1926.
Ribbon: 38mm watered silk mustard yellow.
Metal: Silver gilt.
Size: 41mm (George VI) or 32 mm (Elizabeth II).
Description: Circular with a raised rim of laurel leaves bearing a ring for suspension. (Obverse) crowned effigy of the reigning monarch; (reverse) the emblem of the country with the name round the foot.
Comments: *These medals accompanied certificates of honour awarded to indigenous persons who had rendered valuable service to the colony or protectorate. These awards appear to have been in abeyance since the early 1980s. Exceptionally, the New Hebrides badge was awarded to three British officers (Colonel (now General Sir Charles) Guthrie, Lieutenant-Colonel C. H. C. Howgill and HRH the Duke of Gloucester) in connection with the "Coconut War" in July 1980, instead of a campaign medal.*

VALUE:

George V	Rare
George VI	Rare
Elizabeth II	Rare

349. NAVAL ENGINEER'S GOOD CONDUCT MEDAL

Instituted: 1842.
Ribbon: Originally plain dark blue but later broad blue with whiteedges.
Metal: Silver.
Size: 35mm.
Description: (Obverse) a two-masted paddle steamer with a trident in the exergue; (reverse) a circular cable cartouche enclosing a crowned fouled anchor and the legend FOR ABILITY AND GOOD CONDUCT. Between the cable and the rim the details of the recipient were engraved round the circumference. Considering the rarity of the award, it is even more remarkable that the medals have several unique features. Shaw's medal, for example, had oak leaves in the exergue, flanking the trident, but this feature was omitted from later medals. Medals have been recorded with a straight bar suspender, a steel clip and ring suspender or fixed ring suspension with one or two intermediate rings.
Comments: *This medal was abolished five years after it was instituted, only seven medals being awarded in that period: to William Shaw (1842), William Dunkin (1842), William Johnstone (1843), John Langley (1843), J.P. Rundle (1845), George Roberts (1845) and Samuel B. Meredith (1846). Restrikes were produced in 1875 and at a later date. The original medals have a grooved rim, the 1875 restrikes a diagonal grained rim and the later restrikes a plain, flat rim.*
VALUE:

Original	Rare
1875 restrike	£120–140
Later restrike	£80–100

350. INDIAN RECRUITING BADGE (GEORGE V)

Instituted: 1917.
Ribbon: Plain dark green.
Metal: Bronze.
Size: Height 45mm; max. width 48mm.
Description: A five-pointed star with ball finials, surmounted by a wreathed gilt medallion bearing a left-facing crowned bust of King George V, inscribed FOR RECRUITING WORK DURING THE WAR.
Comments: *Awarded to Indian officers and NCOs engaged in recruitment of troops. It could only be worn in uniform when attending durbars or state functions, but at any time in plain clothes.*

VALUE: George V £50–60 *Miniature* £15–20

351. INDIAN RECRUITING BADGE (GEORGE VI)

Instituted: 1940.
Ribbon: Emerald green divided into three sections interspersed by narrow stripes of red (left) and yellow (right).
Metal: Silver and bronze.
Size: Height 42mm; max. width 39mm.
Description: A multi-rayed silver breast badge surmounted by an imperial crown with a suspension ring fitted through the top of the crown. In the centre is superimposed a bronze medallion bearing the left-facing crowned profile of King George VI, within a collar inscribed FOR RECRUITING.
Comments: *Awarded to selected civilian and military pensioners, full-time members of the Indian Recruiting Organisation, fathers and mothers having at least three children in the armed services, and wives having a husband and at least two children serving in the defence forces.*

VALUE: George VI £40–50 *Miniature* £20–25

352. NAVAL GOOD SHOOTING MEDAL

Instituted: August 1902.
Ribbon: Dark blue with a red central stripe edged in white.
Metal: Silver.
Size: 36mm.
Description: (Obverse) the effigy of the reigning monarch; (reverse) a nude figure of Neptune holding five thunderbolts in each hand. In the background can be seen the bows of a trireme and the heads of three horses, with a trident in the field. The Latin motto VICTORIA CURAM AMAT (Victory loves care) appears round the circumference. Fitted with a straight suspension bar. The recipient's name, number, rank, ship and calibre of gun are impressed round the rim.
Comments: *Instituted to promote excellent gunnery performances in the annual Fleet Competitions, it was first awarded in 1903 but was discontinued in 1914. Subsequent success was marked by the issue of a clasp bearing the name of the ship and the date. A total of 974 medals and 62 bars were awarded. 53 men received one bar, three men got two bars and only one achieved three bars.*

VALUE:			Miniature
Edward VII	£180–200		£50–60 (in silver)
George V	£200–220		£30–35 „

353. ARMY BEST SHOT MEDAL

Instituted: 30 April 1869.
Ribbon: Watered crimson with black, white and black stripes at the edges.
Metal: Bronze or silver.
Size: 36mm.
Description: (Obverse) the veiled diademmed profile of Queen Victoria; (reverse) Victory bestowing a laurel crown on a naked warrior armed with a quiver of arrows and a bow and holding a target, impaled with arrows, in his other hand. Fitted with a straight suspension bar.
Comments: *This medal, sometimes referred to as the Queen's Medal, was awarded annually to the champion in the Army marksmanship contests held at Bisley. It was originally struck in bronze, but was upgraded to silver in 1872. The award ceased in 1882, but was revived in 1923 and thereafter known as the King's Medal. The original reverse was retained, with the appropriate effigy of the reigning sovereign on the obverse. Since 1953 it has been known as the Queen's Medal again. In the post-1923 medals a bar bears the year of the award, with additional year clasps for subsequent awards. Until 1934 a single medal was awarded each year, but in 1935 two medals were granted, for the champion shots of the Regular and Territorial Armies respectively. Subsequently additional medals have been sanctioned for award to the military forces of India, Canada, Australia, New Zealand, Ceylon, Rhodesia, the British South Africa Police, the Union of South Africa, Pakistan, Jamaica and Ghana.*

VALUE:		Miniature
Victoria bronze	Rare	—
Victoria silver	Rare	—
George V	£700–800	£30–40
George VI	£700–800	£30–40
Elizabeth II	£700–800	£10–15

354. QUEEN'S MEDAL FOR CHAMPION SHOTS OF THE ROYAL NAVY AND ROYAL MARINES

Instituted: 12 June 1953.
Ribbon: Dark blue with a red central stripe bordered white.
Metal: Silver.
Size: 36mm.
Description: (Obverse) the effigy of Queen Elizabeth II; (reverse) Neptune (as on the Naval Good Shooting Medal).
Comments: *Instituted as the naval counterpart of the Army best shot medal.*

VALUE:

Elizabeth II	£700–800	*Miniature*	£10–15

355. QUEEN'S MEDAL FOR CHAMPION SHOTS OF THE ROYAL AIR FORCE

Instituted: 12 June 1953.
Ribbon: Broad crimson centre flanked by dark blue stripes bisected by thin light blue stripes.
Metal: Silver.
Size: 36mm.
Description: (Obverse) the effigy of Queen Elizabeth II; (reverse) Hermes kneeling on a flying hawk and holding the caduceus in one hand and a javelin in the other. The recipient's details are engraved on the rim and the medal is fitted with a straight bar suspender.
Comments: *Competed for at the annual RAF Small Arms Meeting at Bisley.*

VALUE:

Elizabeth II	—	*Miniature*	£10–15

356. QUEEN'S MEDAL FOR CHAMPION SHOTS OF THE NEW ZEALAND NAVAL FORCES

Instituted: 9 July 1958.
Ribbon: Crimson centre bordered with white and broad dark blue stripes at the edges.
Metal: Silver.
Size: 36mm.
Description: (Obverse) the effigy of Queen Elizabeth II; (reverse) similar to that of the Naval Good Shooting Medal of 1903-14. Fitted with a clasp bearing the year of the award and a straight suspension bar.
Comments: *Awards were made retrospective to 1 January 1955. This medal is awarded for marksmanship in an annual contest of the New Zealand Naval Forces. Additional clasps are granted for further success.*

VALUE:

Elizabeth II	Rare	*Miniature*	—

357. UNION OF SOUTH AFRICA COMMEMORATION MEDAL

Instituted: 1910.
Ribbon: 38mm orange-yellow with a broad central dark blue stripe.
Metal: Silver.
Size: 36mm.
Description: (Obverse) the effigy of King George V; (reverse) a blacksmith beating on an anvil the links of a chain, symbolising the unification of the four countries (Cape Colony, Natal, Orange Free State and the Transvaal), with the date in the exergue.
Comments: *Awarded to those who played a prominent part in the ceremonies connected with the Union, as well as to certain officers and men of HMS* Balmoral Castle, *a Union Castle liner specially commissioned as a man-of-war to convey HRH the Duke of Connaught as the King's representative to South Africa for the celebrations.*

VALUE:

	Named	Unnamed	*Miniature*
George V	£250–300	£200–240	£15–20

358. LOYAL SERVICE DECORATION (SA)

Instituted: 1920.
Ribbon: A broad dark blue central stripe flanked on one side by a gold bar with a thin red stripe superimposed towards the edge, and on the other side by a yellow bar with a thin white stripe towards the edge. Transvaal recipients wore the ribbon with the red to the centre of the chest; Orange Free State recipients wore the ribbon with the white stripe to the centre of the chest.
Metal: Silver.
Size: 36mm.
Description: (Obverse) the arms of the Transvaal; (reverse) the arms of the Orange Free State. Fitted with a swivel suspender. Recipients wore the medal with the appropriate state arms showing.
Comments: *Awarded by the Union of South Africa to officers of the two former Boer republics for distinguished service during the Second Boer War of 1899-1902.*

VALUE:
Silver (591)   £100–150

359. ANGLO-BOER WAR MEDAL

Instituted: 1920.
Ribbon: Broad green and yellow stripes with three narrow stripes of red, white and dark blue in the centre. Transvaal recipients wore the ribbon with the green to the centre of the chest, while Orange Free State recipients wore it with the yellow towards the centre.
Metal: Silver.
Size: 36mm.
Description: Both sides inscribed ANGLO-BOER OORLOG round the top, with the dates 1899-1902 round the foot. Medallions set in a border of a square and quatrefoil show the arms of the Orange Free State on one side and the Transvaal on the other. The medal was worn with the side showing the arms of the appropriate state uppermost. Fitted with a straight bar swivelling suspender.
Comments: *Awarded by the Union government to officers and men of the former Boer republics for loyal service in the war against the British.*

VALUE:
Silver   £60–70   *Miniature*   £15–20

360. COMMONWEALTH INDEPENDENCE MEDALS

Since the partition of the Indian sub-continent in 1947 and the emergence of the Dominions of India and Pakistan, it has been customary for medals to be issued to mark the attainment of independence. As these medals are invariably awarded to British service personnel taking part in the independence ceremonies, they are appended here, in chronological order of institution, the date of the actual award, where later, being given in parentheses. These medals invariably have symbolic motifs with the date of independence inscribed. The distinctive ribbons are noted alongside. All are 32mm wide unless otherwise stated.

India 1947 (1948) three equal stripes of orange, white and green
Pakistan 1947 (1950) dark green with a central thin white stripe
Nigeria 1960 (1964) three equal stripes of green, white and green
Sierra Leone 1961 three equal stripes of green, white and blue
Jamaica 1962 black centre flanked by yellow stripes and green edges
Uganda 1962 (1963) six stripes of black, yellow, red, black, yellow and red
Malawi 1964 three equal stripes of black, red and green
Guyana 1966 36mm red centre flanked by yellow stripes and broad green edges. The green and yellow separated (left) by a thin black stripe and (right) by a thin pale blue stripe
Fiji 1970 Grey-blue with bars half red, half white, towards each end
Papua New Guinea 1975 Red bordered by thin stripes of yellow and white, with black edges
Solomon Islands 1978 five equal stripes of blue, yellow, white, yellow and green
Gilbert Islands (Kiribati) 1980 half red, half black, separated by a thin white stripe, and edged in yellow
Ellice Islands (Tuvalu) 1980 equal stripes of red, white and red edged yellow. the white stripe bisected by a thin black stripe
Zimbabwe 1980 Silver or bronze 38mm black centre flanked by red and yellow stripes with edges of green or blue
Vanuatu 1980 (1981) 25mm four equal stripes of red, black, yellow and dark brown
St Christopher, Nevis and Anguilla 1983 bars of green (left) and red (right) with a black central bar having two thin white stripes, flanked by yellow stripes

VALUE: From £20   *Miniature*   £10–20

361. MALTA GEORGE CROSS FIFTIETH ANNIVERSARY COMMEMORATIVE MEDAL

Instituted: 1992.
Ribbon: Dark blue with central stripes of white and red (the Maltese national colours).
Metal: Cupro-nickel.
Size: 36mm.
Description: (Obverse) the crowned arms of the island, which include the George Cross in the upper left corner, with the date 1992 at the foot. (Reverse) a replica of the George Cross with the eight-pointed Maltese Cross at the top and the date 1942 at the foot, with a legend BHALA SHIEDA TA'EROIZMU U DEDIKAZZJONI on one side and TO BEAR WITNESS TO HEROISM AND DEVOTION on the other. Suspension is by a fixed bar decorated with laurels, attached to a ring.
Comments: *Sanctioned by the government of Malta to celebrate the fiftieth anniversary of the award of the George Cross by King George VI to the island for its heroic resistance to prolonged Axis attack during the Second World War. The medal has been awarded to surviving veterans who served in Malta in the armed forces and auxiliary services between 10 June 1940 and 8 September 1943. Permission for British citizens to wear this medal was subsequently granted by the Queen. As a number of veterans applied for the medal after the cut-off date of 15 April 1994, the Maltese Government sanctioned a second striking—these medals carry the word COPY below the right arm of the George Cross.*

VALUE:
Cupro-nickel	£80–100	*Miniature*	£8–10
Restrike	£60–70		

362. SHANGHAI VOLUNTEER CORPS MEDAL

Date: 1854
Ribbon:
Metal: Silver.
Size: 38mm
Description:
Comment: *Awarded to the officers and men of the Shanghai Volunteers who took part in the battle of Soo Chow Creek (also known as the battle of Muddy Flats) which took place in April 28, 1854. Examples are of the greatest rarity and the last one to appear at auction was sold in 1991. Further details are sought.*

VALUE: £800–850

363. SHANGHAI JUBILEE MEDAL

Instituted: 1893.
Ribbon: Watered silk half bright red, half white or red with 4mm central white stripe.
Metal: Silver or bronze.
Size: 36mm.
Description: (Obverse) triple-shield arms of the municipality surrounded by a band with thistles, shamrocks and roses round the foot and NOVEMBER 17 1843 round the top. (Reverse) a scrolled shield with the words SHANGHAI JUBILEE and NOVEMBER 17 1843 and inscribed diagonally across the centre with the recipient's name in block capitals. The shield is flanked by Chinese dragons and above is a steamship and the sun setting on the horizon. The rim is engraved 'Presented by the Shanghai Municipality'. Issued with a small suspension ring, but often replaced by a straight bar. This medal has also been recorded with an ornamental silver brooch bearing the dates 1843–1893 on the second type of ribbon.
Comments: *The British settlement in Shanghai was founded in 1843 and formed the nucleus of the International Settlement established in 1854 under the control of an autonomous Municipal Council. In effect the International Settlement functioned as an autonomous City State administered by a Municipal Committee formed from those nations comprising the Settlement. This was abolished when Shanghai was overrun by Imperial Japanese troops in 1941.*

VALUE:	Silver (625)	£250–300
	Bronze (100)	£250–300

364. SHANGHAI FIRE BRIGADE LONG SERVICE MEDAL

Instituted: Before 1904.
Ribbon: Black with broad crimson borders.
Metal: Silver.
Size: 31mm.
Description: (Obverse) an armorial device featuring a Chinese dragon standing on a symbolic high-rise building on which is displayed a flame on a pole crossed by a hook and ladder, with MIH-HO-LOONG SHANGHAI round the top and the motto "Say the word and down comes your house" round the foot; (reverse) blank. It seems strange that no Chinese characters appear on the medal. Ring and double claw suspension, with a broad silver brooch bar at the top of the ribbon.
Comment: *Awarded for a minimum of twelve years regular service with the Municipal Fire Brigade. The award was presumably in abeyance following the Japanese invasion in 1937 and the wholesale destruction of the international commercial metropolis.*

VALUE: £300

365. SHANGHAI VOLUNTEER FIRE BRIGADE LONG SERVICE MEDAL

Instituted: 1904.
Ribbon: Red with white edges.
Metal: Gold, silver or bronze.
Size: 36mm.
Description: (Obverse) the arms and motto of the Municipality surrounded by a collar inscribed SHANGHAI VOLUNTEER FIRE BRIGADE ESTABLISHED 1866. (Reverse) a pair of crossed axes surmounted by a fireman's helmet under which is a horizontal tablet on which are engraved the recipient's dates of service. Round the circumference is inscribed FOR LONG SERVICE (top) and WE FIGHT THE FLAMES (foot) with quatrefoil ornaments separating the two inscriptions. Fitted with a swivelling scroll suspender.
Comments: *The medal in silver was awarded to members of the Volunteer Fire Brigade for five years service, for eight years service a clasp was added to the ribbon and for 12 years service the medal was awarded in gold. Bronze medals exist but are believed to have been specimens only.*

VALUE: Silver   £450–500

366. SHANGHAI VOLUNTEER CORPS LONG SERVICE MEDAL

Instituted: 1921.
Ribbon: Equal bands of red, white and blue, the red bisected by a thin green stripe, the white by black and the blue by yellow.
Metal: Silver.
Size: 36mm.
Description: (Obverse) an eight-pointed radiate star bearing a scroll at the top inscribed 4th APRIL 1854. The arms of the Municipality superimposed on the star and surrounded by a collar inscribed SHANGHAI VOLUNTEER CORPS. Round the foot of the medal is a band inscribed FOR LONG SERVICE. (Reverse) plain, engraved with the name of the recipient and his period of service.
Comments: *The Volunteer Corps was raised in 1853 to protect the British and other foreign settlements. The date on the scroll alludes to the Corps' first engagement, the Battle of Muddy Flat. The Corps was cosmopolitan in structure, although the British element predominated. It was disbanded in September 1942, nine months after the Japanese overran the International Settlement. Awarded for 12 years good service, the last medal was awarded in 1941.*

VALUE: Silver   £250–300   *Miniature* £25–40

367. SHANGHAI MUNICIPAL POLICE DISTINGUISHED CONDUCT MEDAL

Instituted: 1924.
Ribbon: Red with a central blue stripe (1st class); red with a blue stripe at each edge (2nd class).
Metal: Silver or bronze.
Size: 36mm.
Description: (Obverse) arms of the Municipality and the inscription SHANGHAI MUNICIPAL POLICE; (reverse) the words FOR DISTINGUISHED CONDUCT. The recipient's name and rank was engraved round the rim.
Comments: *Awarded to officers and men of the Municipal Police in two classes, distinguished solely by their ribbons and the metal used (silver or bronze). A sliding clasp was fitted to the ribbon to denote a second award; this featured the Municipal crest and was engraved on the reverse with the details of the award. Only six awards were ever made, including two to Europeans.*

VALUE: Silver   £800–900
              Bronze   £650–750

368. SHANGHAI MUNICIPAL POLICE LONG SERVICE MEDAL

Instituted: 1925.
Ribbon: Brown with a central yellow band edged in white.
Metal: Silver.
Size: 36mm.
Description: (Obverse) arms of the Municipality within a collar inscribed SHANGHAI MUNICIPAL POLICE; (reverse) plain apart from the inscription FOR LONG SERVICE in two lines across the centre. The recipient's name and rank were engraved round the rim in upper and lower case lettering. Awards to Indians were named in cursive script with the Hindi equivalent alongside. Fitted with a swivelling scroll suspender.
Comments: *Awarded for 12 years good service in the Shanghai Municipal Police, an international force composed largely of Sikhs, Chinese and White Russians as well as British ex-soldiers and policemen. Dated clasps for further five year periods of service were awarded. The medal was abolished in 1942.*

VALUE:

		Miniature
Silver	£280–300	£45–50
With clasp	£350–400	£50–60

369. SHANGHAI MUNICIPAL POLICE (SPECIALS) LONG SERVICE MEDAL

Instituted: 1929.
Ribbon: Dark brown with three white bars, each bisected by a thin yellow stripe.
Metal: Silver.
Size: 36mm.
Description: (Obverse) the arms of the Municipality with the motto OMNIA JUNCTA IN UNO (all joined in one) round the circumference. (Reverse) inscribed SHANGHAI MUNICIPAL POLICE (SPECIALS) FOR LONG SERVICE in six lines. A unique award to A.L. Anderson (1930) was inscribed on the reverse FOR DISTINGUISHED AND VALUABLE SERVICES.
Comments: *Awarded for 12 years active and efficient service in the Special Constabulary. Some 52 medals and 8 clasps for additional service are recorded in the* Shanghai Gazette, *but the actual number awarded was probably greater. The medal was discontinued in 1942.*

VALUE:

With clasp	Very rare
Without clasp	£450–500

370. SHANGHAI MUNICIPAL COUNCIL EMERGENCY MEDAL

Instituted: 1937.
Ribbon: 38mm bright red, having a broad white central stripe bordered black and yellow edges separated from the red by thin black stripes.
Metal: Bronze.
Size: 40mm.
Description: An eight-pointed star with ring suspension. (Obverse) a central medallion superimposed on the radiate star with the triple-shield arms of the Municipality surrounded by a collar inscribed SHANGHAI MUNICIPAL COUNCIL. (Reverse) a laurel wreath enclosing the words FOR SERVICES RENDERED - AUGUST 12 TO NOVEMBER 12 1937.
Comments: *Awarded to members of the Police, Volunteer Corps, Fire Brigade and civilians for services during the emergency of August-November 1937 when fighting between the Chinese and Japanese in and around Shanghai threatened to encroach on the International Settlement. Issued unnamed, but accompanied by a certificate bearing the name and unit of the recipient. Examples have been seen with the recipient's name engraved on the reverse.*

VALUE:

Bronze star	£80–100	*Miniature*	£25–30

371. AUTOMOBILE ASSOCIATION SERVICE CROSS

Date: 1956.
Ribbon: Yellow with three narrow black stripes.
Metal: Silver.
Size: 36mm.
Description: A silver cross flory terminating in scrolls, with the AA emblem surmounted in the centre.
Comments: *Established in commemoration of the Association's Golden Jubilee, the Cross is the highest award to AA patrolmen and other uniformed members of staff for conspicuous acts of bravery involving an imminent risk of personal injury whilst on duty in uniform, or whilst engaged in an action related to duty. To date only 15 crosses have been awarded. A monetary reward accompanies the Cross.*

VALUE: Rare

372. AUTOMOBILE ASSOCIATION SERVICE MEDAL

Date: 1956.
Ribbon: Half yellow, half black.
Metal: Silver.
Size: 36mm.
Description: A circular medal in the form of the AA badge with wings sprouting from the top and flanking a claw and ring suspension. (Obverse) AA superimposed on a wheel, with the inscription AUTOMOBILE ASSOCIATION/SERVICE MEDAL round the circumference; (reverse) details of the award.
Comments: *Like the Cross, the Medal of the Association was instituted in commemoration of the Association's Golden Jubilee. The medal is awarded to members of the uniformed staff for courageous or outstanding initiative and devotion to duty. To date, only 60 medals have been awarded, including four in 1997, mainly for life-saving and bravery in accidents. A monetary reward accompanies the Medal. A Service Citation is also awarded for lesser acts, a total of 63 having been bestowed so far.*

VALUE: Rare

373. SUFFRAGETTE MEDAL

Instituted: 1909.
Campaign: Votes for women.
Ribbon: Three equal stripes of purple, silver and green.
Metal: Silver.
Size: 20mm.
Clasps: Prison bars surmounted by a broad arrow, or an enamelled bar in the WSPU colours.
Description: A small silver medal suspended by a ring from a bar with scrolled finials, engraved with the date of the award. A similarly scrolled brooch bar at the top of the ribbon is inscribed FOR VALOUR. The plain medal is engraved HUNGER STRIKE in various styles and hallmarked.
Comments: *This medal was awarded by the Women's Social and Political Union (WSPU) to those militant Suffragettes who were imprisoned for various acts of violence and who went on hunger strike while in prison. At first they were forcibly fed under the most barbaric conditions, as a result of which several died. The government then introduced the Cat and Mouse Act, whereby hunger strikers at the point of death were released, but were then re-arrested and returned to prison when they had recovered sufficiently from their ordeal. Bars were awarded in respect of subsequent periods of imprisonment and hunger strike.*

VALUE: £3500–£4000 (unboxed)
                    £5000–£6000 (in personally inscribed case)

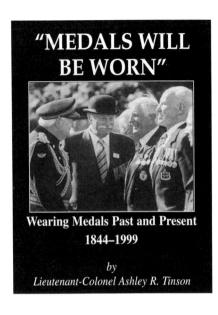

Unofficial
medals

Interest has been steadily growing in recent years in unofficial medals, a subject on the fringes of medal collecting. The term is deliberately vague and encompasses a very wide range of medals, medalets and medallions of a commercial, private or local nature. Such a generic term would, for example, include regimental medals awarded for marksmanship or good conduct, often associated with official medal groups of the 19th century. This is a very esoteric group, often consisting of medals which were specially engraved for the occasion and therefore exceedingly difficult to quantify.

On the other hand, many of the earlier medals, now highly regarded as forerunners of the general campaign series, were unofficial in origin, and relied upon the enterprise of public-spirited indviduals and prize agents such as Alexander Davison (nos. 78 and 85) or Matthew Boulton (no. 84), generals such as Elliot (no. 74), Earl St Vincent (no. 80) or Gordon of Khartoum (no. 133) or even private bodies such as the Highland Society (no. 83).

Then there is the large and fascinating group of civic or institutional medals which were presented to volunteers returning from the Boer War of 1899–1902. M.G. Hibbard, in his splendid monograph *Boer War Tribute Medals* (1982), recorded no fewer than 78 such medals, 40 from towns and cities in England, 25 from other parts of the United Kingdom and 13 from Commonwealth countries. Some of these were fitted with ribbons and were obviously intended for wear alongside the official medals of the war; others were 'danglers' intended to be fitted to watch-chains; and others still were not fitted with any form of suspension and were thus in the nature of commemorative medals intended purely as a memento of volunteer service.

So far as can be ascertained, such tribute medals were not produced in previous conflicts, which were predominantly fought by regular troops; and such was the scale of the involvement of volunteers and later conscripts in the First World War that the cost of providing civic medals of this nature would have been prohibitive. Instead, returning soldiers had to be content with some form of paper testimonial, at best. A notable exception was the gold medal presented by the Lord Mayor of London to the members of the anti-aircraft gun crews which shot down the first Zeppelin (listed below).

Apart from that, the Boer War group therefore constitutes a unique, but clearly defined group. They are, however, generally outside the scope of this YEARBOOK, although it should be noted that several medals in this category have long been accepted in the regular canon: the Kimberley Star (no. 154), the Kimberley Medals (no. 155), the Yorkshire Imperial Yeomanry Medal (no. 156) and the Medal for the Defence of Ookiep (no. 157). The reason for their acceptance is quite arbitrary, and just why the Yorkshire Imperial Yeomanry medal should be so highly regarded while others are not seems to rest on the fact that this medal is more commonly met with than the others—which is hardly a valid criterion.

For the sake of completing the record we have endeavoured to introduce a number of unofficial medals, particularly as groups including certain of these medals are coming onto the market and inevitably some purchasers are curious to know their origins.

In addition there are a number of other unofficial medals available to veterans such as the "Battle for Britain" medal with its various clasps but it is not the intention to make this a definitive guide, so we have decided to limit this section to those medals that were initially commissioned or supported by the relevant veterans associations and mainly produced in recent years in order to fill the gap left in the official series.

Credit for reviving such medals must go to the Mayor of Dunkirk on whose initiative the medal awarded to survivors of the 1940 evacuation was instituted in 1965. Subsequently distribution of this medal was taken over by the Dunkirk Veterans' Association, applications being strictly limited to those who could prove that they had taken part in that historic event. This practice continued with the commissioning of the Bomber Command Medal by their Association in response to the long-standing grievance of veterans of the Second World War who felt that their contribution to the ultimate victory had been deliberately ignored for political reasons. The success of this medal encouraged the production of similar awards for other categories of servicemen, or for campaigns which many felt should have had a distinctive campaign medal.

It must be stressed that all of these medals are available for purchase only by bona-fide veterans or their proven next of kin with sales also benefitting related charities. The wearing of these medals has always been a contentious issue with veterans choosing to wear them below but never alongside their official decorations.

U1. LORD MAYOR OF LONDON'S GOLD MEDAL FOR THE DESTRUCTION OF ZEPPELIN L15

Date: 1916.
Campaign: First World War.
Branch of Service: Royal Artillery.
Ribbon:
Metal: 9 carat gold.
Size: 29mm.
Description: (Obverse) the arms of Sir Charles Wakefield within a double ring inscribed PRESENTED BY THE LORD MAYOR round the top and COLONEL SIR CHARLES WAKEFIELD round the foot; (reverse) An anti-aircraft gun and two scrolls inscribed WELL HIT and MARCH 31st and number L15. It is engraved near the top with the rank and name of the recipient. It was issued unmounted but various ornamental suspensions loops were later fitted privately.
Comments: *The Lord Mayor of London offered a reward of £500 to the first gun crew to shoot down a Zeppelin. On 3 April 1916 Capt. J. Harris submitted a claim on behalf of the Purfleet gun crew that they were responsible for the bringing down of the airship L15, but it later transpired that gun crews from Abbey Wood, Dartford, Erith, North Woolwich, Plumstead and the Royal Arsenal, among others, were also involved. It was decided to use the prize money in procuring these medals, a total of 353 being awarded.*

U2. DUNKIRK MEDAL

Date: 1960.
Ribbon: Orange with one thin and one wide red stripe each side with two very thin black lines bisecting both sides.
Metal: Bronze.
Size: 36mm wide.
Description: (Obverse) a shield bearing the arms of Dunkirk (a lion passant above a heraldic dolphin) mounted on an anchor; (reverse) a circle bearing a burning lamp with DUNKERQUE 1940 beneath, surrounded by a laurel wreath and surmounted by crossed swords; the whole mounted on and surrounded by a laurel wreath.
Comments: *This medal was first made available to veterans of the Dunkirk evacuation and later administered by the now disbanded Dunkirk Veterans Association. It was created by the French National Association of Veterans of the Fortified Sector of Flanders and of Dunkirk and awarded in recognition of the sacrifice of 30,000 combatants between 29 May and 3 June 1940.*

U3. BOMBER COMMAND MEDAL

Date: 1985.
Campaign: Second World War.
Branch of Service: RAF Bomber Command.
Ribbon: Midnight blue with a central flame stripe and blue-grey edges.
Metal: Cupro-nickel.
Size: 36mm.
Description: (Obverse) A Tudor crown surmounting a laurel wreath containing the letters RAF, flanked by smaller wreaths containing the brevet letters of the aircrew signifying courage, team spirit and leadership; (reverse) a Lancaster bomber flanked by the dates 1939 and 1945 with inscription A TRIBUTE TO THE AIRCREW OF BOMBER COMMAND round the circumference.
Comments: *Produced at the behest of Air Vice Marshal Donald Bennett following a design competition in MEDAL NEWS. The competition was the brainchild of author Alan Cooper campaigning on behalf of Bomber Command veterans. The first medal was struck by Lady Harris (widow of the wartime commander of Bomber Command).*

U4. NORMANDY CAMPAIGN MEDAL

Date: 1987.

Campaign: Service in the Normandy campaign between June 6 and August 20, 1944.

Branch of Service: All British and Allied forces.

Ribbon: Dark red with deep navy blue stripes towards the edges and light blue edges, symbolising the three services.

Metal: Cupro-nickel.

Size: 36mm.

Description: (Obverse) insignia of the combined services surrounded by 13 stars (representing the USA) and the inscription BLESSENT MON COEUR D'UNE LANGUEUR MONOTONE ("soothe my heart with dull languor"), a quotation from Verlaine broadcast by the BBC at 21.15 on June 5, 1944 to signal the start of the D-Day operations. (Reverse) a tank landing craft with its ramp on the beaches of France symbolised by fleurs-de lis; NORMANDY CAMPAIGN round the top and the date of the campaign inscribed on the ramp. The medal is fitted with a plain suspension bar while the ribbon bears a clasp inscribed NORMANDY between oak leaves.

Comments: *Commissioned by the Normandy Veterans Association whose Welfare and Benevolent Fund benefited from the proceeds of sales.*

U5. ARCTIC CAMPAIGN MEDAL

Date: 1991.

Campaign: Second World War.

Branch of Service: Personnel of the Russian convoys.

Ribbon: 32mm watered weave in equal bands of blue and white representing ice and sea.

Metal: Cupro-nickel.

Size: 36mm.

Description: (Obverse) a liberty ship framed in the cross-hair of a U-boat periscope, with the inscription FOR SERVICE IN THE ARCTIC ZONE 1939-45 round the top; (reverse) four figures representing merchant seaman, Royal Naval, Army and RAF personnel, with the inscription THE ARCTIC CAMPAIGN round the top.

Comments: *This award was proposed by the Russian Convoy Club in conjunction with the North Russia Club, who are the beneficiaries of the project.*

U6. MERCHANT NAVAL SERVICE MEDAL

Date: 1998.

Campaign: Second World War.

Branch of Service: Merchant Navy and DEMS Gunners.

Ribbon: Dark blue with a central narrow white stripe flanked by broader green and red stripes, representing the navigation lights of an approaching ship.

Metal: Cupro-nickel.

Size: 36mm.

Description: (Obverse) a stockless anchor encompassed by its heavy cable, surmounted by the initials MN; (reverse) a capstan surmounted by a naval crown and flanked by grotesque sea monsters, the whole encircled by a rope tied at the foot in a reef knot. The outer circumferance is inscribed FOR MERCHANT NAVAL SERVICE. The medal is fitted to a plain suspension bar by an ornamental scroll.

Comments: *Veterans were eligible for this medal in respect of at least two years' service in the Merchant Navy. The award was inspired by the fact that although service in the mercantile marine was recognised after World War I it was ignored after World War II. King George's Fund for Sailor's benefits from the sale of this medal.*

U7. ALLIED EX-PRISONERS OF WAR MEDAL

Date: 1991.
Campaign: All wars of the 20th century.
Branch of Service: Prisoners of war.
Ribbon: Green with red edges. The centre has a broad black stripe edged in white, having a white strand of barbed wire running down the middle.
Metal: Cupro-nickel.
Size: 36mm.
Description: (Obverse) a young bird trapped by barbed wire, against a globe of the world, with the inscription INTERNATIONAL PRISONERS OF WAR; (reverse) a twisted barb of wire whose four strands divide the inscription INTREPID AGAINST ALL ADVERSITY. Fitted with a plain suspension bar.
Comments: *This award proposed by the National Ex Prisoners of War Association is applicable to any former PoWs whose countries were allies of Britain at the time of their capture irrespective of whether the United Kingdom was itself involved in the conflict.*

U8. RESTORATION OF PEACE MEDAL

Date: 1995.
Campaign: Second World War.
Branch of Service: Armed forces and civilians involved in the war effort.
Ribbon: Rich claret with a central broad gold stripe.
Metal: High-security HS1 gold-coloured alloy.
Size: 36mm.
Description: (Obverse) the letter V enclosing the date 1945, superimposed on a globe with the inscription A TIME FOR PEACE round the circumference; (reverse) a simple wreath enclosing the inscription FOR ALL WHO STRIVED (sic) FOR PEACE. The plain suspension bar is fitted to the medal by a peace dove on both sides.
Comments: *Produced at the behest of the British Red Cross Society to mark the 50th anniversary of the cessation of hostilities in the Second World War.*

U9. SUEZ CANAL ZONE MEDAL

Date: 1995.
Campaign: Suez Canal Zone, 1945-57.
Branch of Service: British and French forces.
Ribbon: Sand-coloured edged with narrow stripes of red, white and blue. A broad central crimson stripe has a light blue stripe down the middle.
Metal: High-security HS1 gold-coloured alloy.
Size: 36mm.
Description: (Obverse) the Sphinx and Pyramid flanked by the dates 1951-54 and 1956-57, representing the two most recent periods of conflict; (reverse) stylised papyrus grass with the words TO MARK SERVICE IN THE CANAL ZONE at left. Fitted with an ornamental suspension bar in the form of Pharaonic wings.
Comments: *The Ex-Services Mental Welfare Society (Combat Stress) is the beneficiary of this project.*

U10. NATIONAL SERVICE MEDAL

Date: 1991.

Campaign: Period of conscription, 1939-60.

Branch of Service: National Service, both military and civilian.

Ribbon: Dark blue with a narrow central gold stripe and narrow white and red stripes at the edges representing the involvement of the Royal British Legion.

Metal: Cupro-nickel.

Size: 36mm.

Description: (Obverse) the seated figure of Britannia supported by a lion, with the inscription NATIONAL SERVICE 1939-1960; (reverse) a wreath enclosing the inscription FOR CROWN AND COUNTRY. Fitted with scrolled suspension.

Comments: *Between January 1939 when the National Service Act was passed, and December 1960 when it was repealed, some 5,300,000 young people were conscripted into the armed services. The medal was proposed by the Royal British Legion and almost 100,000 have been issued to date.*

U11. JORDAN SERVICE MEDAL

Instituted: April 1997.

Branch of Service: British ex-service personnel who served in the Hashemite Kingdom of Jordan between 1948 and 1957 and again during the 1958 emergency, i.e. the 16th Independent Parachute Brigade and attached units.

Ribbon: Golden sand, edged on both sides with four thin stripes of the Jordanian national colours (black, white, green and red).

Metal: Gilt brass.

Size: 36mm.

Description: (Obverse) Effigy of King Hussein; (reverse) inscription in raised lettering: FOR SERVICE IN THE HASHEMITE KINGDOM OF JORDAN, with or without the date 1958 below.

Comments: *This medal was produced on the initiative of G.E. Harris of Haverfordwest with the approval of the late King Hussein. Sales of the medal benefit the SSAFA Forces Help charity. It was manufactured by the Bigbury Mint, Ermington, Devon. To date 1,183 veterans have applied for the medal (either version), including two of the four female nurses who served in Jordan.*

U12. HONG KONG SERVICE MEDAL

Instituted: 1999.

Branch of Service: All former civil and military personnel who served for a minimum of six months in the Crown Colony of Hong Kong, or their next of kin.

Ribbon: Pale blue with a central yellow stripe.

Metal: Gilt metal.

Size: 36mm.

Description: (Obverse) Bird of Paradise surrounded by the words HONG KONG SERVICE MEDAL 1841–1997; (reverse) HONG KONG in Cantonese characters surrounded by a circular wreath. The medal is suspended from a unique suspender depicting two mythical Chinese dragons.

Comments: *SSAFA Forces Help, the ex-servicemen's charity, benefits from the sales of this medal.*

Now available

from Token Publishing Ltd

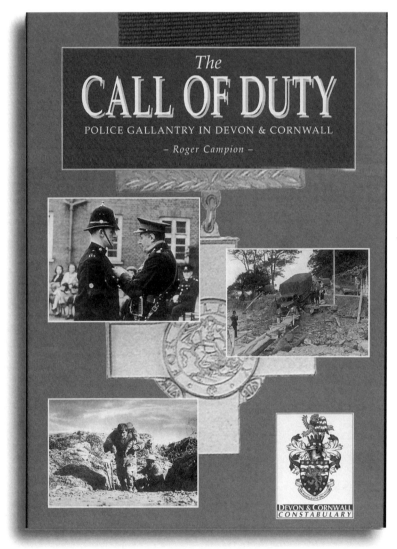

This book records for the first time the fascinating stories of police officers serving in Devon and Cornwall who have received official recognition for acts of selfless courage, above and beyond the call of duty. It includes the formal awards of national decorations, medals or honours and also the awards won by officers serving their country in the military services in times of war, and those who served through the horrors of cities blitzed into ruin. These are the stories of police officers who, without a thought for themselves, upheld the proud tradition of serving and protecting the public

Price £19.95 plus £4 post & packing

Provincial Police medals

In addition to the official medals and decorations awarded to police officers (see nos. 271, etc.) there are a number of medals which have been instituted by county or civic constabularies for long and distinguished service. As the ribbons of these awards are sometimes noted on the tunics of policemen we have decided to include these semi-official awards in a separate section. It is our intention, in a future edition of MEDAL YEARBOOK, to extend this treatment to the semi-official awards made by county and regional fire brigades and the Special Constabulary, on the same basis. It is also the intention to include the current market value of all of these medals where possible.

We are indebted to Roger Campion for furnishing us with details of no fewer than 20 provincial police medals, the result of a long time study of this absorbing subject. Should readers know of any other medals we would be grateful for their details for inclusion in forthcoming editions of the MEDAL YEARBOOK.

The medals have been listed here in alphabetical order by place of origin, irrespective of the date of institution. The Metropolitan Police, founded in 1829, and its neighbour, the City of London Police, are conspicuous by their absence from this survey, and it is suspected that both forces must have produced distinctive awards at some time during their long history.

Accordingly, the first distinctive police medal so far recorded is the Liverpool City Police Order of Merit which dates from 1852. Significantly, several other awards were instituted in 1897, the year of Queen Victoria's Diamond Jubilee, a period when the resources of the police forces must have been stretched to the limit in crowd control. This set the ball rolling, and in the ensuing years many constabularies followed suit. The great majority of the older-established awards ceased by the end of 1951, when the Police LS&GC was introduced. These medals therefore survive as tangible mementoes of the period when distinct constabularies existed at county, city and even borough level. Only one county constabulary—Dunbartonshire—is thought to have awarded a medal to its regular officers to celebrate the coronation of 1902 and this is included for the first time this year, thanks to the knack of Ian Hall in unearthing previously unknown police medals. There may be more out there that we are yet to hear of. If you know of any, please get in touch to ensure that the section is as complete as possible. A few entries are reproduced without pictures and we are keen to put this right, if you can help please let us know.

All the forces in the section are now gone and the medals are one of the few tangible mementoes of the history of policing in the United Kingdom and the days when it was very much a local matter. Most of the medals are attractive in design and feature the city or borough coat of arms, a further reminder of truly local community policing.

P1. ABERDEEN CITY CONSTABULARY MEDAL

Instituted: 5 July 1909.
Branch of Service: Aberdeen City Constabulary.
Ribbon: Royal blue.
Metal: Silver.
Size: 39mm.
Description: (Obverse) The Seal of the City of Aberdeen with the legend AWARDED BY THE TOWN COUNCIL OF ABERDEEN around the circumference; (reverse) a laurel wreath with the inscriptions FOR SPECIAL SERVICE and CITY CONSTABULARY with a space between the two for the rank and name of the recipient and the date of the award. The exergue has a motif of a constable's helmet superimposed on a pair of crossed truncheons. The ribbon was attached by a ring suspender.
Comments: *Awarded to officers who distinguished themselves in the execution of their duty. The first award made in 1909 was cast in gold but further awards were of silver. The medal was discontinued in 1936. The Constabulary was founded in 1818 but became a part of Grampian Police on 16 April 1975.*

P2. BIRKENHEAD CONSTABULARY GOOD SERVICE MEDAL

Instituted: 13 September 1897.
Branch of Service: Birkenhead Constabulary.
Ribbon: Red with two stripes of dark blue all equal in width.
Metal: Silver and Bronze.
Size: 39mm.
Description: (Obverse) left-facing conjoined Young Head and Old Head of Queen Victoria surrounded with the inscription VICTORIA DIAMOND JUBILEE 1837–1897; (reverse) the Arms of Birkenhead and town motto contained within an oak and laurel wreath tied at its base all surrounded by the legend FOR GOOD SERVICE and BIRKENHEAD CONSTABULARY. The recipient's name, rank and number were engraved on the rim. A plain straight swivelling suspender was employed.
Comments: *The medal was issued to all members of the constabulary with 20 or more years service to mark the Diamond Jubilee of Queen Victoria. Silver medals (10) were issued to officers and 12 bronze medals to sergeants and constables. The medals were presented in a black box marked in gold lettering with the recipient's rank and number. Although it wasn't formally abolished until 1951 no more medals were ever issued. Founded in 1833, Birkenhead amalgamated with the Cheshire Constabulary in 1967 and became a part of Merseyside Police on 1 April 1974.*

P3. BOLTON COUNTY BOROUGH POLICE LONG SERVICE MEDAL

Instituted: 30 July 1913.
Branch of Service: Bolton County Borough Police.
Ribbon: Blue with two red stripes (5mm) placed 6mm from each end.
Metal: Silver.
Size: 34mm.
Description: (Obverse) the arms of the City of Bolton surrounded by a raised circle with the legend FOR GOOD SERVICE (above) and BOLTON BOROUGH POLICE (below); (reverse) a laurel wreath surrounding a central field containing the inscription PRESENTED BY THE WATCH COMMITTEE and the date of the award in four lines. The medal is suspended from an ornate bar attached by a claw fitting.
Comments: *Initially awarded for 25 years service without default, the period was reduced to 20 years in 1931. Silver slip-on bars were awarded for each additional five years service. The bars were plain and usually inscribed with OVER 25 YEARS or OVER 30 YEARS although unmarked examples exist. The medals were engraved on the lower rim with the recipient's rank, name and date of appointment. Discontinued at the outbreak of World War II and formally abolished in 1951. The Bolton County Borough Police Force was founded in 1839. In 1969 it joined with several others to form the Lancashire Constabulary but became part of the Greater Manchester Police on 1 April 1974.*

P4. BOOTLE BOROUGH CONSTABULARY GOOD CONDUCT MEDAL

Instituted: August 1897.
Branch of Service: Bootle Borough Constabulary.
Ribbon: Five equal stripes of blue, white, blue, white, blue.
Metal: Silver and bronze.
Size: 32mm.
Description: (Obverse) the Old Head of Queen Victoria with the inscription VICTORIA DIAMOND JUBILEE 1837–1897; (reverse) the Coat of Arms of the Borough with BOROUGH OF BOOTLE above. This is surrounded by an outer ring bearing the words AWARDED FOR GOOD CONDUCT 1837–1897. The rank and name of the recipient was engraved on the lower rim. The medal hung from a plain straight suspender and claw fitting.
Comments: *Initially issued by the Watch Committee to commemorate the Diamond Jubilee and retained for award to members of the force for 15 years service without blemish. Bronze medals were awarded to sergeants and constables and silver medals to officers of the rank of inspector and above. Plain bars were awarded for further unblemished service. It was abolished in 1948. The force was founded on 1 July 1887 but ceased to exist in 1967 on amalgamation with the Liverpool City Police to form the Liverpool and Bootle Police. It now forms part of the Merseyside Police.*

P5. BRIGHTON BOROUGH POLICE MERITORIOUS CONDUCT MEDAL

Instituted: 7 February 1902
Branch of Service: Brighton Borough Police.
Ribbon: Royal blue.
Metal: 22ct gold.
Size: 34mm.
Description: (Obverse) Coat of Arms of Brighton Borough within a
    wreath of laurel; (reverse) engraved with the rank and name of the
    recipient, the date of the award and brief details of the circumstances.
    The medal was hung from a gold suspender ring with a plain brooch
    bar some (but not all) of which were inscribed BOROUGH OF
    BRIGHTON POLICE MEDAL for fixing to the tunic.
Comments: *Issued to all ranks of the force for especially meritorious service.*
    The first medal was awarded for saving life at the scene of a fire with others
    granted later for saving lives at sea, the arrest of an armed criminal and
    destroying a ferocious dog. There is one recorded instance of a bar being
    awarded for a second act of courage. The bar was ornate with laurel leaves at
    the top and sides and inscribed with the name of the recipient and date of the
    award.
      The Brighton Borough Police was founded in 1838 but ceased to exist as a
    separate force on 31 December 1967 when it amalgamated with the Sussex
    Constabulary. It was a part of the Sussex Combined Police from 1 April 1943
    until 31 March 1947 for the duration of the Second World War.

P6. BRISTOL CITY POLICE LONG SERVICE AND GOOD CONDUCT MEDAL

Instituted: 8 December 1926.
Branch of Service: Bristol City Police.
Ribbon: Dark red with a central green stripe 6.5mm wide.
Metal: Silver.
Size: 36mm.
Description: (Obverse) arms of the City of Bristol surrounded by a band
    with the legend FOR GOOD SERVICE above and BRISTOL CITY
    POLICE below; (reverse) a laurel wreath tied with a ribbon with the
    recipient's name, rank and number inscribed in the centre. It was
    suspended from a plain straight swivelling bar
Comments: *Rewarded for 17 years service with exemplary conduct. Bars were*
    awarded for each additional five years service. The bars were also made of
    silver. The medal was discontinued in 1951 on the introduction of the
    National Police Long Service and Good Conduct Medal. A total of 610 were
    awarded, made up as follows: 112 without bars, 359 with 1 bar, 105 with 2
    bars, 23 with 3 bars, 11 with 4 bars. Bristol City Police was founded in 1836.
    On 1 April 1974 the force amalgamated with the Somerset and Bath
    Constabulary and a part of the Gloucestershire Constabulary to form the
    current Avon and Somerset Constabulary.

P7. CAMBRIDGE CITY POLICE LONG SERVICE MEDAL

Instituted: 1913.
Branch of Service: Cambridge City Police.
Ribbon: Red with a blue central stripe.
Metal: Silver.
Size: 36mm.
Description: (Obverse) the Coat of Arms of the City of Cambridge with the legend CAMBRIDGE BOROUGH POLICE FOR LONG SERVICE around the circumference; (reverse) a wreath of laurel tied with a ribbon with the rank and name of the recipient and date of the award inscribed in the centre. The medal was attached by a claw to a plain straight swivelling suspender
Comments: *Awarded to members of the force after 25 years service without blemish. It appears to have been a short-lived medal with no record of any award after 1914. The force was founded in 1836 but ceased to exist in 1965 when it was amalgamated with the Cambridgeshire Constabulary to form the Mid-Anglia Police. It was renamed the Cambridgeshire Constabulary on 1 April 1974.*

P8. CARDIFF CITY POLICE AND FIRE BRIGADE MEDAL FOR CONSPICUOUS BRAVERY

Instituted: 11 May 1908.
Branch of Service: Cardiff City Police Force and Fire Brigade.
Ribbon: Yellow with three red chevrons.
Metal: Silver.
Size: 39mm.
Description: (Obverse) the Coat of Arms of the City of Cardiff with the legend FOR CONSPICUOUS BRAVERY below; (reverse) a seven line inscription PRESENTED BY THE CARDIFF WATCH COMMITTEE TO (rank, number and name) FOR CONSPICUOUS BRAVERY. A claw fitting and ornate swivelling scroll suspender were used.
Comments: *The medal carried a non-pensionable allowance of 2/- (10p) a week for life. Plain silver, slip-on clasps were awarded for any subsequent act of bravery. The unusual ribbon displayed a single chevron when worn in undress uniform. The medal was not awarded after 1929. The Cardiff City Police was founded as the Cardiff Borough Police in 1836 and became a part of South Wales Constabulary on 1 April 1969.*

P8A. DUNBARTONSHIRE COUNTY COUNCIL CORONATION MEDAL 1902

Instituted: 1902.
Branch of Service: Dunbartonshire County Constabulary.
Ribbon: Royal blue.
Metal: Silver and bronze.
Size: 34mm.
Description: (Obverse) the crowned and robed bust of King Edward VII facing right with the words EDWARD VII and the date 1902 on the left and KING OF GREAT BRITAIN & IRELAND EMPEROR OF INDIA in nine lines in the right third of the medal; (reverse) the coat of arms of Dunbartonshire with the date JUNE 26 (left) and 1902 (right) in a scroll on each side. The legend DUMBARTONSHIRE COUNTY COUNCIL lies around the upper circumference. In a scrolled panel in the lower half of the medal is the inscription PRESENTED TO MEMBERS OF THE DUMBARTONSHIRE CONSTABULARY TO COMMEMORATE THE CORONATION OF HIS MAJESTY KING EDWARD VII in five lines. The medal hangs from a plain ring suspender. Issued unnamed.
Comments: Awarded at the time of the 1902 coronation to all members of the Constabulary. Silver medals were given to officers of the rank of inspector and above and bronze to sergeants and constables. No more than 100 of both types were issued. The Dunbartonshire Constabulary was formed in 1840 but ceased to exist in 1975 when it became part of Strathclyde Police.

P9. EXETER CITY POLICE LONG SERVICE AND EFFICIENCY MEDAL

Instituted: May 1928.
Branch of Service: Exeter City Police.
Ribbon: White with two broad (8mm) grass green stripes. A miniature has been seen with the full-size ribbon folded in at each end to leave a green ribbon with a central white stripe all of equal width.
Metal: Silver.
Size: 36mm.
Description: (Obverse) the arms of the City of Exeter with the legend FOR LONG SERVICE AND EFFICIENCY around the circumference; (reverse) hat of maintenance superimposed on two crossed swords of state with the legend CITY OF EXETER POLICE FORCE around the circumference. It was suspended from a straight bar.
Comments: *Awarded for 17 years efficient and zealous service without default. Bars were awarded for each additional five years service at 22, 27 and 32 years. All medals were engraved on the rim with the name of the recipient. About 35 were awarded. Discontinued in June 1939.*
   Exeter City Police was founded in 1836 but ceased to exist as a separate force in 1966 on amalgamation with the Devon Constabulary to form the Devon and Exeter Constabulary. It is now a part of the Devon and Cornwall Constabulary.

P10. GRIMSBY COUNTY BOROUGH POLICE GOOD SERVICE MEDAL

Instituted: November 1914.
Branch of Service: Grimsby County Borough Police.
Ribbon: Dark blue with crimson edges and a crimson central line.
Metal: Silver and bronze.
Size: 35mm.
Description: (Obverse) Coat of Arms of the County Borough of Grimsby inside an oak wreath. Around the circumference is the inscription FOR GOOD SERVICE above and COUNTY BOROUGH OF GRIMSBY POLICE below; (reverse) a laurel wreath tied with a ribbon around a central field containing the legend PRESENTED BY THE WATCH COMMITTEE and the date in five lines. The recipient's rank and name are engraved on the lower rim. The medal employed a claw fitting and plain straight swivelling suspender.
Comments: *The medal was given as a reward for 25 years unblemished service. Officers of the rank of inspector or above were awarded silver medals and sergeants and constables bronze. At least one example exists with the date of the award engraved on the lower rim not the reverse. The medal was discontinued in 1941 although serving holders were permitted to wear them until they retired. The force was founded in 1846 and survived until 1969 when it was amalgamated with the Lincolnshire County Constabulary and Lincoln City Police. It became a part of Humberside Police on 1 April 1974.*

P11. LEAMINGTON SPA BOROUGH POLICE CORONATION MEDAL

Instituted: 1902.
Branch of Service: Leamington Spa Borough Police.
Ribbon: Sea blue.
Metal: Silver.
Size: 32mm.
Description: (Obverse) the conjoined crowned heads of King Edward VII and Queen Alexandra inscribed HM EDWARD VII KING to the left and HM ALEXANDRA QUEEN to the right with PROCLAIMED 1901 at the base; (reverse) inscribed with the words PRESENTED BY ALDERMAN WACKRILL JP TO THE LEAMINGTON BOROUGH POLICE FORCE AND FIRE BRIGADE ON THE OCCASION OF THE CORONATION OF HIS MAJESTY EDWARD VII JUNE 26th 1902 in eleven lines. The medal hung from a plain suspender attached by a ring.
Comments: *Awarded to celebrate the coronation in 1902. The Leamington Spa Borough Police was founded in 1835 and amalgamated with the Warwickshire County Constabulary in 1947.*

P12. LINCOLN CITY POLICE GOOD SERVICE MEDAL

Instituted: 17 June 1926.
Branch of Service: Lincoln City Police.
Ribbon: Dark red with a broad green central stripe.
Metal: Silver.
Size: 32mm.
Description:(Obverse) arms of the City of Lincoln surrounded by a laurel wreath and surmounted by a scroll bearing the motto FLOREAT LINDUM with the legend FOR GOOD SERVICE above and LINCOLN CITY POLICE below; (reverse) a wreath of laurel tied at the base with a ribbon usually with the recipient's name, rank and number inscribed centrally. Examples exist with the central field left blank and the recipient's name inscribed on the lower rim. It was suspended from a swivelling straight bar by a claw.
Comments: *Awarded by the City Watch Committee to officers on completion of 20 years service without default. It was abolished in October 1941 although holders still serving were allowed to wear their medals until they retired. The force was founded in 1836 but ceased to exist on 1 April 1967 on amalgamation with the Lincolnshire Police.*

P13. LIVERPOOL CITY POLICE ORDER OF MERIT

Instituted: October 1851.
Branch of Service: Liverpool City Police Force.
Ribbon: Blue with red edges and a red central stripe.
Metal: Silver.
Size: 32mm.
Description: (Obverse) Coat of Arms of the City of Liverpool surrounded with a laurel leaf and with the city motto DEUS NOBIS HAEC OTIA FECIT in a banner above and the date 9th OCT 1851 along the bottom; (reverse) the inscription PRESENTED BY THE WATCH COMMITTEE TO (engraved name) AS A REWARD FOR GOOD CONDUCT in nine lines in the central field with ORDER OF MERIT (above) and LIVERPOOL POLICE FORCE (below) around the circumference on a raised circle. The medal hung from a plain swivelling suspender bar.
Comments: *Awarded to officers with good conduct records for at least five years to commemorate the visit of Queen Victoria to the city on 9 October 1851. Each period of five years was signified by the award of a bar up to a maximum of three. There were 112 recipients at a parade held on 5 August 1852–72 were awarded with one bar, 26 with two bars and 14 with three. The Liverpool City Police was amalgamated with the Bootle Borough Constabulary in 1967 and became part of Merseyside Police in 1974.*

P14. LIVERPOOL CITY POLICE DIAMOND JUBILEE GOOD SERVICE MEDAL

Instituted: 1897.
Branch of Service: Liverpool City Police.
Ribbon: Blue with red edges and a red central stripe.
Metal: Silver and bronze.
Size: 32mm.
Description: (Obverse) the Old Head of Queen Victoria with the words VICTORIA DIAMOND JUBILEE above and the dates 1837–1897 below; (reverse) the Liver Bird on a shield topped with the royal crown surrounded by a wreath of oak and laurel. A scroll above the shield contains the legend DEUS NOBIS HAEC OTIA FECIT. In addition the words FOR GOOD SERVICE and LIVERPOOL CITY POLICE are found around the circumference above and below the shield. With a claw fitting and straight swivelling suspender.
Comments: *Silver medals were awarded to officers of the rank of inspector and above who had 20 years service with unblemished records on 20 June 1897 or were serving officers on 20 June 1887 and had continued to serve for a further 10 years without default. Bronze medals were awarded to sergeants and constables with 20 years approved service.*

P15. LIVERPOOL CITY POLICE GOOD SERVICE MEDAL

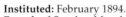

Instituted: 1900.
Branch of Service: Liverpool City Police.
Ribbon: Red with a single blue diagonal stripe (silver medal); blue with a single red diagonal stripe (bronze medal). From 1930 both ribbons were changed to a more conventional design: red with a blue central stripe and a white stripe on either side (silver); blue with a central red stripe and a white stripe on either side (bronze).
Metal: Silver and bronze.
Size: 32 mm.
Description: (Obverse) identical to the reverse of the Liverpool City Police Diamond Jubilee issue (P14); (reverse) a wreath of laurel with a central field containing an inscription with the words PRESENTED BY THE WATCH COMMITTEE, sometimes with the date of the award and the recipient's name engraved on the rim, sometimes with all details on the reverse.
Comments: *Inspired by the medal issued to commemorate the Diamond Jubilee of Queen Victoria in 1897 with the same qualifying criteria appilcable. From 1918 onwards the bronze medal was given after 20 years and the silver medal awarded after 25 years service. A bar was awarded for each additional five years service after the award of the silver medal. Service in excess of 30 years was denoted by a bar with the legend SERVICE OVER 30 YEARS. The medals were discontinued in 1951.*

P16. MANCHESTER CITY POLICE BRAVERY MEDAL

Instituted: February 1894.
Branch of Service: Manchester City Police.
Ribbon: Crimson.
Metal: Silver.
Size: 32mm.
Description: (Obverse) The Coat of Arms of the City of Manchester inscribed above with MANCHESTER CITY POLICE and below with FOR BRAVERY; (reverse) a laurel wreath tied at the base with a ribbon surrounding the central area which was available for the rank and name of the recipient together with the date of the award. The medal was fitted to a swivelling suspender of ornate design by means of a claw and attached to the uniform by a buckle pin.
Comments: *Awarded to members of the City Force in recognition of acts of outstanding bravery. Further acts performed could be rewarded by the granting of a bar. 71 medals were awarded and it is thought that four bars were granted. No medals were granted after 1948. The force was founded in 1839 and amalgamated with the Salford City Police in 1968 until 1 April 1974 when it became a part of the Greater Manchester Police.*

P17. NEW WINDSOR BOROUGH POLICE CORONATION MEDAL 1902

Instituted: 1902.
Branch of Service: New Windsor Borough Police.
Ribbon: Red with green stripe at either edge 6.5mm wide.
Metal: Bronze.
Size: 32mm.
Description: (Obverse) The conjoined heads of King Edward VII and Queen Alexandra facing right with the words KING EDWARD and QUEEN ALEXANDRA around. The designer's name is also visible; (reverse) the coat of arms of the Borough of Windsor and WINDSOR BOROUGH in a scroll beneath and a crown above. The word POLICE is shown below the scroll with an encircling band and the inscription TO COMMEMORATE THE CORONATION 1902. With a claw fitting and straight swivelling suspender.
Comments: *Issued to members of the force who took part in the Coronation. The medals were originally issued unnamed although some exist with the name and rank of the recipient engraved on the lower rim. The New Windsor Borough was founded in 1836 but merged with the Berkshire Constabulary in April 1947. It now forms part of the Thames Valley Police.*

P18. NEW WINDSOR BOROUGH POLICE CORONATION MEDAL 1911

Instituted: 1911.
Branch of Service: New Windsor Borough Police.
Ribbon: Red with green stripe at either edge 6.5mm wide.
Metal: Bronze
Size: 32mm.
Description: (Obverse) the conjoined heads of King George V and Queen Mary facing left; (reverse) very similar to the 1902 medal with the coat of arms of the Borough of Windsor but without the crown—all surrounded by a band containing the words TO COMMEMORATE THE CORONATION 1911.
Comments: *Issued to all officers of all ranks who were on duty during the Coronation.*

P19. PLYMOUTH CITY POLICE CONSPICUOUS BRAVERY AND GOOD SERVICE MEDAL

Instituted: 16 April 1930.
Branch of Service: Plymouth City Police.
Ribbon: Dark red with two broad blue stripes and a central blue line.
Metal: Silver.
Size: 36 mm.
Description: (Obverse) arms of the City of Plymouth surrounded by a laurel leaf wreath topped with an imperial crown to which the suspension ring was attached; (reverse) a rectangular panel for the recipient's name and the legend PLYMOUTH CITY CONSTABULARY above and GOOD SERVICE below. Very few medals were inscribed with the recipient's name.
Comments: *Awarded for 17 years service without default or for an act of conspicuous gallantry. Bars were awarded for each additional five years service. Where an officer who had been awarded a medal for service performed an act of gallantry he was awarded a bar inscribed FOR GALLANTRY. Where the award was for gallantry and the officer subsequently fulfilled the conditions relating to an award for good service he was also entitled to a bar. There are no known instances of this occurring and any inscription on the bar is a matter for conjecture. Approximately 200+ medals were awarded. Discontinued in 1951 on the introduction of the National Police Long Service and Good Conduct Medal. Plymouth City Police was founded in 1836 but ceased to exist as a separate force in June 1967 when it was amalgamated with two other forces to form the Devon and Cornwall Constabulary.*

P20. READING BOROUGH POLICE BRAVERY MEDAL

Instituted: 26 April 1904.
Branch of Service: Reading Borough Police.
Ribbon: Royal blue with a central white stripe 4.5 mm wide.
Metal: Bronze.
Size: 39 mm.
Description: (Obverse) The Arms of the Borough of Reading with the legend READING POLICE above and FOR BRAVERY below on a surrounding raised circle; (reverse) left plain for the recipient's details to be engraved. An ornate scrolled swivelling suspender was used.
Comments: *Instituted at the suggestion of the Chief Constable, Captain John Henderson, and awarded to members of the force for acts of special bravery or for saving life. Most recorded awards were made for stopping runaway horses. A bar was awarded for further acts by the same officer (one such award recorded—to Constable 17 Gillings in 1908 and 1909). Gratuities were usually given to the recipient. It was discontinued in 1951. The Reading Borough Police was founded in 1836 but became part of the Thames Valley Police on 1 April 1968.*

P21. REIGATE BOROUGH POLICE GOOD SERVICE MEDAL

Instituted: September 1913.
Branch of Service: Reigate Borough Police.
Ribbon: Medium blue.
Metal: Silver.
Size: 32 mm.
Description: (Obverse) the Coat of Arms of the Borough with the inscription 25 YEARS GOOD SERVICE above and REIGATE BOROUGH POLICE below; (reverse) a wreath of oak leaves with the recipient's rank and name and the date of the award. The medal hung from a plain straight suspender.
Comments: *Awarded to all members of the force for 25 years good service without a blemish on their records. The medal was discontinued in 1943 when the borough force was combined with the Surrey Constabulary and Guildford Borough Police under the wartime defence regulations to form the Surrey Joint Constabulary.*

P22. ROCHDALE COUNTY BOROUGH POLICE BRAVERY MEDAL

Instituted: 15 November 1928.
Branch of Service: Rochdale County Borough Police Force.
Ribbon: Red.
Metal: Silver.
Size: 35 mm.
Description: (Obverse) the Rochdale Coat of Arms and borough motto surrounded by the legend ROCHDALE COUNTY BOROUGH POLICE; (reverse) a three line inscription AWARDED BY THE WATCH COMMITTEE followed by the rank and name of the recipient. Around the circumference were the words FOR EXTREME BRAVERY. It was suspended from a swivelling suspender with a floral design and attached to the uniform by an ornate pin buckle.
Comments: *Awarded to members of the Borough Police Force for acts of outstanding bravery. It was retained after the Police Long Service and Good Conduct Medal was introduced but finally discontinued in 1969 when the Rochdale County Borough Police was amalgamated with others to form the Lancashire Constabulary. It became a part of the Greater Manchester Police on 1 April 1974.*

P23. ROCHDALE COUNTY BOROUGH POLICE LONG SERVICE MEDAL

Instituted: 14 August 1930.
Branch of Service: Rochdale County Borough Police.
Ribbon: Blue with a central red stripe, all of equal width (silver medal) Blue with two bands of red, all of equal width (bronze medal).
Metal: Silver and bronze.
Size: 35 mm.
Description: (Obverse) Coat of Arms of the Borough of Rochdale with the town motto and the legend ROCHDALE COUNTY BOROUGH POLICE around the circumference; (reverse) a six line inscription in the central field AWARDED BY THE WATCH COMMITTEE TO (rank and name). Around the circumference was the legend FOR LONG AND FAITHFUL SERVICE. The medals were suspended to a plain straight swivelling suspender by a claw.
Comments: *The bronze medal was awarded after 20 years service and the silver after 25 years, both requiring a clean record. They were discontinued in 1949.*

P23A. TAYSIDE POLICE MEDAL FOR MERITORIOUS CONDUCT

Instituted: 1996.
Branch of Service: Tayside Police.
Ribbon: Police blue, with two white stripes towards the centre, fitted with a brooch pin for suspension.
Metal: Silver.
Size: 36mm.
Description: (Obverse) a crowned thistle on a dark blue ground with the motto SEMPER VIGILO (always on guard) at the foot, in red, white, green and blue enamels; (reverse) details of the award.
Comments: *Awarded to police officers and members of the public for actions which fall short of national recognition but which are deemed to be above the standard required for a Chief Constable's commendation.*

VALUE: —

P24. WIGAN BOROUGH POLICE GOOD SERVICE MEDAL

Instituted: —
Branch of Service: Wigan Borough Police.
Ribbon: Dark blue with a red central stripe.
Metal: Silver.
Size: 35 mm.
Description: (Obverse) The Coat of Arms of the Borough of Wigan within an outer circle containing the legend FOR GOOD SERVICE (above) and WIGAN BOROUGH POLICE (below); (reverse) a laurel wreath tied at the base with a bow surrounding a central field containing an inscription with the rank and name of the recipient together with the date he joined the force. The medal has an ornamental scroll suspender attached by a swivelling claw fitting. The ribbon is attached by a brooch fitting.
Comments: *The Wigan County Borough Police was founded in 1836 but later amalgamated with the Lancashire County Constabulary and eleven other borough forces to form the Lancashire Constabulary. It became a part of Greater Manchester Police on 1 April 1974.*

Awards of the British Commonwealth

In recent years many countries of the British Commonwealth have created their own individual systems of Honours and Awards. However, some British awards are still recognised within these systems. The medals and awards of these countries instituted prior to their own systems being introduced, are included in the main section of this book. In this section of the YEARBOOK we include the latest honours and awards of AUSTRALIA, NEW ZEALAND and, new for this edition, SOUTH AFRICA, together with their current Orders of Precedence encompassing their own and former British honours and awards. We also include the Orders of Precedence in Canada. It is anticipated that the latest honours and awards for Canada and selected other countries of the former British Commonwealth will be included at a future date.

THE ORDER OF PRECEDENCE IN AUSTRALIA (including British awards)

Victoria Cross
George Cross
Cross of Valour
Most Noble Order of the Garter
Most Ancient and Most Noble Order of the Thistle
Knight Grand Cross, the Most Honourable Order of the Bath
Order of Merit
Knight, the Order of Australia
Knight Grand Cross, the Most Distinguished Order of St Michael & St George
Knight Grand Cross, the Royal Victorian Order
Knight Grand Cross, the Order of the British Empire
Companion, the Order of Australia
Companion of Honour
Knight Commander, the Most Honourable Order of the Bath
Knight Commander, the Most Distinguished Order of St Michael & St George
Knight Commander, the Royal Victorian Order
Knight Commander, the Order of the British Empire
Knight Bachelor
Officer, the Order of Australia
Companion, the Most Honourable Order of the Bath

Companion, the Most Distinguished Order of St Michael & St George
Commander, the Royal Victorian Order
Commander, the Order of the British Empire
Star of Gallantry
Star of Courage
Distinguished Service Order
Distinguished Service Cross (Australian)
Member, the Order of Australia
Lieutenant, the Royal Victorian Order
Officer, the Order of the British Empire
Companion, the Imperial Service Order
Member, the Royal Victorian Order
Member, the Order of the British Empire
Conspicuous Service Cross
Nursing Service Cross
Royal Red Cross 1st Class
Distinguished Service Cross (British)
Military Cross
Distinguished Flying Cross
Air Force Cross
Royal Red Cross 2nd Class
Medal for Gallantry
Bravery Medal

Distinguished Service Medal (Australian)
Public Service Medal
Australian Police Medal
Australian Fire Service Medal
Member of the Order of Australia
Order of St John
Distinguished Conduct Medal
Conspicuous Gallantry Medal
George Medal
Conspicuous Service Medal
Antarctic Medal
Queen's Police Medal for Gallantry
Queen's Fire Service Medal for Gallantry
Distinguished Service Medal (British)
Military Medal
Distinguished Flying Medal
Air Force Medal
Queen's Gallantry Medal
Royal Victorian Medal
British Empire Medal
Queen's Police Medal for Distinguished Service
Queen's Fire Service Medal for Distinguished Service

Commendation for Gallantry
Commendation for Brave Conduct
Queen's Commendation for Brave Conduct
Commendation for Distinguished Service
War Medals in order of campaign
Australian Active Service Medal
Australian Service Medal
Australian Active Service Medal 1945–75
Australian Service Medal 1945–75
Police Overseas Service Medal
Civilian Service Medal
Polar Medal
Imperial Service Medal
Coronation/Jubilee Medals
Defence Force Service Medal
Reserve Force Decoration
Reserve Force Medal
National Medal
Champion Shots Medal
Long Service Medals
Independence/Anniversary Medals
Approved Foreign Orders, Medals and Decorations

"The Australian and New Zealand troops have indeed proved themselves worthy sons of the Empire."

GEORGE R.I.

AUSTRALIAN MEDALS

Since 1975 Australia has instituted a number of purely Australian awards. Medals and decorations pertaining to Australia, instituted prior to 1975 will be found in chronological sequence within the main text of this book.

The Australian system was inaugurated on February 14, 1975 when the Order of Australia, four bravery awards and the National Medal were established by Letters Patent. Since then a further 27 medals, decorations, commendations and citations have been introduced, which, including the various grades of the Order of Australia, brings the total to 37. A very detailed and comprehensive account of the Australian awards will be found in *The National Honours & Awards of Australia* by Michael Maton (1995). They are listed below in order of precedence. To date few of these new awards have come onto the market, thus we have not always been able to give an accurate valuation other than to indicate that the award is "Rare".

A1. VICTORIA CROSS FOR AUSTRALIA

Instituted: 1991.
Ribbon: Crimson 38mm wide.
Metal: Bronze.
Size: 35mm at each axis.
Description: A cross pattée with raised edges. (Obverse) a crowned lion standing on the royal crown, with the words FOR VALOUR on a semi-circular scroll below; (reverse) a circle containing the date of the action for which it was awarded. The Cross is suspended by a ring attached to the cross and a V-lug below a straight suspension bar ornamented with laurels.
Comments: *The Victoria Cross for Australia is identical to the British award and is awarded, with the approval of the Queen, by an instrument signed by the Governor-General on the recommendation of the Minister of Defence. Some 96 Australians have won the VC since 1856, the most recent being Warrant Officer Keith Payne for bravery in Vietnam (May 1969). No award of the Australian VC has yet been made.*

VALUE: As no. 24

A2. CROSS OF VALOUR

Instituted: 1975.
Ribbon: Magenta 38mm wide with a blood-red central band of 16mm.
Metal: Gold.
Size: 42mm.
Description: A straight-armed Greek cross with diminishing rays between the arms, ensigned by St Edward's crown and an integral suspension bar inscribed FOR VALOUR. The cross is surmounted by the heraldic shield of Australia topped by the Star of the Federation.
Comments: *Intended to replace the British civilian award of the George Cross. To date, only three CVs have been awarded.*

VALUE: Rare

A3. ORDER OF AUSTRALIA

Instituted: 1975.
Ribbon: Royal blue bearing scattered gold mimosa blossoms of various sizes (General Division); similar, but with gold edges (Military Division)

Neck/shoulder badge

Breast badge

KNIGHTS AND DAMES OF THE ORDER

The insignia consists of a neck badge and breast badge. In the case of a Dame there was the option of a neck badge or a shoulder badge, the latter being identical in every respect save the mounting. The neck badge is worn with a 16mm ribbon, while the shoulder badge of the Dame is worn with a 28mm ribbon. The breast badge is worn on the left side of a coat or outer garment.

Neck Badge: A gold disc 60mm in diameter, jewelled and having at its centre the arms of Australia enamelled in full colour on a blue ground decorated with two branches of mimosa. The whole is ensigned by the St Edward Crown in full colour with a suspension ring at the top.

Breast Badge: The emblem of the Order, 80mm in diameter, in gold, jewelled, and having the arms of Australia at the centre, surmounted by the St Edward Crown.

Comments: *There is also a miniature, 20mm in diameter, worn with the 16mm ribbon, a lapel badge, 10mm in diameter for ordinary civilian wear, and a ladies' badge mounted on a brooch bar. Knights and Dames are entitled to the prefix "Sir" or "Dame" and to use the postnominal letters AK or AD respectively. Between May 24, 1976, when the grade of Knights and Dames was introduced, and March 3, 1986 when these grades were abolished, a total of 11 Knights and two Dames were created, excluding the Queen (Sovereign of the Order) and the Prince of Wales.*

VALUE:		
	Breast badge	Rare
	Neck/shoulder badge	Rare
	Miniature badge	—

COMPANION OF THE ORDER

The insignia consists of a gold neck badge (men) or shoulder badge (women) 60mm in diameter, similar to the Knight's badge but having at its centre a circlet of blue enamel edged in gold containing two sprigs of mimosa and inscribed AUSTRALIA at the foot. These badges are worn with a 16mm neck ribbon or 38mm shoulder bow respectively. Miniatures, lapel and brooch badges with jewelled centres identical to those of the Knights or Dames, are also worn. Companions have the postnominal letters AC after their name.

Comments: *Up to 1994 214 Companions had been appointed in the General Division and 17 in the Military Division.*

VALUE:	Neck badge	Rare
	Miniature badge	Rare

Companion's badge.

OFFICER OF THE ORDER

The insignia is a badge similar to that of the Companion but only 55mm in diameter, and in silver-gilt instead of gold. The miniature, lapel badge and brooch badges have a blue enamel centre. Officers have the postnominal letters AO after their name.

Comments: *Up to 1994 1,164 Officers had been appointed, 990 in the General Division and 174 in the Military Division.*

VALUE:	Badge	£800–2000
	Miniature badge	£50-80

Officer's badge.

MEMBER OF THE ORDER

The insignia is a badge consisting of the emblem of the Order, 45mm in diameter in silver-gilt but without the enamelled centre, although the miniature, lapel badge and brooch badges have a blue enamel centre. Members have the postnominal letters AM.

Comments: Up to 1994 3,727 Members had been appointed to the Order, 3,064 in the General Division and 663 in the Military Division.

VALUE:	Badge	£450–1000
	Miniature badge	£50–80

For the Medal of the Order of Australia (see no. A15)

Member's badge.

A4. STAR OF GALLANTRY

Instituted: 1991.
Ribbon: Deep orange with chevrons of light orange, points upwards.
Metal: Silver-gilt.
Size: 37mm.
Description: A seven-pointed Federation Star ensigned by a St Edward crown affixed to a suspension bar inscribed FOR GALLANTRY. (Obverse) a smaller Federation Star 22mm across, surrounded by stylised flames representing action under fire: (reverse) central horizontal panel on a stepped background.
Comments: *Second and subsequent awards are denoted by a silver-gilt 34mm bar with a replica of the Federation Star at the centre. Recipients are entitled to the postnominal letters SG. To date no award has been made.*

VALUE: —

A5. STAR OF COURAGE

Instituted: 1975.
Ribbon: Blood-red 32mm with a magenta central band 16mm wide.
Metal: Silver.
Size: 50mm.
Description: A seven-pointed, ribbed star surmounted by the heraldic shield of Australia and ensigned by a St Edward Crown affixed to a suspension bar inscribed FOR COURAGE.
Comments: *Subsequent awards are denoted by a silver bar bearing a replica of the star. Recipients are entitled to the postnominal letters SC. Since 1976 less than 60 Stars of Courage have been awarded. No awards were made in 1979 or 1982 and the most in any on year was 7 (1988 and 1991). One foreign award has been made, to Flight Lieutenant Holden, RNZAF, for his part in rescuing six trapped passengers from a helicopter crash in 1981.*

VALUE: £5000–12,000

A6. DISTINGUISHED SERVICE CROSS

Instituted: 1991.
Ribbon: Ochre-red flanked by silver-blue bands.
Metal: Nickel-silver.
Size: 41mm.
Description: (Obverse) a modified Maltese cross with a seven-pointed Federation Star at the centre and flames in the interstices. It is ensigned with a St Edward Crown affixed to a plain suspension bar. (Reverse) plain but for a horizontal panel giving details of the award.
Comments: *Nickel-silver bars are granted for subsequent awards and have a Federation Star at the centre. Recipients are entitled to the postnominal letters DSC. So far only two awards have been made (November 1993) to senior Army officers commanding Australian forces assisting the UN peace-keeping operations in Somalia.*

VALUE: Rare

A7. CONSPICUOUS SERVICE CROSS

Instituted: 1989.
Ribbon: 32mm wide, with alternate diagonal stripes of bush green and sandy gold 6mm wide.
Metal: Nickel-silver.
Size: 38mm.
Description: A modified Maltese cross with fluted rays between the arms. (Obverse) the constellation of the Southern Cross within laurel leaves, ensigned with a St Edward's Crown affixed to a plain suspension bar. (Reverse) a horizontal panel for details of the award.
Comments: *Instituted to award all ranks of the armed services for outstanding service and devotion to duty in non-warlike situations. Since its inception only 129 crosses have been awarded (29 to the Navy, 39 to the RAAF and 61 to the Army). Recipients are entitled to the postnominal letters CSC.*

VALUE: £500–1000

A8. NURSING SERVICE CROSS

Instituted: 1991.
Branch of Service: Members of the Nursing Services of the Army, RAN and RAAF.
Ribbon: 32mm red flanked by broad white stripes.
Metal: Silver.
Size: 43mm.
Description: A stepped cross with straight arms, with a red enamelled plain cross at the centre and ensigned with the St Edward Crown affixed to a plain suspension bar. (Reverse) a horizontal panel superimposed on a pattern of fluted rays.
Comments: *Awarded for outstanding devotion and competency in the performance of nursing duties in support of the armed forces. Recipients are entitled to the postnominal letters NSC. To date, only four crosses have been awarded, two each to members of the RAAF and Army Nursing Services.*

VALUE: Rare

A9. MEDAL FOR GALLANTRY

Instituted: 1991.
Ribbon: 32mm light orange with chevrons of deep orange, points upwards.
Metal: Silver-gilt.
Size: 38mm.
Description: (Obverse) Federation Star surrounded by flames and surmounted by a St Edward Crown affixed to a suspension bar inscribed FOR GALLANTRY; (reverse) horizontal panel on a background of fluted rays.
Comments: *Awarded to all ranks of the armed services for acts of gallantry in action in hazardous circumstances. To date 13 medals have been awarded.*

VALUE: Rare

A10. BRAVERY MEDAL

Instituted: 1975.
Ribbon: 32mm with 15 alternating stripes of blood-red and magenta.
Metal: Bronze.
Size: 38mm.
Description: (Obverse) heraldic shield and Federation Star on a circular zigzag border; (reverse) zigzag pattern.
Comments: *Awarded to civilians and members of the armed services in non-warlike conditions for acts of bravery in hazardous circumstances. Recipients are entitled to the postnominal letters BN. Some 307 medals have been awarded since 1976.*

VALUE: £500–2000

A11. DISTINGUISHED SERVICE MEDAL

Instituted: 1991.
Ribbon: 32mm silver-blue with three stripes of ochre-red.
Metal: Nickel-silver.
Size: 38mm.
Description: (Obverse) Federation Star with flames in the angles; (reverse) horizontal panel on a ground of fluted rays.
Comments: *Awarded to all ranks of the armed services for distinguished leadership in action. Recipients are entitled to the postnominal letters DSM. To date 21 awards of the DSM have been made, the first in November 1993 to Corporal Thomas Aitken as a section commander in Somalia during Operation Solace.*

VALUE: Rare

A12. PUBLIC SERVICE MEDAL

Instituted: 1989.
Ribbon: 32mm with 12 alternating stripes of green and gold of varying widths, the widest green on the left and widest gold on the right.
Metal: Nickel-silver.
Size: 38mm.
Description: (Obverse) an inner circle showing four planetary gears spaced equidistant from a central sun gear, surrounded by the inscription PUBLIC SERVICE. An outer circle shows 36 upright human figures representing a wide range of professions and activities. (Reverse) a wreath of mimosa surrounding the text FOR OUTSTANDING SERVICE.
Comments: *Awarded for outstanding public services at Commonwealth, State or Local Government levels. The number of medals allocated to each state is limited annually to 33 (commonwealth), 22 (New South Wales), 17 (Victoria), 11 (Queensland), 6 each (Western and Southern Australia), 3 (Tasmania) and 2 (Northern Territory). Awards may be made to Norfolk Island once every three years. Recipients are entitled to the postnominal letters PSM.*

VALUE: £100–200   *Miniature*   £10–15

A13. AUSTRALIAN POLICE MEDAL

Instituted: 1986.
Ribbon: 32mm white with a central broad dark blue stripes.
Metal: Nickel-silver.
Size: 38mm.
Description: (Obverse) effigy of Queen Elizabeth within a Federation Star, with an outer pattern of fluted rays; (reverse) wreath of golden wattle enclosing the inscriptions AUSTRALIAN POLICE MEDAL and FOR DISTINGUISHED SERVICE.
Comments: *Awarded for distinguished service among members of the Australian Federal Police and the forces of the states and territories. Awards are limited annually to no more than one per thousand members (or proportionately) in each force, plus one additional medal for the whole of Australia. Recipients are entitled to the postnominal letters APM.*

VALUE: £250–400   *Miniature*   £10–15

A14. AUSTRALIAN FIRE SERVICE MEDAL

Instituted: 1988.
Ribbon: 32mm central gold band bearing an irregular pattern of red flames and flanked by green stripes.
Metal: Cupro-nickel.
Size: 38mm.
Description: (Obverse) effigy of Queen Elizabeth superimposed on a Federation Star composed of flames; (reverse) inscriptions AUSTRALIA FIRE SERVICE MEDAL and FOR DISTINGUISHED SERVICE on a background of flames.
Comments: *Awarded for distinguished service among members of the fire services on the basis of one annually for every 1,000 full-time and one for every 25,000 part-time or volunteer firemen. Recipients are entitled to the postnominal letters AFSM.*

VALUE: £250–400   *Miniature*   £10–15

A15. MEDAL OF THE ORDER OF AUSTRALIA

Instituted: 1976.
Ribbon: Royal blue 32mm, with gold mimosa decoration (General Division), or edged with gold (Military Division).
Metal: Silver-gilt.
Size: 40mm.
Description: (Obverse) emblem of the Order of Australia surmounted by St Edward crown affixed to a plain suspension bar.
Comments: *The medal of the Order is awarded for meritorious service. Holders of the medal are entitled to the postnominals OAM.*

VALUE: £250–350   *Miniature*   £20–25

A16. CONSPICUOUS SERVICE MEDAL

Instituted: 1989.
Ribbon: 32mm wide with alternating diagonal stripes of bush green and sandy gold 3mm wide.
Metal: Nickel-silver.
Size: 38mm.
Description: (Obverse) the Southern Cross encircled by laurel leaves; (reverse) a horizontal panel on a ground of fluted rays.
Comments: *Awarded to all ranks of the armed forces for meritorious achievement in non-warlike situations. Recipients are entitled to the postnominal CSM.*

VALUE: £200–350   *Miniature*   £10–15

A17. ANTARCTIC MEDAL

Instituted: 1987.
Ribbon: 32mm snow-white moire with 3mm edges in three shades of blue merging with the white.
Metal: Nickel-silver.
Size: 38mm.
Description: An octagonal medal surmounted by an ice crystal device affixed to a plain suspension bar. (Obverse) a global map of the Southern Hemisphere showing Australia and Antarctica, and the legend FOR OUTSTANDING SERVICE IN THE ANTARCTIC; (reverse) a polar explorer outside Sir Douglas Mawson's hut, leaning into a blizzard and wielding an ice-axe.
Comments: *Awarded to persons who have given outstanding service in connection with Australian Antarctic expeditions. Recipients must have a minimum of 12 months service in Antarctica. Clasps are inscribed with the year of service or with TO 1992 for persons who have served in Antarctica over several years. A total of 50 medals were awarded between 1987 and 1994, 1987 being the commonest date.*

VALUE: £350–500   *Miniature*   £30–35

A18. COMMENDATION FOR GALLANTRY

Instituted: 1991.
Ribbon: Plain orange 32mm wide and 90mm long.
Metal: Silver-gilt.
Size: 22mm.
Description: The insignia consists of a row of flames tapering towards the ends, with a seven-pointed Federation Star superimposed.
Comments: *Instituted for civilian acts of gallantry considered to be of lesser magnitude than those for which the star or medal would be awarded. To date three awards have been made.*

VALUE: **Rare**

A19. COMMENDATION FOR BRAVE CONDUCT

Instituted: 1975.
Ribbon: Blood-red 32mm wide and 90mm long.
Metal: Silver-gilt.
Size: 30mm.
Description: A sprig of mimosa, mounted diagonally near the foot of the ribbon.
Comments: *Intended to reward acts of bravery worthy of recognition but less than those for which the CV, SC or BM would be considered appropriate. Some 474 commendations were awarded between 1975 and 1994.*

VALUE: £150–500   *Miniature*   £5–10

A20. COMMENDATION FOR DISTINGUISHED SERVICE

Instituted: 1991.
Ribbon: Ochre-red 32mm wide and 90mm long.
Metal: Nickel-silver.
Size: 22mm.
Description: A central Federation Star mounted on a row of flames tapering towards the end.
Comments: *Awarded for distinguished performance of duties. To date 33 awards have been made, including six to the RAN (Gulf War) and six to the Army (Somalia).*

VALUE: Rare

A21. AUSTRALIAN ACTIVE SERVICE MEDAL 1975

Instituted: 1991.
Ribbon: 32mm with a central red stripe, flanked by stripes of silver-green, light-green, gold, dark green and brown.
Metal: Nickel-silver.
Size: 38mm.
Description: (Obverse) a seven pointed Federation Star within a laurel wreath; (reverse) FOR ACTIVE SERVICE within a laurel wreath.
Clasps: Kuwait, Somalia, Vietnam 1975, Cambodia.
Comments: *Awarded for active service in various conflicts, denoted in each case by a campaign clasp. The Kuwait clasp recognised service in the Gulf theatre of operations between January 17, 1991 and February 28, 1991. Service before and after those dates was awarded by the Australian Service Medal with the appropriate clasp. The Somalia clasp was awarded for active service between January 10, 1993 and May 21, 1993 during Operation Solace. The Cambodia clasp was awarded for active service with UNTAC between October 1991 to October 1993. In August 1998 the Governor General altered the regulations and the Vietnam 1975 and Cambodia clasps are now awarded to the AASM. Holders of the Australian Service Medal (No. A22) will now receive the AASM.*

VALUE:

	RAN	RAAF	Army
Kuwait	£250–300 (937)	£300–450 (126)	£400–500 (41)
Somalia	£400–500 (20)	—	£250–350 (1016)

Miniature	£10–12

A22. AUSTRALIAN SERVICE MEDAL 1975

Instituted: 1991.
Ribbon: 32mm with a central brown stripe flanked by stripes of dark green, light green, gold and silver-green.
Metal: Nickel-silver.
Size: 38mm.
Description: (Obverse) a modified heraldic shield on a background of the lines of longitude, surmounted by a St Edward crown affixed to a plain suspension bar; (reverse) clusters of mimosa blossom, surrounding a Federation Star inscribed FOR SERVICE.
Clasps: Kashmir, Middle East, Vietnam 1975, Sinai, Uganda, Gulf, Iran-Iraq, Namibia, Peshawar, Kuwait, Iraq, West Sahara, Cambodia, Balkans, Somalia, Bougainville, Guatemala "Special Ops.".
Comments: *For service with multinational peacekeeping forces. In many cases, the appropriate UN medal was also awarded. Some 2,363 medals and clasps have been issued to the RAN, 632 to the RAAF and 2,618 to the Army.*

VALUE: £200–500   *Miniature*   £15–20

A23. POLICE OVERSEAS SERVICE MEDAL

Instituted: 1992.
Ribbon: 32mm with a chequerboard pattern of black and white squares.
Metal: Nickel-silver.
Size: 38mm.
Description: (Obverse) globe surmounted by a branch of wattle, the whole enclosed in a chequerboard pattern and surmounted by a St Edward crown affixed to a plain suspension bar.
Clasp: Cyprus, Cambodia (20), Somalia (2), Mozambique (20), Haiti (30) and Bouganville denoted by a globe emblem on the ribbon bar. Several officers have received two or three clasps and at least five officers have five clasps. A clasp for Timor has recently been authorised.
Comments: *Awarded to members of Australian police forces serving as members of peace-keeping missions under the auspices of the United Nations. Consequently recipients also receive the appropriate UN medals.*

VALUE: £200–500   *Miniature*   £25–30

A24. DEFENCE FORCE SERVICE MEDAL

Instituted: 1982.
Ribbon: 32mm azure blue with two gold stripes.
Metal: Cupro-nickel.
Size: 38mm.
Description: A circular chamfered medal bearing a Federation Star on which appears the insignia of the three defence forces. The medal is ensigned by the St Edward Crown affixed to a plain suspension bar. (Reverse) inscription FOR EFFICIENT SERVICE IN THE PERMANENT FORCES.
Clasp: Awarded for further periods of five years service.
Comments: *The medal is granted for 15 years service in the Defence Force, of which 12 years must have been as a member of the permanent Force.*

VALUE: £75–100   *Miniature*   £10–12

A25. RESERVE FORCE DECORATION

Instituted: 1982.
Ribbon: 32mm azure blue with a broad central band of gold.
Metal: Cupro-nickel.
Size: Oval 44mm high and 36mm wide.
Description: (Obverse) the joint services emblem on a radiate ground within a wreath of wattle; (reverse) inscribed FOR EFFICIENT SERVICE IN THE RESERVE FORCES.
Clasps: bar with the Royal Cypher flanked by sprigs of wattle.
Comments: *Awarded for a minimum of 15 years service as an officers in the Reserve Forces. Clasps for additional service of five years are granted.*

VALUE: £200–250

A26. RESERVE FORCE MEDAL

Instituted: 1982.
Ribbon: 32mm azure blue with narrow gold edges.
Metal: Cupro-nickel.
Size: Oval 44mm high and 36mm wide.
Description: (Obverse) insignia of the joint services on a rayed background; (reverse) inscription FOR EFFICIENT SERVICE IN THE RESERVE FORCES.
Comments: *Awarded to non-commissioned officers and other ranks of the reserve forces on completion of 15 years service. Clasps for further five-year periods of service have the Royal Cypher flanked by sprigs of wattle*

VALUE: £175–250

A26A. AUSTRALIAN DEFENCE FORCE LONG SERVICE MEDAL

Instituted: 1998.
Ribbon: 32mm with central 10mm panel of seven narrow alternating stripes of azure blue and gold flanked by 7mm broad azure stripes and 4mm gold edges.
Metal: Nickel-silver.
Size: 38mm.
Description: A circular medal ensigned with the St Edward Crown attached to the suspension bar. (Obverse) the Australian Defence Force emblem surrounded by two sprays of wattle leaves and blossom; (reverse) a central horizontal panel surrounded by the inscription FOR SERVICE IN THE AUSTRALIAN DEFENCE FORCE.
Clasps: Bar with the Royal Cypher flanked by sprigs of wattle.
Comments: *This medal supersedes the Defence Force Service Medal, the Reserve Force Decoration and Reserve Force Medal. It is awarded on completion of 15 years service, clasps being awarded for further periods of service.*

VALUE: —

A27. NATIONAL MEDAL

Instituted: 1975.
Ribbon: 32mm with 15 alternating gold and blue stripes.
Metal: Bronze.
Size: 38mm.
Description: (Obverse) arms of the Commonwealth of Australia on a ground of mimosa blossom within a recessed circle. Incuse inscription round the edge: THE NATIONAL MEDAL FOR SERVICE. (Reverse) plain.
Comments: *Awarded to members of the various uniformed services for long service and good conduct, being a minimum of 15 years in one service or an aggregate of 15 years in two or more services. An amendment by Letters Patent in 1987 extended the award of this medal to the prison services. Bars for further periods of 10 years service are available.*

VALUE: £75–100   *Miniature*   £8–12

A28. CHAMPION SHOTS MEDAL

Instituted: 1988.
Ribbon: 32mm central dark blue stripe flanked by red and light blue stripes.
Metal: Antiqued brass.
Size: 38mm.
Description: (Obverse) a wreathed vertical panel with the Southern Cross and two crossed rifles; (reverse) plain.
Comments: *Only three medals are awarded annually, to the respective champion shots of the RAN, RAAF and Army. Of the seven RAAF awards, Sgt Philip MacPherson has won the medal three times (1991–3) and Sgt Brett Graeme Hartman has won it four times (1988–90 and 1994).*

VALUE: Rare   *Miniature*   £10–12

A29. CIVILIAN SERVICE MEDAL, 1939–1945

Instituted: 1994.
Ribbon: 32mm ochre-red central stripe flanked by narrow white stripes and broad stripes of opal green towards the edges.
Metal: Bronze.
Size: 38mm.
Description: (Obverse) the Southern Cross superimposed on a globe surrounded by mimosa blossoms; (reverse) horizontal panel for the recipient's name, with 1939 above and 1945 below.
Comments: *Awarded to civilians who had assisted Australia's war effort in a wide variety of organisations and who served under quasi-military conditions for at least 180 days. The medal may be awarded posthumously and presented to the next-of-kin. It is estimated that up to 70,000 people are eligible for this medal.*

VALUE: £100–150   *Miniature*   £8–10

A30. AUSTRALIAN ACTIVE SERVICE MEDAL, 1945–1975

Instituted: 1995.
Ribbon: 32mm central thin red stripe flanked by narrow yellow stripes and broad stripes of pale blue, black and purple towards the edge.
Metal: Nickel-silver.
Size: 38mm.
Description: (Obverse) the seven-pointed Federation star surrounded by the legend THE AUSTRALIAN ACTIVE SERVICE MEDAL 1945–1975; (reverse) a wreath of mimosa sourrounding a plaque for the recipient's details.
Clasp: Korea, Malaya, Malaysia, Vietnam.
Comments: *This medal fills a gap between the Australian Service Medal (no. 190) and the current Australian Service Medal which was instituted in 1975. It is awarded to all ranks of the armed forces for warlike service in theatres of operation between the end of the Second World War and February 13, 1975. The medal is worn immediately after any Second World War awards and before any other campaign awards.*

VALUE·   £150–250   *Miniature*   £10–12

A31. AUSTRALIAN SERVICE MEDAL, 1945–1975

Instituted: 1995.
Ribbon: 32mm central thin yellow stripe flanked by narrow green stripes flanked by grey with wide navy blue stripe at left and pale blue at right.
Metal: Nickel-silver.
Size: 38mm.
Description: (Obverse) the arms of the Commonwealth of Australia surrounded by the legend THE AUSTRALIAN SERVICE MEDAL 1945–1975; (reverse) seven-pointed Federation star with space for recipient's details, surrounded by mimosa leaves.
Clasp: Japan, PNG (Papua New Guinea), Indonesia, Middle East, Berlin, Kashmir, Korea, FESR, Thai-Malay, Thailand, W New Guinea, SW Pacific.
Comments: *This medal fills a gap between the Australian Service Medal (no. 190) and the current Australian Service Medal which was instituted in 1975. It is awarded to all ranks of the Australian Defence Force for non-warlike service in theatres of operation between the end of the Second World War and February 13, 1975. It is estimated that about 65,000 people are eligible for this medal. The medal is worn after campaign awards and before long service and foreign awards.*

VALUE: £100–300   *Miniature*   £12–15

A32. UNIT CITATION FOR GALLANTRY

Instituted: 1991.
Ribbon: Green encased in a silver-gilt rectagular frame with flame decoration. A seven-pointed Federation Star in silver-gilt in worn in the centre.
Comments: *This system was borrowed from the USA, many Australian formations and units receiving American unit citations during the Vietnam War. So far, however, no Unit Citations for Gallantry have been awarded. The citation is worn by all members of the unit receiving the citation for extraordinary gallantry in action, and appears on the right breast (Army and RAAF) or below the medal ribbons on the left breast (RAN). So far no Unit Citations for Gallantry have been awarded.*

VALUE: —

A33. MERITORIOUS UNIT CITATION

Instituted: 1991.
Ribbon: Gold encased in a rhodium-plated silver frame with flame decoration. A rhodium-plated silver Federation Star is mounted in the centre.
Comments: *Awarded to members of a unit for sustained outstanding service in warlike operations. So far only three Meritorious Unit Citations have been issued, all to units of the RAN for service in the Gulf War, 1990–91.*

VALUE: Rare

A34. AUSTRALIAN MERCHANT NAVY SERVICE CROSS

Instituted: 1998.
Branch of Service: Australian Merchant Navy.
Ribbon: Blue with narrow white central stripe and white edges.
Metal: Silver.
Size: 36mm.
Description: A cross fourchée on which is superimposed a small circular medallion bearing the insignia of the Australian Merchant Navy. Fitted with bar suspender.
Clasp: A gold laurel spray.
Comments: *This semi-officialmedal was created in 1998 to mark United Nations Year of the Ocean, September 24 being designated by the UN International Maritime Organisation as Day of the Merchant Mariner. The cross is awarded to officers for 15 years bona fide service on Articles of Agreement. Clasps are awarded for each additional 15 years service.*

VALUE: —

A35. AUSTRALIAN MERCHANT NAVY MERITORIOUS MEDAL

Instituted: 1998.
Branch of Service: Australian Merchant Navy.
Ribbon: Watered silk white with broad blue edges and central stripe.
Metal: Silver.
Size: 38mm.
Description: (Obverse) the crowned insignia of the Merchant Navy; (reverse) AUSTRALIAN MERCHANT NAVY MERITORIOUS MEDAL. Fitted with an ornamental bar suspender.
Comments: *This semi-official medal is awarded for an exceptional contribution to the Merchant Navy over a long period of time, but may also be awarded for an individual act of bravery by a seafarer.*

VALUE: —

A36. AUSTRALIAN MERCHANT NAVY COMMENDATION

Instituted: 1998.
Branch of Service: Australian Merchant Navy.
Ribbon: Watered silk with a dark blue centre, white stripes and light blue edges.
Metal: Silver.
Size: 36mm.
Description: A laurel wreath joined at the top by a merchant navy crown attached to a ring for suspension.
Comments: *This semi-official medal is awarded for an ongoing or individual contribution by a person in one of the many fields of maritime endeavour including education, research and development, maritime business, industrial relations and professional achievement.*

VALUE: —

A37. GALLIPOLI MEDAL

Instituted: 25 April 1990.
Branch of Service: ANZAC veterans of the Gallipoli campaign.
Ribbon: Central broad deep blue stripe, flanked by narrow crimson stripes and broad edges of yellow and light blue respectively.
Metal: Bronze.
Size: 36mm.
Description: A small circular medal superimposed on an eight-pointed star with ring suspension. (Obverse) a Tudor crown surrounded by the inscription GALLIPOLI 1914-15.
Comments: *This medal was originally approved by King George V but was never issued at the time. In April 1990 it was presented to the 200 surviving Gallipoli veterans to mark the 75th anniversary of the ill-fated landings on the Turkish coast.*

VALUE: —

A38. ARMISTICE REMEMBRANCE MEDAL

Instituted: 2000.
Branch of Service: Surviving veterans of the First World War.
Ribbon: Red with a black central stripe and narrow black edges.
Metal: Silver.
Size: 36mm.
Description: (Obverse) a 'Digger' in the uniform of the First World War with the legend 80TH ANNIVERSARY ARMISTICE REMEMBRANCE MEDAL; (reverse) the words LEST WE FORGET in three lines within a wreath of ferns surmounted by a seven-pointed star. Fitted with a suspension bar with a Tudor crown on both sides.
Comments: *Awarded to all veterans of the First World War who were still alive on 11 November 1998, the 80th anniversary of the Armistice.*

VALUE: —

A39. NEW SOUTH WALES CORRECTIVE SERVICE BRAVERY MEDAL

Instituted: 1989.
Ribbon: Dark blue with a broad crimson central stripe.
Metal: Silver-gilt.
Description: A cross pattée with radiations in the angles and surmounted by a St. Edward's crown fitted to a ring for suspension. (Obverse) the arms of New South Wales within a circular band inscribed CORRECTIVE SERVICE N.S.W., with a scroll at the foot inscribed FOR BRAVERY; (reverse) plain.
Comments: *Awarded to prison officers for bravery.*

VALUE: —

A40. NEW SOUTH WALES CORRECTIVE SERVICE EXEMPLARY CONDUCT CROSS

Instituted: 1989.
Ribbon: Navy blue with a broad gold central stripe.
Metal: Silver.
Descrpiton: A seven-pointed star surmounted by a large St. Edward's crown fitted to a suspension ring. (Obverse) the arms of New South Wales within a circular band inscribed CORRECTIVE SERVICE N.S.W., with a scroll at the foot inscribed EXEMPLARY CONDUCT; (reverse) plain.
Comments: *Awarded to prison officers for exemplary conduct.*

VALUE: —

A41. NEW SOUTH WALES CORRECTIVE SERVICE MERITORIOUS SERVICE MEDAL

Instituted: 1989.
Ribbon: Red with a broad central gold stripe.
Metal: Bronze.
Size: 36mm.
Description: An elongated circle fitted with a suspension bar. (Obverse) the arms of New South Wales, with N.S.W. CORRECTIVE SERVICE at the top and LONG SERVICE at the foot; (reverse) FOR TWENTY YEARS SERVICE in four lines within a wreath.
Comments: *Awarded for 20 years service in the New South Wales prison service. Originally a bronze clasp for 30 years service was added after a further ten years, but this was replaced on 14 May 1999 by a bronze clasp for 25 years and silver clasps for 30, 35 and 40 years service.*

VALUE: —

A42. NEW SOUTH WALES CORRECTIVE SERVICE LONG SERVICE MEDAL

Instituted: 1989.
Ribbon: Navy blue with two silver stripes.
Metal: Bronze.
Size: 36mm.
Description: A circular medal fitted with a plain suspension bar. (Obverse) the crowned emblem of the Corrective Service with a wreath at the foot; (reverse) a laurel branch round the left side, with the words FOR FIFTEEN YEARS SERVICE in four lines on the right.
Comments: *Awarded for 15 years service in the New South Wales prison service.*

VALUE: —

A43. COMMISSIONER'S VALOUR AWARD

Instituted: 1987.
Ribbon: Light blue with narrow white stripes towards the edges and dark blue edges.
Metal: Silver.
Description: A cross pattée with a crowned and enamelled centrepiece bearing the insignia of the New South Wales Police Service within a wreath, inscribed FOR BRAVERY.
Comments: *Awarded to police officers where an act of conspicuous merit involving exceptional bravery is in evidence. It is very sparingly awarded, although eight awards were made in both 1993 and 1994.*

VALUE: —

A44. COMMISSIONER'S COMMENDATION FOR COURAGE

Instituted: 1970.
Ribbon: Light blue with a narrow central white stripe and narrow white edges.
Description: The insignia of the New South Wales Police Service affixed directly to the ribbon.
Comments: *Awarded to police officers where the risk to life has been less apparent, but where sufficient courage has been shown under hazardous circumstances to warrant the award. There is no restriction on the number of awards and about 90 are made annually.*

VALUE: —

A45. COMMISSIONER'S COMMENDATION FOR SERVICE

Instituted: 1970.
Ribbon: Light blue with narrow white edges.
Description: The insignia of the New South Wales Police Service affixed directly to the ribbon.
Comments: *Awarded to police officers for outstanding service. About ten commendations are awarded annually.*

VALUE: —

A46. COMMISSIONER'S UNIT CITATION

Instituted: 1994.
Description: A silver bar in the form of a wreath containing a light blue insert.
Comments: *Awaded to units, patrols, groups, squads and commands where outstanding service involving bravery or actions of obvious merit have been evident. The emblem is worn by each member of the unit, while the unit receives a framed citation for display. About five citations are awarded annually.*

VALUE: —

A47. QUEENSLAND PRISON SERVICE SUPERINDENDENT'S LONG SERVICE MEDAL

Instituted: Before 1988.
Ribbon: Dark blue with three narrow silver stripes.
Description: An eight-pointed Maltese cross superimposed on a wreath surmounted by a St. Edward's crown attached to a ring for suspension from a rectangular bar inscribed MERITORIOUS SERVICE. The top of the ribbon has a similar brooch bar with the recipient's details engraved on the reverse. The centre of the cross has the arms of Queensland.

VALUE: —

A48. QUEENSLAND PRISON SERVICE OFFICERS LONG SERVICE MEDAL

Instituted: Before 1988.
Ribbon: Silver with two narrow dark blue stripes.
Description: A circular medal fitted with a loop for suspension via a ring attached to an ornamental rectangular bar. The brooch bar at the top of the ribbon bears the recipient's personal details on the reverse. (Obverse) the crowned and wreathed insignia of the Queensland Prison Service with the inscription LONG AND MERITORIOUS SERVICE round the foot.

VALUE: —

A49. QUEENSLAND POLICE VALOUR AWARD

Instituted: 1993.
Ribbon: Maroon, light blue and dark blue in equal widths.
Metal: Silver.
Description: A Maltese cross superimposed on a wreath, with an enamelled centrepiece featuring the St. Edward's crown within a wreath and surrounded by the inscription QUEENSLAND POLICE VALOUR AWARD.
Comments: *This decoration is apparently similar to the Queensland Police Award which was discontinued in the 1930s.*

VALUE: —

A49. HUMANITARIAN OVERSEAS SERVICE MEDAL

Instituted: 2000.
Ribbon: Green with a central gold stripe.
Metal: Nickel-silver.
Size: 38mm.
Description: A circular medal (obverse) a stylised eucalyptus tree surrounded by a ring of gum nuts; (reverse) a ring of gum nuts with the recipients details engraved in the centre.
Comments: *This medal is intended to be awarded to civilians who have provided outstanding humanitarian service overseas (although service personnel may be considered for the award in exceptional circumstances) and is believed to be the first medal of its kind. As most government employees will be eligible for the Australian Service medals, it is anticipated that this medal will be awarded to non-government employees or volunteers and as there is no time limit to the award it can be awarded retrospectively.*

VALUE: —

THE ORDER OF PRECEDENCE IN NEW ZEALAND
(including British Awards)

Victoria Cross
George Cross
Order of the Garter
Knights Grand Cross, The Most Honourable Order of the Bath
Order of Merit
New Zealand Cross
Baronet's Badge
Knights Grand Cross, The Most Distinguished Order of St Michael and St George (GCMG)
Knights Grand Cross, The Royal Victorian Order
Knights Grand Cross, The Most Excellent Order of the British Empire
Order of Companions of Honour
Order of New Zealand
Knight Commander, The Most Honourable Order of the Bath
Knight Commander, The Most Distinguished Order of St Michael and St George
Knight Commander, The Royal Victorian Order
Knight Commander, The Most Excellent Order of the British Empire
Knight Bachelors badge
Companion, The Most Honourable Order of the Bath
Companion, The Most Distinguished Order of St Michael and St George
Commander, The Royal Victorian Order
Commander, The Most Excellent Order of the British Empire
Distinguished Service Order
Lieutenant, The Royal Victorian Order
Officer, The Most Excellent Order of the British Empire
Queen's Service Order
Imperial Service Order
Member, The Royal Victorian Order
Member, The Most Excellent Order of the British Empire
Royal Red Cross (Member)
Distinguished Service Cross
Military Cross
Distinguished Flying Cross
Air Force Cross
Royal Red Cross (Associate)
Order of St John (All classes)
Albert Medal
Distinguished Conduct Medal
Conspicuous Gallantry Medal
George Medal
Queen's Police Medal for Gallantry
Distinguished Service Medal
Military Medal
Distinguished Flying Medal

Air Force Medal
Empire Gallantry Medal
Queen's Gallantry Medal
Royal Victorian Medals
Queen's Service Medal
British Empire Medal
Queen's Police Medal for Distinguished Service
Queen's Fire Service Medal for Distinguished Service
War Medals in order of campaign
New Zealand General Service Medal
Polar Medal
Imperial Service Medal
Coronation and Jubilee Medals in date order
New Zealand 1990 Commemoration Medal
New Zealand Suffrage Centennial Medal 1993
New Zealand Meritorious Service Medal
New Zealand Armed Forces Award
New Zealand Army Long Service and Good Conduct Medal
Royal New Zealand Navy Long Service and Good Conduct Medal
Royal New Zealand Air Force Long Service and Good Conduct Medal
New Zealand Police Long Service and Good Conduct Medal
New Zealand Fire Brigades Long Service and Good Conduct Medal
New Zealand Prison Service Medal
New Zealand Traffic Service Medal
Colonial Auxiliary Forces Decoration
Colonial Auxiliary Forces Long Service Medal
New Zealand Efficiency Decoration
New Zealand Efficiency Medal
Royal New Zealand Naval Volunteer Reserve Decoration
Royal Naval Reserve Decoration
Royal New Zealand Naval Volunteer Reserve Long Service and Good Conduct Medal
Royal Naval Reserve Long Service and Good Conduct Medal
Air Efficiency Award
Queen's Medal for Champion Shots of the New Zealand Naval Forces
Queen's Medal for Champion Shots of the Military Forces
Queen's Medal for Champion Shots of the Air Forces
Cadet Forces Medal
Rhodesia Medal 1980
Service Medal of the Order of St John
Other Commonwealth Members' Orders, Decorations and Medals in date of award
Approved Foreign Orders, Decorations and Medals in order of date of award

---

At the time of going to press no definitive revised Order of Wear including the new awards and decorations was available. The above list is the Order of Wear prior to the new changes. It is hoped that the new Order of Wear will be published in a future edition of the Medal Yearbook.

New Zealand
medals

Between 1848 and 1996 New Zealanders were eligible for the various British or Imperial honours and awards. The first step towards an independent honours system was taken in 1975 when the Queen's Service Order and Queen's Service Medal were instituted.

Thereafter a range of distinctive New Zealand medals was gradually adopted for the defence forces, the police, fire and prison services, this culminated in the introduction of a totally separate New Zealand Royal Honours System in May 1996. With a few exceptions, all honours and awards are conferred by, or in the name of, the sovereign (Queen Elizabeth) on the advice of Her Majesty's New Zealand ministers. A distinctive feature of many New Zealand orders, decorations and medals is the influence of Maori art forms.

Medals and decorations which were specific to New Zealand but made under Royal Warrants prior to 1975 are listed in the main body of this book. A new range of New Zealand gallantry and bravery awards is in the process of being developed, and this includes the creation of a Victoria Cross for New Zealand as well as the highest non-combatant bravery award, the New Zealand Cross. The new medals and decorations are given below in order of precedence. To date very few of these awards have come onto the market. and information on their rarity and other missing details have not been available, so it has been decided to omit prices in this section. However, it is hoped to include them and the missing information in future editions.

NZ1. VICTORIA CROSS FOR NEW ZEALAND

Instituted: June 1998.
Ribbon: Crimson 38mm wide.
Metal: Bronze.
Size: 35mm at each axis.
Description: A cross pattée with raised edges, identical to the British and Australian Victoria Crosses (MYB24 and A1).
Comments: *Although identical to the existing VC, awards will be made under a New Zealand, as opposed to a British, Royal Warrant. Recipients are entitled to the postnominal letters VC.*

NZ2. NEW ZEALAND CROSS

Instituted: 1998.
Ribbon:
Metal: Silver with gold applique.
Size:
Description: Similar to the original New Zealand Cross of 1869 (MYB25) but incorporating changes which were first proposed in 1885 and only now implemented, viz. fern fronds have replaced laurel leaves.
Comments: *The premier civilian award for bravery, it now supersedes the George Cross so far as New Zealand citizens are concerned. Recipients are entitled to the postnominal letters NZC.*

NZ3. ORDER OF NEW ZEALAND

Instituted: 1987.
Ribbon: Red ochre with a narrow white stripe towards either edge.
Metal: 9 carat gold.
Description: An oval medal decorated with coloured enamels bearing in the centre the heraldic shield of New Zealand within a Kowhaiwhai rafter pattern.
Comments: *Instituted as a first-level non-titular order, it is modelled on the British Order of Merit (1917) and the Order of the Companions of Honour (1917). The Order comprises the Queen as Sovereign and no more than 20 ordinary members who are entitled to the postnominal letters ONZ. Additional members may be appointed in commemoration of important royal, state or national occasions. Honorary membership includes citizens of Commonwealth nations of which the Queen is not Head of State, and of foreign countries. The badge must be returned on the death of the holder. No miniature exists, but a lapel badge was instituted in 1990.*

NZ4. NEW ZEALAND ORDER OF MERIT

Instituted: 1996.
Ribbon: Plain red ochre (kokowai).
Comments: *An order of chivalry designed alongBritish lines and intended to replace the various British orders to which New Zealanders were formerly appointed. It consists of five classes whose insignia are noted separately below. In addition, there is a collar of the order, worn only by the Sovereign of the Order and the Chancellor (the Governor-General of New Zealand). The collar is composed of links of the central badge and gold koru (in the form of the letter S) with a pendant badge featuring the New Zealand arms. Distinctive lapel badges denoting membership of the Order are worn in civilian clothes.*

Breast star

NZ4. NEW ZEALAND ORDER OF MERIT (contd.)

KNIGHTS AND DAMES GRAND COMPANIONS (GNZM)

Badge: A cross in white enamel set in silver-gilt with, in the centre, a medallion comprising the New Zealand arms in coloured enamel surrounded by a circle of green enamel inscribed in gold FOR MERIT / TOHU HIRANGA and surmounted by a royal crown. The badge is worn from a sash over the right shoulder and resting on the left hip.

Star: A gold breast star of eight points, each arm bearing in relief a representation of a fern frond, superimposed in the centre of which is a smaller representation of the badge of the order.

KNIGHTS AND DAMES COMPANIONS (KNZM /DNZM)

A badge and breast star similar to that above, except that the badge is worn from either a neck ribbon or a bow on the left shoulder. The breast star is in silver, with the badge of the order in the centre.

COMPANIONS (CNZM)

A badge similar to that above, worn from a neck ribbon or a bow on the left shoulder.

OFFICERS (ONZM)

A smaller representation of the badge in silver-gilt, with the motto in green enamel. Worn from a ribbon on the left lapel or from a ribbon tied in a bow and worn on the left shoulder.

MEMBERS (MNZM)

Badge as for Officers but in silver.

NZ5. NEW ZEALAND GALLANTRY STAR

Instituted: 1998.
Branch of Service: New Zealand armed forces.
Ribbon: Red with a blue central stripe bordered by thin white stripes.
Metal: Silver and gilt.
Size: 45mm.
Description: A faceted silver 8-pointed star surmounted by a gilt crown surrounded by a wreath of fern. With ring suspension.
Comments: *This decoration supersedes the British Distinguished Service Order, Distinguished Conduct Medal and Conspicuous Gallantry Medal. Recipients are entitled to the postnominal letters NZGS.*

NZ6. QUEEN'S SERVICE ORDER

Instituted: 1975.
Ribbon: Narrow red ochre edges with a centre of alternating diagonal steps in ochre, white and black descending from left to right. The design is based on the Maori Poutama (stepped) pattern used in Tukutuku wall panels to represent the stairway to heaven, but here denoting the steps of achievement.
Metal: Frosted sterling silver.
Description: A badge based on the stylised representation of a manuka flower, consisting of five large and five small stylised petals. Superimposed in the centre is a silver-gilt medallion bearing the crowned effigy of the Queen within a circle of red enamel bearing the name of the sub-division and surmounted by St Edward's Crown. The full name of the recipient is engraved on the reverse.
Comments: *The single non-titular order is divided into two divisions for Community Service and for Public Services respectively. Ordinary membership is limited to 30 appointments per annum. Members of the Royal Family may be appointed as Extra Companions and include so far the Duke of Edinburgh (1981), Prince Charles (1983) and the Princess Royal (1990). Recipients are entitled to the postnominal letters QSO, and appropriate lapel badges for everyday wear.*

NZ7. NEW ZEALAND GALLANTRY DECORATION

Instituted: 1998.
Branch of Service: New Zealand armed forces.
Ribbon: Red with central blue stripe and two equal white stripes.
Metal: Silver and gilt.
Size: 46mm.
Description: A simple faceted silver cross surmounted by the royal crown and fern frond wreath emblem. With ring suspension.
Comments: *This decoration supersedes the British DSC, MC, DFC, AFC, DSM, MM, DFM and AFM. Recipients are entitled to the postnominal letters NZGD.*

NZ8. NEW ZEALAND BRAVERY STAR

Instituted: 1998.
Branch of Service: New Zealand police forces, fire brigades and civilians.
Ribbon: Blue with two narrow red stripes.
Metal: Silver and gilt.
Size: 46mm.
Description: An 8-pointed faceted star with four long and four short points in the angles surmounted by a gilt royal crown and fern frond wreath emblem. With ring suspension.
Comments: *This decoration superseded the British George Medal and is the second grade award for civilian acts of bravery. Recipients are entitled to the postnominal letters NZBS.*

NZ9. NEW ZEALAND BRAVERY DECORATION

Instituted: 1998.
Branch of Service: Civilians and members of the armed forces in non-combat situations.
Ribbon: Blue with three equal stripes of red.
Metal: Silver and gilt.
Size: 45mm.
Description: A cross pattée surmounted by a small faceted four-pointed star with the royal crown and fern frond wreath emblem. With ring suspension.
Comments: *This decoration is awarded for acts of bravery in a non-combat situation. It supersedes the British QGM, QPM, QFSM, AFC and AFM. Recipients are entitled to the postnominal letters NZBD.*

NZ10. NEW ZEALAND GALLANTRY MEDAL

Instituted: 1998.
Branch of Service: New Zealand armed forces.
Ribbon: red with two central blue stripes and two outer white stripes.
Metal: Bronze.
Size: 38mm.
Description: (Obverse) the Rank-Broadley effigy of Her Majesty Queen Elizabeth II with the legend ELIZABETH II QUEEN OF NEW ZEALAND; (reverse) FOR GALLANTRY/MO TE TOANGA surrounded by a fern frond wreath with the royal crown above.
Comments: *This decoration replaces the Mention in Despatches. Recipients are entitled to the postnominal letters NZGM.*

NZ11. NEW ZEALAND BRAVERY MEDAL

Instituted: 1998.
Branch of Service: Civilians or members of the New Zealand armed forces in a non-combat situation.
Ribbon: Blue with four red stripes.
Metal: Bronze.
Size: 38mm.
Description: (Obverse) the Rank-Broadley effigy of Her Majesty Queen Elizabeth II with the legend ELIZABETH II QUEEN OF NEW ZEALAND; (reverse) FOR BRAVERY/MO TE MAIA surrounded by a fern frond wreath with the royal crown above.
Comments: *This decoration replaces the Queen's Commendations for Brave Conduct and Valuable Service in the Air. Recipients are entitled to the postnominal letters NZBM.*

NZ12. QUEEN'S SERVICE MEDAL

Instituted: 1975.
Ribbon: Same as the Queen's Service Order.
Metal: Silver.
Size: 38mm.
Description: (Obverse) effigy of Queen Elizabeth surrounded by the royal styles and titles; (reverse) New Zealand arms with THE QUEEN'S SERVICE MEDAL round the top. Two versions of the reverse exist, inscribed at the foot either FOR COMMUNITY SERVICE or FOR PUBLIC SERVICES. The medal is fitted with a suspension ring.
Comments: *Awards are made for valuable voluntary service to the community or meritorious and faithful services to the Crown or similar services within the public sector. Military service is ineligible. The name of the recipient is engraved on the rim. Recipients are entitled to the postnominal letters QSM.*

NZ13. NEW ZEALAND SERVICE MEDAL 1946–1949

Instituted: 1995.
Branch of Service: New Zealand armed forces, merchant navy and civil airline crews.
Ribbon: 32mm white with a central red stripe and black stripes at the edges.
Metal: Rhodium plated steel.
Size: 38mm.
Description: (Obverse) New Zealand arms; (reverse) FOR SERVICE TO NEW ZEALAND 1946–1949 with a fern frond below.
Comments: *Awarded to about 7300 personnel despatched direct from New Zealand who had not had previous service in the Second World War, as well as about 5,000 troops stationed in Italy at the end of the war who were then sent to the Far East to take part in the police and peacekeeping operations in Japan between March 23, 1946 and March 31, 1949, a minimum of 28 days' service being required.*

NZ14. NEW ZEALAND GENERAL SERVICE MEDAL (WARLIKE OPERATIONS)

Instituted: 1995.
Branch of Service: New Zealand armed forces.
Ribbon: 32mm dark blue with a central black stripe flanked by red stripes.
Metal: Silver.
Size: 38mm.
Description: (Obverse) crowned effigy of Queen Elizabeth; (reverse) THE NEW ZEALAND GENERAL SERVICE MEDAL within a wreath of pohutakawa blossom, fern fronds and kowhai blossom, ensigned by a royal crown affixed to a plain suspension bar.
Clasps: Malaya 1960–64, Kuwait.
Comments: *Awarded for service in warlike operations.*

NZ15. NEW ZEALAND GENERAL SERVICE MEDAL (PEACEKEEPING OPERATIONS)

Instituted: 1995.
Branch of Service: New Zealand armed forces.
Ribbon: 32mm dark blue with a white central stripe flanked by narrow red stripes.
Metal: Bronze.
Size: 38mm.
Description: As above.
Clasps: Mozambique, Cambodia, Peshawar, Somalia, Arabian Gulf, Sinai, Iraq, Bouganville, Korea 1954-57.
Comments: *Awarded for peacekeeping operations. The relevant UN medals were also awarded.*

NZ16. NEW ZEALAND 1990 COMMEMORATION MEDAL

Instituted: 1990.
Ribbon: 32mm nine narrow stripes, black at the centre flanked by alternate white and red ochre.
Metal: Silver-gilt.
Size: 38mm.
Description: (Obverse) effigy of Queen Elizabeth with inscription ELIZABETH II . QUEEN OF NEW ZEALAND incuse on a raised rim; (reverse) stylised Kotuku or White Heron with inscription NEW ZEALAND 1990 COMMEMORATION.
Comments: *Awarded during the sesquicentennial year of British annexation to recognise achievements of New Zealanders in community service and the public services or their contribution to the country. The medal is accompanied by a certificate.*

NZ17. NEW ZEALAND MERITORIOUS SERVICE MEDAL

Instituted: 1985.
Branch of Service: NCOs of the rank of sergeant or petty officer in the armed forces.
Ribbon: 32mm crimson with a narrow green central stripe.
Metal: Silver.
Size: 38mm.
Description: (Obverse) bare-headed effigy of Queen Elizabeth; (reverse) FOR MERITORIOUS SERVICE within a laurel wreath surmounted by a royal crown and the legend NEW ZEALAND.
Comments: *Awarded for a minimum of 21 years full-time service in the armed forces, although this may be reduced to 18 years in the case of those invalided out of the services on grounds of disability.*

NZ18. NEW ZEALAND ARMED FORCES AWARD

Instituted: 1985.
Branch of Service: Officers of the armed forces.
Ribbon: 32mm dark blue, crimson and light blue with a central stripe of black.
Metal: Silver.
Size: 38mm.
Description: (Obverse) crowned effigy of Queen Elizabeth; (reverse) crossed swords, eagle and naval crown with two fronds below and inscription NEW ZEALAND ARMED FORCES AWARD.
Comments: *Awarded to commissioned officers of the armed services for 15 years full-time service back dated to 1977. Clasps for each additional 15 years may be awarded.*

NZ19. ROYAL NEW ZEALAND NAVY LONG SERVICE MEDAL

Instituted: 1985.
Branch of Service: Royal New Zealand Navy.
Ribbon: 32mm dark blue edged in white.
Metal: Silver.
Size: 38mm.
Description: (Obverse) uncrowned effigy of Queen Elizabeth; (reverse) HMS *Victory* surrounded by the inscription FOR LONG SERVICE AND GOOD CONDUCT.
Comments: *Awarded for naval ratings with 15 years service. Clasps may be awarded for each additional 15 years, denoted in undress uniform by a silver rosette on the ribbon bar.*

NZ20. NEW ZEALAND ARMY LONG SERVICE & GOOD CONDUCT MEDAL

Instituted: 1985.
Branch of Service: New Zealand Army, Regular Forces.
Ribbon: 32mm crimson edged in white.
Metal: Silver.
Size: 36mm.
Description: (Obverse) crowned effigy of Queen Elizabeth; (reverse) FOR LONG SERVICE AND GOOD CONDUCT attached to an ornamental title bar bearing the words NEW ZEALAND in raised lettering.
Comments: *Similar to the British Army LS&GC Medal (229) but with a distinctive New Zealand suspension bar. Only soldiers of the Regular Force serving from December 1, 1977 onwards, are eligible for this medal, a minimum of 15 years full-time irreproachable service being required. Clasps for additional periods of 15 years may be granted.*

NZ21. ROYAL NEW ZEALAND AIR FORCE LONG SERVICE MEDAL

Instituted: 1985.
Branch of Service: Royal New Zealand Air Force.
Ribbon: 32mm equal stripes of dark blue and crimson edged in white.
Metal: Silver.
Size: 36mm.
Description: (Obverse) uncrowned effigy of Queen Elizabeth; (reverse) an eagle with outstretched wings surmounted by a royal crown encircled by the inscription FOR LONG SERVICE AND GOOD CONDUCT.
Comments: *This medal replaces the award of the British RAF LS&GC Medal (MY 268). It is, in fact, indistinguishable from the British award except for the recipient's details engraved on the rim.*

NZ22. NEW ZEALAND TERRITORIAL SERVICE MEDAL

Ribbon: 38mm gold edged in crimson.
Comments: *This award is now obsolete, and further details are required. It appears to have been the New Zealand equivalent of the Efficiency Decoration (MY236).*

NZ23. NEW ZEALAND LONG AND EFFICIENT SERVICE MEDAL

Ribbon: 32mm crimson with two white stripes towards the centre.
Comments: *This medal is now obsolete, and further details are required. It appears to have been the New Zealand equivalent of the Efficiency Medal (MY237).*

NZ24. NEW ZEALAND POLICE LONG SERVICE & GOOD CONDUCT MEDAL

Instituted: 1976.
Ribbon: 32mm crimson with a central dark blue stripe flanked with white stripes.
Metal: Silver.
Size: 38mm.
Description: (Obverse) crowned effigy of Queen Elizabeth; (reverse) St Edward's Crown, sceptre and sword on a cushion within a wreath of oak leaves and fern fronds, surrounded by the inscription NEW ZEALAND POLICE—FOR LONG SERVICE AND GOOD CONDUCT.
Comments: *This medal is similar to the NZ Police LS&GC Medal (MY283) issued under Imperial Warrant, but differs in the ribbon and the inscription on the reverse. Awards made to police officers employed on or after January 1, 1976, with a qualifying period of service of 14 years. Clasps for additional periods of seven years are also awarded.*

NZ25. NEW ZEALAND PRISON SERVICE MEDAL

Instituted: 1981.
Ribbon: 32mm crimson with a central dark blue stripe flanked by narrow green stripes.
Metal: Silver.
Size: 36mm.
Description: (Obverse) crowned effigy of Queen Elizabeth II; (reverse) St Edward's crown and inscription NEW ZEALAND PRISON SERVICE FOR LONG SERVICE AND GOOD CONDUCT.
Comments: *Awarded for 14 years service with bars further 7 year periods.*

NZ26. NEW ZEALAND FIRE BRIGADES LONG SERVICE AND GOOD CONDUCT MEDAL

Instituted: 1976.
Ribbon: 32mm vermilion with a central black stripe flanked by narrow yellow stripes.
Metal: Silver.
Size: 38mm.
Description: (Obverse) crowned effigy of Queen Elizabeth (reverse) NEW ZEALAND FIRE BRIGADES— FOR LONG SERVICE AND GOOD CONDUCT above a fern frond.
Comments: *Originally awarded for 14 years full or part time services as a fireman, but amended by Royal Warrant (1981) to include fire brigades maintained or operated by companies as well as the forces under the control of the NZ Fire Service Commission. Clasps are awarded every additional period of seven years service.*

NZ27. NEW ZEALAND SUFFRAGE CENTENNIAL MEDAL

Instituted: 1993.
Ribbon: 32mm purple with narrow central stripes of white, yellow and white.
Metal: Antiqued bronze.
Size: 38mm.
Description: (Obverse) crowned effigy of Queen Elizabeth; (reverse) wreath of fern and camellia enclosing the inscription 1893 THE NEW ZEALAND SUFFRAGE CENTENNIAL 1993.
Comments: *Awarded to selected persons who by their virtues, talents and loyalty have made a recognised contribution to the rights of women in New Zealand or to women's issues in New Zealand. It was only awarded during the centennial year of the granting of votes to women—New Zealand being the first country in the world to do so.*

NZ28. NEW ZEALAND ENFORCEMENT LONG SERVICE MEDAL

Instituted: 1988.
Ribbon:
Metal:
Size:
Description:
Comments: *This medal is now obsolete.*

NZ29. NEW ZEALAND TRAFFIC SERVICE MEDAL

Instituted: 1994.
Ribbon: Bright blue with a narrow central white stripe flanked by black stripes.
Metal: Silver.
Size: 38mm.
Description: (Obverse) crowned effigy of Queen Elizabeth; (reverse) crowned wreath of fern fronds enclosing the word THE NEW ZEALAND TRAFFIC SERVICE MEDAL.
Comments: *Awarded to uniformed traffic officers in service after January 1987 who had completed 14 years service. Clasps for each additional period of seven years are also awarded.*

NZ30. ROYAL NEW ZEALAND NAVAL RESERVE DECORATION

Instituted: 1985.
Ribbon: 38mm green edged with white.
Metal: Silver and gold.
Size: 54mm high and 33mm wide.
Description: A skeletal badge consisting of an oval loop of rope in silver surrounding the Royal Cypher in gold.
Comments: *Awarded to commissioned officers of the Royal New Zealand Naval Reserve, with a minimum of 15 years service. Clasps for each additional period of 10 years are also awarded. The names of recipients are engraved on the reverse. Recipients are entitled to the postnominal letters RD.*

NZ31. ROYAL NEW ZEALAND NAVAL VOLUNTEER RESERVE DECORATION

Instituted: 1985.
Ribbon: 38mm dark blue with a central green stripe flanked by narrow crimson stripes.
Metal: Silver and gold.
Size: 54mm high and 33mm wide.
Description: A skeletal badge, similar in design to the above.
Comments: *Awarded to commissioned officers in the Royal New Zealand Naval Volunteer Reserve, with a minimum of 15 years service. Clasps for each additional period of 10 years are awarded. The names of recipients are engraved on the reverse. Recipients are entitled to the postnominal letters VRD. These decorations replaced the British RD and VRD, the latter being obsolete and the organisation of the Royal New Zealand Navy being such that the British Admiralty Board regulations were no longer applicable.*

NZ32. ROYAL NEW ZEALAND NAVAL VOLUNTEER RESERVE LONG SERVICE AND GOOD CONDUCT MEDAL

Instituted: 1985.
Ribbon: 32mm dark blue with a central broad stripe of green between narrow crimson stripes.
Metal: Silver.
Size: 36mm.
Description: (Obverse) uncrowned effigy of Queen Elizabeth; (reverse) a battleship with the motto DIUTURNE FIDELIS (faithful of long duration).
Comments: *Awarded to RNZVR ratings serving on or after December 1, 1977, with a minimum of 15 years service. Clasps for each additional period of 10 years are awarded.*

South African medals

Apart from the various British campaign medals from 1834 onwards, distinctive medals relating to military service in South Africa date from 1896 when a version of the Meritorious Service Medal (MYB210) was provided with the name of the Cape of Good Hope on the reverse. This was accompanied by similar versions of the Distinguished Conduct Medal (MYB42) and the Long Service and Good Conduct Medal (MYB229). The following year similar awards were instituted for Natal. Moreover, there were also a number of military and naval medals issued under Dutch, and later Boer, administrations which are outside the scope of this Yearbook.

Cape and Natal colonists received British awards from the earliest days of the British occupation, and numerous instances have been recorded of awards to South Africans of both the orders of chivalry and gallantry decorations. This situation coninued after the formation of the Union of South Africa in 1910. As a rule, these were identical to the British versions in every respect but there were a few notable exceptions. The Victory Medal (MYB170) was struck with a bilingual (English and Dutch) reverse for award to South African forces. Distinctive medals for the police, railway and harbour police and prison services (MYB284–285 and 290–291) were awarded but as they were instituted by Royal Warrant they are included in the main body of this Yearbook.

Other South African awards which will be found in the main section are the King's Police Medal for gallantry or bravery (MYB49), the Africa Service Medal (MYB189), the South African Medal for War Service (MYB192) and the South African Medal for Korea (MYB196). There were also South African versions of the Efficiency Decoration (MYB236), Efficiency Medal (MYB254), the Permanent Force LS&GC (253) and Air Efficiency Award (MYB270). Finally, there are three miscellaneous medals: the Union of South Africa Commemoration Medal of 1910 (MYB357), the Loyal Service Decoration of 1920 (MYB358) and the Anglo-Boer War Medal instituted at the same time (MYB359).

In 1952 the Union of South Africa instituted its own system of awards for gallantry in action, bravery in a non-combat situation and for distinguished service. Nine of these awards had a standard reverse showing the arms of the Union of South Africa surmounted by the royal cypher. In 1961, when South Africa became a republic and left the Commonwealth, the republican arms, without royal cypher, was substituted. The tenth award was the Union Medal which was completely redesigned and renamed the Permanent Force Good Service Medal (SA11 below).

Subsequently other awards, as well as changes in design, have been made from time to time. The Republic of South Africa was re-admitted to membership of the Commonwealth on June 1, 1994, following the holding of free elections which brought Nelson Mandela to power. The medals are listed here in order of institution, as several were subject to wholesale revision or supercession, notably in 1974–76 and 1980–81. Medals SA72-76 were abolished in 1990 when South West Africa became an independent republic within the British Commonwealth under the name of Namibia.

The data given here derives from *South African Orders, Decorations and Medals* by E. G. M. Alexander, G. K. B. Barron and A. Bateman, published in 1986. Since that date at least 60 other awards have been created: about 40 in the period up to 1994 when South Africa rejoined the Commonwealth, and about a score since then, with further awards in the pipeline. At this stage we are still collating information on South African medals and it is intended to feature more illustrations and to enlarge this section as well as to include authoritative valuations in future issues of the Yearbook.

SA1. CASTLE OF GOOD HOPE DECORATION

Instituted: 1952.

Ribbon: 44.5mm green.

Metal: Gold.

Description: A pentagonal (five-sided) medal fitted with a ring for suspension. (Obverse) a circular medallion at the centre showing Van Riebeeck's ship *Dromedaaris* in Table Bay, surrounded by a garland of Protea (the national flower) and the inscription: CASTEEL DE GOEDE HOOF DEKORASIE round the top and CASTLE OF GOOD HOPE DECORATION round the foot. (Reverse) the recipient's details.

Comments: *A gold miniature of the decoration is worn on the ribbon on the tunic. This is South Africa's highest gallantry award but to date it has not been awarded.*

SA2. LOUW WEPENER DECORATION

Instituted: 1952.

Ribbon: 35mm divided into equal stripes, six orange and five white.

Metal: Silver.

Description: Scene at the battle of Thaba Bosigo, Basutoland (now Lesotho) in 1865 in which Louw Wepener, shown in the foreground, was the hero. Inscribed LOUW WEPENER round the top and DECORATION DEKORASIE round the foot. Fitted with a scrolled suspension bar.

Comments: *Further awards were to have been denoted by a silver button inscribed with the initials LWD, but to date none has been manufactured.*

SA3. STAR OF SOUTH AFRICA

Instituted: 1952.

Ribbon: 44.5mm orange with three 3mm green stripes in centre, 6mm apart.

Metal: Silver.

Description: A multi-facetted five-point star, fitted with a ring for suspension.

Comments: *Further awards were to be denoted by a silver five-pointed star, but none was ever manufactured.*

SA4. VAN RIEBEECK DECORATION

Instituted: 1952.
Ribbon: 32mm sky blue.
Metal: Silver-gilt.
Description: A five-pointed star on which is superimposed a circular medallion depicting Jan van Riebeeck, founder of the Dutch colony at the Cape of Good Hope in 1652, surrounded by the inscription: UITNEMENDE DIENS DISTINGUISHED SERVICE. The tip of the star is fitted with an ornamental mount for ribbon suspension.
Comments: *Further awards were to have been indicated by miniature silver-gilt cannon but none was ever manufactured. This award was discontinued in August 1975.*

SA5. HONORIS CRUX

Instituted: 1952.
Ribbon: 32mm leaf-green with 3mm red outer and 2mm white inner edges.
Metal: Silver gilt and enamels.
Description: An eight-pointed cross with eagles in the interstices, surmounted by a large laurel wreath for suspension. The Latin inscription HONORIS CRUX (cross of honour) is inscribed on a circular band in the centre.
Comments: *Further awards were to have been denoted by a miniature silver-gilt eagle but none was ever manufactured. This decoration was replaced by the Honoris Crux Decoration in 1975 (see SA42 below).*

VALUE:

SA6. VAN RIEBEECK MEDAL

Instituted: 1952.
Ribbon: 32mm sky blue with 6mm white central stripe.
Metal: Silver.
Description: *Very similar to the Van Riebeeck Decoration (above) but differing in the ribbon. It, too, was discontinued in August 1975.*

SA7. SOUTHERN CROSS MEDAL

Instituted: 1952.
Ribbon: 32mm dark blue with 3mm orange and white central stripes.
Metal: Silver and enamels.
Description: A circular medal with a raised rim in the form of a laurel wreath, fitted with a beaded suspension bar. Within the wreath the field of dark blue enamel shows the Southern Cross constellation.
Comments: *This decoration was superseded in 1975 by a medal of the same name but quite different design (see SA45 below).*

SA8. UNION MEDAL

Instituted: 1952.
Branch of Service: Union of South Africa Permanent Defence Force.
Metal: Silver.
Size: 38mm,
Description: A scalloped medal with an ornamental suspension bar. (Obverse) arms of South Africa; (reverse) the Royal Cypher.
Comments: *This medal was awarded to members of the Union Defence Force Permanent Force, irrespective of rank, for a minimum of 18 years service of an impeccable character. Clasps were awarded for further periods of 12 years service. It was superseded in 1961 by the Permanent Force Good Service Medal.*

SA9. JOHN CHARD DECORATION

Instituted: 1952.
Ribbon: 32mm dark red with 3mm dark blue (outer) and 2mm white (inner) edges.
Metal: Silver.
Description: An upright oval medal fitted with a ring for suspension. The centre shows a view of Rorke's Drift in 1879. At the top is the inscription JOHN CHARD and at the foot DECORATION DEKORASIE.
Comments: *This decoration replaced the Efficiency Decoration and Air Efficiency Award and was named in memory of Lieutenant John Chard, VC who commanded the garrison at the defence of Rorke's Drift during the Zulu War, 1879. The medal ribbon is worn with a silver button embossed with the initials JCD.*

SA10. JOHN CHARD MEDAL

Instituted: 1952.
Ribbon: As above, but no silver button worn.
Metal: Bronze.
Description: Identical to SA9 except for the inscription MEDALJE MEDAL round the foot.
Comments: *This medal replaced the Efficiency Medal.*

SA11. PERMANENT FORCE GOOD SERVICE MEDAL

Instituted: 1961.
Ribbon: 32mm consisting of nine stripes alternating orange, white and blue.
Metal: Silver and bronze.
Description: A scalloped medal, similar in shape to the Union Medal (SA8) but having the arms of the Republic on the obverse. Reverse inscribed VIR LANGDURIGE DIENS EN GOEIE GEDRAG / FOR LONG SERVICE AND GOOD CONDUCT.
Comments: *Awarded for a minimum of 18 years service. A silver device in the form of the republican arms was added to the ribbon for further periods of 12 years service.*

SA12. SOUTH AFRICAN POLICE CROSS FOR BRAVERY

Instituted: 1963.
Ribbon: 44.5mm dark blue with a central gold stripe flanked by narrow white stripes.
Metal: Silver.
Description: A pyramidal cross surmounted by a laurel wreath enclosing a circle divided into quandrants and inscribed in Latin VIVIT POST PUNERA VIRTUS.
Clasp: A bar may be awarded for further acts of bravery.

SA13. SOUTH AFRICAN POLICE STAR FOR DISTINGUISHED SERVICE

Instituted: 1963.
Ribbon: 31.25mm white with narrow green and red stripes towards each edge.
Metal: Silver.
Description: A six-pointed radiate star having at the centre a star of David entwined with a circle enclosing the insignia of the police service. The top of the star has a radiate mounting affixed to the suspension bar.
Clasp: A clasp was awarded for further periods of distinguished service.
Comments: *This decoration was superseded by a new award in 1979 but retaining the same name (see SA53 below).*

SA14. SOUTH AFRICAN POLICE STAR FOR MERIT

Instituted: 1963.
Ribbon: 32mm orange, with 3mm white central stripe flanked by 3mm blue stripes.
Metal: Silver.
Description: A six-pointed radiate star with suspension bar affixed to the topmost point. Towards the centre is a circle enclosing a triangle with stylised hands holding a flame above a V-shaped altar.
Clasp: *Further awards are denoted by a bar.*

SA15. SOUTH AFRICAN POLICE MEDAL FOR FAITHFUL SERVICE

Instituted: 1963.
Ribbon: 32mm royal blue with 3mm old gold central stripe.
Metal: Silver.
Description: A laurel wreath enclosing the arms of the republic. The ornamental letters TD (initials of 'faithful service' in Afrikaans) at the top of the medal linked the rim to the plain suspension bar.
Clasp: A bar denoting further awards was authorised up to 1979.
Comments: *This medal replaced the Police Good Service Medal (MYB284).*

SA16. COMMANDANT GENERAL'S MEDAL

Instituted: 1965.
Ribbon: 32mm orange with sky blue edges and a broad dark blue central stripe.
Metal: Silver.
Description: A laurel wreath enclosing a five-sided polygon divided into sectors. In the centre is a circle enclosing crossed rifles above a circular target and bushveld scenery. In the exergue is the inscription KOMMANDANT GENERAALS MEDALJE COMMANDANT GENERALS MEDAL. The top of the polygon has a fluted bar connecting it to the suspension bar decorated with laurel sprays.
Comments: *This medal was awarded for outstanding marksmanship. Further awards were denoted by a circular silver button inscribed with the year of the award. This medal was superseded in 1975 by the SADF Champion Shot Medal (see SA48 below).*

SA17. DE WET DECORATION

Instituted: 1965.
Ribbon: 32mm orange with a broad blue central stripe and 3mm green edges separated from the orange by narrow white stripes.
Metal: Silver.
Description: Two sprays of Protea blossom enclose a vignette of General Christiaan De Wet, leader of Boer forces in 1901-2, on horseback with the inscription DEKORASIE DE WET DECORATION round the top of the field. Foliate spurs link the top of the rim to a plain suspension bar.
Comments: *Further awards were denoted by a circular silver button embossed with the letters DWD.*

SA18. PRISONS DEPARTMENT FAITHFUL SERVICE MEDAL

Instituted: 1966.
Ribbon: 31mm broad deep blue central stripe flanked by narrow white stripes and broad green edges.
Metal: Silver.
Description: As 291 but with the arms of the Republic in place of the arms of the Union of South Africa.
Comments: *Conditions for this award were the same as for 291. It was replaced by the South African Prisons Service Medal for Faithful Service in 1968 (see SA30 below).*

SA19. CADET CORPS MEDAL

Instituted: 1966.
Ribbon: 32mm orange with 5mm blue edges separated from the orange by narrow white stripes.
Metal: Silver.
Description: A prancing Springbok enclosed in a laurel wreath with the inscriptions CADET CORPS MEDAL and KADETKORPSMEDALJE at the sides.
Comments: *Awarded for 20 years service as an officer in the Cadet Corps. Further awards were to have been denoted by a circular silver button bearing the prancing Springbok motif but none was ever produced. It was abolished in August 1976 when the Cadet Corps ceased to exist as a separate force, being absorbed into the Commandos or Citizen Force.*

SA20. SOUTH AFRICAN RAILWAYS POLICE CROSS FOR VALOUR

Instituted: 1966.
Ribbon: 44.5mm old gold with a broad white central stripe flanked by narrow black stripes and black edges.
Metal: Silver.
Description: An eight-pointed star mounted on a circular base with radiate points in the interstices. At the centre is a small medallion showing a lion enclosed by a laurel wreath. At the top, a building surmounted by a cross is linked to a suspension loop.
Comments: *This decoration was replaced by an entirely new design in 1980 (see SA56 below).*

SA21. SOUTH AFRICAN RAILWAYS POLICE DECORATION FOR DISTINGUISHED SERVICE

Instituted: 1966.
Ribbon: 32mm white with a central stripe of old gold flanked by narrow black stripes. At the edges are narrow stripes of green (inner) and black (outer).
Metal: Silver.
Description: A circular medal on which is superimposed a five-pointed star with radiate points in the angles. At the centre is a tiny medallion with a laurel wreath enclosing a device of an upraised hand grasing thunderbolts. A stylised railway station building affixed to the top of the rim joins the medal to the plain suspension bar.
Comments: *This decoration was superseded in 1980 by the South African Railways Police Decoration for Outstanding Service (see SA51 below).*

SA22. SOUTH AFRICAN RAILWAYS POLICE STAR FOR MERIT

Instituted: 1966.
Ribbon: 32mm white with a broad old gold central stripe edged in blue, with narrow black stripes at the outer edges.
Metal: Silver.
Description: A circular medal with a five-pointed star having the spokes of a wheel showing in the angles. A small medallion in the centre has a laurel wreath enclosing a pair of hands holding a flame. The stylised railway station at the top is attached to a plain suspension bar.
Comments: *This award was replaced in 1980 by a new design, but retaining the original name (see SA52 below).*

SA23. SOUTH AFRICAN RAILWAYS POLICE MEDAL FOR FAITHFUL SERVICE

Instituted: 1966.
Ribbon: 32mm old gold with a broad central white stripe edged in red and having narrow black stripes at the outer edges.
Metal: Silver.
Description: A circular medal with a tiny central medallion enclosing a trek wagon in a laurel wreath from which radiate the spokes of a wheel.
Comments: *This medal superseded the Railway Police Good Service Medal (284) and was, in turn, replaced by an entirely new design in 1980.*

SA24. STATE PRESIDENT'S SPORTS AWARD

Instituted: 1967.
Ribbon: 38mm in three equal parts of orange, white and blue.
Metal: Silver.
Description: A circular medal with 32 faceted points extending from the rim, and fitted at the top with a loop for suspension. The centre has a laurel wreath enclosing a bird in flight over a five-sided emblem. The inscription STAATSPRESIDENT SPORTTOEKENNING appears at the sides.
Comments: *Awarded for outstanding achievement in team or individual sports.*

SA25. PRO MERITO MEDAL

Instituted: 1967.
Ribbon: 32mm sky blue with a dark blue centre flanked by narrow white and orange stripes.
Metal: Silver.
Description: A circular medal depicting a Protea blossom surrounded by a wreath of Protea flowers. The foliate spurs at the top are connected to a plain suspension bar.
Comments: *Awarded for meritorious service.*

SA26. LOUW WEPENER MEDAL

Instituted: 1967.
Ribbon: 35mm orange with four narrow white stripes.
Metal: Silver.
Description: A circular medal identical to SA2 except for the inscription round the foot which reads MEDALJE MEDAL.
Comments: *Further awards were to be denoted by a circular bronze button embossed with the letter LWM but none was ever produced. This medal was superseded in 1975 by the Honoris Crux Decoration (see SA42 below).*

SA27. MENTION IN DESPATCHES

Instituted: 1967.
Metal: Bronze.
Description: A miniature replica of the coat of arms of the Republic, worn directly on the tunic and not affixed to any medal ribbons.

SA28. SOUTH AFRICAN PRISONS SERVICE DECORATION FOR VALOUR

Instituted: 1968.
Ribbon: 35mm red with broad green edges separated from the red by very narrow gold stripes.
Metal: Silver.
Description: A five-sided medal mounted on a six-pointed plain star, with a lifebelt ring at the top for suspension. In the centre is a plain cross with the scales of justice at the top and a lifebelt at the foot. Round the sides of the pentagon is the inscription PRISONS DEPARTMENT DEPARTEMENT VAN GEVANGENISSE.
Comments: *This medal, replacing earlier medals of the Union of South Africa (290-1), was in turn superseded in 1980 by no fewer than 11 new medals (see SA65–75 below).*

SA29. SOUTH AFRICAN PRISONS SERVICE MEDAL FOR MERIT

Instituted: 1968.
Ribbon: 35mm with a broad red centre having a very narrow white stripe down the middle. Towards each edge are white stripes and broad blue edges.
Metal: Silver.
Description: A circular medal with a lifebelt at the top for suspension. The field bears the arms of the Republic with DEPARTMENT VAN GEVANGENISSE round the top and PRISONS DEPARTMENT round the foot.
Comments: *Superseded in 1980 by medals SA56–63 below.*

SA30. SOUTH AFRICAN PRISONS SERVICE MEDAL FOR FAITHFUL SERVICE

Instituted: 1968.
Ribbon: 35mm broad green centre flanked by white stripes and broad blue edges.
Metal: Silver.
Description: A cone-shaped medal rising to a point surmounted by a lifebelt for suspension. The field has a wreath of protea enclosing an open book surmounted by crossed keys, with the scales of justice at the top and a lifebelt at the foot. Towards the rim are the inscriptions DEPARTMENET VAN GEVANGENISSE at the top and PRISONS DEPARTMENT at the foot.
Comments: *This long service medal was replaced in 1980 by a series of three medals of the same name but in gold, silver and bronze classes (see SA63 below).*

SA31. COMMANDANT GENERAL OF THE SOUTH AFRICAN DEFENCE FORCE COMMENDATION

Instituted: 1968.
Ribbon: None.
Metal: Bronze.
Description: A Protea emblem sewn on to the tunic and not worn on medal ribbons.
Comments: *Awarded for mention in despatches. It was superseded in 1974 by the Chief of the South African Defence Force Commendation Medal (see SA39 below).*

SA32. DANIE THERON MEDAL

Instituted: 1970.
Ribbon: 32mm green with three narrow yellow stripes.
Metal: Silver.
Description: An eagle hovering over mountain peaks, with three stars on either side and DANIE THERON round the top and MEDALJE MEDAL at the foot. Scrolling spurs secure the medal to the plain suspension bar.
Comments: *This medal was named in memory of one of the heroes of the Boer War (1899-1902).*

SA33. JACK HINDON MEDAL

Instituted: 1970.
Ribbon: 32mm yellow with a narrow central green stripe and broad green stripes at the edges.
Metal: Bronze.
Description: An upright oval medal showing the sun rising over a mountain peak. In the foreground Jack Hindon and two companions unfurling the Vierkleur (Boer flag) during the battle of Spioen Kop on January 24, 1900. Inscription JACK HINDON round the top, with MEDALJE MEDAL at the foot. Fitted with scrolled spurs to a plain suspension bar.
Comments: *This medal, named in honour of Captain Oliver John Hindon who fought for the South African Republic (Transvaal) against the British in the Boer War, was awarded to NCOs and other ranks of the Commandos of the South African Defence Force "for exceptionally diligent and outstanding service in peacetime or war". It was superseded by the Danie Theron Medal (above) in October 1975.*

SA34. WOLTEMADE DECORATION FOR BRAVERY

Instituted: 1970.
Ribbon: 44.5mm blue with orange edges.
Metal: Gold or silver.
Description: (Obverse) Wolraad Woltemade riding through the raging sea; (reverse) the arms of the Republic. The design is otherwise identical to the Union of South Africa King's or Queen's Medals for Bravery (40) which it superseded.
Comments: *Awarded in gold or silver for heroism in the saving of life.*

SA35. DECORATION FOR MERITORIOUS SERVICE

Instituted: 1970.
Ribbon: 38mm blue with white (inner) and orange (outer stripes at the sides).
Metal: Silver.
Description: A radiate star on which is superimposed an enamelled bifurcated five-branched cross, with similar bifurcations projection in the interstices. At the centre of the cross is a small enamelled medallion bearing the Protea emblem. Fitted with a loop for suspension.
Comments: *Awarded for meritorious service at provincial or national level.*

SA36. STATE PRESIDENT'S SPORTS MERIT AWARD

Instituted: 1971.
Ribbon: 37.47mm in three equal parts of orange, white and blue.
Metal: Silver.
Description: Identical to the State President's Sport Award (SA24 above), which it replaced, apart from the emended inscription round the foot: STATE PRESIDENT'S SPORTS MERIT AWARD.

SA37. ORDER OF GOOD HOPE

Instituted: 1973.
Ribbon: Green with gold stripes towards the edges, differing in size and position according to class.
Metal: Gold, silver and enamels.
Description: A radiate eight-pointed star with a central medallion showing two birds in flight and having the Latin inscription SPES BONA (good hope) round the top.
Comments: *This order was awarded mainly to civilians and military personnel of foreign countries who had rendered service to the Republic. It was divided into five classes, distinguished by the ribbon:*
> *Special Class: Grand Collar. No ribbon worn*
> *First Class: Grand Cross. 101mm green with a 24mm gold stripe 3mm from each edge.*
> *Second Class: Grand officer. 40mm green with a 9mm gold stripe 1.5mm from each edge.*
> *Third Class: Commander. 40mm green with a 9mm gold stripe 1.5mm from each edge.*
> *Fourth Class: Officer. 40mm green with a 9mm gold stripe 1.5mm from each edge.*

SA38. SOUTH AFRICAN POLICE MEDAL FOR COMBATING TERRORISM

Instituted: 1974.
Ribbon: 31.75mm red with a central silver stripe and narrow silver stripes towards each edge.
Metal: Silver.
Description: A six-pointed star mounted on a beribboned wreath with a device containing three Protea flowers at the top linked to a plain suspension bar.
Comments: *Awarded for participation in police actions which, in the broadest terms, might be described as combating terrorism, including quelling anti-Afrikaans demonstrations by black schoolchildren. Clasps were granted for subsequent awards.*

SA39. CHIEF OF THE SOUTH AFRICAN DEFENCE FORCE COMMENDATION MEDAL

Instituted: 1974.

Ribbon: 32mm orange centre flanked by sky-blue stripes and dark blue edges.

Metal: Silver.

Description: A circular medal with concave curves between twelve points and a plain ring for suspension from a rectangular bar. In the centre, a beaded medallion surrounded by Protea flowers contains the insignia of the South African Defence Force.

Comments: *This medal superseded the Commandant General's Commendation (SA31 above).*

SA40. PRO PATRIA MEDAL

Instituted: 1974.

Ribbon: 32mm orange with a broad central band of dark blue divided by a thin central orange stripe, with narrow white stripes towards the edges.

Metal: Silver.

Description: An eight-sided medal with rectangular motifs in each sector, and a central medallion depicting a stylised aloe plant. It has a plain ring attached to a straight suspension bar with a Protean emblem flanked by laurel sprays.

Comments: *This medal, awarded for outstanding service to the state, was modified in June 1976.*

SA41. ORDER OF THE STAR OF SOUTH AFRICA

Instituted: 1975.

Ribbon: Blue, 37mm (neck ribbon), 80mm (sash), 44mm (breast ribbon) or 20mm (miniature). A narrow central white stripe denotes the second class (redesignated silver award in 1977).

Metal: Enamelled gold or silver depending on class.

Description: An eight-pointed Maltese cross with an eight-pointed star superimposed at the centre and having a circular Protea wreath behind. *First Class:* A Protea ornament at the top joins the star to a five-pointed badge in the form of a ground plan of a fort, enclosing a circular device featuring the insignia of the Defence Force. This is linked by a chain to circular medallions embellished with eight-pointed stars forming the neck collar of the order. *Second Class:* A similar star but in silver and enamels and suspended by a loop from a neck ribbon.

Comments: *This order superseded the Star of South Africa (SA2) and was, in turn, substantially modified in 1978 (see SA51 below).*

SA42. HONORIS CRUX DECORATION

Instituted: 1975.
Ribbon: 32mm orange with additional white stripes according to
class.
Metal: Enamelled gold or silver, according to class.
Description: An eight-pointed Maltese cross superimposed on a
wreath with crossed swords in the angles, fitted with an
ornamental suspension bar
Comments: *This award replaced the Honoris Crux (SA5 above) and
was divided into four classes, distinguished by their ribbons.*
Honoris Crux Diamond. Plain orange ribbon, 32mm.
Honoris Crux Gold. Orange with a 1mm central white stripe.
*Honoris Crux Silver. Orange with a 1mm white stripe 13mm from
each edge.*
*Honoris Crux. Orange with 2mm white edges and 1mm white stripe
5mm from each edge.*

SA43. SOUTHERN CROSS DECORATION

Instituted: 1975
Ribbon: 32mm blue with 1mm white stripes 13mm from each
edge.
Metal: Silver and enamels.
Description: An eight-pointed Maltese cross superimposed on a
larger, broader cross of the same form, with a beaded
enamelled medallion at the centre bearing the constellation of
the Southern Cross. Fitted with a Protea emblem for
suspension from a straight bar.
Comments: *This award was instituted as part of the range of decorations
introduced in 1975 as the national state of emergency deepened. It was
intended as a higher class of the previous Southern Cross medal of
1952, awarded for services to the state.*

SA44. PRO MERITO DECORATION

Instituted: 1975.
Ribbon: 32mm blue with a 4mm white central stripe.
Metal: Enamelled silver.
Description: An eight-pointed Maltese cross with a central
medallion depicting a stylised Aloe plant.
Comments: *This award divided the previous Pro Merito into two
classes.*

SA45. SOUTHERN CROSS MEDAL

Instituted:1975.
Ribbon: 32mm blue with 2mm white edges and two 1mm white stripes 13mm from each edge.
Metal: Enamelled silver.
Description: A five-pointed radiate star with circular radiate sectors between the arms, having a beaded central medallion depicting the constellation of the Southern Cross. Fitted with a plain ring for suspension from a straight bar.
Comments: *This medal replaced the Southern Cross Medal of 1952 (see SA7 above) when this decoration was divided into two classes.*

SA46. PRO MERITO MEDAL

Instituted: 1975.
Ribbon: 32mm blue with 2mm white edges and 4mm white central stripe.
Metal: Enamelled silver.
Description: A five-pointed radiate star with circular radiate sectors between the arms and a central beaded medallion depicting a stylised Aloe plant.
Comments: *This medal replaced the original Pro Merito of 1967 when that decoration was divided into two classes.*

SA47. SOUTH AFRICAN DEFENCE FORCE GOOD SERVICE MEDAL

Instituted: 1975.
Ribbon: 32mm green with different stripes according to class and branch of service.
Metal: Gold, silver or bronze.
Description: A scalloped medal bearing the coat of arms of the Republic. Fitted with ornamental spurs to a plain suspension bar.
Comments: *This medal superseded the Permanent Force Good Service Medal of 1961 (see SA11 above) and was divided into three classes, each having distinctive ribbons as follows:*
Gold Medal:
    Permanent Force. *Three narrow white stripes towards each edge*
    Citizen Force. *Three narrow blue stripes towards each edge*
    Commandos. *Three narrow orange stripes towards each edge*
Silver Medal:
    Permanent Force. *Two narrow white stripes towards each edge*
    Citizen Force. *Two narrow blue stripes towards each edge*
    Commandos. *Two narrow orange stripes towards each edge*
Bronze Medal:
    Permanent Force. *One narrow white stripe 2mm from each edge*
    Citizen Force. *One narrow blue stripe 2mm from each edge*
    Commandos. *One narrow orange stripe 2mm from each edge*

SA48. SADF CHAMPION SHOTS MEDAL

Instituted: 1975.
Ribbon: 32mm orange with a broad central dark blue stripe and broad sky blue edges.
Metal: Silver.
Description: Very similar to the Commandant General's Medal (SA16) except for the inscription in the exergue which now reads: SAW KAMP1OENSKUTMEDALJE / SADF CHAMPION SHOT MEDAL.
Comments: *Awarded annually to the champion shot, it replaced SA16. Further awards were denoted by a circular silver button inscribed by the year of the award.*

SA49. CIVIL DEFENCE MEDAL FOR BRAVERY

Instituted: 1976.
Ribbon: 32mm red with narrow white and yellow stripes towards each edge.
Metal: Silver.
Description: A cross with curved ends and a laurel wreath in the angles. The oval centre features the cruciform insignia of the Civil Defence service with tiny florets in the angles. Fitted with a small ring for suspension from a plain bar.
Comments: *Awarded for brave conduct in the course of natural disasters, fire, flood, etc.*

SA50. CIVIL DEFENCE MEDAL FOR MERITORIOUS SERVICE

Instituted: 1976.
Ribbon: 32mm yellow with narrow red stripes towards each edge, flanked by narrow white stripes.
Metal: Silver.
Description: A circular medal with a ring of enamel surrounding the cruciform insignia of the Civil Defence service, without the florets in the angles. The top of the medal has a circular device showing an Aloe plant surmounted by a ring for suspension from a plain bar.
Comments: *Awarded for distinguished service in the Civil Defence formations.*

SA51. ORDER OF THE STAR OF SOUTH AFRICA

Instituted: 1978.
Ribbon: Blue 80mm (sash), 40mm (breast ribbon), 37mm (neck ribbon) and 20mm (miniature).
Description: As SA41.
Comments: *This order was re-organised into an exclusively military division and a division which could be awarded to either military personnel or civilians. The exclusively military classes are:*
    Order of the Star of South Africa. *Ribbon and decoration as SA41 First Class.*
    Order of the Star of South Africa Silver. *Order and ribbon as SA41 Second Class.*
    The new classes, which can be awarded to civilians and military personnel alike, are:
      Class I: Grand Cross. *Ribbon as above, but with gold edges; decoration and collar as above.*
      Class II: Grand Officer. *Blue ribbon with silver edges; decoration similar and worn from a neck ribbon.*
      Class III: Commander. *Blue ribbon with silver edges and a central gold stripe; decoration similar and worn from a neck ribbon*
      Class IV: Officer. *Blue ribbon with a central gold stripe and narrow silver stripes on either side; decoration similar and worn from a ribbon on the breast.*
      Class V: Knight. *Blue ribbon with a 2mm silver stripe in the centre, flanked by 1mm silver stripes and silver edges; decoration similar and worn from a ribbon on the breast.*

SA52. SOUTH AFRICAN POLICE STAR FOR DISTINGUISHED LEADERSHIP

Instituted: 1979.
Ribbon: 37mm gold with a broad central blue stripe flanked by thin white stripes.
Metal: Silver.
Description: A facetted eight-point cross with the points of a star in the angles. In the centre is a circular device depicting a stylised Aloe plant. The top of the decoration is fitted with a large plain ring for suspension.
Comments: *Awarded to senior police officers for distinguished service.*

SA53. SOUTH AFRICAN POLICE STAR FOR DISTINGUISHED SERVICE

Instituted: 1979.
Ribbon: 31.25mm white with narrow stripes towards the edges and red edges.
Metal: Silver.
Description: A six-pointed radiate star with a star of David entwined with a circular band at the centre, enclosing the insignia of the police service. The top of the star has a vertical decorative bar for suspension.
Comments: *Awarded to all ranks.*

SA54. SOUTH AFRICAN POLICE STAR FOR OUTSTANDING SERVICE

Instituted: 1979.
Ribbon: 36mm gold with green edges and two broad white bands, each of which has a narrow blue stripe in the centre.
Metal: Silver.
Description: A radiate cross with curved ends, with a spear-pointed star in the angles. The top rises to a point to which is attached a V-shaped suspension bar.
Comments: *Awarded for outstanding service, including specific acts of bravery or gallant conduct.*

SA55. SOUTH AFRICAN POLICE STAR FOR FAITHFUL SERVICE

Instituted: 1979.
Ribbon: 36mm gold with a broad green centre, narrow green stripes towards the edges and two narrow blue stripes flanking the centre.
Metal: Silver.
Description: A circular medal on which is superimposed an eight-point radiate star with a circular centre enclosing a cruciform geometric device. The fluted top is connected to a V-shaped suspension bar.
Comments: *Awarded for long and faithful service, further awards being denoted by a clasp.*

SA56. SOUTH AFRICAN RAILWAYS POLICE CROSS FOR VALOUR

Instituted: 1980.
Ribbon: 44.5mm old gold.
Metal: Silver.
Description: An eight-point Maltese cross superimposed on a shorter but broader Maltese cross, with a small medallion at the centre depicting a stylised Protea plant. A similar ornament at the top is affixed to a small ring attached to a plain suspension bar.
Comments: *This decoration replaced the issue of 1966 (SA20).*

SA57. SOUTH AFRICAN RAILWAYS POLICE STAR FOR DISTINGUISHED LEADERSHIP

Instituted: 1980.
Ribbon: 37mm bronze-green.
Metal: Silver.
Description: A 16-point star, with a small eight-point star at the centre, suspended from a collar with a five-pointed badge bearing the arms of the Republic at the centre and linked medallions bearing laurel wreaths.
Commenta: *Arguably the most elaborate decoration ever devised for any railway service.*

SA58. SOUTH AFRICAN RAILWAYS POLICE STAR FOR DISTINGUISHED SERVICE

Instituted: 1980.
Ribbon: 36mm bronze-green with broad gold edges.
Metal: Silver.
Description: Collar as above, but only an eight-point star, with the same small eight-point star at the centre.
Comments: *Awarded for distinguished service in the Railway Police.*

SA59. SOUTH AFRICAN RAILWAYS POLICE DECORATION FOR OUTSTANDING SERVICE

Instituted: 1980.
Ribbon: 31.8mm white with a broad gold centre flanked by narrow green stripes and having edges of black (outer) and green (inner).
Metal: Silver.
Description: A circular medal on which is superimposed a filve-point star with a five-point radiate star in the angles. At the centre is a laureated medallion bearing the insignia of the railway service. The stylised railway station mount at the top is affixed to a plain suspension bar.
Comments: *Awarded for outstanding service in the Railways Police. Further awards are denoted by a clasp. This medal replaced the Distinguished Service Decoration of 1956 (SA21).*

SA60. SOUTH AFRICAN RAILWAYS POLICE STAR FOR MERIT

Instituted: 1980.
Ribbon: 32mm old gold with a white centre with a narrow red stripe, flanked by broad green stripes.
Metal: Silver.
Description: An octagonal medal with an inner octagon and an eight-point star having at its centre a medallion showing two hands holding a flame. An ornamental fitment at the top is connected to a plain suspension bar.
Comments: *This star replaced the award instituted in 1966 (SA22).*

SA61. SOUTH AFRICAN RAILWAYS POLICE STAR FOR FAITHFUL SERVICE

Instituted: 1980.
Ribbon: 32mm white central stripe flanked by thin red stripes, broader silver stripes and broad green edges.
Metal: Silver.
Description: Obverse similar to the above, but with a different inscription on the reverse.
Comments: *Awarded for long service and good conduct, further awards being denoted by a clasp.*

SA62. SOUTH AFRICAN RAILWAYS POLICE MEDAL FOR FAITHFUL SERVICE

Instituted: 1980.
Ribbon: 32mm old gold with a green central stripe flanked by black and having narrow red edges.
Metal: Silver.
Description: An octagonal medal containing a laurel wreath enclosing the coat of arms of the Republic. Fitted to a plain suspension bar.
Comments: *Awarded for long service, further periods being denoted by clasps. This medal replaced the medal of 1966 (SA23).*

SA63. SOUTH AFRICAN RAILWAYS POLICE MEDAL FOR COMBATING TERRORISM

Instituted: 1980.
Ribbon: 32mm white with a narrow green central stripe and edges. Two bands of thin blue stripes with thin red stripes on either side appear towards the edges.
Metal: Silver.
Description: A circular medal with a laurel wreath enclosing an upright sword.
Comments: *Further service in combating terrorism on the railways is marked by a clasp.*

SA64. SOUTH AFRICAN PRISONS SERVICE CROSS FOR VALOUR (DIAMOND)

Instituted: 1980.
Ribbon: 32mm red.
Metal: Silver.
Description: A double Maltese cross with a diamond centre, affixed to a plain suspension bar by a laurel wreath.
Comments: *Further awards are denoted by a clasp.*

SA65. SOUTH AFRICAN PRISONS SERVICE STAR FOR EXCELLENCE

Instituted: 1980.
Ribbon: 44mm green.
Metal: Silver.
Description: A 12-point cross surmounted by a laurel wreath.
Comments: *Awarded for good conduct. No clasps for further periods of service are granted.*

SA66. SOUTH AFRICAN PRISONS SERVICE CROSS FOR VALOUR

Instituted: 1980.
Ribbon: 32mm red with a white central stripe.
Metal: Silver.
Description: A Maltese cross of frosted silver with a plain circular centre and an inverted V attachment to a plain suspension bar.
Comments: *Awarded for length of service, a clasp being granted for additional periods.*

SA67. SOUTH AFRICAN PRISONS SERVICE STAR FOR DISTINCTION

Instituted: 1980.
Ribbon: 32mm green with a white central stripe.
Metal: Silver.
Description: A 12-point cross similar to SA57 but with a plain ring for suspension.
Comments: *Awarded for distinguished service, but no clasps granted for further service.*

SA68. SOUTH AFRICAN PRISONS SERVICE STAR FOR MERIT

Instituted: 1980.
Ribbon: 32mm green with a white central stripe and white stripe towards the edges.
Metal: Silver.
Description: A 10-point cross with Protea flowers in the angles and a plain ring for suspension from a straight bar.
Comments: *No clasps awarded for additional service.*

SA69. SOUTH AFRICAN PRISONS SERVICE CROSS FOR MERIT

Instituted: 1980.
Ribbon: 32mm green with three 2mm white stripes and broad white edges.
Metal: Silver.
Description: A cross pattee very similar to the German Iron Cross in appearance, but without any detail on the front. Fitted with a plain ring for suspension from a straight bar.
Comments: *No clasps granted for additional awards.*

SA70. SOUTH AFRICAN PRISONS SERVICE MEDAL FOR MERIT

Instituted: 1980.
Ribbon: 32mm green with white edges and two (commissioned officers) or three (NCOs) thin white stripes in the centre.
Metal: Silver.
Description: A radiate star with a floriate centre and an inverted V and ring for suspension from a straight bar.
Comments: *The only distinction between the medals awarded to commissioned and non-commissioned officers lies in the pattern of thin white stripes on the medal ribbon.*

SA71. SOUTH AFRICAN PRISONS SERVICE MEDAL FOR FAITHFUL SERVICE

Instituted: 1980.
Ribbon: 32mm yellow with two sets of three green stripes (gold), two sets of two green stripes (silver) or two green stripes (bronze) towards either side.
Metal: Gold, silver or bronze.
Description: A circular medal with the arms of the Republic in the centre and a garland of Protea blossom round the circumference.
Comments: *Awarded in three classes, by metal and appropriate ribbon, according to length of service. A clasp denoting a further period of service is added to the gold medal.*

SA72. NATIONAL INTELLIGENCE SERVICE CROSS FOR VALOUR

Instituted: 1981.
Ribbon: 40mm violet.
Metal: Silver.
Description: A cross with spear shaped finials, lions in the interstices and a central medallion bearing the insignia of the National Intelligence Service. An ornamental loop at the top is affixed to a plain ring for suspension.
Comments: *Awarded to members of the Intelligence Service for bravery in action against enemies of the state.*

SA73. NATIONAL INTELLIGENCE SERVICE DECORATION FOR DISTINGUISHED LEADERSHIP

Instituted: 1981.
Ribbon: Turquoise 37mm (ceremonial) or 44mm (other).
Metal: Silver
Description: As above but having the lion emblem at the centre.
Comments: *No clasps awarded.*

SA74. NATIONAL INTELLIGENCE SERVICE DECORATION FOR OUTSTANDING LEADERSHIP

Instituted: 1981.
Ribbon: 44mm turquoise with 20mm white central stripe.
Metal: Silver.
Description: Very similar to the above, but with appropriately worded inscription on the reverse.
Comments: *No clasps awarded.*

SA75. NATIONAL INTELLIGENCE SERVICE MEDAL FOR DISTINGUISHED SERVICE

Instituted: 1981.
Ribbon: 44mm turquoise with two broad white stripes towards the centre.
Metal: Silver.
Description: A medal with the cross as SA66 superimposed. Fitted with the same ornamental loop and plain ring for suspension.
Comments: *No clasps awarded.*

SA76. NATIONAL INTELLIGENCE SERVICE MEDAL FOR FAITHFUL SERVICE

Instituted: 1981.
Ribbon: 36mm red flanked by white on which are two sets of three narrow green stripes (gold), or two sets of two stripes (silver) or two narrow green stripes (bronze).
Metal: Gold, silver or bronze.
Description: Circular medals with a broad rim enclosing a shield bearing the floral emblem of the National Intelligence Service. At the top is a lion passant gardant holding a large scrolled S, from which is attached a plain ring for suspension.
Comments: *No clasps awarded for additional periods of service.*

SA77. NATIONAL INTELLIGENCE SERVICE DECORATION

Instituted: 1981.
Ribbon: 40mm turquoise with a red centre flanked by two narrow white stripes (gold) with an additional sentral stripe (silver) or two additional central stripes (bronze).
Metal: Gold, silver or bronze.
Description: A cross with rounded ends with geometric ornament in the angles. The lion emblem appears at the centre and an ornamental loop is fitted at the top for ring suspension.
Comments: *Awarded in gold, silver or bronze according to the length and quality of service. No clasps awarded for additional periods of service.*

SA78. NATIONAL INTELLIGENCE SERVICE CIVIL DECORATION

Instituted: 1981.
Ribbon: 40mm white with a 16mm central turquoise stripe.
Metal: Silver.
Description: A circular medal with a small central medallion bearing the insignia of the Intelligence Service and having 16 points radiating to the rim. The lion emblem is affixed to the top and attached to a plain ring for suspension.
Comments: *Awarded to civilian staff of the Intelligence Service, employed on clerical or administrative duties.*

SA79. SOUTH AFRICAN POLICE SILVER CROSS FOR GALLANTRY

Instituted: 1985.
Ribbon: 36mm blue with broad white edges, each having a narrow central red stripe.
Metal: Silver.
Description: A cross pattée with an outlined rim and a laurel wreath at the centre enclosing the police emblem. Affixed to a straight suspension bar by an ornamental yoke.
Comments: *Awarded for individual acts of heroism. A clasp is granted for additional awards.*

SA80. SOUTH WEST AFRICAN POLICE STAR FOR OUTSTANDING SERVICE

Instituted: 1981.
Ribbon: 36mm red with a central gold stripe and white edges.
Metal: Silver.
Description: A Maltese cross with a laurel wreath in the angles. In the centre a view of a stone fortress tower.
Comments: *This and the following medals were authorised by the South West Africa Official Gazette in December 1981 when South West Africa was under South African administration. A clasp for further periods of service was authorised.*

SA81. SOUTH WEST AFRICAN POLICE STAR FOR DISTINGUISHED SERVICE

Instituted: 1981.
Ribbon: 36mm blue with a gold central stripe and white stripes towards the edges.
Metal: Silver.
Description: A circular medal with a 22-point star and a laurel wreath enclosing a view of Bogenfels Rocks.
Comments: *A clasp was authorised for further periods of service.*

SA82. SOUTH WEST AFRICAN POLICE STAR FOR FAITHFUL SERVICE

Instituted: 1981.
Ribbon: 36mm green with broad white bands towards the edges, each having a narrow central gold stripe.
Metal: Silver.
Description: An irregularly shaped medal showing the sun beating down on the Namib Desert. Fitted with an inverted V mount for suspension.
Comments: *Further awards were to be denoted by a clasp.*

SA83. SOUTH WEST AFRICAN POLICE MEDAL FOR FAITHFUL SERVICE

Instituted: 1981.
Ribbon: 36mm brown with two sets of narrow green stripes towards the edges.
Metal: Silver.
Description: A circular medal with a raised rim, enclosing the same motif as the star SA74.
Comments: *No clasps awarded.*

SA84. MEDAL FOR THE ESTABLISHMENT OF THE SOUTH WEST AFRICAN POLICE

Instituted: 1981.
Ribbon: 36mm orange with broad blue stripes towards either edge.
Metal: Silver.
Description: A radiate star with a decorative surround. Superimposed on the intersection of the lines is the famous landmark known as the Finger Rock.
Comments: *This medal was issued to all serving personnel when the South West African Police was inaugurated. Most instituted in South Africa itself since 1994 in the next edition of this Yearbook.*

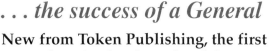

Indian
medals

From its independence from British rule in 1947, India has consciously evolved its own distinctive set of civilian and military awards. Within the changing legal constraints of governmental form, as a self-governing dominion from 1947 to 1950 and as a secular republic since 1950, India has sought to achieve an egalitarian, non-class-based set of awards which still reward achievement and service in tangible form. At times in conflict with aspects of India's culture which call for nonviolence, India has maintained one of the largest armies in Asia and has experienced a number of conflicts, many of them with her sibling and neighbor, Pakistan. Moreover, Indian has since the earliest days of independence supported and participated in a wide range of international peacekeeping efforts and these, too, are represented in medals and awards.

A recurring image through India's awards is the national emblem (shown above). The national emblem is a replica of the lion capital of Sarnath, near Varanasi in the northern Indian State of Uttar Pradesh. The lion capital was erected on a column in the third century BC by the Mauryan Emperor Ashoka to mark the spot where Buddha first proclaimed his message of peace and emancipation to the universe. The national emblem is thus seen as symbolic of contemporary India's reaffirmation of its ancient commitment to world peace and goodwill.

The four lions (one is hidden from view) – symbolising power, courage and confidence – rest on a depiction of the chakra or wheel of Ashoka and the Buddhist law which he tried to implement; this chakra also appears on the Indian flag and is a recurring motif on Indian awards. The motto "Satyameva Jayate" inscribed below the emblem in Devanagari/Hindi script means "truth alone triumphs".

We are indebted to Professor Ed Haynes of Winthrop University for supplying the information and valuations for this section. It is anticipated that the next edition of the YEARBOOK will include illustrations of most if not all of the medals listed.

I1. BHARAT RATNA

Instituted: 1954.
Branch of Service: Indian nationals, though it has been awarded to non-Indians.
Ribbon: 50mm, white moiré.
Metal: Bronze and silver-gilt.
Size: 58mm x 47mm.
Description: (Obverse) a dull bronze pipal (Ficus religiosa) leaf design, stem downwards. In the centre, a burnished bronze sunburst with the name of the decoration in silver-gilt in Sanskrit/Hindi "Bharat Ratna" below; (reverse) in the centre, the national emblem in burnished bronze. Worn around the neck from an oval suspender.
Comments: *The Bharat Ratna (or, roughly translated, "Jewel of India") is India's supreme decoration and honor, awarded for the highest degrees of national service. This service includes artistic, literary, and scientific achievement, as well as "recognition of public service of the highest order." Throughout the history of the decoration, it has been very carefully stressed that the award of the Bharat Ratna carries with it no title, no "knighthood," and no particular status.*

VALUE: **Extremely rare**

I2. PARAM VIR CHAKRA

Instituted: 1950.
Branch of Service: All members of the Indian Armed Forces.
Ribbon: 32mm, medium purple.
Metal: Bronze.
Size: 35mm.
Description: (Obverse) on a raised circle, the national emblem. Surrounding this, four replicas of Indra's Vajra (the all-powerful mythic thunderbolt weapon on the ancient Vedic god of war); (reverse) around a plain centre, two legends separated by lotus flowers, above the name of the decoration in Hindi and below in English "PARAM VIR CHAKRA". The decoration is suspended from a straight swivelling suspension bar. It is named and dated on the edge.
Comments: *The name translates (roughly) as "Highest Bravery Medal". Awarded to officers and enlisted personnel of all military branches for the highest degree of valor or self-sacrifice in the presence of the enemy. It may be awarded posthumously and, indeed, most of the awards have been posthumous. In many ways, the Param Vir Chakra can be seen as a post-Independence equivalent of the Victoria Cross.*

VALUE: **£7500–8000**

I3. ASHOKA CHAKRA

Instituted: 1952.
Branch of Service: All Indian citizens, both military and civilian personnel.
Ribbon: 32mm, dark green with a 2mm central saffron stripe.
Metal: Silver gilt.
Size: 35mm.
Description: (Obverse) the chakra of Ashoka, surrounded by a lotus wreath and with an ornate edge; (reverse) blank in the centre, with the name of the decoration in Hindi along the upper edge on the medal and the same name in English along the lower rim "ASHOKA CHAKRA", on either side is a lotus-flower design. Suspended by a swivelling straight bar suspender. The medal is named on the edge.
Comments: *The name translates (roughly) as "Ashoka Medal". Awarded for the "most conspicuous bravery or some daring or pre-eminent valour or self-sacrifice" other than in the face of the enemy. The decoration may be awarded either to military of civilian personnel and may be awarded posthumously. The medal was originally established as the "Ashoka Chakra, Class I" and was renamed in 1967. In many ways, the Ashoka Chakra can be seen as a post-independence equivalent of the George Cross.*

VALUE: **£6000+**

I4. PADMA VIBHUSHAN

Instituted: 1954
Branch of Service: All Indian citizens, both military and civilian personnel.
Ribbon: 32mm, medium pink (officially, "lotus-colored").
Metal: Burnished bronze and white gold.
Size: 30mm.

continued

Description: (Obverse) a "mainly circular" badge with geometrical patterns and, in the centre, a lotus flower with four major petals embossed in white gold, above and below this flower, the name of the decoration in Hindi in white gold; (reverse) the national emblem, with motto below, in white gold. The badge is suspended by a ring.

Comments: *The name translates (roughly) as "High Decoration of the Lotus". The Padma Vibhushan is awarded to recognize exceptional and distinguished service to the nation, in any field, including services rendered by government servants. In practice, most initial appointments have been to Padma Shri, with subsequent promotions to Padma Bhushan and Padma Vibhushan representing continued national service of an increasingly high order, although direct appointments to higher levels of the award have been rarely noted.*

VALUE: £1000–2000

I5. PADMA BHUSHAN

Instituted: 1954.
Branch of Service: All Indian citizens, both military and civilian personnel.
Ribbon: 32mm, medium pink (officially, "lotus-colored") with a 6mm central white stripe.
Metal: Burnished bronze and white gold.
Size: 30mm.
Description: (Obverse) a "mainly circular" badge with geometrical patterns and, in the centre, a lotus flower with three major petals embossed in white gold, above and below this flower, the name of the decoration in Hindi in white gold; (reverse) the national emblem, with motto below, in white gold. The badge is suspended by a ring.
Comments: *The name translates (roughly) as "Decoration of the Lotus". The Padma Bhushan is awarded to recognize distinguished service of a high order to the nation, in any field, including services rendered by government servants. In practice, most initial appointments have been to Padma Shri, with subsequent promotions to Padma Bhushan and Padma Vibhushan representing continued national service of an increasingly high order, although direct appointments to higher levels of the award have been rarely noted.*

VALUE: £800–1000

I6. SARVOTTAM YUDH SEVA MEDAL

Instituted: 1980.
Branch of Service: All members of the Indian Armed Forces.
Ribbon: 31mm, orange, with a central 2mm red stripe.
Metal: Unknown.
Size: Unknown.
Description: Unknown.
Comments: *The name translates as "Supreme Battle Service Medal". Awarded for the highest degree of distinguished services in an operational context. In many ways, this is an operational version of the Param Vishisht Seva Medal which, since 1980, has been restricted to non-operational awards. To date, this has apparently not been awarded.*

VALUE: Rare

I7. PARAM VISHISHT SEVA EDAL

Instituted: 1960.
Branch of Service: All members of the Indian Armed Forces.
Ribbon: 32mm, yellow, with a 2mm central stripe of dark blue.
Metal: Silver gilt.
Size: 35mm.
Description: (Obverse) a five-pointed star; (reverse) the national emblem with the name of the decoration in Hindi above (until 1967, this would have been "Vishisht Seva Medal", the class being implied by the metal in which the decoration was produced, after 1967, the name was altered, predictably, to "Param Vishisht Seva Medal"). Suspended from a swivelling straight bar suspender. Named on the edge.
Comments: *The name translates as "Highest Distinguished Service Medal". The Param Vishsish Seva Medal is awarded to recognize "distinguished service of the most exceptional order" to all ranks of the armed forces. In practice, however, the award tends to be granted only to the most senior officers of the various branches of the Indian military. The medal was originally established as the "Vishisht Seva Medal, Class I" and was renamed in 1967.*

VALUE:
Vishisht Seva Medal, Class I (1960–67)	£800–1500
Param Vishisht Seva Medal (1967–)	£700–1250

I8. MAHA VIR CHAKRA

Instituted: 1950.
Branch of Service: All members of the Indian Armed Forces.
Ribbon: 32mm, half white, half orange-saffron.
Metal: Silver and silver-gilt.
Size: 35mm.
Description: (Obverse) a five-pointed star. On the centre of this star. a domed gilded national emblem; (reverse) around a plain centre, two legends separated by lotus flowers, above the name of the decoration in Hindi and below "MAHA VIR CHAKRA". The medal is suspended from a swivelling straight bar suspender. The medal is almost always seen named and dated on the edge.
Comments: *The name translates as "Great Bravery Medal". Awarded for the acts of valor in the presence of the enemy. It may be awarded posthumously.*

VALUE: £2000–3000

I9. KIRTI CHAKRA

Instituted: 1952.
Branch of Service: All Indian citizens, both military and civilian personnel.
Ribbon: 30mm, dark green with two 2mm saffron stripes.
Metal: Silver.
Size: 35mm.
Description: (Obverse) the chakra of Ashoka, surrounded by a lotus wreath and with an ornate edge; (reverse) for pre-1967 awards, the medal is blank in the centre, with the name of the decoration in Hindi along the upper edge on the medal and the same name in English along the lower rim, "ASHOKA CHAKRA", on either side is a lotus design, there is no indication of the class on the pre-1967 awards; for the post-1967 awards, the names are changed to "KIRTI CHAKRA". Suspended by a swivelling straight bar suspender. The medal is named on the edge.
Comments: *The name translates as "Glory Medal". Awarded for "conspicuous gallantry" in non-combatant situations. The Kirti Chakra can be awarded to military personnel as well as to civilians. The medal was originally established as the "Ashoka Chakra, Class II" and was renamed in 1967.*

VALUE:
      Ashoka Chakra, Class II (1952–67)   £1000–2500
      Kirti Chakra (1967–)   £800–2000

I10. PADMA SHRI

Instituted: 1954.
Branch of Service: All Indian citizens, both military and civilian personnel.
Ribbon: 31mm, medium pink ("lotus-colored") with two 6mm white stripes.
Metal: Burnished bronze and white gold.
Size: 30mm.
Description: (Obverse) a "mainly circular" toned bronze badge with geometrical patterns and, in the centre, a lotus flower with five major petals embossed in white gold, above and below this flower, the name of the decoration in Hindi is embossed in white gold; (reverse) the national emblem, with motto below, in white gold. The badge is suspended by a ring.
Comments: *The name translates (very roughly) as "Honour of the Lotus". The Padma Shri is awarded to recognize distinguished service to the nation, in any field, including services rendered by government servants. In practice, most initial appointments have been to Padma Shri, with subsequent promotions to Padma Bhushan and Padma Vibhushan representing continued national service of an increasingly high order, although direct appointments to higher levels of the award have been rarely noted.*

VALUE: £300–500

I11. SARVOTTAM JEEVAN RAKSHA PADAK

Instituted: 1961.
Branch of Service: Civilians.
Ribbon: 32mm red with light blue edge stripes and a 1mm green centre stripe.
Metal: Gold.
Size: 58mm.

continued

Description: (Obverse) a hand in the Abhai Mudra and, above "Ma Bhaih" in Hindi and below in Hindi "Jevan Rakash Padak" or on later issues "Sarvottam Jeevan Rakash Padak"; (reverse) the national emblem.

Comments: *The name translates as "Supreme Life Saving Medal". Awarded to civilians to recognize acts of lifesaving, including cases of drowning, fire, or mine accidents "for conspicuous courage under circumstances of very great danger to the life of the rescue." The only cases in which members of the armed forces, police, or fire services can be awarded the medal is when such acts take place outside the course of their duty. The medal was originally established as the "Jeevan Raksha Padak, Class I" but was later renamed.*

VALUE:

Jeevan Raksha Padak, Class I	£400–600
Sarvottam Jeevan Raksha Padak	£200–400

I12. UTTAM YUDH SEVA MEDAL

Instituted: 1980.
Branch of Service: All members of the Indian Armed Forces.
Ribbon: 31mm, orange with two equally spaced 2mm red stripes.
Metal: Not known.
Size: Not known.
Description: Not known.
Comments. *The name translates (roughly) as "Best War Service Medal". Awarded for a high degree of distinguished services in an operational context. In many ways, this is an operational version of the Ati Vishisht Seva Medal which, since 1980, has been restricted to non-operational awards. To date, this only appears to have been awarded twice.*

VALUE: **Rare**

I14. ATI VISHISHT SEVA MEDAL

Instituted: 1960.
Branch of Service: All members of the Indian Armed Forces.
Ribbon: 32mm, yellow with two 2mm dark blue stripes.
Metal: Silver.
Size: 35mm.
Description: (Obverse) a five-pointed star in the centre; (reverse) the national emblem with the name of the decoration in Hindi above (until 1967, this would have been "Vishisht Seva Medal", the class being implied by the metal in which the decoration was produced; after 1967, the name was altered, predictably, "Ati Vishisht Seva Medal"). Suspended from a swivelling straight bar suspender. Named on the edge.
Comments: *The name translates (roughly) as "Higher Distinguished Service Medal". The Ati Vishsish Seva Medal is awarded to recognize "distinguished service of an exceptional order" to all ranks of the armed forces. The medal was originally established as the "Vishisht Seva Medal, Class II" and was renamed in 1967.*

VALUE:

Vishisht Seva Medal, Class II (1960–67)	£700–900
Ati Vishisht Seva Medal (1967–)	£600–800

I15. VIR CHAKRA

Instituted: 1950.
Branch of Service: All members of the Indian Armed Forces.
Ribbon: 32mm, half dark blue and half orange-saffron.
Metal: Silver.
Size: 35mm.
Description: (Obverse) a five pointed star, with the *chakra* in the centre, and, on this, the domed gilded national emblem; (reverse) around a plain centre, two legends separated by lotus flowers: above the name of the decoration in Hindi and below "VIR CHAKRA". The decoration is suspended from a swivelling straight bar suspender and is almost always named and dated on the edge.
Comments: *The name translates as "Bravery Medal". Awarded for acts of gallantry in the presence of the enemy.*

VALUE: £800–1200

I16. SHAURYA CHAKRA

Instituted: 1952.
Branch of Service: All Indian citizens, both military and civilian personnel.
Ribbon: 30mm, dark green with three 2mm orange stripes.
Metal: Bronze.
Size: 35mm.
Description: (Obverse) in the centre, the *chakra* of Ashoka, surrounded by a lotus wreath and with an ornate edge; (reverse) for pre-1967 awards, the medal is blank in the centre, with the name of the decoration in Hindi along the upper edge on the medal and the same name in English along the lower rim, "ASHOKA CHAKRA", on either side is a lotus design; there is no indication of the class on the pre-1967 awards, for the post-1967 awards, the, names are changed to Shaurya Chakra in Hindi above and "SHAURYA CHAKRA" below. Suspended by a swivelling straight bar suspender. The medal is named on the edge.
Comments: *The name translates as "Heroism Medal". Awarded for gallantry other than in the face of the enemy. The medal was originally established as the "Ashoka Chakra, Class III" and was renamed in 1967.*

VALUE:

Ashoka Chakra, Class III (1952–67)	£500–700
Shaurya Chakra (1967–)	£300–500

I17. YUDH SEVA MEDAL

Instituted: 1980.
Branch of Service: All members of the Indian Armed Forces.
Ribbon: 31mm, orange with three equally spaced 2mm red stripes.
Metal: Unknown.
Size: Unknown.
Description: Unknown.
Comments: *The name translates as "War Service Medal". Awarded for a high degree of distinguished services in an operational context. In many ways, this is an operational version of the Vishisht Seva Medal which, since 1980, has been restricted to non-operational awards.*

VALUE: £450–550

I18. PRESIDENT'S POLICE AND FIRE SERVICES MEDAL FOR GALLANTRY

Instituted: 1951.
Branch of Service: The organized police, Central Intelligence Bureau, or organized fire services.
Ribbon: 32mm, half dark blue, half white, with a 2mm red central stripe.
Metal: Silver.
Size: Unknown.
Description: (Obverse) the embossed flag of the President of India on a shield in gilt and the legend "PRESIDENT'S POLICE AND FIRE SERVICES MEDAL" above and "INDIA" below, these two legends are separated by five-pointed stars; (reverse) the national emblem in the centre with "FOR GALLANTRY" above and a wreath below.
Comments: *Awarded to those who have performed acts of exceptional courage. In normal circumstances, no more than forty-five presidential police medals for gallantry may be awarded in any single year.*

VALUE: £500–550

I19. PRESIDENT'S POLICE MEDAL FOR GALLANTRY

Instituted: Unknown.
Branch of Service: The organized police and Central Intelligence Bureau.
Ribbon: 32mm, half dark blue, half white, with a 2mm red central stripe.
Metal: Silver
Size: Unknown.
Description: (Obverse) a five-pointed star within a wreath; (reverse) within a wreath, the national emblem, surrounded by a legend. Suspended by a swivelling straight bar suspender.

continued

Comments: *This Medal is awarded for conspicuous gallantry in saving life and property, or in preventing crime or arresting criminals. All police personnel of the country irrespective of rank and length of service are eligible for this award.*

VALUE: £500–550

I20. PRESIDENT'S FIRE SERVICES MEDAL FOR GALLANTRY

Instituted: Unknown.
Branch of Service: The organized fire services.
Ribbon: Unknown.
Metal: Unknown.
Size: Unknown.
Description: Unknown.

VALUE: £600–700

I21. PRESIDENT'S HOME GUARDS AND CIVIL DEFENSE MEDAL FOR GALLANTRY

Instituted: 1974.
Branch of Service: All members of the home guards, civil defense, and mobile civil defense emergency forces.
Ribbon: 32mm, black with an 8mm white centre, these stripes are separated by 4mm saffron-orange stripes.
Metal: Silver.
Size: 35mm.
Description: (Obverse) the national emblem and motto in gilt and, below, the emblem of the Home Guards, surrounding it the name of the medal in Hindi and "PRESIDENT'S HOME GUARDS AND CIVIL DEFENCE MEDAL"; (reverse) the *chakra* of Ashoka in the centre, surrounded by the Hindi legend "Vitra" or "Gallantry" and "GALLANTRY". The medal is named on the rim.
Comments: *Awarded to those who have performed acts of exceptional courage and skill.*

VALUE: £600–700

I22. SENA MEDAL

Instituted: 1960.
Branch of Service: All members of the Indian Army.
Ribbon: 32mm, red, with a 2mm white central stripe.
Metal: Silver.
Size: 35mm.
Description: (Obverse) a bayonet, point upwards; (reverse) a standing soldier with the legend in Hindi "Sena Medal" above. The medal is suspended by a swivelling straight bar suspender and is named on the edge. The medal is also often dated on the edge as well.
Comments: *The name translates as "Army Medal". Awarded to members of the army, of all ranks, "for such individual acts of exceptional devotion to duty or courage as have special significance for the Army." In effect, the Sena Medal serves as a sort of general commendation medal for the Indian Army. In some cases, it is also awarded for gallantry.*

VALUE: £100–170

I23. NAO SENA MEDAL

Instituted: 1960.
Branch of Service: All members of the Indian Navy.
Ribbon: 32mm, dark blue with a 2mm white central stripe.
Metal: Silver.
Size: 35mm.
Description: (Obverse) the naval crest (a naval crown); (reverse) crossed anchors, partially surrounded by a

chain cable. Above, "Nao Sena Medal" in Hindi. The medal is suspended by an ornate swivelling straight bar suspender and is named and usually dated on the edge.

Comments: *The name translates (roughly) as "Navy Medal". Awarded to all members of the Indian Navy "for such individual acts of exceptional devotion to duty or courage as have special significance for the Navy." In effect, the Nao Sena Medal serves as a sort of general commendation medal for the Indian Navy. In some cases, it is also awarded for gallantry.*

VALUE: £250–350

I24. VAYU SENA MEDAL

Instituted: 1960.
Branch of Service: All members of the Indian Air Force.
Ribbon: 30mm, alternating 2mm diagonal (lower left to upper right) stripes of grey and orange-saffron.
Metal: Star.
Size: Unknown.
Description: (Obverse) a four-armed star with the points shaped like lotus blooms, in the centre, the national emblem; (reverse) a Himalayan Eagle with wings spread, and the legend, above and below, "Air Force / Medal" in Hindi. Suspended by a swivelling (?) straight bar suspender and normally named and dated on the edge.
Comments: *The name translates (roughly) as "Air Force Medal". Awarded to all members of the Indian Air Force "in recognition of such individual acts of exceptional devotion to duty or courage as have special significance for the Air Force." In effect, the Vayu Sena Medal serves as a sort of general commendation medal for the Indian Air Force. In some cases, it is also awarded for gallantry.*

VALUE: £200–300

I25. VISHISHT SEVA MEDAL

Instituted: 1960.
Branch of Service: All members of the Indian Armed Forces.
Ribbon: 32mm, yellow with three 2mm dark blue stripes.
Metal: Bronze.
Size: 35mm.
Description: (Obverse) a five-pointed star in the centre; (reverse) the national emblem with the name of the decoration in Hindi above, "Vishisht Seva Medal". Suspended from a swivelling straight-bar suspender. Named on the edge.
Comments: *The name translates as "Distinguished Service Medal". The Vishsish Seva Medal is awarded to recognize "distinguished service of an exceptional order" to all ranks of the armed forces. The medal was originally established as the "Vishisht Seva Medal, Class III" and was renamed in 1967.*

VALUE: £100–200

I26. INDIAN POLICE MEDAL FOR GALLANTRY

Instituted: 1932.
Branch of Service: Members of a recognized Indian police force, the Central Intelligence Bureau, or an organized fire service.
Ribbon: 34mm, dark blue with a 10mm medium red central stripe, 5mm white edge stripes, and a 1mm white stripe just in from these edge stripes.
Metal: Bronze.
Size: 36mm.
Description: (Obverse) the crowned head of King George VI, facing left, there is some question whether the medal was ever issued with the post-1947 royal titles; (reverse) within a crowned wreath, the words "INDIAN / POLICE" and on a ribbon tying the sides of the wreath "FOR GALLANTRY". Suspended by a swivelling straight-bar suspender and named on the edge.
Comments: *This medal was awarded for acts of bravery by members of the Indian Police. This represents a continuation of the pre-Independence colonial medal into the period of time when India was a dominion, 1947-50. (This is the same as MYB59 in the UK listings.)*

VALUE: £150–250

I27. POLICE MEDAL FOR GALLANTRY

Instituted: 1951.
Branch of Service: Members of a recognized Indian police force, the Central Intelligence Bureau, or an organized fire service. With the creation of a separate Fire Services Medal for Gallantry, those personnel were no longer eligible for this award.
Ribbon: 34mm, dark blue with a 10mm medium red central stripe, 5mm white edge stripes, and a 1mm white stripe just in from these edge stripes.
Metal: Bronze.
Size: 36mm.
Description: (Obverse) the national emblem in the centre and the legend "Police Medal" above and "POLICE MEDAL" in English below; (reverse) two horizontal lines, above and below the legend "Indian / Police" and, in the centre, "For Gallantry", the entire reverse is contained within a wreath. Suspended by a swivelling straight bar suspender and named on the edge.
Comments: *Awarded to those members of the police who have performed services of conspicuous gallantry.*

VALUE: £100–200

I28. FIRE SERVICES MEDAL FOR GALLANTRY

Instituted: Unknown.
Branch of Service: The organized fire services.
Ribbon: 32mm, half yellow, half brown.
Metal: Unknown.
Size: Unknown.
Description: Unknown.
Comments: *Awarded to those members of the fire services who have performed services of conspicuous gallantry.*

VALUE: £150–250

I29. HOME GUARDS AND CIVIL DEFENCE MEDAL FOR GALLANTRY

Instituted: 1974.
Branch of Service: Awarded to members of the home guards, civil defense, and mobile civil emergency force.
Ribbon: 32mm, five stripes, three 8mm white and two 4mm black, the central white stripe has a thin (1mm) black stripe down the centre.
Metal: Bronze.
Size: 35mm.
Description: (Obverse) the national emblem and motto and surrounding this the name of the medal in Hindi and English "HOME GUARDS AND CIVIL DEFENCE MEDAL"; (reverse) the Home Guards emblem, surrounded by the Hindi legend "Virta" or "Gallantry" and "GALLANTRY" in English. The medal is suspended from a ring and named on the edge.
Comments: *Awarded to those members of the home guards and organized civil defence who have performed services of conspicuous gallantry.*

VALUE: £200–300

I30. UTTAM JEEVAN RAKSHA PADAK

Instituted: 1961.
Branch of Service: Civilians.
Ribbon: 32mm red with 4mm light blue edge stripes and two 1mm green centre stripes.
Metal: Silver.
Size: 58mm.
Description: (Obverse) a hand in the *Abhai Mudra* and, above in Hindi "Ma Bhaih" and below, also in Hindi, "Jeevan Rakash Padak" or later "Uttam Jeevan Rakash Padak"; (reverse) the national emblem.
Comments: *The name translates (roughly) as "Best Life Saving Medal". Awarded to civilians to recognize acts of lifesaving, including cases of drowning, fire, or mine accidents "for courage and promptitude under circumstances of very great danger to the life of the rescue." The only cases in which members of the armed forces, police, or fire*

services can be awarded the medal is when such acts take place outside the course of their duty. The medal was originally established as the "Jeevan Raksha Padak, Class II" and was later renamed.

VALUE:
Jeevan Raksha Padak, Class II   —
Uttam Jeevan Raksha Padak   —

I31. PRIME MINISTER'S LIFE SAVING MEDAL

Instituted: 1958.
Branch of Service: All members of the Indian police forces.
Ribbon: Unknown.
Metal: Unknown.
Size: Unknown.
Description: Unknown.
Comments: *Awarded to police personnel within the territory of India who have done outstanding work in saving life.*

VALUE: £100–120

I32. WOUND MEDAL

Instituted: 1973.
Branch of Service: All members of the Indian military, including reserve and territorial forces, and members of the Railway Protection Force, police, Home Guards, civil defense, or any other organization specified by the government.
Ribbon: 32 mm, white, with a 10mm red central stripe.
Metal: Silver.
Size: 35mm.
Description: (Obverse) the national emblem in the centre, to the left, the name of the medal in Hindi and to the right "WOUND MEDAL"; (reverse) within a circle, Ashoka's *chakra*. The medal is suspended by a ring and is named on the edge with impressed capital letters.
Comments: *Awarded for those who sustain "wounds as in result of direct enemy action in any type of operations or counter-insurgency actions." Eligible categories include all ranks of the Indian military, including reserve and territorial forces, and members of the Railway Protection Force, police, Home Guards, civil defense, or any other organization specified by the government. Aircrews who, in the course of bailing out of an aircraft destroyed by hostile action may be awarded if they sustain injuries (and not, specifically, "wounds"). The medal may not be awarded posthumously.*

VALUE: £30–40

I33. GENERAL SERVICE MEDAL 1947

Instituted: 1950.
Campaign: For general service in campaigns from 1947 to 1965.
Branch of Service: Indian armed forces, including reserve forces, territorial army, Indian States' Forces, militia, nursing services, and enrolled or uniformed civilians. It some cases, it appears to have also been awarded to police personnel.
Ribbon: 31mm, red with five 1mm dark green stripes.
Metal: Cupro-nickel.
Size: 35mm.
Description: (Obverse) the Bhavani, or divine sword of justice and true discrimination, point upward and within a halo; (reverse) a lotus flower with buds with the legend above "GENERAL SERVICE" and, below, "INDIA". Suspended by a non-swivelling straight bar suspender to which the bar is attached. The medals are usually named on the edge with impressed capital letters.
Clasps: Seven bars: Jammu and Kashmir (1947-49), Overseas Korea 1950–53, Naga Hills (1955–56), Goa 1961, Ladakh 1962, NEFA 1962, Mizo Hills (1966-75)
Comments: *Awarded for service with the Indian armed forces (including reserve forces, territorial army, Indian States' Forces, militia, nursing services, and enrolled or uniformed civilians) in circumstances of active service. The individual active service events are each represented by a bar. Throughout, and regardless of the specified time periods for qualification decoration, wounds resulting in evacuation, or death in circumstances of active service result in automatic eligibility for the medal and appropriate bar. Likewise, time spent as a prisoner-of-war is allowed to count toward the qualifying period. In 1965, the medal was superseded by the Samanya Seva Medal.*
continued

I33. *continued*

VALUE:

Jammu and Kashmir (1947–49)	£20–35	Ladakh 1962	£35–50
Overseas Korea 1950–53	£200–250	NEFA 1962	£20–30
Naga Hills	£20–30	Mizo Hills	£25–30
Goa 1961	£25–35		

Multi-bar medals should be considered scarce, perhaps £20 for each extra bar.

I34. SAMANYA SEVA MEDAL 1965

Instituted: 1975.

Campaign: For general service in minor campaigns since 1965.

Branch of Service: Indian armed forces, including reserve forces, territorial army, militia, nursing services, and enrolled or uniformed civilians. It some cases, it appears to have also been awarded to police personnel.

Ribbon: 30.5mm, medium green with three, equally spaced, 3.5mm stripes of red, dark blue, and light blue.

Metal: Cupro-nickel.

Size: 35mm.

Description: (Obverse) the national emblem and, to the left the name of the medal in Hindi and to the right "SAMANYA SEVA MEDAL", at the bottom, the date "1965"; (reverse) the Indian elephant badge, drawn from the design of the flag of the Indian president. The medal is suspended by a non-swivelling straight bar suspender to which the bar is attached and is usually named on the edge.

Clasps: The clasps are always in Hindi, but the English versions of their names are given here. To date, there have been five bars: Kutch Khargil 1965, Nathula Chola (1967), Nagaland (1975), Mizoram (1975), Tirap (19??).

Comments: *The name translates as "General Service Medal, 1965". Intended as a successor for the General Service Medal 1947, the Samanya Seva Medal, 1965 was awarded for specific services in specified actions which were represented by bars attached to the medal. Throughout, and regardless of the specified time periods for qualification decoration, wounds resulting in evacuation, or death in circumstances of active service result in automatic eligibility for the medal and appropriate bar. Likewise, time spent as a prisoner-of-war is allowed to count toward the qualifying period.*

VALUE:

Kutch Khargil 1965	£20–35
Nathula Chola	£20–30
Nagaland	£15–25
Mizoram	£15–25
Tirap	£15–25
Manipur	£20–30

Multi-bar medals should be considered scarce, perhaps £20 for each extra bar.

I35. SAMAR SEVA STAR

Instituted: 1967.

Campaign: For combat service in the 1965 Indo-Pakistani War.

Branch of Service: Indian armed forces, including reserve forces, territorial army, militia, nursing services, and enrolled or uniformed civilians. It some cases, it appears to have also been awarded to police personnel.

Ribbon: 30mm, red, dark blue, and light blue, with five thin 1mm white stripes.

Metal: Bronze.

Size: 39mm.

Description: (Obverse) a five-pointed star with the national emblem with the surrounding legend of the name of the medal in Hindi; (reverse) the naming details are impressed in the centre of the plain reverse. Suspended by a ring.

Comments: *Awarded for ten days of service in an area defined as a "battle zone" during the 1965 war between India and Pakistan (5 August 1965–25 January 1966), or for one day of service in actual combat conditions, or for three operational sorties or three operational flying hours (five hours for air observation post personnel). It was awarded to all members of the Indian armed forces, as well as to reserve, territorial, and militia personnel, as well as to civilians who served in combat areas in support positions. The name translates (roughly) as "Battle Service Star".*

VALUE: £15–25

I36. POORVI STAR

Instituted: 1973
Campaign: For combat service in the eastern theater of operations in the 1971 Indo-Pakistani War.
Branch of Service: Indian armed forces, including reserve forces, territorial army, militia, nursing services, and enrolled or uniformed civilians. It some cases, it appears to have also been awarded to police personnel.
Ribbon: 33mm, green with an 11mm central stripe of yellow.
Metal: Bronze.
Size: 40mm.
Description: (Obverse) a five-pointed star. In the domed circular centre, the national emblem with the surrounding legend "POORVI STAR" and the name of the medal in Hindi; (reverse) the naming details are impressed in the centre of the plain reverse. Suspended by a ring.
Comments: *Awarded to all ranks of the Indian armed forces, police forces, and civilians employed in support of the armed forces during the 1971 Indo-Pakistani War. The Poorvi Star was awarded to those who served in the eastern theater of war for one day in a battle zone (3 December–16 December 1971 in Bangladesh or the Bay of Bengal), for ten days in another qualifying area (25 March 1971–25 March 1972 in specified areas of West Bengal, Bihar, Assam, Meghalaya, Tripura, Mizoram, and specified airfields and ports), or who carried out one operational sortie or three flying hours in the zones and periods specified. The name translates as "Eastern Star".*

VALUE: £20–30

I37. PASCHIMI STAR

Instituted: 1973.
Campaign: For combat service in the western theater of operations in the 1971 Indo-Pakistani War.
Branch of Service: Indian armed forces, including reserve forces, territorial army, militia, nursing services, and enrolled or uniformed civilians. It some cases, it appears to have also been awarded to police personnel.
Ribbon: 31mm, medium pink with three 2mm white central stripes.
Metal: Bronze.
Size: 40mm.
Description: (Obverse) a five-pointed star. In the domed circular centre, the national emblem with the surrounding legend "PASCHIMI STAR" and the name of the medal in Hindi; (reverse) the naming details are impressed in the centre of the plain reverse.
Comments: *Awarded to all ranks of the Indian armed forces, police forces, and civilians employed in support of the armed forces during the 1971 Indo-Pakistani War. The Paschimi Star was awarded to those who served in the western theater of war for one day in a battle zone (3 December–16 December 1971 in specified "battle zones" in Jammu and Kashmir, Punjab, Rajasthan, Gujarat, and the Arabian Sea), for ten days in another qualifying area (25 March 1971–25 March 1972 in specified areas of Jammu and Kashmir, Punjab, Rajasthan, Gujarat, and specified airfields and ports), or who carried out one operational sortie or three flying hours in the zones and periods specified. The name translates as "Western Star".*

VALUE: £15–25

I38. SIACHEN GLACIER MEDAL

Instituted: 1987.
Campaign: For the ongoing clashes since 1984 between Indian and Pakistani troops on the Siachen Glacier of the High Himalayas.
Branch of Service: Indian armed forces, including reserve forces, territorial army, militia, nursing services, and enrolled or uniformed civilians. It some cases, it appears to have also been awarded to police personnel.
Ribbon: 31mm, equal stripes of medium blue 10mm, white 11mm, and medium blue 10mm.
Metal: Cupro-nickel.
Size: 36mm.
Description: (Obverse) the national emblem, surrounded by the name of the medal in Hindi and the English; (reverse) a stylized scene of the mountains with standing figures and a helicopter. Suspended by a non-swivelling straight bar suspender and is usually named on the edge.
Comments: —

VALUE: £15–25

I39. SPECIAL SERVICE MEDAL

Instituted: 1986.
Campaign: Awarded for a range of special operational assignments.
Branch of Service: Indian armed forces, including reserve forces, territorial army, militia, nursing services, and enrolled or uniformed civilians. It some cases, it appears to have also been awarded to police personnel.
Ribbon: 30mm, medium blue-grey with 6.5mm red edges.
Metal: Cupro-nickel.
Size: 35mm.
Description: (Obverse) within a sunburst (outer) and wreath (inner), the National emblem. Above and below, there is the name of the medal in Hindi and the legend "SPECIAL SERVICE MEDAL"; (reverse) within a sunburst (outer) and wreath (inner), a dove flying to the left above a mountain range. Suspended by a non-swivelling straight bar suspender to which the bar is attached and it is usually named on the edge.
Clasps: The clasps are in Hindi, but are given here in translation: Rakshak (1984–), Sri Lanka (1987–90).
Comments: *Instituted to recognize special services by the Indian military which could not easily be recognized by existing medals.*

VALUE:
   Rakshak   —
   Sri Lanka   £15–25

I40. RAKSHA MEDAL 1965

Instituted: 1967.
Campaign: For service in the 1965 Indo-Pakistani War.
Branch of Service: Indian armed forces, including reserve forces, territorial army, militia, nursing services, and enrolled or uniformed civilians. It some cases, it appears to have also been awarded to police personnel.
Ribbon: 31.5mm, orange with three, equally spaced, 3.5mm stripes of red, dark blue, and light blue.
Metal: Cupro-nickel.
Size: 36mm.
Description: (Obverse) the national emblem; (reverse) the depiction of a rising sun, with a half-wreath below and, above, the name of the medal in Hindi "Raksha Medal/1965". Suspended by a non-swivelling straight bar suspender. The medal is usually named on the edge.
Comments: *Awarded for service in the 1965 war with Pakistan. The medal was awarded to any armed forces personnel, paramilitary forces under military command (including police forces in many cases) who were borne on the effective strength of their unit on 5 August 1965 and who had, as of that date, served for at least 180 days. The medal was also awarded to anyone who qualified for the Samar Seva Star. The name translates as "Defence Medal"*

VALUE: £10–15

I41. SANGRAM MEDAL

Instituted: 1973.
Campaign: For service in the 1971 Indo-Pakistani War.
Branch of Service: Indian armed forces, including reserve forces, territorial army, militia, nursing services, and enrolled or uniformed civilians. It some cases, it appears to have also been awarded to police personnel.
Ribbon: 32mm, maroon-brown with three 1mm white stripes.
Metal: Cupro-nickel.
Size: 35mm.
Description: (Obverse) the national emblem in the centre with the surrounding name of the medal in Hindi and English; (reverse) the depiction of a rising sun, with a half-wreath below. Suspended from a ring suspender. The medal is normally named on the edge.
Comments: *The name translates (roughly) as "Battle Medal" Awarded for service during the 1971/72 war with Pakistan. The medal could be given to all categories of personnel who served in the military, paramilitary forces, police, and civilians in service in the operational areas of Jammu and Kashmir, Punjab, Gujarat, Rajasthan, West Bengal, Assam, Meghalaya, Mizoram, or Tripura between 3 December 1971 and 20 December 1972 (both dates inclusive).*

VALUE: £8–12

I42. SAINYA SEVA MEDAL

Instituted: 1960.
Branch of Service: Indian armed forces.
Ribbon: 32mm, orange-saffron, with two 1mm stripes, white and green.
Metal: Cupro-nickel.
Size: 36mm.
Description: (Obverse) an image of the Nanda Devi mountain peak with a bamboo stand in the foreground; (reverse) the gate to a medieval fort (actually the gate at Purana Quila in New Delhi), above, the Hindi legend "Sainya Seva Medal". Suspended by a non-swivelling straight bar suspender to which the bar is attached. The medal is normally named on the edge.
Clasps: Clasps exist only in Hindi, but the names have been translated here. To date, six clasps have been observed: Jammu and Kashmir, NEFA, Himalaya (not awarded after 1986, when it was replaced by the High Altitude Service Medal), Bengal-Assam, Andaman and Nicobar, and Desert.
Comments: *The name translates (roughly) as "Military Service Medal" Awarded in recognition of non-operational services under conditions of special hardship and severe climate.*

VALUE:

Jammu and Kashmir	£10–12
NEFA	£15–20
Himalaya·	£10–12
Bengal–Assam	£12–15
Andaman and Nicobar	£40–50
Desert	£20–30

Multi-bar medals should be considered scarce, perhaps £20 for each extra bar.

I43. HIGH ALTITUDE SERVICE MEDAL

Instituted: 1986.
Branch of Service: Indian armed forces, including reserve forces, territorial army, militia, nursing services, and enrolled or uniformed civilians. It some cases, it appears to have also been awarded to police personnel.
Ribbon: 32mm, medium blue with a series of 1.5mm white chevrons, approximately 6mm apart. The ribbon is observed with a great deal of variation, but never of consistent high quality. Many specimens are produced from what seems to be thin plasticized paper, while others are made from a coarse, almost plastic, material (where the medium blue almost seems to have been painted on); all ribbons observed are distinctly one-sided.
Metal: Cupro-nickel.
Size: 35mm
Description: (Obverse) the national emblem in the centre, on either side, the name of the medal in Hindi, of the left in Hindi and on the right in Roman characters "UCCHH TUNGTA MEDAL" (High Altitude Service Medal); (reverse) a somewhat stylized scene of the Himalayan mountains. Suspended from a non-swivelling straight bar suspender. Usually named on the edge.
Comments: *Awarded for service in the high Himalayas, above 9000 feet (approximately 2700 m). This medal replaces the earlier "Himalaya" clasp to the Sainya Seva Medal.*

VALUE: £15-25

I44. POLICE (SPECIAL DUTY) MEDAL

Instituted: 1962.
Branch of Service: The Indian police forces.
Ribbon: 34.5mm, white, with a series of 4mm stripes: red, yellow, green, red, yellow, green.
Metal: Cupro-nickel.
Size: 39mm.
Description: (Obverse) the national emblem within an ornate wreath; (reverse) a low-relief depiction of the high Himayalas, labeled below left in English as "GANGOTRI", above, the curved Hindi legend "Police Katin Seva Padak" appears. Suspended by an ornate non-swivelling straight bar suspender to which the bar is attached. The medal has not been observed named.
Clasps: To date, ten clasps have been reported, all in English: Jammu and Kashmir, J&K, Mizoram, Nagaland, Punjab, Rajasthan, Tripura, Gujarat, Himachal Pradesh, Manipur.
Comments: *Awarded in recognition of services by police personnel under conditions of special hardship and/or severe climate. Multi-bar medals do not exist, as separate medals are awarded for each period of qualifying service (even if it duplicates an earlier award).*

continued

I44. *continued*

VALUE:

Chandigarh	£20–25	Meghalay	£20–25
Gujarat	£15–25	Mizoram	£15–20
Himachal Pradesh	£20–25	Nagaland	£15–20
J&K	£25–35	Punjab	£15–20
Jammu and Kashmir	£10–12	Rajasthan	£10–12
Manipur	£15–20	Tripura	£20–25

I45. VIDESH SEVA MEDAL

Instituted: 1960.

Branch of Service: Indian armed forces, including reserve forces, territorial army, militia, nursing services, and enrolled or uniformed civilians. It some cases, it appears to have also been awarded to police personnel.

Ribbon: 32mm, medium blue with five equally spaced 1mm white stripes.

Metal: Cupro-nickel.

Size: 35mm.

Description: (Obverse) the national emblem and, below the name of the medal in Hindi; (reverse) an ancient Indian ship on the open stormy seas. Suspended by a non-swivelling straight bar suspender to which the bar is attached. The medal is normally named on the edge.

Clasps: To date, at least forty bars have been issued and more can be expected to be forthcoming. All bars observed have been in Hindi, but their names are translated here

Comments: *The name translates as "Foreign Service Medal". Awarded to military personnel for services outside of India. Personnel assigned to diplomatic missions are excluded from awards. In many cases, the clasps are awarded either for service with the United Nations or other multi-national missions or for detached service on loan to foreign governments.*

VALUE:

Korea (NNRC, 1950–54)	£20–35	Iran–Iraq (UNIIMOG, 1988–91)	scarce
Nepal (1952–)	£25–40	Afghanistan	rare
Indo-China (ICSC, 1954–)	£25–40	Zambia	rare
Indonesia (1955–)	rare	Sudan	rare
United Arab Republic (UNEF, 1956–)	£20–35	Namibia (UNTAG, 1989–90)	rare
Ethiopia (1957–)	rare	Central America (ONUCA, 1989–92)	rare
Lebanon (UNOGIL, 1958)	rare	Angola (UNAVEM and MONUA, 1989–)	scarce
Iraq (1959–)	rare	Cambodia (UNAMIC and UNTAC, 1991–93)	scarce
Ghana (1959–)	rare	El Salvador (ONUSAL, 1991–95)	rare
Congo (ONUC, 1960–64)	£20–35	Iraq–Kuwait (UNIIKOM, 1991–)	rare
Bhutan (1961–)	£25–40	Western Sahara (MINUSRO, 1991–)	scarce
Nigeria	rare	Mozambique (ONUMOZ, 1992–94)	rare
New Guinea (UNTEA and UNSF, 1962–63)	rare	Yugoslavia (UNPROFOR, 1992–95)	rare
Yemen (UNYOM, 1963–64)	scarce	Somalia (UNOSOM, 1992–95)	scarce
Algeria (1963–)	rare	Haiti (UNMIH, 1993–96)	rare
Cyprus (UNFICYP, 1964–)	rare	Rwanda (UNAMIR, 1993–96)	rare
Bangladesh	rare	Liberia UNOMIL, (1993–)	rare
Mauritius	rare	Bosnia and Herzegovina (UNMIBH, 1995–)	rare
Sri Lanka (1987–90)	£25–30	Angola (MONUA, 1997–)	rare
Maldives (1988)	rare	Sierra Leone (UNOMISL, 1998–)	rare
		Multi-bar medals should be considered rare.	

I46. PRESIDENT'S POLICE AND FIRE SERVICES MEDAL FOR DISTINGUISHED SERVICE

Instituted: 1951.

Branch of Service: The organized police, Central Intelligence Bureau, or organized fire services.

Ribbon: 32mm, half dark blue, half white.

Metal: Silver and silver-gilt.

Size: Unknown.

Description: (Obverse) the embossed flag of the President of India on a shield in gilt and the legend "PRESIDENT'S POLICE AND FIRE SERVICES MEDAL" above and "INDIA" below, these two legends are separated by five-pointed stars; (reverse) the national emblem in the centre with "FOR DISTINGUISHED SERVICE" above and a wreath below.

Comments: *Awarded to those who have performed acts of conspicuous devotion to duty.*

VALUE: £200–250

I47. PRESIDENT'S POLICE MEDAL FOR DISTINGUISHED SERVICE

Instituted: Unknown.
Branch of Service: The organized police and Central Intelligence Bureau with twenty-one years of service.
Ribbon: 32mm, half dark blue, half white.
Metal: Silver.
Size: Unknown.
Description: (Obverse) a five-pointed star within a wreath; (reverse) within a wreath, the national emblem surrounded by a legend. Suspended by a straight-bar suspender.
Comments: *Every year about 125 Medals are awarded on the occasion of Independence and Republic Day in recognition of a special distinguished record in Police service or in the Central Police/ Security Organisation.*

VALUE: £200–250

I48. PRESIDENT'S FIRE SERVICES MEDAL FOR DISTINGUISHED SERVICE

Instituted: Unknown.
Branch of Service: The organized fire services.
Ribbon: Unknown.
Metal: Unknown.
Size: Unknown.
Description: Unknown.

VALUE: £250–350

I49. PRESIDENT'S HOME GUARDS AND CIVIL DEFENCE MEDAL FOR DISTINGUISHED SERVICE

Instituted: 1974.
Branch of Service: Awarded to members of the home guards, civil defense, and mobile civil emergency force.
Ribbon: 32mm, black with an 8mm white centre, these stripes are separated by thin 4mm saffron-orange stripes.
Metal: Silver.
Size: 35mm.
Description: (Obverse) the national emblem and motto in gilt and, below, the emblem of the Home Guards, surrounding it the name of the medal in Hindi and in English "PRESIDENT'S HOME GUARDS AND CIVIL DEFENCE MEDAL"; (reverse) the *chakra* of Ashoka in the centre, surrounded by the Hindi legend "Sarahaniy Seva" or "Distinguished Service" and "DISTINGUISHED SERVICE". Suspended by ???. The medal is named on the rim.
Comments: *Awarded to those who have exhibited conspicuous devotion to duty.*

VALUE: £300–400

I50. MERITORIOUS SERVICE MEDAL

Instituted: 1957.
Branch of Service: Non-commissioned personnel of the Indian armed forces.
Ribbon: (First ribbon, 1957–69) 33mm, claret, with 4mm white edges and a 3mm white centre stripe; (second ribbon, 1969–) 33.5mm, medium grey with 1.5mm white edge stripes and three 1.5mm stripes of red, dark blue, and light blue. *continued*

Metal: Silver.
Size: 36mm.
Description: (Obverse) the national emblem within an ornate rim; (reverse) within an ornate lotus wreath, the legend "FOR/MERITORIOUS/– SERVICE –" and the same legend in Hindi. Suspended from an ornate swivelling straight bar suspender. The medal is normally named on the edge.
Comments: *Awarded to non-commissioned officers of the rank of dafadar/havildar, chief petty officer/petty officer, or warrant officer, flight sergeant/sergeant for eighteen years of distinguished service. In 1970, the requisite period of service was reduced to fifteen years.*

VALUE: £25–35

I51. LONG SERVICE AND GOOD CONDUCT MEDAL

Instituted: 1957.
Branch of Service: Non-commissioned personnel of the Indian armed forces.
Ribbon: (First ribbon, 1957–69) 33mm, claret with 4mm white edge stripes; (second ribbon, 1969–) 32mm, medium grey with 2.5mm white edge stripes and narrow (2mm) edge stripes (reading inward) of red, dark blue, and light blue.
Metal: Silver.
Size: 36mm.
Description: (Obverse) the national emblem within an ornate rim; (reverse) within an ornate lotus-wreath, the circular legend "FOR LONG SERVICE AND GOOD CONDUCT" and, within this circular legend, the Hindi name of the medal. Suspended from an ornate swivelling straight bar suspender. The medal is normally named on the edge.
Comments: *Awarded to non-commissioned officers below the rank of dafadar/havildar or below the ranks of petty officer/corporal and to enlisted personnel for fifteen years of distinguished service. When originally established in 1957, the requirements for award were eighteen years in the army and air force and only fifteen years for the navy; in 1970, the requisite period of service was standardized across services at fifteen years.*

VALUE: £20–25

I52. COAST GUARD MEDAL FOR MERITORIOUS SERVICE

Instituted: Unknown.
Branch of Service: Unknown.
Ribbon: White with two blue stripes (?).
Metal: Unknown.
Size: Unknown.
Description: Unknown.

VALUE: £30–45

I53. INDIAN POLICE MEDAL FOR MERITORIOUS SERVICE

Instituted: 1932.
Branch of Service: Indian police and fire services.
Ribbon: 35mm, dark blue, with 5mm white edge stripes and a 13mm claret central stripe.
Metal: Bronze.
Size: 36mm.
Description: (Obverse) the head of King George VI, it is unclear whether the medal was ever issued with the post-1947 royal titles; (reverse) within a crowned wreath, the words "INDIAN / POLICE" and on a ribbon tying the sides of the wreath "FOR MERITORIOUS SERVICE". Suspended by a non-swivelling straight bar suspender and named on the edge.
Comments: *This represents a continuation of the pre-Independence colonial medal into the period of time when India was a dominion, 1947–50. (This is the same as MYB59 in the UK listings.)*

VALUE: £150–100

I54. POLICE MEDAL FOR MERITORIOUS SERVICE

Instituted: 1951.
Branch of Service: Indian police and fire services with at least fifteen years of service.
Ribbon: 35mm, dark blue, with 5mm white edge stripes and a 13mm claret central stripe.
Metal: Bronze.
Size: 36mm.
Description: (Obverse) the national emblem in the centre and the legend "Police Medal" above; (reverse) two horizontal lines, above and below the legend "Indian/Police" and, in the centre, "For Meritorious Service", the entire reverse is contained within a wreath. Suspended by a non-swivelling straight bar suspender and named on the edge.
Comments: *Awarded to those who have performed services of conspicuous merit. No more than 750 such medals may be awarded in any one year.*

VALUE: £150–200

I55. FIRE SERVICES MEDAL FOR MERITORIOUS SERVICE

Instituted: Unknown.
Branch of Service: Unknown.
Ribbon: 31.5mm, brick red with 2.5mm gold edge stripes and three 2.5mm black stripes.
Metal: Unknown.
Size: Unknown.
Description: Unknown.

VALUE: £250–350

I56. HOME GUARDS AND CIVIL DEFENCE MEDAL FOR MERITORIOUS SERVICE

Instituted: 1974.
Branch of Service: Awarded to members of the home guards, civil defense, and mobile civil emergency force.
Ribbon: 32mm, five stripes, three 8mm white and two 4mm black, the central white stripe has a thin (1mm) black stripe down the centre.
Metal: Bronze.
Size: 35mm.
Description: (Obverse) the national emblem and motto. Surrounding, the Hindi legend "Home Guards and Civil Defense Medal" and, in English, "HOME GUARDS AND CIVIL DEFENCE MEDAL"; (reverse) the Home Guards emblem, surrounded by the Hindi and English legends "MERITORIOUS SERVICE". The medal is suspended from a ring and named on the edge.
Comments: *Awarded for meritorious service.*

VALUE: £250–350

I57. JEEVAN RAKSHA PADAK

Instituted: 1961.
Branch of Service: Civilians.
Ribbon: 32mm red with 4mm light blue edge stripes and three 1mm green centre stripes.
Metal: Bronze.
Size: 58mm.
Description: (Obvrese) a hand in the *Abhai Mudra* and in Hindi, above "Ma Bhaih" and below "Jevan Rakash Padak"; (reverse) the national emblem.
Comments: *The name translates as "Live Saving Medal" Awarded to civilians to recognize acts of lifesaving, including cases of drowning, fire, or mine accidents "for conspicuous courage under circumstances of very danger of grave bodily injury to the rescue." The only cases in which members of the armed forces, police, or fire services can be awarded the medal is when such acts take place outside the course of their duty. The medal was originally established as the "Jeevan Raksha Padak, Class III" and was later renamed.*

VALUE: £50-80

I58. TERRITORIAL ARMY DECORATION

Instituted: 1952.
Branch of Service: Officers of the Territorial Army.
Ribbon: 30mm, dark blue with a 10mm central orange stripe; the blue stripes have 1mm white stripes at the centre and between the blue and orange parts.
Metal: Silver.
Size: Unknown.
Description: (Obverse) an oblong medal with a five-pointed star in the centre, surrounded by an oblong wreath; (reverse) a Hindi legend translating as "For Good Service". Suspended by a ring and the national emblem. A square bar "TERRITORIAL" is used to suspend the ribbon.
Comments: *The medal is awarded to officers of the Territorial Army for twenty years of efficient service.*

VALUE: £70–80

I59. TERRITORIAL ARMY MEDAL

Instituted: 1952.
Branch of Service: Enlisted personnel of the Territorial Army.
Ribbon: 29mm, dark blue, with a 1mm orange central stripes and, on each side, two equally spaced 1mm white stripes.
Metal: Silver.
Size: 43 x 32mm.
Description: (Obverse) an oblong medal with the national emblem in the centre; (reverse) around the upper edge, a Hindi legend translating as "For Good Service". Suspended from an ornate non-swivelling straight bar suspender carrying a ribbon bearing the legend "TERRITORIAL". The lower portion of the reverse is blank (not, apparently, for naming since the medal is named on the edge). The medal is usually named on the edge.
Comments: *The medal is awarded to junior commissioned officers, non-commissioned officers, and enlisted personnel of the Territorial Army for twelve years of efficient service during which they have attended a minimum of twelve training sessions; recipients also must be specifically recommended for the award. A bar is awarded for eighteen years of service and a second bar may be awarded for twenty-four years of service. The bar is made of silver and bears Ashoka's chakra.*

VALUE: £30–40

I60. INDIAN INDEPENDENCE MEDAL 1947

Instituted: 1949.
Branch of Service: "All Indian Nationals and Nepalese Gurkhas, male and female, on the strength of units or formations of the Indian Armed Forces on 15 August, 1947 and the Ruling Princes and State Forces of States acceeding to the Dominion of India by 1 January, 1948."
Ribbon: 30mm, three equal orange, white, green stripes.
Metal: Cupro-nickel.
Size: 36mm.
Description: (Obverse) Ashoka's *chakra*, crowned (for the only time) with the surrounding legend: "GEORGIUS : VI D : G : BRITT : OMN : RED : FID : DEF"; (reverse) the national emblem, without motto, and the legend "INDIAN INDEPDNDENCE/15TH AUGUST 1947". Suspended by a non-swivelling straight bar suspender. The medal is normally named on the edge.
Comments: *Awarded to all members of the Indian armed forces (including those rulers and State Forces of those "Princely" States that had acceded to India before 1 January 1948) who were serving on 15 August 1947. It was also awarded to British service personnel who remained in India after Independence to assist in the reformulation of the armed forces of India after Partition and who were still serving on 1 January 1948.*

VALUE: £10–15

I61. INDEPENDENCE MEDAL 1950

Instituted: Unknown.
Branch of Service: Indian police forces.
Ribbon: 32mm, red with a 9mm orange central stripe; a 2mm dark blue stripe separates the red and orange on each side.
Metal: Cupro-nickel.
Size: 36mm.

Description: (Obverse) the national emblem in the centre surrounded by the legend "INDEPENDENCE MEDAL/26th JANUARY 1950"; (reverse) within a lotus wreath, the *chakra* and, below, the legend "POLICE". Suspended by a non-swivelling straight bar suspender. The medal is normally not named.

Comments: *Awarded to all members of the Indian police forces who were serving on 26 January 1950, the date of the proclamation of India's status as a republic (and, in effect, of full independence, as India had been a dominion since 15 August 1947).*

VALUE: £15–20

I62. FIFTIETH INDEPENDENCE ANNIVERSARY MEDAL

Instituted: 1997.
Branch of Service: Indian armed forces and police services.
Ribbon: 32mm, yellow with central 3mm stripes of orange, white, and green.
Metal: Cupro-nickel.
Size: 35mm.
Description: (Obverse) the Lahori Gate of the Red Fort in Delhi with the legend above "50th INDEPENDENCE ANNIVERSARY" and below "1947-1997"; (reverse) a pebbled map of India with the Hindi legend above "50th Anniversary of Independence" and, below, "1947-1997". Suspended by a non-swivelling straight bar suspender. Official issues are named on the edge.
Comments: *Instituted to commemorate the fiftieth anniversary of India's independence, 15 August 1997. . The medal was awarded to all members of the armed forces, paramilitary forces, and police forces (broadly defined) who were serving on that date.*

VALUE: £15–20

I63. TWENTY-FIFTH INDEPENDENCE ANNIVERSARY MEDAL

Instituted: 1973.
Branch of Service: Indian armed forces and police services.
Ribbon: 32mm, maroon with central stripes of orange, white, green (4mm each).
Metal: Cupro-nickel.
Size: 35mm.
Description: (Obverse) the national emblem in the centre, surrounded by the legend in English and Hindi "25th INDEPENDENCE ANNIVERSARY MEDAL"; (reverse) the *chakra* with the dates "1947 / 1972" above and below. Suspended by a ring. Usually named on the edge.
Comments: *Awarded to commemorate the twenty-fifth anniversary of Indian independence in 1972. The medal was awarded to all members of the armed forces, paramilitary forces, and police forces (broadly defined) who were serving on 15 August 1972.*

VALUE: £8–12

I64. THIRTY YEARS LONG SERVICE MEDAL

Instituted: 1980.
Branch of Service: All members of the Indian armed forces.
Ribbon: 31mm, orange, with a central strips of red, dark blue, light blue (each 3mm).
Metal: Cupro-nickel.
Size: 35mm.
Description: (Obverse) the national emblem in the centre, surrounded by the Hindi and English legends above "LONG SERVICE" and, below, "30 YEARS"; (reverse) a depiction of the joint armed services emblem of crossed swords, anchor, and eagle with a rising sun above. Suspended by a non-swivelling straight bar suspender. Usually named on the edge.
Comments: *Awarded to all armed services personnel for thirty years of service. In almost all cases, this medal would – of course – be awarded to very senior officers or Junior Commissioned Officers.*

VALUE: £20–30

I65. TWENTY YEARS LONG SERVICE MEDAL

Instituted: 1971.
Branch of Service: All members of the Indian armed forces.
Ribbon: 30mm, equal stripes of red, dark blue, light blue.
Metal: Cupro-nickel.
Size: 35mm.
Description: (Obverse) the national emblem in the centre, surrounded by the Hindi and English legends above "LONG SERVICE" and, below, "20 YEARS"; (reverse) a depiction of the joint armed services emblem of crossed swords, anchor, and eagle with a rising sun above. Suspended by a non-swivelling straight bar suspender. Usually named on the edge.
Comments: *Awarded to all armed services personnel for twenty years of service*

VALUE: £10–15

I66. NINE YEARS LONG SERVICE MEDAL

Instituted: 1971.
Branch of Service: All members of the Indian armed forces.
Ribbon: 34mm, green with nine equally spaced 1mm black stripes.
Metal: Cupro-nickel.
Size: 35mm
Description: (Obverse) the national emblem in the centre, surrounded by the Hindi and English legends above "LONG SERVICE" and, below, "9 YEARS"; (reverse) a depiction of the joint armed services emblem of crossed swords, anchor, and eagle with a rising sun above. Suspended by a non-swivelling straight bar suspender. Usually named on the edge.
Comments: *Awarded to all armed services personnel for nine years of service*

VALUE: £8–12

I67. HIGH DEFENCE SECURITY CORPS MEDAL

Instituted: 1964.
Branch of Service: Members of the Defence Security Corps.
Ribbon: 32mm, light blue with two 1mm yellow stripes, 2mm apart, toward each edge.
Metal: Bronze (?).
Size: 35mm.
Description: (Obverse) the national emblem; (reverse) two crossed swords with a five-pointed star above and the Hindi legend indicating the name of the medal (which altered in 1968). Suspended from a swivelling ornate straight bar suspender. Usually named on the edge.
Comments: *The medal is awarded annually to officers and enlisted personnel of the Defence Security Corps (Raksha Suraksha Corps) who have served for a minimum of seven years in the Defence Security Corps and for a total of fifteen years in combined armed services and Defence Security Corps service. The medal is awarded on a scale of two per thousand enlisted personnel in the Defence Security Corps. It carries with it a pension of Rs. 25 per year. Personnel who meet the qualifications but are not awarded this medal will be awarded the Defence Security Corps Medal.*

VALUE:
Defence Security Corps Medal, Class I (1964–68)   £25–35
High Defence Security Corps Medal (1968–)   £25–35

I68. DEFENCE SECURITY CORPS MEDAL

Instituted: 1964.
Branch of Service: Members of the Defence Security Corps.
Ribbon: 32mm, light blue with a 1mm yellow stripe toward each edge.
Metal: Bronze.
Size: 35mm.
Description: (Obverse) the national emblem; (reverse) two crossed swords with a five-pointed star above and the Hindi and English legend indicating the name of the medal (which altered in 1968). Suspended from a swivelling ornate straight bar suspender. Usually named on the edge.

Comments: *The medal is awarded annually to officers and enlisted personnel of the Defence Security Corps (Raksha Suraksha Corps) who have served for a minimum of seven years in the Defence Security Corps and for a total of fifteen years in combined armed services and Defence Security Corps service. This medal is awarded to those who have met the conditions of award for the High Defence Security Corps Medal but have not received that medal (and its pension). The medal is awarded on a scale of two per thousand enlisted personnel in the Defence Security Corps.*

VALUE:
Defence Security Corps Medal, Class II (1964–68)	£20–30
Defence Security Corps Medal (1968–)	£20–30

I69. NATIONAL CADET CORPS LONG SERVICE MEDAL FOR FOURTEEN YEARS

Instituted: Unknown.
Branch of Service: Officers of the National Cadet Corps.
Ribbon: Unknown.
Metal: Cupro-nickel.
Size: 35mm.
Description: (Obverse) the national emblem with, above in Hindi and English "NATIONAL CADET CORPS" and below in Hindi and English "FOURTEEN YEARS LONG SERVICE MEDAL"; (reverse) a small domed wreathed circle with "NCC" and below in Hindi "Unity and Discipline". Suspended by a non-swivelling straight bar suspender and named on the edge.
Comments: *Awarded to officers seconded to the National Cadet Corps (usually university professors) for fourteen years of service.*

VALUE: £35–45

I70. NATIONAL CADET CORPS LONG SERVICE MEDAL FOR SEVEN YEARS

Instituted: Unknown.
Branch of Service: Officers of the National Cadet Corps.
Ribbon: Unknown.
Metal: Cupro-nickel.
Size: 35mm.
Description: (Obverse) the national emblem with, above in Hindi and English "NATIONAL CADET CORPS" and below in Hindi and English "SEVEN YEARS LONG SERVICE MEDAL"; (reverse) a small domed wreathed circle with "NCC" and below in Hindi "Unity and Discipline". Suspended by a non-swivelling straight bar suspender and named on the edge.
Comments: *Awarded to officers seconded to the National Cadet Corps (usually university professors) for seven years of service.*

VALUE: £20–30

Foreign medals
found in British
groups

There are a number of awards and decorations issued by Foreign Governments which are frequently encountered in groups of medals awarded to British servicemen. These awards have usually been officially conferred by the foreign power and make an interesting addition to the service history of the recipient.We list below just a few of the awards most commonly encountered in groups of the World War I period, obviously there are many, many more examples from other periods and most can be identified using standard reference works. For further details of many of these award listed here we would recommend reading, amongst many other publications, *The Medals, Decorations & Orders of the Great War 1914–1918* by Alec A. Purves, available from Token Publishing Ltd, price £16. The prices quoted in this section are for single examples of the medals alone; when they are included with a group of British medals the price can often be many times the quoted figure.

BELGIUM

Commander's neck badge, Order of Leopold II

ORDER OF LEOPOLD II
Commander's neck badge   £100–150
Knight's badge   £35–50

Miniature   £20–25

BELGIUM *continued*

Officer's badge, Order of the Crown

ORDER OF THE CROWN
Officer's badge   £15–25
Knight's badge   £15–25

Miniature   £15–20

CROIX DE GUERRE   £12–15

Miniature   £8–10

FRANCE

LEGION d'HONNEUR 1870–1951
Neck badge   £185–200
Breast badge   £35–60

Miniature   £25–30

MÉDAILLE MILITAIRE 1870   £20–30

Miniature   £20–25

FRANCE *continued*

GREECE

1914–18 reverse

CROIX DE GUERRE

1914–16 reverse	£15–20
1914–17 reverse	£15–20
1914–18 reverse	£12–15
for each star or palm add £3	
Miniature	£10–12

ORDER OF THE REDEEMER

Commander's badge	£275–400
Knight's badge	£225–275
Officer's badge	£120–180
Miniature	£40–50

ITALY

AL VALORE (unnamed)

Bronze	£30–40
Silver	£50–60
Miniature, silver	£25–30

Restrikes are also known. They can be distinguished from the originals by the omission of the initials FG at the bottom on the obverse.

ORDER OF THE CROWN 2nd Class

Breast badge	£90–125
Officer's badge	£60–90
Knight's badge	£45–60
Miniature	£20–30

In addition to the above medals, the Messina Earthquake Medal, awarded by the King of Italy in 1908 to British personnel who went to the aid of victims of the tragic earthquake at Messina, can be found under Medal No. 163A

ITALY *continued*

WAR CROSS	£15–20
Miniature	£8–10

King Victor Emmanuel III of Italy pictured in uniform, 1918.

JAPAN

ORDER OF THE RISING SUN

3rd Class	£500–600
4th Clas	£375–425
5th Class	£280–350
6th Class	£200–300
7th Class	£50–75
8th Class	£20–40
Miniature	£30–40

ORDER OF THE SACRED TREASURE

3rd Class	£400–450
4th Clas	£200–250
5th Class	£120–150
Miniature	£40–50

RUSSIA

ORDER OF St STANISLAUS (illustrated)

Gold	£450–£500
Silver-gilt	£160–185
Miniature	£50–60

ORDER OF St ANNE

Gold	£250–350
Miniature	£50–60

CROSS OF St GEORGE

3rd Class	£90–110
4th Class	£50–70
Miniature	£30–40

MEDAL OF St GEORGE

3rd Class	£90–110
4th Clas	£40–60
Miniature	£10–15

SERBIA

ORDER OF KARAGEORGE
  4th Class   £200–300

ORDER OF THE WHITE EAGLE WITH SWORDS
  Knight's badge   £100–150

  Miniature   £40–50

TURKEY

ORDER OF THE MEDJIDIEH
1st Class	£480–500
2nd Clas	£350–400
3rd Class	£150–200
4h Class	£85–125
5th Class	£65–85

ORDER OF THE OSMANIEH
1st Class	£480–500
2nd Clas	£380–420
3rd Class	£170–200
4th Class	£85–125
5th Class	£65–85

Abbreviations and initials

O Observer

The medal collector is constantly coming across initials and abbreviations on medals and in documents—many of which are commonplace and easily decipherable. However, there are many more which can cause problems when trying to identify a medal recipient. The following list represents only a small selection of the inexhaustible number of abbreviations encountered, but hopefully it will be of some assistance to the collector. The *"Token Book of Militarisms"* contains literally hundreds more if you cannot find the abbreviation you are looking for here.

1 E Ang   1st East Anglian Regiment
1 R Dgns   1st Royal Dragoons
1 QDG   1st Queen's Dragoon Guards
11H   11th Royal Hussars
12L   12th Royal Lancers
13/18H   13th/18th Royal Hussars
14/20H   14th/20th Royal Hussars
15/19H   15th/19th Royal Hussars
3 E Ang   3rd East Anglian Regiment
4 QOH   4th Queen's Own Hussars
4H   4th Royal Hussars
5 DGds   5th Royal Inniskilling Dragoon Guards
7QOH   7th Queen's Own Hussars
7GR   7th Gurkha Rifles
A/   Acting
A Avn   Army Aviation
Abn Inf   Airborne Infantry
A/CWEM   Acting Chief Weapons Engineering Mechanic
A/LMEM   Acting Leading Marine Engineering Mechanic
A/LRO(G)   Acting Leading Radio Operator (General)
A/PO   Acting Petty Officer, Acting Pilot Officer
A&SH   The Argyll and Sutherland Highlanders
AAC   Army Air Corps
AAU   Air Ambulance Unit
AB   Able Seaman; Airborne
ABDS   Army Bomb Disposal Squad
AC1   Aircraftman 1st Class
ACC   Army Catering Corps, Armoured Car Company
ACF   Army Cadet Force
ADALS   Assistant Director, Army Legal Service
AE   Army Education Officer, Air Efficiency Award
AER   Army Emergency Reserve
AFC   Air Force Cross
AFM   Air Force Medal
AGS   Africa General Service Medal
AIY   Ayrshire Imperial Yeomanry
ALO   Air Liaison Officer
ALS   Army Legal Services

AM   Albert Medal
AM1   Air Mechanic 1st Class
AMA   Acting Master at Arms
AMS   Assistant Military Secretary; Army Medical Staff
AOC   Army Ordnance Corps
APC   Army Pay Corps
APL   Aden Protectorate Levies
APTC   Army Physical Training Corps
AQ   Assistant Quartermaster; Administrative Quartermaster
Armd   Armoured
ASC   Army Service Corps; Air Service Command
ATO   Ammunition Technical Officer
B&H   The Bedfordshire & Hertfordshire Regiment
B&R   Blues & Royals
BAAT   British Army Advisory Team
BATT   British Army Training Team
BAO   British Army of Occupation
Bdr   Bombadier
BDU   Bomb Disposal Unit
BEM   British Empire Medal
BF   British Forces
BGS   Brigadier, General Staff
BIY   Bedford Imperial Yeomanry
BM   Brigade Major
BORD.R   Border Regiment
BR   British
Brig   Brigadier
Br Coy   Bearer Company
BSA Police   British South Africa Police
Buffs   The Buffs (Royal East Kent Regiment)
BW   Black Watch (Royal Highland Regiment)
BWM   British War Medal
C&TC   Commissariat and Transport Corps
C/Sgt   Colour Sergeant
C&S   Command & Staff
CAC   Canadian Armoured Corps
CADAC   Canadian Army Dental Corps
CAEA   Chief Air Engineering Artificer
CAHTC   Cape Auxiliary Horse Transport Corps
CAMN HIGH   Cameron Highlanders
Capt   Captain

CAR Central African Rifles
CASC Canadian Army Service Corps
CATO Commander Ammunition Technical Officers
CB Commander of the Order of the Bath
CBE Commander of the Order of the British Empire
CBF Commander British Forces
CC Cadet Corps; Coastal Command; Combat Command
CCAEA Charge Chief Air Engineering Artificer
CCCC Cape Colony Cyclist Corps
CCF Combined Cadet Force
CCMEA Charge Chief Marine Engineering Artificer
CCS Casualty Clearing Station
C de G Croix de Guerre
Cdr Commander
CE Canadian Engineers
CEO Chief Executive Officer; Chief Education Officer
CG Coast Guard; Commanding General
CGC Conspicuous Gallantry Cross
CGM Conspicuous Gallantry Medal
Cheshire The Cheshire Regiment
CI Crown of India, Imperial Order; Counter-Intelligence
CIV City Imperial Volunteers
CIE Companion of the Order of the Indian Empire
CLY County of London Yeomanry
CMEM Chief Marine Engineering Mechanic
CMFR Commonwealth Monitoring Force Rhodesia
CMG Companion of the Order of St Michael and St George
CMM Commander of the Order of Military Merit
CMO Chief Medical Officer
CMMP Corps of Military Mounted Police
CMP Corps of Military Police
CMSC Cape Medical Staff Corps
CMR Cape Mounted Riflemen
CO Commanding Officer
Col Colonel
Coldm Gds Coldstream Guards
Comd Commander
COS Chief of Staff
CP Cape Police
Cpl Corporal
CPO Chief Petty Officer
CPOAEA Chief Petty Officer Air Engineering Artificer
CPOWEA Chief Petty Officer Weapons Engineering Artificer
CSI Companion of the Order of the Star of India
CSM Company Sergeant Major; Campaign Service Medal
CT, C/T, Ch Tech Chief Technician
CVO Commander of the Royal Victorian Order
D Diver
D Comd Deputy Commander
D&D The Devon and Dorset Regiment
DAD Deputy Assistant Director
DADOS Deputy Assistant Director of Ordnance Services
DADVRS Deputy Assistant Director Veterinary & Remount Section
DAMA Department of the Army Material Annex
DANS Director of Army Nursing Services
DAPM Deputy Assistant Provost Marshall
DAT Director of Army Training

DBE Dame Commander, Order of the British Empire
DCLI The Duke of Cornwall's Light Infantry
DCM Distinguished Conduct Medal
DCMG Dame Commander of the Order of St Michael and St George
DCO Duke of Cambridge's Own; Duke of Connaught's Own
DCOS Deputy Chief of Staff
DCVO Dame Commander of the Royal Victorian Order
DDSD Deputy Director Staff Duties
DEO Duke of Edinburgh's Own
DERR The Duke of Edinburgh's Royal Regiment (Berkshire & Wiltshire)
Det Detached; Detachment
Devon The Devonshire Regiment
DFC Distinguished Flying Cross
DFM Distinguished Flying Medal
DG Dragoon Guards
DI Defence Intelligence
DLI The Durham Light Infantry
DMT District Mounted Troops
Dorset The Dorset Regiment
DOS Director of Ordnance Services
DS Defence Secretary; Deputy Secretary; Defensive Section
DSC Distinguished Service Cross
DSM Distinguished Service Medal
DSO Distinguished Service Order
DWR The Duke of Wellington's Regiment
EAR East African Rifles
ED Efficiency Decoration
EF Expeditionary Force
EGM Empire Gallantry Medal
EM Edward Medal; Efficiency Medal
EOD Explosive Ordnance Disposal
ERD Emergency Reserve Decoration
ERE Extra Regimentally Employed
FA Field Ambulance
FANYC First Aid Nursing Yeomanry Corps
FBRA Field Battery Royal Artillery
FC Fighter Command
Fd Field
FELF Far East Land Forces
FF Field Force
FFL French Foreign Legion
FFR Frontier Force Rifles
FL, F/L, Flt Lt Flight Lieutenant
FM Field Marshal
FMR Frontier Mounted Rifles
FO, F/O, Fg Off Flying Officer
FS Fighter Squadron; Field Security
FS, F/S, F/Sgt Flight Sergeant
Fus Fusilier
G Howards Green Howards (Alexandra, Princess of Wales's Own Yorkshire Regiment)
G Or General Operational Requirements
GBE Grand Cross, Order of the British Empire
GC George Cross, Group Captain
GCB Knight Grand Cross Order of the Bath
GCH Knight Grand Cross Hanoverian Order
GCIE Knight Grand Commander Order of the Indian Empire
GCLH Grand Cross Legion of Honour
GCM Good Conduct Medal

GCMG   Knight Grand Cross Order of St Michael
and St George
GCSI   Knight Grand Commander Order of the Star
of India
GCVO   Knight Grand Cross Royal Victorian Order
Gdsmn   Guardsman
GLI   Guernsey Light Infantry
Glosters   The Gloucestershire Regiment (28th/61st
Foot)
GM   George Medal
Gnr   Gunner
GOC   General Officer Commanding
Gordons   The Gordon Highlanders (75th/92nd
Regiment)
GPR   Glider Pilot Regiment
GR   Gurkha Rifles
GS   General Service
GSC   General Service Corps
GSM   General Service Medal
GSO   General Staff Officer
HA   Horse Artillery
HAC   Honourable Artillery Company
IIBM   Her Britannic Majesty
HCR   Household Cavalry Regiment
HG   Home Guard; Horse Guards
HLI   The Highland Light Infantry
HQ   Headquarters
IAOC   Indian Army Ordnance Corps
IASC   Indian Army Service Corps
IC   In Charge
IDSM   Indian Distinguished Service Medal
IE   Order of the Indian Empire
IG   Irish Guards
Int   Intelligence
Int Corps   Intelligence Corps
Int & Sy Coy   Intelligence and Security Company
IO   Intelligence Officer
IOM   Indian Order of Merit
IRC   Infantry Reserve Corps
ISM   Imperial Service Medal
ISO   Imperial Service Order
IY   Imperial Yeomanry
JSSC   Joint Services Staff College
KAR   King's African Rifles
KB   Knight Bachelor
KBE   Knight of the Order of the British Empire
KC   Knight Commander
KCB   Knight Commander Order of the Bath
KCH   Knight Commander of the Royal Hanoverian
Guelphic Order
KCIE   Knight Commander Order of the Indian
Empire
KCIO   King's Commissioned Indian Officer
KCMG   Knight Commander Order of St Michael
and St George
KCSI   Knight Commander Order of the Star of India
KCVO   Knight Commander Royal Victorian Order
KDG   King's Dragoon Guards
KG   Knight of the Order of the Garter
KGCB   Knight Grand Cross Order of the Bath
KGL   King's German Legion
Kings   The King's Regiment (Liverpool)
KLH   Knight of the Legion of Honour
KM   King's Medal
KOM   Knight of the Order of Malta
KORB   The King's Own Royal Border Regiment

KOSB   The King's Own Scottish Borderers
KOYLI   The King's Own Yorkshire Light Infantry
KPM   King's Police Medal
KRRC   The King's Royal Rifle Corps
KSG   Knight of the Order of St George
KSLI   The King's Shropshire Light Infantry
KT   Knight of the Order of the Thistle
L/Cpl   Lance Corporal
L/Sgt   Lance Sergeant
LAC   Leading Aircraftman
Lanc Fusiliers   The Lancashire Fusiliers
Lanc R   The Queen's Lancashire Regiment
LC   Labour Corps
Leic   The Royal Leicestershire Regiment
LG   Life Guards; London Gazette
LI   Light Infantry
Linc   The Royal Lincolnshire Regiment
LM   Legion of Merit
LMA   Leading Medical Assistant
LS   Leading Seaman
Lt   Lieutenant
Lt-Cdr   Lieutenant Commander
Lt-Col   Lieutenant-Colonel
MA   Military Attache
Maint   Maintenance
Maj   Major
Maj-Gen   Major-General
Mal.LBC   Maltese Labour Corps
MBE   Member of the Order of the British Empire
MC   Military Cross
MEM   Marine Engineering Mechanic
MFA   Mercantile Fleet Auxiliary
MFS   Medical Field Service
MGC   Machine Gun Corps
MH   Medal of Honour
MI   Mounted Infantry
MID   Mentioned in Despatches
MKW   Military Knights of Windsor
MM   Military Medal; Medal of Merit
MMGS   Motor Machine Gun Service
Mne   Marine
MMR   Mercantile Marine Service
MR   Middlesex Regiment
MRCVS   Member Royal College of Veterinary
Surgeons
MSC   Medical Staff Corps
MSM   Meritorious Service Medal
MTO   Motor Transport Office
MVO   Member of the Royal Victorian Order
NACS   Naval Air Commando Squadron
NAS   Naval Air Squadron
NCO   Non-Commissioned Officer
NFA   Natal Field Artillery
NGS   Naval General Service (Medal)
NZEF   New Zealand Expeditionary Force
OBE   Officer of the Order of the British Empire
OBLI   Ox and Bucks Light Infantry
OC   Officer Commanding
OCS   Officer Cadet School
OEO   Ordnance Executive Officer
OHBMS   On Her Britannic Majesty's Service
OM   Order of Merit
OR   Operational Requirements; Other Ranks;
Organised Reserve
Ord   Ordnance
OS   Ordinary Seaman; Ordnance Survey

PAOCVA Prince Albert's Own Cape Volunteer Rifles
PAVG Prince Albert's Volunteer Guard
Para The Parachute Regiment
PO Petty Officer
PO/AC Petty Officer Aircrewman
POMA Petty Officer Medical Assistant
POMEM Petty Officer Marine Engineering Mechanic
PR Public Relations
PSO Personnel Selection Officer
Pte Private
PVCP Permanent Vehicle Check Point
PWO The Prince of Wales's Own Regiment of Yorkshire
Q Ops Quartermaster General Branch Operations
QARANC Queen Alexandra's Royal Army Nursing Corps
QCBC Queen's Commendation for Brave Conduct
QFSM Queen's Fire Service Medal
QDG The Queen's Dragoon Guards
QGM Queen's Gallantry Medal
QLR The Queen's Lancashire Regiment
QM Quartermaster
QMAAC Queen Mary's Auxiliary Ambulance Corps
QPM Queen's Police Medal
QRIH Queen's Royal Irish Hussars
QSA Queen's South Africa (Medal)
Queens The Queen's Regiment—Queen's Division
R Anglian Royal Anglian Regiment
R Fus Royal Fusiliers (City of London Regiment)
R Innis Royal Inniskilling
R Signals Royal Corps of Signals
RA Royal Artillery
RAC Royal Armoured Corps
RAChD Royal Army Chaplains Department
RAEC Royal Army Educational Corps
RAFVR Royal Airforce Volunteer Reserve
RAMC Royal Army Medical Corps
RAOC Royal Army Ordnance Corps
RAPC Royal Army Pay Corps
RARO Regular Army Reserve of Officers
RASC Royal Army Service Corps
RAVC Royal Army Veterinary Corps
RB The Rifle Brigade
RCT Royal Corps of Transport
RE Corps of Royal Engineers
RECC Reconnaissance Corps
REME Corps of Royal Electrical and Mechanical Engineers
RF Royal Fusiliers
RFA Royal Field Artillery
Rfmn Rifleman
RGJ Royal Greenjackets
RHA Royal Horse Artillery
RHF The Royal Highland Fusiliers
RHG Royal Horse Guards
RI Royal Irish Rangers (27th (Inniskilling), 83rd and 87th)
RI Regt Royal Irish Regiment
RIC Royal Irish Corps
RIF The Royal Irish Fusiliers
RM Royal Marines
RMA Royal Military Academy
RMC Royal Military College

RMLI Royal Marine Light Infantry
RMP Corps of Royal Military Police
RNF The Royal Northumberland Fusiliers
RNR Royal Naval Reserve
RNVR Royal Naval Volunteer Reserve
RO Radio Operator
RPC Royal Pioneer Corps
RRC Royal Red Cross (Medal)
RRF Royal Regiment of Fusiliers
RRW Royal Regiment of Wales
RS The Royal Scots (The Royal Regiment)
RSDG Royal Scots Dragoon Guards
RSF Royal Scots Fusiliers
R Sig Royal Signals
RSM Regimental Sergeant Major
RSO Regimental Supply Officer
RTR Royal Tank Regiment, Royal Armoured Corps
RUR The Royal Ulster Rifles
RVM Royal Victorian Medal
RVO Royal Victorian Order
RWF The Royal Welsh Fusiliers
RWK The Queen's Own Royal West Kent Regiment
RW Kent R Royal West Kent Regiment
S/L, S/Ldr, Sqn Ldr Squadron Leader
S/Sgt Staff Sergeant
SAC Senior Aircraftman
SAS Special Air Service Regiment
SC Staff College; Staff Captain; Second in Command; Signal Corps
SF Special Forces
SG Scots Guards
SGM Sea Gallantry Medal
Sgmn Signalman
Sgt Sergeant
SI Star of India (Order)
SJAB St John Ambulance Brigade
SMIO Special Military Intelligence Officer
SMIU Special Military Intelligence Unit
Smn Seaman
SO1 Staff Officer, Grade 1
Som LI Somerset Light Infantry
SWB The South Wales Borderers
TA Territorial Army
T&AVR Territorial and Army Volunteer Reserve
TD Territorial Decoration
TEM Territorial Efficiency Medal
TF Territorial Force
TG Town Guard
Trg Gp Training Group
UKLF United Kingdom Land Forces
UNM United Nations Medal
UNSM United Nations Service Medal
V&A Victoria and Albert (Order)
VC Victoria Cross
WAAF Women's Auxiliary Air Force
WAFF West Afican Frontier Force
W/C, W/Cdr, Wg Cdr Wing Commander
W&S Worcestershire & Sherwood Foresters
WEA Weapons Engineering Artificer
WG Welsh Guards
Wilts Wiltshire Regiment
WO Warrant Officer
WOI Warrant Officer Class I
WOII Warrant Officer Class II
WRAC Women's Royal Army Corps
WRAF Women's Royal Air Force

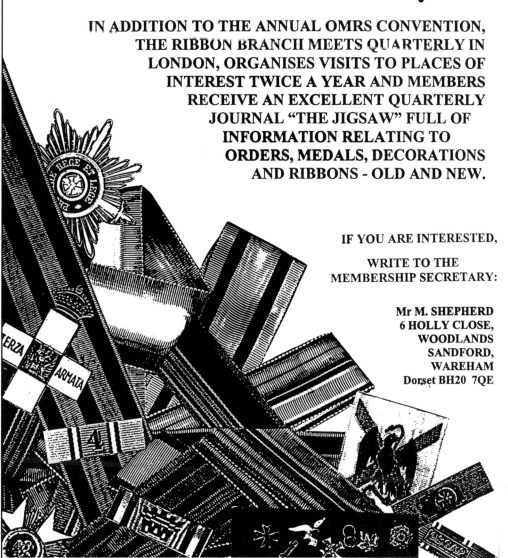

# **Researching your medals**

The fact that many British medals are named enables the serious collector to engage in researching both the life and service history of the recipient as well as being able to learn about the history of the regiment/ship/unit or whatever with which he served. There is no easy or definitive guide to the range of research materials that are available, nor to the range of information likely to be found. The sort of information available varies greatly depending on whether the recipient was an officer or other rank, the service and unit with which he served, and the period during which he served. The experience and perseverance of the researcher can also affect the outcome. For those who are new to research, or who live a long way from the original sources, it may be wise to employ a professional researcher, at least initially. The PRO keeps a list of independent researchers who undertake this kind of work

When researching a medal and its recipient, experienced collectors regularly refer to a mixture of manuscript and printed sources:

Manuscript Sources

The Public Record Office (PRO, Ruskin Avenue, Kew, Surrey TW9 4DU) and the Oriental & India Office Collections (OIOC, British Library, 96 Euston Road, London NW1 2DB) are the two major depositories of official records of interest to the medal collector. Generally speaking the collector of medals to the British Armed Services will find the PRO records essential to their enquiries, whilst anyone interest in the Indian Army and Navy (formerly the armed services of the Honourable East India Company), also the participation of British Forces in Indian campaigns, will find the OIOC to be an essential source of information. County Record Offices, National Libraries and Museums, and also Regimental Museums can also have important holdings of manuscript records.

A first visit to the PRO and the OIOC can be daunting. The range of records held by both Record Offices is also awe-inspiring once research has gone beyond consulting medal rolls and service papers.

Whilst there is no substitute for *experience* in learning successfully to branch out from the main stream of records, it is essential to be well prepared. It is important to have some idea of where to start looking and to realise the scope and limitations of the documents—it should be noted that the PRO is subject to the standard 30 year closure rule for records, with many personal records being closed for longer periods. A great deal of time can be spent in simply locating the relevant references. To help you be more informed and to help eliminate time-wasting there are a number of important guides available that will aid in the location of the most relevant documents:

Cox, J. and Padfield, T., *Tracing your Ancestors in the Public Record Office* (1983).
Farrington, A., *Guide to the Records of the India Office Military Department* (1981).

Hamilton-Edwards, Gerald, *In Search of Army Ancestry* (1977).
Holding, N., *The Location of British Army Records: A National Directory of World War I Sources* (1984).
Holding, N., *World War I Army Ancestry* (1982).
Rodger, N.A.M., *Naval Records for Genealogists* (1988).

In addition it is worth noting that
1. The Public Record Office produces a range of leaflets which provide useful information about particular classes of records—records relating to military, naval and air services are particularly well-covered. The leaflets are free to visitors to the PRO.
2. The Mormons have published a wide range of guides to genealogical research which cover subjects of interest to medal/military researchers.
3. The National Army Museum occasionally holds a study day on the subject of military research.
4. New information is becoming available all the time and in new forms: for example, the PRO has been producing a video on genealogical research.

Additionally, it is important to be aware that new documents are released periodically to public access. Probably the most important in recent years are those at the Public Record Office relating to World War I. Although the PRO and other record offices produce regular leaflets and guides to new records, **MEDAL NEWS** *now includes a regular feature which enables all collectors to remain abreast of the many records as they become available.*

Medal Entitlement/Verification

Most collectors start their research by checking with the campaign medal roll (if available) that the recipient is indeed entitled to the medal and any clasps. It is a logical point at which to begin. This is often regarded as a simple, routine procedure, but for the unwary there are pitfalls and complications. The following points should always be borne in mind:

1. Printed medal rolls will always contain errors in transcription, thus any discrepancies between a medal and the roll should, whenever possible, be checked

back with the original manuscript roll. The more complex the original roll, the more transcription errors are likely to occur (for example, the claimaints' lists for the Naval General Service Medal 1793-1840 and even the Military General Service Medal 1793-1814 are good examples of rolls where difficulties are likely to arise).

2. Some rolls have not survived—for example that for the Gwalior Campaign 1843. In such instances prize or bhatta rolls may exist at either the Public Record Office or the India Office. The inclusion of a recipient's name will at least indicate that he was most likely "entitled" to a medal and/or clasp (prize rolls indicate the share of money—realised from the loot captured in an action and then sold—allocated to each participant; bhatta is an extra allowance of pay made for field service).

3. Some medal rolls are incomplete, as with some of the regimental rolls for the Crimea Medal 1854–56.

4. With some campaign medal rolls, supplementary lists and late claimants' documentation have not survived.

5. Some medal rolls are difficult to search and therefore one has to take time in understanding the background to the documents one is looking at—the various lists of recipients for the Military General Service Medal 1794–1814 is a case in point.

It is important to note that the establishment of a recipient's entitlement is not the same thing as verifying a medal. Verification also requires the numismatic knowledge to know that the medal and clasps appear genuine. Where entitlement cannot be confirmed from the medal rolls, some collectors may be happy to rely on their numismatic knowledge to assure themselves that a medal is "genuine".

Published Sources

The published literature on medals is far-reaching and diverse, ranging from simply-produced booklets to detailed studies published in several volumes. A full bibliography of medallic and related works would in itself fill several volumes, particularly if fully cross-referenced.

The references which follow seek to provide a useful list of publications which either relate to orders, decorations and medals in general or to specific items in particular; the list includes medal rolls and casualty lists. No attempt has been made to include journal articles, as this would be an immense task; however a list of useful periodicals, some of which publish regular indexes, appears at the end.

Suggestions for other works that might be considered for inclusion in the next Yearbook *are welcomed.*

Most collectors seek to build up a solid library which reflects their main interests, but inevitably there are always books that have to be consulted elsewhere. Major libraries and national museums, such as the British Museum Library, the National Army Museum, the Imperial War Museum, the Hendon Royal Air Force Museum, the Greenwich Maritime Museum, and the Portsmouth Naval Musuem have extensive holdings of relevant material which can be consulted on the premises. City and County Reference Libraries are important for collectors who rarely visit London. Some Regimental

Museums have libraries attached. Most libraries of any size will have a subject index to their collection of books (and sometimes manuscripts and photographs).

ORDERS, DECORATIONS AND MEDALS

GENERAL WORKS
(listed in alphabetical order by author)

Alexander, E. G. M., Barron, G. K. B. and Bateman, A. J., *South African Orders, Decorations and Medals* (1986).

Blatherwick, Surg. Cmdr. F. J., *Canadian Orders, Decorations and Medals* (4th edition, 1994).

Brine, F., *British Decorations from 1348 to the Present Time, Together with Those Given by Allies* (1880).

Burke, J. B., *The Book of Orders of Knighthood and Decorations of Honour of All Nations* (1858).

Central Office of Information, *Honours and Titles.* Part of the Aspects of Britain series.

Downey, M., *The Standard Catalogue of Orders, Decorations and Medals Awarded to Australians* (1971).

Dymond, Steve, *Researching British Military Medals, a Practical Guide* (1999).

Eaton, Col. I Ion. I.F. (later Lord Cheylesmore)., *Naval and Military Medals* (1897).

Elvin, C.N., *A Handbook of the Orders of Chivalry, War Medals and Crosses with Their Clasps and Ribbons and Other Decorations* (1892).

Floyd., J. B. (ed), *United States Decorations Awarded to the Armed Forces of the British Empire in World War II, Part I* (1997).

Gibson, J.H., *British War Medals and Other Decorations, Military and Naval* (1866).

Gibson, J.H., *British Military and Naval Medals and Decorations* (1880).

Gordon, Major L.L., *British Orders and Awards* (1959).

Hall, D.C. (in association with Wingate, C.), *British Orders, Decorations and Medals* (1973).

Hastings, Irwin D., *War Medals and Decorations* (1910).

Hieronymussen, Paul, *Orders, Medals and Decorations of Britain and Europe* (1967).

Hayward, J. B. & Son (pub.) *Honours and Awards of the Army, Navy and Air Force 1914-20* (1979).

Irwin, Ross W. , *War Medals and Decorations of Canada* (1969).

Jocelyn, A., *Awards of Honour* (1956).

Johnson, S. C., *Medals of our Fighting Men* (1916).

Johnson, S. C., *The Medal Collector* (1921).

Johnson, S. C., *Everybodys Medals: Including Medals, Decorations, Honours and Orders* (1914).

Joslin, E., C., *The Observers Book of British Awards and Medals* (1974).

Letcher, Owen., *Medals and Decorations of the British Commonwealth of Nations - Medaljes en Dekorasies van de Britse Gemenebes van Nasies* (1941).

Litherland, A. R. and Simpkin, B. T., *Spink's Standard Catalogue of British Orders, Decorations and Medals* (1990).

McClenaghan, Tony, *Indian Princely Medals: A Record of the Orders, Decorations and Medals of the Indian Princely States* (1997).

Maton, Michael, *The National Honours & Awards of Australia* (1995).

Mayo, J. H., *Medals and Decorations of the British Army and Navy* (1897).

Mericka, V., *Book of Orders and Decorations* (1975).

Monick, S., *South African Military Awards 1912-1987* (1988).

Monick, S., *Awards of the South African Uniformed Public Services 1922-1987* (1988).

Narbeth, Colin, *Collecting Military Medals* (1971).

Nicolas, N.H., *History of the Orders of Knighthood of the British Empire; of the Order of the Guelphs of Hanover, and of the Medals, Clasps and Crosses, Conferred for Naval and Military Services* (1842).

Pamm, Anthony M., *Honours and Rewards of the British Empire and Commonwealth*, 2 vols. (1996).

Payne, A.A., *A Handbook of British and Foreign Orders, War Medals and Decorations awarded to the Army and Navy* (1911).

Purves, A.A., *Collecting Medals and Decorations* (1968).

Purves, A.A., *The Medals, Decorations and Orders of the Great War 1914-18* (1975).

Purves, A.A., *The Medals, Decorations and Orders of World War II 1939-45* (1986).

Purves, Alec A., *Orders, Decorations and Medals, a Select Bibliography* (1958).

Seedie's Roll of Naval Honours & Awards 1939-1959.

Seedie's List of Submarine Awards for World War II.

Seedie's List of Fleet Air Arm Awards 1939–1969.

Seedie's List of Coastal Forces Awards for World War II.

Seedie's List of Awards to the Merchant Navy for World War II (1997).

Steward, W.A., *War Medals and Their History* (1915).

Steward, W.A., *The ABC of War Medals and Decorations* (1918).

Tancred, G., *Historical Record of Medals and Honorary Distinctions* (1891).

Taprell-Dorling, Captain H. (ed. Alec A. Purves), *Ribbons and Medals* (1983).

Tinson, Lt-Col. Ashley R., *"Medals Will Be Worn", Wearing Medals Past and Present 1844–1999* (1999).

ORDERS
(listed by the Order of Precedence)

GENERAL

CB Printers Group (Pubr)., *Orders of Chivalry and Gallantry Awards* (1963).

De la Bere, Sir I. *The Queen's Orders of Chivalry* (1961).

Harbord, R.E., *Supplement to the Royal Family Orders, Badges of Office, Royal Household Medals and Souvenirs* (1954)

Hunter, John., *A Concise Description of the Insignia of the Orders of British Knighthood*

James, G.P.L., *The Royal Family Orders, Badges of Office, Royal Household Medals and Souvenirs* (1951)

Neville, D.G. *A History of the Early Orders of Knighthood and Chivalry.*

Patterson, Stephen, *Royal Insignia* (1996).

Risk, J.C., *British Orders and Decorations* (1973).

ORDER OF THE GARTER

Anstis, J., *The Register of the Most Noble Order of the Garter* (1724).

Ashmole, E., *The Institution, Laws and Ceremonies of the Most Noble Order of the Garter* (1672).

Ashmole, E., *History of the Most Noble Order of the Garter* (1715).

Beltz, G.F., *Memorials of the Most Noble Order of the Garter* (1839).

Buswell, J., *An Historical Account of the Knights of the Most Noble Order of the Garter* (1757).

Dawson, T., *Memoirs of St George The English Patron: And of the Most Noble Order of the Garter* (1714).

Fellowes, Rev. E.H., *The Knights of the Garter 1348-1939* (1939).

Harrison, A.P., *Order of the Garter: Armorial Registry of the Sovereign and the Knights of the Most Noble Order of the Garter—Their Names, Titles, Election, Installment and Demise* (1845).

Heylyn, P., *The History of that Most Famous Saint and Soldier of Christ Jesus: St George of Cappadocia...The Institution of the Most Noble Order of St George, named The Garter. A Catalogue of all the Knights Thereof Until this Present* (1631).

Hope, W.H. St J., *The Stall Plates of the Knights of the Order of the Garter 1348-1485* (1901).

Leake, S.M., *The Statutes of the Most Noble Order of The Garter* (1766).

ORDER OF THE THISTLE

Innes of Learney, Sir T., *The Foundation of the Most Ancient and Most Noble Order of the Thistle* (1959).

Lyon King of Arms, Lord, and Warrack, J., *The Knights of the Most Ancient and Most Noble Order of the Thistle* (1911).

ORDER OF ST PATRICK

Galloway, Peter, *The Order of St Patrick* (1983).

Galloway, Peter, *The Most Illustrious Order* (1996).

Grierson, G.A. & Grierson, J.F., *Statutes and Ordinances of the Most Illustrious Order of St. Patrick* (1831).

ORDER OF THE BATH

Anstis, J., *Observations Introductory to an Historical Essay Upon the Knighthood of the Bath* (1725).

Perkins, Canon J., *The Most Honourable Order of the Bath* (1913).

Risk, J.C., *The History of the Order of the Bath and its Insignia* (1982).

ORDER OF ST MICHAEL AND ST GEORGE

Abela, A.E., *The Order of St Michael and St George in Malta* (1988).

ROYAL VICTORIAN ORDER

Galloway, P., Martin, S. and Stanley, D., *Royal Service. Volume I* (1996).

Malloch, R. J., *The Royal Victorian Chain and Other Honors of the Sovereign,* (The Orders and Medals Society of America 1990).

Royal Victorian Order: Statutes and Lists of Members (1930).

ORDER OF THE BRITISH EMPIRE

Burke, *Handbook to the Order of the British Empire* (1921).

Galloway, Peter, *The Order of the British Empire* (1996).

Thorpe, A. Winton (ed.), *Burke's Handbook to the Most Excellent Order of the British Empire* (1921).

ORDER OF ST JOHN OF JERUSALEM

Bedford, W.K.R., and Holbeche, R., *The Order of the Hospital of St John of Jerusalem* (1902).

Fincham, H.W., *The Order of the Hospital of St John of Jerusalem and its Grand Priory of England* (1915).

The Grand Priory in the British Realm of the Venerable Order of the Hospital of St John of Jerusalem, *Roll of the Order 1931; Centenary Issue* (1936).

King, Col. E.J., *The Knights of St John in England* (1924).

King, Col. E.J., *The Knights of St John in the British Empire, Being the Official History of the British Order of the Hospital of St John of Jerusalem* (1934).

Luke, Sir H., *An Examination of Certain Claims to be an Order of St John* (1965).

Puddy, E., *A Short History of the Order of the Hospital of St John of Jerusalem in Norfolk* (1961).

Renwick, E.D., *A Short History of the Order of St John* (1959).

Tozer, C.W., *The Insignia and Medals of the Grand Priory of the Most Venerable Order of the Hospital of St John of Jerusalem* (1975).

DECORATIONS
(listed in alphabetical order by name of medal)

GENERAL

Abbott, P.E. and Tamplin, J.M.A., *British Gallantry Awards* (1981).

Abela, A.E., *Maltas George Cross and War Gallantry Awards*.

Bles, G (pub.) *Naval Honours and Awards 1939-1940* (1942).

Brown, G.A., *Commando Gallantry Awards of World War II*.

Campbell, G.L., *Royal Flying Corps (Military Wing)—Honours, Awards and Casualties 1914 17* (1917)

Chatterton-Dickson, W.W.F., *Seedie's List of Coastal Forces Awards for World War II*.

Chatterton-Dickson, W.W.F., *Seedies List of Fleet Air Arm Awards 1939-1969*.

Chatterton-Dickson, W.W.F., *Seedie's Roll of Naval Honours & Awards 1939-59* (1990).

Clarke, John D., *Gallantry Medals and Awards of the World* (1993).

Escott, Beryl, *20th Century Women of Courage* (1999).

Greenhill (pub.) *South African Honours and Awards 1899-1902*.

Hayward J. B. & Son (pub.) *Honours & Awards to the Indian Army 1914-21* (1992).

Hayward J. B. & Son (pub.) *Honours & Awards of the Old Contemptibles* (1992).

Housley, C., *British Gallantry Awards to Sherwood Foresters* (1999).

Hypher, P.P., *Deeds of Valour Performed by Indian Officers and Soldiers During the Period from 1860 to 1925* (1927).

Jacob, J.R., *Court Jewellers of the World* (1978).

McInness, I. and Webb, J.V., *Contemptible Little Flying Corps* (1991).

Midland (pub.) *Tank Corps Honours & Awards 1916-1919* (1982).

O'Shea, P., *An Unknown Few: The Story of Those Holders of the George Cross, the Empire Gallantry Medal, and the Albert Medals Associated with New Zealand*.

Pamm, Anthony N., *Honours and Rewards in the British Empire* (1995) (2 vols.).

Royal Flying Corps: *Casualties and Honours During the War of 1914-17* (1987).

Stanistreet, A. *'Gainst All Disaster: Above and Beyond the Call of Duty* (1986).

Wilson, Sir A., and McEwen, Capt. J.H.F., *Gallantry* (1939).

ALBERT MEDAL
Henderson, D.V., *For Heroic Endeavour* (1988).

CHIEFS' MEDALS
Jamieson, A.M., *Indian Chief Medals and Medals to African and Other Chiefs* (1936).

CONSPICUOUS GALLANTRY MEDAL
Cooper, A.W., *In Action With The Enemy: The Holders of the Conspicuous Gallantry Medal (Flying)*.

Brown, G. and Penhall, R., *Conspicuous Gallantry Medal* (1977).

McDermott, P., *For Conspicuous Gallantry*.

DISTINGUISHED CONDUCT MEDAL
Abbott, P.E., *The Distinguished Conduct Medal 1855-1909* (1987).

Ashton, M., *The Canadian Medal Rolls—Distingushed Conduct and Military Medal (1939-45 & 1950-53)*.

Brown, George A., *For Distinguished Conduct in the Field: The Register of the DCM 1939-92* (1993).

Mackinlay, Gordon, *True Courage: The Distinguished Conduct Medal to Australians 1939-1972* (1993).

McDermott, P., *For Distinguished Conduct in the Field: The Register of the DCM 1920-92* (1994).

Polaschek, A.J., *The Complete New Zealand Distinguished Conduct Medal* (1978).

Walker, R.W., *The Distinguished Conduct Medal 1914-20(1981)*.

DISTINGUISHED CONDUCT MEDAL (AFRICAN)
Arnold J., *The African DCM to the King's African Rifles and the West African Frontier Force* (1998).

DISTINGUISHED FLYING CROSS
Carter, N. and C., *The Distinguished Flying Cross and How it was Won 1918–1995*, 2 vols. (1998).

DISTINGUISHED FLYING MEDAL
Ashton, M., *The Canadian Medal Rolls—Distinguished Flying Medal (1939-1945)*.

Tavender, Ian, *The Distinguished Flying Medal: A Record of Courage* (1990).

Tavender, Ian, *The DFM Registers for the Second World War* (1999).

DISTINGUISHED SERVICE CROSS
Fevyer, W. H., *Distinguished Service Cross 1901-1938* (1990).

Witte, R. C., *Fringes of the Fleet and the Distinguished Service Cross* (1997).

DISTINGUISHED SERVICE MEDAL
Fevyer, W.H., *The Distinguished Service Medal, 1914–1920* (1982).

Fevyer, W.H., *The Distinguished Service Medal, 1939-1946* (1981).

DISTINGUISHED SERVICE ORDER
Creagh, General Sir O'Moore and Humphris, H.M., *The D.S.O.: A Complete Record of Recipients* (1978).

EDWARD MEDAL
Henderson, D.V., *For Heroic Endeavour* (1988).

EMPIRE GALLANTRY MEDAL
Henderson, D.V., *For Heroic Endeavour* (1988).

GEORGE CROSS
Bisset, Lieut. Colonel Ian, *The George Cross* (1961).

Campion, Roger, *The Call of Duty* (1997).

Dowling, Dr C., *The Victoria Cross and George Cross* (1970).

Hare-Scott, K., *For Gallantry—The George Cross* (1951).

Smyth, Sir J., *The Story of the George Cross* (1968).
This England (pub.), *The Register of the George Cross* (1990).

GEORGE MEDAL
Fevyer, W.H., *The George Medal*.
Henderson, D.V., *Dragons Can Be Defeated* (1984).
Henderson, D.V., *Fashioned into a Bow* (1995).

INDIAN ORDER OF MERIT
Hypher, P.P., *Deeds of Valour of the Indian Soldier Which Won the Indian Order of Merit During the Period From 1837 to 1859* (1925).
Peterson, C., *Unparalleled Danger Unsurpassed Courage: Recipients of the Indian Order of Merit in the Second World War* (1997).

KING'S POLICE MDAL
Farmery, J. P., *Police Gallantry: The King's Police Medal, The King's Police and Fire Service Medal and the Queen's Police Medal for Gallantry 1909–1979* (1995).

MILITARY MEDAL
Abbink, H. and C., *The Military Medal: Canadian Recipients 1916-1922.*
Ashton, M., *The Canadian Medal Rolls—Distingushed Conduct and Military Medal (1939-45 & 1950-53).*
Bate, Chris and Smith, Martin, *For Bravery in the Field: Recipients of the Military Medal 1919-1939, 1939-1945* (1991).

VICTORIA CROSS
Biggs, M., *The Story of Gurkha VCs.*
Clayton, Ann, *Chavasse, Double VC* (1992).
Clayton Ann, *Martin-Leake, Double VC* (1995).
Cooksley, Peter, *The Air VCs* (1998).
Creagh, General Sir O'Moore and Humphris, H.M., *The Victoria Cross 1856-1920* (1993).
Crook, M.J., *The Evolution of the Victoria Cross* (1975).
Dowling, Dr C., *The Victoria Cross and George Cross* (1970).
Gerard, M., *The Victoria Cross* (1892).
Hare-Scott, K., *For Valour—The Victoria Cross* (1949).
Harvey, David, *Monuments to Courage* (1999).
Haydon, A.L., *The Book of the Victoria Cross* (1906).
Laffin, John, *British VCs of World War 2: A Study in Heroism* (1997).
Lee, P.H., *The Victoria Cross* (1912).
Lennox, Lord W., *The Victoria Cross: The Rewarded and Their Services* (1857).
Leyland, R., *For Valour: The Story of the Victoria Cross.*
Little, M.G., *The Royal Marines Victoria Crosses.*
Muddock, J.E., *For Valor—the Victoria Cross 1856-1895* (1895).
Mundell, F., *Stories of the Victoria Cross* (1890).
Mulholland, J. and Jordan, A., *Victoria Cross Bibliography* (1999).
Napier, Gerald, *The Sapper VCs* (1998).
O'Byrne, R.W., *The Victoria Cross* (1865).
Pillinger, D. and Staunton, A., *Victoria Cross Locator* (1991).
Parry, D.H., *Britain's Roll of Glory, or the Victoria Cross, Its Heroes and Their Valour* (1895)
Parry, D.H., *The Victoria Cross, Its Heroes and Their Valour* (1913).
RAMC Historical Museum, *The Medical Victoria Crosses.*

Sarkar, D., *Guards VC: Blitzkrieg 1940* (1999).
Smyth, Brig. Sir John, *The Story of the Victoria Cross* (1964).
Snelling, Stephen, *VCs of the First World War: Gallipoli* (1995).
Stewart, Lt.Col.Rupert., *The Victoria Cross: The Empire's Roll of Valour* (1916).
This England (pub.), *Register of the Victoria Cross* (1988).
Toomey, T.E., *The Victoria Cross and How Won 1854-1889* (1889).
Toomey, T.E., *Heroes of the Victoria Cross* (1895).
Turner, J.F., *VCs of the Air* (1961).
Turner, J.F., *VCs of the Army 1939-51* (1962).
Turner, J.F., *VCs of the Royal Navy* (1956).
Wilkins, P.A., *The History of the Victoria Cross* (1904).

CAMPAIGN MEDALS
(listed in chronological order by date of campaign medal)

GENERAL
Carter, T. and Long, W.H., *War Medals of the British Army 1650-1891* (1972).
Dickson, Bill Chatterton, *Seedie's List of Awards to the Merchant Navy for World War II* (1997).
Douglas-Morris, Captain K.J., *Naval Medals 1793-1856* (1987).
Douglas-Morris, Capt K.J. *Naval Medals Vol. II 1856-1880.*
Johnson, Derek E., *War Medals* (1971).
Joslin, E.C., Litherland, A.R. and Simpkin, B.T., *British Battles and Medals* (1988).
Kerr, Major W.J.W., *Notes on War Medals 1794-1840* (1948).
Laffin, J., *British Campaign Medals.*
Long, W.H., *Medals of the British Navy* (1895).
Poulsom, Major N.W.A., *Catalogue of Campaign and Independence Medals Issued During the Twentieth Century to the British Army* (1969).
Power, J.R., *Identification Data on British War Medals and Their Interpretation* (1962).
Power, J.R., *Addenda and Corrigenda to Identification Data on British War Medals and their Interpretation* (1963).
Purves, A.A., *Some Notes on War Medals for the Collector* (1958).
Steward, W., Augustus, *War Medals and their History* (1915).
Vernon S.B., *Collector's Guide to Orders, Medals and Decorations* (With Valuations) (1990).
Williams, R.D. *Medals to Australians: with Valuations.*

MILITARY GENERAL SERVICE MEDAL
1793-1814
Foster, Col. Kingsley O.N., *The Military General Service Medal Roll 1793-1814* (1947).
Mullen, A.L.T., *The Military General Service Medal 1793-1814.*
Newnham, A.J., *The Peninsula Medal Roll 1793-1814* (privately produced).
Vigors, Lieutenant Colonel D.D. and Macfarlane, Lieutenant Colonel A.M., *The Three Great Retrospective Medals 1793-1840 Awarded to Artillerymen* (1986).
Wilson, B., *Canadian Recipients of the MGS, Egypt (1882-9) and NW Canada Medals.*

NAVAL GENERAL SERVICE MEDAL
1793-1840

Douglas-Morris, Captain K.J., *The Naval General Service Medal Roll, 1793-1840* (1982).

Hailes, Colonel D.A., *Naval General Service Medal Roll 1793-1840* (privately produced).

MacKenzie, Col R.H., *The Trafalgar Roll: The Ships and the Officers* (1989).

Message, C.W., *Alphabetical Naval General Service Medal Roll 1793-1840* (1995).

Newnham A.J., *Naval General Service Medal Roll 1793-1840* (privately produced).

O'Byrne, William, *Naval Biographical Dictionary* (2 vols, 1849).

Roberts, *The Trafalgar Roll* (1995).

Vigors, Lieutenant Colonel D.D. and Macfarlane, Lieutenant Colonel A.M., *The Three Great Retrospective Medals 1793-1840 Awarded to Artillerymen* (1986).

ARMY OF INDIA MEDAL 1799-1826

Gould, R.W. and Douglas-Morris, Captain K.J., *The Army of India Medal Roll 1799-1826* (1974).

Vigors, Lieutenant Colonel D.D. and Macfarlane, Lieutenant Colonel A.M., *The Three Great Retrospective Medals 1793-1840 Awarded to Artillerymen* (1986).

WATERLOO MEDAL

Dalton, C., *The Waterloo Roll Call* (1904).

Haythornthwaite, P. J., *Waterloo Men* (2000).

Lagden, A. and Sly, J., *The 2/73rd at Waterloo: Including a Roll of All Ranks Present, with Biographical Notes* (1998).

INDIAN CAMPAIGN MEDALS

Biddulph, Major H., *Early Indian Campaigns and the Decorations Awarded for Them* (1913).

Cook, H. C. B., *The Sikh Wars 1845–6, 1848–9* (1975).

Stone, A.G., *The First Afghan War 1839-1842 and Its Medals* (1967).

Stiles, Richard G. M., *The Story of the India General Service Medal 1908–35* (1996).

SOUTH AFRICA MEDAL 1835-53

Everson, Gordon R., *The South Africa 1853 Medal Roll* (1978).

Sole, T.E., *The Military Casualties of south Africa: Vol 1 1834-1878.*

NEW ZEALAND MEDAL 1845-66

Cowan, J., *The New Zealand Wars* (2 volumes) (1969).

Gudgeon, T.W., *Heroes of New Zealand and Maori History of the War* (1887).

Longley, H.G., *The New Zealand Wars 1845-1866* (1967).

Stowers, R., *The New Zealand Medal to Colonials: Detailed Medal Rolls of Officers and Men in Colonial Units Who Received the New Zealand Medal for Service in the New Zealand Wars 1845–72* (1999).

INDIA GENERAL SERVICE MEDAL 1854-95

Parritt, Colonel B.A.H., *Red With Two Blue Stripes* (1974).

CRIMEA MEDAL 1854-56

Cook, F. and Cook, A., *Casualty Roll for the Crimea 1854-55* (1976).

Duckers, P. and Mitchell, N., *The Azoff Campaign 1855* (1997).

Lummis, Canon W.M., *Honour the Light Brigade* (1973).

Mitchell, N. and Duckers, P., *Presented to the Queen: The Crimea Medal Award Ceremony, 18 May 1855* (1996).

Research Publications and Productions (pub.), *Returns Relating to Officers of the Army in the Crimea* (1989).

Savannah Publications (pubs.), *Casualty Roll for the Crimea 1854-55* (1999).

INDIA MUTINY MEDAL 1857-59

Asplin, K. J., *Indian Mutiny Medal Roll (British Forces)* (1999).

Tavender, I.T., *Casualty Roll for the India Mutiny 1857-59* (1983).

CANADA GENERAL SERVICE MEDAL 1866-70

Neale, G. N. and Irwin, R. W., *The Medal Roll of the Red River Campaign in 1870 in Canada* (1982).

Thyen, R., *Canada General Service Medal Roll 1866–70* (1999).

ABYSSINIAN WAR MEDAL 1867–68

Bates, Darrell, *The Abyssinian Difficulty* (1979).

SOUTH AFRICA MEDAL 1877-79

Forsyth, D.R., *South African War Medal 1877-8-9: The Medal Roll.*

Holme, N., *The Silver Wreath. The 24th Regiment at Isandhlwana and Rorke's Drift 1879* (1979).

Knight, Ian, *Brave Men's Blood* (1990).

Knight, Ian, *Zulu: Isandlwana and Rorke's Drift 22nd–23rd January 1879* (1997).

Mackinnon, J.P. and Shadbolt, S.H., *The South Africa Campaign of 1879* (1882).

Sole, T.E. *The Military Casualties of South Africa: Vol 1 1834-1878.*

Tavender, I.T., *Casualty Roll for the Zulu and Basuto Wars, South Africa 1877-79* (1985).

Whybra, J., *The Roll Call for Isandhlwana and Rorke's Drift* (1990).

Holme, N., *The Noble 24th, Biographical Records of the 24th Regiment in the Zulu War and the South African Campaigns 1877–1879* (2000).

AFGHANISTAN MEDAL 1878-80

Farrington, A., *The Second Afghan War 1878-80 Casualty Roll* (1986).

Robson, Brian, *The Road to Kabul: The Second Afghan War 1878–1881* (1986).

Shadbolt, S.H., *The Afghanistan Campaigns of 1878-80* (1882).

CAPE OF GOOD HOPE GENERAL SERVICE MEDAL 1880-97

Forsyth, D.R., *Cape of Good Hope General Service Medal: The Medal Roll.*

EGYPT MEDAL 1882-89

Maurice, Colonel J.F., *The Campaign of 1882 in Egypt.*

Webb, J.V., *Abu Klea Medal Roll.*

KHARTOUM STAR 1884

Fearon, D., *General Gordon's Khartoum Star* (1967).

NORTH WEST CANADA MEDAL 1885

Pacific Publishing Co (pub.), *North-West Canada Medal Roll (The Riel Rebellion 1885)* (1974).

BRITISH SOUTH AFRICA COMPANY MEDAL 1890-97
Forsyth, D.R., *British South Africa Co. Medal 1890-1897.*
Owen, C.R., *British South African Company Medal Roll 1890-1897.*
Roberts (pub.), *The British South Africa Company Medal Rolls 1890-1897* (1993).

HONG KONG PLAGUE MEDAL
Platt, J. J., Jones, M. E. and Platt, A. K., *The Whitewash Brigade: The Hong Kong Plague 1894* (1999).

INDIA MEDAL 1895–1902
Farrington, A., *India General Service Casualty Roll* (1987).
Barthorp, Michael, *The Frontier Ablaze: The North-West Frontier Rising 1897–98* (1996).

ASHANTI STAR 1896
McInnes, Ian and Fraser, Mark, *The Ashanti Campaign 1896.*

QUEEN'S & KING'S SOUTH AFRICA MEDAL 1899-1902
British Naval Brigades in the South Africa War 1899-1902 (Reprint).
Dooner, M.G., *The Last Post: A Roll of All Officers Who Gave Their Lives in the South African War 1899-1902* (1980).
Fevyer, W.H. and Wilson, J.W., *The Queen's South Africa Medal to the Royal Navy and Royal Marines* (1983).
Gray, S., *The South African War 1899-1902 - Service Records of British and Colonial Women.*
Hayward, J. B. & Son (pub.), *List of Casualties of the South Africa Frontier Force* (Reprint 1972).
Hayward, J. B. & Son (pub.), *South African War Casualty Roll: Natal Field Force* (1980).
Lusted, C.A (pub.), *The Queens South Africa Medal 1898-1902* (1974).
Mitchell, Dr F.K., *Roll Of The Bar, Defence of Mafeking, on the Queen's Medal for South Africa, 1899-1902* (1963).
Palmer, A., *The Boer War Casualty List* (1999).
Stirling, J., *British Regiments in South Africa 1899-1902* (reprint) (1994).
Stirling, J., *The Colonials in South Africa* (1990).

CAPE COPPER COMPANY'S MEDAL 1902
Forsyth, D.R., *Medal Roll of the Cape Copper Company's Medal.*

CHINA MEDAL 1900
Fevyer, W.H. and Wilson, J.W., *The China War Medal 1900 to the Royal Navy and Royal Marines* (1985).
Narbeth, C., *Taku Forts* (1980).

OOKIEP DEFENCE MEDAL
Kieran, Brian L., *O'okiep* (1996).

AFRICA GENERAL SERVICE MEDAL 1902
Fevyer, W.H. and Wilson, J.W. *African General Service Medal to the RN and RM.*
Magor, R.B., *African General Service Medals.*
TIBET MEDAL 1903–04
Fleming, Peter, *Bayonets to Lhasa* (revised 1985).
Roberts (pub.), *The Tibet Campaign 1904 and the Royal Fusiliers.*

NATAL REBELLION MEDAL 1906
Forsyth, D.R., *Natal Native Rebellion 1906: The Medal Roll.*
Roberts Medals Publications Ltd (pub.), *The Natal Zulu Rebellion 1906.*
INDIA GENERAL SERVICE MEDAL 1908–35
Styles, Richard G. M., *The Story of the India General Service Medal 1908–35* (1992).
Naval & Military Press (pub.), *India General Service Medal 1908–1935 to the Royal Air Force* (1994).

FIRST WORLD WAR MEDALS 1914-19
Adler, Revd. M (ed.), *British Jewry Book of Honour 1914-1918* (1922 and reprint 1997).
Bell, E.W., *Soldiers Killed on the First Day of the Somme* (1977).
Christie, N.M. *Officers of the Canadian Expeditionary Force who Died Overseas 1914-1919.*
Fevyer, W. H. and Wilson, J. W., *The 1914 Star to the Royal Navy and the Royal Marines* (1995).
Hayward, J. B. & Son (pub.), *Officers Died in the Great War* (1988).
Hayward, J. B. & Son (pub.), *Soldiers Died in the Great War* (80 parts).
Hobson, C., *Airmen Died in the Great War 1914-18: The Roll of Honour of the British and Commonwealth Air Services of the First World War* (1995)
Imperial War Museum (pub.), *Drake, Royal Naval Division Roll of Honour.*
Imperial War Museum (pub.), *Hawke, Royal Naval Division Roll of Honour.*
Imperial War Museum (pub.), *Hood, Royal Naval Division Roll of Honour.*
Imperial War Museum (pub.), *Howe, Royal Naval division Roll of Honour.*
Imperial War Museum (pub.), *Nelson, Royal Naval division Roll of Honour.*
Jarvis, S.D. and Jarvis, D.B., *The Cross of Sacrifice* (1990-1994) (several volumes).
Laslo, A.J., *The Interallied Victory Medals of WWI* (1986).
Merewhether, Lt-Col L. A., CIE and Smith Sir F., Bart., *The Indian Corps in France* (1919).
Mitchell, F.K., *Medals of the Great War Awarded to South Africans* (1983).
New Zealand Expeditionary Force Roll of Honour (Reprint).
Parks, Major Edwin, *The Royal Guernsey Militia* (1993).
Ruvigny, Marquis de., *The Roll of Honour 1916-1919.*
Walker, R., *To What End Did They Die?—Officers Died At Gallipoli.*
Williams, R.D., *Guide to Collecting and Researching Campaign Medals of the Great War* (1993).
Williamson, H.J., *The Roll of Honour, Royal Flying Corps and Royal Air Force for the Great War 1914-18* (1992).

SECOND WORLD WAR MEDALS
Devereux, J. and Sacker, G., *Roll of Honour, Land Forces World War 2 Volume I* (Cavalry, Yeomanry, RAC, Reconnaissance Corps, RTR and Brigade of Guards—other volumes to follow) (1999).
Hayward, J. B. & Son (pub.), *Prisoners of War (British, Empire and Commonwealth Forces)* (3 volumes, reprint).
Purves, A. A., *The Medals, Decorations & Orders of World War II* (1986).
Savannah Publications (pubs.), *Roll of Honour Land Forces WWII* (2000).

NAVAL GENERAL SERVICE MEDAL 1915
Fevyer, W.H. and Wilson, J.W., *NGS Medal 1915-1962 to the Royal Navy and Royal Marines for the Bars Persian Gulf 1909-1914, Iraq 1919-1920, NW Persia 1920* (1995).

KOREA MEDALS 1950-53
Dyke, P., *Korea 1950-53: Mentions-in-Despatches* (1989).
Gaston, P., *Korea 1950-1953, Prisoners of War, The British Army*.
Harding, Colonel E.D., *The Imjin Roll* (1976).
Ingraham, Kevin R., *The Honors, Medals and Awards of the Korean War 1950-1953* (1993).

MERITORIOUS SERVICE MEDALS
Chamberlain, Howard, *Service Lives Remembered, The MSM in New Zealand and its Recipients 1895–1994* (1995) and *Supplement* (1997).
McInnes, Ian, *The Meritorious Service Medal to Aerial Forces* (1984).
McInnes, Ian, *The Meritorious Service Medal to Naval Forces* (1983).
McInnes, Ian, *Meritorious Service Medal to Naval Forces* (1983).
McInnes, Ian, *Meritorious Service Medal. The Immediate Awards 1916-1928* (1992).
McInnes, Ian, *The Annuity Meritorious Service Medal* (1994).
Sainsbury, Major J.D., *For Gallantry in the Performance of Military Duty* (1980).

LONG SERVICE & GOOD CONDUCT MEDALS
(listed alphabetically by author)
Douglas-Morris, Captain K.J., *The Naval Long Service Medals* (1991).
Lees, J.R., *Recipients of the Long Service & Good Conduct Medal 1833-1916 to the Somerset Light Infantry (Prince Alberts)*.
McInnes, I. and Gregson, J. B., *The Army Long Service & Good Conduct Medal 1830–1848* (1996).
Pallas, S.M., *Canadian Recipients of the Colonial Auxiliary Forces Officers Decoration and the Colonial Auxiliary Forces Long Service Medal*.
Tamplin, J.M.A., *The Army Emergency Reserve Decoration and the Efficiency Medal (Army Emergency Reserve)* (1989).
Tamplin, J.M.A., *The Colonial Auxiliary Forces Long Service Medal* (1984.)
Tamplin, J.M.A., *The Colonial Auxiliary Forces Officers' Decoration: the Indian Volunteer Forces Officers' Decoration* (1981).
Tamplin, J.M.A., *The Efficiency Decoration Instituted 1930* (1987).
Tamplin, J.M.A., *The Imperial Yeomanry Long Service and Good Conduct Medal* (1978).
Tamplin, J.M.A., *The Militia Long Service and Good Conduct Medal* (1979).
Tamplin, J.M.A., *The Special Reserve Long Service and Good Conduct Medal* (1979).
Tamplin, J.M.A., *The Territorial Decoration 1908-1930* (1983).
Tamplin, J.M.A., *The Territorial Force Efficiency Medal 1908-1921 and the Territorial Efficiency Medal 1922-1930* (1980).

Tamplin, J.M.A., *The Volunteer Long Service Medal* (1980).
Tamplin, J.M.A., *The Volunteer Officers' Decoration* (1980).
Williams, R.D., *The Victoria Volunteer Long and Efficient Service Medal & the Volunteer Officers' Decoration* (1976).

LIFESAVING MEDALS
Barclay, C., *Royal Humane Society Medals* (1999).
Brown, G., *Lloyds War Medal for Bravery at Sea* (1992).
Cox, Barry, *Lifeboat Gallantry: The Complete Record of Royal National Lifeboat Institution Gallantry Medals and How They Were Won 1824–1996* (1998).
Cumming, Sir J., *Literature of the Life-Boat 1785-1947* (1947).
Dibdin, C., *History of the Institution's Gold and Silver Medals* (1909).
Fevyer, William H., *Acts of Gallantry, Vol. I, 1830–71* (1996).
Fevyer, William H., *Acts of Gallantry, Vol. 2, 1871–1950* (1997).
Gawler, J., *Lloyds Medals 1836-1989*.
Jeffery, S., *The Liverpool Shipwreck and Humane Society 1839-1939* (1939).
Lamb, Sir J.C., *The Life Boat and Its Work* (1911).
Mundell, F., *Stories of the Royal Humane Society* (1895).
Scarlett, R., *Under Hazardous Circumstances: Lloyds War Medal for Bravery at Sea*.
Young, L., *Acts of Gallantry: Being a Detailed Account of Each Deed of Bravery in Saving Life from Drowning in All Parts of the World for which the Gold and Silver Medals and Clasps of the Royal Humane Society Have Been Awarded from 1830-1871.*

ANIMAL AWARDS
Le Chene, Evelyn, *Silent Heroes: The Bravery and Devotion of Animals in War* (1994).

OTHER MEDALS
Balmer, Major J.L., *TD, British and Irish Regimental and Volunteer Medals 1745-1895.*
Borts, L.H., *UN Medals and Missions* (1998).
Cole, H. N., *Coronation and Royal Commemorative Medals 1887-1977* (1977).
Condon, Major J.P.B., MBE, *The Kings and Queens Medals for Shooting (Regular Army).*
Dalzell, M. and Riches, P., *Mentioned in Despatches 1948-1968* (1999).
Duckers, P., *The Delhi Durbar Medal 1911 to The British Army* (1995).
Hibbard, M.G., *Boer War Tribute Medals* (1982).
James G.P.L., *The Royal Family Orders, Badges of Office, Royal Household Medals and Souvenirs* (1951).
Owen, D., *The King's and Queen's Medal for Shooting* (1999).
Poulsom, Major N.W., *The White Ribbon: a Medallic Record of British Polar Expeditions* (1968).
Poulsom, Major N.W.A., *Catalogue of Campaign and Independence Medals Issued During the Twentieth Century to the British Army* (1969).
Scarlett, R.J., *The Naval Good Shooting Medal 1903-1914* (1990).
Wilson, J.W. and Perkins, R., *Angels in Blue Jackets: The Navy at Messina, 1908.*

Societies
for medal
collectors

Listed here are some of the many societies around the world that cater for the medal collector or those interested in military history. The addresses given are mostly the private addresses of the membership secretaries to whom all correspondence should be sent. *We would appreciate information from other Societies who would like their details included in the next YEARBOOK.*

Association de Collectionneurs de Decorations et Médailles (MEDEC) (Paasbloemstraat 81, 2060 Merksem, Belgium).

Birmingham Medal Society (229 Rednal Road, King's Norton, Birmingham B38 8EA).

Bund Deutscher Ordenssammler e.v. (Postfach 1260, Eisenbergstr 10, D-6497 Steinau a.d. Str., Germany).

The Crimean War Research Society (4 Castle Estate, Ripponden, West Yorkshire HX6 4JY).

Crown Imperial (history, traditions, regalia, insignia) (37 Wolsey Close, Southall, Middlesex UB2 4NQ).

Indian Military Historical Society (37 Wolsey Close, Southall, Middlesex UB2 4NQ).

Life Saving Awards Research Society ("Little Sadlers", 10 Upper Edgeborough Road, Guildford, Surrey GU1 2BG).

London Medal Club (Jim Lees, 020 8560 7648).

Medal Society of Ireland (1 The Hill, Stillorgan, Co. Dublin, Ireland).

Mid-Western Orders & Medals Society (MIDOMS) (5847 Gilbert Avenue, La Grange, IL 60525, USA).

Military Collector's Club of Canada (MCCofC) (PO Box 64009, RPO Morse Place, Winnipeg, MB, R2K 4K2, Canada).

Military Medal Society of South Africa (1 Jacqueline Avenue, Northcliff 2195, South Africa).

Naval Historical Collectors and Research Association (17 Woodhill Avenue, Portishead, Bristol BS20 9EX).

Orders & Medals Society of America (OMSA) (PO Box 484, Glassboro, NJ 08028, USA).

Orders & Medals Research Society (OMRS) (21 Colonels Lane, Chertsey, Surrey KT16 8RH).

Orders & Medals Research Society, Australia Branch (Sydney) (10/8 Pacific Parade, Dee Why 2099, NSW).

ditto, Canada Branch (Ottawa) (17 Ella Street, Ottawa, Ontario, Canada K1S 2S3).

ditto, Canada Branch (Toronto) (273 Corner Ridge Road, Aurora, Ontario, Canada L4G 6L6).

ditto, Hong Kong Branch (Flat 23, 11/F Mt Nicholson Gap, 103 Mt Nicholson Road, Hong Kong).

ditto, New Zealand Branch (Wellington) (54 Lohia Street, Khandallah, Wellington, New Zealand).

ditto, Northern Branch (Manchester) (7 St Michael's Avenue, Great Lever, Bolton, Lancs BL3 2LP.

ditto, Scottish Branch (21 Hartington Place, Edinburgh EH10 4LF).

ditto, Sussex Branch (9 Merryfield Drive, Horsham, West Sussex RH12 2AA).

ditto, Cotswold Branch (Cheltenham) (12 The Verneys, Cheltenham, Glos GL53 7DB).

ditto, Northumbrian Branch (41 Ashdown Avenue, Durham DH1 1DB).

ditto, Medal Ribbon Branch (7 Durham Way, Rayleigh, Essex SS6 9RY).

ditto, Miniature Medals Branch (54 Priory Bridge Road, Taunton, Somerset TA1 1QB).

Ordenshistorik Selskab (Falkoneralle 79, DK 2000 Frederiksberg, Denmark).

Société Suisse de Phaleristique (Box 1, CH-1137 Yens, Switzerland).

Stockport Militaria Collectors Society, Stockport Armoury (Clive Williams 0161 368 3128).

Victorian Military Society (20 Priory Road, Newbury, Berks RG14 7QN).

MUSEUMS AND COLLECTIONS

The majority of the museums listed below are the regimental museums of the British Army, Militia, Yeomanry and Territorials, but we have included other museums pertaining to the Royal Navy, the Royal Marines and the Royal Air Force where medals form a significant part of the collections. So, too, the museums of the police forces, fire brigades, Red Cross, Royal National Lifeboat Institution and similar bodies have been included where relevant. Readers should also bear in mind that many general museums in our towns and cities boast fine collections of military medals pertaining to their local regiments. We have included those of which we are aware. The date of foundation is shown in brackets after the name.

Some service museums have been undergoing refits, relocations and amalgamations. We would welcome further information from readers about these changes and about other general museums in their areas with a good coverage of medals to local regiments.

Space prevents us from going into details regarding the scope of individual museum holdings. We give the postal address, telephone number, and the name of the curator wherever possible, also the hours of opening and admission charges (where applicable) at the time of going to press. Where two charges are listed, the first denotes the full adult price and the second the concessionary charge (OAPs, students and children). Where three charges are given the first is the full adult price, the second the OAP concession and the third the children's charge. It is always sensible, particularly before travelling long distances to visit a museum or collection, to telephone and check that the published details are still correct.

Some museums may have libraries holding archival material; this should be checked out and the conditions for use ascertained as such holdings will not have the resources to answer detailed research enquiries.

Where museums are devoted to one particular regimental/service/unit or whatever, they are listed by title in alphabetical order. This may not always accord with the exact official name of the museum which is given on the address line. The well-known national museums are listed alphabetically by name. More general museums which include medal collections are listed by the name of the town. If you cannot see the name of the museum you require at first glance, it may be worth searching through the full list, as some museums escape neat classification and would require extensive cross-referencing to do them full justice.

Aberdeen Maritime Museum (1984)
Provost Ross's House, Shiprow, Aberdeen. 01224 5857888. Monday–Saturday, 10am–5pm. Admission free.

Airborne Forces Museum (1969)
Browning Barracks, Aldershot, Hants GU11 2BU. 01252 349619. £1.25/60p. Tuesday–Sunday, 10am–4.30pm. Major D. M. Cuthbertson–Smith.

Aldershot Challenge (1989)
Wavell House, Cavans Road, Aldershot, Hants GU11 2LQ. 01252 21048. Only by appointment at present.

Aldershot Military Museum (1984)
Queen's Avenue, Aldershot, Hants GU11 2LG. 01252 314598. £1.50/£1/50p. March–October, 10am–5pm; November–February 10am–4.30pm daily. Closed Christmas and New Year. Ian Maine.

Argyll and Sutherland Highlanders Regimental Museum (1945)
Stirling Castle. 01786 475165. Free. Easter–September, Monday–Saturday, 10am–5.30pm; Sunday, 11am–5pm. October–Easter, Monday–Saturday, 10am–4.30pm; Sunday, 11am–4pm.

Army Physical Training Corps Museum (1949)
Army School of Physical Training, Queen's Avenue, Aldershot, Hants GU11 2LB. 01252 347131. Free. Monday–Friday, 8.30am–12.30pm; 2pm–4pm. Weekends by appointment. Closed in August, and two weeks each at Easter and Christmas. A. A. Forbes and J. Pearson.

Army Transport Museum (1983)
Flemingate, Beverley, Humberside HU17 0NG. 01482 860445. £2.50/£1.50. Daily, 10am–5pm. Closed 24–26 December. David Dawson.

Arundel Toy and Military Museum (1978)
Dolls House, 23 High Street, Arundel, West Sussex.
01903 507446/882908. £1.25/90p. June–August,
10.30am–5pm daily. Otherwise open on Bank
Holidays and weekends in winter.

**Aylmer Military Collection and Isle of Wight Home
Guard Museum (1984)**
Nunwell House, Brading, Isle of Wight PO36 0JQ.
01983 407240. £2.30/£1.80/60p (children
accompanied by adults). July–September, Sunday–
Thursday, 10am–5pm. Otherwise by appointment.
J. A. Aylmer.

Ayrshire Yeomanry Museum
Rozelle House, Monument Road, Alloway by Ayr
KA7 4NQ. 01292 264091. Monday–Saturday, 10am–
5pm, Sundays, April–October, 2–5pm.

Bangor, Museum of Welsh Antiquities (1898)
Ffordd Gwynedd, Bangor, Gwynedd, LL57 1DT.
01248 353368. 50p. Tuesday–Friday, 12.30pm–4.30pm;
Saturday, 10.30am–4.30pm. Includes medals and
militaria of the Welsh regiments. Patricia
Benneyworth.

Bath Police Museum (1985)
Manvers Street, Bath, Avon BA1 1JN. 01225 444343.
Free, by appointment only. Sergeant Mike Stanton.

Bedale, Badges and Battledress Museum (1990)
The Green, Crakehall, Bedale, North Yorkshire DL8
1PH. 01677 424444. £1/80p/50p. Easter–September,
Tuesday–Friday, 11am–5pm; Saturday and Sunday,
1pm–5pm. Barrie Morris.

**Bedfordshire and Hertfordshire Regimental
Museum**
Luton Museum, Wardown Park, Luton, Beds LU2
7HA. Monday–Friday, 10am–5pm, Sunday, 1pm–
5pm.

Black Watch Museum (1924)
Balhousie Castle, Perth PH1 5HR. 01738 21281 ext
8530. Free. Easter–September, Monday–Friday, 10am–
4.30pm; Sundays and Bank Holidays, 2pm–4.30pm.
Major A. R. McKinnell, MBE.

**Border Regiment and King's Own Royal Border
Regiment Museum (1973)**
Queen Mary's Tower, The Castle, Carlisle, Cumbria
CA3 8UR. 01228 32774. £2/£1.50/£1. April–
September, Monday–Saturday, 10am–4pm; Sunday,
10am–6pm. October–March, 10am–4pm daily. Stuart
Eastwood.

British Red Cross Museum and Archives (1984)
Barnett Hill, Wonersh, Guildford, Surrey GU5 0RF.
01483 898595. Free, by appointment. Monday–Friday,
9.30am–4.30pm. Margaret Poulter.

**Burnley, Towneley Hall Art Gallery and Museum
(1902)**
Burnley, Lancs BB11 3RQ. 01282 424213. Free.
Monday–Friday, 10am–5pm; Sunday, 12pm–5pm.
Small collection including two VCs, other unique
items seen by appointment. Susan Bourne.

Bygones
Fore Street, St Marychurch, Torquay, Devon TQ1
4PR. 01803 326108. Daily (except Christmas Day).
Summer, 10am–10pm, Winter 10am–4pm.

Caenarfon Air Museum
Caernarfon Airport, Dinas Dinlle, Caernarfon,
Gwynedd LL54 5TP. £2.50/£1.50. March–November
9.30am–5.30pm.

**Cambridge, Scott Polar Research Institute Museum
(1920)**
Lensfield Road, Cambridge CB2 1ER. 01223 336540.
Free. Monday–Saturday, 2.30pm–4pm. Robert
Headland.

**Cameronians (Scottish Rifles) Regimental Museum
(1928)**
Mote Hill, off Muir Street, Hamilton, Lanarkshire
ML3 6BY. 01698 428688. Free. Monday–Wednesday,
Friday–Saturday, 10am–1pm; 2pm–5pm. John
McGourty.

Chester, Cheshire Military Museum (1972)
The Castle, Chester CH1 2DN. 01244 327617. 50p/
25p. Daily, 9am–5pm. Lieut. Colonel R.C. Peel.

City of London Police Museum (1964)
37 Wood Street, London EC2P 2NQ. 0171 601 2705.
Free, by appointment only. Roger Appleby.

Colchester, Military Miniatures Museum (1978)
13 Cheveling Road, Old Heath, Colchester, Essex CO2
8DL. 01206 794473. Free, by appointment only. Daily,
9am–5pm. Anthony Debski.

Coldstream Museum
13 Market Square, Coldstream. 01361 82600. Easter–
end October, Monday–Saturday 10am–5pm, Sunday
2–5pm.

Colne, British in India Museum (1972)
Newtown Street, Colne, Lancs BB8 0JJ. 01282 613129/
870215. £1.20/50p. Monday–Saturday, 10am–4pm.
Closed December, January and Bank Holidays.

Devonshire Regiment Museum
Wyvern Barracks, Barrack Road, Exeter, Devon EX2
6AE. Monday–Friday, 10am–4.30pm. Closed Bank
Holidays. Lieutenant Colonel D.R. Roberts.

Dingwall Museum (1975)
Town Hall, High Street, Dingwall, Ross–shire IV15
9RY. 01349 65366. 50p/25p. May–September,
Monday–Saturday, 10am–5pm. Otherwise by
appointment only. Includes medals and militaria of
the Seaforth Highlanders, Duke of Ross-shire's Buffs.
Dr Anthony Woodham.

Diss, 100th Bomb Group Memorial Museum (1978)
Common Road, Dickleburgh, near Diss, Norfolk. 0379
740708. Medals and memorabilia of the Eighth Air
Force and 100th Bomb Group. Free. May–September,
Saturday, Sunday and Wednesday, 10am–5pm.
October–April, weekends only, 10am–4.30pm. S. P.
Hurry.

Dorchester, The Keep Military Museum (1927)
The Keep, Bridport Road, Dorchester, Dorset DT1
1RN. 01305 264066. £2.50/£1.50. Monday–Friday,
9.30am–5pm. Sat./Bank hols 9.30am–1pm and 2pm–
5pm. Sundays in August 10am–4pm. Major J. Carroll.

**Duke of Cornwall's Light Infantry Regimental
Museum (1925)**
The Keep, Bodmin, Cornwall PL31 1EG. 01208 72810.
£1/50p. Monday–Friday, 8am–5pm. Major W. H.
White.

Duke of Wellington's Regiment Museum (1960)
Bankfield Museum, Boothtown Road, Halifax HX3
6HQ. 01422 352334/354823. Free. Tuesday–Saturday,
10am–5pm; Sunday, 2.30pm–5pm.

Durham Light Infantry Museum (1969)
Aykley Heads, Durham DH1 5TU. 0191 384 2214.
Free. Tuesday–Saturday, 10am–5pm; Sunday, 2pm–
5pm. Stephen D. Shannon.

East Lancashire Regimental Museum (1934)
Blackburn Museum and Art Gallery, Museum Street,
Blackburn, Lancs BB1 7AJ. 01254 667130. Free.
Tuesday–Saturday, 10am–5pm.

Essex Regimental Museum (1973)
Oaklands Park, Moulsham Street, Chelmsford, Essex
CM2 9AQ. 01245 260614. Free. Monday–Saturday,
10am–5pm; Saturday, 2pm–5pm. Ian Hook.

Feltham, Army Museums Ogilby Trust (1954)
Falklands House, Elwood Avenue, Feltham,
Middlesex TW13 7AA. 0181 844 1613. Free, Daily,
9am–4pm. Colonel P. S. Walton.

Fleet Air Arm Museum (1962)
RNAS Yeovilton, Somerset BA22 8HT. 01935 840565.
£4.80/£3.50/£2.70. Daily, 10am–4.30pm. Open all
year exept Christams Eve, Christmas Day and
Boxing Day. Graham Mottram.

Glasgow Art Gallery and Museum (1854)
Kelvingrove, Glasgow G3 8AG. 0141 359 3929. Free.
Monday–Saturday, 10am–5pm; Sunday, 11am–5pm.
Includes medals of the Glasgow Yeomanry,
Highland Light Infantry and regiments associated
with the city.

Gloucestershire Regiments Museum (1989)
Gloucester Docks, Gloucester GL1 2HE. 01452
522682. £2.50/£1.50/£1.25. Tuesday–Sunday and
Bank Holidays, 10am–5pm. Christine Beresford.

Gordon Highlanders' Regimental Museum (1961)
St Lukes, Viewfield Road, Aberdeen AB15 7XH.
01224 311300. April–October, Tuesday–Saturday
10.30am–4.30pm (closed Mondays). November–
March: by appointment only. Melanie Brooker, MA
(Hons), MA, FSA (Scot).

Green Howards Regimental Museum
Trinity Church Square, Richmond, Yorkshire DL10
4QN. 01748 822133. £1/75p/50p. April–October,
Weekdays 9.15am–4.30pm, Sundays 2–4.30pm.
Restricted hours the rest of the year

Guards Museum (1988)
Wellington Barracks, London SW1E 6HQ. 0171 414
3271. £2/£1. Monday–Thursday, weekends, 10am–
4pm. Captain David Horn.

Gurkha Museum (1974)
Peninsular Barracks, Romsey Road, Winchester,
Hants SO23 8TS. 01962 842832. £1.50/75p. Tuesday–
Saturday, 10am–5pm. Brigadier C. Bullock.

Hawkinge, Kent, Battle of Britain Museum (1969)
Hawkinge, Kent CT18 7AG. 0130 389 3140. £2.50/£2
£1.50. Easter–end of May, October, 11am–4pm. July–
September, 10am–5pm. Mike Llewellyn.

Hertford Regiment Museum
8 Bull Plain, Hertford SG14 1DJ. Tuesday–Saturday,
10am–5pm.

Hertfordshire Yeomanry Museum
Paynes Park, Hitchin, Herts SG5 1EQ. 01462 434476.
Free. Monday–Saturday, 10am–5pm; Sunday, 2pm–
4pm. Closed Bank holidays.

Hornsea Folk Museum (19780
Burn's Farm, 11 Newbegin, Hornsea, East Yorkshire
HU18 1BP. 01964 533443. £1.50/£1. Easter w/e, 1
May–30 September, Monday to Saturday, 11am–5pm
and Sunday 2–5pm. E. Yorkshire Regt, E. Riding
Yeo., Royal Artillery, The Home Front. Dr J. E. S.
Walker.

Honourable Artillery Company Museum
Armoury House, City Road, London EC1 2BQ.
Apply in writing for a visit.

Imperial War Museum (1917)
Lambeth Road, London SE1 6HZ. 0171 416 5000.
£3.70/£2.70/£1.85. Daily, 10am–6pm.

Imperial War Museum (1976)
Duxford Airfield, Duxford, Cambridge CB2 4QR.
01223 835000. £5.50/£3.80/£2.75. March–October,
10am–6pm daily; October–March, 10am–4pm daily.

Inns of Court and City Yeomanry Museum (1947)
10 Stone Buildings, Lincoln's Inn, London WC2A
3TG. 0171 405 8112. Free. Monday–Friday, 10am–
4pm. Major R. J. B. Gentry.

Intelligence Corps Museum
Defence Intelligence and Security Centre,
Chicksands, Nr Shefford, Beds SG17 5PR. 01462
752340. Free. Monday–Friday, 10am–3.30pm.
Appointment necessary. Major (Retd) R. W. M.
Shaw.

Kent and Sharpshooters Yeomanry Museum
Hever Castle, Tonbridge, Kent TN8 7NG. April–
October 12–6pm.

King's Own Royal Regt (Lancaster) Museum (1929)
City Museum, Market Square, Lancaster LA1 1HT.
01524 64637. Free. Monday–Saturday, 10am–5pm.

**King's Own Scottish Borderers Regimental
Museum (1954)**
Berwick Barracks, The Parade, Berwick-upon-Tweed
TD15 1DE. 01289 307426. £1.80/40p. Monday–
Friday, 9.30am–4.30pm; Saturday, 9.30am–12pm.
Lieut. Colonel C. G. O. Hogg.

**King's Own Yorkshire Light Infantry Regimental
Museum (1932)**
Museum and Art Gallery, Chequer Road, Doncaster,
South Yorkshire DN1 2AE. 01302 734293. Monday–
Saturday, 10am–5pm; Sunday, 2pm–5pm. Major
C. M. J. Deedes.

King's Regiment (Liverpool) Museum
William Brown Street, Liverpool L3 8EN. 0151
2070001. Daily, 10am–5pm, Sunday 2pm–5pm. G. S.
Boxer.

**15th/19th King's Royal Hussars (Light Dragoons)/
Northumberland Hussars**
Tyne & Wear Museums, Newcastle Discovery,
Blandford Square, Newcastle-upon-Tyne NE1 4JA.
0191 232 6789. Monday–Friday, 9am–4pm.

King's Royal Hussars Museum in Winchester (1980)
Home Headquarters (South): Peninsula Barracks, Romsey Road, Winchester. 01962 828541. Free admission. Tuesday–Friday, 10am–4pm; weekends and Bank holidays, 12pm–4pm. Major P. J. C. Beresford, Regimental Secretary.

Lamanva Military Vehicles
Lamanva, Nr Mabe, Falmouth, Cornwall TR10 9BJ 01326 72446. £2,75/£1.50. Easter–October 10am–5pm, Rest of year 10am–4pm.

Lancashire Fusiliers Regimental Museum (1933)
Wellington Barracks, Bury, Lanc BL8 2PL. 0161 764 2208. 50p/25p. Monday–Saturday (closed Wednesday), 9.30am–4.30pm.

17th/21st Lancers Regimental Museum (1964)
Belvoir Castle, Grantham, Lincs NG 31 6BR. 01476 870161. £3.20/£2.20. April–October, Tuesday–Thursday, Saturday and Sunday, 11am–5pm. Bank Holiday Mondays, 11am–5pm. Major W. M. Walton.

Light Infantry Museum (1990)
Peninsular Barracks, Romsey Road, Winchester. 01962 828530. £1.50/75p. Tuesday–Saturday, 10am–5pm; Sunday, 12pm–4pm. Patrick Kirby.

Liverpool Scottish Regimental Museum
Forbes House, Score Lane, Childwell, Liverpool L16 6AN. 0151 6474342. By appointment. D. Reeves.

London Fire Brigade Museum (1967)
94A Southwark Bridge Road, London SE1 0EG. 0171 587 4273. Free. Monday–Friday, 9am–4.30pm. John Rodwell.

London Scottish Regimental Museum (1935)
Regimental Headquarters, 95 Horseferry Road, London SW1P 2DX. 0171 630 1639. Free, by appointment only.

Manchesters Museum (1987)
Town Hall, Ashton–under–Lyne, Lancs. 0161 342 3078 or 0161 343 1978. Free. Monday–Saturday, 10am–4pm. Dr Alan Wilson.

Metropolitan Police Historical Museum (1969)
New Scotland Yard, Broadway, London SW1H 0BG. 0181 305 1676. By appointment only. Paul Dew.

Monmouth, The Castle and Regimental Museum (1989)
The Castle, Monmouth, Gwent NP5 3BS. 01600 772175/712935. Free. Summer daily, 2pm–5pm; winter weekends 2pm–5pm. Other times by appointment. Dr Eric Old.

The Muckleburgh Collection
Weybourne, Norfolk. 01263 588210. £4/£3/£2. Daily (February–November) 10am–5pm.

National Army Museum (1960)
Royal Hospital Road, Chelsea, London SW3 4HT. 0171 730 0717. Free. Daily, 10am–5.30pm. Ian G. Robertson.

National Maritime Museum (1934)
Romney Road, Greenwich, London SE10 9NF. 0181 858 4422. £7.45/£5.45. Summer, Monday–Saturday, 10am–6pm; Sunday, 12pm–5pm. Winter, Monday–Saturday, 10am–5pm; Sunday, 2pm–5pm. Richard Ormond.

National Museum of Ireland (1877)
Kildare Street, Dublin 2, Republic of Ireland. 01 618811. Free. Tuesday–Saturday, 10am–5pm; Sunday, 2pm–5pm. Includes medals of the former Irish regiments.

National War Museum of Scotland
The Castle, Edinburgh. 0131 220 4733. Free (but entrance fee to the castle). April–Nov. 9.45am–5.30pm/Dec.–March 9.45am–4.30pm.

Newark Air Museum (1968)
Winthrop Airfield, Newark-on-Trent NG24 2NY. 01636 707170. £2.50/£1.50. April–October, Monday–Friday, 10am–5pm; weekends, 10am–6pm. November–March, daily 10am–4pm. Mike Smith.

Northamptonshire Regimental Museum
Abington Park Museum, Abington, Northampton. 01604 35412. Colonel J. P. Wetherall.

Order of St. John of Jerusalem Museum
St. John's Gate, St. John's Lane, Clerkenwell, London EC1M 4DA. 0171 253 6644. Tuesday–Friday 10am–5pm, Saturday 10am–4pm. Pamela Willis.

Oxfordshire & Buckinghamshire Light Infantry
TA Centre, Slade Park, Headington. Oxford OX3 7JL. 01865 716060. Free. Monday–Friday 10am–4pm.

Polish Institute and Sikorski Museum
20 Princes Gate, London SW7 1QA. 0171 589 9249. Monday–Friday 2pm –4pm.

Preston, County and Regimental Museum (1987)
Stanley Street, Preston, Lancs PR1 4YP. 01772 264075. £1/children free. Monday–Saturday (closed Thursday), 10am–5pm. Stephen Bull.

Prince of Wales's Own 9th /12th Lancers Regimental Museum (1972)
City Museum and Art Gallery, The Strand, Derby DE1 1BS. 01332 255581. Free. Monday, 11am–5pm; Tuesday–Saturday, 10am–5pm; Sunday and Bank Holidays, 2pm–5pm. Nick Forder.

Prince of Wales Regiment of Yorkshire and Regimental Museum of the 4th/7th Royal Dragoon Guards (1925)
3A Tower Street York YO1 1SB. 01904 642 038. 50p/25p. Monday–Friday, 9.30am–4.30pm; Saturday, 10am–4.30pm. Brigadier J. M. Cubiss.

Princess of Wales's Regimental Museum (1987)
Inner Bailey, Dover Castle, Kent CT16 1HU. 01304 240121. £5/£3.70/£2.50. Summer, 10am–6pm daily; winter, 10am–4pm. Lieut. Colonel L. M. Wilson, MBE.

Princess Patricia's Canadian Light Infantry Museum Hatch Court, Hatch Beauchamp, Taunton, Somerset TA3 6AA. 01823 480120. £2.80/£1. June–September, Tuesday and Bank Holiday Mondays, 2.30–5pm. Otherwise by appointment. Dr and Mrs Odgers.

Queen Alexandra's Royal Army Nursing Corps Museum (1953)
Regimental Headquarters, Royal Pavilion, Farnborough Road, Aldershot, Hants GU11 1PZ. 01252 349301/349315. Free. Monday–Friday, 9.30–12 noon; otherwise by appointment. Major McCombe.

Queen's Dragoon Guards Regimental Museum
Cardiff Castle, Cardiff, South Glamorgan CF1 2RB.
01222 222253. £3/£2/£1.50. March, April and
October, 10am–5pm daily. May–September, 10am–
6pm. Nov.–February, 10am–4.30pm. Gareth Gill.

Queen's Lancashire Regiment (1929)
Fulwood Barracks, Preston, Lancs PR2 4AA. 01772
260 362. Free. Tuesdays to Thursdays only, 9.30am–
4.30pm. Major A. J. Maher, MBE.

Queen's Own Highlanders Regimental Museum
Fort George, Ardersier, Inverness–shire. 01463
224380. Free. April–September, Monday–Friday,
10am–6pm; Sunday, 2pm–6pm. October–March,
Monday–Friday, 10am–4pm.

Queen's Royal Lancers
Belvoir Castle, nr Grantham, Lincs, NG31 6BR. £5/
£4/£3, family ticket £14. March–September, every
day, 11am–5pm (except Mondays and Fridays). Capt
(Ret) J. M. Holtby.

**Queen's Own Royal West Kent Regimental
Museum (1966)**
St Faith's Street, Maidstone, Kent ME14 1LH. 01622
754497. Free. Monday–Saturday, 10.30am–5.30pm;
Sunday, 2pm–5pm. Colonel H.B.H. Waring, OBE.

Queen's Royal Surrey Regimental Museum (1979)
Clandon Park, Guildford, Surrey GU4 7RQ. 01483
223419. April–October, closed Monday, Friday,
Saturday. 12–5pm. Penny James.

Royal Air Force Museum (1963)
Grahame Park Way, Hendon, London NW9 5LL.
0181 205 2266. £4.50/£2.25. Daily, 10am–6pm. Dr M.
A. Fopp. Medal queries: A. Cormack.

Royal Air Force Regiment Museum (1965)
Royal Air Force Regiment Depot, Royal Air Force
Honington, Bury St Edmunds, Suffolk IP31 1EE.
01359 269561. Initially by appointment. Ask for
Museum Director/staff.

**Royal Air Force Museum Reserve
Collection (1965)**
RAF Cardington, Beds MK42 0TH. 01234 742711.
Free, by appointment only. Bruce James.

Royal Armouries Museum (1996)
Waterfront, Leeds City Centre. 0113–245 6465.
£6.95+concessions. Daily (except Christmas Eve,
Christmas Day and New Year's Day). 10am–5pm
(winter), 10am–6pm (summer).

**Royal Army Chaplains' Department Museum
(1968)**
Bagshot Park, Bagshot, Surrey GU19 5PL. 01276
471717, ext. 2845. Free. Monday–Friday, 10am–4pm,
by appointment. Closed in August. Major Margaret
Anne Easey.

Royal Army Dental Corps Museum (1958)
Headquarters RADC, Evelyn Woods Road,
Aldershot, Hants GU11 2LS. 01252 347782. Free.
Monday–Friday, 10am–12pm; 2pm–4pm. Closed on
bank holidays. Major Vincent Ward.

Royal Army Educational Corps Museum (1967)
Wilton Park, Beaconsfield, Bucks HP9 2RP. 01494
683290. Free, by appointment only. Simon Anglim.

Royal Army Medical Corps Museum (1952)
Keogh Barracks, Ash Vale, Aldershot, GU12 5RQ.
01252 340212. Free. Monday–Friday, 8.30am–4pm;
weekends and evenings by appointment. Lieut.
Colonel Roy Eyeions, OBE.

Royal Artillery Regimental Museum (1946)
Old Royal Military Academy, Woolwich, London
SE18 4DN. 0181 781 5628. Free. Monday–Friday,
12.30pm–4.30pm. Brigadier Ken Timbers.

Royal Corps of Signals Outstation Museum (1987)
Helles Barracks, Catterick Garrison, North Yorkshire
DL9 4HH. 01748 873778. Free. Mon.–Thurs., 10am–
4pm; Friday, 10am–3pm. Lieut. Col. F. M. Orr, OBE.

Royal Devon Yeomanry (1845)
Museum of North Devon, The Square, Barnstaple,
Devon EX32 8LN. 01271 46747. £1/50p .Tuesday–
Saturday, 10am–4.30pm. Jerry Lee.

**Royal East Kent Regiment, Third Foot (The Buffs)
Museum (1961)**
Royal Museum and Art Gallery, High Street,
Canterbury, Kent CT1 2JE. 01277 452747. Free
admission Monday–Saturday, 10am–5pm. Kenneth
Reedie.

**Royal Electrical and Mechanical Engineers
Museum (1958)**
Isaac Newton Road, Arborfield Garrison, Reading,
Berks, RG2 9LN. 01734 763567. Free. Monday–
Friday, 9am–12.30pm; 2pm–4pm. Weekends by
appointment. Closed on Bank holidays. Lieut.
Colonel Larry LeVar.

Royal Engineers Museum
Brompton Barracks, Chatham, Kent ME4 4UG. 01634
406397. £1/50p. Tuesday–Friday, 11.30am–5pm,
Spring/Summer Bank holidays 10am–5pm. Colonel
G. W. A. Napier.

Royal Fusiliers Museum (1962)
HM Tower of London, EC3N 4AB. 0171 488 5612.
25p. Daily, 9.30am–4.30pm. Maj. B. C. Bowes-Crick.

**Royal Gloucester, Berkshire, Wiltshire (Salisbury)
Regimental Museum (1982)**
The Wardrobe, 58 The Close, Salisbury, Wilts SP1
2EX. 01722 414 536. £1.80/£1.50p. Major J. H. Peters,
MBE.

Royal Hospital Chelsea
Hospital Road, Chelsea, London SW3 4SL. 0171 730
0161. Free. Daily, 10am–12pm; 2pm–4pm. Major
R. A. G. Courage, CVO, MBE.

Royal Green Jackets Museum
Peninsular Barracks, Romsey Road, Winchester.
01962 863846. £2/£1. Monday–Saturday, 10am–5pm;
Sunday, 12pm–4pm.

Royal Hampshire Regimental Museum (1933)
Serle's House, Southgate Street, Winchester, Hants
SO23 9EG. 01962 863658. Free. All year Monday–
Friday 10am–12.30pm, 2pm–4pm. Weekends/Bank
holidays April to October only, midday–4pm. Lt–
Col. H. D. H. Keatinge.

**Royal Highland Fusiliers Regimental Museum
(1960)**
518 Sauchiehall Street, Glasgow G2 3LW. 0141 332
0961. Free. Monday–Thursday, 9am–4.30pm; Friday,
9am–4pm. W. Shaw, MBE.

13th/18th Royal Hussars (Queen Mary's Own) Regiment (1957)
Cannon Hall Museum, Cawthorne, Barnsley, South Yorkshire S75 4AT. 01226 790270. Free. Tuesday–Saturday and Bank holiday Mondays, 10.30am–5pm; Saturday and Sunday, 2.30pm–5pm. Brian Murray.

Royal Inniskilling Fusiliers Regimental Musuem (1938)
The Castle, Enniskillen, Co. Fermanagh, Northern Ireland BT74 7BB. 01365 323142. £1 / 75p. Summer, Monday–Friday, 9.30am–5pm; weekends, 2pm–5pm. Winter, Monday–Friday, 930am–12.30pm; 2pm–5pm. Major George Stephens, MBE.

Royal Irish Fusiliers
Sovereign's House, The Mall, Armagh BT61 9AJ. 01861 522911. Weekdays 10am–4.30pm. Major M. Wright.

Royal Irish Regiment Museum (1993)
Regimental Headquarters, Royal Irish Rangers, St Patrick's Barracks, Ballymena, BFPO 808, Northern Ireland. 01266 661388. Free. Monday–Friday, 10am–4.30pm. Lieut. Carol Liles.

Royal Leicestershire Regiment Museum (1969)
The Magazine, Oxford Street, Leicester. 0116 2473220. Free. Monday–Thursday, Saturday, 10am–5.30pm; Sunday, 2pm–5.30pm. Y. C. Courtney.

Royal Logistic Corps Museum (1995)
Blackdown Barracks, Deepcut, near Camberley Surrey GU16 6RW. 01252 340871. Free. Monday–Friday, 10am–4pm; Saturday 10am–3pm; closed Sundays and public holidays. Admission free. Major T. R. Lill, MBE.

Royal Lincolnshire Regimental Museum (1985)
Burton Road, Lincoln LN1 3LY. 01522 528468. £1/50p. May–September, daily, 10am–5.30pm. October–April, Monday–Saturday, 10am–5.30pm; Sunday, 2pm–5.30pm.

Royal Marines Museum (1956)
Southsea, Hants PO4 9PX. 01705 819385. £2.50/£1.50/£1.25. Whitsun–September, 9.30am–5pm. Winter, 9.30am–4.30pm. Col. K. N. Wilkins, OBE.

Royal Military Police Museum (1979)
Rousillon Barracks, Broyle Road, Chichester, West Sussex PO19 4BN. 01243 786311 ext 4225. Free. April–September, Tuesday–Friday, 10.30am–12.30pm; 1.30pm–4.30pm; Sat–Sunday, 2pm–6pm. October–March, Tuesday–Friday, 10.30am–12.30pm; 1.30pm–4.30pm. Closed January. Lt-Col. Maurice Squier.

Royal National Lifeboat Institution Museum (1937)
Grand Parade, Eastbourne, East Sussex BN21 4BY. 01323 730717. Free. April–December, 9.30am–5pm daily. January–March, Monday–Friday, 9.30am–5pm. J. M. Shearer.

Royal National Lifeboat Institution Museum (1969)
Pen-y-Cae, Barmouth, Gwynedd. Free. Easter–October, 10.30am–6.30pm, daily.

Royal Naval Museum (1911)
HM Naval Base, Portsmouth PO1 3LR. 01705 733060. £2/£1.75. Daily, 10.30am–5pm. H. Campbell Murray.

Royal Norfolk Regimental Museum (1945)
Shirehall, Market Avenue, Norwich NR1 3JQ. 01603 223649. 80p/40p. Monday–Saturday, 10am–5pm; Sunday, 2pm–5pm. Kate Thaxton.

Royal Northumberland Fusiliers Regimental Museum (1970)
The Abbot's Tower, Alnwick Castle, Alnwick, NE66 1NG. 01665 602152 / 510211. Easter–October, 11am–5pm daily. Captain Peter H. D. Marr.

Royal Scots Regimental Museum (1951)
The Castle, Edinburgh EH1 2YT. 0131 310 5016. Free. March–September, Monday–Saturday, 9.30am–4.30pm; Sunday, 11am–4.30pm. October–April, Monday–Friday, 9.30am–4pm. Major Dick Mason.

Royal Signals Museum (1967)
Blandford Camp, Blandford, Dorset DT11 8RH. 01258 482086. Free. Monday–Friday, 10am–5pm; Saturday, Sunday (June–September only) 10am–4pm.

Royal Sussex Regimental Museum (1930) also the 4th Queen's Own Hussars; 8th King's Royal Irish Hussars; Queen's Royal Irish Hussars Museums
Redoubt Fortress, Royal Parade, Eastbourne, East Sussex BN21 4BP. 01323 410300. £1.50/£1. April–October. Other times by appointment. B. R. Burns.

Royal Tank Regiment Museum (1923)
Bovington Camp, near Wareham, Dorset BH20 6JG. 01929 403463/403329/463953. £4/£2. Daily, 10am–5pm. Closed at Christmas. Colonel J. Woodward.

Royal Ulster Constabulary Museum (1983)
Brooklyn, Knock Road, Belfast BT5 6LE. 01232 650222. Free. Monday–Friday, 9am–5pm. Robin Sinclair.

Royal Ulster Rifles Museum (1935)
Regimental Headquarters, The Royal Irish Rangers, 5 Waring Street, Belfast BT1 2EW. 01232 232086. Free. Monday–Friday, 10am–12pm; 2pm–4pm. Major M. B. Murphy.

Royal Warwickshire Regimental Museum (1928)
St John's House, Warwick CV34 4NF. 01926 491653. Free. Tuesday–Saturday, 10am–12.30pm; 1.30pm–5.30pm; Sunday, 2.30pm–5pm. Brigadier J. K. Chater.

Royal Welch Fusiliers Museum (1955)
Caernarfon Castle, Gwynedd LL55 2AY. 01286 673362. 9.30am–6pm daily; winter 9.30am–4pm; Lieut-Col P. A. Crocker.

St Helier, Elizabeth Castle and Militia Museum
St Helier, Jersey, Channel Islands. 01534 23971. £2/£1. April–October, daily, 10am–5pm.

Sandhurst Royal Military Academy (1960)
Royal Military Academy Sandhurst, Camberley GU15 4PQ. 01276 63344 ext 2457. Free, by appointment only.

School of Infantry and Small Arms School Corps Weapons Museum (1953)
School of Infantry, Warminster, BA12 0DJ. 01985 842487. Free. Daily, 9am–4.30pm. Lieut-Colonel Tug Wilson, MBE.

Scottish Horse Museum
The Cross, Dunkeld, Perthshire. 50p Easter–September 10am–5pm.

Sherwood Foresters Regimental Museum (1923)
The Castle, Nottingham. 0115 946 5415. Monday–Friday free; weekends and Bank holidays. £1.50/80p. Daily 10am–5pm except Friday between November and February when 1–5pm. Closed Christmas Day and Boxing Day.

Shropshire Regimental Museum (1985)
The Castle, Shrewsbury, S71 2AT. 01743 262292. £3/£1. Open every day except Monday April–September, October–March closed Sundays and Monday. 10am–4.30pm. Peter Duckers.

South Lancashire Regiment (Prince of Wales's Volunteers) and the Lancashire Regiment Museum (1934)
Fulwood Barracks, Preston, Lancs PR2 8AA. 01772 716543. Free. Tuesday–Thursday, 9am–4.30pm. Otherwise by appointment. Major Glover.

South Nottinghamshire Hussars Museum (1974)
TA Centre, Hucknall Lane, Bulwell, Nottingham NG6 8AB. 0115 9272251. Free, by appointment only.

South Wales Borderers and Monmouthshire Regimental Museum (1934)
The Barracks, Brecon, Powys LD3 7EB. 01874 623111 ext 2310. £1. October–March, Monday–Friday, 9am–1pm; 2pm–5pm. April–September, daily except Sunday, same hours. Major Bob Smith.

South Wales Police Museum (1950)
Police Headquarters, Cowbridge Road, Bridgend, Mid Glamorgan CF31 3SU. 01656 655555 ext 427. Free. Monday–Thursday, 10am–1pm; 2pm–4.30pm; Friday, 10am–1pm; 2pm–4pm. Jeremy Glenn.

Staff College Museum (1958)
Staff College, Camberley, Surrey GU15 4NP. 01276 412662/412647/412650. Free, by appointment only. Colonel Philip S. Newton, MBE.

Staffordshire Regimental Museum (1962)
Whittington Barracks, Lichfield, Staffs WS14 9PY. 0121 311 3240/3229. Free. Monday–Friday, 9am–4.30pm. Major E. Green.

Suffolk Regimental Museum (1967)
The Keep, Gibraltar Barracks, Bury St Edmunds, Suffolk IP33 1HF. 01284 752394. Free. Weekdays, 10am–12pm; 2pm–4pm. Major A. G. B. Cobbold.

Sussex & Surrey Yeomanry Museum (1993)
Also Royal Observer Corps' Museum
Newhaven Fort, Newhaven, East Sussex. Tel: 01273 611055; April–October, other times by appointment. Hon. curator Keith Fuller.

Tangmere, Military Aviation Museum (1992)
Tangmere, near Chichester, West Sussex PO20 6ES. 01243 775223. £3/50p. February–November, daily, 11am–5.30pm. Andy Saunders.

Taunton, Somerset Military Museum (1974)
County Museum, The Castle, Taunton, Somerset TA1 1AA. 01823 255504. £1.20/80p/30p. Monday–Saturday, 10am–5pm. Brigadier A. I. H. Fyfe.

Welch Regiment Museum (1927)
The Black and Barbican Towers, Cardiff Castle, Cardiff, South Glamorgan CF1 2RB. 01222 229367. £2/£1. Daily 10am–6pm (April–October), 10am–4.30pm (November–March). Lieut. Bryn Owen, RN.

Wellington Museum
Apsley House, 149 Piccadilly, Hyde Park Corder, London W1V 9FA. 0171 499 5676. £2/£1, Tuesday–Sunday 11am–5pm. J. Voak.

West Midlands Police Museum (1991)
Sparkhill Police Station, 641 Stratford Road, Birmingham B11 6EA. Free, by apppointment only.

Woodbridge, 390th Bomb Group Memorial Air Museum (1981)
Parham Airfield, Parham, Woodbridge, Suffolk. 01359 51209. Free. Sundays and Bank Holidays, 11am–6pm.

Worcestershire Regimental Museum (1973)
City Museum and Art Gallery, Foregate Street, Worcester. 01905 25371. Free. Monday–Wednesday, Friday, 9.30am–6pm; Saturday, 9.30am–5pm. Col. John Lowks. Archives: 01905 354359, by appointment.

York, Divisional Kohima Museum (1991)
Imphal Barracks, Fulford Road, York YO1 4AY. 01904 662381. Free, by appointment only.

York, Yorkshire Air Museum and Allied Air Forces Memorial (1984)
Halifax Way, Elvington, York YO4 5AU. 01904 605595. £2.50/£1.50. Monday–Friday, 10.30am–4pm; weekends, 10.30am–5pm. Peter Douthwaite.

York and Lancaster Regimental Museum (1947)
Brian O'Malley Central Library and Art Gallery, Walker Place, Rotherham, Yorkshire S65 1JH. 01709 382 121 ext 3625. Free. Tuesday–Saturday, 10am–5pm. Don Scott.

Professional directory

On the following pages are the names and addresses of auctioneers, dealers, booksellers and fair organisers, all of whom will be of assistance to the medal collector. Most are full time and many have retail shops and the collector is usually welcome during normal business hours. Some have extensive stocks of medals whilst others include medals in a more diverse inventory. A number of dealers are part time or work from small premises or from home and appointments are necessary as many keep their stock in the bank for security. Telephone numbers have been included where known and it is always sensible to make contact before travelling any distance.

AUCTIONEERS

The following hold regular medal auctions or feature medals in general numismatic or militaria sales.

Bosleys
The White House, Marlow, Bucks SL7 1AH. 01628 488188 (fax: 01628 488111). Specialist auctioneers of medals and militaria. Website: www.bosleys.co.uk.

Dix Noonan Webb
1 Old Bond Street, London W1X 3TD. 020 7499 5022 (fax 020 7499 5023). Auctioneers and valuers. Regular auctions of medals. E-mail: auctions@dnw.co.uk.

Downie's Militaria
7th Floor, 343 Little Collins Street, Melbourne, Vic 3000, Australia. (03) 670 0500 (fax 03 670 0311). Sales with emphasis on Australian and UK medals.

Floyd, Johnson & Paine
PO Box 9791, Alexandria, VA 22304, USA. (312) 777 0499 (fax 312 777 4017). Auctions of medals and militaria.

Glendining's
101 New Bond Street, London W1Y 9LG. 020 7493 2445 (fax 020 7491 9181). Auctioneers and valuers of medals. Approximately four sales per year. Website: www.phillips-auctions.com.

Jeffrey Hoare Auctions Inc.
319 Springbank Dr., London, Ontario, Canada, N6J 1G6. (519) 473 7491 (fax (519) 473 1541). Regular sales of medals, badges and militaria.

Imperial Auctions
10 Water Street, Accrington, Lancs BB5 6PX. Tel/ fax: 01254 393323. Regular sales of medals and badges.

Lockdales
36 Upper Orwell Street, Ipswich, IP4 1HR. Tel: 01473 218588. Regular sales. Call for venue.

Postal Auctions
PO Box 4087, Hornchurch, Essex RM11 2BP. Eight sales of medals and related items per year. Website: www.medalauctions.demon.co.uk.

Sotheby's
34–35 New Bond Street, London W1Y 2AA. 020 7293 5709. Auctioneers and valuers. Regular sales of medals and militaria.

Spink & Son Ltd (Christie's International)
69 Southampton Row, Bloomsbury, London WC1B 4ET. 020 7563 4009 (fax 020 7563 4066). Auctioneers and valuers. Regular sales of medals and militaria.

Wallis & Wallis
West Street Auction Galleries, Lewes, Sussex BN7 2NJ. 01273 480208 (fax 01273 476562). Regular sales of militaria, arms, armour and medals.

Ware Militaria Auctions
The Function Rooms, Hertford Rugby Club, Hoe Lane, Ware, Herts. Bi-monthly auctions, for details call 01920 871901.

Whytes Auctioneers
30, Marlborough Street, Dublin 1, Ireland. Tel: (+3531) 874 6161 (fax: +3531 874 6020). Auctioneers and valuers. Regular sales. E-mail: whytes@iol.ie, Website: www.whytes.ie.

INTERNET AUCTIONS

Amazon/Sothebys
amazon.sothebys.co.uk
E-bay
www.ebay.co.uk
Speedbid
www.speedbid.com
QXL
www.qxl.com

DEALERS

Ackley Unlimited
PO Box 82144, Portland, Oregon, USA 97282-0144. (503) 659 4681. Orders, medals and decorations. Free quarterly lists on request.

Armoury of St. James's
17 Piccadilly Arcade, Piccadilly, London SW1Y 6NH. 020 7493 5082 (fax 020 7499 4422). Orders, decorations, medals, militaria.

Ashley, Brooks & Jervis
Flat 2, 75 High Street, Rochester, Kent ME1 1LX. 01634 827225. British and foreign medals and badges. Lists.

Michael Autengruber
Schillstrasse 7B, D-63067 Offenbach, Germany. (69) 88 69 25 evenings. Orders, medals, literature. Catalogues $US3 (Europe), $US6 (elsewhere).

Bonus Eventus
Aartshertoginnestratt 27, 8400 Oostende, Belgium. (059) 801696. Medals and miniature medals. Free medal lists (specify full-size or miniatures).

Bostock Militaria
"Pinewood", 15 Waller Close, Leek Wootton, near Warwick CV35 7QG. 01926 856381. British orders, medals and decorations. Sae for free current lists. Callers welcome by appointment.

Award Productions Ltd
PO Box 300, Shrewsbury, SY5 6WP. 01952 510053 (fax: 01952) 510765). Suppliers of unofficial medals for veterans.

Paul Boulden
Parade Antiques Market, 17 The Parade, The Barbican, Plymouth, Devon. 01752 221443. Fax: 01589 632686. Medals and militaria. 6 lists p.a. (£3, £6 overseas).

Boyne Coins & Medals
Trim Road, Navan, Co. Meath, Ireland. (00353 46) 21079. Coins and medals. Many Irish medals stocked.

British Military Badges
The Castle Armoury, 18 Castle Street, Dover, Kent CT16 1PW. 12pp list of British Military Badges. UK & BFPOs £2, Europe £2.40, Elsewhere £3.

Philip Burman
Blackborough End, Middleton, King's Lynn, Norfolk PE32 1SE. 01553 840350. Large and varied stock of orders, medals and decorations. Send large sae for lists, issued 6 times a year. Website: www.military-medals.co.uk.

John Burridge
91 Shenton Road, Swanbourne, Western Australia 6010. British and Commonwealth medals and decorations.

Mark Carter
PO Box 470, Slough SL3 6RR. 01753 534777. British and foreign orders, medals, decorations and miniatures. Fairs organiser. Lists £5 (UK and BFPO), £7.50 (overseas airmail).

Central Antique Arms & Militaria
Smith Street Antiques Centre, Warwick CV34 4JA. 01926 400554. British orders, decorations, medals and militaria. Lists 50p.

Chelsea Military Antiques
Unit N13/14, Antiquarius, 131–141 King's Road, London SW3 4PW. 020 7352 0308. Medals and militaria. Monday–Saturday, 10am–6pm. E-mail: richard@chelseamilitaria.co.uk, Website: www.chelseamilitaria.co.uk.

Chester Militaria
6 Chirk Close, Newton, Chester CH2 1SF. 01244 344268. Medals and militaria.

Coldstream Military Antiques
55a High Street, Marlow, Bucks. Tel/fax 01628 822503. Medals, badges, insignia.

Collector's Lair
#205 - 15132 Stony Plain Road, Edmonton, Alberta, Canada T5P 3X8. (403) 486 2907. Medals, badges and uniforms.

Norman W. Collett
PO Box 235, London SE23 1NS. 020 8291 1435 (fax 020 8291 3300). British medals and decorations, and military books. Regular catalogues issued. Send 50p in stamps for the current 48 page medal list or 32 page book list. Medals website: www.medalsonline.co.uk. Books website: www.militarybookworm.co.uk.

Command Post of Militaria
1306 Government Street, Victoria, British Columbia, Canada V8W 1Y8. (250) 383 4421. Medals, badges and uniforms.

Conglomerate Coins & Medals
206 Adelaide Street, Brisbane, Queensland 4000, Australia. (07) 2211217 (fax 07 2299128). Medals and medallions.

Peter R. Cotrel
7 Stanton Road, Bournemouth, Dorset BH10 5DS. Mail order only—callers by appointment. 01202 388367. British, American and general foreign medals and decorations. Medal albums etc.

Jamie Cross
PO Box 73, Newmarket, Suffolk CB8 8RY. Specialist in Third Reich medals, badges and decorations.

C. J. & A. J. Dixon Ltd
23 Prospect Street, Bridlington, East Yorkshire YO15 2AE. 01262 676877 (fax 01262 606600). British and world orders, medals and decorations. 4 large lists a year £8 (UK), £12 (overseas). Email: chris@dixonsmedals.co.uk. Website: www.dixonsmedals.co.uk

D.M.D. Services
6 Beehive Way, Reigate, Surrey RH2 8DY. 01737
240080. Victorian campaign medals and
decorations.

Frank Draskovic
PO Box 803, Monterey Park, CA 91754, USA.
Worldwide orders and medals, especially
European and Far Eastern.

M. J. Dyas Coins and Medals
Unit 3, 42 Stratford Road, Shirley, Solihull B90
3LS. 0121 733 2225. All medals—memorial
plaques a speciality. Lists £1 (UK), £2 (overseas).

Edinburgh Coin Shop (Hiram T. D. Brown)
11 West Crosscauseway, Edinburgh EH8 9JW.
0131 668 2928 (fax 0131 668 2926). British medals
and decorations. 4 lists a year and postal
auctions.

Andy Garrett
1 St Peters Gate, Brackley, Northants NN13 7NL.
01280 700180. British and foreign medals, groups
and collections, badges and militaria.

Gateway Militaria
Box 24049, 13 - 1853 Grant Avenue, Winnipeg,
Manitoba, Canada R3N 1ZO. (204) 489 3884 (fax
204 489 9118). Medals and badges.

Glance Back
17 Upper Church Street, Chepstow, Gwent NP6
5EX. 01291 626562. Large stock of Medals, badges
and military books.

Gordons Medals & Military Collectables
Grays Antiques Centre,Davies Mews, Davies
Street,London W1K 5AB. 020 7495 0900 (fax 020
7495 0115). Monday–Friday, 10.30am–6pm.
Campaign medals, militaria, German and 3rd
Reich. Catalogues £6 (UK), £12 (overseas air).
E-mail: sales@gordonsmedals.co.uk,
Website: www.gordonsmedals.co.uk.

Louis E. Grimshaw
612 Fay Street, R.R. #1 Kingston, Ontario, Canada
K7L 4VI. (613) 549 2500. Military antiques and
collectables, including medals. Catalogues of
arms, medals and militaria . Single copies $C5
(Canada), $US4 (USA), $US6 (elsewhere).

Great War Medals
22 Selborne Road, Southgate, London N14 7DH.
Mainly WW1 medals and books. 36 page
catalogue of medals and decorations, £7.50 (UK),
£11 (overseas).

W. D. Grissom
PO Box 12001, Suite 216, Chula Vista, California,
USA 91912. American medals. Free lists.

Tom Halpin
268 Gilmore Street, Mineola, NY 11501, USA. 516-
248-4673. Fax: 516 248 6082. Worldwide awards
with other military (all services) items. Large
newspaper-style list.

A. D. Hamilton & Co.
7 St Vincent Place, Glasgow G1 2DW. 0141 221
5423 (fax 0141 248 6019). British and foreign
medals, groups and collections, badges and
militaria. Monday-Saturday, 9am - 5.30pm.
Email:jeffrey@hamiltons.junglelink.co.uk.Website:
www.adhamiltons.com.

Raymond D. Holdich
Trafalgar Square Collectors' Centre, 7 Whitcomb
Street, London WC2 7HA. 020 7930 1979.
Monday–Friday, 11am–5.30pm. Saturday by
appointment only. British gallantry awards,
campaign medals, cap badges, medals and
decorations. E-mail: rdhmedals@aol.com Website:
www.rhmedals.com.

Invicta International
740 Gladstone Avenue, Ottawa, Ontario, Canada
K1R 6X5. (613) 232 2263. Worldwide medals,
badges, insignia, wings, books and prints.

Steve Johnson
USA: PO Box 745, Batavia, IL 60510, USA. (630)
761 4004 (fax (630) 761 4006). UK: Woodbridge,
Derwent Avenue, Rowlands Gill, Tyne & Wear
NE39 1BZ. All world orders, medals, decorations
and militaria.

Paul Laycock
6 Poplar Terrace, Moldgreen, Huddersfield, W.
Yorks HD5 8AB. British medals and decorations.
Regular lists.

Liverpool Medal Company Ltd
42 Bury Business Centre, Kay Street, Bury, Lancs
BL9 6BU. 0161 763 4610/4612 (fax 0161 763 4963).
British and world medals and decorations. Regular
lists.
E-Mail: liverpoolmedals@online.rednet.co.uk,
Website: www.liverpoolmedals.co.uk.

March Medals
199 Springthorpe Road, Erdington, Birmingham
B24 0SJ. 0121 373 2020. Orders of chivalry,
decorations, campaign medals, military antiques,
books, ribbons and accessories. Regular lists.
Monday-Friday, 10am–5pm; Saturday, 10am–
2pm.

Medals of Service
926 Old Northern Road, Glenorie NSW 2157,
Australia. 61 02 9652 2022 (fax 61 02 9652 2950).
Specialising in replica medals.

Merseyside Collectors Centre
Unit C110-111, Market Hall, Grange Precinct,
Birkenhead, Merseyside L41 2YH. Tel/fax: 0151
666 1431. Medals and militaria.

Militaria House
238 Davenport Road, PO Box 99, Toronto, Ontario
Canada M5R 1J6. Mail bid auctions of decorations,
medals, insignia and militaria. 4 catalogues per
year $25 (US and Canada), $30 (overseas).

Miniature Medals
MC Miniature Medals, PO Box 1512, Warwick
CV35 9YX. Tel/fax 01926 651500. Miniature medal
specialist. Lists.

Peter Morris
1 Station Concourse, Bromley North Railway
Station, Kent. Postal: PO Box 223, Bromley, Kent
BR1 4EQ. 020 8313 3410 (shop hours), 020 8466
1762 (other times). Monday-Friday, 10am–6pm;
Saturday, 9am–2pm. Free quarterly lists. E-mail:
info@petermorris.co.uk,Website:www.petermorris.co.uk

Neate Militaria & Antiques
PO Box 3794, Preston St Mary, Sudbury CO10 9PX.
01787 248168 (fax 01787 248363). Monday-Friday,
9am-6pm. Lists available, £6 (UK, EC), £10
(overseas). E-mail: gary@neatemedals.fsnet.co.uk.

Detlev Niemann
Ballindamm 9, V Floor, 20095 Hamburg 1,
Germany. 0049 40 3252 5354 (fax 0049 40 3252
5454). Specialist in German orders, decorations,
militaria, etc. Catalogue subscription £20 for 4
issues. E-mail: Detlev-Niemann@t-online.de
Website: www.Detlev-Niemann.de.

Pieces of History
PO Box 4470, Cave Creek, AZ 85331, USA. (602)
488 1377 (fax 602 488 1316). Worldwide medals
badges, patches, accessories etc. Lists available.

Q & C Militaria
22 Suffolk Road, Cheltenham, Gloucestershire
GL50 2AQ. Tel/fax 01242 519815. British and
Commonwealth orders, medals, decorations and
miltaria.

R & M International
PO Box 6278, Bellevue, Washington, USA. 98008-
0278. Well illustrated 64 page lists of medals and
decorations of the world, $US2.50. Website: www.
randminternational.com.

Barbara Radman
Westfield House, 2G Westfield Road, Witney,
Oxon OX8 5JG. 01993 772705. British and Foreign
orders, medals and decorations. Specialist in
Serbia, Montenegro, Russian and Baltic States.

Romsey Medals
5 Bell Street, Romsey, Hampshire SO51 8GY.
01794 512069 (fax 01794 830332). Orders, medals
and decorations.

S. E. Sewell
PO Box 104, Ipswich, Suffolk IP5 7QL. 01473
626950. A wide variety of medals, mainly British.

George M. Shank
1574 Arnold Ct., Huntingdon, W. Va. 25705, USA.
304-736-8730. Worldwide orders, medals and
decorations. Large lists.

E. C. Snaith & Son Ltd
20 Vale Street, Denbigh, Denbighshire LL16 3BE.
Tel: 01745 812218 Fax: 01745 816367. Wholesalers
to the Medal Trade.

Southern Medals
16 Broom Grove, Knebworth, Herts SG3 6BQ. 32
page lists of British and Commonwealth medals
and decorations. £6 (UK), £9 (overseas).

Spink & Son Ltd (Christie's International)
69 Southampton Row, Bloomsbury, London WC1B
4ET. 020 7563 4009 (fax 020 7563 4066). Dealers,
auctioneers. The Medal Gallery, Monday-Friday,
9am–5.30pm (Tues. to 7.30pm). Publishers of *Spink
Medal Quarterly*, £8 (UK), £15 or $US25 (overseas).
E-mail: info@spinkandson.com,
Website: www.spink-online.com.

Sunset Militaria
Dinedor Cross, Herefordshire HR2 6PF. 01432
870420 (fax: 01432 870309). Military research and
world medal ribbons. SAE for list.

Suttle Medals and Militaria
50 Lackey Street, Summer Hill, NSW 2130,
Australia. Tel/fax 61 02 9798 6113. Medals,
militaria, books, uniforms, etc.

Jeremy Tenniswood
28 Gordon Road, Aldershot, Hants GU11 1ND.
01252 319791 (fax 01252 342339). Orders, medals
decorations and militaria and related books.

Third Arm Militaria
PO Box 121, Market Rasen, Lincs LN8 3GF. 01673
828081. Specialising in Campaign Medals and
British Army Insignia.

Toad Hall Medals
Court Road, Newton Ferrers, near Plymouth,
South Devon PL8 1DH. 01752 872672 (fax 01752
872723). Lists available.
E-mail: th.medals@virgin.net.

Toye, Kenning & Spencer Ltd
Regalia House, Newtown Road, Bedworth,
Warwickshire CV12 8QR. 01203 315 634 (fax 01203
643 018). Manufacturers of miniature medals,
medal ribbons, badges, etc.

Treasure Bunker Militaria Shop
21 King Street, The Trongate, Glasgow G1 5QZ.
Tel/Fax: 0141 552 4651, E-mail: treasure
bunker.com, Website: info@treasurebunker.com.

Eugene G. Ursual
PO Box 8096, Ottawa, Ontario, Canada K1G 3H6.
(613) 521 9691 (fax 613 523 3347). Medals, orders,
decorations, miniatures and militaria. 10 lists a
year $12 (Canada), $15 (USA), $20 (overseas)

Vernon
Box 1560MN, Wildomar, California, USA 92595.
Worldwide orders, medals and decorations. Lists
10 times a year, $3 (USA), $20 (oversea airmail).

Welsh Medals & Militaria
1 Mortimer Road, Cardiff CF1 9JZ. 01222 374202.
Medals, coins and militaria.

Fred S. Walland
17 Gyllyngdune Gardens, Seven Kings, Essex IG3
9HH. 020 8590 4389. Orders, medals and decorations. Lists £7.50 (UK and BFPO), £15 (overseas).

Worcestershire Medal Service Ltd
56 Broad Street, Sidemoor, Bromsgrove, B61 8LL.
01527 835375 (fax: 01527 576798). Specialists in
ribbons, full size and min. medals, mounting and
cases. E-mail: WMS@WORCMEDALS.COM,
Website: www.worcmedals.com.

Yeovil Collectors Centre
16 Hendford, Yeovil, Somerset BA20 1TE. 01935
433739. Medals, badges, etc. Occasional lists.

**The information appearing in this
section is correct at the time of going
to press. If any of the details
included are not correct as printed,
please telephone 01404 46972.**

BOOKSELLERS/DEALERS

In addition to the names listed below, it should be noted that a number of the medal dealers listed above regularly or occasionally include books on their medal lists.

Articles of War
8806 N. Bronx Avenue, Skokie, IL60077-1896, USA. 847 674-7445 (fax 847 674-7449. e-mail warbooks@aol.com). Dealer in military books, domestic and imported, both new and secondhand.

Aviation Bookshop
656 Holloway Road, London N19 3PD. 020 7272 3630. Aviation history—books, magazines, posters and videos.

Battlefield Military Bookstore
3915 Highway 7, Minneapolis, MN 55416, USA. 612 920-3820. Wide range of military books.

Buffo Books
32 Tadfield Road, Romsey, Hants SO51 8AJ. 01794 517149. Mainly 20th century military history, especially Second World War.

Bunker to Bunker Books
PO Box 342, 1631 St Mary's Road, Winnipeg, Canada MB R2N 3X9. General but with a focus on Canadian-related material.

Andrew Burroughs
24 St. Martins, Stamford, Lincolnshire PE9 2LJ. 01780 51363. Military history. Lists available.

Buttercross Books
2 The Paddock, Bingham, Nottingham NG13 8HQ. Tel/fax 0115 9 837147. Napoleonic era and First World War. Lists available.

Caliver Books
816/818 London Road, Leigh-on-Sea, Essex SS9 3NH. Tel/fax 01702 73986. Military history up to 1900. Shop and mail order. Lists available.

Chelifer Books
Todd Close, Curthwaite, Wigton, Cumbria CA7 8BE. General military history, including unit histories. Lists available.

The Collector
36 The Colonnade, Piece Hall, Halifax, West Yorks HX1 1RS. Military, naval and aviation history, all periods.

Q. M. Dabney & Company
PO Box 42026-MH, Washington, DC 20015, USA. Military books of all periods. Lists $US1 each.

Peter de Lotz
20 Downside Crescent, Hampstead, London NW3 2AP. 020 7794 5709. (fax 020 7284 3058). Military, naval and aviation history, with emphasis on regimental and divisional histories.

Tom Donovan Military Books
52 Willow Road, Hampstead, London NW3 1TP. 020 7431 2474 (fax 020 7431 8314). Printed works, documentation and manuscript material relating to the British Military Services. Regular lists.

Francis Edwards
13 Great Newport Street, Charing Cross Road, London WC2H 4JA. 020 7379 7669 (fax 020 7836 5977). All aspects of military history. Lists available.

Chris Evans Books
Unit 6, Jervoise Drive, Birmingham B31 2XU. Tel/fax 0121 477 6700. General military history. Lists available.

Falconwood Transport and Military Bookshop.
5 Falconwood Parade, The Green, Welling, Kent DA16 2PL. 020 8303 8291. Military, naval and aviation history.

Kenneth Fergusson
The Book Room, The Post Office, Twyning, Tewkesbury, Glos GL20 6DF. 01684 295855. Military and aviation history.

Ken Ford Military Books
93 Nutshalling Avenue, Rownhams, Southampton SO1 8AY. 023 8073 9437. British colonial wars. Lists available.

John Gaunt
21 Harvey Road, Bedford MK41 9LF. 01234 217686. Numismatic books including medal reference works.

GM Services
98 Junction Road, Andover, Hampshire SP10 3JA. Tel/fax 01264 362048. Postal auctions of military books.

Tony Gilbert Antique Books
101 Whipps Cross Road, Leytonstone, London E11 1NW. 020 8530 7472. Military, naval and aviation history.

Martin Gladman
235 Nether Street, Finchley, London N3 1NT. 020 8343 3023. Military, naval and aviation history.

G. L. Green.
18 Aldenham Avenue, Radlett, Herts WD7 8HX. 01923 857077. Naval and maritime history.

George Harris
Heathview, Habberley Road, Bewdley, Worcs DY12 1JH. 01299 402413. Napoleonic, Victorian campaigns and the First World War.

Derek Hayles Military Books
35 St. Marks Road, Maidenhead, Berks SL6 6DJ. 01628 39535. Regular lists.

Hersant's Military Books
17 The Drive, High Barnet, Herts EN5 4JG. Tel/fax 020 8440 6816. General military history. Lists available by period.

Michael Hicks Beach
99 York Mansions, London SW11 4BN. 020 7622 2270. British and Imperial military history.

Jade Publishing Ltd
5 Leefields Close, Uppermill, Oldham, Lancs OL3 6LA. 01475 870944. British and imperial military books.

Jerboa-Redcap Books
PO Box 1058, Highstown, N.J. 08520, USA. (609) 443 3817. British military books (all services), including collectables. Catalogues $US2.

Keegan's Bookshop
Merchant's Place, Reading RG1 1DT. Phone/fax 01734 587253. Secondhand booksellers with good stock of military titles. Shop in town centre. Parking nearby.

Roger Knowles
26 Church Road, Norton Canes, Cannock, Staffs WS11 3PD. 01543 279313. Military history

John Lewcock
6 Chewells Lane, Haddenham, Ely, Cambs CB6 3SS. 01353 741152. Naval history.

Liverpool Medal Company Ltd
42 Bury Business Centre, Kay Street, Bury, Lancs BL9 6BU. 0161 763 4610/4612 (fax 0161 763 4963). Medal dealers, but publish an occasional separate book catalogue.

London Pride
14E Fort Lee Road, Bogota, NJ 07603, USA. 201 525-1828 (fax 201 525-0815). General military books.

Ian Lynn
258 Upper Fant Road, Maidstone, Kent ME16 8BX. 01622 728525. Military history.

Marcet Books
4a Nelson Road, Greenwich, London SE10 9JB. 020 8853 5408. Naval history.

G. & D. I. Marrin & Sons
149 Sandgate Road, Folkestone, Kent CT20 2DA. 01303 253016 (fax 01303 850956) Specialises in material relating to the First World War.

McLaren Books
91 West Clyde Street, Helensburgh, Dunbartonshire G84 8BB. 01436 676453. Naval history.

Midland Counties Publications
Unit 3, Maizefield, Hinckley, Leicestershire LE10 1YF. 01455 233747. Aviation books.

Military Bookman
29 East 93rd Street, New York, NY 10128, USA. (212) 348 1280. Large stock of military history relating to all services worldwide and all periods.

Military Bookworm
PO Box 235, London SE23 1NS. 020 8291 1435. Decorations & medals, regimental & divisional histories, and campaign histories. Subscription to lists £9 (approx 9 per year)

Military History Bookshop
2 Broadway, London N11 3DU. Tel/fax 020 8368 8568. Lists, subscription £2.50 (4 issues).

Military Parade Bookshop
The Parade, Marlborough, Wilts SN8 1NE. 01672 515470 (fax 01980 630 150). Wide ranging new and secondhand books. Lists available.

Motor Books
St Martins Court, London WC2N 4AL. 020 7836 5376 (fax 020 7497 2539). Comprehensive stock of military books in print.

Military & Naval History
54 Regis Road, Tettenhall, Wolverhampton WV6 8RW. 01902 756402. British Military history. Lists available.

Roberts
PO Box 1, Brimpton, Reading, RG7 4RJ. 0118 971 4044. New and secondhand military history.

Savannah Publications
90 Dartmouth Road, Forest Hill, London SE23 3HZ. 020 8244 4350 (fax 020 8244 2448) e-mail savpub@dircon.co.uk. Publisher and distributor of works of reference relating to British Army, Navy and RAF history/medals/biography and service histories/genealogy. Free catalogues. Website: www.savannah-publications.com.

Selous Books
40 Station Road, Aldershot, Hants, GU11 1HT. 01252 333611 (fax: 01252 342339). Specialists in military books. SAE for catalogue, plus £1 stamp)

Anthony J. Simmonds
23 Nelson Road, Greenwich, London SE10 9JB. 020 8853 1727. Naval and maritime history. Occasional catalogues.

Andrew Skinner
42 Earlspark Avenue, Newlands, Glasgow G43 2HW. 0141 632 4903 (fax 0141 632 8453). General military history stock with special emphasis on Scotland. Monthly lists.

Frank Smith Maritime Aviation Books
98/100 Heaton Road, Newcastle upon Tyne. 0191 265 6333. Naval, maritime and aviation history.

Spink & Son Ltd (Christie's International)
  69 Southampton Row, Bloomsbury, London WC1B 4ET. 020 7563 4000 (fax 020 7563 4066). Specialist Book Department.
  Email: info@spinkandson.com.
  Website: www.spink-online.com.

Stephen Tilston
  37 Bennett Park, Blackheath, London SE3 9RA. Tel/fax 020 8318 9181. General stock, but specialising in the First World War. Lists available

THCL Books
  185 Lammack Road, Blackburn, Lancs BB1 8LH. Military book specialist aand publishers of collectors' cards of medal heroes. Lists available.

Token Publishing Ltd.
  Orchard House, Duchy Road, Heathpark, Honiton, Devon EX14 1YD. 01404 46972 (fax 01404 44788). E-mail info@token-publishing.com. Publishers of *Medal News* and *Coin News* and related titles.

Ken Trotman Ltd
  Unit 11, 135 Ditton Walk, Cambridge CB5 8QD. 01223 211030 (fax 01223 212317). Large, wide-ranging stock. Lists available: 3 per year.

Brian Turner Military Books
  1132 London Road, Leigh-on-Sea, Essex SS9 2AJ. Tel/fax 01702 78771. Printed works and documentation relating to military, naval and aviation history, specialising in the First World War, India and Africa.

Robin Turner
  30 Great Norwood Street, Cheltenham, Glos GL50 2BH. 01242 234303. Military, specialising in the Napoleonic period.

Mark Weber
  35 Elvaston Place, London SW7 5NW. 020 7225 2506 (fax 020 7581 8233). Specialises in official war histories and books by and about Sir Winston Churchill.

Ray Westlake Military Books
  53 Claremont, Malpas, Newport, South Wales NP9 6PL. 01633 854135 (fax 01633 821860). General military books.

Terence Wise
  Pantiles, Garth Lane, Knighton, Powys LD7 1HH. Military history especially regimental and divisional histories. Lists available.

Woodford Books
  The Lodge, Well Street, Docking, King's Lynn, Norfolk PE31 8LQ. 01485 518700. Medal and military books, photograph albums, letters, ephemera. Lists available.

Woolcott Books
  Kingston House, Higher Kingston, Nr Dorchester, Dorset DT2 8QE. 0135 267773 (fax 01305 848218). Military and colonial history, specialising in India, Africa and 19th century campaigns.

World War Books
  Oaklands, Camden Park, Tunbridge Wells, Kent TN2 5AE. 01892 538465. Military, naval and aviation books and documents, particularly First World War, regimental histories, maps, diaries and photographs. Lists available.

World War II Books
  PO Box 55, Woking, Surrey GU22 8HP. 01483 722880 (fax 0483 721548). Second World War military history. 12 lists per year.

R.J. Wyatt.
  33 Sturges Road, Wokingham, Berks RG11 2HG. 01734 780325. All aspects of British military history, with an emphasis on the First and Second World Wars, Volunteers, and the Territorial Army.

FAIRS

Many fairs are held regularly and organised by professionals, in addition a number of societies organise fairs for the public (Victorian Military Society, Aldershot Militaria Society, etc.). The dates are usually well advertised in MEDAL NEWS and other publications, however, times and venues are liable to change so it is advisable in every instance to telephone the organisers beforehand. Listed below are the major fair organisers and the events known to us.

Aldershot Militaria and Medal Fair
Princes Hall, Barrack Road, Aldershot, Surrey. Mark Carter, 01753 534777.

Arms, Shooters, Militaria and Medal Fair
The Premier, Compton and Manx Suites, The National Motorcycle Museum, Birmingham. Up to 150 tables. Central Arms Fairs, 11 Berwick Close, Warwick CV34 5UF. 01926 400554/497340.

Bedford Arms Fair
The Corn Exchange, Bedford. Arms & Armour UK, 58 Harpur Street, Bedford MK40 2QT. 01234 341831.

Bolton Militaria Fair
Horwich Leisure Centre, Victoria Road.Bolton. Northern Arms Fair. 01423 780940 or 0113 2716180.

Britannia Medal Fair
Victory Services Club, 63-79 Seymour Street, Marble Arch, London W2. Six p.a. Britannia Enterprises, 28 Raglan Place, Burnopfield, Gateshead NE16 6NN. 01267 71869.

Bromley Medal and Militaria Fair
Civic Centre, Bromley, Kent. Ray Brough. 020 8766 0329.

Cheshunt Militaria Fair
Wolsey Hall, Windmill Lane, Cheshunt, Herts. Hands Militaria Fairs. Tel/Fax: 01892 730233.

Chessington Militaria Fair
Community Sports College, Garrison Lane, Chessington, Surrey. Hands Militaria Fairs. Tel/Fax: 01892 730233.

Collectors' Market
London Bridge Main Line Station, London SE1. Every Saturday. Over 60 stands comprising medals, badges and militaria. 020 8398 8065.

Didcot Militaria Fair
Civic Hall, Britwell Road, Didcot, Berks. Hands Militaria Fairs. Tel/Fax: 01892 730233.

Dorking Militaria Fair
Dorking Halls, Reigate Road, Dorking, Surrey. Hands Militaria Fairs. Tel/Fax: 01892 730233.

Dunstable Arms & Armour Fair
The Queensway Hall, Dunstable. Arms & Armour UK, 58 Harpur Street, Dunstable MK40 2QT. 01234 344831.

Farnham Annual Militaria Fair
The Maltings, Bridge Street, Farnham, Surrey. Aldershot Militaria Society. 01705 839400/831804.

Farnham Militaria Fair
The Maltings, Bridge Square, Farnham, Surrey. Hands Miliatria fairs. Tel/Fax: 01892 730233.

Fleet Militaria Fair
The Harlington Centre, Fleet Road. Hands Militaria Fairs. Tel/Fax: 01892 730233.

Ipswich Medal and Militaria Fair
Kesgrave Community Centre. Steve Sewell. 01473 626950.

Leeds Militaria Fair
Pudsey Civic Hall (off main Leeds to Bradford ring-road). Northern Arms Fair. 01423 780940 or 0113 2716180.

London Arms Fairs
The Paragon Hotel, Lillie Road, London SW6. 4 shows p.a. Douglas Fryer. 01273 475 959.

London Military Market—Islington
Angel Arcade, Camden Passage, Islington, London N1. Every Saturday, 8am–2pm. Over 35 stands. 0162882 2503 or 01455 556971.

Maidenhead Medal and Militaria Fair
The Magnet Leisure Centre, Maidenhead, Kent. Ray Brough. 020 8766 0329.

Midhurst Militaria Fair
The Grange, Bepton Road, off the A286, Midhurst, Surrey. Hands Militaria Fairs. Tel/Fax: 01892 730233

Newcastle-upon-Tyne Militaria Fair
Park Hotel, Grand Parade, Tynemouth. Northern Arms Fair. 01423 780940 or 0113 2716180.

North Kent Military Collectors' Fair
The Inn on the Lake Hotel, Shorne, Gravesend, Kent. For further details phone Keith or Veronica Reeves on 01634 375098

Stratford Upon Avon Militaria & Medal Fair
Leisure Centre. Mark Carter. 01753 534777.

Stockport Arms Fair
The Armoury Hall (TA), Greek Street, Stockport. For details Tel: 0161 485 6908.

Tunbridge Wells
The Camden Centre, Market Square, Camden Road. Ray Brough. 020 8766 0329.

Victorian Military Fair
Victorian Military Society, 49 Belsize Park, London NW3 4EE. 020 7722 5542.

Watford Arms, Militaria and Medal Fair
Bushey Hall School, London Road, Bushey, Herts. Sovereign Fairs. 01438 811657 or 01923 448903.

West Country Militaria and Medal Fair
Yate Leisure Centre, Kennedy Way, Yate, near Chipping Sodbury, Bristol. Mark Carter. 01753 534777.

INDEX TO
MEDAL NEWS

Here we include the complete **Cumulative Subject Index** to the parent magazine MEDAL NEWS, commencing with the March 1989 issue, when it became a separate publication.

MEDAL NEWS was born in 1981 from the amalgamation of *Medals International* and *Coins & Medals*, into the popular title *Coin & Medal News*. However, the success of this magazine and the continuing growth of both the coin and the medal collecting hobbies prompted the separation of the two sections in March 1989. Since then both *Coin News* and MEDAL NEWS have grown from strength to strength and today are the hobby's leading publications, not only in the UK but MEDAL NEWS is the *only* independent magazine in the world devoted to the collecting and study of medals. Most later issues of MEDAL NEWS are still available, price £3—please enquire whether we have the issue you require (if not then photocopies of articles can be supplied at £5 per article).

NOTES

References are indicated **year, month: page,** for example 9004.18 means April 1990 issue, page 18; 9306.24 means June/July 1993 issue, page 24.

Each year runs from February to December. For example the year 1990 includes the December 1990/January 1991 issue.

Names of ships are indicated in italics.

Names of people have been included where they appear to be the major subject of an article or where more than trivial information is included.

Abbreviations used:
(cr)   Indicates the inclusion of a full or partial casualty list.
(mr)   Indicates the inclusion of a medal roll.
(nr)   Indicates nominal roll.
(i)   Indicates that the reference gives information rather than the object itself. For example it tells you where to find a medal roll rather than reproducing the roll itself.
(p)   Indicates that the reference is to a picture of a person or object where little or no other information is given.
(mp)   Same as (p) except that the picture is of medals.
(br)   Indicates Book Review.

Bainbridge, James Scott, Yorkshire Regt (WWI) 9002.10
Baker, Samuel, Sir: Nile explorations 9312.21-22
Balabac, sinking (mr) 9002.20-22
Balaclava 8908.15-18
    Crimea Medal clasp 9002.28
    Light Brigade & Policemen 8909.05
Balkans: clasp to Australia Service Medal (1975) 9403.11
Ball, B.M., Maj 39/Foot 9308.24-25
Ball, Frederick Markam, Flt Lt RAFVR: MC Java (1945) 9605.13
Ball, Stanley: *Wanderer* 9006.10-12
Ball, William: *Wanderer* 9006.10-12
Ballard: Guadalcanal 9209.20-21
balloonists medals 9005.21, 9008.28
Baltic Medal (1854-55): naming 9003.23
Baluch Horse: badge 9410.22
Banks, N.L.R. 'Over the Front' (br) 9303.23
Bannister, John, Pte: 'The Life and Death of. . . . .' service in India (backround) 9803.23-25
'Baptism of Fire' (br) Marsay, Mark 9906.24
Barber, C., Sgt Maj R. Regt Fus (p) 8904.25
Barber, W.H. Tpr 44 Reconnaisance Regt 9906.27
Barker, Ralph 'The RFC in France—From Bloody April 1917 to Final Victory' (br) 9511.19
Barker, Ralph 'Royal Flying Corps in France 1914-16' (br) 9503.19
Barker, William Lt Col, VC: biography published 9803.06
Baronet's Badge of Nova Scotia (mp) 9503.07
Barracouta: Boer War 9108.21
Barrett, J., Flt Lt 204 Squad: DFC *Kensington Court* (1939) 9410.12-13
Barrington-Kennett Medals 9310.16-17, 9402.26
Barrow, Percy, Lt Col: El Teb (1884) 8906.19
Baskeyfield, Jack Sgt South Staffordshire Regt. VC 9705.28-29
Bassett, Paul, Capt R.E. MC (1993) 9502.11
Bassett, Samuel J., Col RM: WWI/WWII 9603.18-19
Bate, C.K. 'For Bravery in the Field: recipients of the MM (1919-39)' (br) 9306.21
battlefields code of conduct 9105.07
Baxter, I. 'India Office Library & Records' (br) 9104.25
Bear of Oakland, meeting with *Discovery II* 8904.12
Beatham R. Pte. highest price paid for medal to an Australian for his VC 9906.07
Beatty, John L, Capt *Madura*: OBE WWII 9504.19
Bedfordshire Regt:Badges 9702.29-30
Bedfordshire & Hertfordshire Regt: name of 9111.25

Bedfordshire Yeomanry: Badges 9712.26
Bee, William Henry Askew, Lt RN: 9709.15-16
Belben, George Devereux, Lt RN: [I]Glatton[i] (1918)
    8909.16-17
Belgian ribbon emblems: Belgian 9006.25
Bell, D.M., PO: George Medal (p) 9006.09
Bell, Donald S., Lt 9/Green Howards: Footballer VC 9012.27
Bell, Frederick W., W Australian Mounted Inf 9211.21-22
Bell, Henry, Yorkshire Regt (WWI) 9002.09
Belle Hill: rescue (1875) 9403.18-19
Bellona (1944) 9412.13-15
Belmont, battle of (Boer war) (cr) 9911.18-21
Bengal Army
    (nri) 9003.20
    researching officers 9210.14-16
Bengal Co British Mounted Infantry: Somaliland (1903-04)
    9006.15
Bennett, David, F.O 617 Squad RAF 9503.21
Bennett, Donald CB, CBE,DSO Air Vice Marshall
    'Pathfinder' (br) 9906.24
Bennett, G.W., Pte: Albert Medal (p) 9403.07
Bennett, James Mallett, Sgt Australian Flying Corps:
    London to Australia flight (1919-20) 9509.16-17, 22
Bennett, R.W. 'Badges of the Worcestershire Regiment
    9503.19-20
Berenice (Persian Gulf) (1857) 9502.13-14
Beresford, Rebecca, Nurse: Memorial Plaque (mp) 9402.09
Bereton, J.M. & Savory, A.C.S. 'History of the Duke of
    Wellington's Regt 1702-1992' (br) 9502.21
Berkeley, A.P.F.M., Sqdn Ldr: *Eagle* 9110.17-18
Berkshire Yeomanry:Badges 9712.27
Berkshire and Westminster Dragoons: Badges 9712.28
Berlin Airlift: clasp to British Army of the Rhine (unofficial
    medal) 9511.24
Beryl: Mediterranean WWII 9608.16-17, 9609.23
Besant, T.F., Lt Cmdr RN (AE-1) 9306.12-13
Betham, ?: Gyantse Fort (1904) 9404.21
Bethell, C.A., Brev. Maj.: *SS Arandora* Star WWII 9009.14-17
Bevan-John, D.R.S., FO 228 Squad: *Kensington Court* (1939)
    9410.12-13
Bews, John, 73/Foot 9212.28
Bezar, Edwin, Sgt Maj 62/57 Foot 9010.11-12, 9011.25
Bhutan War (1864-65): Dewangiri 8910.15-19
Bikanir Camel Corps: Somaliland (1903-04) 9006.15
Bin Chee, Bidin, Capt MV *Brunei*: King's Commendation for
    Brave Conduct (1942) 9504.21
Binney Memorial Medal 9808.20-21
Bingham, E.W., Surgeon Cmndr RN (Antarctic) 9003.11-14
Birchall, F.T., Artificer RN: CGM group (mp) 9410.07
Bird, J., Pte West Aus: Slingersfontein (1900) 8909.19-20
Birmingham Loyal Association: gorget 9310.25
Birmingham Pals: badge 9012.21
British Empire Medal: PRO records 9206.14-15
British German Legion9908.18-21
Bishop, B. 'The Hell, the Humour & the Heartbreak' (br)
    9111.23
Bishop, G.N., Sgt West Aus: Slingersfontein (1900) 8909.19-
    20
Bishop, William, Col Sgt 37/ Regt: MSM (p) 9612.10
'Black Boots': Support unit of the BSAP 9704.16-17
Blackheath & Woolwich Battn: badge 9111.26-27
Blackpool Volunteers: badges 8912.21-22
Black Watch
    badges 9505.20-21
        piper's 9003.25
        shoulder-belt plate 9011.21
        tropical helmet 9405.23
Black Watch of Canada: badge 9106.26
Blair Mayne, Robert, Lt Col SAS (WWII) 9508.12-13
Blaydon, Sgt: MM WWII 9402.21
Bletchley Park: 9801.05
Blood Donor Medals
    Britain 9011.24
    Hungary 9011.24
'Bloody Red Tabs' (br) 9609.22
'Blood Tub, The: General Gough and the Battle of
    Bullecourt 1917' (br) Walker, Jonathon 9904.29
'Blue Bonnets, Boers and Biscuits. the Diary of Private
    William Fessey, DCM serving in the King's Own Scottish

Borderers During the Boer War ' (br) Wilson, Heather
    9905.26
Blue Max (Prussia)
    Military Air Service WWI 9411.12-13
    photo correction 9412.24
Blue Ribbon Merit Medal (Japan) 9002.26-27
Blues and Royals: badge 9309.23
Bobbie, 66/ Foot mascot 9503.20
Boer War (1899-1902)
    Belmont, battle of (cr) 9911.18-21
    Kimberley, siege of and 'Long Cecil' 9908.24-26
    Imperial Hospital Corps 9906.20-21
    Naval activity 9108.19-22
    Okiep (1902) 9108.21-22
    O'Reilly, Bill 0001.20-21
    Talana, battle of (1899) (mr) 9909.24-26 & 9910.23-26
    Volunteer Service Companies 9104.15-17
Boer War Project bibliography (i) 9403.05
Boer War Star (proposed) 9502.20
Bogdan Khemelnitsky, Order of (USSR) 9409.17-19
Bolton, Ernest: served Four different countries (1891-1919)
    9511.15
03/ Bombay Light Cavalry: Persian Gulf (1856-57) 9502.13-
    14
18/ Bombay Native Infantry: Abyssinia (1868) 9502.14
Bombay Grenadiers: Somaliland (1903-04) 9006.15
Bombay Pioneers: Somaliland (1903-04) 9006.15
Bomb Disposal: Germany (1946) 9412.19
Bomber Command
    aircraft loss reports (nr) 9410.15-17
    WWII 9208.14-15
Bomber Command Medal: overseas entitlement 9112.28
Booth, Henry, Col. Sgt. 80th Foot: Ntombe River (1879)
    8906.16-18
Border Mounted Rifles: Wagon Hill (1900) (cr) 9306.14-18
Border Regt
    badges
        Cap badges 9711.26-27
        Lonsdale Battn WWI 9012.22
        Musician 9403.24
        Officer's 9710.30-31, 9711.26-27
        Territorial Battn 9108.25-26
        Volunteer Bttn. 9710.30-31, 9711.26-27
Borneo,1965 Australian National Servicemen 0001.16-17
Borton, Richard E. , Capt SS *Vyner Brooke*: MBE (1942)
    9504.12
Bosely, J., Pte 19/Hussars: DCM (1884) 8906.19
Bosnia Medal: debate re eligibility 9612.13-14
Boulton: Trafalgar Medal 9705.20-21 (entitlement)
Bouque, Simone: SOE French Sect 9303.20-21
Bourne, Henry, Lt RN: NGS (p) 9512.06
Bower, Tom 'Heroes of World War II' (br) 9508.19
Bowman, J.A. 'Pickelhaube Vol 2' (br) 9208.26
Boyd, Capt: Tayleur Fund Medal 9403.18
Boyd, John, Lt (Canadian Overseas Railway Construction
    Corps): MC WWI 9611.12-13
Boyden Peter B. and Guy, Alan J. Editors:'Soldiers of the
    Raj: The Indian Army 1600-1947' (br) 9810.26
Bradfield J.T. Capt (SLI) in Iraq 1920 9910.20-21
Bradley, Joe, 10 Squadron: MM WWII 9402.22
Bradshaw, Alfred H., Sgt RAF WWII 9110.21-22
Brain, Lester J. Capt: Qantas Empire Airways
    9408.19-20
'Brassey's Companion to the British Army' (br) 9605.23
Brecknockshire Battalion (SW Borderers): badge 9606.21
Brentini, Terry, Glider Pilot Regt 9205.13-14, 9210.28
Breslau: WWI 9302.18-19
Brewster, S., 'Accrington Pals' (p) 8912.07
Brian (parachuting alsation): Dickin Medal 9511.07
Bridge, Toby, Maj: Medal of Bravery (Canada) (Bosnia)
    9606.05
Bridge on the River Kwae (Kwai): Buddhist temple 9210.20-
    21
Briers, John, 11/Hussars: VC Crimea 9311.25
Britannia: loss (1941) (mr) 8909.25
Britannia:loss (1941) 8906.21-22
Britania Medal Fair 9703.26-27
British Antarctic Survey 9003.12-13
'British Army Mutineers 1914-1922' Putkowski, Julian,: (br)
    9903.27

British Army of the Rhine (unofficial medal) 9511.24
British awards to Allied Armies: PRO records 9206.15
British-Bahawalpur Alliance Medal (1833-1933) (p) 9512.07
'British Battles & Medals' (Spink): 6th Edn update 8904.19,
   20, 8910.23
British Button Society (i) 9204.28
British Commonwealth Air Training Plan (mr) 9112.15-18
British Empire Medal 9303.26
   Air Training Plan WWII (mr) 9112.16
   elimination of 9412.10-11
   medal stats 9304.23
   to QMAAC (mr) 9302.15-17
British Forces
   abbreviations
      home guard insignia 9105.25
      naval rating titles (current) 9202.20-21
   commissions from ranks 9002.09-10
   demobilisation papers WWI 9404.25
   rankers info in PRO 9112.27
   rank structures; proposed changes 9505.05
   Regiments garrisoned Scotland (i) 9404.25
   reserve forces definitions 8904.27
   service record fakes 9102.18-19
   Warrant Officers Class III 9112.23
British Newspaper Library 9506.18-19
British Red Cross & St John's Enquiry List No. 14 8908.06-07
British Somaliland (1903-04) (mr) 9006.14-17
British South African Police. support unit 9704.16-17
British War Medal (1914-20)
   & numismatics 9308.19-21
   entitlement 8912.28
   King's Head variations 9005.19, 9006.28
   miniatures 9005.19
   naming 9002.18, 9004.18
   ribbon 8908.26
'British VCs of World War 2, A study in Heroism" bt John
   Laffin (br): 9802.25
Brocklebank, W.H. 2/5th Welch: SS Arandora Star 9012.27
Bromhead family 8908.22
'Bromsgrove School Worcestershire VC Holders' (br)
   9612.06
Bronze Medal for Valour (Italy): 6/Gordon Highlanders
   WWI (mr) 9411.17
Bronze Star (USA): Australian awards (Vietnam) 9602.13
Bronze Star for Valor (USA): Australian awards (Vietnam)
   9602.13
brooches to medals 9202.27, 9204.28
Brown, F.C., AB Beryl: MID WWII 9609.23
Brown, Malcolm 'The Imperial war Museum Book of the
   Somme' (br) 9706.24
Brown, P., Gnr RMR: killed Ohio (1942) 9602.25
Browne, Sidney, Dame QAIMNS (p) 9609.09
Brunei: scuttled (1942) 9504.13
Brunei: operationsin, 1962 9804.13
Buchanan, Cecil Douglas, Polar Medal George VI 8904.11-13
Buckingham Palace Co: badge 9105.25
Buckinghamshire Yeomanry (Royal Buckinghamshire
   Hussars): Badges 9712.28
Buffs: tropical helmet badge 9405.22
Bulkeley, John D., Lt US Navy Torpedo boats WWII 9112.13
Bullock, Jim, Romsey medals (p) 9505.06
Bulwark sinking (1914) (cr) 9109.15-17
Bunton, J., Pte: medal group (mp) 9610.09
Burant, Alec B., Capt SS Kinta: MBE (1942)
   9504.12-13
Burgon, Robert, Berwick on Tweed Lifeboat (p) (mp)
   9411.07
Burke, T, Sgt 550 Squad (1944) 9410.15-16
Burma
   (1890) KRRC (mr) 9312.15-18
   WWII 9004.11-12, 9008.20
Burma Gallantry Medal 9202.26
Burma Star: ribbon 8908.26
Burns, David, Lt Col: OBE citation 9509.12
Burns, Robert J., Lt Cmdr Melbourne: George Medal 9404.18
Burton, Elizabeth J.: sons & Indian Mutiny
   9205.21-22
Burton, Richard F.: Nile explorations 9312.21-22
Burton, Richard DSC, RM. 9902.20-21 (mr)
Busaco, battle of (1810) 8906.11

Bush, George J. RN: Zeebrugge (1918) 9104.19-20
Bushire (Persian Gulf) (1856): 3rd Bombay Light Cavalry
   9502.13
Buxton, D. ' Honour to the Airborne, Pt I 1939-48' (br)
   9504.22
Byng, J.H.G, Field Marsh. (p) 9511.07
Byrne, Thomas, Pte, 21st Lancers: VC (p) 9602.08

C

Cabul Medal (1842): naming 9003.22
Cadet Forces Medal (1950): ribbon 8909.26
Caernarvon Castle: battle with Thor WWII 8906.22
Caesar's Camp (1900) (cr) 9306.14-18
Caffyn, Frederick, Capt Dunera: OBE WWII 9504.19
Caithness & Sutherland Home Guard: badge 9105.24
Calcutta: re SS Balabac (mr) 9002.20-22
Caldwell, George and Cooper, Robert 'Rifle Green in the
   Peninsula' Vol 1 (br) 9910.36
Caledon: Heligoland (1917) (mr) 9303.16-17
Calgary Highlanders: badge 9106.26
Calypso: Heligoland (1917) (mr) 9303.16-17
Cambodia: clasp to Australia Service Medal (1975) 9403.11
Cambrai (1917): 29th Divisional Artillery (MM mr) 8910.10-
   12
Cambridgeshire Regt: badge 9108.25-26
   Territorial Regt: badges 9703.31-32
Cameron, George E.E Gordon, Maj Gordon High 9411.11
Cameron Highlanders
   badge 9506.22-23
   Sudan (1898) (mr Khedive's Sudan Medal)
      9504.14-17
Cameron Highlanders of Ottawa: badge 9106.26
Cameronians
   badges 9511.22-23
      helmet plate 9006.23
      piper's 9003.24-25
      Territorial Battn 9108.25
      tropical helmet 9405.22
Campaign Service Medal (1962) 9006.18, 9009.27
Campbell, John, Capt: W Australians (Boer War) 9211.21-22
Campion, Roger 'The Call of Duty: Police Gallantry in
   Devon and Cornwall' (br) 9801.29
Canada General Service Medal (1866-70): naming 9003.23
91st Canadian Highlanders: badge 9106.26
Canadian awards 9308.26
Canadian Corps Cyclist Bn: badge 9104.23
Canadian Divisional Cyclists: badge 9104.23
Canadian Expeditionary Force: Infantry badges 9010.24-25
Canadian Lifeboat Institution: Patron's medal introduction
   9804.05
Canadian Medal of Bravery 9503.05
Canadian Militia: Red River (1870) 9012.18-20
Canadian Overseas Railway Construction Corps (WWI)
   9611.12-13
Canadian Scottish: badges 9106.26-27
Canadian Scottish Regiment Museum: obtains William
   Metcalf VC 9811.07
Canal Zone (1952): GSM (1918-28) 8905.28
Canberra: in the Falklands 1982 9804.19-21 (mr)
Cane, Edith: Britannia 8909.25
Candia, Crete 1898 (cr, mr) 0001.24-25
Canterbury Brigade, N Zealand Mounted Rifles 9008.22-23
Canterbury Regt: badge 9203.24-25
cap badges: Royal Sussex Regt 9412.22-23
Cape Breton Highlanders: badge 9106.26
Cape Colony (1901): Sybille 9108.20
Cape Copper Company Medal: Boer War 9108.21-22
Cape Mounted Rifles
   Port Natal 8912.15
   (cr) 9004.26-27
Cape St Vincent (1797) 9206.16-17
captain-class frigates (Royal Navy) 8904.23
Captain Matthew Webb Silver Medal for Bravery (mp)
   9312.09
Capture of Ghuznee Medal see Ghuznee Medal
Carabiniers
   badges 9309.22
   musician 9402.25
Caradoc: Heligoland (1917) 9303.16

Malaya 9602.25
PRO records 9206.14-15
Reconnaissance Corps (mr) 9106.21
to New Zealanders (i) 9406.26
WWI Collecting 9909.15-17
Military Medal for Gallantry (Ireland) 9204.21, 9206.28, 9208.28
Military Medical Cross (Germany) 8909.12
Military Merit, Cross for (Germany): Brunswick WWI 8908.10
Military Order of the Tower and Sword (Portugal) (mp) 9104.10
Military Police, Campaign Service Medal (1962) 9006.18
Military Ribband 9012.24
militia
  definition of 8904.27
  shako plates 9103.11-12, 9211.24-25
Militia bar to Efficiency Medal (T) 8904.27-28
Millar, Francis H., Cpl (14859) Royal Scots/North Staffs: WWI medals 9604.25
Miller, J., Pte: Somaliland DCM 9006.14-17
Mills Company: the "Roo Club" 9703.19-21
Mills, Wayne, Cpl 1/ Duke of Wellington's Regt: CGC citation 9509.11
Mills, Wayne, Cpl Duke of Wellington's Regt: CGC (Gorazde) 9608.11
Mine Rescue Service Decoration (Germany) 8903.09
miniatures
  British War Medal (1914-20) 9005.19
  medal suspensions 8910.24
  researching 9901.20
  Victory Medal 9008.24
Mitcham Town Guard: badges 8912.21-22
Mitchell, Capt *Othello*: rescue re *Trimountain* 9605.15
Mitchinson, K.W. 'Cotton Town Comrades: Story of Oldham Pals' (br) 9310.21, 9402.04
Mitchinson, K.W. 'Gentleman And Officers' (London Rifle Brigade WWI) (br) 9506.07
Moar, May: RNLI Medal 8905.20
Modeste (Suez) 8912.10-11
Moffatt, James, Sgt 1/Yorkshire Regt 9002.09
Mohammerah (Persian Gulf) (1857) 9502.13-14
Mohommed-bin-Abdullah Hussan: Somaliland (1903-04) 9006.14-17
Molife, Jabez: Isandhlwana 9008.11-13, 9012.26
Monmouthshire Regiment: badges 9608.20-21
Monmouthshire Regt: badge 9108.25-26
Mons: VCs 9603.26
Montgomerie, Archibald J. (1855-1908) RN 9308.15-16
Montgomerie-Charrington, Victor R. (1887-1939) 2/Life Guards 9308.16
'Monty's Marauders'; Black rat and Red Fox (br): 9801.29
'Monuments to Courage' Harvey, David (br) 9908.37
Moor, H.G., Capt. Western Australians: Slingersfontein (1900) 8909.19-20
Moore, A.G.H., Maj.: obituaty 9304.05
Moore, Douglas, PO *Voyager*: George Medal 9404.17
Moore, Geoffrey: obituary 9302.04
Moore, Percy 2nd Lt: The last Jameson Raider? 9811.24-26
Moore, R.L.G., Sgt 550 Squad (1944) 9410.15-16
Moore, William A., LS *Beryl*: DSM WWII 9608.16
Morell, Sgt: GM Iranian Embassy Siege 9503.11
Moriarty, David, Capt 80/Foot: Ntombe River (1879) 8906.15-18
Moriarty, David J., Flt Sgr RNZAF: CGM(F) WWII 9609.15
Morris, Noel:published history of the casualties remembered on the war Memorial at Reedham (Norfolk) 9901.06
Most Eminent Order of the Indian Empire: miniatures 8911.27
Most Excellent Order of the British Empire 9412.10-11
Motherhood Medals 9011.24
Motor Gunboats WWII 9112.13
Motor Torpedo Boats WWII 9112.13
Mounted Infantry Co KRRC: Somaliland (1903-04) (mr) 9006.14-17
Mounted Rifles, New Zealand: badges 9008.22-23
Moyse, Robert, Lancashire Fusiliers: DCM WWI 9510.19
Mozambique: clasp to Australian Service Medal (1945-75) 9511.11

Mudie, J. "National Series" medals 8906.11-13
Mudie, William D., Capt *Thibet* 9002.26-27
Muir, Cyril V., East Surrey Regt 9310.19
Muir, Robert C., 605 Squadron 9310.18-20
Muir, Robert C.: 2 sets of WWI Medals 9610.26
mulct: definition 9404.26
Mullen, A.L.T. 'Military General Service Medal (1793-1814)' (br) 9011.28
Mullins, Capt ILH: VC Elandslaagte (1899) 9510.15
Murgu, I.G., Sgt. WWI & II (p) 9303.10
Murinda, Fraser Kaboko, Sgt-Maj: Southern Rhodesia 9710.16
Murphy, John: DSC (Gallipoli) medal group (mp) 9612.09
'Murphy': PRO Dog National Charity Lifesaver Award 9504.05
Murray, H.W., Capt (13/AIF 8912.19
14/ Murray's Jat Lancers: badge 9409.23
Muskets and Musketry 9811.16-18
Muster Books: names of 19/ Foot missing (1854) (nr) 9611.17
Myer's Drift (1879) 8906.15-18
Myler, Matthew Joseph: Pte !st Newfoundland Regt 9703.29
Myngs: *Glatton* (1918) 8909.15-17
Mystery ships WWII 9705.13-14

N

Nakhimov, Order of (USSR) 9409.17-19
Namibia: clasp to Australia Service Medal (1975) 9403.11
Napier, Gerald 'Sapper VCs, The' (br) 9807.29
Napier, R.F.L., Maj 1/ Cameron Highlanders: Sudan (1898) 9504.14-17
Napoleonic Wars 9003.15-16
Napoleon, legacy of:The French Legion of Honour 9702.24-25
Nares, George S., Capt: Arctic expedition (1876) 9312.20
Natal Hotchkiss Detachment: Wagon Hill (1900) (cr) 9306.14-18
Natal Native Horse: Isandhlwana (1879) 9008.11-13
Natal Volunteer Ambulance Corps: Spion Kop (1900) (cr) 9408.14-17
National Ex-Service Association: possible creation of 9606.24
National Maritime Museum: picture research room 9611.05
National Memorial Arboretum 9504.06
National Reserve 1914-1920 9704.21-24
National Service Medal 9611.18
Native Infantry: Bhutan War (1864-65) 8910.16-17
Nato Medal: Former Yugoslavia; permission to wear 9511.05
Naval Actions (Victorian) 9910.28-29
Naval Brigade: Crimea Medal (1854-56) awarded 1855 (mr) 9612.18-21
Naval Brigade Actions (Victorian) 9905.24-25
Naval General Service Medal (1915-62): Persian Gulf 1909-14 clasp 9611.20
Naval General Service Medal (1793-1840) naming 9002.18-19, 9003.22
  Persian Gulf (1909-14) (mr) 9309.13-17
'Naval General Service Medal Roll' (br) 9609.19
Naval General Service Medal: entitlement to clasps 9807.20-21
Naval General Service Medal: Rolls and research 9809.24
Naval Historical Collectors and Research Association 8903.27
Naval and Military Reward (1685) (p) 9305.08
Naylor, C., Cmdr *Penhurst* (p) 9111.07
Near East (1956): clasp to GSM 9508.10-11, 9510.26
Neghelli, 1st Cavalry Group (Italy) 8912.28
Neilson, W.G., Col. A & SH: DSO Magersfontein (p) 9010.09
'Nelson: an Illustrated History' (br) 9602.22
Nelson, Horatio
  Cape St Vincent (1797) 9206.17
  Maritime Museum Exhibition 9602.07
Nelson, K.J, 'Spitfire RCW'; exploits of Wing Cmdr Wilkinson' (br) 9504.23
Nelson Battalion: badge 9102.23
Neptune: rescue (1861) 9403.18-19
Netherlands East Indies (1945-46) 9005.16-17
Neville, S.H., Pte: WWI medal group (p) 9608.09

R

records release 9803.29 & 9909.28
records, Army Officers' 9911.35
Worledge, cyril, Sgt RAF: DFM WWII 9609.15
Worth, Geoffrey P., PO [I]Voyager[i]: BEM 9404.17
'Wotsit': PRO Dog National Charity Lifesaver Award
9504.05
Wright R. and Rawnsey C.F.'Night Fighter'(br) 9908.37
Wusthoff, K, Lt German Air Force: Blue Max 9411.12-13
Wyatt (?Wylie), Lt RA (Port Natal) 8912.15
Wynn, K.G. 'Men of the Battle of Britain Supp Vol' (br)
9208.26
Wyon, William: medal designs 9102.24

Y

Yangtse River: *Peterel* 9509.13-14
Yarra Borderers (1912-18): badge 9005.25
Yatternick, F/OE 550 Squad (1944) 9410.15-16
Yellow Ribbon Medal (Japan) 9311.19
Yellow Ribbon Merit Medal (Japan) 9002.26
Yeomanry: arm badges 9004.24
Yeomanry badges
Bedfordshire 9801.27
Berkshire 9801.27
Berkshire and Westminster Dragoons 9801.28
Royal Buckinghamshire Hussars 9801.28
Cheshire (Earl of Chester's) 9801.28
Derbyshire 9802.26
Royal North Devon 9802.26
Queen's Own Dorset 9802.26
Queen's Own Dorset and West Somerset 9802.27
Essex 9802.27
Royal Gloucestershire 9802.26
Hampshire Carabiniers 9803.26-27
Herefordshire 9803.26-27
Hertfordshire and Bedfordshire 9803.26-27
Inns of Court and City 9803.26-27
Royal East Kent 9803.26-27
West Kent (Queen's Own) 9803.26-27
Kent and County 9803.26-27
King's Colonials 9803.26-27
    Welsh 9704.25-26
King Edward's Horse 9804.26-27
Duke of Lancaster's Own 9804.26-27
Lancashire Hussars 9804.26-27
Leicesteshire (Prince Albert's Own) 9804.26-27
Leicesteshire and Derbyshire (Prince Albert's Own)
9804.26-27
Lincolnshire 9804.26-27
London 9804.26-27
City of London (Rough Riders) 9804.26-27 and 9805.27-28
2nd County of London (Westminster Dragoons) 9805.27-
28
3rd County of London (Sharpshooters) 9805.27-28
4th County of London 9805.27-28
London and Territorials 9805.27-28
Royal Mercian and Lancastrian 9805.27-28
Middlesex (Duke of Cambridge's Hussars) 9805.27-28
Norfolk (King's Own Royal Regt.) 9807.25-26
Northamptonshire 9807.25-26

Northumberland Hussars 9807.25-26
Nottinghamshire (Sherwood Rangers) 9807.25-26
South Nottinghamshire Hussars 9807.25-26
Queen's Own Oxfordshire Hussars 9807.25-26
Queen's Own 9807.25-26
Royal 9807.25-26
Shropshire 9808.27-28
North Somerset 9808.27-28
North Somerset and Bristol 9808.27-28
West Somerset 9808.27-28
Staffordshire (Queen's Own Royal Regt.) 9808.27-28
Duke of York's Own Loyal Suffolk Hussars 9808.27-28
Suffolk and Norfolk 9808.27-28
Surrey (Queen Mary's) 9808.27-28
Sussex 9809.27-28
Warwickshire 9809.27-28
Queen's Own Warwickshire and Worcestershire 9809.27-
28
Wessex 9809.27-28
Westmoreland and Cumberland 9809.27-28
Royal Wiltshire 9809.27-28
Queen's Own Royal Worcesteshire 9809.27-28
Yorkshire 9809.27-28
York & Lancaster Regt
Haspres War Memorial (nr) 9512.13
Sheffield Pals badge WWI 9012.22
Yorke, Robert, Act Capt Coldstream Grds QGM 9502.11
York and Lancaster Regiment: badge 9603.20-21
York Militia: gorget 9310.25
Yorkshire Brigade: badges 9603.20-21, 9709.27-28
Yorkshire Regt
1st, New Zealand Hill (1900) (cr) 9011.15-17
Givenchy (1915) 9204.15-18
Green Howards Badges 9602.20-21
Somaliland (1903-04) 9006.15
tropical helmet badge 9405.22
Yorkshire Volunteers: badges 9603.20-21
Yorkshire Yeomanry: badges 9206.24-25, 9809.27-28
Young, Dennis ("Chick"): Invasion of Sicily 9710.23-24
Young, H.W., Maj Indian Army: KCMG/DSO (p) 9510.08
Young, Martin Cortlandt de Bude, 2/Lt KOSB: Loos 9404.13
Young, St John, Lt RTR: George Cross (1944) 9402.14
Young Citizens Volunteers Battn badge WWI 9012.22
Yser Medal (Belgium) 9005.22

Z

Zakynthiote Liberation Medal (1811) 9505.16
Zamoyski, Adam 'The Forgotten Few' (br) 9508.19
Zeebrugge (1918) 9009.27
Royal Australian Navy 9104.19-20
VC (mr) 9005.13-14
Zeppelins, raids on (1914) 9111.09-11
Zulu Wars
Eshowe: siege and relief of (1879) (cr) 9809.20-23
Isandhlwana (1879) 9008.11-13
Islandhlwana survivors medal 0001.18-19
Ntombe River (1879) (c) 8906.15-18
120th Anniversary commemorations 9906.07

MEDAL RIBBONS

In this section we feature the majority of the ribbons for the medals included in the main section of the book.
Where the same ribbon is used for more than one medal, only one is illustrated here.

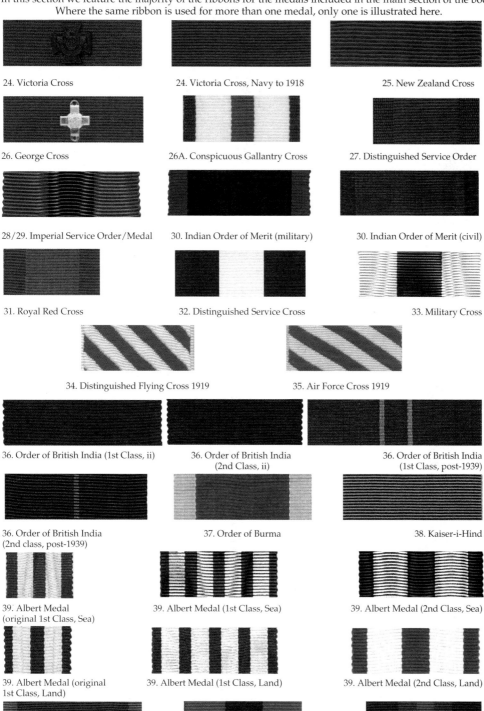

24. Victoria Cross

24. Victoria Cross, Navy to 1918

25. New Zealand Cross

26. George Cross

26A. Conspicuous Gallantry Cross

27. Distinguished Service Order

28/29. Imperial Service Order/Medal

30. Indian Order of Merit (military)

30. Indian Order of Merit (civil)

31. Royal Red Cross

32. Distinguished Service Cross

33. Military Cross

34. Distinguished Flying Cross 1919

35. Air Force Cross 1919

36. Order of British India (1st Class, ii)

36. Order of British India (2nd Class, ii)

36. Order of British India (1st Class, post-1939)

36. Order of British India (2nd class, post-1939)

37. Order of Burma

38. Kaiser-i-Hind

39. Albert Medal (original 1st Class, Sea)

39. Albert Medal (1st Class, Sea)

39. Albert Medal (2nd Class, Sea)

39. Albert Medal (original 1st Class, Land)

39. Albert Medal (1st Class, Land)

39. Albert Medal (2nd Class, Land)

40. SA Queen's Medal for Bravery

41/42. Distinguished Conduct Medal

43. DCM (KAR and WAFF)

449

44. Conspicuous Gallantry, Navy

44. Conspicuous Gallantry, RAF

45. George Medal

46/49. King's Police Medal 1916

46. King's Police Medal (Gallantry)

47. Queen's Police Medal

48. Queen's Fire Service Medal

50/51. Edward Medal

52. Indian Distinguished Service Medal

53. Burma Gallantry Medal

54. Distinguished Service Medal

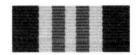

55. Military Medal

56. Distinguished Flying Medal

57. Air Force Medal

58. Constabulary Medal Ireland 1872

59. Indian Police Medal
(Meritorious Service)

60. Burma Police Meritorious Service Medal

61. Colonial Police Medal (Gallantry)
62. Colonial Fire Brigade Medal (Gallantry)

61. Colonial Police Medal (Meritorious Service)
62. Colonial Fire Brigade (Meritorious Service)

63. Queen's Gallantry Medal

64. Allied Subjects Medal

65. King's Medal for Courage
in the Cause of Freedom

66. King's Medal for Service in the
Cause of Freedom

67/68. Sea Gallantry Medal

79. Seringapatam

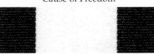

93. Naval Gold Medal

94. Naval General Service Medal

95. Army Gold Cross/96. Maida Gold
Medal/97. Army Gold Medal

98. Military General Service Medal

99. Waterloo Medal

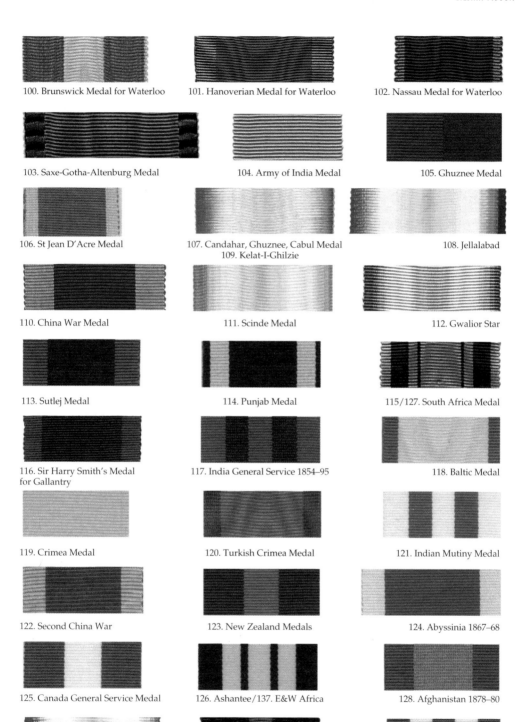

100. Brunswick Medal for Waterloo

101. Hanoverian Medal for Waterloo

102. Nassau Medal for Waterloo

103. Saxe-Gotha-Altenburg Medal

104. Army of India Medal

105. Ghuznee Medal

106. St Jean D'Acre Medal

107. Candahar, Ghuznee, Cabul Medal
109. Kelat-I-Ghilzie

108. Jellalabad

110. China War Medal

111. Scinde Medal

112. Gwalior Star

113. Sutlej Medal

114. Punjab Medal

115/127. South Africa Medal

116. Sir Harry Smith's Medal
for Gallantry

117. India General Service 1854–95

118. Baltic Medal

119. Crimea Medal

120. Turkish Crimea Medal

121. Indian Mutiny Medal

122. Second China War

123. New Zealand Medals

124. Abyssinia 1867–68

125. Canada General Service Medal

126. Ashantee/137. E&W Africa

128. Afghanistan 1878–80

129. Kabul to Kandahar Star

130. Cape of Good Hope GSM

131. Egypt Medal

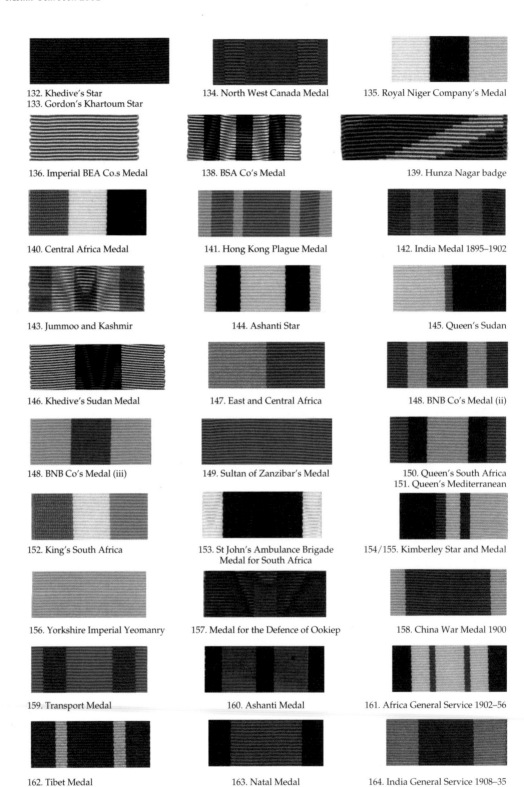

132. Khedive's Star
133. Gordon's Khartoum Star

134. North West Canada Medal

135. Royal Niger Company's Medal

136. Imperial BEA Co.s Medal

138. BSA Co's Medal

139. Hunza Nagar badge

140. Central Africa Medal

141. Hong Kong Plague Medal

142. India Medal 1895–1902

143. Jummoo and Kashmir

144. Ashanti Star

145. Queen's Sudan

146. Khedive's Sudan Medal

147. East and Central Africa

148. BNB Co's Medal (ii)

148. BNB Co's Medal (iii)

149. Sultan of Zanzibar's Medal

150. Queen's South Africa
151. Queen's Mediterranean

152. King's South Africa

153. St John's Ambulance Brigade Medal for South Africa

154/155. Kimberley Star and Medal

156. Yorkshire Imperial Yeomanry

157. Medal for the Defence of Ookiep

158. China War Medal 1900

159. Transport Medal

160. Ashanti Medal

161. Africa General Service 1902–56

162. Tibet Medal

163. Natal Medal

164. India General Service 1908–35

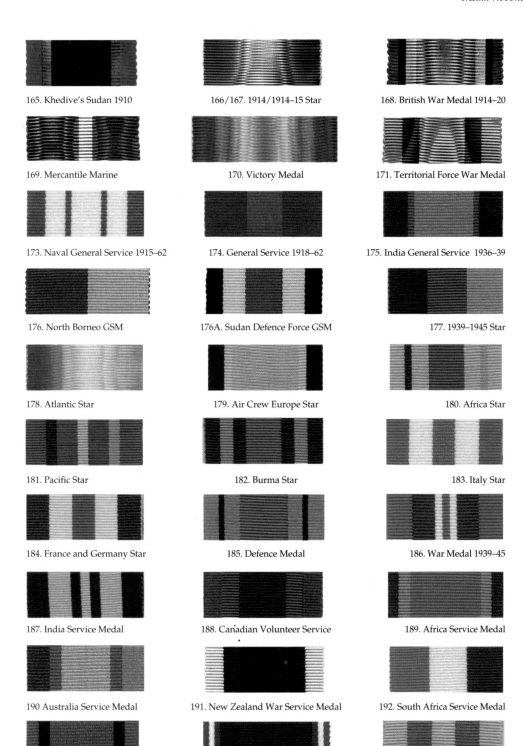

165. Khedive's Sudan 1910

166/167. 1914/1914–15 Star

168. British War Medal 1914–20

169. Mercantile Marine

170. Victory Medal

171. Territorial Force War Medal

173. Naval General Service 1915–62

174. General Service 1918–62

175. India General Service 1936–39

176. North Borneo GSM

176A. Sudan Defence Force GSM

177. 1939–1945 Star

178. Atlantic Star

179. Air Crew Europe Star

180. Africa Star

181. Pacific Star

182. Burma Star

183. Italy Star

184. France and Germany Star

185. Defence Medal

186. War Medal 1939–45

187. India Service Medal

188. Canadian Volunteer Service

189. Africa Service Medal

190 Australia Service Medal

191. New Zealand War Service Medal

192. South Africa Service Medal

193. Southern Rhodesia War Service

194. Newfoundland Voulunteer War
Service Medal

195. Korea Medal

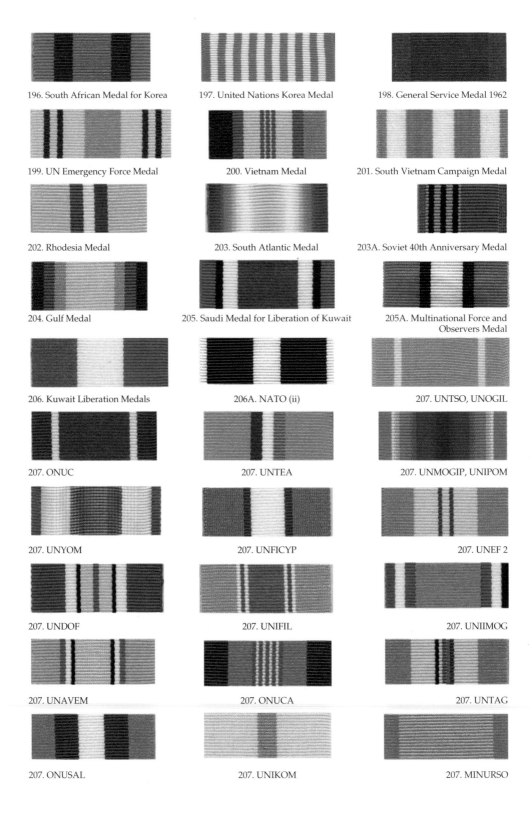

196. South African Medal for Korea

197. United Nations Korea Medal

198. General Service Medal 1962

199. UN Emergency Force Medal

200. Vietnam Medal

201. South Vietnam Campaign Medal

202. Rhodesia Medal

203. South Atlantic Medal

203A. Soviet 40th Anniversary Medal

204. Gulf Medal

205. Saudi Medal for Liberation of Kuwait

205A. Multinational Force and Observers Medal

206. Kuwait Liberation Medals

206A. NATO (ii)

207. UNTSO, UNOGIL

207. ONUC

207. UNTEA

207. UNMOGIP, UNIPOM

207. UNYOM

207. UNFICYP

207. UNEF 2

207. UNDOF

207. UNIFIL

207. UNIIMOG

207. UNAVEM

207. ONUCA

207. UNTAG

207. ONUSAL

207. UNIKOM

207. MINURSO

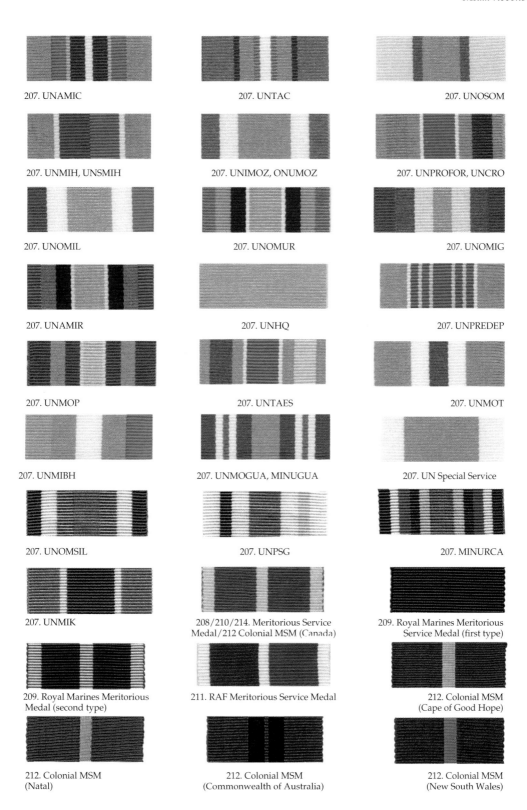

207. UNAMIC

207. UNTAC

207. UNOSOM

207. UNMIH, UNSMIH

207. UNIMOZ, ONUMOZ

207. UNPROFOR, UNCRO

207. UNOMIL

207. UNOMUR

207. UNOMIG

207. UNAMIR

207. UNHQ

207. UNPREDEP

207. UNMOP

207. UNTAES

207. UNMOT

207. UNMIBH

207. UNMOGUA, MINUGUA

207. UN Special Service

207. UNOMSIL

207. UNPSG

207. MINURCA

207. UNMIK

208/210/214. Meritorious Service Medal/212 Colonial MSM (Canada)

209. Royal Marines Meritorious Service Medal (first type)

209. Royal Marines Meritorious Medal (second type)

211. RAF Meritorious Service Medal

212. Colonial MSM (Cape of Good Hope)

212. Colonial MSM (Natal)

212. Colonial MSM (Commonwealth of Australia)

212. Colonial MSM (New South Wales)

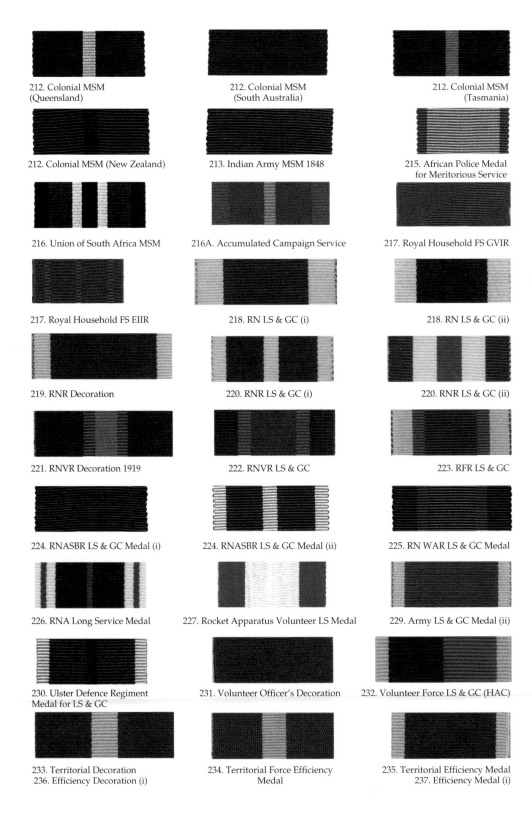

212. Colonial MSM
(Queensland)

212. Colonial MSM
(South Australia)

212. Colonial MSM
(Tasmania)

212. Colonial MSM (New Zealand)

213. Indian Army MSM 1848

215. African Police Medal
for Meritorious Service

216. Union of South Africa MSM

216A. Accumulated Campaign Service

217. Royal Household FS GVIR

217. Royal Household FS EIIR

218. RN LS & GC (i)

218. RN LS & GC (ii)

219. RNR Decoration

220. RNR LS & GC (i)

220. RNR LS & GC (ii)

221. RNVR Decoration 1919

222. RNVR LS & GC

223. RFR LS & GC

224. RNASBR LS & GC Medal (i)

224. RNASBR LS & GC Medal (ii)

225. RN WAR LS & GC Medal

226. RNA Long Service Medal

227. Rocket Apparatus Volunteer LS Medal

229. Army LS & GC Medal (ii)

230. Ulster Defence Regiment
Medal for LS & GC

231. Volunteer Officer's Decoration

232. Volunteer Force LS & GC (HAC)

233. Territorial Decoration
236. Efficiency Decoration (i)

234. Territorial Force Efficiency
Medal

235. Territorial Efficiency Medal
237. Efficiency Medal (i)

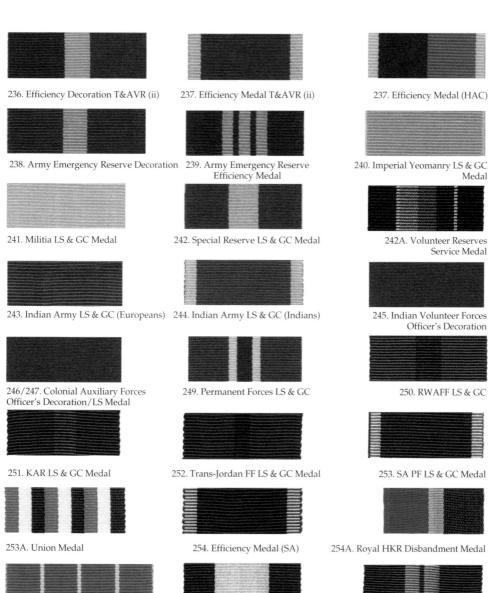

236. Efficiency Decoration T&AVR (ii)

237. Efficiency Medal T&AVR (ii)

237. Efficiency Medal (HAC)

238. Army Emergency Reserve Decoration

239. Army Emergency Reserve Efficiency Medal

240. Imperial Yeomanry LS & GC Medal

241. Militia LS & GC Medal

242. Special Reserve LS & GC Medal

242A. Volunteer Reserves Service Medal

243. Indian Army LS & GC (Europeans)

244. Indian Army LS & GC (Indians)

245. Indian Volunteer Forces Officer's Decoration

246/247. Colonial Auxiliary Forces Officer's Decoration/LS Medal

249. Permanent Forces LS & GC

250. RWAFF LS & GC

251. KAR LS & GC Medal

252. Trans-Jordan FF LS & GC Medal

253. SA PF LS & GC Medal

253A. Union Medal

254. Efficiency Medal (SA)

254A. Royal HKR Disbandment Medal

255. Canadian Forces Decoration

256. Victoria Vol. Long & Efficient Service Medal

257. New Zealand Long & Efficient Service Medal

258. NZ Volunteer Service Medal

259. NZ Territorial Service Medal (i)

259. NZ Territorial Service Medal (ii)

261/261A. Ulster Defence Regiment Medal

262. Cadet Forces Medal

263. Royal Observer Corps Medal

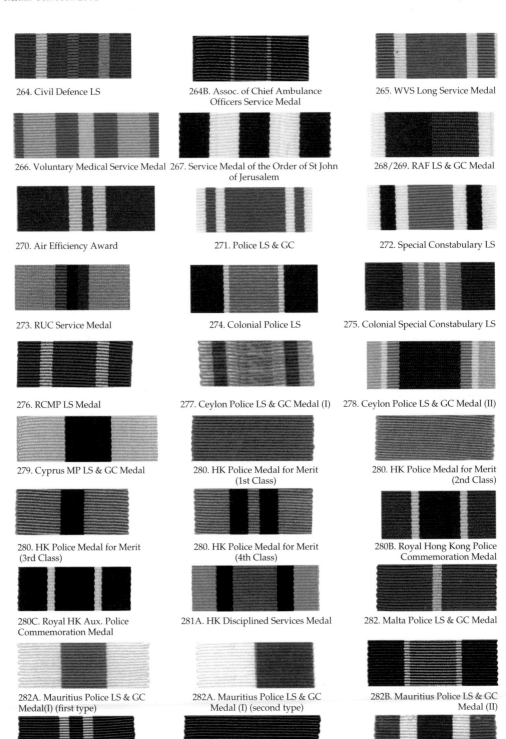

264. Civil Defence LS

264B. Assoc. of Chief Ambulance Officers Service Medal

265. WVS Long Service Medal

266. Voluntary Medical Service Medal

267. Service Medal of the Order of St John of Jerusalem

268/269. RAF LS & GC Medal

270. Air Efficiency Award

271. Police LS & GC

272. Special Constabulary LS

273. RUC Service Medal

274. Colonial Police LS

275. Colonial Special Constabulary LS

276. RCMP LS Medal

277. Ceylon Police LS & GC Medal (I)

278. Ceylon Police LS & GC Medal (II)

279. Cyprus MP LS & GC Medal

280. HK Police Medal for Merit (1st Class)

280. HK Police Medal for Merit (2nd Class)

280. HK Police Medal for Merit (3rd Class)

280. HK Police Medal for Merit (4th Class)

280B. Royal Hong Kong Police Commemoration Medal

280C. Royal HK Aux. Police Commemoration Medal

281A. HK Disciplined Services Medal

282. Malta Police LS & GC Medal

282A. Mauritius Police LS & GC Medal(I) (first type)

282A. Mauritius Police LS & GC Medal (I) (second type)

282B. Mauritius Police LS & GC Medal (II)

282. NZ Police LS & GC Medal (second type)

283A. Seychelles Police LS & GC Medal

284. SA Police Good Service Medal

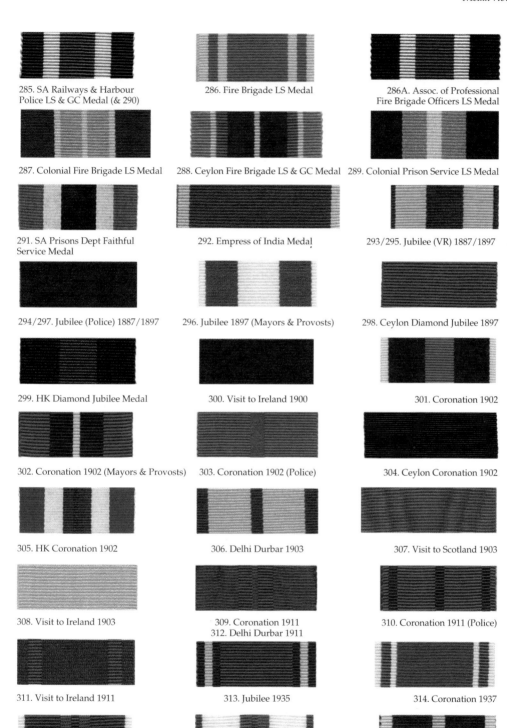

285. SA Railways & Harbour Police LS & GC Medal (& 290)

286. Fire Brigade LS Medal

286A. Assoc. of Professional Fire Brigade Officers LS Medal

287. Colonial Fire Brigade LS Medal

288. Ceylon Fire Brigade LS & GC Medal

289. Colonial Prison Service LS Medal

291. SA Prisons Dept Faithful Service Medal

292. Empress of India Medal

293/295. Jubilee (VR) 1887/1897

294/297. Jubilee (Police) 1887/1897

296. Jubilee 1897 (Mayors & Provosts)

298. Ceylon Diamond Jubilee 1897

299. HK Diamond Jubilee Medal

300. Visit to Ireland 1900

301. Coronation 1902

302. Coronation 1902 (Mayors & Provosts)

303. Coronation 1902 (Police)

304. Ceylon Coronation 1902

305. HK Coronation 1902

306. Delhi Durbar 1903

307. Visit to Scotland 1903

308. Visit to Ireland 1903

309. Coronation 1911
312. Delhi Durbar 1911

310. Coronation 1911 (Police)

311. Visit to Ireland 1911

313. Jubilee 1935

314. Coronation 1937

315. Coronation 1953

316. Jubilee 1977

317. Royal Humane Society (1921)

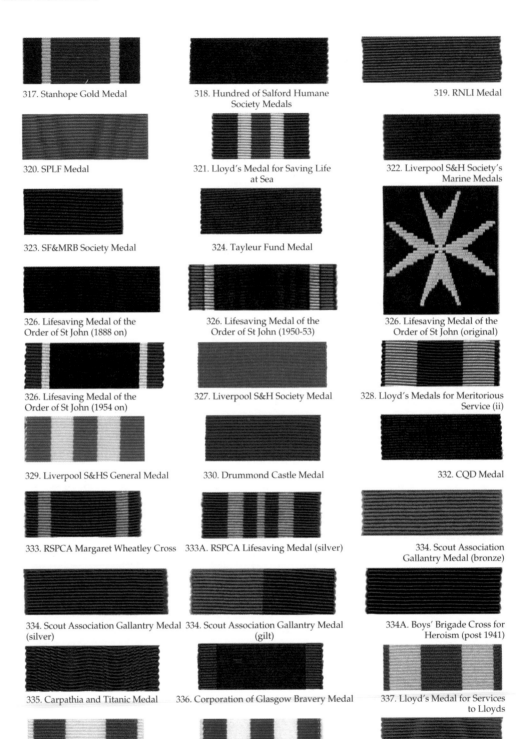

317. Stanhope Gold Medal

318. Hundred of Salford Humane Society Medals

319. RNLI Medal

320. SPLF Medal

321. Lloyd's Medal for Saving Life at Sea

322. Liverpool S&H Society's Marine Medals

323. SF&MRB Society Medal

324. Tayleur Fund Medal

326. Lifesaving Medal of the Order of St John (1888 on)

326. Lifesaving Medal of the Order of St John (1950-53)

326. Lifesaving Medal of the Order of St John (original)

326. Lifesaving Medal of the Order of St John (1954 on)

327. Liverpool S&H Society Medal

328. Lloyd's Medals for Meritorious Service (ii)

329. Liverpool S&HS General Medal

330. Drummond Castle Medal

332. CQD Medal

333. RSPCA Margaret Wheatley Cross

333A. RSPCA Lifesaving Medal (silver)

334. Scout Association Gallantry Medal (bronze)

334. Scout Association Gallantry Medal (silver)

334. Scout Association Gallantry Medal (gilt)

334A. Boys' Brigade Cross for Heroism (post 1941)

335. Carpathia and Titanic Medal

336. Corporation of Glasgow Bravery Medal

337. Lloyd's Medal for Services to Lloyds

338. Lloyd's Medal for Bravery at Sea

339. Liverpool S&HS Swimming Medal

340A. Order of Industrial Heroism

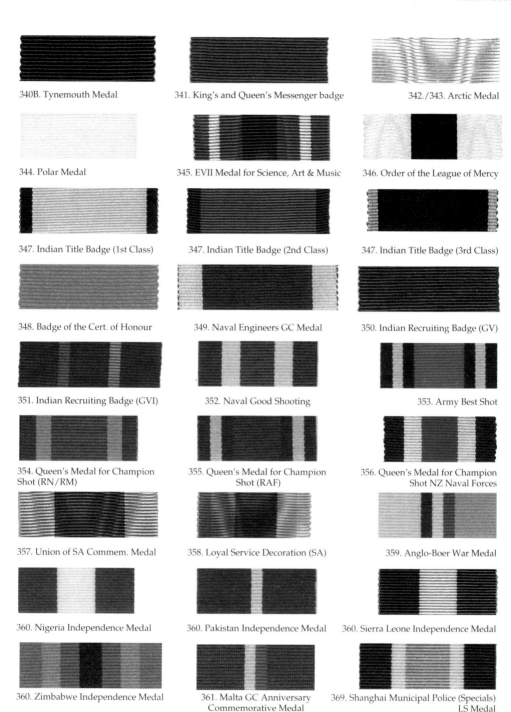

340B. Tynemouth Medal

341. King's and Queen's Messenger badge

342./343. Arctic Medal

344. Polar Medal

345. EVII Medal for Science, Art & Music

346. Order of the League of Mercy

347. Indian Title Badge (1st Class)

347. Indian Title Badge (2nd Class)

347. Indian Title Badge (3rd Class)

348. Badge of the Cert. of Honour

349. Naval Engineers GC Medal

350. Indian Recruiting Badge (GV)

351. Indian Recruiting Badge (GVI)

352. Naval Good Shooting

353. Army Best Shot

354. Queen's Medal for Champion Shot (RN/RM)

355. Queen's Medal for Champion Shot (RAF)

356. Queen's Medal for Champion Shot NZ Naval Forces

357. Union of SA Commem. Medal

358. Loyal Service Decoration (SA)

359. Anglo-Boer War Medal

360. Nigeria Independence Medal

360. Pakistan Independence Medal

360. Sierra Leone Independence Medal

360. Zimbabwe Independence Medal

361. Malta GC Anniversary Commemorative Medal

369. Shanghai Municipal Police (Specials) LS Medal

370. Shanghai Municipality Council Emergency Medal

371. AA Service Cross

372. AA Service Medal

AUSTRALIAN MEDAL RIBBONS

A1. Victoria Cross for Australia

A2. Cross of Valour

A3. Order of Australia (General)

A3. Order of Australia (Military)

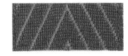

A4. Star of Gallantry

A5. Star of Courage

A6. Distinguished Service Cross

A7. Conspicuous Service Cross

A8. Nursing Service Cross

A9. Medal for Gallantry

A10. Bravery Medal

A11. Distinguished Service Medal

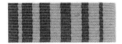

A12. Public Service Medal

A13. Australian Police Medal

A14. Australian Fire Service Medal

A16. Conspicuous Service Medal

A17. Antarctic Medal

A21. Australian Active Service Medal 1975

A22. Australian Service Medal 1975

A23. Police Overseas Service Medal

A24. Defence Force Service Medal

A25. Reserve Force Decoration

A26. Reserve Force Medal

A27. National Medal

A28. Champion Shots Medal

A30. Australian Active Service Medal
1945–1975

A31. Australian Service Medal
1945–1975

NEW ZEALAND MEDAL RIBBONS

NZ4. New Zealand Order of Merit

NZ6. Queen's Service Order and Medal

NZ13. NZ Service Medal 1946–49

NZ14. NZ General Service Medal (Warlike Operations)

NZ15. NZ General Service Medal (Peacekeeping Operations)

NZ16. NZ 1990 Commemoration Medal

NZ17. NZ Meritorious Service Medal

NZ18. NZ Armed Forces Award

NZ19. RNZN Long Service Medal

NZ20. NZ Army LS&GC Medal

NZ21. RNZAF Long Service Medal

NZ22. NZ Territorial Service Medal

NZ23. NZ Long & Efficient Service Medal

NZ24. NZ Police LS&GC Medal

NZ25. NZ Prison Service Medal

NZ26. NZ Fire Brigades LS&GC Medal

NZ27. NZ Suffrage Centennial Medal

NZ28/29. NZ Enforcement LS Medal/ NZ Traffic Service Medal

Miss out on MEDAL NEWS and miss out on an exciting read

Subscribe today! See page 25 for further details

Index
of medals

NOTES

NOTES